Capturing the Horizon

CAPTURING THE HORIZON

The Historical Geography of Transportation
since the Sixteenth Century

James E. Vance, Jr.

The Johns Hopkins University Press
Baltimore and London

Originally published as *Capturing the Horizon: The Historical Geography of Transportation since the Transportation Revolution in the Sixteenth Century* in 1986 in a hardcover edition by Harper & Row, Publishers, Inc. Reprinted by arrangement with James E. Vance, Jr.

Softshell Books edition, 1990

The Johns Hopkins University Press, 701 West 40th Street,
Baltimore, Maryland 21211
The Johns Hopkins Press Ltd., London

The paper used in this book meets the minimum requirements of American National Standard for Information Sciences—Permanence of Paper for Printed Library Materials, ANSI Z39.48-1984.

Library of Congress Cataloging-in-Publication Data

Vance, James E.
    Capturing the horizon: the historical geography of transportation
since the sixteenth century / James E. Vance, Jr.—
Softshell Books edition, 1990
        p.   cm.
    Reprint. Originally published: New York: Harper & Row, ©1986.
    Includes bibliographical references (p.
    ISBN 0-8018-4012-0 (pbk)
    1. Transportation—History. I. Title.
[HE151.V29   1990]
388'.09—dc20   89-71675
                                                         CIP

To those with a surpassing geographical curiosity:

The late Samuel Van Valkenburg, who showed me the fascination and value of geographical comparison;

Raymond and Marion Murphy, who brought to that interest a measure of order and the wish to convey it;

Many of my students, over thirty years, and Tiffany Vance, who brought purpose and pleasure to that work;

Jean, whose patience has endured the filling of a great number of locks, the slow progress of a multitude of watched trains, and the long discussion by others on how to reach and capture a myriad of horizons;

and to the memory of Cache who was very good company, and herself geographically curious;

this book is affectionately dedicated.

Contents

Preface

Common sense tells us that geographical features and events within a limited time period and a compact area will be strongly interrelated. Far less obvious are the connections that might exist over half a millennium and across oceans. It was to look at interrelatedness within the Western world and for the last five hundred years that I set out to write this book, braving all the pitfalls that lie across the pursuit of such generalization, particularly in such a field as transportation where there is a virtual army whose common banner is the accumulation of the especially arcane knowledge concerning "their" particular railroad, canal, aircraft, or corner of the world. This is not their book, as my intent here is to seek out common, continuous, and geographically comprehensive patterns, on the land and in time. To gain that end, comparisons must be drawn and, at times, considerable detail given; but the objective is always the broadly effective process and the evolution of transportation technology and its geographical research.

Any such extensive goal forces compromise—in being precisely correct and complete within the parochial example, in using national terms in what is an international study, in searching for an understanding of process rather than the detail that demonstrates it, in selecting one example to serve for the multitude, and in many other ways. This is particularly the case in the handling of Great Britain. It is an aphorism that Americans and Britons are divided by a common language, and I fear that will be most clear here. Even such a common and simple thing as a rail-guided pavement for steam—later electric and diesel—locomotives is commonly called a *railway* in Britain and a *railroad* in the United States. Which term should be used in a comparative study? Partly because it comes more naturally from my typewriter, but mainly because it serves comparative analysis better in standing specifically for a standard common-carrier heavily built rail guideway, I have employed *railroad* here, even when writing about such facilities in Britain, so that I might reserve *railway* to serve as the generic term for light constructions, often in streets, and frequently serving either a specialized freight or a restricted passenger demand. In the technology of railroads—like that of canals, civil aviation, and most other aspects of transportation—the descriptive nouns were first colloquial and thus often various by region. Here I have attempted to use those terms as in common practice in the United States—as, for example, in naming the timber maintaining the base and gauge of a railroad, here *ties* rather than the English *sleepers*.

That adoption of American terminology raises a point that must be dealt with directly—chauvinism. A study of the evolution of technology provides a fertile culture for the propagation of charges of chauvinism, as few things are seen as reflecting the central genius of a people more than their contributions to the technology of transportation. Think of the heated arguments that arise over automobiles of various national origins. Most writing about the evolution of technology has been distinctly *national*. It is little questioned that an American book on civil aviation pays scant attention to British and French planes, or that British books on canals tend to disregard what the French were doing a century before the Duke of Bridgewater, and to overlook completely those Hollanders and Italians who were floating along slackwater navigations even several centuries earlier. In this book I attempt to look at the generally significant events, and the locales where they took place, without reference to any national interest. As an American, I have biases, and they must show. A lifetime of thinking about railroads has convinced me that there is such a thing as "the American railroad," and that it is not a Siamese twin but rather a most distant cousin of the British railroad. About all they share is the use of the expansive quality of steam and a "standard gauge." Some may think this mere chauvinism: I hope at least to show that it is highly informed. One final point to be corrected in this regard, and one fault shared by Americans and Britons, is a reverberant disregard in most of the English-language literature of what the French have been about during this half millennium. Here I must come away with a full measure of respect for what the French have done to capture horizons, even though those compatriots of Nicolas Chauvin have commonly strongly favored their own ones.

This search for the historical geography of transportation within the western world is predicated on the belief that the horizons of that realm are as extensive geographically as they are in time. The past is seldom lost: rather it is transformed and geographically expanded. This is as much true of the spread of American technology and experience to Europe as it is of the more widely appreciated diffusion of the European experience and culture to the "New Lands." The indebtedness of nineteenth-century America to the canal technology of Europe is incontestable, but by the middle of the last century the borrowing became reciprocal. The electric trolley followed on the horse-car as an American contribution to European, as well as to domestic, urbanization. That quick and enthusiastic borrowing was related to a particular structural change in settlement that is very recent in human history—the rise of urbanization.

For any of us living today, the city is our largest artifact, so it seems natural that we would seek to understand the relationship that exists between the obvious evolution of cities and of transportation. In an earlier book, *This Scene of Man: The Role and Structure of the City in the Geography of Western Civilization* (Harper & Row, 1977), I sought an understanding of the evolution of the urbanization process. To pair with that evolution, I here wish to look at the development of transportation over a shorter period, the last five hundred years. As these two books were conceived of as the two pillars to support a common superstructure, the different time span needs some explanation. In *This Scene of Man* nearly three thousand years of time were considered, mainly because the city has grown slowly as both a physical and a social entity, and human institutions tend to evolve at a very moderate pace, if more continuously than many appreciate. In transportation there were changes in the past, but for a complexity of reasons here considered most of the technical evolution in transportation has occurred quite rapidly during the last half millennium. As evolution rather than time, geography rather than history as such, are the concerns of this pair of books, the two pillars need not be of the same time-length to support what I hope is a level and sound conclusion.

The initial purpose in presenting these two works—*This Scene of Man* and *Capturing the Horizon*—was to seek an answer to the question of the nature of transportation-settlement relationships. When I wrote a Ph.D. thesis thirty-five years ago, I posed myself that question with respect to a single metropolis, Boston, and ever since I have worked to try to formulate and present a more encompassing answer that might serve for Western society as a whole. There is, of course, no simple, immutable statement of such transportation-settlement relations; but there can be broad conclusions concerning the demands that urbanization places on contemporary transportation and the role that transportation evolution plays in reshaping cities. Here I have attempted to relate that evolution of transportation to several aspects of urban geography—the onset of the commercial revolution of the seventeenth and eighteenth centuries and the

beginning of the modern metropolis, the advent of the Industrial Revolution and the vast increase in urbanization it unleashed, and more recently the creation of the morphologically complex metropolis with its heavy dependence on both greater mobility and more personalized transport—that help to delineate such relationships. This is not the place to attempt to spell out the interrelated processes (that is done in the eighth and final chapter); this is, however, the place to emphasize that the interrelatedness mentioned at the beginning of this preface attaches equally to transportation-settlement interaction. At times cities have engendered transport, as did the cities of the Po Basin and the Low Countries in the canal era and the steaming factory towns of Britain in the 1840s, whereas at other times the development of transportation encouraged the initiation and growth of cities, both the railroad towns of interior North America and the suburbs and satellites that clustered in thick bands around the early industrial towns. The relationship of cities and transportation can be observed and stated, but not for all times or every place. There can be no elegant simplicity in the detail of the relations; but there can be the strong and confident assertion that the interaction is always present and normally of extreme significance in any attempt to explain how cities begin or grow and, in turn, why we must search for the horizon and in what ways we do so at any particular time.

No book can be written without critical dependence on the work and thought of others, and this study shows that need. Certain persons have had a long-term influence on my thinking about transportation; most notable were two of my good friends through much of my professional life, the late Edward Ullman and the most vigorously present Harold Mayer. Their work opened many doors, and their enthusiasm for the geographical study of transportation convinced me that I was walking a nearly empty road, but certainly a main artery of research necessary for a general understanding of geographical relationships.

During the three decades that I have lectured variously on the geography of transportation, I have depended significantly on my students both to sharpen my ideas and to give purpose to that effort. All have been important to me; a few have contributed more than they perhaps realize and thus deserve singling out here. Roger Barnett of the University of the Pacific has been for twenty years the sort of verbal companion most devotees of trains, trolleys, and the other facilities of mobility come to depend on critically. Chuck Sargent of Arizona State University began by correcting my misperceptions of gandy dancing and has continued for many years as an ingenious scout for me of transportation evolution. Vic Ryerson and Rich Tower, though less committed to geography than those already mentioned, worked hard to help me understand American railroading, which they came to know professionally. If I have any feeling for civil aviation, I owe in full measure that ability to Alan Bender. Many others have aided in my education, among them Marsha Dillon of Sacramento State University with respect to ports, Peter Rees of the University of Delaware on West Indian and Mexican transportation, and Jean Cermakian of the Université de Québec in the matter of canals. Clare Cooper, then at Nebraska but now at Berkeley, long ago opened my eyes to direct railroad settlement; John Reps at Cornell has taught me much more. Mel Webber at Berkeley invigorated my interest in automotive transportation, and Bill Garrison there in the need for a thought as to the future. Jan De Vries in history at Berkeley widened my view and set me a proper standard for what history can tell us about the meaning of

mobility in the past. Bill Wallace at the University of New Hampshire has frequently shown me what a geographer should know about railroads. Many others—among them a number of locomotive engineers whose response to my lectures have been more helpful to me than I suspect I was to them—have worked to give me an understanding of how things work. That kindly indulgence in the interest of education, mine, on the part of several freighter captains and Canadian bush pilots, and numberless railroad brakemen and conductors, and even a few locomotive engineers, in North America, Europe, and South Africa has played an important role for which I wish to extend thanks.

In writing this book a number of people have aided greatly with editorial encouragement and advice, which I deeply appreciate. First among them is Don Meinig at Syracuse whose interest in this work started it and carried it forward when most needed. Second, my editor, Logan Campbell, deserves credit and thanks for his help and understanding. These people, good friends in considerable measure because of a shared interest in transportation, have given this work much of its worth; the failings are entirely mine.

I wish to single out Adrienne Morgan for her most substantial, and I believe successful, cartographic contributions to this book. She has taken my rough ideas and made of them clear, forceful, and graphic presentations that show how useful a well-constructed map can be in geographical analysis. Her responses to my importunate wishes have been kind and calming, making of collaboration an honorable and productive relationship. She has my strongest thanks.

The illustrations for this book have been chosen with two objectives in mind: first, to illustrate points made in the text, and, second, to suggest the look of transportation features at the time under discussion. This is not easy, as in the heyday of much of the material in this book photography did not exist—for example, when the canals and early railroads were in active use and the country roads and city streets were as bad as they actually could be. For that reason I have sought contemporary, or at least fairly old, illustrations to avoid the loss that the constant modernization of transportation brings about when we use pictures from our own day. Where I have had to use present-day materials, I have sought out those that were least unrepresentative of the form of transportation at its most important time of use.

Those who have supplied me with pictures deserve my sincere thanks. Trans-World Airlines and Pan American World Airways have been particularly generous in supplying pictures of the planes they respectively pioneered; American Airlines has furnished me with pictures of the DC-4s, DC-6s, DC-7s, and *Electras* that were their particular interest. The Port of Oakland and the Port Authority of New York and New Jersey have kindly lent pictures, as have the Chicago Transit Authority and the Massachusetts Bay Transit Authority. The French Embassy in Washington has been of great help in securing pictures of several aspects of transportation in which France was a pioneer. The Union Pacific Railroad Museum in Omaha has fully supported the distinction of its parent corporation in finding and furnishing pictures of construction of the world's greatest railroad. Professor Jan De Vrees of the University of California, Berkeley, has been generous in allowing me to reproduce two maps from his important study of seventeenth-century Dutch canals. The French National Railroads (SNCF) have shown the interest in the whole field of transportation that I would anticipate and have allowed me to use several of their photographs. I wish to acknowledge this help and express thanks for it, and for the permission to publish these pictures. Unfortunately, there have been dead ends, such as British Airways' unwillingness to furnish pictures of their characteristic planes, leaving the impression that I have deliberately disregarded British contributions to civil aviation.

I wish to acknowledge the kindness of Little, Brown and Company, publishers of Carl Solberg's *The History of Commercial Aviation in America*; of the Mystic Seaport Museum Incorporated, publishers of Robert Albion, William A. Baker, and Benjamin Labaree's *New England and the Sea*; and of The Cambridge University Press, publishers of R. H. Thornton's *British Shipping*, and thank them for permission to publish extended passages from those works.

Finally, no book can reach the press without the hard and careful work of a number of typists and technical persons. This is no exception. I wish particularly to thank Peggy Lincoln and Natalia Vonnegut, who typed large parts of the manuscript over a number of years, and to express appreciation for the work of Charlie Hadenfeldt and J. Folger-Brown, who always made usable to the printer my changes of mind. And Don Johnston of the Library Photo Service of the University of California has been ingenious and helpful in securing phots of a wide variety of materials. Piper Gaubatz was invaluable to me in preparing a comprehensive index. To all who have been so generous of their attention and skill, I extend my deep appreciation.

chapter *1*

Introduction
The Transportation Revolution of the Sixteenth Century

Society, for a great part of its existence, has had little more than the land within the visual horizon as its effective realm of activity. To begin with, the low natural productivity of such a narrowly circumscribed space meant that human groups had to migrate with their flocks slowly over the landscape, equally slowly shifting that horizon along with their wandering. Few people could hope for much freedom or ease of movement. Life became even more confined and parochial when agriculture was developed, permitting a human group to occupy the same spot continuously and avoid the rigors of a migratory existence. This gain, however, came at the cost of losing the shifting horizon that migratory organization brought. Fixed abode meant fixed horizon, narrow experience, localized natural economy, provincial political viewpoint, and very low demand for transportation. From the discovery of agriculture until well on in human history, the narrow perspective of a group placed the act of transportation well down among human undertakings.

The Middle Ages was a time of expansion of commercial activity, of growth in local economies, and of an increasing curiosity about the world outside. Trade broke the isolation of the natural economy and of feudal society. It brought goods over greater distances and turned the interests of local groups outward, beyond their actual horizon. Along with that increase in geographical perspective came the inability of individuals in a community to carry out all their needs for transportation themselves, as they had done throughout most of human history. Transporting goods, and later people, became a specialized occupation, requiring increasingly large vehicles. The concentration of interest among those so occupied led to a search for improvement in the vehicles themselves and in the draft animals used to pull them, as well as an effort to harness the forces of nature to provide less costly propulsion—by wind, by river currents, and (in a more arcane fashion) by the force of gravity—to substitute for the dragging of loads by muscle power.

In many ways the Middle Ages marked the beginning of an effort to regain the accomplishments of the Romans. In transportation, however, that was far from the case. Quite early, medieval transportation technology began to outdistance Classical accomplishments. By the sixteenth century, the onset of modern times, human transportation was far advanced over what had existed a thousand years before.

It is that Transportation Revolution of the sixteenth century, in its several manifestations, that first concerns us here. In seeking the cause of that fundamental transformation and of subsequent shifts in transportation technology, we must recall the eternal human desire to "capture the horizon" by reaching it and pushing it ever farther away through harnessing to human needs the forces of muscle power, of nature, and finally of machine power. These forces magnify the individual's modest ability to move about the earth's surface and to bear the burden of goods, until by now our control of the earthly horizon is essentially complete. Every spot on earth is within economic reach for those who live in prosperous and developed countries. No terrestrial economic horizons remain closed to those who have carried the Transportation Revolution almost to its ultimate fulfillment. That transformation, and its geographical impact, is the subject of this book.

THE TWO PILLARS OF TRANSPORTATION-SETTLEMENT RELATIONSHIPS

Geography, like history, appears to have a simple purpose. Yet acquaintance with either field shows how hard it is to define this purpose. Etymologically, *geography* is the description of the earth's surface, which Merriam-Webster recasts in modern terms as "a science that deals with the earth and its life; esp.: the description of land, sea, air, and the distribution of plant and animal life including man and his industries." The effort of geographers in the twentieth century has been not merely to describe but also to explain the distribution of various tangible features of the human and natural landscapes. In the mainstream of geographic research, the emphasis has always been on the observable—in geographers' terms, the *mappable*—feature and its explanation. Thus, in a recent book—*This Scene of Man: The Role and Structure of the City in the Geography of Western Civilization*—I set out to describe and explain the largest human artifact, the city, as it arose and has evolved since Classical times. In doing so, I was operating within the traditional geographer's framework—studying physical occurrences on the earth's surface in an effort to understand whence they came and how they evolve. My method was both natural to the profession and desirably simple and straightforward. The only difficulty lay in the unreality attached to examining pattern without process. Clearly, the analysis presented in that book implied that a fundamental component of the broad range of morphogenetic forces was one process that had to remain for the time being a strong but silent partner in the shaping of cities.

In this book I wish to have the silent partner appear on its own account. Many years ago I set for myself the question of precedence in transportation-settlement relations. After thirty years of various approaches to the question, the answer remains as it was after my first effort at understanding: that in the explanation of that greatest of human features in geography—settlement—transportation is a silent partner whose gift to humanity—geographical mobility—is crucial. Settlements cannot exist unless people have some mobility. And shifts in the availability of mobility provide, in all likelihood, the most powerful single process at work in transforming and evolving the human half of geography.

Thus transportation and settlement are symbiotically intertwined. *This Scene of Man* should not stand by itself, other than in anticipation of the present volume. Here I set out to discuss the role and structure of transportation and the evolution of the process of mobility in shaping human geography. This book is intended to complement my earlier study of urban morphogenesis by supplying the corresponding consideration of transportation morphogenesis. We must be concerned with both the role transportation plays and the facilities and technologies it employs at various times and under different circumstances. But we always should view the transportation as a process brought into demand and transformed by the needs of human occupation of the earth's surface—that is, by a human geography whose greatest measure is to be found in settlement, particularly in its most advanced form—in cities.

The study of transportation can be justified by its inherent interest and scale. But when we seek to explain the patterns taken by canals, turnpikes, railroads, roads, shipping lanes, and airways, we can no more isolate transportation than we can study settlement without considering the mobility that permits it. Here, our attention will focus on why various forms and routes of movement arose and changed. That will necessitate a repeated reconsideration of the transportation-settlement relationship. Yet the detail on settlement must be furnished by passing reference to *This Scene of Man* rather than full explanation here.

Because *mobility* has come to mean more than human auto-motive abilities—to imply some harnessing of the motive force of the lower animals, the atmosphere, gravity, or fossil fuels—it is particularly pertinent to consider the evolution of transportation at this time. Human society is passing from a time of cheap energy back toward the state of more expensive energy that ruled human mobility until this century. Thus, in seeking to deal with energy decrementation, it is useful to learn how society existed and settlement functioned under other conditions of energy availability than those of our generation. By examining transportation morphogenesis, we can find tangible and understandable examples of the mobility associated with various levels of energy consumption.

More than four thousand years of recorded human history could be considered in studying the evolution of the technology of transportation, but only in the Middle Ages did much transformation take place. The rapid technological development that began toward the end of the fifteenth century ushered in the period of transportation morphogenesis that concerns us here. Before we begin our story in detail, however, it is helpful to go back a bit and examine the nature of transportation and human mobility in earlier times.

HUMAN MOBILITY IN CLASSICAL AND MEDIEVAL TIMES

The central geographical characteristic of the feudal system of the Middle Ages was immobility. Common people were legally tied to the land they tilled; trade was severely restricted to local barter, save for a few luxuries consumed in minuscule quantities by the overlord class. Movement was so uncommon that it was seen as a strange activity, setting those with mobility apart from the common lot. A separate system of law, known as *piepowder law* in English, was needed to deal with traveling merchants in their infrequent contacts with those local residents ruled by the customary law of the manor or of the specific town. The greatest measure of religious devotion was provided by the pilgrimage, such as that to Santiago de Compostela, which tested and tried medieval men and women as no native obligation could do. The Middle Ages were a time of local castles loosely held by distant and frequently disregarded sovereigns; of the autarkic natural economy of the manor; and of the geographical restraint of serfdom, which left most people imprisoned in a village—not by walls but by space and a true fear of the unknown beyond the visible horizon. Medieval transportation was a primitive undertaking innate to daily life— but only to the extent that human beings have the ability and the need to move in most of their waking acts. The narrow range of movement of the individual in daily activity tended to become the practical extent of economic, social, and even military and political life for the self-defined feudal community.

The medieval pattern of movement was so primitive largely because that era of geographical atomization witnessed a sharp retrogression from Roman times, when certain broadly defined human activities did elicit extensive geographical ties. If we classify those activities as economic, social, religious, and political-military, then in Roman times several concerns engendered rather extensive movement, notably the last, and only to a considerably reduced degree was there movement for economic and social purposes. A substantial factor in restricting travel to military-political activity was the considerable effort required for mobility and the simple technology of Roman transport, which relied mostly on *inherent movement*. All true human beings could walk erect; and, despite the considerable engineering accomplishments of the Romans, it was largely walking that moved troops and emissaries about the empire. Roman engineers did facilitate that inherent

movement by paving narrow roads, bridging streams, and even cutting short tunnels or great switchback paths over mountain passes. Thus even in Classical times we should distinguish between the *technology of movement* and the *facilities* that conduct it along particular geographical lines. The Romans were great innovators in the provision of facilities, but they accomplished little in the actual technology of transportation. For them, the main technology employed was the inherent movement of individuals required by their jobs to be mobile.

Unfortunately, with the fall of the Roman Empire the routes the Romans had constructed passed slowly into disrepair. Up to the time of Charlemagne there seems to have been a coherent system of facilities. In the dismemberment of his empire, however, the Roman routes were disrupted to the extent that passing over any great distance became economically too costly to be undertaken often. In the Dark Ages that followed on Charlemagne's glory, people did not walk differently from the Romans, but they lacked the integrated system of facilities that the Roman engineers had built. In this situation, feudalism (with its retreat to the local entity in most activities) was encouraged if not absolutely assured. Only the feeble efforts of medieval religious orders worked against the decay of routes. With the political dismemberment of the empire and the creation of new sovereignties with different desired flows, new alignments of facilities were required, but for several centuries they remained unprovided for. The Western economy stagnated for lack of transportation and then declined, further encouraging the parochial tendencies always present in human society.

It was this situation that obtained during the early Middle Ages, when the needs for transportation were small but the chance of employing it economically were perhaps

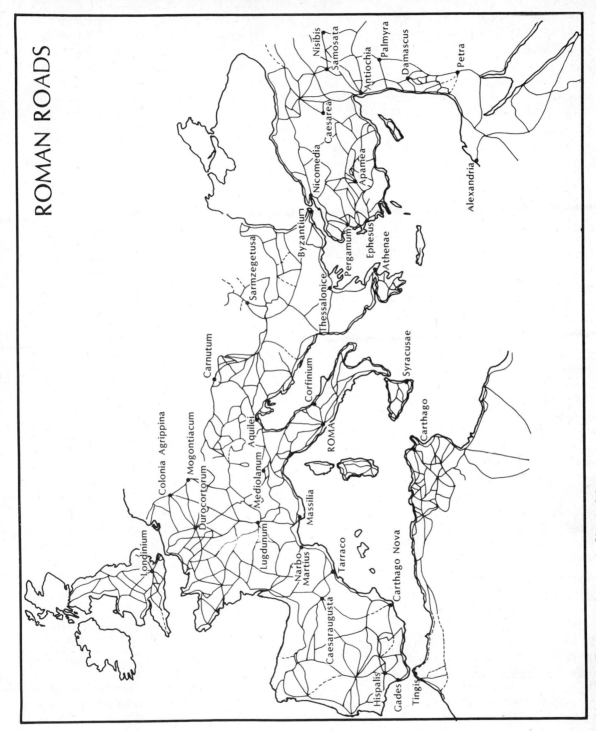

ROMAN ROADS

Map of the Roman road system in Classical times.

even more limited. It may well have been a fight against that adversity to movement that fostered the considerable efforts made by medieval people to improve the actual technology of transport, as distinct from the facilities used to pass over the ground. The Middle Ages witnessed no appreciable improvement in facilities—at least until the very last decades of that epoch, when primitive rail-guided ways were introduced in German mines—but they did see a fundamental improvement in the technology of transport. This came in the form of harnessing the greater muscle power of draft animals (than humans) as the tractive force to be employed. The Romans had used horses for chariots and oxen for wagons, but no harness was available that could employ the full effort those poor beasts could actually produce. Oxen were harnessed by their horns and horses by straps that tended to choke them if they pulled hard. Only in the twelfth century were the breast and girth bands attached to a yoke and pole supplanted by the padded collar and shafts or traces that have ever since been used to secure the maximum effort of horses.[1] The Romans had possessed vehicles—chariots inherited from the Greeks and wagons from the Celtic *carpentum*; the latter, according to the Theodosian Code, was capable of transporting 726 pounds when translated into English measure.[2]

Perhaps the greatest failing of the Roman wagon was found in its fixed axles (similar in operation to the fixed axles of most freight cars found even today on European railroads), which necessitated superior facilities for practical operation. In contrast, as early as the first century B.C. the Celts are known to have built wagons with pivoted fore-axles, which were altogether more efficient vehicles, rolling over the surface rather than plowing a shallow furrow as the rigid-frame wheels tended to do. Only as these swiveling

fore-axles (known colloquially as *bogies* in the north of England, whence the term entered general use when a similar feature was employed in early colliery railways) came into wider use, as they did only at the end of the Middle Ages, was the wagon made capable of efficient use with animal traction, then the only sort available. Until then the two-wheeled cart seems to have been the main vehicle of freight transport, as Brueghel's paintings show as late as 1564. These rolled rather than plowed because a single axle could more easily be turned. It was the late-medieval combination of proper harness and the swiveling fore-axle that finally improved the technology of road transport to the point economic movement was encouraged and the more commodious four-wheeled wagon could be employed.

What began the trend toward movement? A likely answer is found in the reasons that led people to move. As already noted, these were political-military, economic, religious, social, and intellectual, of which the first was probably the earliest factor. The Greeks, Persians, Romans, and other ancient peoples seem to have conquered distant areas, and conquest facilitated trade, the spread of religion, and the introduction of culture and customs. A principal explanation of the primacy of political conquest probably can be found in the auto-motive nature of mankind. Furthermore, it is always more feasible to mount a brief effort at costly transport than a sustained one. Troops and their materiel could move when continuing trade could not. Once conquest is accomplished, however, it is essential to maintain communication between the homeland and the conquered area, so efforts must be made to provide the facilities that would cheapen the effort-cost of transportation.

In the Classical world, that was about all that was done. The Greeks did it by developing practicable vessels and leaving land transport in a primitive state. Thus the Greek states were *thalassic*. The Romans, perhaps because by chance they made more areal conquests, created a land system suited to human transport but of limited value for goods. As a result, they maintained their empire as long as troops and governors could move, but it declined rapidly when the communications system was disrupted by the barbarians—a disruption not intended by those invaders, who sought merely to take over Rome. In the process, however, many bands attacked. As each conquered its bit, the overall transportation system on which the empire had been based was disrupted, leaving the state broken in parts and the sum of the parts less than it had been in earlier times.

The decline of the Roman Empire destroyed military-political travel as it had existed and, along with it, most other movements. The Dark Ages were shaded, in transportation terms, because society's atomization made travel unnecessary—save for the one encompassing institution that remained. The Roman Church survived the bear hug of the barbarians, and was dependent on funds gained from the tithing of communicants in the entire Christian West. Thus ties of modest sort were continued throughout the extent of what had been the Roman Empire of the west, with emissaries of the church—oddly, often Syrian and Jewish traders—serving as tithe carriers for the papacy. As western Europe began to emerge from the early medieval political and social atomization, religious orders were at the forefront of a transportation revival. These monks were the first men since Roman times to look toward the facilitation of movement beyond the immediate community in which people lived and to see that good Christian souls would be encouraged and sustained through social intercourse among the residents of the kingdom of faith.

The medieval orders—the *Fratres Pontifices*, the Benedictines, and others—began the work in transportation *innovation*.

THE RETURN OF ENGINEERING AND THE RELIEF OF STRESS

As medieval people began to move about more readily, they did so in response to a psychological objective—the veneration of relics—that was peculiarly medieval. The Catholicism of the time was mystical and characterized by fears and ills, the solution for which was not at all clear. The faithful observed miracles and created sites that became shrines for veneration alongside the burial places of the Apostles. The graves of Church Fathers and leading saints were considered generally beneficial shrines at which to pray for relief from diseases the nature of which were beyond comprehension and to seek to allay the terror of death that seems to have become the mark of medieval Christianity. Such powerful religious forces were the first that could draw people to face the real hazards of travel in these times. It was in great part to overcome the rigors of the pilgrimage and to facilitate the flow of tithes and authority between Rome and the local sees and parishes that the orders of monks took up the improvement of transportation. In doing so, they were adopting a practice that can be summarized here by the notion that there is a fundamental process in the historical geography of transportation that we may designate as the *relief of stress*. In other words, the innovation in transportation comes not where the previously available facilities are least but, rather, where they are likely to be most developed but commonly overtaxed.

In the Middle Ages there existed what economists today call an *infrastructure* of transport, inherited in this case from the

Romans and thereby preserving in stone the engineering skills of those conquerors and administrators. Once the empire collapsed, the physical fabric and the construction skills that produced it wasted—the latter more rapidly. Roman bridges did survive to serve diminished demands; but eventually most fell, as arched structures are likely to do if poorly maintained. A further problem arose from the fact that the mercantile and political geographies of the Middle Ages were quite different from those of the earlier empire: States were smaller, and trade was reoriented to the point that new routes were established and new towns grew up along them. We have already seen that the one area in which medieval people considerably outdistanced the Romans was the technology of harnessing and wagon building, perhaps because Celtic influence was stronger among them. As a result, by the twelfth century land transport came to tax the remaining transport infrastructure, notably at the points of greatest stress, which tended to be the river crossings. At Trier in Germany a Roman bridge remained in service, as others did in a number of places in Italy and a few in France and Spain. But elsewhere, as the lines of movement strengthened with the return of distant connections, ferries and fords had to serve, though generally rather badly. Robbers tended to infest such spots, preying on medieval travelers. High water made both fords and ferries inoperable; in some places, old, rickety bridges were used to extract excessive tolls from traders and pilgrims.

It was in this situation that the *Fratres Pontifices* and other orders undertook the "pious work" of bridge construction and mountain-pass road building. St. Bernard's fame is universal, and many know of St. Bénézet and the bridge he built at Avignon. Other monks who sought with facilities and shelters to encourage movement of people are less well known, although they were numerous and

their works represented the return of professional engineering to Western society. Because the stress points of the Middle Ages were at river crossings, it is the engineering works there that provide us with evidence of this technical renaissance. The Roman roads themselves had survived somewhat better than the Roman bridges; additionally only in the Middle Ages did a substitute for construction by a corps of slaves in the imperial employ have to be devised. That replacement was found in the *corvée*, which had existed in most societies from ancient times. This was the duty of small land holders to furnish labor to the state—later, in the Middle Ages, to their immediate feudal lord—in order to accomplish desirable work from which all were assumed to benefit. In particular, this meant the building and repair of roads, which became a critical matter with the fall of Rome and the system of slavery it used for such labor. Throughout the second half of the first Christian millennium, some feeble efforts were made at road maintenance. Only with the better organization of the High Middle Ages was much accomplished, however, when a specific corvée for road repair came into use in France, England, and other centralizing states. For them, the demonstrable need for an interconnected road system suggested recourse to this traditional labor duty as the agency of provision. There were two main problems. First, the workers had almost no engineering knowledge; thus they often merely scraped the spring mud off the surface of the road to gain firm footing, thereby creating a potential stream course the next time it rained. Second, they clearly worked more earnestly on roads of local rather than long-distance importance, leaving gaps in the national system. Nevertheless, the corvée became the standard source of labor for road building in most Western countries until the beginning of the twentieth century, and it remains nominally in force in some areas even today.

The corvée was, however, no adequate solution to the problem of providing river and mountain crossings: for that, the religious orders had to be created.

ADVANCES IN BRIDGE BUILDING

The efforts at medieval bridge building were most fruitful in two areas where centralizing states found it essential to provide reasonable year-round connections—in France in the west and in the Turkish Empire evolving in the Balkans. It is significant that these were the two areas where the greatest expertise was evolving in vaulted construction, from the Byzantine church base in the east and from the truly innovative Gothic church architecture of France in the west. The latter was particularly important, because—in terms of engineering and the conservation of materials—the Gothic arch and vault were much more daring. Starting in the early twelfth century, the Abbot Suger at St. Denis and other monks worked out a church architecture that could span greater distances and with higher vaults. The purpose was to enlarge and illuminate the church in an era when preaching was replacing ritual alone in church services, but in bridge building the experience of the architectural monks was of equal, if different, value. There the experience with establishing the footings for the tall weight-bearing columns of cathedrals must have contributed to the greatly improved foundations for the abutments and stream piers of bridges. Further, the arched vaults of the medieval bridges were lighter, broader, and generally more daring in engineering than were those of the Romans. The lighter quality, along with improved foundations, meant that bridges could be attempted across wider streams and those with more difficult footing problems.

The renaissance of bridge building in the West seems to have come in southern France, where several outstanding examples survive, giving us a fairly clear idea of the nature of such structures. Apparently one of the earliest of these bridges was that across the river Tarn at Ste. Enimie, with the high-pointed ogival arched bridge across the Lot at Espalion following soon after, in the eleventh or early twelfth century.[3] The Pont St. Esprit twenty miles above Avignon was begun in 1265 and completed in 1307, to be carried on twenty-three arches across the Rhône.

The most famous bridge of the Middle Ages was, however, the one recalled by the children's *chanson*, the bridge at Avignon itself. There is much controversy about the origin and original structure of this bridge. Legend has it that when a total eclipse of the sun was witnessed in the lower Rhône valley on September 14, 1178, the bishop of the severely frightened city of Avignon began to preach to the townspeople collected in the market square. In the course of that sermon, a shepherd, Benoît, interrupted the prelate to say that God had commanded him to build a bridge across the Rhône, the most variable large river in Europe. Driven out of town for his presumptousness, Benoît returned and, on repeating his words, was ordered to display his divine support by carrying a stone too heavy for a man to the bank of the river. When he did so easily, the crowd turned to his support and he was commissioned to build a bridge westward across the Rhône. The completed structure was a wonder of the time. There is some doubt about its precise fabric—Viollet-le-Duc thought it possessed twenty-one arches, others hold for twenty, and all but four have actualy fallen to the seasonal wrath of the river—but there is no question that the task was completed and the Church canonized Benoît as St. Bénézet.

As the remnant shows, this bridge was fairly novel. It possessed cutwaters both before and astern the piers, in contrast to the Roman's bow shields, which Alberti showed were actually far less necessary than those built to protect against the turbulence behind the pier; and its arches seem to have been three-centered rather than semicircular like the Romans'.[4] Multiple centering offers a considerable advantage over the full-centered arch in that the openings can be enlarged with respect to the piers, thus permitting more of the river bed to be free of encumbrances. On the turbulent Rhône this would be crucial.

A medieval bridge that gained fame for its poor rather than its fine fabric was the first stone bridge to be built across the Thames at London. The children's verse notes that London Bridge is falling down, as in fact it did, numerous times. Peter of Colechurch, who constructed the bridge, seems to have had far less understanding of engineering than did Benoît—or perhaps less divine intercession. He built a bridge of poor design, with pointed arches that apparently had no advantage over semicircular ones, poor footings, and an attempt at too great closure of the river by a bridge that was as much a dam as it was a river crossing. As one author notes: "The end result was something for which neither a Gothic architect nor a Roman engineer would have claimed credit. The bridge was a miracle [but only] of asymmetry." All its piers were different in shape and size; most of the nineteen arches were unlike others, with the widest only 34 feet 5 inches and the narrowest no more than 15 feet. Although the river was 936 feet wide at the crossing, the open water between the piers at low tide when the water level dropped below the starlings was only 194 feet, or 20 percent, which explains why boating on the Thames tended to operate in two parts—that above London Bridge and that below—with goods and passengers being transferred across the "portage" at the bridge.[5] All one can say for this structure is that it did last for six centuries, being replaced only in 1831 by the New London Bridge—that structure now

transported to Arizona to span an artificial and Pacific "Thames" built to plan.

At the dawn of the late Middle Ages, bridge building made great strides over both the efforts of the Romans and those of the monks. Some fine specimens of true medieval bridges, such as the Pont Valentré at Cahors in southern France, impress us with their fortifications; but only as learning quickened and mental speculation gained acceptance did great changes occur that caused historians in the last century to apply the term *Renaissance* to the very close of medieval times. During the earlier Middle Ages defense had been a primary consideration in the building of any bridge, so that most had military features, though few perhaps as many as the Pont Valentré. The exigencies of defense required that bridges be constructed so that a span might be destroyed without destroying the whole structure. This meant massive mid-river piers, which in engineering terms were also abutments that would contain the thrust of the arches left standing.

Only when the defense of a town shifted to massive walls built against cannon fire could bridges also evolve. In Florence in 1345 the decision was made to try to build a stone-arch bridge across the Arno—the first attempt to construct a bridge with an arch wider than a semicircle. Instead, a segment of a large circle was carried on piers that not only bore its weight but as well balanced its lateral thrust. The Ponte Vecchio, using segmental arches of 90 feet at the side and 100 feet in the middle, managed to cross the river with only two piers as well as maintaining a much lower rise, which permitted vehicles to cross the bridge. This was in contrast to Venice and its new bridge at the Rialto, built 150 years later, which, though again a segmental arch, as a foot bridge was allowed to rise 20 feet for a span of 88 feet.

It was this segmental arch, or the complex

multicentered arches that came later, that finally permitted fairly light bridging of turbulent streams. The Romans' massive, many-arched bridges across such streams frequently were swept away in floods because those numerous weight-bearing piers so dammed the river. Late-medieval (early Renaissance) engineers—by using the segmental arch that transformed downward bearing to lateral thrust and, in turn, carried that thrust successively across the stream to the abutments on the bank—were able to reduce the number of piers as well as their thickness and obstruction of the river. These bridges with a lower profile also, for the first time, permitted river crossings in flat country to be carried out without massive approaches or bridge slopes too steep for vehicles.

Thus the transportation problem introduced by a stress point—in this case, the river crossing in or at the edge of a city—was first attacked with the existing technology. Ultimately, however, as either the stress remained unrelieved or the technology proved inadequate, experimental work was undertaken to find a better technical solution. The low-rise, segmental arch remained the solution to the bridging problem in cities down to the present. Only in the last generation have continuous-girder and other recent forms made possible the replacement of the segmental arch in city bridges. In the countryside, greater space and the frequent presence of steeper banks of streams have permitted simple semicircular arches—or their modern equivalent, the parabolic arch—to be used. At the hand of Gustave Eiffel these high-rise arches rendered in steel (as at Oporto or in the imcomparable Garabit Viaduct across the Truyère in the Massif Centrale of France) show a wonderful lightness and grace unknown until the advent of continuous girders and prestressed concrete road bridges.

In the late nineteenth century when the great French engineer was working, a new form of stress existed, that of transporting heavy minerals from isolated mountainous areas, which posed a novel problem—the level crossing of deep river valleys in plateau country—for which a classic high arch would serve well. The result was the parabolic arch topped by the girder-supported rail line. The stability of this form was ideal for railroads, as heavy loads could be supported and the pounding of the driving wheels of locomotives endured. In different conditions of stress, the crossing of wide rivers in low country by the increasing rail net, the same need for a reasonably level line existed. As there it was impossible to place the arch below the deck on which the trains operated, the structure was reversed: the arch soared high, but the deck was slung below it as a chord kept only the minimum distance from the surface of the water that would permit passage of river boats or ships.

From this discussion it should be apparent that stress and solution are constantly changing and interacting forces. The high arch has come and gone from the engineer's toolbox because of these varying conditions. The same could be said for other technical solutions. The Greeks used ruts to guide the wheels of vehicles, although the practice seems to have disappeared for over a millennium only to return in the mines of medieval Germany. In the form of the railroad such guideways began to decline with the advent of the automobile. Now, however, problems of energy conservation and population clustering have called the guideway back from retirement; the so-called light railway is fashionable among engineers as a solution to transportation across stress points of the present, those constructions of traffic common to metropolitan areas.

We have, however, gotten ahead of our story in making this general point about the likelihood that innovation will take place geographically at the point where contemporary stress on transportation is at its greatest. Now we should return to the question of why the late Middle Ages witnessed such a rise of transportation to a dominant position in the minds of Western people—that is, those in Europe and later in European settlement and colonial activity overseas.

THE TRANSPORTATION REVOLUTION BEGINNING IN THE FIFTEENTH CENTURY

As the Middle Ages closed in what we have come to call the Renaissance, though the term is far more appropriate to Italy than it is to other parts of Europe, transportation was beginning to change in such fundamental ways that we are justified retrospectively in calling the period a time of *transportation revolution*. We have already seen a number of the elements that accomplished that structural change. Among the facilities for transport, the earliest canal locks were being developed and the bridge for road transport was being built at critical stress points. Wagons were coming into use that were more efficient than any in the past and it seems the suspended passenger wagon that probably began as the Hungarian *kocsi* was being employed by personages of note.[6] Thus, not only were the facilities for transport rapidly being improved, but the technology of transport as well. Many legal impediments to travel and transportation were beginning to be relaxed somewhat at this time. Commercial law was entering as common law, though only in Massachusetts in the seventeenth century was it actually codified.[7] Piepowder courts to deal with strangers, passports to permit them to travel, bookkeeping practices that allowed control of business to be vested elsewhere, and a system of banking to permit trade other than by barter or gold were among the institutional changes that came in this transition from the Middle Ages to modern times. The craving for mobility both encouraged and ultimately paid for the expansion of transportation. The Age of Discovery further supported that expansion by opening to Europeans a knowledge of the world that for the first time was much greater than that of the Arabs or the Chinese. In the three centuries after 1500 the world's coastlines outside the frozen seas of polar regions were charted and made known to all who could read a map, finally destroying the "natural order" to geography that the Greeks had created simply by mental speculation. After the devastation by the plagues of the thirteenth and succeeding centuries, the demographic recovery of European society, particularly in the seventeenth century, provided the human base for the geographical explosion of population from Europe to all habitable continents, three of which were so Europeanized that in cultural and ethnic terms the Western society that was concentrated in western Europe in 1500 had, by 1900, spread to include the Americas and Australia in a permanent way and south and east Asia and southern Africa (though probably in a more ephemeral fashion).

In retrospect it is clear that the dynamism of western Europe, as it recovered from the plagues and as nation-states replaced the chained economies of feudal society, for the first time brought to that area such a demand for improvements in transportation that from 1600 on most of the innovation in transport can be found in the Western society of Europe and its diaspora. The Chinese had canals with locks probably before these Westerners, but they lacked many of the social and political institutions that made the canal a Western facility in modern times. Although horses, wagons, the rigging and navigation of sailing ships, and other components of the technology of transport might first have come from beyond Europe, after Jamestown most development took place in the West, with all the components of present transportation strongly rooted there. To imagine modern society (even in Asia or Africa) without the railroad, the automobile, or the airplane is impossible. Even apparently isolated folk cultures are quite modern in their transportation support, as attested by the weekly shipments of fresh bread from Edmonton to the remote settlement of Sachs Harbour on Banks Island in the Canadian Arctic Archepelago 1,500 route miles to the north.

The Transportation Revolution, as we shall style the three centuries from 1500 to 1800, is distinguishable from earlier and later times by the trends it set in motion rather than by the total transformation of transport and society. Horses, wagons, river navigations, and coastal sailing all existed before the onset of this revolution, but during the three centuries under consideration such trends were established that fundamental structural changes occurred both in facilities and in the technology of transport itself. These meant that humanity could expand its horizon; could expect to move farther and more cheaply than in the past; and could begin to establish social, political, and economic institutions more demanding of mobility than ever before. The Spanish and Portuguese colonial empires began the Europeanization of that newly found world; but even during the three centuries of the Transportation Revolution, France, England, Scotland, Holland, Denmark, and Sweden joined in this political expansion.

Intimately involved in this revolution was the emergence of an economic philosophy, *mercantilism*, that could not grow and be implemented without such structural transformations. Mercantilism was rooted in the broad geographical sweep of trade, for which improved transport was essential. In turn, once transport was improved, a wider range for trade became possible, so that we are now painfully aware that the modern world experiences a nearly global trading system in which the efficient and continuing operation of ships, railroads, and planes determines not merely prosperity but actual survival. The mercantilist era, which corresponds rather well with our three centuries of technical revolution, saw the beginning of trade wars, which were primarily attacks on the moving vehicles of the trade itself. And both World Wars I and II were contests of transport as well as of land armies. Thus the Transportation Revolution is distinguishable not as a fully discrete set of events but instead as the inception of processes that have, in most cases, continued down to the present.

Developments during that revolution allowed the growth of transportation and an increasing dependence on it. New points of stress were created, which in turn required further evolution of facilities and transportation technology. During the half millennuim since the onset of the Transportation Revolution, the creation and relief of stress has been continuous—so much so that we have come to expect an ever-expanding transportation and a continuous effort to improve facilities and technology. Only in the last decade have we begun to question whether that evolution can continue unabated—or, for that matter, whether it should. The philosophical argument concerning the supersonic transport plane has taken on qualities distinct from those that attended the introduction of railroads, automobiles, and the earlier airplanes. Arguments concerning the economic cost of the SST, its impact on human health, and its role in assigning scarce resources to the needs of a minuscule element of society are quite different from Dr. Dionysius Lardner's contemporary concern that the early locomotive's speed would deny sufficient air to the passengers transported.

The era of the Transportation Revolution was also the time of the final determination of the political and economic dominance in most of the Atlantic fringe of Europe. In Roman Gaul what is today Lyon was the administrative capital, with a network of highways radiating therefrom to the military and administrative frontiers of that great province. In the Middle Ages the counts of Paris began to organize a French state, centering militarily on their seat, which by the time of the Transportation Revolution was finally emerging as a political reality. To defend and administer that increasingly powerful French realm, a system of highways centering on Paris had to be formed. Late in the Middle Ages the net of royal routes began to take shape; by the sixteenth century France had become the single most powerful nation, in political and military terms, in Western society. Throughout the *ancien régime*, which corresponded almost exactly with the era of most fundamental transportation transformation, the efforts by the ministries of the Most Christian King were continuous to cement Parisian dominance and defend its security by fortifications on the national frontier—both undertakings that called into being the first national transportation system since the fall of Rome.

It is important to understand the timing of this effort to fix the dominance of particular cities and to secure the national boundaries. It came in western Europe a century or more before the full flower of industrialization because that florescence required the actual contribution of the improved facilities and improved technology that political and military exigencies induced. France as the most centralized and most populous of monarchies was the leader in the creation of a national transportation system, first with the *route royale* but subsequently with the first coherent plan for canal building.

At the time France was actively planning and shaping its national system on land, England was seeking the route to national power on the sea. England was not a very significant maritime power in the Middle Ages, when the Norse and the Italians were far more dominant as well as technically superior. Only in the sixteenth century, as notions of mercantile expansion arose in London and the other ports, did Parliament and the English crown begin to foster a merchant marine, understanding that thence came the basic provenance and support for a naval supremacy. The trade wars with the Dutch during the late sixteenth and the seventeenth century confirmed both the need for a merchant marine and the ultimate political-military weapon it provided. The lesson was well learned by the rather dull-witted British monarchs—so well, in fact, that Britian had no national transportation policy on land until the close of World War I. But the ships of the Red Ensign demonstrated clearly that after the Transportation Revolution it was possible for an active and coherent transport policy at sea both to defend the frontiers of the state and to fix urban dominance at the center. While Paris was becoming Europe's greatest administrative-political city, London grew as its greatest economic center by controlling the most elaborate and extensive trading system. Because it was so much easier and cheaper to extend trade rapidly by sea—nature provided the facilities, so humans had only to improve the transport technology—trade could most easily be nurtured from a port. And London became and remained Europe's greatest port from about 1600 until 1945.

Elsewhere on the Continent the contrast between a national system by land and one by sea can be observed. In Italy and Germany, which remained politically fractionated for over three hundred years after 1500, no national system by either land or sea was possible. The technical superiority of the Hansa and Venetian-Genoan captains and ships was lost in this period; on land, no German or Italian state had enough extent to make much of an impression in the development of land transport. Only Spain, Portugal, and the Low Countries offered much scope for such a development. The Iberian monarchies did show considerable energy and accomplishment at sea, forging trade routes completely around the globe and providing ships to return material riches in a volume never before witnessed. On land they were less skillful, leaving the peninsula rather in a later-medieval state until the nineteenth century.

THE CHRONOLOGY OF TRANSPORTATION MORPHOGENESIS

This consideration of the several expressions of innovative facilities and practices that so transformed Europe's transportation as to allow us to look upon this period, 1500 to 1800, as a true revolution should suggest to us the main components of any discussion of that era. This earliest developments undoubtedly were those that came in wagons, carriages, and coaches, and in the roads over which they operated, as symbolized in the work of late-medieval bridge-building. Next in time came the transformation of waterways that had existed for other purposes—largely drainage of excessive water in the north and relief of seasonal drought in the south—to transportation purposes. Most fundamental to that shift was the development of a practical canal lock that could permit changes in level without the turbulence associated with steep grades in a watercourse.

Once the lock was known, the canal became the first facility and technology used to try to solve the increasing transportation problems engendered by the rise of industry and commerce in western Europe. For most of the time encompassed by the Transportation Revolution, it was the improvement of roads and the provision of canals that engaged the attention Europeans gave to land transit. At sea, contemporaneous efforts sought in an absolute sense to expand the known seas while improving the nature of ships, so as to permit increased speed under sail to make movement over those increasing distances practical. By 1800, or shortly thereafter in the case of the technology of sail, most of the gains that could be won with the traditional technology of transport—the use of draft animals and their vehicles on roads or canals and the dependence on sail for movement about the seas—had reached its ultimate refinement. In nearly two hundred years since the Napoleonic Wars, and the rapid expansion of economic activity thereafter, traditional transport was quickly overtaxed on both land and at sea, though initially more so in the first realm. The result was the beginning of an effort to use *heat* in its various physical expressions as the motive power.

The era that saw the physics of heat employed for tractive effort clearly elevated transportable fuel to a dominant position in facilitating such power. This is as true of the early steam road vehicles, such as Cugnot's artillery tractor in France in the 1770s, as it is of the nuclear-powered ship *Savannah* or the rockets that launch Soviet and U.S. satellites. Each new stage in transportation technology in this era of heat as power has tended to be associated with a new fuel that would make possible a technology previously impracticable. The steam engine being developed in England, France, and the United States at the end of the period of actual revolution in transport was made possible mainly by the successful utilization of coal as a source of heat. This utilization came not from the new discovery of coal, which had been known and narrowly used as a fuel since Classical times, but rather from the production of iron in sufficient strength and quantity to harness and use the physical property of water's expansion with rising temperature. Other fuels could be used, as wood was in America; but in Europe from the beginning, and in

America as the poor quality of wood as boiler fuel was appreciated, coal was the real driving force. As long as coal and steam were the related sources of power, however, it proved difficult to employ them save in heavy vehicles such as steamships or locomotives that required water flotation or iron-rail support for effective working.

Conditions changed with the development of petroleum-derived fuels, first outgrowths of the refining of crude oil to produce "coal oil" for illumination. Two lines of technical development were followed: (1) substituting "coal gas" or "coal oil" itself (kerosene) for coal, thus gaining some weight saving with the more thermally efficient gas or liquid; and (2) using one or several of the other petroleum fractions, naphtha or gasoline in particular, not for the production of simple heat but rather through their nearly instantaneous combustion for the production of an explosive force that might equally be used to drive a piston. The steam automobile depended on the first, whereas the internal combustion engine grew from the second. The greater efficiency of combustion within a chamber soon turned most attention to that technology, although the use of heat itself also was advanced by Parson's development of the steam turbine, which shaped most of the marine engineering from the turn of the century on to World War II.

The vastly improved tractive effort secured from petroleum and the internal-combustion engine returned the attention of Western society to roads, which had been serving only a very local role, much as the Roman system became a local-service, disconnected thing during the earlier Middle Ages. But just as the development of better harness and wagons joined with increasing trade to encourage a resurrection and ultimate improvement of the Roman system, so the automobile, and later the truck, resurrected the prerail European system.

In North America there had been such a limited net of roads before the railroad era that resurrection is hardly the appropriate word to use: here instead it was the creation of a road system de novo, so it is not surprising that the first true system of automobile roads was shaped in the United States in the 1920s. With that system of highways in hand, it was only a short time before motor trucking was introduced to bring the efficiencies of automotive transportation to the movement of freight as well as people and mail. Europe, with its denser net of rails and poorer road system, did not experience this prewar trucking development. It waited until the last twenty years to turn to trucks, which ultimately clogged its marginally adequate roads.

Power and technology joined in different fashion at sea and in the air. Heat was still the source of power; but, as we have seen in ships, it was used mainly for creating steam that could be used either in pistons or in turbines. Only just around the time of World War II was internal combustion, in diesel engines, brought widely to shipping, gaining fuel efficiencies and more compact power plants. That same goal was advanced by the substitution of nuclear reactors to produce heat to generate electricity or to create steam to run turbines, but as yet such fuel is used mainly for naval rather than commercial vessels.

In the air the internal-combustion engine was absolutely the key to heavier-than-air craft. Gasoline-fired engines were lighter than steam plants, which earlier had been applied to gas-filled balloons and airships, so they held out hope for a machine that could actually lift itself off the ground. We know the Wright brothers' success in 1903, but we are less likely to give full attention to the role of technology in determining the introduction of various air services. In the three centuries of the Transportation Revolution it was mostly the improvement of facilities (for the passage of rather traditional vehicles) that changed the shape and access to the economically integrated land realm, although at sea it was mostly technical improvement of shipping that worked the change. In the nearly two hundred years since the close of that revolution, the tables have been reversed: on land, and over it, it has been mostly the improvement of technology of vehicles that has transformed movement, whereas at sea the greatest shifts have been in facilities—the construction of ship canals, the laying out of new ports, and the provision of navigation aids.

For transportation on land, which will be the main concern of this book, it is valid to speak of two basic eras since the considerable improvement of transport began around 1500: the first (1500 to 1800) we have already called the Transportation Revolution; the second (1800 to the present) we may term the Era of Technological Advance. During the Transportation Revolution the efforts were particularly concentrated on the improvement of land-based facilities and inland navigation; in relieving stress within the medieval road system first with the earliest canals; and then, a century later, in undertaking new national projects of road building tied to the nation-state and the cities it elevated to importance (in contrast to the Roman system and the Classical system of cities). Only at sea, where the geographical facilities for transport were naturally provided from the beginning, was the emphasis on transportation technology rather than geographical facility. This situation was reversed during the Era of Technological Advance, when the emphasis fell on vehicular improvement rather than route pioneering with respect to land transport, with emphasis on the route more than the vehicle showing up at sea. If we accept that air transportation was mainly a case of devising a vehicle that could lift itself off the ground and sustain itself in the air, more than creating a new set of geographical facilities, air

transport is a particularly striking case of development typical of the Era of Technological Advance.

RECONSTRUCTION THROUGH TECHNOLOGY

The decades of the Napoleonic Wars in Europe stand as an important divide in the progress of transportation. Before the French Revolution most attention focused on improving *facilities* for fairly traditional media of transport. Great changes occurred, and they were particularly signaled by constructions that can be examined morphologically. After the Napoleonic period development took on a far more technological cast, making a consideration of geographical facilities alone inadequate. During this era we must look at the actual *operating qualities of the vehicles* involved to begin to reconstruct what developers had in mind and how they set about accomplishing their goal. To a considerable degree, save for air transport, the medium of transport already existed by Napoleonic times. Canals, surfaced roads, rail-guided ways, and ocean shipping lanes were well known and used. What has changed is the technology of operation along those routes. Horse and gravity traction were replaced by steam and much later by various turbine and internal-combustion engines. No one, again save in the case of airplanes, has devised a new form of transport until very recently (with the so-called ground-effect vehicles, for which great claims have been made but with which little has been accomplished) so development since the return of peace to Europe and North America in 1815 has been concerned with *vehicular evolution*. Thus, when we attempt to understand that evolution, we must seek to reconstruct the forces that brought change and the subsequent transformations induced by innovations in transport technology.

The one totally new medium has been air transport. Within it, both facilities and technology have had to be shaped during the last eighty years. But most of the conscious acts have focused on the vehicles and their navigation system. There are differences between a level grass field in 1910 and the Dallas–Fort Worth airport in 1980, but not great fundamental structural contrasts. Taking off and landing are influenced more by the application of power or drag than by the surface involved, so even air transport is properly a part of the Era of Technological Advance. Thus, when we attempt to analyze the evolving geographical patterns of air transportation, we must focus mainly on innovation through technology rather than through morphology as was the case in the earlier centuries of the Transportation Revolution.

MEASURES OF RELATIONSHIP

A study of morphology and technology needs measures that can be applied to all forms of transportation in order to allow us to draw analytical contrasts among them. Clearly, all transport moves, so it is in the various qualities of that movement that we find the most evident measures. These qualities again fall basically into the division we have noted with respect to time. There are *measures of the facility itself*—its relationship to terrain, preexisting settlement, resources, goods that move, and the like—and there are *measures of technological capacity* and accomplishment—such as the size of the vehicle, its operating characteristics, its energy consumption, and other aspects of motion.

Two measures of facility stand out as most indicative of the geographical pattern and utility of a transportation route. The first we may call *conformity to terrain*—the degree to which the alignment and grade of the line of transport matches the natural terrain surface over which it must pass. In pioneering routes such as the Oregon Trail, there will be an almost absolute conformity to terrain; in fact, it will be one of the requisites in laying out the trail that it pass over ground usable by whatever vehicle is envisaged for the service. Only as time passes, operating costs mount, and the long-term economic benefits of transforming the natural route become apparent will the degree of conformity tend to decline. In extreme cases such as the recently constructed trans-Alpine routes via the Grand St. Bernard pass or Mont Blanc tunnel, there will be a major transformation of terrain to allow service along the route to be operated more economically. In extreme cases as well, totally new lines of movement may be shaped that cannot operate in the absence of that facility. In June, 1978, a blockage of the Mont Blanc road tunnel led to a queue of trucks more than 50 miles long between east of Aosta and the Italian portal of the tunnel to the west of Courmayeur because no other route across the western Alps could handle trucks with such heavy loads, requiring the drivers to await the reopening of the tunnel.

The second measure of geographical pattern and utility is another *conformity*, that *to preexisting settlement*. Again, as with terrain, the likelihood is that the earliest, most pioneering routes, will conform closely to the location of towns intermediate between more distant large city pairs. Historically, there have been two aspects to conformity to settlement. In the case of Roman roads little effort was made to reflect the location of any but the larger settlements, for which in most cases the Romans had selected the site. To a considerable degree it may be said that the Romans worked out the location of roads and towns at the same time, allowing roads to be direct over great distances and often placing towns at critical stress points on the general line of movement. Both London and Paris in the Roman Period were bridging sites at major rivers that lay across the general direction of movement. It seems probable that the Roman network of roads was actually superimposed on an older, more typical system, which had grown up through the eventual interconnection of short segments of road that initially had simply connected close pairs of villages or other settlements. Just as narrow bricks can make a towering wall, so such short intervillage units can be assembled into a through route over a considerable distance. And, like a brick wall during an earthquake, the small-unit incrementation along a route proves weak and easily interrupted in times of stress. That was why the Romans shaped their own road system, which could be of use in such times of trial. Once the Roman purpose disappeared, however, the tendency was for Europe to revert to the highly conformal pioneering pattern, abandoning the Roman network where it failed to serve fairly local purposes. Pierre Fustier believes that a rather extensive *réseau local* was of necessity shaped during the Middle Ages to care for movements that had not been comprehended by the Romans' use of Gaul.[8] Although the types of vehicles employed will have some bearing on the road itself, to a much more considerable degree that route will change in response to the desired conformity to settlement. The interstate highway system in the United States is thoughtfully and correctly named: what sets it apart from all previous road systems is its long-distance function. And that function makes it far less conformal to settlement than was the previously ruling Federal Aid Primary System shaped in the 1920s.

In either expression of conformity—terrain or settlement—the trend is toward the lessening of degree. This trend is as true within the self-contained history of a medium of transport as to all transport history. The medieval *réseau local* of French roads was as fitted to the landscape as lines drawn on one's skin, but as time passed a network of royal routes was shaped that no

longer hugged the land so intimately. Instead, roads were carried on causeways up the sides of hills in order to reduce the severity of the opposing grade, or cut through the crest to reduce the total climb. With the coming of automobiles, roads required even greater cutting and filling—not because a car cannot climb a steep hill but because it cannot do so swiftly or cheaply. Finally, with motor trucking the hills themselves had to yield, as in the Alps, the Pyrenees, the Vosges, the Rockies, and even the Folded Appalachians, where tunnels were driven through such obstructions—this because drivers would pay to avoid the hill altogether.

In similar fashion, the canal systems that represented the first major improvement on traditional roads were highly conformal, but less so than the medieval highway system had been. During the life of the canal-building era, those waterways became increasingly less conformal to terrain, until in nineteenth-century England Thomas Telford showed what aqueducts and tunnels could accomplish in reducing operating costs, a demonstration carried even farther by the French and Belgians in their later works near Marseille and on the Albert Canal. It seems justified to generalize that *conformity to terrain declines with increasing economic use of the route.*

Adherence to on-line settlement also tends to decline with economic growth. The early rail lines in most places showed a tendency to pick up as many intermediate towns as possible—though, interestingly, not on the first true railroad, the Liverpool and Manchester, which passed directly between those two cities. Little was done until the use of rail transport grew, and congestion and redundant distance became more costly. Then "fast lines" were constructed around congested spots, as in the recently constructed Palmdale Cut-off on the Southern Pacific, or "air-lines" run straight between two large cities. Currently the French are building such a specialized line in the new high-speed route from Paris to Lyon. Because economic support still depends on total loading throughout the entire route, only in the most heavily traveled corridors can the large generator of intermediate traffic be grandly disregarded. For every North Philadelphia bypass there are considerably more Route 128s, Metro Parks, or Watfords, suburban stations at which express trains stop to build up rather than speed by potential traffic. For truly long-distance traffic, there is always the desire to avoid delays and roundabout routing. Yet those two objectives may be in conflict. In the era of cheap energy the bypass came to be favored because time was more highly valued: whether increasing energy costs will lead to more direct routing is still undetermined.

This tendency to seek to avoid intermediate delay shows up graphically in the historical geography of air transportation, which we will examine in some detail later on. For a medium where speed is of the essence, the tendency to create bypasses and great-circle routes is noteworthy. It is actually faster to fly nonstop in a subsonic plane from San Francisco to London than it is to fly to New York and, making the best possible connection, go on to Europe by *Concorde*. In the summer of 1984 the scheduled flying time in a 747 was just over 10 hours San Francisco to London, whereas it was 15 hours for the closest possible connection via New York and the *Concorde*. This fact, along with the virtual certainty that supersonic planes will not be permitted to operate at full speed across U.S. airspace and the abysmal operating economics of the plane, has dampened carriers' interest in the *Concorde*. It lacks the ability to fly nonstop effectively beyond the range of Washington to London. Even with the *Concorde* refueled and operating at 95 percent of the speed of sound (the legal possible limit in the United

States), it is probable that nonstop subsonic flying would be faster to most destinations beyond the effective 3,800-mile range of this plane. From this example it should be clear that conformity to settlement remains an important consideration in the structuring of air transport, as in other media, and that the size and operating characteristics of aircraft with respect to conformity remain important considerations in the purchasing of planes.

A third measure of the facilities of transportation exists in the actual carrying *capacity* of the line. This shows up most directly at points of stress, where capacity may become overtaxed. To care for that load, duplicate facilities are often constructed, in important instances allowing us to substitute morphological information, which is directly observable, for flow information, which is not. In his classic study of U.S. railroads, Edward Ullman prepared a map of facilities in order to gain an understanding of possible flows.[9] Here we shall also occasionally fall back on facilities as a measure of possible movement.

In times past, there was often a strong seasonal influence on transportation. Movement along the earth roads and rivers of the Middle Ages was effectively forfended for extensive periods by high, turbulent water or by mud. In colder regions, ice halted winter navigation, although land transport was often easier on frozen than on ill-drained earth. Even today, transportation in northern Canada is much more extensive in winter than in summer, with a considerable network of so-called winter roads reaching from the frontier of settlement to the Arctic coast and across the Barren Ground from Hudson Bay to the Mackenzie. The question of the all-weather route is one of time more than of geography, since most parts of the world have some naturally available transport route if the right moment can be chosen. But most human acts must come at a particular time; waiting for the naturally auspicious moment may be an insupportable burden. To overcome it, an all-weather route is devised, though often not until considerable economic pressure has built up to justify the cost of lengthening the workable season of the route. In some cases, as with canals in the northern United States, where extension of the working season was nearly impossible, alternative forms of transportation were encouraged. New York state limited railroad building along the route of the Erie Canal and, when such lines were eventually built, levied a toll against tonnage carried by rail, except in the wintertime when the Erie water was frozen.

A more limited measure of facilities concerns their *availability*. Some routes are public because they are natural; a general legal principle holds that their continued use creates a public domain within which access is open to all. Unimproved land has traditionally been treated as common land, although a group may seek to defend it against outsiders for the resources it yields. In Western society, however, nature's route was normally considered to belong to all people as well. In periods of political fragmentation and disintegration, that principle tended to be abridged: mountain passes or narrow river valleys capable of closure were often made sites for exacting tolls simply because such tolls could be enforced. Even as late as the mid-nineteenth century, the Danish kingdom felt free to exact Sound Dues for passage from the North Sea to the Baltic; only American reluctance to submit to this vestige of medieval banditry caused the Danes to begin remitting the dues. After United States protests in 1843 and 1853, the Americans agreed to only a single year's extension in 1856, leading to an international treaty in 1857 that extinguished the toll for 30,476,325 rix-dollars (then about $20 million U.S.).[10] Ultimately almost everywhere at sea the right of free and innocent passage was established, particularly by pressure in

the last century. On land however, the practice was different.

The contrast grew out of the fact that land transport, unlike that at sea, normally required considerable improvement on the natural endowment. The sea may be restless but it is also essentially immutable by human efforts, whereas on land human works require investment of labor and capital that must be repaid. Thus the priciple arose that the cost of works of improvement is reimbursed by those benefiting from their use. This practice is implicit in all land transport, even canals. It may be a simple repayment through tolls, as with the seventeenth-century canals in France and turnpikes in England, or it may be through a charge on the royal or public purse, as with the royal routes of the *ancien régime*. In all cases the investment comes through an expectation of return, either directly or in the rise in the common wealth. If the latter, then access to the route by all is normally assured; if a more particularized benefit seems likely, then a specific user charge is characteristically made. We find this distinction clearly drawn within American cities even today, when general tax levies (by property taxation) are used to maintain residential streets, thus offering to the abutters a connection with everyone who might wish to reach them or whom they might seek to visit, whereas user taxes (gasoline taxes in particular) are used to provide arterial streets and long-distance roads. In extreme cases, where the cost is inordinate and the benefit narrowly available, actual access tolls are charged in recognition of that narrow service.

A fundamental distinction must be drawn between the naturally provided routes—paths through virgin ground, the seas and uncanalized rivers, and the airspace above us—and those that must be built to serve. In the era when roads were little improved on nature and were of mainly local use, the recourse was to a general responsibility for their construction and maintenance through the operation of the corvée. But once direct economic benefit could be perceived to flow from their improvement, a more restricted levy became essential, and the turnpike roads of the seventeenth century were undertaken. The contrasting measure of particular and general benefit emerges again with the development of safety bicycles in the 1870s. Then the numbers of potential users rose, to increase even faster at the turn of the century when automobiles followed in the wake of the wheelmen. Suddenly the popular demand for better roads made it plain that the corvée could no longer provide adequate mileages or surfaces. First recourse was to general tax monies, particularly those levied on property whose owners might benefit from such improvements. California even took the novel step of imposing a so-called road poll tax of $3.00 on all males between 21 and 50, presumably because they would be the prime beneficiaries, since even in California at the turn of the century women were considered ill-suited to solo driving.[11] American states appropriated considerable sums of money, as did most Western countries, but the funds availablable from general taxes were too meager. Even the most adequately served state, Massachusetts, in 1904 had only 46 percent of its road mileage improved (in contrast to 7 percent nationally).[12] Although access to roads was to be public, it was clear that some measure of beneficial interest was needed. Fortunately, the shift to automobiles from horse-drawn vehicles and bicycles offered an opportunity to measure benefit directly, through miles driven. That chance came from the measurement that fuel afforded; the heavier the car, the more it was used, and the farther one drove, the larger the bill at the pump. In 1909 Britain began to levy a petrol tax, and although American states resisted for a time, Oregon

became the pioneer in the imposition of such an indirect user charge when it adopted a gasoline tax in 1919.[13]

The arrival at a user charge for roads simply reflected conclusions that had been drawn earlier with respect to railroads, although there the decision was hidden by the practice of the companies serving as providers both of the routeway and of the vehicles and service operated thereon. That duality of interest was not envisaged at first, as in 1825 the Stockton and Darlington Railway furnished a route initially open to all. It was soon discovered, however, that, because rail-guided ways do not permit easy passing of one vehicle by another, an overall plan for the working of the line is essential, and could best be provided by the rail company's operation of the vehicles on the line. With that conjunction, the user charge for the line is hidden in the transportation charge for the vehicle and its movement. Rail lines have remained essentially unique in this conjunction and in the queuing problems cited.

The canals built between the sixteenth and mid-nineteenth centuries and the turnpikes begun in the seventeenth century had economically controlled access from the beginning, although the boats and coaches on them were run independently of the private or quasi-public organizations building the line. Thus the user charges clearly distinguished between that for facilities and that for transportation. At sea, on natural waterways, and later in the air, the principle of free access to a legally "free good" was traditionally asserted—most forcefully by the private entrepreneurs of transportation who made the American sailing packet the wonder of the oceans and the American river steamboat the harbinger of powered navigation in the first half of the nineteenth century.

This extension of the general notion of

space as a free good to roads and canal-izations of rivers has confused the econo-mics of transportation and created problems for other transport media. All sorts of social benefits were assigned to the construction of roads such that general tax monies were used, and continue to be employed, in their construction. To the extent that there is general benefit from treating roads as a free good, this is no doubt supportable. But roads often become an intergral part of profit mak-ing by the operators of vehicles—notably buses and trucks—that are able to compete rather unfairly with a form of transport, the railroad, that in North America still stands as the private provider of the line as well as of the vehicle. The free-good quality also at-taches to inland navigation in many coun-tries, the United States and Canada among them, and to the use of airspace. If water-ways were furnished complete by nature and airspace required no control or navigation aids, then treating each as a free good would place all on equal footing; but such is not the case. Locks and dredging of river courses cost large sums of money, and air navigation facilities are extremely costly. Yet Canada is the only important nation charg-ing for the use of airspace, as distinct from airports, so that a nonstop flight from San Francisco to London must pay for passing through Canadian airspace, though never landing there. Otherwise, airlines and barge lines on canalized rivers in general operate without user charges for their route. And even though buses and trucks pay user charges, it is demonstrable that these are heavily subsidized by ordinary car drivers' contributions to the total cost of building and maintaining the route. In this context it is logical to argue, as some are beginning to do, that the only way to find the competitive contribution of various media of transport is for the governments to provide the route as a partially free good to rail-car operating

companies—just as they do for buses, trucks, barges, airplanes, and ships using nationally provided navigation aids to enter and leave ports or navigate along a country's coast.

In such terms the measurement of access—or, more particularly, of differences in access—becomes a critical analytical tool in the historical geography of transporta-tion.

RELATIONSHIP OF ROUTE AND TECHNOLOGICAL ADVANCE

Facilities of transportation clearly exist to provide a route for movement. Such move-ment is an attribute of virtually all organ-isms, so what we are considering is not those natural facilities—the original surface of the land or sea or the three-dimensional volume of air or water—but those facilities that humans have shaped from the primal el-ements. The degree of technological advance involved in such transformations is far sur-passed by the technological change neces-sary in the provision of vehicles to use the facilities. Thus it is arbitrary to restrict the term *transportation technology* to the things that move. Nevertheless, I believe that re-striction is justified on two grounds: first, that *vehicular technology* is an awkward term, and, second, that since the beginning of the nineteenth century most technical innova-tion has actually come in the vehicle, with only a derivative shift in the route facility as a consequence of that development.

This sort of devolution of technology from the vehicle to the route is true even in the case of railroad development, wherein we discover that the first efforts to use steam for locomotion—those of Cugnot, Oliver Evans, William Murdock, and Richard Trevithick, all in the eighteenth century—were for road-based vehicles. Only because of the low mechanical efficiency of these engines—

their weight was excessive in relation to their tractive effort—was resort made to a railroad on which the heavier weights could be borne. Granting that the technology of the railroad combined a specialized supporting pavement and a guideway (which came to influence the development of the medium), still it was the vehicular technology that had really brought the steam railroad into existence. In that advent we observe many changes from the older route-based technology of the tramroad or plateway, very much creatures of the previous era of route—rather than vehicular—innovation. Medieval wagons could operate on the tramroads, but hardly on the earliest steam railroads.

To complete this dichotomous analysis, we may look at the recent development of ground-effect vehicles, or Hovercraft. These lumbering giants represent an oddly anachronistic contribution to technical advance. Specifically, the Hovercraft represents the ultimate abnegation of the Transportation Revolution, with its great emphasis on the provision of geographical facilities for movement. The ground-effect vehicle requires no prepared way; in fact, it is likely to destroy anything but the most sturdily constructed way, as attested by the constant efforts necessary to restore the surface disrupted by the high-velocity air cushion on which the giant rides. In truth, the Hovercraft is logically a pioneering vehicle, to be used before developed routes are available, or beyond the frontier where they have not yet been built. Strangely, however, the place these brutal machines have been employed is in crossing the most developed waterway in the world, the narrow seas between Britain and the Continent. There is obvious appeal in finally divorcing the vehicle from the route—taking the Era of Technological Advance to its ultimate—but like most extreme positions this is more abstractly than practically valid. Speed on water is more comfortable and cheaper in a hydrofoil vehi-

cle, and the relatively small cost of docks can easily be borne in any developed service. The engineering logic of the ground-effect vehicle is not matched by any economic or geographical logic in its present employment. Twenty years of promotional activity has failed to convince most people that the Transportation Revolution did not predate the Era of Technological Advance considered here. Thus the use of Hovercraft has been restricted to an odd chauvinist pattern.

MEASURES OF TRANSPORTATION

To appraise the contribution of the various media and the vehicles characteristic of various times, we need simple measures of transportation character and contribution, measures that permit the comparison of one form with another and one period with its predecessors and successors. Such measures may seem simplistic, but they assess relationships that are important, though largely uncompared.

Unit of Service

The first measure of vehicular character is a simple one of size. Let us call it *unit of service* because our interest in vehicles is not that of the engineer but rather of the observer of what transportation does for people. The units of service vary greatly, from a person's back to supertankers carrying hundreds of thousands of tons. Units vary because technology advances but also because jobs differ. A jeweler's pocket can carry his wares but hardly those of Exxon. Thus technological advance should not rule out the use of past forms of transport possessed of particular characteristics, such as a particular unit of service. Any developed nation will need many forms, not all of them very advanced. There is a constant doubling back in transportation development, some of which grows out of human desires rather than economic or engineering efficiency. A case in point is the passenger car, which in the abstract is not an efficient way to move people about; but it may induce many desirable social effects that engineering and economic efficiency tend to destroy. There is a sound social case that can be made for the American suburb, a good economic argument for the American supermarket, and a solid psychological justification for the mobility of American employment of men *and* of women: all these benefits would be impossible without the small unit of service offered by the American car. We may not be able to continue its use, but we should not deny its virtues, particularly if we must plan for a change that will tend to deny those virtues to us and for which we must make compensating efforts.

Frequency of Service

The unit of service tends to play a major role in shaping a second determinative characteristic of transportation more than of its vehicles—the *frequency of service*. It is a truism of transportation that the ideal form would furnish us with service the instant we realized we desired it. That immediacy of satisfaction is innate to human beings because our first transport was on our own two feet, which patently we could move at will. For millennia people could physically command their available movement at any time. So mobile, in fact, were humans that the elaborate structures of slavery and feudalism were erected to keep persons from moving. Since the manumission of those persons during the centuries of the Transportation Revolution (for feudalism) and the Era of Technological Advance (for black slavery) it has indeed been hard to keep people "down on the farm," or for that matter in one country rather than another.

From a utilitarian viewpoint, probably nothing is as important as frequency of service, given the facts of human impatience and the desire for mobility. It is the almost infinite frequency of private automobile travel that has such strong appeal. With a well-nigh ubiquitoius road net, such as exists in most developed Western countries, the near-infinite frequency of car travel means that for the first time human beings have at their call a form of powered transport with virtually all the advantages of pedestrian movement—infinite access and perpetual availability—and none of the required effort. Furthermore, excellent road systems render the speed of travel equal to that of all but the most specialized transport systems, the sort that only a few markets can support. High-speed rail and air services of great frequency are so unusual that only a minute number of transportation needs can be met with them. Only in the rarest utopia could these rapid alternatives to car travel represent a *geographically* acceptable replacement for that private unit of service with near-infinite frequency. The fact that Boston to Washington, London to Bristol, Tokyo to Osaka, and Paris to Lyon may be able to have high-speed rail services should not be thought in any way to demonstrate that most regions (even of wealthy Western countries) will have such service on a frequency sufficient to compete in actual service with the car. We may have to accept a lower level of service but we should not delude ourselves that "less is more," or claim that such represents better service of human needs.

Distance Decay

Even with manumission, certain geographical restraints remained. During the Middle Ages those restraints were unappreciated because the geographical fixity of serfdom held families to a very localized area. The result was the so-called natural economy of the manor and the elaborately parceled trading system that the German geographer Walter Christaller denominated the "central-place system."[14] With the granting of the right to mobility, which came in western Europe and England by the sixteenth century— though only in the early nineteenth century in Bavaria—people began to realize that space is itself a restraint on movement. Once persons could not reach the edge of their permitted realm in a morning's walk, time became a constraining factor in transportation.

With freedom to move, persons sought to move increasing distances. Vehicular transport ultimately had to be adopted, and with that acceptance arose the question of timing. A person can walk whenever the spirit moves, but even a wagon cannot. As units of service increased in size—the canal barge, the coach, the steam train, and onward—the tendency was for frequency of service to decline, although this was not a single-direction affair. If trade grew rapidly, frequency probably went up as well. Still, a problem existed; it is worth while to note that when the American transcontinental railroad opened in 1869 it was soon found that one passenger train in each direction each week would serve, leaving daily service to so-called mixed trains that were mostly freight.

Speed

Part of that secular improvement in transportation service has come in *speed of movement*, which stands as another measure of transportation effect. Again, the basal level is that of the sturdy walker, say some 4 miles an hour over open surface. Such a level was not improved on at first by the use of either wagons or canal barges, each of which moved at about the same rate as the pedestrian. In fact, only late in the Transportation Revolution was much movement faster than on foot. When the Pilgrims sailed to Ply-

mouth, they made the trip at an average speed of under 2 miles an hour, covering the 3,400 statute miles in 66 days. In doing so, of course, they sailed at a somewhat higher speed, 6 to 7 knots when the wind was fresh; but between tacking and becalming their actual progress was only about 50 miles per day,[15] a distance a sturdy walker could have covered had there been land between Cape Cod and Land's End.

By the eighteenth century efforts were underway to improve the basal speed of travel. The stagecoach operating over constructed roads steadily improved the speed of land travel. From taking 4 days to cover the 200 miles from London to York (about the walker's speed) in 1754, the journey was shortened to 36 hours in 1776 (5.5 mph), to 31 in 1796 (6.5 mph), and ultimately to 20 hours (10 mph) as railroads came into operation.[16] During this same period sailing speeds began to increase with better designed hulls and better sails. This improvement came first on American ships, which began after 1783 to compete very successfully with the former monopolists who operated British shipping. From the 6 to 7 knots of the *Mayflower,* speeds increased slowly until the early decades of the nineteenth century. Then fast sailing earned a high premium, so ships were built to secure it. The ultimate for sail came in the North Atlantic with the *Lightning* of 1854 which in 24 hours covered 436 miles, or a speed of 18.5 knots, a record never exceeded and one worthy of most modern freighters. Two years later the *James Baines* made a 420-mile day and in doing so was clocked at a speed of 21 knots, a figure unmatched by more than a select few powered liners.[17]

The division between the period of the Transportation Revolution and the Era of Technological Advance is well borne out in the matter of speed. With the exception of stagecoaches a few decades earlier, few vehicles plying the roads or waters before the end of the eighteenth century moved at speeds very much greater than that of a fast walker. At sea speed was increasing, but the circuity of most navigations and the calm periods reduced overall journeys to a timing similar to that still found on land. But the vast technological effort at improving land vehicles between about 1780 and 1830 worked a great change in speed. Even the early railroads had trains that could go faster than any vehicle before their time. At the Rainhill trials in 1829, the Liverpool and Manchester Railway sought to find out if locomotive engines were capable of drawing trains consistently and at a reasonable speed. It seems that the *Rocket*, Stephenson's entry in the contest, won, "her speed being frequently 18, and occasionally, upwards of 20 miles an hour."[18] Others report even one set of the trials when "Its speed varried at different parts of the journey: its swiftest motion being rather above twenty-nine miles an hour; and its slowest pace about eleven miles and a-half an hour."[19] Certainly by the end of the first decade of rail travel the faster trains were operating at around 30 miles an hour. At the same time efforts were being made to operate steam-powered "locomotives" over the better roads that connected closely adjacent towns possessed of important ties. In 1831 Gurney put such a locomotive carriage in service between Gloucester and Cheltenham. Ogle soon thereafter fielded a steam carriage that was reported in a parliamentary enquiry to have sped "between thirty-two and thirty-five miles an hour; that it has attained sixteen and a-half miles an hour on a slope rising one in six; that thirty-six persons have been in one carriage; and that it has drawn five times its own weight at from five to six miles an hour."[20]

The Era of Technological Advance so emphasized speed that we may begin to distinguish between various forms of transit on this basis. Finally, travelers had a choice.

The canal boat operated best at about 2 miles an hour, and was thought in the first half of the nineteenth century to be limited to such speeds, although progress up to twice that figure could be accomplished, but only with massive increases in the needed tractive effort and in bank erosion from the greater wash of the faster boats. Because of such speed constraints the canal boat had never been the match for stagecoaches operating over good roads. And canal barges were virtually abandoned as passenger vehicles by the late 1830s, when railroads began to provide relatively cheap mass transportation. As the network of rail lines spread, that service also cut badly into the coaching runs. The victory of the steam train over road transport thus came from two qualities it possessed: it could carry people and goods faster than any other then available medium, and it could carry them at lower cost than any other land transport.

This victory, though it lasted for just about a century, was a limited one. By 1930 the airplane was beginning to outstrip the train for speed, something it could hardly do in its own infancy. As the earlier planes operated at speeds no greater than those already attained by the fastest train runs, the original air services tended to be located where water or mountains intervened between two important cities in a route of heavy travel. There the detachment of the plane from surface conditions, and necessary transshipment, gave it an operating advantage it could not earn from speed itself. Only when the speed of planes crept significantly ahead of the great expresses, as it did with the new flying machines introduced in the late 1920s, was air competition of any significance. Ultimately such speed won, but again only when the increasing scale of air travel allowed a lowering of fares to be competitive with those by rail. Thus, for the first-class trade air travel began to compete in the 1930s; but only in the late 1950s and early

1960s, with the introduction of more cheaply operated jets, did the masses begin to move by air. It seems that speed is a desirable attribute of transportation, and one that serves to draw sharp contrasts among media, but it is often far from a controlling measure.

Stage

Fairly directly related to speed is a measure that is not readily apparent to the traveler, though it influences the journey considerably. This quality is properly called the *stage* of such a journey, a term that seems to have entered the language in the seventeenth century, at the beginning of road improvement. Stages are the distance (and indirectly time) intervals between necessary stops. Originally this meant changing horses (or waiting overnight while they rested), an intrinsic need for the operation of extended services. Stagecoaches are an obvious example introduced with the relatively fast *and* continuous running of those vehicles in the eighteenth century.

Sailing ships, free of fuel needs, had stages determined only by needs for water, food, and possibly wood for cooking. But generally sailing could be carried on continuously between very distant ports. With the arrival of the steam railroad, however, stage reentered with a vengence. The early locomotives were mechanically so inefficient that fuel and water had to be restocked very frequently, a fact that made numerous way stops no real impediment to speed. The same was true for the earliest steamboats, which of necessity had to operate on rivers or short coastal reaches. On the Ohio and Mississippi, for example, the earliest boats simply tied up to the bank, where woodcutters, constantly at work on the gallery forest, loaded very green wood on deck in large quantities. The inefficiency of such a fuel joined with that of the huge, slow-rotating, low-pressure steam engines to make the stages of steamboat travel too short for crossing any great body of water.

Ultimately improvements in fuel and engine efficiency, with the substitution of dry coal and higher-pressure engines, meant that a longer stage (and thereby a broader water) could be crossed. But only when considerable technical advances in steam engines had taken place, around the late 1830s, were the services that had begun on rivers in the first decade of the nineteenth century extended to trans-Atlantic passage. Even then it was many years before the efficiency and stage length of marine steamboating was sufficient for wide use in direct navigation to India, China, and Australia, leaving those markets for at least another generation to the sailing captains. Thus the last epoch of sail was in this trade, with sail ruling in immigrant passenger service well through the last century and in the wheat trade well beyond. In fact, the last sailing ships in the wheat trade disappeared only with the outbreak of World War II.

These sailing ships had to be huge. The *Great Republic*, launched for the Australia trade at Boston in 1853, was the largest wooden ship ever built, 335 feet long with four masts.[21] Iron and steel sailers were its successors. The five-masted barque *France*, 430 feet long with a 55-foot beam, was the largest sailing ship ever built at its launch in 1913 and was never exceeded in size. "The growth in size at the end of the nineteenth century was accompanied by a reduction in relative sail area and by a demand for cargo-carrying capacity and economical working rather than extreme speed."[22] This survival well into recent decades of the traditional ship, which had been sailing in one form or another for six thousand years, came from a cheapness of operation that also permitted extremely long stages impossible in any other types of ship before the nuclear-

The Martin flying-boat M-130. *Source*: Pan American World Airways photo.

powered *Savannah* launched in 1959, which was built to operate 1,230 days without refueling.[23]

Stage came to be even more critical in the development of commercial aircraft. If we take the Wrights' first successful flight, on December 17, 1903, with a "stage" of 120 feet, as the beginning, improvements came quickly. By late 1905 they had flown 24.25 miles, and by late 1909 Henri Farman had flown 144.2 miles at Mourmelon in France.[24] Still, these were experimental, noncommercial flights, which show the state of the art but not its utility. By the close of World War I planes were flying between London and Paris, Berlin and Weimar, and other similar distances. Progress was slow. By the early 1930s the possible range of commercial aircraft had risen to about 500 miles, and even the striking advances made with the introduction of the DC-3 to commercial service in 1936 did not improve on that figure.[25] In fact, it was only the Boeing planes being constructed at this time that showed much improvement in stage, a fact that delayed trans-Atlantic service until well after the inauguration of that across the Pacific because Britain, with no longer-stage aircraft, refused Americans the landing rights in Newfoundland that were crucial for such service. Gibbs-Smith notes wryly that "England kept to a very conservative tradition in biplanes in her air transport during most of this period, and Imperial Airways seems to have adopted the slogan 'slow but sure'."[26] As he generously notes, "it was in the United States that the modern airliner was born, and many of the basic features arrived at in the first years of design and operation are still in force today."[27] This is true particularly in the concern for stage length.

In the latter half of the 1930s stage length became a critical concern in U.S. commercial aviation because transcontinental service in the United States was the first mass long-distance air market. As developed by the DC-3, this service required at least three and usually four intermediate stops. To overcome that problem, U.S. airline companies sought a plane with longer stages, which was found first in the DC-4 (introduced to the military in 1942) and the Lockheed *Constellation* (1943). These were the first land-based planes that could fly across the Atlantic as well as across the United States with one stop. The result was that once the war was over, North Atlantic service was introduced with these land-based planes, although they required several intermediate stops between London and New York. This was particularly true of the DC-4, which by 1945 had had its stage lengthened to about 1,850 miles (400 miles less than that of the *Constellation*).

A plane capable of nonstop operation across the United States came in 1947 with the DC-6, capable of a stage of 3,000 miles, still only partially a transcontinental plane. That goal was ultimately reached in 1953 with the introduction to service of the DC-7. Now the stage length was adequate for all-weather transcontinental service, but still not for trans-Atlantic flights. Such capability was found finally in the DC-7C and the *Superconstellation*, both introduced in the mid-1950s. With these planes most ocean routes could be crossed nonstop, with only

the longest routes requiring a single refueling.[28]

When jet planes were introduced, their speed seemed to indicate that they should be used for such long-haul service. Thus the first successful jet, the Boeing 707, was given a long stage length, 3,300 miles, and operating characteristics related to it. The result was an aircraft inefficient for shorter hauls, which nevertheless soon began to be served by these jets. The need for a plane with short-haul characteristics led to the development of the 727 (2,600 miles), followed by the shorter-haul 737 (1,600 miles). Thus the recent differentiation among aircraft has been based on two characteristics, modular stage length and passenger capacity, with stage just as important as capacity. As we examine the various media that have been used in various periods of transportation history, such a consideration of modular stage length for each will help us to understand the reasoning that lay behind innovations in transport over the years.

Competence

Another measure of a transportation vehicle is its ability to carry particular loads, something we might term its *competence*. To use an extreme example, when society had to depend on the porterage of human backs and mules' packs, only relatively small units of freight might be sent over land. Anything larger had to be carried by ship, a fact that leads us to surmise that the great monoliths in Egypt and other ancient societies must have been moved along rivers and then tediously warped up ramps by dozens or hundreds of individual hands. Land transport was so exceptional as to become possible only for items of great religious significance. Even in the nineteenth century when Western society became intrigued by Egyptian obelisks, it was a major undertaking to move them to Paris (1831), London (1877), and New York (1879). Even more difficult had been the transport of the tallest of all of these by the Emperor Constantine, who had it erected in Rome's Circus Maximus, to be reerected in 1552 at the order of Pope Sixtus V in what ultimately became St. Peter's Square. These movements of obelisks, as well as the sarcens of Stonehenge, the great figures on Easter Island, and other monoliths, demonstrate that societies have the ability to provide high competence in transport for unusual items and journeys. But for most of those times there was a modular upper limit of what can be moved economically.

That limit has grown fairly continuously since the beginning of the Transportation Revolution, and certainly the power exists to enlarge it even today. Unfortunately, a normal control is exerted by what is termed the *loading gauge* on a railroad—that is, the outside dimensions of the vehicle or load that may be passed along a particular right of way. Even on modern highways there is a fairly effective loading gauge, given particularly by the modular height of overpasses, set in the American Interstate Highway system at about 17 feet; the width of those overpasses, up to four 12-foot lanes in some but not all cases; and the nature of access roads and permitted interruptions of traffic flow. Anything larger can only move by water, where the ultimate load is almost unlimited, as the movement of Texas Towers for offshore oil drilling demonstrates. Still, for general purposes limits of load tend to determine not merely the nature of the ultimate individual load but also, to a lesser degree, the cost of transportation. Much as the railroad brought exceptional advantages in freight transportation, it had a lower competence than the canal barge with which it initially competed. The result was a much greater time utility for the freight car but a higher line cost for moving freight over distance. Similarly we find inland navigation repeatedly proposed as a cheaper way of transporting goods as well as a way to handle vast quantities of goods, which might overtax the individual and collective competence of railroads.

Orientation of Service

This contrast between rail and inland navigation lines serves to introduce still another aspect of comparison among the various media of transportation—the orientation of the particular form. The earliest and most primitive forms tend to be rather undifferentiated; people could carry loads as well as move themselves about. Horses were perhaps more person- than goods-carriers in Roman times; but during the Middle Ages, with better harness, the horse became the worker's as well as the aristocrat's steed. As we have seen, canals were virtually always freight-oriented, whereas railroads were ambivalent; airlines for many years served largely passengers, although their earliest commercial use tended to be for mail transport. Orientations can change, but the initial ones tend to be geographically compelling. Because air service in its formative years was mainly for passengers, airports were set up to serve the needs of individual travelers. As air freight came into greater use, it was discovered that certain kinds of goods handling—notably in wholesale trade—had to move from traditional freight-oriented locations near railroad sidings in the central city to proximity to airports.[29] Increasingly today certain industries and wholesaling activities have had to be relocated to respond to the reorientation of air travel. Similar relocations in the early railroad era did not grow out of a reorientation of a single medium, but stemmed from the substitution of a new form, with its own particular geographical facilities, for an older form with different facilities. In recent years we have witnessed the effect of a reorientation in ocean shipping, which has seen the almost complete departure of passenger service save for a few tourist-oriented cruise operations. The great passenger docks are gone from Le Havre, Southampton, London, New York, and San Francisco. The few cruise facilities that exist are as likely to be in Port Everglades, Florida, as in the traditional liner ports. Large port cities no longer cater much to people, only to goods. Even in goods transport, the wide adoption of container cargo handling has greatly reduced the number of freighters that carry any passengers or that dock in traditional port areas such as the London docks, those on the Hudson in New York, or those in San Francisco—each with its cramped quarters and crowded street access.

Financial and Energy Cost

A final measure of all forms of transportation, for comparative purposes, is actual operating cost in terms of both money and energy. The greatest single force for innovation and transformation in transportation has always been that of lowering the money cost of movement, either by removing the points of greatest stress on previously existing transportation or by encouraging an increase in the capacity of the route such that economies of scale will lower unit costs and permit a larger market to be tapped. Commonly, both work together to encourage change. To prompt the investment of capital necessary for the construction of major works, both an impediment to a previously substantial movement and a developable further market are necessary.

As we shall see, the nineteenth-century governments of the United States and Canada were too impatient to gain physical access to the developable parts of their countries to wait for market forces to provide transportation through private investment. Transcontinental railroads at first, and western and northern railroads later on, might not be potentially profitable for some years after completion; but the U.S. and Canadian governments couldn't wait. First one and then subsequent "frontier lines" were financially encouraged by the governments. In the United States four transcontinental railroads (out of seven) were built with substantial government subsidies. In Canada all three were so subsidized. By the time of World War I it became clear that Canada could not support three transcontinentals, so two reverted, through bankruptcy, to the control of the federal government, which made essentially one out of the last two, creating no more than two effective systems for the country.

THE ORGANIZATION OF THE STORY

The fundamental problem in describing and analyzing the historical geography of transportation since the revolution of that activity at the onset of the sixteenth century lies in the fact that human beings have gained command of an increasingly diverse set of transportation systems. Where in the time of Columbus most people spent their lives walking and carrying what goods they consumed, few of us do either of those things in a continuous or even a common fashion; instead, within a single day we may call to our use planes, trains, automobiles, and even ferries. Virtually all of us would find our lives unacceptably localized if we were able to use only foot transport. Never would we appear able to capture the horizon whose mysteries constantly intrigue us.

The increasing complexity of transportation is nothing new; people and animals as beasts of burden began to win some relief in the sixteenth century, when canals were built to extend nature's waterways and improve on them by reducing or obliterating the often strong currents that rivers interposed against upstream journeys. Thus in chronological terms we must always consider at least two media of transport for each period. This might seem to suggest a chronological division of this book into sections on the transportation of early modern times, of the Industrial Revolution, of the era of American expansion in the nineteenth century, and so on. But the strong role of technology, evolving seamlessly often over long periods of time, argues against such a structure. There is much to be said for considering canal building and navigation en bloc covering a period from the time of Leonardo to that of Thomas Telford and De Witt Clinton, or for examining the railroad from its primitive roots in medieval Germany to France's new high-speed T.G.V. line from Paris to Lyon. But this consideration of individual media of transportation could mask a desirable awareness of the succession of innovation, with subsequent competitive substitutions of different media, in the evolution of transportation. The reason for the rise of a competitor—or for evolution within an existing medium, for that matter—is important in our analysis. We seek to understand the geographical basis of transportation development and, in turn, the way that activity shapes our successive human geographies. Only by handling both time and technology, more or less in parallel, can we gain analytical insight.

Fortunately, there is a rough chronological progression in the introduction of the various media. We have already considered the nature of transportation up to the close of the Middle Ages, and the slower and more modest changes before 1500. From that watershed date we may consider forms of transport largely in terms of a chronology of inceptive adoption. The sixteenth century saw the introduction of the canal, with the height of technology represented by the pound lock, as the main evolutionary force in both human mobility and geography. For a full three centuries canals remained the most advanced form of transportation, the one to be built wherever the money was available. For the most part road-building was regarded as a cheap alternative where the canal was physically or financially impracticable.

In the end, however, economic life could not be constrained by such a simple dichotomy between the high technology and the ancient one. There were places where the water demands of canals could not be met or the high cost of construction could not be borne, yet where something better than roads was needed. To meet that demand, the railed-road was developed. As early as the fifteenth century an initial form of railed-roads were built, but only with the development of steam traction did the potential flexibility and expansibility of the railroad make of it the high technology of the time. This supersession was particularly encouraged because steam propulsion on canals is made difficult by the speed restraints those narrow waterways force on steam navigators. From 1825 on, the steam railroad's wonderful qualities—potential ubiquity, construction costs cheaper than those for canals, greater independence of terrain, and nearly limitless expansibility to meet a growing market's demands—severely slowed further construction of canals.

The staged development of transportation suggested by this example continued during the last century and a half. Initially railroads were a long-distance (that is, largely rural) carrier, but the spatial spread of cities necessitated a serious effort to apply rail technology to the urban area. By the late nineteenth century the effort bore fruit, allowing cities to make startling extensions of their area and thus shaping one of the fundamental revolutions in human geography. If for no other reason, that revolution forces us to consider in a coherent and chronological manner the introduction of mechanical transport to the cities of developed countries. Although general railroad development continued, it was urban railroading that represented both the advanced technology of its time and the most geographically evolutionary force. Thus, after a full discussion of long-distance rail transportation—one chapter concerned with the evolution of British rail technology and its spread in Europe, and a second chapter given over to the origin of American rail technology and its geographical underpinnings—we turn in chapter 5 to this consideration of the urban transport problem and its modern solution.

Contemporaneous with the various aspects of this rail era (1825–1925) was the application of steam power to ocean navigation. After sketching the medieval changes in navigation, with the consequent Age of Discovery and Age of Mercantilism, the evolution of the geography of ocean shipping is considered from the onset of increasingly fast, reliable, and frequent voyages first under the ultimate technology of sail (as developed particularly in New England), and then using the evolving technology of steam as came in the merchant marine of the northwest European countries during the last century and a half. Chapter 6 presents this tale, which runs on sea alongside the development of rail on land.

The constraints on steam-powered transport, particularly at the interface where transshipment was required, led to the earliest air services. Once originated in the 1920s, those air transport undertakings sought to enter competitively in a true race with trains and steamships beyond the narrow waters that became the site of the earliest air hops. As technology was advanced—most strikingly in the United States after the late 1920s—flying services became well established before World War II and in-

creasingly dominant in long-distance travel after 1945. Their evolution down to the present is the subject of chapter 7.

The one form of transport that does not fit easily in this timed sequence (from the medieval canal to the most modern jet plane) is transport by road, because roads have always been the backstay of local travel, and thus are ever present in the total transportation picture. That supporting role has changed in recent times; starting with the development of integrated highways in the 1920s, the substitution of automotive for rail transport became an actuality such that the period after World War II has been one of the internal-combustion engine, and later the turbine, calling forth the construction of great airports and a specialized system of long-distance, free-flowing highways. Outside of western Europe and Japan, the advanced nations have tended to abandon technical innovation on railroads and to concentrate such activities in the automotive and aviation spheres. Road transportation thus has been ever present, though often stagnant and ancillary. The periods of technical, and thereby geographical, innovation have been quite separated in time. In the sixteenth and early seventeenth centuries western Europe witnessed efforts at the development of long-distance road systems—the turnpikes of England and the National Routes of France. These are considered in a vignette between chapter 2 and chapter 3 in order to place this highway consideration in its appropriate time location. Again, in nineteenth-century North America the road was used as a pioneering device—a story presented in a vignette between the fourth and fifth chapters. Finally, in modern times the adoption of automotive transport has further transformed the highways on which those vehicles operate and the *geographical impact* of road transportation. This matter is presented in a transitional section between chapter 6 on urban transportation and chapter 7 on air transport. In the final chapter the shared processes of transportation evolution are noted and their interaction assessed, to emphasize the complexity of human efforts and instruments used to capture the horizon during the last five hundred years.

NOTES

1. E. M. Jope, "Vehicles and Harness," in Singer, Holmyard, Hall, and Williams, eds., *A History of Technology,* vol. 2 (New York: Oxford University Press, 1958), p. 538
2. Ibid., p. 540.
3. Joseph Gies, *Bridges and Men* (New York: Grosset & Dunlop, 1963), p. 32.
4. David Steinman calls these "three-centered arches" [*Bridges and Their Builders* (New York: Dover Publications, 1957), p. 59]. L. Sprague Camp terms them "probably of the semicircular type" [*The Ancient Engineers* (Cambridge, Mass.: MIT Press, 1970), p. 343].
5. Gies, op. cit., p. 40.
6. László Tarr in the *History of the Carriage* (Budapest: Corvina Press, 1969), p. 185, tells that "although the earliest written reference to *kocsi* in the Hungarian sense can be traced as far back as the end of the Middle Ages—most of the important data regarding the development of this vehicle date from the beginning of modern times."
7. Lawrence M. Friedman, *A History of American Law* (New York: Simon and Schuster, 1972), p. 69.
8. Pierre Fustier, *La Route: Voies Antiques, Chemins Anciens, Chaussées Modernes* (Paris: Ed. A. et J. Picard, 1968), p. 154.
9. Edward L. Ullman, "The Railroad Pattern of the United States," *Geographical Review* 39 (1949): 242–256.
10. "The Sound," *Encyclopaedia Britannica*, 11th ed. (New York: Encyclopaedia Britannica Company, 1910).
11. John E. Brindley, *History of Road Legislation in Iowa* (Iowa City: The State Historical Society of Iowa, 1912), p. 298.
12. Ibid., pp. 76–77.
13. H. J. Dyos and D. H. Aldcroft, *British Transport* (Leicester: Leicester University Press, 1971), p. 367; John B. Rae, *The American Automobile* (Chicago: University of Chicago Press, 1965), p. 89.
14. For a detailed discussion of the role that feudalism played in constraining movement, see the chapters on the Middle Ages in James E. Vance, Jr., *This Scene of Man: The Role and Structure of Cities in the Geography of Western Civilization* (New York: Harper & Row, 1977).
15. George F. Willison, *Saints and Strangers* (New York: Reynal and Hitchcock, 1945), p. 128.
16. W. H. Boulton, *The Pageant of Transport through the Ages* (London: Sampson, Low, Marston & Co., n.d.), p. 38.
17. Romola Anderson and R. C. Anderson, *The Sailing-Ship* (New York: Bonanza Books, 1963), p. 191.
18. James Scott Walker, *An Accurate Description of the Liverpool and Manchester Railway* (Paterson, N.J.: D. Burnett, printer, 1830), p. 20.
19. James Scott Walker, *The Roads and Railroads, Vehicles, and Modes of Travelling of Ancient and Modern Countries: with Accounts of Bridges, Tunnels, and Canals in Various Parts of the World* (London: John W. Parker, 1839), p. 312.
20. Ibid., p. 299.
21. Anderson and Anderson, op. cit., p. 192.
22. Ibid., p. 198.
23. W. A. Baker and Tre Tryckare, *The Engine Powered Vessel* (New York: Grosset & Dunlop, 1965), p. 208.
24. Charles H. Gibbs-Smith, *The Aeroplane: An Historical Survey* (London: Her Majesty's Stationery Office, 1960), pp. 276–279.
25. Ronald Miller and David Sawers, *The Technical Development of Modern Aviation* (New York: Praeger, 1970), p. 19.
26. Gibbs-Smith, op. cit., p. 109.
27. Ibid., p. 110.
28. Miller and Sawers, op. cit., pp. 22–25.
29. For a discussion of this shift, see James E. Vance, Jr., *The Merchant's World: The Geography of Wholesaling* (Englewood Cliffs, N.J.: Prentice-Hall, 1970).

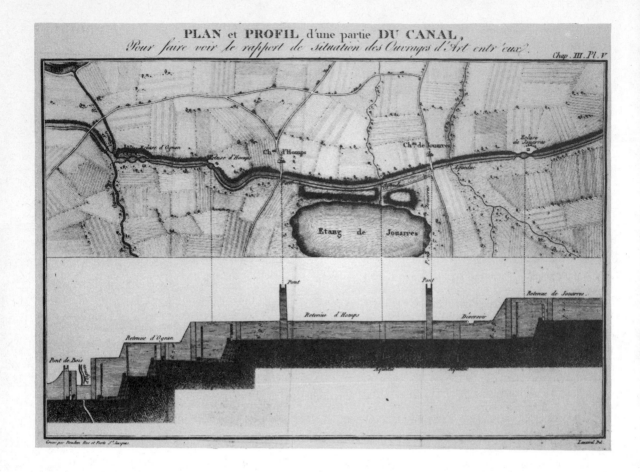

PLAN et PROFIL d'une partie DU CANAL,
Pour faire voir le rapport de situation des Ouvrages d'Art entr'eux.

Chap. III. Pl. V

Etang de Jouarres

Pont
Pont
Retenue de Jouarres
Retenue d'Homps
Déversoir
Retenue d'Ognon
Pont de Bois
Aqueduc
Aqueduc

chapter 2

Canals of the Renaissance and Industrial Periods

The burden of movement has always been as real as the craving to undertake it. It is unnecessary to explain the origin of the search for assistance in transportation to anyone who has carried so much as a shopping bag from a supermarket. From earliest times people have sought relief in the carrying of loads, not usually from sloth but rather from necessity. There was an ever-present desire to move larger loads than humans were competent to carry, and over distances that could not be borne with their porterage skills taxed to the limit. For millennia—in fact, very widely in a geographical sense up to the beginning of the Transportation Revolution—slavery was employed to supply the competence the individual lacked or, rather, wished to apply to other pursuits. The Greek, Roman, and later Venetian galleys of the Mediterranean would have been unthinkable without slave labor. Without that transport, the glories of Classical architecture, engineering, learning, and education would have been impossible.

I do not intend this as a justification for slavery in ancient times; there is never a justification for slavery. I do intend to bring into focus the critical nature of burden bearing and the moral ambiguity it forced on the humanist societies of the past. Thinking, sensitive, and basically upright people could temporize to the extent necessary to tie human muscle involuntarily, but surely, to transport. Only upon the development of forms of transportation that could rely on beasts of burden or, preferably, on inanimate power, was the manumission of human slaves finally begun.

The Transportation Revolution grew out of such an employment of animal power and the winds and waters. The so-called barbarians were considerably less barbarous than the Romans they replaced when it came to slavery—in some measure, certainly, because they were far more adept at using horses and oxen, wagons and carts in transport than had been the Roman conquerors. As we have seen, by the High Middle Ages harness had been notably improved and the tracking of vehicles enhanced through the development of the swiveling front axle. Thus, when our ancestors in the fourteenth and fifteenth centuries confronted the transportation problem, they did not automatically think in terms of great gangs of slaves, as the ancients had, but instead sought ways to harness beasts or nature to increase human competence to move over distances.

During these centuries the effort to harness nature began to bear fruit. Sails were applied more successfully to navigation in both the narrow and the pelagic seas. Unlike the Romans and Greeks, the late-medieval Venetian and Genoan navigators were able to sail somewhat against the wind and on a complex course that could be maintained only through the use of the newly discovered magnetic compass, introduced by the Arabs. Hulls were improved to allow for greater capacity and speed and thus reduce the labor input per ton transported.

Tons themselves tell us another advance wrought by these late medieval navigators. Originally a ton was a large wine cask, a *tun*, which became one of the more important commodities to move during the Middle Ages—particularly to Britain, which lay too far north to produce potable wine at home. These bulky tuns filled with wine grown in English possessions in southwestern France could be moved with reasonable dispatch, moderate cost, and general success in the ships then coming into use to carry several million gallons of wine a year to Bristol, Southampton, London, and other ports. Because this high-volume wine trade was among the first to develop with a standard cargo, *tuns* or *tons* came to be a measure of the carrying capacity of ships. Even today we speak of *register tons* for ships—that is, a subsequently standardized measure of internal capacity of the hull (at 100 cubic feet)—which refers back to the space taken by the medieval wine tun in the ships of the time.

The *Mayflower* of 1620 was rated at 180 tons burden; that is, it could have stored below decks something like 180 medieval tuns. This may not sound large to us in an era of tankers that can carry a quarter of a million tons, but to the people of the late Middle Ages the ability to move dozens or even hundreds of tons at one time was impressive. Among other things, that ability allowed the medieval English to enjoy the pleasures of reasonably priced wine in their barren land.

In terms of the ability to move goods and even people, in the fourteenth and fifteenth centuries, there was no possibility of a renaissance of transportation as there was in learning, architecture, and art. Instead, the greatest development in transportation had only begun in the era just then closing, setting the stage for a true leap forward, which on reflection we can abundantly perceive as a Transportation Revolution of the early modern era. During that emerging epoch perhaps the greatest contribution to change, and to the advancement of human material life, came in the matter of harnessing inanimate energy as had never been possible before. At first inanimate energy was tied in as a helper for the existing energy provided by animals, but eventually it came to work alone on land as it already did at sea. In the late Middle Ages animals as beasts of burden could not be greatly increased in numbers, and the food-producing capacity of Western agriculture was still very limited; therefore, there was an inestimable value in tying what burden-bearing humanity had possessed for several millennia to a new source of energy—to be secured from the winds, flowing water, and the low friction and weight-bearing capacity of slackwater ponds.

Greater efficiency in transportation is fundamentally measured by a reduction in the energy it takes to move a unit weight a specific distance: thus, if one person or one horse could draw a particular load in a cart over the unsurfaced roads of the late Middle Ages, anything that would increase the possible load drawn would automatically increase transportation efficiency. Doing so became crucial for several reasons. Perhaps most fundamental was the increase in trade such that material flows grew both in volume and in the distance covered. From the fourteenth century on, the conditions of technological advance were such that great preferential benefit attached to coastal trade, which could make use of the rapidly improving ships of the time. Another factor turing the attention of the West to increasing the efficiency of transport was the scarcity, cost, and often poor health of draft animals. William Petty estimated at the end of the seventeenth century that animals could be valued at one-quarter the sum of all agricultural land.[1] Yet numbers were not large, and there were certainly more jobs for the horses and mules to accomplish than those numbers permitted. Times of epizootic further complicated the problem, withdrawing from Europeans much of the already scarce animate power they could command.[2]

A further encouragement of increasing efficiency came from the urbanization then taking place in Western society. As the Greeks and Romans had discovered, cities cannot exist without the transportation of food, clothing materials, the constituents of buildings, and (in some areas) fuels. To collect people together means rapidly stripping the land of the local provision of these commodities, a scourge that would destroy the city save for its citizens' ability to call on such goods from a distance. But greater distance meant greater costs, so there was an increasing pressure introduced to lower costs (by increasing efficiency) as the search for provender had to spread outward from the city.

This effort was further required by the increasing demands placed on transport by those human activities that led to urbanization. Two activities that tended to depend on the agglomeration of people and their labor led to medieval and early modern urbanization: the conduct of long-distance trade and the transformation of raw materials through various types of artisan manufacture. As Florence expanded in the production of fine woolen textiles, it also had to extend its trade, both to secure fleeces for transformation and to command markets for sales. Banking followed in turn as a specialized means of facilitating both these efforts. There was a circularity between basic economic activity and urbanization, one engendering the other; but there was a remorseless linearity in the increasing demand for transport to keep the system operating.

That demand was first expressed where urbanization reached its highest level relative to local resources; where particular stress existed within existing transport faced with carrying food for a large population, raw goods for a busy mercantile and manufacturing force, and building materials for a burgeoning city. The largest European city of the High Middle Ages was probably Milan, which the Friar Bonvesin della Riva in 1288 estimated to have 200,000 people within its walls and in the dependent area surrounding them.[3] Until the growth of Paris at the beginning of the modern era, the city on the Po Plain stood as the largest place to arise in the West since classical Rome in its florescence. The Eternal City had depended on a massive system of slavery and the seasonally navigable Tiber to gather the requisite food and other materials from its vast empire to its equally overgrown capital. Milan, too far from the sea to be reached by river navigation, had to find some other way of coping with its rapid growth during late-medieval times.

Without slavery or an empire, Milan could not become so large—in the Middle Ages it may have been no more than one-tenth as

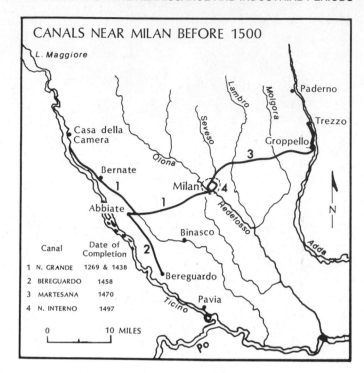

CANALS NEAR MILAN BEFORE 1500

Canal	Date of Completion
1 N. GRANDE	1269 & 1438
2 BEREGUARDO	1458
3 MARTESANA	1470
4 N. INTERNO	1497

0   10 MILES

Source: Singer, Holmyard, Hall, and Williams, eds., *A History of Technology*, vol. 2 (New York: Oxford University Press, 1958), p. 538.

populous as imperial Rome—yet it reached a size that began to require something beyond the traditional means and practices of transportation. The solution was found in the creation of artificial rivers—navigations—reaching from the producing regions at some distance from the city to its gates, or even within the walls.

THE DEVELOPMENT OF THE NAVIGLIA GRANDE

The earliest canal is undoubtedly lost to human history; filled up with weed, silt, or sand; and obliterated from both the landscape and our knowledge. The Greeks and Romans knew how to cut ditches wide and deep enough to permit the passage of small boats. The isthmus of Corinth had one, as did the low country of Lincolnshire in Roman Britain. It is often hard to determine

the purpose for which such ditches were dug—sometimes for drainage of too wet lands, as in Lincolnshire or Holland; sometimes for the irrigation of too dry lands, as in the Po Plain or the Saracen lands; sometimes for the creation of a moat to stem invasion, as may have been true of some British and Greek ditches—but waterways have always shown the proclivity to be employed for a number of uses. Multipurpose development was not discovered with the canalization of the Tennessee River during the Tennessee Valley Authority days of the 1930s. Once water was there, its multiplicity of uses to mankind would suggest a likely complexity of employment.

The Po Basin stands as an area of colluvial accumulation carried southward over geologic time from the impressive heights of the Alps. Each season's flood added its bit to the buildup of great sloping surfaces descending from one to two thousand feet in the north to near sea level where the river Po drained eastward to the Adriatic. The gravelly nature of the colluvium combined with a sharp seasonality of precipitation to produce a late-summer and fall drought that could be destructive to the wine, oil, and grain crops that had, since Roman times, been the essence of Mediterranean agriculture and the staple of Latin life. To overcome that possible blight, farmers had learned in antiquity to engage in simple ditch irrigation, which diverted the continuing flow of the rivers, maintained by the warm-season meltwater of the snows and glaciers of the Alps, onto the gently sloping riparian plains.

As Milan grew even in the High Middle Ages, a need was felt for supplies of food and building material brought from a distance. Given the excessive cost of transporting goods over roads, it is not surprising that already in the twelfth century a larger version of the riparian ditch was proposed to carry boats that might more economically transport those increasing volumes of goods. To understand this project it is necessary to be aware that, when the Galli Insubres founded Melpun or Mediolanum, a site on the low interfluve between the Ticino and the Adda was selected. Thus, when the Romans took over this apparently Celtic settlement in 222 B.C., they inherited a site probably first occupied by a people using horses and carts to the extent they had any transportation available to them. After a set of vicissitudes that cause us to wonder how what we now call Milano could survive for 1,500 years, it was the rapid urbanization at this dry-land site that badly needed the support of cheaper transportation in the twelfth century.

That assistance came first in the period 1179–1209, when Cistercian monks constructed an irrigation diversion from the Ticino River, which drains Lake Maggiore southward across the colluvial fans that push the Po toward the south side of the basin in which it flows. In 1257 this riparian canal was carried from Abbiategrasso eastward for some 15 miles to connect with the moat ringing the outer walls of what had come to be called Milano. Not too much is known about the early structure of these two sections, which collectively came to be known as the *Naviglio Grande*. It seems certain that the fall of water, conditioned by the slope of the ground southward, was controlled through sluices, which as a result of the considerable seasonal variation between high water (late spring and early summer) and low water (fall and winter) probably could be opened to permit easier flow. Such openings would almost certainly have suggested to the economically observant Italians the idea of using these irrigation canals as transportation routes for the sort of boats that had navigated the natural waterways of the Po, its tributaries and its deltaic distributaries, and the other streams of high volume that coursed down the slope from the Alps. On the Po, navigation could be carried upstream to Pavia and even Turino in season, on the Adige to Verona, on the Brenta to Padua, on the Moncio to Mantua, and on the Adda to Lodi—all approachable by small craft. Among the larger Lombard towns, only Milan was high and dry.

With the completion of the irrigation works from Lake Maggiore, that isolation was partially removed. With the later construction of a canal link from Abbiategrasso to Pavia, completed in 1458,[4] the most powerful city of the plain was accessible to water transport and thus no more isolated than any of the other north Italian cities. It could join with them in providing the first positive demonstration of the interaction of economic development and urban growth.

Milan, to gain access to the Ticino, could depend on minor changes in the facilities afforded by the riparian irrigation canal constructed in the twelfth century; but to be connected to Pavia and the Po navigation required somewhat more technological complexity. The 12-mile section of canal from Abbiategrasso to Bereguardo, which with a portage into the navigable lower Ticino gave access to the usable lower course of the Po, posed considerable problems. There a drop of about 80 feet—over 7 feet per mile—had to be comprehended. To that end the pound lock, an only recently appreciated structure, was employed. As is the case for so many facilities and vehicles in transportation, the origin of the pound lock is in dispute.

THE ORIGIN OF THE LOCK: HOLLAND AND FLANDERS

Primitive examples of what might be called locks dated from some seventy-five years earlier in Flanders and Holland, not to mention still older but less direct examples from China. In 1373 at Vreeswijk, Holland, at the place where the canal from Utrecht joins the Lek River, a facility was built to provide an adjustment of the varying levels of the river and canal. Apparently it was a simple adaptation of the much older Dutch contrivance, the sluice, which was a single gate intended to control the flow of water from one ditch to another. In an enlarged version at Vreeswijk a sluice separated the canal from a commodious basin capable of holding several boats. In turn, the basin was separated by a second sluice from the river. "From regulations of 1378 and 1412 we learn that the Vreeswijk lock was operated three times weekly, at 2 o'clock in the afternoon."[5] First one sluice was opened and boats from the river were admitted. Then, with the sluice closed, the water in the lock was permitted to adjust to the level of the canal; when this was accomplished, the other sluice was opened and the boats began to move on toward Utrecht on that artificial waterway. Other examples of this large tide-lock were constructed at Delfshaven in 1389, Schiedam in 1395,

and one with three gates existed at Gouda in 1413.

The first true model for the locks eventually adopted on the Bereguardo Canal came at Damme, on the canal that had to be built to maintain the connection of the early medieval port of Bruges to the sea in the Scheldt estuary. At Damme in 1394–1396 a lock was devised that could be used frequently, with such continuity coming from its smaller size and greater ease of filling. A masonry chamber was substituted for the grass-banked basin at Vreeswijk, and two vertically lifted gates closed it at opposite ends. Thus a lock 34 by 100 feet was obtained. Everywhere in Flanders and Holland these earlier locks were intended more for drainage than for navigation. Normally single locks were used to pass from a canal to a river or from one canal to another, rather than to overcome changes in the elevation of the surface. Throughout the polder lands levels of drainage vary by relatively small amounts, and there are not even low hills to interrupt the level skyline. But the complex technology involved in draining this only partially unwatered foreshore and making it arable was such that any use of its drains for navigation usually necessitated small shifts in level. The pound lock in particular came to serve that purpose, notably after its success at Damme, because the water required to operate the more confined locks was minimized to avoid returning any more water than critically necessary to the polders that lay below sea level, and this necessitated endless and difficult pumping to maintain dryness.

THE STECKNITZ CANAL CROSSES A WATERSHED

Once the lock had been developed for this particular purpose, it came into adaptive use elsewhere. The first use of the lock to overcome variations in the surface of the land apparently occurred on the canal built to

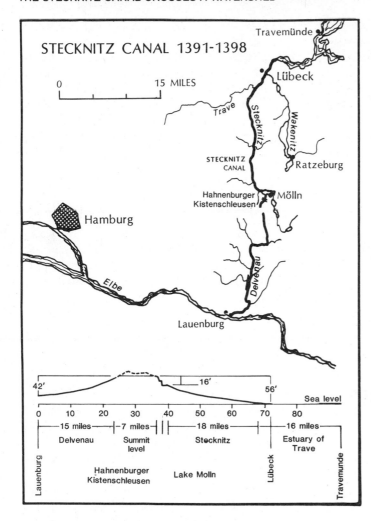

STECKNITZ CANAL 1391-1398

0   15 MILES

Travemünde
Lübeck
Trave
Stecknitz
Wakenitz
STECKNITZ
CANAL
Ratzeburg
Hahnenburger
Kistenschleusen
Mölln
Hamburg
Delvenau
Elbe
Lauenburg

42'   16'
                                              56'
                                    Sea level
0   10   20   30   40   50   60   70   80
— 15 miles — — 7 miles — | | — 18 miles — | — 16 miles —
Delvenau   Summit   Stecknitz   Estuary of
              level   Trave

Lauenburg
Hahnenburger   Lake Molln   Lübeck
Kistenschleusen   Travemünde

Source: Singer, Holmyard, Hall, and
Williams, eds., *A History of Technology*,
vol. 2 (New York: Oxford University
Press, 1958), p. 538.

connect the Hanseatic port of Lübeck with the river Elbe above Hamburg. Such a canal would have been particulary desired as a way of circumventing payment of the so-called Sound Dues that the Danes exacted of all shipping passing between the Baltic and the North Sea. By cutting this ditch across the base of the isthmus of Kiel, the German merchants tied the great river system of Germany itself, the Elbe, to that vestibule of eastern trade that the Baltic provided.

In the fourteenth century the Stecknitz River, which flowed into Lübeck harbor from the south, was made navigable for 18 miles, over a rise of 40 feet, to Lake Mölln. This navigability was obtained through the use of stanches, the first water-control device to be shaped in the Middle Ages. Initially these were probably merely sections of a low wooden dam, which might be removed on occasion to relieve the pressure on that dam in times of high water or to permit the passage through the barrier by a boat that was floated on a flash of water rushing through the opening thus afforded. Subsequently the stanch evolved into the sluice already mentioned. In the Middle Ages these were great lifting gates raised on some sort of head frame in order to open a connection between the water ponds on either side. If only small differences in level were involved, as in Flanders, the turbulence was controlled sufficiently to allow the boat to be winched through the opening. We know of a *magna slusa* at Nieuport in Flanders, mentioned in 1184; one at Governolo on the Mincio between Lago di Garda and Mantua in Lombardy, built between 1188 and 1198; and one at Gouda in Holland just after 1200. Clearly, in those areas where primitive navigation first developed, the sluice—or stanch as it was called in England —was rapidly evolved by the quickening technology of the Middle Ages. The control of the Stecknitz by such a contrivance would have been more tolerable than desirable: it represented an initial effort at expanding water transport in the hinterland of what was the most important trading city of the Hanseatic League. That expansion was greatly advanced by the Elbe connection, which would open up much of central Europe to those energetic merchants. Its greatest importance came in providing a connection largely independent of the lower Elbe, with its heavy tolls, between the salt workings at Lüneburg and the Baltic port of Lübeck, which dispatched salt widely throughout the Scandinavian herring trade.

To gain a connection to the Elbe, two natural barriers intervened south of Lake Mölln: the first was a part of the second. Between the lake and the headwaters of a southward-flowing affluent of the Elbe, the Delvanau, some 7 miles of upland existed, rising to a terrain divide 28 feet above the lake. The undertakers of the extension of Lübeck's hinterland decided on a canal to cross this divide and located it in a cut that was 12 feet below the surface at its lowest point. Even then the 7-mile ditch was still 16 feet above the lake level at its north end. There the developers constructed two locks,

the Hahnenburger Kistenschleusen, to tie the canal to the lake. To complete the waterway to the Elbe, the river Delvanau was controlled by eight stanches to handle the 42-foot drop in the 15 miles to Lauenburg on the Elbe.[6] As completed in 1398 the Stecknitz canal is apparently the first artificial waterway to cross a terrain divide, and certainly the earliest to use a proper pound lock to gain or lose elevation. Its main problem came from a shortage of water in the 7-mile summit "pond" where seepage from the sandy ground was at first thought adequate to fill the cut and supply the lockage water. The result was the imposition of periodic operation on the Kistenschleusen, once every two or three days when enough water had seeped into the summit pond. As a result, large basins to contain up to ten 35-foot barges had to be built, so the model employed had to be that of Vreeswijk rather than Damme.

The Stecknitz Canal seems to have been of sufficiently limited utility not to lead to a major transformation of European transportation. The combination of stanches and the periodic lock at Hahnenburg must have made this a difficult route to use. Still, as a canal crossing a watershed it was innovative, leaving only the perfection of the pound lock to provide a functioning model of what might be accomplished in a human transformation of hydrography to create new routes that would be the cheapest to traverse for their time.

THE INVENTION OF THE POUND LOCK

The use of water for power was far more extensive in the Middle Ages than many people appreciate. The grist mill to grind grain into flour was, if not ubiquitous (because of the absence of potential dam sites in areas such as Flanders), at least commonplace. In addition, forges and fulling mills were water-powered. The result was that most potentially navigable streams were interrupted by mill dams wherever settlement was at all dense, and by rapids or falls wherever they crossed hard geologic strata. Hence most rivers were navigable only in those segments of water of reasonable gradient: where grade was steep, nature interposed an interruption similar to that added in the Middle Ages by the millers of various sorts. As the economy quickened in the High Middle Ages, greater recourse to rivers came from the buildup of long-distance trade, both in range and in volume. Boatmen were increasingly recorded as providing transit service where nature and human design permitted. The existence of gaps meant that transport had to be broken off at those interruptions or else the goods transhipped around them. The stanch with its opening was a primitive method of passing through man-made barriers, but it was of no value at the natural breaks, where only at flood time could there be enough water for even a hazardous crossing, such as the shooting of the rapids at the Long Sault on the St. Lawrence or the Falls of the Ohio at Louisville-Portland. There was no primitive technology for passage of vertical falls.

It is a truism of transportation that most innovations begin as a partial solution to a locally appreciated problem and commonly trend toward either (1) a more radical solution to a geographically localized problem or (2) a modest solution to a more general problem. So it was in the attempts to deal with the gaps in river navigation. There were some efforts at the modest solution of the general problem—for example, the broaching of dams by requiring stanches for the passage of boats. Other efforts led to the radical solution of the geographically limited problem of overcoming falls or gradients too steep to navigate—for example, in the efforts to create improved portages and, ultimately, the pound lock.

There is little doubt that the rudiments of a successful inland navigation were present when, during the Middle Ages, successfully designed boats were available and the technology for propelling them existed. By then, the use of the flow of water to carry boats downward was well developed: it seems that the use of crude ropes to drag the boat upward against the flow had begun during that period. We know that the river Severn in England had gangs of hauliers, whose job it was to draw boats back toward the headwaters. Other streams seem to have had similar gilds. In this way the means of propulsion and the nature of the boat were developed for inland navigation well before the Transportation Revolution. What developed during the period 1450–1600 was a solution for the geographical problem associated with river navigation—specifically, the removal of the absolute barrier to movement and the beginnings of the attack on the traction problem that still existed even after the hauliers gild had, in places, begun the use of horses towing from the bank.

That traction problem was an oddly balanced one. Boats headed downstream were difficult to steer in a following current, often rather strong, which severely reduced the time available for maneuver. In the reverse direction the problem also related to the speed of the current, which forced exhausting effort on the hauliers even for fairly moderate velocities of water. Clearly the problem with traction lay in the existence of any considerable velocity in the water; yet it was axiomatic that any natural stream would have to have such a flow to exist. This was particularly evident in the effort to extend the river navigations headward, as in the Po Basin, where the use of the Alpine left-bank tributaries of the main river almost immediately encountered increasing velocities even within the area of colluvial fans below the foothill line.

Taking the Milanese canal system as an example of the evolution of the solution to the geographical problem, we must first distinguish the two areas of attack: the over-coming of stream velocity and the overcoming of variations in elevation. The two are, of course, intimately related; any reduction in drop—that is, in gradient—will automatically reduce water velocity, which is almost wholly a function of gradient. Thus the two problems could be solved simultaneously, although that was not done in the earlier centuries of river navigation. Stanches were first introduced simply to allow passage through a physical barrier in the river, although they did slow velocities in their "ponds." The existence of those dams opened by stanches meant that in fact both the gradient and the velocity at that precise spot were aggravated over natural conditions. The rush of water through the opening was commonly so great that boats were in danger of being stove in passing downward (when they might easily crash against the jambs of the stanch). In struggling upward, herculean efforts were necessary to draw the boat through the wall of water cascading down from the higher mill pond to the uncontrolled river below. The sluices of the Ticino Canal would clearly have suffered from these trying conditions when all control of flow was thus contained. For irrigation the sluice was acceptable; for navigation it soon was not.

As in Flanders and Holland, it began to be understood in the High Middle Ages that some way had to be found to lower the surface of the water without introducing high turbulence. The Dutch had found the way in their large basin locks that were operated at infrequent intervals. The Germans on the Stecknitz followed the practice, possibly in direct imitation of the Dutch, as the Hansa merchants were intimately familiar with Holland and its topography. The Italians probably were not; in any event, the periodic lock would hardly serve their purpose. There was neither the space to build such basins each time a shift of levels of 6 to 8 feet was

needed, nor the possibility of detaining boats repeatedly in the 40 kilometers between the intake from the Ticino River and the end of the Naviglia Grande at the Porta Ticinese beneath Milan's walls. One periodic lock may be tolerable; a dozen are not. The solution obviously lay in the adoption of the Flemish box or trunk lock, such as that at Damme, but again it is doubtful that the north Italians knew of its details.

The most probable origin of the pound lock put to use during the fifteenth century on the Milanese canals was the rational invention of the facility by the increasingly well-educated "engineers" of the Italian Renaissance. A number of these men have been proposed as the inventor of the pound lock. Not surprisingly, Leonardo da Vinci has an incontestable claim through a sketch contained in the *Codice Laurenziano* (Milan, c. 1495), as does Leone Battista Alberti through a description of a lock with two gates separated by a distance equal to the length of a boat, contained in *De re aedificatoria*, which was written in the 1460s.[7] We now know that Bertola da Novate between 1456 and 1459 actually constructed five pound locks on a right-bank tributary of the Po flowing northward from the Apennines through Parma.[8] Without doubt the intellectual analysis of what must have been a general problem facing all those architects and engineers working for palatine dukes in northern Italy—that of controlling velocity of flow and overcoming elevation—would lead these intelligent and educated men to similar solutions, in this case the pound lock.

Although that structure may now seem to have been simple and self-evident, there were refinements on the *Kistenschleusen* of the 1390s that were crucial in the broad geographical adoption of such facilities. The advances came specifically in the reduction in the volumes of lock water required and in the operation of the enclosing gates. Shifting from periodically operated locks to those opened more frequently meant that the amount of water per opening had to be reduced drastically. To accomplish that, the water capacity of locks had to be massively reduced, a requirement that ever since the fifteenth century has meant the tailoring of the lock to the modular vessel expected to operate through the structure. The small boats of the Middle Ages led to small locks, just as desires to increase the size of boats has brought on structures on the important waterways of Europe that today are built to handle 1,300-ton vessels (in rare cases even 3,000-ton ones). A 1,300-ton boat in medieval times would probably have been beyond the competence of builders, and it almost certainly would have far outdistanced any need for transport then expressed.

By linking the size of locks to the size of boats, a vast improvement in the frequency of service was accomplished: there was no reason to delay the passage of a single boat if that was all the lock could handle. Taking a specific case, the existence of the periodic locks at places like Vreeswijk would have forefended the operation of the express, passenger-carrying canal boats, the *trekschuit*, which came into operation at the end of the sixteenth century and continued to ply special high-speed Dutch canals, *trekvaart*, down to the coming of the railroad. We will examine these later in the chapter, but here it is well to appreciate that speed and frequency of service were concerns of our ancestors as they are ours.

The lock conformal to the modular boat also produced the least possible consumption of a scarce commodity, lockage water. On the Naviglio Grande there was no real shortage of water at most times—Lago Maggiore was a splendid canal reservoir—but once cuts with poorer headwater supplies, or no such supplies (because the canal crossed a land divide) were built, conservation of lockage water became critical. The

pound lock proportional to the canal boat came in this indirect fashion to shape the boats in relation to the quantities of water available, and ultimately to constrain the total utilization of the canal to the total volume of water available to operate the locks. When water became scarce, restraints on use had to be introduced or other sources of water secured. Toward the close of the canal era, canal reservoirs were enlarged if possible or replenished by pumping back already-used lockage water where such enlargement was impossible. As we shall see, it was this water-supply problem that delayed the most important of all European canal projects—the effort to connect the Mediterranean with the Atlantic in France proposed by Leonardo and Francis I in the early sixteenth century.

Leonardo proved a central figure in the evolution of canal facilities because it was his analysis and design solution that finally created reasonably efficient gates to close the pound locks. It seems that before the last decade of the fifteenth century those gates had been lifting ones, a single plane raised in a head frame rather akin to the smaller sluices used to this day on drainage and irrigation facilities. These portcullis or guillotine gates were mechanically inefficient, the water pushing against them made them hard to open, and the amount of force required to raise a large heavy oaken closure can easily be imagined. When Leonardo was appointed engineer to the Duke of Milan in 1482, he became responsible for a number of canals as well as other civil works. A century earlier plans had been set to construct in this burgeoning city a great church in the style then fashionable—a church that remains, albeit cloaked in Italianate decoration, the world's largest Gothic cathedral. The prodigious amounts of stone required had to come from Lago Maggiore along the Naviglio Grande, but for delivery to the building site the former moat surrounding

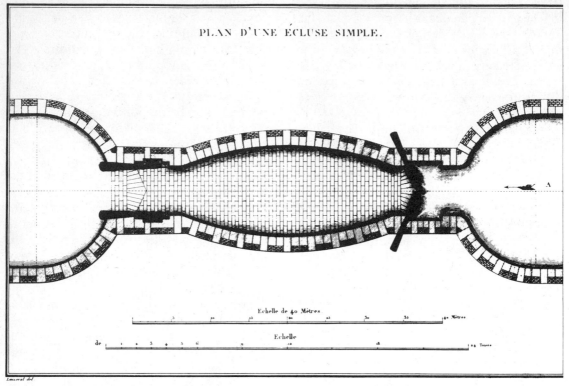

PLAN D'UNE ÉCLUSE SIMPLE.

Echelle de 40 Mètres

Echelle

Pound lock on the Canal du Midi. *Source*: Andreossy, *Histoire du Canal du Midi* (Paris, 1804).

the earlier city walls was adopted in part as a canal within the city. As expanded over the succeeding century this Naviglio Interno became a ring tying the earlier Naviglio Grande to a later canal of similar form, the Martesana, finished in 1470, to provide a connection to the river Adda, which flowed from the Alps to the Po some 15 miles east of the Lombard metropolis. The Interno integrated this Milanese canal system, but this required several changes in level within the city itself. The final stages of this work, until its completion in 1497, were conducted under the superintendancy of Leonardo.

His design called for six new locks on the Naviglio Interno, for which he devised what has come to be called the *miter gate*. In such

a gate the opening is shifted from a vertical to a horizontal plane, with obvious reduction in the force needed to carry out the operation. Instead of a flat single plane the gates became two planes, meeting at an obtuse angle and mitered so as to fit tightly at the forward edge one against the other. As the angle points upstream, any water pressure against the gates causes them to close more tightly, making this as good a device for conserving water as was possible at the time. Similarly, the butt edges of the gates were let into a groove in the side walls of the lock so that a similar seal was made by the pressure of water on the gates themselves. As a final refinement to ease operation, Leonardo put small sluices in the gates them-

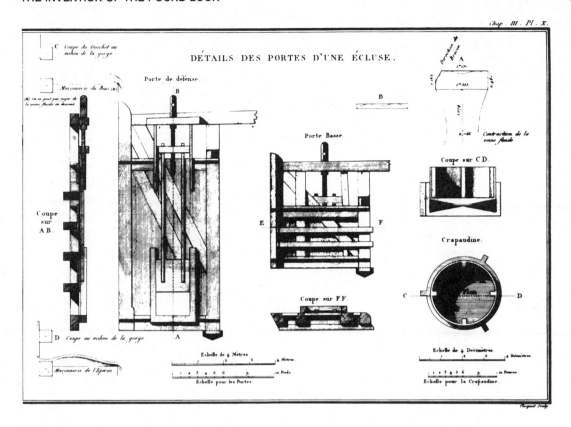

DÉTAILS DES PORTES D'UNE ÉCLUSE.

selves through which the water was let out into the lower level. Once these easily opened apertures had succeeded in lowering the level in the lock to the lower pond (or, in reverse operation, in filling the lock to the level of the upper pond), it would be fairly easy to swing the miter gates on pivots at their butt edge, aligning them with the side walls of the lock chamber. Such a maneuver would be accomplished in slack water with the same level found on either side of the gate.

The combination of the proportionally chambered lock and the miter gate represented such an improvement in facilities that we have not changed the fundamental design of this structure since Leonardo devised it in 1497. Thus for nearly five hundred years most effort on inland navigation has come in improving the vehicles operating on these waterways, and in reducing redundant lockage, through the more elaborate engineering of the canal by a greater use of cuttings, tunnels, and aqueducts. There is great justification in commencing our Transportation Revolution in 1500, when the perfected lock was known to those responsible for laying plans for such internal improvements. Among those most interested in the development was Francis I of France, who inherited suzerainty of the Milanese, which had been captured by Louis XII in 1500. While the French held Milan (1500–1512), Leonardo had readily accepted the patronage of the foreigners, to such an extent that when they were evicted he fell out of favor with the Italians. In 1515, when Francis I succeeded in recapturing Milan, Leonardo joined his court and returned with it to France to end his days at the Chateau of Amboise on the Loire. There he and Francis discussed a system of canals for France, particularly emphasizing the desirability of one to tie France's "deux mers"; but when Leonardo died in 1519 such a gradiose plan was beyond both the purse of that ill-starred king and the water-supply technology of the time. A century of experimentation in canal building had to intervene before such an ambitious project could be proposed seriously.

THE CUTTING OF ARTIFICIAL WATERWAYS: SPECIALIZATION OF TREKVAARTEN IN HOLLAND

Throughout the Middle Ages most of the improvement in navigation that led directly to the creation of canals seemed to take place either in Flanders-Holland or in the Po Basin. In other places—Germany, France, and Britain in particular—there was some activity associated with the strong reliance on river boats as the carriers of heavy or mass quantities of goods. But the technical advances made by the Low Countries and northern Italy overshadowed those of the other burgeoning economies. First those areas experimented with controlling shifts in level, jointly shaping the pound lock by the year 1500. The Flemings. Dutch, and Lombards also came to appreciate another desirable advance in inland navigation—the substitution of the artificial cut for the natural river. No doubt this substitution was at first inadvertent; drainage and irrigation canals were dug in the Low Countries and Lombardy, and their use for boats must have demonstrated how much less tractive effort was needed to propel boats along these cuts than it took to move in ad-

jacent rivers. Navigation even downslope was easier because of the better control of boats in the slack water ponds found between the stanches, or later locks. Thus, although the Naviglia Grande began as an irrigation cut, the extension of that system in the Berguardo Canal was undertaken primarily for navigation.

In Holland and Flanders the first waterways were made for drainage, but by 1500 cuts were being made for navigation purposes. In a detailed study of the Dutch canal system, Jan de Vries has shown that in the Dutch Republic there came ultimately to be three separate components of the network.[9]

There were, in fact, three overlapping shipping networks in the lowlying regions of the Republic. Most basic were the routes of the market boats connecting villages to their market towns. Then came the beurteveren, offering intercity connections between each city and its important trading partners. Finally came the trekvaart network.... The beurtveer and trekvaart networks overlap somewhat: marginal cases exist that seem to belong to both categories. But far more noteworthy than this is the essential difference in the nature of the service provided by the beurtveren and trekshuiten [boat services].

The beurtveren endowed each city with a more or less complete set of direct services to other cities[: t]he frequency and timing of the sailings were geared to suit the requirements of the city markets. It is true that the rays emanating from each city would, when the routes of all cities are superimposed on one map, form a network far more complete than the trekvaart network . . . , but the market orientation of the services and the infrequency of sailings over any given route made this network difficult for through travel. Here the trekvaart system was ideal. While the beurtveren served the cities as competing central places, the trekshuiten served them as members of an urban system. The fact that this "third network" was built when a second already existed makes an important statement about the economy of the mid-seventeenth century Republic.

That construction also reinforces the other evidence supporting the notion that central places as such were remnants of an earlier time, when natural economies existed within extremely confined areas focusing on a local barter-trading center. When long-distance trade began to encourage the expansion of the economy and its extension over considerable distances, a mercantile model of settlement took over. The trekvaarten provide us with tangible evidence of that wider system of urban places.[10]

The trekvaarten that de Vries analyzes were distinctive:[11]

> The newly dug canals were generally drawn as straight as possible across the landscape to connect two cities in the shortest distance. Because of their straightness and their indifference to intermediate villages, these trekvaarten stand out on seventeenth- and eighteenth-century maps in the same way that limited access highways stand out on today's maps. Since the movement of heavy freight via the trekvaarten was generally expressly forbidden, most of them took a form which limited their usefulness to trekschuiten and similar light vessels.... The profile of the Haarlem-Leiden trekvaart [has been] measured in Amsterdam *voeten*, about the length of English feet. The breadth of the canal at water level was thus 18.3 meters, while its depth was 2.4 meters. Since the water level could be expected to rise right up to normal ground level in this low-lying region, the contractor had to use a portion of the excavated earth to build an embankment on one side of the rather shallow canal. On the other side a much larger embankment was to be built to accomodate a 6.4 meters wide towpath. Beyond the towpath embankment the contractor was to dig a drainage ditch. The total breadth of this right of way was 124 voeten, or 37.8 meters.

> One other important characteristic of the trekvaarten was their physical isolation from the previously existing canal network. This was actually only true of the newly dug canals. A fixed bridge with dimensions that would admit nothing larger than a trekschuit prevented large vessels on the Leiden-Utecht trekvaart (the Oude Rijn River) from entering the Gouda-Amsterdam trekvaart where they intersected near Alphen, ... forcing passengers to transfer to waiting barges on the opposite side of the obstacle.... The physical remains of the 658 kilometer trekvaart network are still with us. ... What have vanished, however, are the vessels which for two centuries carried millions of passengers in (what most contemporary writers agree was) homelike comfort. The trekschuiten were long, narrow vessels with a covered area in which the passengers were seated on benches that extended along the sides. The barge possessed a short, movable mast to which a line was attached. The line led to a horse on the towpath which pulled the barge along. This general description applies as well to 1632 as to 1839: no technical changes of any significance occurred during the intervening two centuries.

In this seventeenth-century example we discover the tendency toward specialization in facilities that comes with amplification of demand. Initially most types of transportation have been experimental in both a financial and a technological sense. Once a facility is proved financially viable, there is an ever-possible specialization such that particular demands can be met by small, or even considerable, variations in the initial form given to the facility. The initial navigation on the drainage or irrigation ditch— de Vries's market boats operating on the drainage canal and the carriers of stone for the first phases in the building of Milan cathedral—is followed by an improved facility caring for a now-expressable need, the market-oriented beurtveer of Holland and the Martesana or Bereguardo canals of

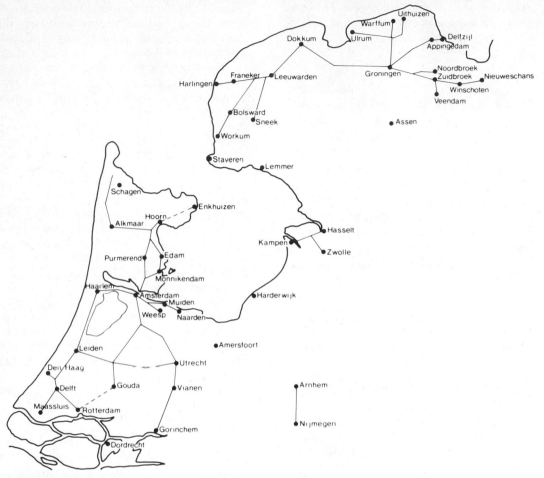

Map of trekvaarten in Holland in the seventeenth century. *Source*: Jan de Vries, *Barges and Capitalism: Passenger Transportation in the Dutch Economy, 1632–1839* (A.A.G. Bijdragon 21, 1978).

Lombardy, possessed of locks and an alignment dictated by navigation needs alone. In the case of the trekvaart, specialization was carried a step farther, to provide rapid passenger lines unencumbered by freight boats.

It is significant that such trekvaart canals were the first to go with the coming of the railroad. This was also the case with the stagecoach lines that came into operation on roads in the early nineteenth century. The most specialized facility is the one most prey to competitive replacement. This truth can

be observed later in the cases of the all-Pullman train, the luxury liners of the 1930s on the North Atlantic, and—we may hope—the *Concordes* operating under rising fuel prices. In the last instance it is unlikely to be a technological advance in speed that will lead to replacement; instead, it will be the fact that wide-bodied jets are four to five times more energy-efficient for nearly the same service as the supersonic plane. This, nevertheless, is a case of technological supersession in a time when energy efficiency must take priority over generally unproductive speed.

FRANCE AND THE DEVELOPMENT OF THE WATERSHED CANAL

Contemporaneous with the specialization of waterways into constructed canals, and even particular types of cut, came the effort to overcome terrain in a more radical fashion. In the cases cited in the Low Countries and in the Po Basin, political factors influenced by geography assured that the earliest canal systems would lie within a single drainage basin (as in Italy) or in basins the limits of which were so indistinct as to make of the polder region a single terrain entity. Efforts to overcome differences in level were not normally thwarted by great shortages of water. In Flanders there was generally too much water; in Italy the vast mountaintop reservoir of the Alpine glaciers and snowfields provided adequate lockage water for much of the year.

In France, however, conditions were quite different because of the different political geography. France joined England in the earliest efforts in Europe at the creation of a linguistically encompassing state. By the late Middle Ages the area that was the nominal fief of the king of France came as well to be under his sovereignty. Burgundy remained outside the realm until 1363; Provence until 1481; and the Franche Comté, Lorraine, and the Duchy of Savoy until well after the onset of the canal era (1674–1678, 1670, and 1860, respectively). By the time Francis I and Leonardo were discussing the use of canals to tie together the various parts of the Most Christian King's realm — that is, the second decade of the sixteenth century — that realm extended over all but the eastern reaches of modern France. Thus one of the earliest nation-states well predated the rise of nationalism in the last century, and had needs for an economic unification of areas that had stood in autarkic, feudal parcels for the previous five hundred years.

The efforts at the economic unification of France faced a realm whose drainage, and thereby earliest navigation, was radially outward. The Po united northern Italy as the polders did Flanders and Holland. In contrast, the French rivers were naturally divisive of the linguistic state. The Escaut and Meuse flowed northward into the Low Countries; the Moselle eastward into Germany; the Doubs, Saône, and Rhône southward into the Mediterranean; and the Garonne, Loire, and Seine westward into the Atlantic quite distant one from the other. This natural endowment could easily support a provincially divided France—that is, the medieval one—but hardly a unified state. To that end had been the speculative consultations of the Bourbon monarch with the Tuscan engineer-painter—speculations that foundered on the fact that the French situation differed from that of the Po Basin. To unify France it was necessary to tie together distinct river systems by providing navigation across the divides that separated the major watersheds. Specifically, this meant tying the Seine to the Loire and Saône, and the Mediterranean to the Atlantic via the Garonne. Not until 1648 and the Treaty of Westphalia did France acquire the Sundgau northwest of Basel, which made possible a connection of the French system of canals with the Rhine.

Watershed canals had been attempted earlier, as in the case of the Stecknitz in the last decade of the fourteenth century. These early instances were fortuitous—the close approximation of the headwaters of two usable streams in low-lying country. Obviously the development of the true pound lock and the solution of the summit-level water-supply problem were necessary before any general construction of watershed canals could be undertaken. By the time of the discussions at Amboise (1515–1519) the lock was in hand, notably because of Leonardo's own work at Milan; but the summit-water solution was yet to be attacked. The Wars of

Religion almost immediately intervened, and it was not until the lull that came with the ascension to the throne of the House of Bourbon-Navarre under Henry IV in 1594, that any advances in the solution of that problem began.

The miter-gated pound lock had appeared in France, not very far from Amboise, when in 1550 river navigations along the Yevre, the Auron, and the Cher adjacent to Bourges were fitted with such locks with "rectangular chambers measuring 90 feet by 13 feet."[12] Again, these Berrichonne navigations were an initial form of the facilities necessary to the creation of a system of inland waterways. They tied together the various agricultural districts within a rich landscape, which we still know from the lush pictures contained in the illustrated manuscripts of the duke of Berry. As France sought what we would now call development, it was such small-scale works that first came into use. By canalizing a river the flow of goods to such a barter-trading town as Bourges could be facilitated. But the Berry lay south of the Loire and was separated from Paris by the watershed between that river and the Seine. The lush production of the Loire Valley was tantalizingly distant from Paris in an era when the costs of wagon transport would have consumed any possible value of many of the products by the time they reached the city. It was partly in this economic-geographic context that the court migrated to the Touraine and other parts of the Loire valley to construct châteaux within a smiling countryside—palaces of the sort in which Francis and Leonardo dreamed of tying the area to Paris by waterway.

The first attempt at a watershed canal came during Francis's reign, when he had Nicholas Bachelier survey a route across Languedoc for a Canal des Deux Mers.[13] The religious wars, which incidentally found the Languedoc considerably interested in

the Reformation, stopped any practical efforts toward construction. Instead, practical attention first turned to the connection between the Loire and the Seine. By then Henry IV had ascended the throne, and in a lull in the Wars of Religion he had been able to appoint the able but Protestant duc de Sully his chief minister. Sully examined the plans for canalization and quickly urged delay on the Deux Mers canal, which required passage over a 620-foot summit in an area of summer drought. He replaced such an undertaking with one across the Seine-Loire divide. In an encompassing survey of the possibilities for canal building in France, the Dutch Royal Dikemaster, Humphrey Bradley, had found what he considered a practical route for a canal to connect the two northern rivers. One attraction of this canal was that it might begin the development of a second route tying the Atlantic and the Mediterranean together across France. Francis and Leonardo had made such a proposal to tie the Loire and the Seine, flowing to the Atlantic, to the Saône-Rhône, draining to the Mediterranean. A canal extending northward from Briare on the Loire to Montargis on the Seine would forge the first link in this greater chain. "Sully's decision was a wise one, for although the Canal de Briare which ultimately resulted from it was only 21¼ miles long it was to serve as a working model for those who would ultimately engineer the Canal du Midi."[14] We shall examine that claim later when we take up the Languedoc canal; for the moment we should look at the Briare as the first important watershed canal in Western civilization.

As first proposed in 1603, the Canal de Briare was rather timid in its design, still basing its connection on the river Trezée for 10 miles between the Loire at Briare and the village of Breteau. Again the line employed navigation on the Loing tributary of the Seine for 26 miles, from Rogny down to Montargis. Fortunately, before construc-

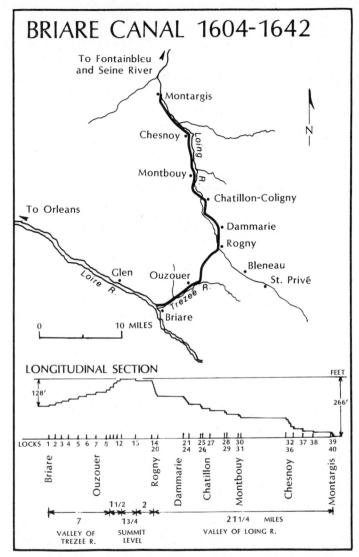

BRIARE CANAL 1604-1642

To Fontainbleu
and Seine River

Montargis

Chesnoy

Montbouy

Chatillon-Coligny

Dammarie

Rogny

Bleneau

St. Privé

To Orleans

Glen

Ouzouer

Loire R.

Trezeé R.

Briare

N

0　　　10 MILES

LONGITUDINAL SECTION

FEET

128'

266'

LOCKS 1 2 3 4 5 6 7 8 12 15　14 20　21 24 25 26 27 28 29 30 31　32 36 37 38 39 40

Briare　Ouzouer　Rogny　Dammarie　Chatillon　Montbouy　Chesnoy　Montargis

11/2　2

7　13/4　21 1/4　MILES

VALLEY OF TREZEÉ R.　SUMMIT LEVEL　VALLEY OF LOING R.

Source: Singer, Holmyurd, Hull and Williams, eds. *A History of Technology*, vol. 2 (New York: Oxford University Press, 1958), p. 538.

tion was begun, the brilliant engineer Hughes Cosnier—"who was more than a century advanced on his time, and who could not be likened to a simple entrepreneur; he both conceived and executed"[15]—was given charge of planning. As he revised the design, the total distance between Briare and Montagris, 43 miles, was to

be taken in a canal with forty locks.

The locks Cosnier constructed were a considerable advance on the simple pound chambers. He may well have been the first to propound the idea that to cluster the locks would lead to more efficient operation from the time viewpoint. Over the years this has proved to be the case, though with some

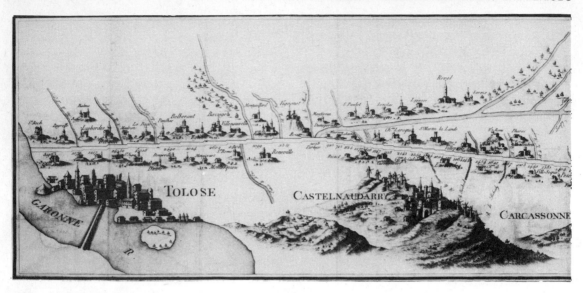

Map of the canal between the seas, the ocean, and the Mediterranean. *Source*: Andreossy, *Histoire du Canal du Midi* (Paris, 1804).

limitations, notably that in double or multiple locks a boat must complete its passage before one going in the opposite direction can enter the flight. And in ascending locks such a staircase makes a heavy demand on the water in the pond at its head—each staircase used in descent takes only one lock of water, which is passed downward ahead of the barge; but each lock within the staircase takes a full lock of water on ascent, meaning that a six-lock staircase, as at Rogny on the Canal de Briare, would require six locks of water to raise one barge over the flight. Only by keeping the pond at the head of the flight long, and thus of considerable storage capacity, could such an amount of water be let down the staircase without greatly reducing the depth of water in the head pond. Fortunately, Cosnier made long ponds; but his need to rise over a summit of 266 feet, with forty locks altogether on the two slopes of the canal, meant that the Canal de Briare was always plagued by a shortage of water.[16]

The construction of the Canal de Briare

began in 1604, and the state provided the labor of some six thousand troops to accomplish the task. For the next seven years the efforts were vigorous; by 1611 three-quarters of the canal had been completed, and thirty-five of the forty locks constructed. In 1610 Henry IV was assassinated, leaving the duc de Sully, as a Protestant, politically exposed when the new regime proved much more rigidly Catholic. A year later he was dismissed as minister and the work on the canal was suspended. For twenty-eight years the weeds grew, but in 1638 Guillaume Boutheroue and Jacques Guyon were issued letters patent permitting them to recommence construction and obtain ownership of the canal by paying off the crown's debts contracted in the earlier construction and by completing the route. Under this arrangement the Briare was completed and opened in 1642, exactly following Hughes Cosnier's design, which proved very successful save in the matter of water supply. Four years later a 13-mile feeder canal was added to that

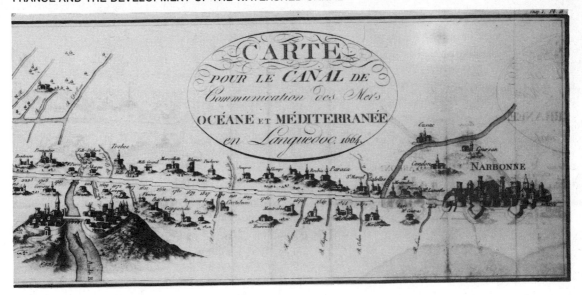

already in place, bringing the supply more or less in keeping with the heavy traffic that was developing.[17] Even with that improvement in supply there was a period of three months, according to the registers of the company, when the canal could not operate for a shortage of lock water, a situation aggravated by the then excessive size of the Briare locks.[18] This lesson was to prove essential to the successful design of the larger Languedocian canal, as the crown would not authorize its commencement until a plan with sufficient water at the summit was devised.

The Canal du Briare was an immediate financial success. Soon it was earning 13 percent on its capital, and over the next century and a half it averaged some 200,000 tons of transit traffic a year.[19] Even today it is an active canal, and one where Cosnier's generous lock size has finally been fully justified. We should appreciate, however, that in these early watershed canals there had to be rather conservative predictions of the

potential traffic: to overdesign these waterways was normally to outdistance the supply of water available.

The Great Work of the Sun King: Riquet and the Canal des Deux Mers

The great financial success of the Canal de Briare, and its obviously beneficial role in providing Paris with access to the wine country of the Loire—where wines superior to those previously tied to Paris by natural navigations (those of the Champagne brought along the Marne) could be had—strongly encouraged others to attempt further cross-watershed diversions of long-established inland navigations. Just as Leonardo and the king had dreamed of a canal across Languedoc, tying the Mediterranean to the Atlantic without the long and politically difficult circumnavigation of the Iberian peninsula, so did seventeenth-century magnates see such a route as desirable.

One of these was Pierre-Paul Riquet de Bon-repos, a tax farmer in the Languedoc. In that office he had prospered handsomely, as was common, but he had to travel widely to earn that competence. The job of *fermier général* existed because the central administration could not enforce taxes since it resided too far from the agricultural population that provided almost the entire king's purse under the *ancien régime*. To be successful as a tax farmer, retaining a percentage of an ever-increasing tax take, meant unremitting pursuit of a population for whom taxes seem culturally abhorrent. Speaking of the men of Roussillon, and seemingly by extension to all those of Languedoc, Riquet told Colbert, the French minister of finance: "No human power could prevent this kind of men killing each other, and you may therefore infer that the tax collectors are subject to the same fate. In this country, the tax collectors are always on the lookout: they kill just as they are killed; it is the only way to carry out their function."[20] Such a sharp attention to the region had convinced the *fermier général* of Languedoc that a canal could be built to connect the Mediterranean with the Atlantic; and his demonstrated ability, even at gunpoint, to extract tax money from the peasantry of the Midi suggested to him how it might be financed.

Before seeking authority to advance such a plan, Riquet carefully examined the land between Narbonne and Toulouse.

As his predecessors, he had understood the critical role played by the Rocks of Naurouze, the watershed [between the Atlantic and Mediterranean] in the construction of the canal; but in place of holding to the inadequate supply of water from the river Ariége, he sought to use there the system applied in a very satisfactory manner at Briare. The objective was then the search for small rivulets on the southern slope of the Montagne Noire, capable of being diverted to the watershed [at Naurouze]: the problem of reservoirs would be less critical.[21]

With the *fontainier* of Revel, an official vaguely responsible for water policy in the vicinity, he set out to examine the Montagne Noire, which rises to over 3,000 feet on the north side of the Col de Naurouze, in search of such a supply. On the river Sor and its tributaries sufficient catchment areas seemed available, which by damming and subsequent diversion could be turned south-ward toward the watershed in the Col. At his estate at Bonrepos, Riquet had constructed a model of the *rigole* he would use to bring water from the Montagne to the summit level of any canal that might be constructed between the seas. Having solved to his own satisfaction what had seemed to be the fundamental problem in the building of such a canal, Riquet, with the assistance of the archbishop of Toulouse, turned to Colbert, writing him that "the facility and assurance of this navigation will be such that the Strait of Gibraltar will cease to be a necessary passage, the revenues of the King of Spain at Cadiz will be diminished, and those of our King augmented a great deal in the leases deposited in the treasury and in the entrance of goods into the kingdom. In addition the tons which will be taken upon the said canal will rise to immense sums and His Majesty's subjects will profit from a thousand new commerces and will secure great advantages from this navigation."[22]

This letter of November 26, 1662, whetted Colbert's interest, no doubt with its mercantilist appeal, which fitted so well into his economic thinking. On his advice Louis XIV issued an *arrêt du Conseil* on January 18, 1663, calling for an investigation to be made by a commission drawn from the States of Languedoc and the king's ministry, including Jean Cavalier, the Geographer Royal, and an engineer, François Andreossy, and Henri de Boutheroue de Bourgneuf, son of the contractor François Boutheroue, who finished the Canal de Briare. The latter became the chief expert of the commission, who, in Riquet's company, gave particular attention to the nature and extent of the water supply for the summit level. This attention was essential, as the operation of the twenty-six locks ultimately to be built ascending between Toulouse and the summit at Naurouze and the eighteen descending locks from Naurouze to the Fresquel River near Carcassone would have to depend on that supply entirely. On January 19, 1665, the commission reported favorably, and an *arrêt du Conseil* was issued on May 27, 1665, authorizing the construction of the trial ditch seeking to supply water to the summit point.[23] By October there seems to have been enough assurance of the success of that trial to lead the king and his financial councillors to issue several edicts confirming Riquet as the contractor for the canal, conferring on Riquet and his heirs the fief of the canal, and establishing financial support for the undertaking.

What was the canal that Riquet set out to build? As it was finished, the Canal des Deux Mers—or, as it is commonly called today, the Canal du Midi—extended for 149 miles from its entrance lock to the Garonne River at Toulouse, eastward over the Col de Naurouze to les Onglous, where it enters the Bassin de Thau for access to the new port of Sète (originally, Cette) located just halfway between the mouth of the Rhône and the Spanish border. On the Mediterranean section, the 114 miles between the Écluse de la Mediterranée and les Onglous, there were seventy-five locks, which raised a boat 623 feet from the sea-level Bassin de Thau to the summit pond on the Col de Naurouze. The navigation across the Bassin de Thau would be about 6 miles to the port of Sète. The summit-level pond is just over 3 miles in length, with the outfall of the *rigole* bringing water from the Montagne Noir standing just midway between Ségala (Écluse de la Mediterranée) and Avignonet (Écluse de l'Océan), where the respective slopes begin. From the Écluse de l'Océan to Toulouse and the entrance to the Garonne, the fall was 203 feet in twenty-six locks, spread over a distance of 49 miles.[24] The water in the *rigole* was secured from a number of rivulets in the Montagne Noir, which with 50 miles of feeder canal was capable of supplying more than seven times the total water contained in the "canal prism" at any one time, [25] some 22 million cubic meters.

The grave concern for the water supply of the Canal du Midi was due to climate and experience. The summer drought of the Mediterranean and the three-month late-summer closure of the Canal de Briare gave the developers pause. Even more, they were concerned with providing a true ship canal rather than some mildly transformed inland navigation. The intention was to offer an alternative route to that around Iberia, which caused Riquet to build large locks and to fill his canal with a considerable depth of water. As planned and built, though not as it exists today, the Canal du Midi was to have a canal prism 56 feet across the surface, 30 feet at the bottom, and 6 feet deep. Because this did not give enough width to permit the passing of two of the 18-foot beam boats they envisaged traveling along the canal, the width was enlarged to 72 to 90 feet at the surface and 42 to 48 feet at the bottom. As always happens in canals, the design prism was encroached on by silting and bank slump to the point that by 1778 the surface was on the average 60 feet wide and the bottom only 32 feet. Today the average is 53 feet at the surface, 33 at the bottom, and 1.6 meters depth (5′4″).[26]

The ample size of the Canal du Midi did permit some sailing along the waterway. The first boats all seem to have had sails; it appears that this was initially thought to be the logical means of propulsion, probably build-

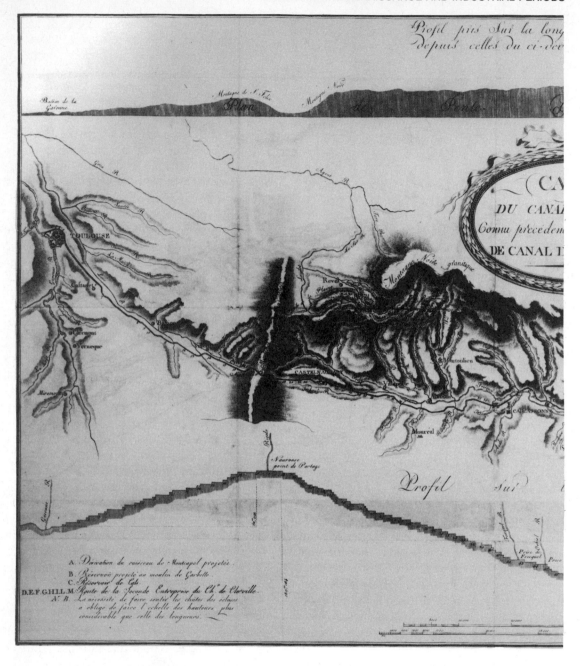

Map and profile of the Canal du Midi. *Source*: Andreossy, *Histoire du Canal du Midi* (Paris, 1804).

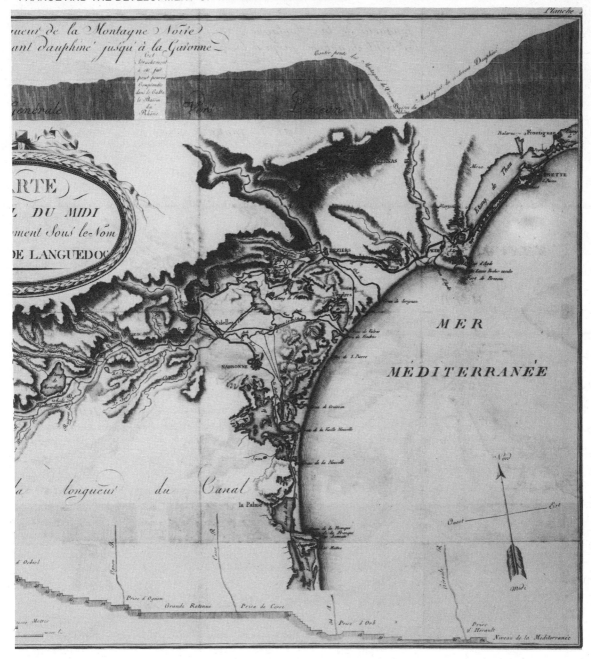

ing on the image of this as a ship canal. But soon after the canal opened it was found that its tortuous course, as it clung to the sinuosities of the contour lines of the country through which it passed, was impossible to sail. Horses on the towpath were substituted even though the boats retained masts and sails to cross the Bassin de Thau, where there was no towpath. The amplitude of the canal showed its importance to national power when, during the American Revolution, France and Spain found themselves at war with England. Little happened in Europe save the beseiging of Gibraltar by the two Catholic kings' armies. In what is perhaps the most elaborate and extended siege of all time, the navigation of the straits was fiercely contested by England and the Continental powers. The result was a great reliance on the Canal du Midi, then called the Canal Royal, for passage between the Mediterranean and the Atlantic. In this intended use of this Canal des Deux Mers, so much traffic passed that the water supply was severely taxed in the late 1770s and early 1780s, although it sufficed; and the annual tolls were at a rate of 1.8 million francs in 1782 before rumors of peace, signed in Paris in 1783, somewhat reduced this volume.[27] In this instance the strategic nature of the canal between the seas was fully demonstrated.

The canal that Riquet brought into being was modeled on experience in Italy and in France. Riquet assigned most of the model to the Canal de Briare, which he had visited in his search for understanding of waterways; François Andréossy, his engineering deputy, after completing his education in Paris traveled to Italy to visit family connections and in the process studied the canals in Lombardy and at Padua in the Venetian Republic, so he viewed the design as an outgrowth of Italian practice. In any event there was much that had to be original in the work. The miter-gated pound lock was certainly firmly established in European prac-

tice by the last half of the seventeenth century, but in the hands of Riquet it was modified better to suit the needs of a canal with an amplitude unknown elsewhere. Because this was intended as a ship canal to handle the ships of the time, its locks as begun near Toulouse were deeper and wider than was the established practice. We know that at least one of these failed because the sidewalls of the chamber were pushed inward by the pressure of the wet ground against the empty chamber. As a result Riquet had the structure so redesigned that the sidewalls became elliptical, essentially creating the much stronger structure of a horizontal arch in place of the straight vertical wall. This elliptical plan also seems to have been dictated by the notion that two of the broad river boats then operating on the Rhône, *caponts* or *capons*, with a maximum beam of 16 feet, could lie in the lock for a single rise or fall. Thus the oval locks were 36 feet across at midpoint but had gate openings of only 19 feet 8 inches at their ends. The advantages of this design were considerable, but they did suffer from the fact that with straight-sided barges considerably more water was employed to operate the locks than would have been required by a more conventional rectangular lock.[28] The scale of these structures can be appreciated from the fact that they were 137.7 feet long, 36 feet at their widest point, and 6 feet deep. Gates were of oak, operated by *flèches* 14 feet long.[29]

In addition to the locks there were perhaps the first instances of other features that came to be more common as the canal era advanced: aqueducts were commonly used to carry the canal trough over intervening streams and, in one case, a stream over the canal; a pontoon aqueduct was employed at Libron because the level of the canal there was only 3 feet 11 inches above the normal level of the Mediterranean, yet an aqueduct was needed to keep the sand from the river

Libron from entering the waterway;[30] at Malpas west of Beziers a 492-foot tunnel was driven through the crest when the canal was led from a lateral position in the valley of the Orb to a similar position in the next valley to the east.[31] Also on the Midi the first long pond was built; this *grand bief* followed the contours for 35 miles, producing a sinuosity that at first seems undesirable. The explanation lies in the fact that at its eastern end, at the Fonséranes locks, where a staircase of eight locks carried the canal traffic downward 70 feet to the river Orb, there was such a demand for lockage water that a large reservoir was needed at the head of the flight. Riquet secured this by shaping the long pond so that even a considerable drawdown of water would neither lower the level of the pond nor create the current that would result from such a removal in a shorter *bief*, or reach.[32] In shaping this long pond, Riquet was forced into the construction of the Malpas Tunnel through the Enserune Ridge, already mentioned, to continue his navigable reservoir of the Grand Bief. Other features that came with the Canal du Midi included the development of a siphon to handle excess water in the canal. Only as the surface level of the canal rose would the crest of the siphon be reached and outward flow commence. The device was thought out by "M. Garipuy, young inventor of siphon drains" and applied near Capestang and Ventenac on the canal route.[33]

Two foundation stones for the canal were laid at the entrance lock between the Garonne River and the waterway in Toulouse on November 17, 1667. Work progressed reasonably rapidly on the excavation and the building of the twenty-six locks rising to the summit pond adjacent to Naurouze. Within a year or so the oval design of the locks had been settled on and a general lift of 8 feet per chamber established, although it was varied by circumstance. The width of the waterway also varied but stood, as we have seen, on the

average between 70 and 90 feet. On steep slopes where the canal was carried on a bench, the width would be reduced; where possible, it might be expanded to allow easier passing of fast boats overtaking slower ones and those moving in opposite directions. By 1672 the locks and ditch as far as Naurouze were complete, allowing the water to be let in from the Rigole de la Plaine, filling the 49 miles of canal in about six days.[34] Almost immediately the use of the canal for transport convinced the undertakers that the waterway would be a commercial success.

Progress on the construction east of Naurouze continued apace. The largest single facility on the canal between Toulouse and Trèbes was the staircase of four locks at St. Roch in Castelnaudary. "As this draws on a pound only 2½ miles long which terminates at the single lock of Laplanque, Riquet realized that additional water capacity would have to be created in this pound to supply the St. Roch staircase. Hence the provision of the magnificent *Grand Bassin* at Castelnaudary, an area of water spacious enough to contain several Atlantic liners and a permanent asset to the town in a region comparatively waterless."[35] By 1668 the canal was completed to Trèbes, and on May 14 Riquet and his heirs, as a consequence of their holding of the fief for the canal, were granted the right to levy a toll. Thus, the first section of the canal authorized by the first royal edict was complete. On August 20 a new edict authorized Riquet to continue the project, giving him eight years to open a waterway to the Bassin de Thau.

Eastward from Trèbes the first 18 miles were easy and determinate. Then the question arose whether the canal should pass through Narbonne, as seems to have been assumed, or else northward thereof through Beziers, Riquet's birthplace. His decision to take the northerly route was much criticized both for the more difficult construction and for its avoidance of the regional metropolis.

His argument was that the Narbonne route would overtax his water supply, as experience bore out when later it proved necessary to call on Vauban to expand the mountain water-collection system before such a Narbonnaise branch was added in the 1680s. Passing via Beziers did involve him in the great octuple staircase at Fonséranes, the Malpas tunnel, and the sinuous Grand Bief already noted; but it also conserved the water in a supply that was proving barely marginal. East of Beziers the construction was relatively easy as it passed down the gentle slope of the Languedocian coastal plain. Unfortunately, Riquet, at the age of 77 and after fifteen years of continuous trial in the building of the greatest civil work ever undertaken before the Erie Canal, died on October 1, 1680. Just before he collapsed, he asked his son Jean Mathias, who had become the director of the project on his being taken ill, "'Where is the canal?' Jean Mathias answered sadly, 'Just one league from the Étang de Thau.' 'One league' repeated his father sadly. They were the last words he ever spoke."[36]

By 1681 the Canal des Deux Mers—soon to become the Canal Royal and today known as the Canal du Midi—was finished after fifteen years of constant labor by thousands of workers. It had cost 15,249,399 livres, some 50 million gold francs—just 2.5 times what had been estimated in 1667. Of that investment, 7,484,051 had come from the royal treasury; 5,807,631 from the taxes secured at least in part through Riquet's continuing role as *fermier général* of Languedoc from the states of that province; and 1,957,571 from Riquet's own fortune.[37] Although his family was badly in debt at his death, ultimately the Riquets were greatly enriched by the tolls or rents they received from the canal between the initiation of tolls in 1668 and their sale of the fief to the French Republic in 1897. By then, under their aegis, the Canal du Midi had been further im-

proved by the building of a lateral canal from Toulouse alongside the Garonne to the point at Castets where the estuary of the Gironne is reached. This 120-mile canal, added to the 149 miles of the Midi, finally completed the greatest work that man had ever undertaken in improving on nature's provision of inland navigation. When the Canal Lateral de Garonne was opened in 1856 it utilized another 53 locks to complete the slackwater navigation from the Mediterranean to the Atlantic. Thus this vast waterway of 269 miles and 154 locks was on a scale that was never equaled during the next century and a half. In fact, not until the canal era had closed with the coming of railroads in the early nineteenth century was any larger project proposed. The Erie Canal was longer, 363 miles, but required far fewer locks, 83 in all. Even the Suez Canal, the first more massive civil engineering work was, when it opened in 1869, a much larger ditch albeit one without the great constructed facilities of the Canal des Deux Mers. In truth, the Deux Mers was a work of such imagination and investment that it represented the creation of a finished art almost with the inception of the basic form.

State Construction of Canals

The success of the Canal Royal was both technical and geographical: it was generously enough constructed to be usable for all but a couple of weeks in summer, and it effectively advanced the geographical integration of the formerly regionally divided economy. Undoubtedly it was the call on the purse of the king and of the province of Languedoc that made the waterway successful. In that era there was not nearly enough private capital available to do a proper job in carrying out such an extensive project. Yet for success the project had to be ample in scale, particularly in the matter of the summit water supply, which was from the beginning seen as the key to the project. Fortunately, Louis XIV so sought glory that he was willing to undertake such a construction if only for its audacity and size. Royal support made enough money available to do the job right, without the need for initial expedients that would make the use of the route only partially successful. Save for moderate additions to the summit-level water supply—occasioned by the construction of branches, such as that to Narbonne, as much as anything—the canal has served down to the present with remarkably little reconstruction.

French Canals after Riquet

Much of the subsequent canal development in France, and on the Continent in general, must be understood in a precapitalist framework. Once the Canal Royal had proved successful in reshaping the economic geography of France there was an obvious force at work to transform the connectivity of other regions of the kingdom. With the Garonne tied to the Mediterranean and the Seine to the Loire, there were still other barriers to breach, notably the connection between the Seine-Loire and the Saône-Rhône.

The Rhône was hardly the ideal waterway. Of steep gradient and interrupted by rapids, plagued by great changes in water level as a result of the extremely variable flow of the Rhône headwaters fed by snowmelt and Alpine glaciers, and whipped by the Mistral pouring southward in its confined valley, the Rhône was perhaps the worst river in western Europe for natural navigation, and the hardest to "improve." Even today that improvement is only partial, though it has been accomplished as far north as Lyon. Until the construction of the Donzère-Mondragon Canal in the worst section of the river, between Valence and Pont St. Esprit, in the post-World War II years, the connection between the Languedocian system of waterways and those of the rest of France was rather tenuous.

Outside Languedoc the French sought goals similar to those obtained there by 1680. Of greatest concern was a connection from the Seine and Loire to the Mediterranean drainage of the Saône. In what seems an un-Gallic extravagance, three canals were begun in the last years of the *ancien régime* to that end. The Canal de Bourgogne, begun in 1775, was commenced at Migennes just upstream on the river Yonne (a tributary of the Seine) from Joigny and carried in 189 locks over a distance of 150 miles. With a summit level, at the crest of the Côte d'Or, of some 3 miles, that eminence is pierced by a tunnel of just over 2 miles, keeping the elevation only to a still-heavy 1,232 feet. The pull up from the Seine-Yonne is the heavier, 115 locks, whereas to the Saône the drop is taken in 76. In the course of the waterway it passes through Dijon, tying that ancient city to the navigation of the Saône. When finished in 1832, the Canal de Bourgogne greatly facilitated transport of the wine of the Côte d'Or, loaded at Dijon, and that of the Chablis, loaded adjacent to the summit tunnel at Rouilly-en-Auxois, to the vast Parisian market.[38] But because it took fifty-nine years to finish the Canal de Bourgogne, the other waterway constructed across the water-parting of the Atlantic and the Mediterranean, the Canal du Centre, though less direct in tying Paris with the southeast, assumed equal importance. This canal through the Bourbonnais tied the Loire, reached from Paris by the Canal du Briare, at Digion, to the river Saône at Chalons-sur-Saône. Seventy-two miles long, on the Centre the rise from the west was easier because the Loire was there well toward its headwaters. Thus there were 26 locks toward Digion but 37 toward Chalons-sur-Saône on sides of a summit lower than that on the Canal de Bourgogne, 987 feet, and requiring no tunnel. This easier crossing of the Morvan than the Côte d'Or allowed the Canal du Centre to be completed quite rapidly, 1784–1790. An additional advantage was its passage through the basin around Le Cruesot, where France's modern metallurgical industry arose.

In the Napoleonic Era France was only partially developed with internal navigation. The canal connections of the Mediterranean and Atlantic, via the Midi, and the Rhône-Saône valley with the Atlantic, via either the Loire (Canal du Centre) or the Seine (Canal de Bourgogne), were in place. In addition there were two crossings of the basin divide between those latter rivers, the older at Briare and the newer via Nevers, and the Canal du Nivernaise. The Midi system and that tributary to the Rhône-Saône were loosely tied together by the extremely difficult navigation on the section of the Rhône below Lyon. In the north of France a number of basically navigable rivers—the Seine, Oise, Eschaut (Scheldt), Aisne, Meuse, Marne, Yonne, and upper Moselle—were used locally, but that employment was not national because of the radial nature of French rivers. Particularly in the north the rivers flowed parallel with the rock structures in Picardy and Artois, carrying the streams directly to the English Channel rather than inward toward Paris. This same radial flow also affected the larger rivers of northeastern France, the Sambre and the Meuse, which in France flowed separately north-northeasterly into Belgium, and the Moselle, trending northeasterly into Germany to join the Rhine at Coblenz. Although each of these rivers might have *biefs* usable for local transportation, there was no extensive system. To provide that, the French had to build a series of relatively short, though not always simple, canals across the rolling divides of these basins. Using the rivers Oise and Marne, tributaries of the

Seine flowing from northeast to southwest and joining that river respectively just downstream from Paris near Pontoise and upstream in the outskirts of the city, connections were made across the Oise-Somme divide via the Canal de St. Quentin, completed in its initial state as the Picardy Canal in 1738,[39] and across the Marne-Aisne divide in the Canal de l'Aisne à la Marne. Begun under Louis XV, the St. Quentin Canal was completed under Napoleon I, providing a double watershed crossing—the Canal Crozat from the Oise tributary of the Seine across to the Somme, a river flowing northwestward directly into the Channel, and the older St. Quentin canal proper from that stream across the divide into the valley of the Eschaut (Scheldt), the main navigable river of Flanders, flowing to the sea in a joint delta with the Rhine. When the St. Quentin Canal was completed, France for the first time had a possible system extending from the Flemish and Dutch waterways to Lyon, and tenuously to the Mediterranean. It is not surprising that the St. Quentin remains the most heavily used canal of France, the key to the integration of the many industrial waterways of Nord, Pas de Calais, and even Loraine, and in turn their connection to the extensive system related to the Scheldt and the Rhine. Because the crowding on this none-too-ample canal was severe, a modern relief canal, the Canal du Nord, was constructed to the west of it in the years after World War II. This modern canal from Noyon to the Oise to Arleux on the Sensée (Eschaut) allows larger barges (350 tons) to cover the distance in half the time.[40]

Coal makes the canalization of the rivers of northern France important in the national economy; but we should appreciate that these are generally deeply concealed coal seams, so the extensive system that now exists north of the low divide between the Somme and the Eschaut was of late develop-

PROPOSED CANAL NETWORK FOR FRANCE 1829

——— Canals of the first class

——— Canals of the second class

- - - Canals of the first class completed or under construction in 1829

+-+-+ Railroads (chemin de fer) as part of the system

Source: Corps de Ponts et Chaussées, map, 1824, overprinted with the canal plan, 1829.

ment. Originally, when Louis XV encouraged the construction of the Canal de St. Quentin, the coal fields that lie just south of the Belgian border were undeveloped, and the kingdom, for what coal it used, depended on small coal basins tucked into embayments in the flanks of the Massif Central and the Morvan, particularly in the Loire coal basin, which straddled the water parting between the Rhône and the uppermost Loire containing both the Rive de Gier and the St. Étienne fields. In the Morvan the Blanzy field, near Le Creusot and Montceau-les-Mines, was of less importance but did export some coal to Paris.

The complexity of the transport of coal from the upper Loire basin to Paris, and from the Blanzy basin to the eastern part of the country, encouraged an elaboration of the original waterways strategy of the government under the *ancien régime*—that is, the interconnection of the major drainage basins by watershed canals. France was still plagued by an industrial development that was located far from Paris, and commonly peripheral to the state—in the Vosges; in the textile centers of the Belgian border region, particularly Lille; in Loraine; and in the industrial valleys adjacent to the Massif Central and the Morvan (Le Creusot, St. Étienne, Decazeville, etc.)—and a coal supply equally far from the center. Under the restored monarchy, Becquey, the director-general of the Corps des Ponts et Chausées, whose job it was to design and carry out civil works related to bridges and roads, was asked to prepare a report on the potential waterway system of France. His report of August 16, 1820, is reminiscent of the American Secretary of the Treasury's report twelve years before, considered at the end of this chapter. In it Becquey presented a comprehensive plan for tying all parts of France together with waterways and for lending considerable assistance to the industrialization of the nation.

The Becquey Report of 1820 and the Rebuilding of Rivers

This report gives us an example of the way canal building evolved with the onset of greater long-distance movement. To go back a moment, we may recall that the first epoch of canal building—say, 1600 to 1815—had been predicated on supplementing the long-standing navigation of rivers by tying their headwaters together to create an extended inland navigation system. With that goal in mind, the various French governments had built about 800 miles of canal, but only about 120 miles under the First Empire of Napoleon I. The restored Bourbon monarchy constructed 577 miles before it fell in the Revolution of 1830; the Orléans monarchy that followed added another 900 miles before mid-century.[41]

The second epoch of French waterway construction, from Becquey's 1820 report to about 1850, added over 1,500 miles to the system and went beyond radically transforming the natural waterways system (in pegging together river navigations with moderate-length watershed canals) through starting to "rebuild" the rivers themselves. In his report Becquet had called for making an economically effective system of what was only a nominally integrated system. The rivers were to be rebuilt in one of two ways, the first by cutting an artificial waterway alongside the stream itself to avoid the shifting sands that plagued many French rivers, rocky sills that created rapids, and water too shallow to navigate. This *lateral canal* was simply the extension of a technology that had of necessity been devised for the watershed canals for the creation of reasonable navigation along the valleys thus interconnected. Under such a plan the Garonne was paralleled by a lateral canal from Toulouse to Castets (completed in 1856), the Loire by the Canal Latèral à la Loire from Digion (at the double junction with the Canal du Centre from the

Saône and the coal-carrying canal up the Loire to Roanne) parallel to that turbulent river to the great aqueduct connecting to the Canal de Briare and on to the Seine (completed in 1836–1837), and the lateral canal built along the Oise north of Paris (completed in 1831).

In other places the rivers were generally sufficiently supplied with water, though interrupted with rapids or choked with sand bars, so what was indicated was not the construction of a lateral canal but instead the canalization of the actual river course. The classic example is to be found in the Seine. From the outlet of the Nivernaise and Bourgogne canals near Auxerre to Paris was about 65 miles. "Boats could be sent down only by shooting a sudden flood of water [the "flash" of water used in the Middle Ages] out of the Nivernaise canal"[42] This upper part of the Seine was partially canalized, for 27 miles above Paris, between 1840 and 1846. In part this was accomplished by the successful application of a movable dam, designed by the engineer Poirée, to La Morue rapids near Marly-sur-Seine. Previously it had taken the combined traction of eight to ten horses on the towpath to breast these rapids. The movable dam was not portable as a structure; rather, the gates could be opened to allow the free flow of the river in times of flood and closed to create a navigation pond with an adjacent lock when low water set in. After 1846 the Poirée dam was applied in six places on the Seine between Paris and tidewater at Rouen to secure reasonable navigation of the stream throughout its whole navigable course. Contemporaneous with this canalization of the Seine under the July Monarchy of the Orléanists went that of the lower Oise, completing the line to the coalfields of Valenciennes and the north in 1836. Subsequently the Sambre, the French Moselle, the Marne, and the Saône were all canalized, finally tying together the artificial summit and lateral canals that interconnected them.

The Industrial System of the North and Northeast

What remained was to add one other type of canal to the French waterways system, the industrial feeder and branch, and to extend the watershed canal into the northeast of France between the Oise and the Sambre, from the Oise (Aisne) to the Marne and the Meuse, and the Marne to the Saône and the Rhine. Under the Becquey plan and other programs of the monarchies restored after 1815, a complex network of waterways was shaped from the rivers of Nord and Pas de Calais, with canal interconnections extending from the Eschaut (Sheldt) at Valenciennes in the east to Calais and Dunkerque in the west. To the east the main stem of the Meuse was canalized from Mouzay for 95 miles to the Belgian border, and then in Belgium on to Visé below Liège, where a canal takes over. This canalized river is tied to the integrated French canal system via the Canal des Ardennes from the Aisne to Point à Bar just below Sedan, crossing a summit of 530 feet (typical of the fairly low divides on the northern edge of the Île de France), and the Canal de l'Est from the Saône to the Marne and the Meuse. The Canal des Ardennes uses the river entering the Seine just below Paris, the Oise, to offer a through route to the east, which passes at 530 feet over the edge of the Paris basin in the northern Forest of Argonne near le Chesne in the Rethelois. To reach this summit 57 locks arise from the Aisne, whereas toward the Meuse only seven locks drop the canal down to that canalized river.

The second access from Paris to the east is afforded by its traditional opening in that direction, that along the canalized Marne, reaching 113 miles due east to Épernay. At that point a lateral canal is required, as the water available in the river is insufficient for extended navigation. This 41.5-mile waterway reaches to Vitry-le-François, which became a junction for two canals dug thence to the Saône at Heuilley (Canal de la Marne à la Saône) and to the Rhine at Strasbourg (Canal de la Marne au Rhin). The Marne-Saône canal was projected across the edge of the Paris Basin, this time over the Plateau of Langres where a 3-mile tunnel keeps the summit level to a still considerable 1,115 feet. This was a late construction, carried out only when it became desirable to integrate the great arc of French industrialization, which extends from the Lyonnaise in the southeast through Loraine to the region du Nord and the Channel coast.

The late development of the Marne-Saône and Est canals came from their main uses to encourage French industrialization, rather than to tie together the various agricultural regions of the realm (as was true of Briare, du Midi, and Bourgogne).

The final examples of mainline canal in France are the Canal de la Marne au Rhin and the Canal du Rhône au Rhin built under the July Monarchy to integrate the rapidly industrializing Vosges region to the rest of France. When the Marne-Rhine canal was completed in 1853, after fifteen years of construction, it was the longest and one of the most important waterways of France. Unfortunately, within seventeen years its eastern end was lost to the Germans as a result of the Franco-Prussian war.

The other canal to tie Alsace to France was that from St. Symphorien on the upper Saône to Strasbourg, a distance by the waterway of exactly 200 miles. The canal crossed the saddle of the Gap of Belfort at an elevation of 1,118 feet, somewhat south of that great fortified city, and then continued from the eastern end of that sag as a distant lateral canal to the upper Rhine for some 65 miles to Strasbourg. From Montbeliard to Strasbourg the Rhône-Rhine canal passed through industrializing country, notably at Montbeliard, Belfort, Mulhouse, Colmar, and in the environs of Strasbourg. When the canal was completed in 1833 this region was a great center of much of the French textile, chemical, and engineering industries. Within pre-1870 France the coal supply for this eastern industrial region had to come from the Blanzy and Loire coal fields so the waterway from the Rhône-Saône was of critical importance in encouraging a quickening of economic activity. Only when the Marne-Rhine canal was completed twenty years later was there any relief from this distant dependence. Like that waterway, the Rhône-Rhine canal was truncated at its eastern end when the country to the east of Belfort was lost to Germany in 1870.

The General Nature of French Canals

When the canal was first introduced under Henry IV just after 1600, French authorities saw it as an instrument for the geographical integration of the emerging national state. At this time, and throughout the *ancien régime*, the canal's purpose was to transport agricultural products from areas of heavy production to those of heavy consumption. The Loire valley, agriculturally the richest in the kingdom, was tied by the Canal de Briare to the great emerging metropolis at the heart of the Paris Basin. The second, much more elaborate undertaking in Languedoc, provided a contrast. Riquet put forward his canal as a great economic route as well as a strategic necessity to a European state with "deux mers." It seems likely that the king's ministry was more interested in the military than the commercial qualities of this waterway. Their willingness to provide it as a fief to the Riquets would support that view, particularly as the later Orléanists of the July Monarchy carefully maintained the royal interest in the Canal d'Orléans, which was built to capture part of the trade from the

Loire to the Seine, and the Canal du Loing, which provided the link from Montargis at the northern end of both those canals and the navigable Seine 30 miles to the north. It was the excessive charges of these royally owned canals that made St. Étienne coal so expensive in Paris in the years of their monarchy.

The strategic use for canals does not immediately strike us in an era with far more militarily effective transportation, but even in the last century a number of strategic canals were constructed. The French, seeking to gain transportation safe from British naval blockade, constructed a canal from Nantes on the Loire all the way to the Rade de Brest on which stood the nation's main western naval base. This 223-mile waterway, with a 53-mile branch to the Rance estuary adjacent to St. Malo on the north coast of Brittany, had a rather small economic role, as evident from its virtual abandonment today. During the nineteenth century in Scotland, other strategic canals were built, the Crinan adjacent to the Clyde and the Caledonian through the vale of Loch Ness. These were essentially ship canals of the sort presaged by the ancient Greek's construction at the Isthmus of Corinth, rebuilt by the modern Greeks in the nineteenth century, and several Roman barge canals. In Canada, after the War of 1812, the British government contributed heavily to the construction of the Rideau Canal from Bytown (Ottawa) to Kingston on Lake Ontario, a route that avoided the potential for interruption enjoyed by the Americans in the International Rapids section of the St. Lawrence River, where several short canals existed around the worst of the Saults.

The pioneering quality of French canals should not be overlooked. Not only did they undertake the earliest serious and effective watershed canals, the first modern strategic canals, and the earliest use of canals to extend the hinterland of the metropolis of a national state; France also was the first country to put forward a national policy of waterway construction and improvement. From Francis I down to the coming of the railroad there was a continuous interest in shaping a national system of waterways. No doubt the large size of France, which meant that there were rivers of considerable volume and length, contributed to this goal. Certainly, the initial phase of planning and construction was to fill the gaps between rivers, leaving navigation on those streams as nature had provided it. Briare and Midi in the seventeenth century, St. Quentin and Centre in the eighteenth, exemplify this effort. Even before 1815 there had been some attention to improving the now weak links in the system, the rivers themselves. But only in the second phase of canal building, as signaled by the plans contained in the Becquey report of 1820, was an effective national system undertaken. Rivers came to be canalized through the construction of Poirée dams in their better-watered parts and to be paralleled by lateral canals in less ample stretches.[43]

The main gap in this national system of waterways came in the failure to construct the proposed Loire-Garonne waterway, an omission probably due to the fact that by the second phase of canal building the effort was aimed at supporting industry rather than agriculture. The southwest was then, as it largely remains, a region of mainly agricultural production. With canals from the metropolis to various parts of the Paris Basin, to Burgundy and the Rhône valley, and to the Loire, there was hardly an urgent need to add Aquitaine to the agricultural hinterland of Paris. Its Bordeaux and Cognacs could stand more costly transportation and did not move in vast quantities. The other stricture in the national sytem existed in the difficult navigation of the Rhône. The cost of that work was so great that it remained unaccomplished until hydroelectric power generation (as a joint undertaking) could help bear the cost when construction began after 1945.

Although a national undertaking for the most part, the earlier canals were turned over to proprietors who were permitted to charge tolls for passage. Even when the state became directly engaged in both the construction and operation of canals, particularly with the restoration of 1815, tolls remained. Railroad competition was a definite moderating influence on the levying of tolls, which were finally abolished on all national waterways in 1898.[44]

Motive Power on French Canals

The motive power on the canals evolved over three hundred years, with France showing far more innovative experimentation than any other country. Riquet had first envisaged sailing along the Canal du Midi. The narrow and winding reaches of that waterway put an end to the practice save on the Étang de Thau between Sète and the first lock on the canal. Subsequently human hauliers operating on the towpath seem to have been the most common tractive effort. Horses and donkeys were used by some boats as time passed but human traction remained down to the end of the nineteenth century at least for some boats on most waterways. Paddle boats were used on the canalized rivers by the 1820s and steam tugs for the passage of canal tunnels from then on. On the Seine, Rhône, and several other rivers, chains resting on the river bottom were run over by steam-operated cog wheels on the boats to gain positive traction by tugs operating on the more fast-flowing streams. On the canals themselves there was some steam operation, but it was frowned on because of the wash from the propellers, which eroded the banks of these narrow cuts. Instead, by 1873 the French were

attempting towing with a four-ton steam engine which had two guiding wheels on rails and two driving wheels on the ballast [of the towpath]. A more successful effort was made about 1880 [on the industrial canals of the Region du Nord] over a distance of 77 kilometers. The engines worked to a timetable, and it was up to the boat owners to 'catch the train.' . . . The service lasted until 1886. Failure resulted from a number of causes: the economic running speeds of engines and boats did not coincide, the towing path had to be shared with all comers including horses, and above all there was intrigue against the new system.

Subsequently electric haulage was introduced between Dijon and Lock 57 on the Canal de Bourgogne, based on hydroelectric generation at Lock 57. On this line "a three-wheel electric horse ran on the bank without rails after the manner of the modern trolley-bus." The cost of improving the towpaths for the use of such wandering "electric horses" was too great, so a rail guideway for them was introduced, again in the industrial canals of the north. "During the 1914–18 war electric traction on rails was developed on the Oise Lateral Canal and on the St. Quentin [which led from Paris to the more active part of the western front]." Electric traction was widely adopted in the north after 1918 and in the east, particularly on the Marne-Rhine canal as it crossed the sandstone Vosges to reach Strasbourg and on the Rhône-Rhine canal between that city and Mulhouse.[45]

The great advantage of bank haulage is succinctly expressed in the maxim of the French Companie Générale de Traction sur les Voies Navigables that "one horse on the bank is worth four in the water," mainly because of the positive quality of bank traction over that in the water.[46] It might be useful to note that one horse can move "on the road a load of 150 kilograms, on rail 500

INLAND WATERWAYS OF FRANCE

∿ Navigable river (depth 6 ft. and over)

⌒ Navigable river (depth under 6 ft.)

– – – Canal (depth 6 ft. and over)

------ Canal (depth under 6 ft.)

0   100 MILES

The canal system of France (Belgium and the Netherlands) as completed.

kilograms, and on water 4,000 kilograms. Thus by using haulage from the bank on rails the waterways [of France] make the utmost economy of fuel and power."[47] It is no doubt for this reason as much as any other that we still find that the great industrial band that extends from the Vosges through Loraine to the English Channel, in France, and onward through Belgium, Holland, and Germany to the East German border remains a realm of active canal utilization.

SPECIALIZATION IN CANALS IN THE LOW COUNTRIES

Flanders and Holland share with Italy the earliest roots of canal building in Europe, but they differ in having an active time of construction in the period 1550–1700 and again during the last century and a half. Drainage canals were introduced in the Middle Ages, but their construction became both necessary and widespread when the line of dunes that had protected the peaty marshes and lagoons of the coastal region were breached in the fifteenth century and water regulation over the whole polder region became essential. The problem was two-sided: as the peaty areas began to sink, they had to be protected against the flooding that came with the rather high tides of the Rhine-Maas delta. When enclosed in dykes and pumped out by windmills, the polders dropped even farther below the high-tide level, as the peaty soils shrank when somewhat dried out. Thus the band some 25 miles wide between the dunes and the *geest* of the eastern Netherlands, bounded on the south by the West Scheldt estuary of that river and on the north by the embayment of the Zuiderzee, was subject to diurnal flooding as it lay below the mean tidal line, in many places below the low-tide line. North of the Zuiderzee the band was even wider, up to 50 miles including the Zuiderzee itself. As the land along the coast continued to sink in a

zone extending from the north slope of the upwarping that formed the French side of the Strait of Dover, Cap Gris Nez and the wolds of Artois, and the northernmost part of Holland, it was necessary throughout this band to engage in active diking and drainage. South of the West Scheldt the land, with only minor areas in the Netherlands Zeeland, was all above the mean tidal level, though often not above the extreme high-tide level.

If we term all the coastal belt between Dunkerque and the Scheldt estuary as Flanders and the belt north of that river mouth as far as the West Frisian Islands as Holland, we may draw certain contrasts that help us to understand the evolution of the canal system in each of these areas. Flanders is today Belgian, save for the part between Gravelines and the present Belgian border at de Panne, which was annexed to France in the period 1668–1679, and a fringe of ten miles just south of the West Scheldt estuary, which remained in the Netherlands after 1830. In turn, what we have called Holland is in the Netherlands. Flanders lay above mean sea level, though subject to flooding from wind-driven waves and extremely high tides. Holland lay below mean sea level and was subject to flooding on every high tide. Thus the coastal belt was subject to inundation from the sea and had to be protected to the west. Furthermore, because this belt lay so near to or even below sea level, the large rivers flowing through it—from the south (the Scheldt), the southeast (the Maas-Meuse), and from the east (the Rhine, called the Waal in the Netherlands)—all had to be carried across the band in diked courses that would keep the river water from ponding up in the drained polders. As in all streams toward their mouths, where the velocity of flow usually drops, the composite delta of the Scheldt-Maas-Rhine was characterized by an aggrading of the bed of the distributaries such that the rivers tended over the centuries to flow higher and higher above the level of the drained polders, and thus to require even more elaborate diking and lockage to interconnect the drainage canals of the polders with the rivers crossing the coastal band and providing access to the open sea to the west.

Canal Service Carried to the Ultimate: Trekvaarten

We have discussed the way canals emerged in Holland in the Middle Ages and the development of the pound lock to permit navigation between the drainage canals in the polders and the rivers crossing the coastal belt at higher elevations. In this development we find an example of a condition in transportation development that we will see repeated later in the case of railroad operation, highway development, and the evolution of air travel—that is, the progressive specialization of the service by separation of its components into different routes and independent facilities. In Holland there was a ubiquity of waterways not to be found anywhere else. For the most productive parts of the Low Countries to be used, they had automatically to be drained; those drainage canals were both widespread and obviously interconnected, but they also were unspecialized for transportation use. The early pound locks, as at Vreeswijk in 1373, represented the cautious beginnings of specialized facilities intended to aid navigation rather than drainage. As the use of canals for movement of boats as well as of the flood of water that plagued the polder lands advanced, there was a call to provide specialized transportation facilities between the locks— that is, waterways intended primarily for transport and not for drainage.

The evolution of the Dutch canal system before the early seventeenth century seems to have come entirely in terms of water control. Dikes were built to contain the outfall of the Scheldt-Maas-Rhine (Waal) that tended to fix the distributaries of this complex delta, determining the necessary places where the discharge of water pumped from the polders must take place. The drainage canals of the polders leading to those discharge points had of necessity to take on a somewhat dendritic quality, with field drains collecting into larger secondary drains and those in turn flowing into major collectors to carry the water to the pumps by the riverside. No doubt there was some navigation on each of these elements, but the greater emphasis must have rested on the main collectors, and the place where they intersected the rivers must have stood as an important juncture in the transport as well as the water-control system. This situation seems to have held up to the mid-seventeenth century, when the desire to create a passenger-carrying canal system was expressed.

To improve on this situation, there seemed to be a need to innovate in both propulsion and geography. As long as basically natural waterways were used, there would be wide *meeren*—undrained sections of the polderlands subject to gusty conditions and yet traversable only by sailing ship, tortuous but fixed distributaries of the delta rivers, and the need to cross streams by sailing. With such a combination of adventitious elements sailing was the only possible way to traverse the polder belt; yet sailing under such conditions was difficult as well as commonly interrupted by becalming or weather too severe to venture into. It was obvious that a dependence on totally artificial waterways would much improve not only the directness of the route between two cities but also the means of propulsion. In place of the variable winds might come the plodding but predictable traction of bank haulage by humans or beasts. In this way the *trekvaarten* already noted were shaped, in response to the desire to improve passenger transportation by speeding it up and making it more reliable. The pattern of intercity connection already in existence on the *beurtveer* network of natural waterways had demonstrated the *scale* of the market; what remained was to improve on the service provided.

In Holland, nature had gone far toward providing the pioneering transportation system capable of initiating a demand that could better be met through innovation. "The trekvaart as an innovation in passenger transport can be compared to the railroad which proceeded through several forms between the wooden tracks of the coal mines and the Liverpool and Manchester Railway [of 1830]." Scheduled passenger barges began to navigate the Willebroek Canal between Antwerp and Brussels in 1618, to connect with river boats on the Scheldt that took passengers from the river Ruppel to the great port city. "At the same time canals were being dug between Ghent and Bruges and Oostende with a view of providing the Flemish cities with an access route to the sea that bypassed territories controlled by the Dutch. These canals were thus not built primarily to carry passengers, but in 1623 (apparently) daily passenger barges began connecting Ghent with Bruges and Bruges with Oostende."[48] In Holland the first *trekschuiten*, drawn boats, passed along the canal from Groningen to Zuidbroek in the northeast, a waterway cut between 1618 and 1622 to open up peat digging in the Veenkoloniën of Friesland, and secondarily a canal that provided about the only practicable route across the high moors of the area. "In the Holland-Utrecht urban heart of the [Dutch] Republic trekvaart development began in 1626–28 with the construction of towpaths along the Vecht and the cutting of new canals to shorten the distance from Utrecht to Amsterdam."[49]

There were several periods during which most of the Dutch system of trekvaarten were constructed. De Vries shows that between 1632 and 1647 fifteen cities in the

Dutch Republic invested 1.5 million guilders in 150 miles of trekvaarten, which fell mainly into four integrated systems around the cities of Groningen and Leeuwarden east of the Zuiderzee and Amsterdam and Delft in Holland proper.[50] A second boom began in 1656, when the two separate systems in the northeast were tied together by the completion of a trekvaart from Dokkum to Groningen, opening inland passenger boat navigation fom the Ems estuary of the eastern border of the Netherlands to the Zuiderzee. In 1658 a similar through connection was opened from Amsterdam and the Zuiderzee southward to the complex of delta distributaries, first at Rotterdam on the lower Lek and then at Gouda on the IJssel. In succeeding years most of Holland proper came to be served with trekvaarten, even the Noorderkwatier in the peninsula between Amsterdam and Hoorn.

In 1665, with the outbreak of the Second Anglo-Dutch [Trade] War, trekvaart construction stopped, never to be resumed. The network of lines extended from the north side of the complex delta through to the Zuiderzee, resuming between that embayment and the estuary of the Ems on the German border. Thus all of Holland and the lower sections of the northeast were served by a waterways network deliberately designed for fast, direct service. Probably the directness was more important than the speed, which was little advanced over the speed of sailing boats, perhaps 5.5 kilometers an hour as opposed to 4. At the close of the era of trekvaart building, the polder regions of the Netherlands possessed a transportation system that remained unrivaled for cheapness and competence to handle large cargoes until the coming of the railroad nearly two centuries later. Even in the early nineteenth century, observers favorably compared the trekvaart system with that of overland travel in France, Germany, or England. Yet there had been virtually no

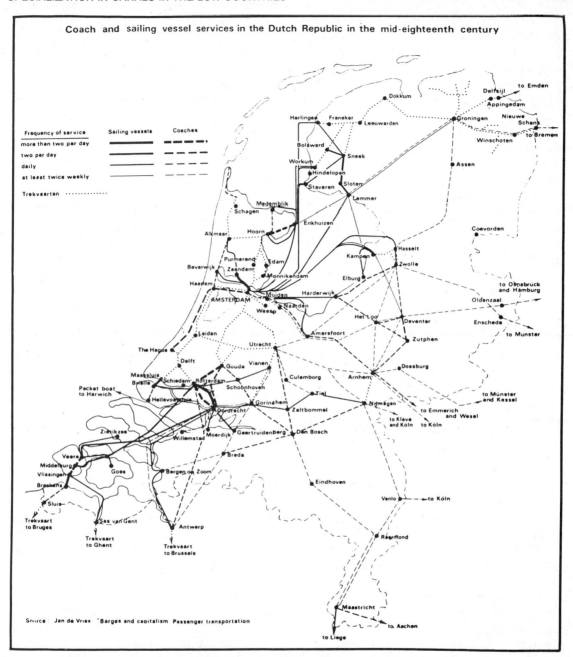

Map of frequency of service on Dutch transportation routes. *Source*: Jan de Vries, *Barges and Cap-italism: Passenger Transportation in the Dutch Economy, 1632–1839* (A.A.G. Bijdragon 21, 1978).

change either in the facilities or the vehicles since the completion of the system around 1665.

From Agriculture to Industry: Belgian Canalization

There is no need to examine the earlier years of Belgian canal building in detail, as those qualities are similar in both Holland and Flanders. To understand the pattern in general terms, we should remember that Flanders had some five major ports—Dunkerque, Oostende, Bruges, Ghent, and Antwerp—and many minor ones. Each save Antwerp had what we might call minor access to the sea. Dunkerque and Oostende were on what we would probably call tidal creeks on a duned coastline backed by marshy areas subject to inundation on higher tides. Bruges was on a more elongated inlet lying more or less behind the dunes and giving access to the West Scheldt estuary rather than to the North Sea coast directly. Antwerp and Ghent were both on the much larger Scheldt above its estuarine portion, though the first lay just at the head of that sea flooding. In each case the medieval scale of the connection to the sea should be emphasized. Boats were tiny at this time—perhaps 50 tons would have served as an upper limit for any that might seek to dock—and the tidal creeks seem to have served adequately the needs of these increasingly flourishing and competitive ports. Flanders was one of the two leading areas of medieval industrialization—the other being Italy from Florence northward—so the port towns were not simple transportation places but also literally centers of manufacture. Manufacturing necessitated five bustling ports, both to receive the staple for fabrication and to export the surplus beyond the possibility of local consumption. Antwerp, for example, in the Middle Ages was the site of a trading organiza-

tion, the English Nation, handling English fleeces—the finest available to the medieval wool trade—and making therefrom woolens of a quality unavailable in Britain or anywhere else but Florence (itself a customer for Cotswold fleeces). Ghent and Bruges shared in this manufacture and the trading voyages that backstayed it.

From the sixteenth century on, several things happened to force the Flemings to undertake various elements of canalization. At the beginning of the chapter we noted the lock at Damme on the tidal creek that had given Bruges access to the sea. The construction of that facility was necessitated by two conditions then obtaining in that part of Flanders: the undertaking of drainage to make possible agricultural use of the marshy coastal belt, which led to the construction of dikes and the control of water levels, and the silting on the lower sections of the river Reye that formed the access to the sea for medieval Bruges. The result was the regulation of the hydraulic regime in the area and the construction of drainage canals and subsequently of navigation canals, such as passed through Damme and Sluis farther north toward the West Scheldt coastline.

The rise of the several important towns in what was variously the Spanish and Austrian Netherlands led to desires to interconnect one with another. Ghent and Antwerp were both on the riverine Scheldt, so nature had provided their connection even to the extent that ocean ships could navigate upstream as far as Ghent. There was a desire for a waterway from Ghent westward to Bruges and then onward to Oostende and Dunkerque near the French border. The section between Ghent and Bruges was dug to ample dimensions in the period 1613–1623, whereas the further extension to Oostende and Dunkerque was opened only in 1640.[51] A further extension to the French border at Gravelines was completed by the end of the century, so that there was a trekvaart throughout Flanders by that year. It would be inaccurate to assume that only then did such regional navigation become possible. Medieval maps suggest that between Ghent and the river Reye below Bruges, the course of the Lieve was used to provide some sort of water connection, probably with minor portaging.[52] No doubt the rivers of Flanders were widely used even before the end of the Middle Ages. Both the Scheldt (the Eschaut in France) and the Lys flowed from south to north across Flanders, the Escheldt passing through such important towns as Tournai and Oudenaarde as well as Ghent and Antwerp and the Lys through Armentières, Lille (by a tributary), Menen, Kortrijk (Courtrai), and Deinze before joining the Scheldt at Ghent. It seems that the first phase of waterway development in Flanders depended on river navigations, in contrast to the drainage canals in the polders found in Holland. The two low areas, however, shared the next phase with the building of the trekvaarten such as that from Dunkerque to Ghent.

Belgium outside of Flanders was similarly provided with water transport along the Meuse (Maas) and its branch, the Sambre. In this way Liège, Huy, Namur, and Dinant could be joined along the Meuse, and in turn along the Sambre above Namur, to Charleroi. The main areas not served were in the very low plateau between the Sambre-Meuse depression on the east and the edge of Flanders in the west. There Brussels, Mons, Mechelen (Malines), and Leuwen (Louvain) were the important places. Only in the sixteenth century did this low plateau region gain political significance with the shift of the political capital of Spanish Netherlands to Brussels. At that point Brabant required improved transport, which was provided by a canal from the Rupel, a minor tributary of the Scheldt entering above Antwerp, to Brussels. This Canal de Willebroek, named for the place on the Rupel where it gained

access to the Flemish waterway system, was 18.5 miles long, rising 33 feet to the canal basin in the capital, with five locks. Singer and his colleagues tell us: "Of the canals built in the sixteenth and seventeenth centuries, the Brussels canal was the first of importance to be constructed outside of Italy. Navigation had long existed between Brussels and Antwerp along the rivers Senne, Rupel, and Scheldt. From time to time during the Middle Ages improvements were made in the Senne navigation, but in 1531 it was decided to cut a canal from Brussels to Willebroeck" that would be half so long as the stream navigation.[53] When opened in 1561 this canal became the model for the north.

As the economy of Hainaut to the south of Brussels expanded, particularly with the rise in coal mining, the need for a canal to connect the capital with that field around Charleroi was intensely felt. It was undertaken in 1826 and, when finished, provided a connection from Antwerp through Brussels to the Sambre and its easterly extension in the Meuse. Further coal canals came with the construction of the waterway from Pommeroeul, in the Borinage coal field, to Antoing, just above Tournai on the Scheldt, avoiding shipment of that coal through France to reach Antwerp.[54]

Industrialization was the key to most of the nineteenth-century digging of canals in Belgium, although the shaping of a national state after the break with the Dutch kingdom in 1830 was an important secondary consideration. Belgium was in many ways an unknown state. Divided from the Netherlands, Belgium faced a difficult problem of access from its industrial areas to the sea. Of the five Flemish ports mentioned earlier, only the poorest, Oostende, retained its direct access. Dunkerque had been lost in 1658 to Louis XIV, who gave it to the English crown after the Restoration of 1660. The profligate Stuarts had to sell it back to raise money shortly thereafter. As the Belgian-Dutch boundary was drawn in 1830, it left the lower course of the Reye, north of Damme, and of the Scheldt in Dutch control, as well as handing over parts of Limburg to the northern kingdom. Although the war ended in 1830, there was such opposition to the peace imposed by the five great powers that the Dutch obstructed its peaceful resolution until 1839. It became evident that something had to be done to give the emergent Belgium a transportation system leading to usable ports and not cut by French or, more particularly, Dutch territory. Until the legalistic conflict with the Dutch was resolved, Bruges, Ghent, Antwerp, and the Meuse (Maas) access to the sea could be closed, as they essentially were.

The solution lay along two lines: to make of Oostende a more useful port than had previously been the case, and to attempt to open access via the Scheldt estuary to the sea. The latter course was not easy; the Dutch had closed the West Scheldt with its two Dutch shores despite its considerable width to Belgian commerce for much of the two hundred years before 1830. Thus the emphasis fell on devising improved east-west routes from industrial Belgium in Namur and Liège provinces to the sea. The king's ministry early settled on building a railroad to accomplish as rapid an overland connection through Belgian territory as possible, making Belgium the oldest railroad builder after England and the United States.

The east-west canals of Belgium came in two places: southward from Brussels to Charleroi, where juncture was made with the navigable Sambre-Meuse, and the effort to carry a canal from Antwerp and the Scheldt to the Meuse downstream from Liège by crossing the northern part of Belgian Brabant. The canal to Charleroi, begun in 1826, was rushed to completion, and efforts toward a canal in the north were advanced. The Bocholt-Herenthals (Kempen) Canal was too slow in completion (1850) to serve the immediate purpose, but in the long run it did help Belgium divert traffic from the Meuse westward just short of the Dutch border.[55] Along with the national railroad plan implemented in the earlier 1830s, these waterways furnished the necessary domestic connection from the industrial belt extending from Mons in the west to Liège and Verviers in the east. Certainly by 1850 Belgium had more of the necessary transportation infrastructure for an industrial revolution than any other continental country.

The problem of the Belgian seaports was still unresolved in the 1830s. In 1825, while Belgium was part of the United Kingdom of the Netherlands, William I initiated the construction of a canal due northward from Ghent to Terneuzen on the shore of the West Scheldt estuary, this avoiding the difficult navigation of the river course between Ghent and Antwerp. When completed in 1827, this ship canal encouraged a considerable effort at building dock basins at Ghent, finished in 1828, to make that medieval river port a modern seaport reached by a ship canal.[56] With the Belgian Revolution, however, this work was cut by creation of the international boundary just a short distance north of Ghent.

The final elements of the modern Belgian canal system were set in place with the completion of the Leopold Canal from Heist on the coast adjacent to Zeebrugge to intersect the Bruges-Ghent Canal just west of the latter place and to reach, at Deinze, the river Lys and the navigation that connected southward to Kortrijk (Courtrai) and the French system near Lille. This waterway was intended as an all-Belgian route to the sea and to the new out-port of Zeebrugge, though it is not a ship canal as such but a 2,000-ton barge canal. The line of waterway was carried eastward by the navigation along the Scheldt between Ghent and Antwerp, which was originally tidal so that at high tide about 8 feet of water were available. In seeking to continue this all-Belgian route east of Antwerp, the canal opened to the Meuse in 1850 was too small for a truly industrial traffic. Between 1930 and 1939 the Albert Canal was under construction, providing a wide waterway with 9 feet of water and locks that could handle barges up to 446 by 43 feet, commonly displacing 2,000 tons. The waterway was also touted as a defensive feature similar to the Maginot Line in France, which would provide a line along which to check a German invasion of Belgium. Less than a year after it was completed, the Albert Canal proved little more than a minor interruption in the invasion of Belgium the Nazis began on May 10, 1940. The economic history of the facility has been much more successful. It allows 2,000-ton barges to navigate from the heavy industrial area of Liège province to the Belgian ports of Antwerp, Ghent, Bruges-Zeebrugge, and Oostende, finally assuring unimpeded access to the sea. Less than twenty years after the opening of the Albert Canal, the creation of the European Common Market, following on the immediately postwar Benelux customs union, made such a Belgian national system less crucial. The rapid growth of the Common Market economies have, however, made such a multiplicity of access routes to the sea desirable for economic rather than political reasons.

The Belgian canal era, like that of the Dutch, has continued down to the present. Even in the last century the Belgian system was more important in industry than in agriculture. The Kempen (Campine) and Sambre-Meuse coalfields could be heavily developed because water transport was available. The Liège district maintained its industrial dominance not by a system of local canals, as in the north of France, but by improving its access to the world of international trade both outside and within Europe.

The course of development of the other waterways on the European continent is beyond the scope of this book. It must suffice to note that in Germany river improvement dominated over canalization. The Rhine was generally navigable to Strasbourg even in medieval times, and with difficulty above there to the falls of that river at Schaffhausen. The Elbe was navigable into Bohemia and the Weser into Thuringia. The only intense development of canals came with the rapid development of the Ruhr coal field, where canals were used to transport the coal to connections with the Rhine River or Dortmund-Ems Canal and the port of Emden on the North Sea. Starting in 1905 a branch was begun near Rheine and carried 202 miles eastward through Minden on the Weser, the outskirts of Hannover on the Leine, Wolfsburg, and reaching the Elbe just below Madgeburg. This integrating waterway could handle 1,000-ton barges when it was opened in 1938. This alignment of waterway just north of the central uplands of Germany was continued eastward from the Elbe by the Havel Canal eastward to Berlin, and by other canals thence to the Oder. The intersection of the Mittelland Canal by the inter-German boundary just east of Wolfsburg has limited its current utility. In 1895 the 61-mile ship canal to provide direct access from the Baltic to the North Sea, from Kiel to the Elbe estuary at Rendsburg, was opened with a depth of 29 feet of water, a width of 213 feet, and a continuous level save for the locks at either end which are 45.9 feet high.

Elsewhere in Europe the Danube is the main navigable stream and one of increasing importance. The project to connect the Rhine via the Main River to the Danube just above Regensburg is well on its way, but even before its completion navigation is possible from Ulm to the mouth of the Danube in Rumania. In the past the main impedence to the use of the river was political rather than physical, although the 162-yard-wide Cazane defile was difficult to navigate (because of its current, not its depth, which is about 150 feet), and farther on the Iron Gate was made hazardous by rocks. Post-World War II facilities there have made navigation easy.

In Russia river navigation had to substitute for a largely absent road and rail system. Even in Soviet times the railroads remain inadequate, so river transport assumes great importance. To facilitate inter-basin navigation, canals have been built between Moscow and the Volga, from the Volga to the Don, and from the upper Volga to Leningrad. From the Czarist capital canals have been built to interconnect the great lakes, Onega in particular, and to gain access to the White Sea. On the European borders of Russia canals connect the headwaters of the Neman and Dvina, flowing to the Baltic with the Dnieper flowing to the Black Sea. As yet there is no interconnection of the Volga and Dnieper systems save via the Baltic or the Black Sea.

BUSINESS INTERESTS INTRODUCE THE CANAL TO BRITAIN

One of the stranger features of economic history is the pride of place often afforded to British canal building. The impression is frequently left that James Brindley, Josiah Wedgewood, and the Duke of Bridgewater strove against incalculable odds of an absent technology and with an innovation of an unimagined boldness in shaping their first English canals. Ignorance and opposition may have existed in England, but that was merely provincialism by the eighteenth

century when Brindley labored. His single-level canal of 10 miles was built five hundred years after the Flemings had devised locks and three hundred years after the Lombards had constructed the Naviglia Grande. Riquet had built several viaducts of considerable length—not to mention a tunnel, extensive dams and water-supply systems, a new port, river weirs, and assorted features of a 150-mile canal—nearly a century before. The Duke of Bridgewater's Canal, which essentially introduced the canal era to England, was far less of a technical accomplishment than the Canal de Briare begun 150 years before in France. So it is hard to understand all the fuss about British canals. It seems that their distinction lies in two aspects rather different from the technical ones normally cited. First, British canals were the first instance in the modern world of private capitalist enterprise applied to waterway construction (and really to development of transportation facilities, as the slightly earlier turnpike roads were what we would today call mixed enterprise of the state and individuals). Second, British canals were intimately tied in to the successful transformation of the scale, organization, and operation of manufacture that we call the Industrial Revolution. Thus it is in business history and secular change in broad-scale economic life that the British canal era gains its significance, not in any considerable way in true invention. I have deliberately discussed the Continental waterways before those of Britain to emphasize how badly focused has been much of the English-language writing on the subject.

In our consideration of British canals, we do well to start with the economic conditions that changed sufficiently in the seventeenth and early eighteenth centuries to bring about a canal era. J. R. Ward has provided us with a useful appraisal of *The Finance of Canal Building in Eighteenth-Century England:*[57]

This chronology accords well with our current understanding of the nature of England's economic development [in the seventeenth and eighteenth centuries]. Its course was determined in the first instance by demographic circumstances. The growth of population had added to the demand, thus inducing technical innovations and increases of output within agriculture and also redistributing income to landowners and capitalist tenant farmers, whose propensity to buy manufactures and other traded goods was high, from wage labourers, with whom this propensity was low. Therefore when rapid population growth occurred agricultural prices rose or at least remained firm in the face of a rapidly increasing volume of output, landlords' rents and farmers' profits rose, the real wages of labourers stagnated or fell, and trade flourished. When it did not, then the opposite conditions held. This mechanism operated in a manner favourable to the growth of output during most of the first seven decades of the seventeenth century, from the 1690s to the later 1720s, and from the 1750s onwards without any serious interruption.

In this analysis Ward argues that in the seventeenth century "successful navigation schemes were few, limited in scale, and subject to long delays in their completion. In the eighteenth century river improvements and canals were both more numerous and more ambitious; it became rarer for works to be abandoned uncompleted."[58] In seeking the origin of this change, we find that it was not a greater infusion of capital from London that brought this quickened pace of inland navigation construction, but rather changes that were taking place in the English provincial towns.

In the seventeenth century "[m]ost provincial townsmen were engaged in trade or manufacture. Therefore not only was their wealth limited in amount, but it was also constituted in such a way as to make its diversion to secondary employments difficult and even hazardous. A high proportion of their assets were usually accounted for by trade goods and debts from customers, and a low proportion by cash and easily negotiable securities." In this situation the ease with which an unwise investment could throw a small merchant into bankruptcy, with its truly draconian punishments at this time, was sufficient to create caution to go along with small resources.[59]

During the seventeenth and early eighteenth centuries all these factors tended to inhibit investment in river improvement. Their force was weakened by degrees and with the passage of time as the same growth of economic activity which created a need for improved communications provided, after some delay, through the process of accumulation in the provincial towns, the means with which that need might be met. By the middle of the eighteenth century men's capabilities had been brought more closely into balance with their aspirations than in the past. It is as testimony to this fact that the historical significance of the canal promotions in part consists.

Thus we see that canal building in England, and Britain in general, displays in sharper focus two forces that were only faintly discernible on the Continent. In England the canal system was geographically determined by the needs and the investment capabilities of various provincial manufacturing towns, avoiding any real suggestion of a national or even regional plan or policy. Second, the English canal system was completely the child of investment capitalism: capital had to be accumulated in Birmingham or Leeds through the operation of what Marxist commentators see as the unjust diversion of the labor surplus from the wage laborers to the manufacturers, whose propensity, like that of "landowners and capitalist tenant farmers," was also toward the purchase of manufactures and other traded goods. And capital had to be earned by the canals to assure their survival.

If we accept this wholly capitalist quality to canal undertakings in England, we still must ask where canals will be built and of what sort they will be? To answer those questions, it is necessary to summarize the base on which canal building came to the British Isles.

The traditional navigation that had been truly natural in the Middle Ages and was improved by human effort in the seventeenth and early eighteenth centuries could not handle the shift in the economic geography of Britain that accompanied industrialization. The technology of hydraulic power was sufficiently modest in the earlier years of the Industrial Revolution to encourage the first phase of power development on the smaller headwaters of rivers rather than on their larger lower courses. High heads and low volumes of flow were easier to harness than were small falls possessed of great discharges. The presence of these easily developed water-power sites away from the parts of the river traditionally navigated combined with the tendency for exposed coalfields to lie in hillier regions or else close to the foothills of the Pennine arch to make a new sort of watershed problem, different from earlier experiences in both England and France.

Britain's coal mining and its early factories were private undertakings. The mines tended to be the property of the landed class (for the simple reason that rural land was narrowly and aristocratically held as a consequence of England's feudalism in the Middle Ages). In contrast, most manufacturing grew out of actual productive labor, of facing problems of artisan production and solving them both technically and economically. Who more than the skilled artisan could make those improvements, which when successful could also considerably enrich the new manufacturer?

As we have seen from Ward's summation of the economic background of the Industrial Revolution, successful enterprise brought increasing amounts of capital onto the account books of these manufacturers, for the first time creating a monied class distinct from that of landholding. Although the source of the money might vary, however, its effective enlargement called for the same efforts from either class: that is, to expand this capital either group would have to cheapen the cost of producing their product and of getting it to market. In production the main concern for the manufaturer and the coal lord was in obtaining food for the workers as cheaply as possible so that wages could be kept low (with the labor surplus kept on his own books). The manufacturer in addition would wish to keep the cost of his raw materials, to the extent they came from a distance, as low as cheap transportation would permit. In the selling of their product the conjunction of interests of the Tory coal lords and the Whiggish manufacturers was nearly absolute; each saw in cheap and extensive transportation the outlet for an expanding production that could otherwise easily flood a local market and depress prices.

The English canal network as it existed at the coming of the railroad was intricate but fairly homogeneous in design and purpose. Thus we need not examine all its components. Instead, we may gain an overall understanding of the system by first looking at its earliest components and then at the shaping of functional categories in the evolved system.

The Cut Comes to England as River Improvement

The arrival of the canal in Britain was as tentative and indirect as in other countries. As already noted, the main effort in the earlier decades of the era of improvement

The Thames and Medway Canal tunnel. *Source*: William Strickland, *Reports on Canals, Railways, Roads, etc. Made to the Pennsylvania Society for Internal Improvements* (Philadelphia, 1826).

came in remaking the rivers better to serve the needs of boats. Of the two thousand miles of waterway in England at the end of the eighteenth century, about one-third came from these river improvements, mostly undertaken between 1600 and 1760. The remainder was divided equally; one-third came in open rivers naturally navigable at the beginning of the period and one-third in canals, mostly built between 1760 and 1800.[60] To improve the rivers, the main device used was that of the pound lock. The first in Britain was used on a short lateral canal built between 1564 and 1566 alongside the river Exe between Exeter and tidewater below Countess Weir. This canal was 1¾ miles long and 3 feet deep over a width of 16 feet. The three locks were probably provided with vertically rising gates more like stanches than the more advanced miter gates of the Lombard canals.[61] This canal was undertaken by the city corporation of Exeter to overcome obstructions in the tidal river Exe that had been added by noble grantees partly in search of water power and partly to force goods intended for Exeter to be landed and required to pay the Earl of Exeter's dues at Topsham Quay. The parochialism and private gain involved in this development may serve as key points to understanding the subsequent development of canals in England.

Hadfield tells us: "In Elizabeth's reign the pound-lock was introduced into England . . .; this invention made possible the improvement of river navigation beyond the point to which it could be taken by dredging and the removal of obstructions, and effected so great an economy in the use of water compared with the old flash-lock that a compromise with the millers sometimes became possible."[62] It seems that in general the number of mill dams in existence across streams was sufficient to assure virtual slackwater navigation between dams—what the English call weirs—but also large enough to make navigation by flashes of water, released by millers to permit passage through their dams, both expensive for the tolls they charged and hazardous in the transit of the turbulent sluices.

When the quickening of economic activity increased the demand for transportation and the shift toward the power sources—water and coal—extended the area needful of inland navigation, the partial technological advance of the canalized river proved inadequate to satisfy the new demands.

We may take the improvement of a river on the northwest slope of the Cotswolds in Gloucestershire as an example of the tentative approach to canal building that typified the earliest efforts at artificial waterways. In

1730 an act of Parliament was passed permitting that the river Stroud be canalized between the Severn and the town of Stroud, but such opposition from the textile mill owners along the river was voiced with respect to a feared shortage of water that nothing happened. A second time, in 1759, efforts were made to build a waterway to serve this important textile area, and again the owners forced on the canal company a scheme so bizarre that it had to be abandoned—a series of dams with cranes that could lift goods out of boats permanently circulating on a lower pool to those doing the same on the next higher pool. Finally in 1779 a standard canal was opened with twelve locks capable of handling the Severn trows (small sailing boats).[63]

THE CANAL COMES TO BRITAIN

The first British canal came into existence at a distance from the areas where established water power made innovation difficult. It came in Northern Ireland, where there was need for transportation from the Tyrone coalfield to the port of Newry on the Irish Sea. Authorized in 1729 by the Irish Parliament, its construction began under the guidance of a French Huguenot, Richard Castle, who had studied Continental waterways after becoming a refugee from his homeland. In three years he made progress, building a stone pound lock that was the first in Ireland. In 1736 Henry Steers became chief engineer of the undertaking and after five years had completed a canal 18 miles long, 45 feet wide, 5 to 6 feet deep, and with fourteen locks capable of handling 50-ton barges.[64] Apparently this canal was a financial and technical success. When its engineer, Steers, became dock engineer for the port of Liverpool and, in 1739, mayor of that town, practical knowledge of canal building came to Lancashire. In 1754

Steers's assistant, Henry Berry, was commissioned by the Liverpool Common Council to examine a small stream, Sankey Brook, which flowed from St. Helens in the Lancashire plain to join the Mersey near Warrington, with the idea of canalizing it to expand the accessible hinterland of the Mersey port to include the St. Helens coalfield. Berry concluded the brook was insufficient in size to be canalized, although it provided a useful valley to be followed. In part because the English Parliament seemed indisposed to granting rights to construct canals, commonly because of opposition from established land and transport interests—and in part because the investors might have been frightened away by too bold a scheme—Berry and the most important single investor, John Ashton, who held 51 of the 120 shares, quietly agreed to utilize the subsidiary powers of the parliamentary grant, that to make "such cuts ... as they shall think proper and requisite" to run an entirely artificial cut alongside nature's Sankey Brook.

As constructed, the Sankey Brook Navigation, opened in 1757, comprised a canal some 12 miles long with three additional branches to coal workings. It had twelve locks to handle the difference in elevation between the collieries and the main river Mersey. Coal began to move in considerable quantities to the salter Ashton's works on the Mersey or to other salt works on the river Weaver around Northwich and Winsford. So successful was this undertaking that it paid 33⅓ percent per annum on capital for the next eighty years.[65]

Certainly little further inducement was needed to lead those possessed of capital into canal investments, particularly if, as was the case with Ashton, they might gain even further through the stimulation of their other economic activities that might benefit from improved transportation. In that class of doubly benefiting capitalists fell both Francis Egerton and Josiah Wedgewood. Egerton as a boy of twelve ascended to his father's title as Duke of Bridgewater and to his estates in the Lancashire plain, known to be underlain by coal. His Worsley estate lay 10 miles from Manchester, a distance that by road transportation made his coal uncompetitive with the product of closer mines in the burgeoning market of the great textile town. When the Sankey Brook Canal was opened in 1757, the St. Helens mines gained an edge in the Manchester market over those at Worsley. It was evidently in this context that Francis Egerton took his decision to build a canal from the Worsley coal mines to Salford.

The Bridgewater Canal

Before looking at that undertaking, it is historically necessary to lay a few ghosts, among them the gushy tale of Egerton's motives for his investment in inland navigation. As the third son of the second Duke of Bridgewater, he seems to have been little regarded by his family, to the extent that he was largely uneducated and considered by his mother of feeble intellect. At twelve, succeeding to the second son of the family, who had briefly inherited the title before dying very young, Francis was possessed of the title as third Duke of Bridgewater and of a very considerable fortune, heavily involved in the coal mines around Worsley in Lancashire. For three years he was enrolled at Eton to make up for some of his past intellectual neglect and at seventeen was dispatched with a tutor, Robert Wood, for a grand tour of the Continent that took him to France, Italy, and Holland. It is known that he visited, and was interested by, the Canal du Midi. It seems most likely that as a rich visitor in Holland he must have ridden on the trekvaarten; certainly money was not spared. While in Rome he had been encouraged by Wood to buy marble statuary to enhance his understanding of art, and later in life he dedicated a then considerable fortune of £150,000 to the purchase of pictures. The marbles were still in the crate on his death, and the pictures were apparently viewed only as an investment. But the canals he saw seem to have made a deep impression.

Returning to London, Egerton pursued the purposeless life of a scion of an aristocratic family—racing at Newmarket, where his weedy physique led observers to believe he would be blown from the entry he rode, and seeking marriage. He fell in love with Jane Revell, who chose instead to marry and endow with her considerable fortune a Cheshire squire, George Warren. He became engaged to the widowed Duchess of Hamilton, one of the Gunning sisters; but she chose instead the future Duke of Argyll. Francis Egerton abandoned London, giving a "final ball" interpreted by the romantic as his departure from women and frivolity but perhaps more accurately, and prosaically, as a celebration of the third reading of the bill permitting his undertaking of a canal from Worsley to Manchester. At any event, he was well into this scheme even when apparently fatally smitten by Elizabeth Gunning.

At Worsley Hall in 1757 Egerton had had long conversations with John Gilbert, the brother of his agent on that estate. Gilbert was the son of a lime maker in Staffordshire who was apprenticed to the father of Matthew Boulton, perhaps the most astute and ingenious manufacturer of the early industrial era in Britain. From the elder Boulton he gained a grounding in what we now call civil and mechanical engineering. With that ability he was hired in June, 1757, to come to Worsley and assist Egerton in planning his canal. Apparently his job was in particular to prepare the considerable quantity of justification for such a canal that must be submitted to Parliament to secure the necessary act to permit its construction.

The most powerful arguments for the canal all seem to have been economic, particularly that coal could be discharged at the canal dock in Salford near Manchester for 4 d. per ton as opposed to the 7–8 d. per ton then obtaining. Petitions from merchants and manufacturers in Salford and at Hollins Ferry, where the canal line would cross the Mersey, called the highly prejudiced members to approve this undertaking.[66]

In 1759 the parliamentary act was passed, Egerton held his celebratory "final ball" in London, and Gilbert set to work building the Duke of Bridgewater's Canal. In the past it has been customary to assign most of the credit for this vaunted canal to James Brindley. Recent research, however, indicates that the planning was done primarily by John Gilbert, with Brindley acting as what we would call a consulting engineer. In the original plan a cut would be made from Worsley to Barton, where the line of the canal must cross the course of the river Irwell that drains from Manchester into the Mersey above Liverpool. It was planned to take some 30 to 35 feet of drop in locks and to rise on the other side a similar height and in the same fashion. But Brindley sensibly proposed building an aqueduct to carry the canal across the river without losing the general level of the waterway. This 38-foot-high bridge was parochially considered the marvel of its age and the waterproofing of its trough through clay-puddling a great invention of Brindley's—a notion that would indeed have struck Pierre-Paul Riguet as a good example of English conceit.

From the east bank of the Irwell the cut was continued into Manchester, instead of the original destination at suburban Salford, to avoid the haulier's charges and tolls that would have arisen from use of the earlier terminus. Thus the level canal was 10.5 miles long and distinguished only by embankments over Stretford Meadows and Trafford Moss and the Barton Aqueduct. It was completed by July 17, 1761, when the first boatload of Worsley coal was laid down on the docks at Manchester, which were connected to the higher level of the center of the city by a tunnel and a shaft up which the loaded boxes of coal could be lifted for direct sale to retail customers. In turn, at the Worsley mine Brindley and Gilbert had constructed a series of some 40 miles of tunnels that reached to most of the working faces. Eventually four different levels were involved, with changes in level accomplished underground over inclined planes capable of taking the boxes up or down to the third level, which connected directly with the Bridgewater Canal itself. It is not surprising that Worsley coal could quite successfully be unloaded at Manchester for less than 4 d. per hundredweight, as was required for a period of forty years in the parliamentary act authorizing the construction.

This low price created a great demand for Worsley coal and made Egerton extremely wealthy. He had risked a fortune in financing his canal, but the experience with the Sankey Brook Canal cannot have left the ultimate outcome quite so much in doubt as some accounts would have it. When we examine the financial benefits derived from this early example of capitalist investment in English transportation, we encounter some difficulty in sorting out Egerton's affairs. It seems that he invested around £220,000 in all his canal undertakings—the Worsley-Manchester canal, its extension some 5 miles westward from Worsley to Leigh, and the 25.75-mile extension of the original canal from Stretford westward alongside the Irwell and Mersey to an outfall to the tidal estuary at Runcorn Gap—or about £5,269 per mile of canal, although this included very expensive dock and warehouse construction in several places. One estimate has it that the original 10.5-mile Bridgewater Canal cost 1,000 guineas a mile. In turn, an estimate, the value of which is not certain, had it that

Egerton's income was £80,000 per year.[67] That sum was compounded of earnings from his coal mines as well as from the canals of which he was the sole proprietor. This intermixing of returns from several functionally related business undertakings brought on the Canal Era in Britain, supplied its capital, and determined its routes and methods of operation. The network was explicable only in terms of the geography of Britain's Industrial Revolution and of the perceptions that the middle and upper classes had of personal benefit. There was hardly a hint of any national canal building, as typical of the Dutch or, later, the Americans.

Francis Egerton became both wealthy and eccentric. As money flowed in from coal sales and canal tolls, he became almost single-minded about the benefits of waterways to landowners and manufacturers. Because the Irwell Navigation, a river improvement trust, would not provide him special rates less than those charged for the navigation of the full distance between Manchester and the tidal Mersey at Runcorn (as his canal joined the river 2.75 miles from the city), Egerton set about building a true canal the 25 miles to tidewater.

Egerton evidently wished to dominate the complex of economic activities the canal induced. He set up brick and lime-burning works at his Castlefield, Manchester, docks; established passenger service on his canals, even experimenting (perhaps at Robert Fulton's suggestion) with a steamboat run from Runcorn to Castlefield in 1797; enlarged his mines to the point of becoming one of the greatest of colliery owners; and ran a very considerable barging operation.

All the while the money poured in, and Egerton turned peculiar. When he found that his workmen at Worsley were slow in returning from lunch at one o'clock, arguing that they often failed to hear the single strike of the bell in the works tower, he had the clock fixed to strike thirteen times at that hour. He was said to be none too clean in his person. Although extremely punctilious about the worker rendering absolutely full measure in his labor, Egerton was mean and oblivious in providing the benefits his wealth and dominance in the lives of his workers made just: "A sidelight on this side of the Duke's character is given in an account of the period which tells us that although Worsley had grown industrially, its religious, educational and social needs were sorely neglected. Every evil attendant on neglect flourished—drunkenness, swearing, Sabbath breaking, cock fighting, gambling and bull baiting." Even more deplorable would seem to be the low wages, long hours, and inhumanity associated with this accumulation of wealth. Not until 1837 were women and children finally excluded from employment in Egerton's mines; even then, human haulage was not banned from either the underground or the open-air canals.[68] One of Egerton's employees dealt forthrightly with the former's sententious advice. When told that the worker was returning late from lunch because his wife had just had twins, Egerton told him unfeelingly, "Aye, well, we have to have what the good Lord send us." But that man noted honestly, "Ah notice He sends all t'babies to our house and all t'brass to yores."[69]

Canals after Bridgewater

It was brass that shaped the pattern of waterways in Britain after the Duke of Bridgewater's startling success. Almost immediately, a rash of canal promotions began. For the next thirty years investment and construction activity were on a scale never before seen in Britain, shaping the first system of transportation predicated on supporting an Industrial Revolution and paid for by user charges. Charles Hadfield has distinguished two phases in this Canal Era—the first between 1761 and 1772, when canals were proposed and undertaken to provide the transportation infrastructure for industrialization and the supply of coal both for export and to supply large urban populations; and the second, between 1790 and 1797, a boom when diverse cuts were proposed to create competition to those already completed and to provide inland navigation to some of the richer agricultural areas.[70]

The Silver Cross   The first major canal to be promoted after the completion of the Bridgewater cut was the backbone of what contemporaries saw as "the great silver cross" that would tie together the four major navigations of England: (1) the Mersey in the west, where the Sankey Brook Canal and Egerton's efforts had begun to shape a locally integrated network of industrial canals of the sort the French were building in the same decades in Artois and Flanders;[71] (2) the Trent, draining the East Midlands; (3) the Severn, draining the Welsh border country and the edges of the West Midlands; and (4) the Thames, with its access to the Metropolis. In many ways this Silver Cross was a French type of canal, one connecting across watersheds the main river basins of the realm. If we were to adopt the classification of canals contained in an *Essay upon the General System of French Inland Navigation*—written by Brisson of the Corps des Ponts et Chaussées, the French department of public works, and published in 1829—this cross would stand at the very forefront of the first class.[72] Its construction would have united the two northern river basins in inland navigation, as well as opening much of the way to the Severn and the Thames, necessitating relatively short branches for completion of the Silver Cross.

The key to that complex connection came in a canal proposed by the salt boilers of Cheshire, those who had supported the Sankey Brook Canal, Thomas Bentley and

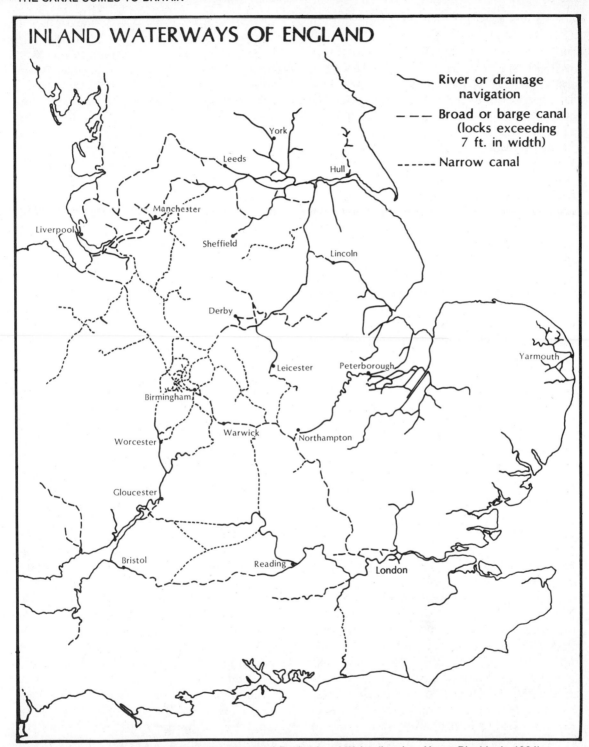

INLAND WATERWAYS OF ENGLAND

River or drainage navigation

Broad or barge canal (locks exceeding 7 ft. in width)

Narrow canal

York
Leeds
Hull
Manchester
Liverpool
Sheffield
Lincoln
Derby
Yarmouth
Leicester
Peterborough
Birmingham
Worcester
Warwick
Northampton
Gloucester
Bristol
Reading
London

Source: Bradshaw's Canals and Navigable Rivers of England and Wales (London: Henry Blacklock, 1904).

Josiah Wedgewood of the Potteries, Matthew Boulton of Birmingham, and Doctor Erasmus Darwin of Litchfield—seemingly as representatives of the commercial and bourgeois interests of the northwest of England. Ultimately the Duke of Bridgewater and his relative Earl Gower entered into the company that sought a parliamentary act to build this waterway, but their participation seems to have been valued as much as anything for the effect it might have in influencing the local landowners to accept the passage of the cut through their fields. Josiah Wedgewood became the acknowledged spokesman for the proposal and certainly one of its ardent protagonists. By the early 1760s, when this canal from the Trent to the Mersey was being bruited, Wedgewood had become a leader in the scientific manufacture of pottery in the traditional ceramic region of North Staffordshire. Local clay and coal had initially encouraged the trade; but efforts to improve the fineness of the product had led the search for raw materials much farther afield, to Cornwall for the finest china clays (kaolin) shipped by sea to the Mersey thence by the Weaver Navigation to Winsford Bridge and then by pack horse to the Potteries. Other materials came from different but extended vectors outward from Burslem, where his factory stood. In turn his ware and that of other potters had to move to market by pack horse and transshipment, obvious disadvantages in the shipment of fragile wares.[73]

The Trent and Mersey As finally approved the Silver Cross was shorn of two of its branches, the line to the upper Severn and that to the headwaters of the Thames. Still, it was by far the most ambitious cut ever undertaken in Britain up to that time, 1766. As completed the Trent and Mersey Canal was 93.375 miles long between Preston Bridge in northern Cheshire just south of the Mersey, where it made junction with the Bridgewater

Canal line from Stretford to Runcorn, and Derwent Mouth in Derbyshire, where it joined the navigable section of the river Trent. Between the two the canal wound about the contours of the ground, keeping cutting and filling to the minimum, reducing the need for aqueducts to those rivers that must be crossed, and (it was proposed) affording direct access to a larger number of farms. With a contour canal the labor also would be reduced. The English feared such constructions would drain the countryside of the rural wage labor on which British agriculture depended. It was even proposed that canal construction must be interrupted at harvest time to assure that plenty of workers would be available to cut and collect the grain at reasonably low wages. That fear proved unfounded, however, as the work on the navigations drew not only the unattached rural poor of England but also large groups from Scotland and particularly Ireland. The *cutters,* as they were first called, came over the length of the Canal Era to be called *navvies,* a term that in English came to stand for casual manual labor.

A contour canal keeps costs down, but only in an area like Flanders can it avoid intervening hills. On the Trent and Mersey there was the watershed between those two rivers to be dealt with, at Harecastle on the alignment selected. To keep the summit lockage down and also to solve the water-supply problem there, Brindley decided to bore a long tunnel, 1.6 miles long, under Harecastle Hill, not merely to reduce the number of locks needed but also to tap the coal measures interbedded there and the considerable volumes of water that could be drained from the mines into the canal trough through the tunnel. As at Worsley the production of coal could help to amortize some of the canal's cost. To reach Harecastle from Preston Bridge three other tunnels, the longest of 0.7 mile at Preston, and thirty-five locks were built in an uninterrupted rise of

326 feet to the north portal of the summit tunnel.

From the Derwent Mouth just south of Derby to Harecastle there was only one very short tunnel; but the river Dove had to be crossed on an aqueduct of twenty-three arches, the upper Trent twice, once by six arches near Rugeley and at grade at Alrewas, and the Dane by a three-arch bridge. In addition, the rise in elevation of 316 feet was taken in forty locks. Fortunately, the undertakers had increased Brindley's original underbuilt plan of 3 feet of water by 50 percent. Even then the Trent and Mersey was very modest in dimensions compared with the older Continental canals. Although each end was larger—to permit the Bridgewater boats of wider beam to use it without reloading as far as the salt workings at Middlewich and the Trent boats to reach to the up-river town of Burton—the middle stretch of the canal could handle only boats of narrow-beam, 7 feet, with a length of 70 feet, and drawing about 4 feet of water. Thus the canal was only about 29 feet at the surface and 4.5 feet deep. In this confined space two "narrow boats" could pass. It was these dimensions on the Trent and Mersey that established the standards for the narrow-boat canals of England, which became the standard right down to the present.[74]

Completion of the Silver Cross The experience with the Grand Trunk, as the Trent and Mersey was commonly called, was less effulgent than the radiance of the Bridgewater cut. For about five years after its completion in 1777, the receipts fell below costs; then the balance shifted, and by 1790 the waterway was paying 6.5 percent—hardly the 33⅓ percent of the Sankey Brook but still quite a respectable sum in that era of low general interest rates.[75] The benefit to the users was virtually instantaneous, fully justifying the immodest motto chosen for the company seal, *Pro patriam populumque fluit.*

In our cynical age we may doubt that the promoters were quite so high-minded as to have *built* the line simply for the country and its people, but there can be no question that the canal flowed in such a way as to unite the internal navigation of England and to be of great, albeit well-rewarded, use to the English people. Towns along the route of the canal prospered as those feudal central places away from it did not. Freight rates between Manchester and Litchfield (just north of Birmingham) dropped from £4 to £1 per ton.[76] Coal became more widely distributed throughout the northwest, supporting small-scale industries well away from the minehead. Slates moved into the area from North Wales, replacing the thatch so subject to vermin and fire. It was argued that the canal reduced the regrating practices of the corn merchants, no longer supportable with the introduction of the postfeudal mercantile economy. Whatever the costs in low wages of construction and handsome returns to the investors in the canal company's shares, there can be no question that the Trent and Mersey greatly stimulated the economy of its region and nurtured the Industrial Revolution in Britain, which largely transpired in the vicinity of this Grand Trunk of navigation.

The opening of the Grand Trunk in 1777 began the Canal Era in earnest. Although the Silver Cross plan had been made more modest to gain private support for the Trent and Mersey, its thinking was not abandoned. Instead, other capitalists took up the Severn connection and that to the Thames at Oxford. The Staffordshire and Worcestershire Canal, that arm of the Cross reaching to the Severn in the southwest, was authorized by Parliament at the same time as the Trent and Mersey, although it opened five years earlier, in 1772. In part this was because the southwestern connection was only half as long, 46.125 miles, and in part because it did not require the tunneling of the Grand Trunk.

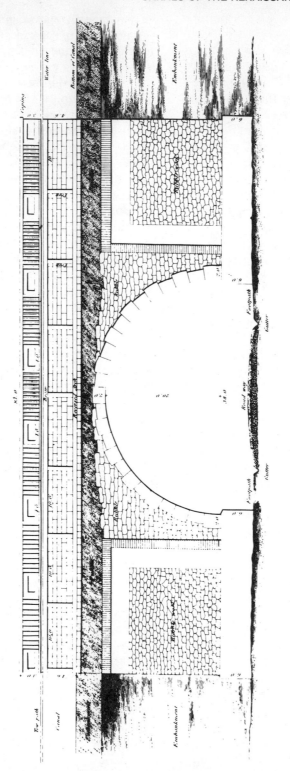

An English canal aqueduct. *Source: William Strickland, Reports on Canals, Railways, Roads, etc. Made to the Pennsylvania Society for Internal Improvements* (Philadelphia, 1826).

Making junction with that larger canal at Great Haywood, the Staffordshire and Worcestershire had only twelve locks rising southward to its summit at Gailey, followed by an uninterrupted descent from Compton in thirty-one locks to the newly built town of Stourport on the river Severn.[77]

A considerable mythology about Stourport had grown up, which has recently been laid to rest.[78] It has been held that the town had to be built only because the old Severn river port at Bewdley refused to have such an innovation as a canal. Porteous has shown that it would have introduced redundant grades, with opposing lockage, to have crossed out of the Stour valley, down which the canal was being carried, over the 350-foot ridge lying to the west between it and Bewdley. In addition the Stour Valley was one of the more important iron-working districts in England and an area likely to benefit greatly from a lateral canal along its steeply graded course. That gradient had proved ideal in securing water power for the forges clustered there, but it served badly for the transport of their pig iron and finished projects. Pig-iron from Halesowen, 12 miles northeast of Wilden Forge, cost 7 s. per ton to move by road, whereas the same pig from Redbrook on the Wye, 80 miles away, cost no more to bring by the Wye and Severn navigations.[79]

It was a wonder to eighteenth-century Britons that canals so transformed the geography of transport that entirely new settlements were required. Worsley, only a village before Egerton built his canal, became a town. Stourport came to replace Bewdley and even Bridgenorth and Shrewsbury as the important upper-river junction on the Severn. Port Dundas at the junction of the Forth and Clyde Canal with the Monkland Canal became a sizable industrial satellite for Glasgow. Coalport on the Severn became a port in 1791 when the Shropshire Canal there made junction with the stream that traditionally carried the heaviest inland

navigation of a river in the British Isles, gaining through that canal access to the coal mines to the north and west. Yet in all cases the British canal towns were small and so pale by comparison with the North American examples of canal towns—Cleveland, Ottawa, and Chicago, for example—that it hardly seems worth the space here to do more than note them.[80]

Perhaps the greatest contribution of the Staffordshire and Worcestershire Canal was that it connected to the western edge of the Black Country, the great coalfields west and northwest of Birmingham. Even in the Middle Ages this district had had an industrial importance because of the iron ores found there interbedded with the coal measures. These Clay-Band ores gained even greater significance by the time of the English Canal Era because the iron makers of Coalbrookdale—adjacent to Coalport but long predating it—had discovered how to smelt iron with coal (coke) in 1713. By mid-century the process was well in hand, so the interbedding of coal and iron in the Black Country provided an unusually strong resource base for modern metallurgy. What was missing was access to other raw materials and to markets. Birmingham had never been an iron-producing town as such—that activity came in the Stour and other valleys draining to the south from the Midland Plateau on which Birmingham stood, or the tributary valleys of the middle course of the Severn between Shrewsbury and Gloucester. This trade had given the Severn its premier place as a navigation with large numbers of hauliers whose back-breaking work drew the trows and other river boats up the shallow stream—often requiring those overtaxed men to wade in the stream itself, since no towpath was completed along the Severn until the beginning of the nineteenth century. Between the environs of the middle Severn and the Black Country, these districts became the true seat of the iron revolution that formed, with textile manufacture, the base for Britain's vanguard position in the Industrial Revolution.

To advance that quickening of commercial and manufacturing activity, it was essential to open out to a wider world the connections from the dales of Shropshire, Worcestershire, and Gloucestershire and to overcome the isolation of the low plateaus of Staffordshire and Worcestershire—the Black Country. The availability of the Severn in an area of iron and coal resources had made a start possible. For further development, artificial canals were essential. At Aldersley, west of Wolverhampton, the emergining network of cuts first came close to the Black Country. In 1767 a group in Birmingham, then a town of 30,000, asked James Brindley to do for them what he had already accomplished for the Grand Trunk and Staffordshire and Worcestershire—to survey their district and come up with a practicable route between the heart of the West Midland metropolis and the latter canal. On June 4 he made a proposal that was remarkably typical of his work: the line wandered along the contours westward from Birmingham through the Black Country to Wolverhampton, for some miles along a contour of 453 feet, then rising in six locks over a 491-foot summit at Smethwick before dropping, in three locks, to 473 feet, a level the canal was to maintain in a very sinuous course all the way to Wolverhampton Top Lock before there descending twenty-one locks in four adjacent flights to Aldersley Junction with the Staffordshire and Worcestershire Canal. This clustering of locks, extension of what the English called *pounds* for as many miles as possible, and unswerving adherence to the contours were all marks of Brindley's work. There was little difficulty in raising the £50,000 capital needed in such an industrious place as Birmingham. Local worthies such as Samuel Garbett, William Small, Samuel Galton, and Matthew Boulton all backed their confidence in the canal as a necessary transportation innovation by considerable investments.

The tendency of canals to destroy local monopolies was well attested by this undertaking. The preamble to the parliamentary bill contained a statement, insisted on by the coal owners of the Black Country, "That the Primary and Principal Object of this Undertaking was and is to obtain Navigation from the [Black Country] Collieries to this Town [of Birmingham]."[81] Much as that may have been the objective, canals cannot be made to transport in only a single direction. Manufactures began to leave the Midland Hardware District in increasing numbers, food could be transported from America to compete with the overpriced grain of English landowners, and coal could be brought from elsewhere if the Black Country magnates became too grasping. Much as the Earl of Dudley and other coal-mine owners might try to constrain the economy of the West Midlands in the way that difficulty and high cost of movement in earlier times had (what some have called the "friction of space"), they could not succeed in the long run. Rather more successful along such questionable lines was the effort of the promoters to beat down a provision that they could not be paid more than a 6 percent return on their shares. Their defense is too disingenuous for the modern ear:[82]

> the Subscribers [to shares] are not so sanguine as to expect profit near so great, and . . . they are quite convinced the quantity of Goods they can now realize [*sic*] as coming to Birm^m or passing thro' such a part of the Country as may be convenient for the Navigation, would not afford common Interest upon their Capital, and that the Supposition of a considerable increase of Tonnage would pay them no more than 6 per cent.[82]

One wonders, if the eventuality were so remote, why they struggled so against it.

Authorized in 1768, the Brindley plan was carried out with only one change. His original notion had been to dig a tunnel through the Smethwich Hill, but "running sand" had discouraged that work until much later when Telford's revision of the Birmingham Canal Navigations (B.C.N.) replaced the numerous locks over the hill by a deep cutting. Within a year a 10-mile section of the canal to the coal mines at Wednesbury was cut and filled with water. The Birmingham Canal Navigations quickly organized the coal trade, paying producers at their docks for the fuel and then transporting it to Birmingham and distributing it by carts within the town. Loud were the protests that they made only "5 per Cent Interest on the money employ'd. But that such Profit do not exceed one farthing per Hundred [weight] on the Coal."[83] The B.C.N. was completed to Aldersley Junction in 1772, essentially at the same time the Trent and Mersey Grand Trunk was opened. Thus, by then the rudiments of the canal system in the West Midlands and Merseyside were in hand. What remained to be done was to make of these alignments useful systems for the support of manufacture and trade on a greatly enlarged scale. Numerous branches, some of them in long tunnels such as the Netherton and Dudley tunnels—1.7 and 1.8 miles long, respectively—were built in the 1790s to gain access to the heart of the Black Country and the Dudley mines. Eventually the B.C.N. had over 70 miles of canal throughout the Black Country and in Birmingham, and there were a number of separate canals—the Dudley, the Worcester and Birmingham, the Birmingham and Fazeley, and others—in a dense network of cuts that could place most factories on or near the canal bank and in easy access to the local mines and the distant markets.

The fourth arm of the Silver Cross—that from the main network directly southeastward to the upper Thames and London—was the last to be undertaken. Only in 1790 was this route opened, in large part because the act to permit the building of the Coventry Canal, which formed the northern section of the connection, came in 1768, just at the end of the first phase of canal construction in England. As was the case with other undertakings in that period, the Coventry Canal was overtaken by economic decline associated with, among other things, the American Revolution. Although the Coventry and B.C.N. were authorized at the same time, the speed with which the latter was completed (just four years), saved it from the painful gestation the route directly to London experienced. It is hard to know exactly why the two companies that made up the southeastern arm of the Silver Cross encountered so much more difficulty in finishing their line, other than that they found trouble in raising the capital.[84] Coventry was an ancient industrial town, but most of the rest of the route passed through the rural shires of the East Midlands—an area where local capital would not have been so plentiful or so liquid as in the manufacturing-trading districts to the west. Again we encounter evidence that supports the notion that the English canals were the creation of capitalist investment, not of national plan. Certainly in such integrated plans the main line between the seat of manufactures, particularly the West Midlands and southern Lancashire, and the national metropolis would have taken a high priority.

Once the Conventry and Oxford canals were opened in 1790, the route to the southeast was passable but not particularly efficient. The Coventry and Oxford cuts were typical of Brindley, who had a hand in each. They wandered like a slack firehose across the countryside, finally reaching Oxford where junction with the Thames navigation took place. That river improvement had been underway for five hundred years in a situation where water-power and navigation interests had been almost continuously in confrontation. The result was an awkward assemblage of facilities that served badly when there was plenty of water in the river and, when there was too little water, worked even less well.

Over the Hills by the Navigation

In this first phase of English waterway development, one final canal must be considered—the Leeds and Liverpool, a cut that ultimately connected those large northern cities over what became Britain's longest canal. By then, however, forty-six years had passed and the Canal Era was ending. The purpose of this canal was to provide reasonable transportation costs between the rapidly growing industrial districts of southern Lancashire on the west and the West Riding of Yorkshire on the east—notably, to provide access from the textile towns on the east slope of the hills to the increasingly important port of Liverpool.

The route was finally located on the ground by James Brindley, so we can easily imagine its features. Length was the most notable, as it was 127 miles from the junction with the Aire and Calder Navigation in the West Riding westward over the crest of the Pennines to the Pall Mall Basin in Liverpool, where the cut gained access to the port. Five years after construction commenced in 1770, the ends of the canal were opened to Newburgh from Liverpool, and a year later to Holmbridge from Leeds. The line over the crest, however, was delayed as a result of many interruptions stemming from wars— the American Revolution and the conflicts following on the French Revolution—and shortages of capital. The line across the height of land required a long, high embankment and aqueduct over the Calder at Burnley and two substantial tunnels. In 1816 the route was finished and connections were secured to Manchester; the original purpose of tying the two northern industrial districts together was accomplished. Unfortunately for the promoters of the Leeds and Liverpool, that objective had been secured earlier by two canals, the Rochdale and the Huddersfield, that began later but progressed more determinedly. As their nature was more in keeping with the second phase of canal building, we may best leave their consideration for later.

The second type of cut developed during and after the Canal Mania of the 1790s was one seeking to improve on success. By the 1790s some canals were already becoming overtaxed; relief was sought through enlarging and improving the original lines, most of which were narrow-boat waterways with clustered locks and sinuous course. Another form of relief was offered by competitive undertakings seeking to divert some of the trade of a sucessful line.

The group of canals that were overtaxed by traffic responded in two different ways: some sought to use their monetary power to restrain competition, so palliative improvements might suffice to maintain their geographical monopoly; others honestly attempted to add capacity to their cut while seeking to keep it alone in its field. The Bridgewater waterways tended to exemplify the first approach—an abdication of responsibility that would in the long run have repercussions of great historical import when the first true steam railroad was built along the route of Egerton's lines. The Birmingham Canal followed a different approach, adopting a policy of activity rather than complacency—a story that needs to be discussed briefly. In 1802 the Stratford-upon-Avon Canal was built between King's Norton, just south of Birmingham, and a juncture with the Worcester and Birmingham Canal at Kingswood. This was the last link in a chain of canals that provided an alternative to the Birmingham Canal in gaining access from the iron-working district on the middle Severn to London via the Oxford Canal and the Thames.[85] In response the Birmingham Company began an extended reconstruction of its waterway, which was particularly advanced in the years 1824–1834 when Thomas Telford carried out a fundamental reconstruction of the company's lines. As Telford saw it, Birmingham was ill served by its now fifty-year-old canal system:[86]

> I found adjacent to this great and flourishing town a canal little better than a crooked ditch, with scarcely the appearance of a haling-path [hauling path], the horses frequently sliding and staggering in the water, the haling-lines sweeping the gravel into the canal, and the entanglement at the meeting of boats incessant; while at the locks at each end of the short summit crowds of boatmen were always quarelling, or offering premiums for a preference of passage, and the mineowners, injured by the delay, were loud in their just complaints.

Unfortunately, the work was hardly completed when the first rail lines reached the West Midland's metropolis.

The second phase of canal construction began as the American Revolution was drawing to a close in 1780 and was longer-lived than had been the first phase in the late 1760s and early 1770s, lasting until the close of the Napoleonic Wars. During that thirty-five years activity varied considerably between the rush during the canal mania of the early 1790s, when the more elaborate projects were proposed or first advanced, and the early nineteenth century, when construction continued more from its own momentum than from a continuing push for canals.

Space allows only a brief summary of this second phase. Perhaps the most striking undertakings were those that sought to compete in the emerging main lines of trade in England, which led to the construction of the Grand Junction Canal to make the route to London from the Midlands efficient and direct as it had never been; to the driving of two additional cuts across the Pennines between the great northern industrial districts; and to the paralleling of the leaky Thames and Severn by a more usable east-west canal across southern England. Beyond these great trunk lines the pattern was largely that of ramifying the networks of waterways within the important coalfields of Britain.

The Grand Junction, completed in 1805, was surveyed in a very different way from the cuts of the first generation: it was possessed of relatively straight ponds that were carried through low ridges in cuts and across the shallow valleys on embankments or aqueducts, as at Wolverton across the Ouse, in order to reduce the lockage. This approach had been developed by Brindley's successors, notably Thomas Telford, when they could combine an increased understanding of the conditions of operation of canals with an improved engineering technology that could build much more daring works in order to reduce the time and cost of operation on the waterways. Just as Brindley was the consulting engineer on many of the first phase canals, so Telford, Rennie, Whitworth, Henshall, and Jessop were the leading engineers of the second phase. They commonly used cuts, aqueducts, tunnels, and later inclined planes to speed up, simplify, and maximize the utilization of the canal and its water supply.

The success of the Grand Junction was immediate, in part because its locks were wider than those on most of the earlier canals. These broad-boat canals could handle two narrow boats (70 feet by 6 feet 10 inches, drawing just under 3 feet of water and carrying about 25 tons) side by side in the locks, or one broad boat (55 to 80 feet long and 12 to 21 feet wide, with 14 feet being perhaps the most standard, and capable of transporting between 50 and 70 tons). The competition for the Thames and Severn, the Kennet and Avon Canal, was just such a broad canal—one that grew directly out of the Canal Mania. Authorized in 1794, this cut was to tie together the navigable part of the Bristol Avon and the Kennet tributary of the Thames at Newbury. At first lateral to the Avon above its terminus at Bath and Devizes, this cut rose in twenty-nine locks over the escarpment of the Wiltshire Downs. Eastward it crossed the Vale of Pewsey on the upper Wiltshire Avon before cresting the divide to the Thames at Crofton and Stibb Green and descending to the Kennet at Hungerford. Pumps supplied water to the Crofton Summit. This canal proved very costly to build over its 57-mile length, as it was generous in its dimensions and construction problems were encountered before it was completed in 1810. Still, it carried more than five times as much tonnage at the height of its use (1838–1839) as did the parallel Thames and Severn.[87] Such experience seemed to justify the more generous investment that the second phase of cutting brought, though not long after this peak the opening in 1841 of the Great Western Railway to Bristol from London radically reduced the importance of any waterway between the southwest and London.

The Pennine Canals

Lancashire and Yorkshire were much more the native heath of the Canal Era. The construction of three canals across the chain should not surprise us. We have already observed the first of the triumvirate, the Leeds and Liverpool, noting its slow progress to completion only in 1816. During the mania, enough money was available that the proponents of a canal from Manchester to Leeds and Bradford via the Rochdale in Lancashire and the Calderdale in the West Riding of Yorkshire were successful in floating their company in 1794. The 33 miles from the

Bridgewater basin in Manchester at Castle Field to the Calder and Hebble Navigation in the West Riding carried the Rochdale Canal over the summit of the Pennines at Warland, 20 miles out of Manchester. This considerable rise was taken in fifty-six locks to the summit pond, there being no tunnel as here intersecting glacial valleys opened a broad sag in the crest of the hills, while the lesser drop to the Calder came in thirty-six locks to Sowerby Bridge.[88] These broad-boat locks (74 by 14) were capable of carrying a heavy trade across the Pennines, although the company had to have extensive reservoirs in the upper reaches to allow such density of traffic as the 556,711 tons carried in 1832.[89] The success of the Rochdale Canal speaks of the requisites for effective operation at this time.

The Decline of British Canals

It was the demonstrable and specific needs for canals to move the goods of industry and a burgeoning trade that allowed the British government to pursue a laissez-faire policy with respect to waterways. So when a second generation of canal construction began in the late 1780s, there was a direct capitalist interest involved, that of gaining rapid return on invested money. The canal mania of the early 1790s worked several changes. Some costly canals could be commenced in areas where the local benefit was demonstrable but the investment funds were scarce. In those places where canals of the first generation were becoming overtaxed, either improvements on that system to increase its capacity or additional routes along the same alignment were easy to finance. As technological experimentation became possible, considerable improvements in facilities were secured, although these tended to raise the cost of canal transport to the extent competition by other forms of transport became possible. Once those competitive forms were developed in any degree, the whole analysis of personal transportation benefit and investment return tended to come to a different conclusion: that canals were less useful than railroads because they were always more geographically constrained and less easily enlarged, and that the return on investment in railroads was likely to be higher than in canals.

Almost overnight, private investment in canals dropped so low that all but a relatively few lines were either abandoned outright or else put out to die by slow and unrepaired deterioration. The longevity of the British canals speaks well for the Brindleys, Telfords, and Rennies; they lasted far longer as a morphological entity than they did in the consciousness of Britons. This last point needs emphasis as today canals have returned to attention in an era of great interest to recreation, which finds the Shropshire Union or the Kennet and Avon appealing relics.

I still vividly recall spending a very long day in 1960 walking from the eastern outskirts of Birmingham completely across that very large city to Smethwick in the west, always along the towpath of the Birmingham Canal Navigations. In that entire time I met not a soul on the towpath save one city garbage boat drawn by a single horse and steered by a lone elderly man at the tiller. For this period of five or six hours I hardly saw anyone as the canal crawled under streets, behind buildings with windows often bricked up, and always walled away from the currently used part of the city. In one place there was a slight suggestion of interest in the canal, as a door in a wall was open and a canvas hose was dropped into the green motionless water of the canal. The local fire brigade was using that nearly forgotten source to extinguish a fire. But no one was looking at the canal.

When I returned to the world of 1960 Birmingham I was even more surprised to discover that few knew the canals were there and almost no one could understand why I would take the time to look at them. All that changed in succeeding years, when the BBC and others began romanticizing the Canal Era and painting the canals as bucolic if not truly idyllic.

THE CANAL IN NORTH AMERICA

The Potamic Phase: The First Effort in American Transportation and Settlement

The European economy developed over a very long period, even if we begin our consideration only when the Romans integrated that activity over an extensive area. Leonardo was working a millennium and a half after the Classical world had begun the economic development of the Po Basin. Thus in Europe the Canal Era was not a time of initial organization of areas, but rather a time when the minute geographical dismemberment found during the feudal era was being overcome, first on a regional scale in Italy and then on a national scale in France, the Low Countries, and England. These activities were organized by increasingly central governments or, in the case of England, sheltered by laissez-faire economic policies advanced by those central governments. The basic pattern of economic activity and human settlement had already been established. What was missing was any ease of transportation among the historically severed parts. The Canal Era effectively brought that connection, by the beginning of the nineteenth century in most places. The impact on the national economy was vast; in truth, as Paul Mantoux saw in England, it was canal building that made the Industrial Revolution possible.[90] Adam Smith had much earlier noted the geographical association of extension of inland navigation and industrial development: "As by means of water-carriage, a more extensive market is opened to every sort of industry than what land-carriage alone can afford, so it is upon the sea coast, and along the banks of navigable rivers, that industry of every kind begins to subdivide and improve itself."[91] So in Europe first the canal served to create a nationally "extensive market," and then industry quickly set out to "subdivide and improve itself" in the Industrial Revolution.

In North America, in both Canada and the United States, the canal was part of the heritage of the settlers, who first came in the seventeenth century when canal building was gaining increasing attention in Europe. In coming to North America those settlers were at first constrained to repeat the historical geography of inland navigation in Europe. The cause was the same: that in the beginning the most logical and efficient *first effort* comes in improving on nature, rather than replacing it. It is not surprising that those European persons planted on the American shore, as practitioners of national mercantilism, adopted what elsewhere I have termed a "mercantile model of settlement"; that is, they settled in a geographical pattern that would be logical for the creation of mercantile links between the newly developing North American colonies and the homelands in Europe.

In Canada, after early experiments with settlements in the present Maritime Provinces, the French focused most of their efforts along the great river of the north, the St. Lawrence, between its lowest rapids at Lachine and the point on the estuary where arable marine sediments become too small in extent to encourage the development of seigneurial settlement of the sort the Gallic planters had in mind. In the English area there was no great river of the south; instead, there were many rather coequal rivers each flowing down from the Appalachian crest to the not-too-distant sea. The two major exceptions were the Connecticut, which in its central section had a great structural valley tying together ends that were probably glacially enlarged, and the Hudson, which was nothing more than a glacial fjord cut completely across the controlling Appalachian structures that determined the small-river-basin grain of the coastal and piedmont areas where first English settlement took place.

Within this natural endowment the English and French set about shaping planted settlements. Because the French and English interest in the New World was mainly that of a mercantilist nation seeking to expand its trading frontiers, the early settlements—that is, before the American Revolution—were virtually all on the coast, accessible to ocean navigation.

Wherever one looked, the mercantile nature of the English and French colonies was so strong that settlement had to conform to the exactions of the economic system and be accessible to ocean shipping. The result was that no French settlements were out of reach of tidewater down to the time of the English Conquest in 1763, and no English settlements of any size—save for Worcester, Massachusetts, and Lancaster, Pennsylvania—were away from access to the sea down to the outbreak of the Revolution.[92]

The first effort at transportation development in the North American colonies had taken this easiest of courses by clinging to the coast. Later mercantile settlements in Australia and Africa followed the practice. Under such a settlement pattern relatively little initial effort was required to begin trading. The sea gave access to the home markets, and the rivers gave access to the interior depots of staple collection. As long as the unalloyed mercantilist economy held sway—until the American Revolution in North America and until the late nineteenth or even the twentieth century in Australia and Africa—the supply of staples tended to come from areas accessible to naturally available water transportation. Canada under the French spread widely into the interior of North America—to the Great Lakes Country, the Illinois Country, the Mississippi Valley, and the Gulf Coast—but always in response to the controlling waterways, the St. Lawrence–Great Lakes and the Mississippi. Even when the French couriers du bois pushed farther into the continent, they did so tied to rivers and the more efficient portages across their headwaters. The alignment of settlements in the American Middle West reflected this potamic expansion of the mercantilist Europeans. The Toledo, Chicago-Peoria, and Green Bay portages carried the French from the St. Lawrence drainage to that of the Mississippi; in doing so they determined where the larger settlements of the region would come, even those that would not rise for a century or more. In various ways the waterways established that Detroit, Toledo, Green Bay, Milwaukee, Chicago, St. Louis, Pittsburgh, Memphis, and New Orleans, the largest among far more such riverine places, would dominate the settlement even of a country no longer either controlled by the French or possessed of a Gallic culture.

The English held no river to rival the St. Lawrence or the Mississippi, so they must instead create not two dominant colonies centered on great rivers—Canada and Louisiana—but more than a dozen such first efforts strung along discrete rivers from the edge of French Canada, in Nova Scotia, to the limits of Spanish Florida, in Georgia. It was unusual to find a colony possessed of more than a single important river leading either to a significant agricultural or natural resource producing area. Maine was certainly an exception to this generalization, though its frontier site, like that of Georgia, made use of the back country difficult throughout most of the colonial period.

The Transformation of the Economy

The independence of the United States, acknowledged by the British in the Treaty of Paris of 1783, forced on the new republic a major reexamination of this natural provision of river transport. The system had depended mainly on gaining ties among some twenty rivers spread among the colonies, which afforded access to the areas producing staples for export and the ports whence that export could be sent to the consumers of the metropolitan country, England and Wales. With peace came a major dislocation of the economic system that had ruled before 1776; in place of mercantilism had come invasion as the British flooded the American market with all the products the colonials had embargoed since 1776, while at the same time refusing to permit Americans to pursue their traditional triangular trade with Canada and the West Indies. The result of that dislocation was even greater because the thirteen colonies had had rather little economic integration before 1776: each dealt with England, not with its neighbors. With Canada and the West Indies gone, the neighbors became more important and the needs of interprovincial trade and transport far more crucial. In 1789 those provinces, loosely confederated in 1783, established a stronger federal government as the United States of America—as much to gain that economic integration in law as for any other reason. Still, the physical integration of the thirteen states could not be accomplished by signing a document. Instead, the first decade of the new nation was taken up with trying to transform the American economy in several important ways.

The most significant transformation came within less than two years when, in 1791, Samuel Slater opened what became the first long-term success as a cotton textile mill to operate within the United States. In this early phase of industrialization the Americans were favored by nature with respect to power, that of falling water in a heavily glaciated landscape, but sorely tried by the transportation problems introduced. Slater had set up his mill at the lowest falls of the Blackstone River in the northern outskirts of the important colonial port of Providence. At such a site transportation was no great problem, particularly as the cotton was being brought by riverboat and ship via Charleston and Savannah from the riverine plantations of South Carolina and Georgia. As the search for more power came with the growth of the machine-spinning industry, New England could provide a hundred sites with ease, but those sites were mostly away from the coast and thus increasingly less accessible to the traditional American mode of transportation, that by water between the fall line and the river-mouth ports.

Other transformations of the American economy came with the opening of the trans-Appalachian country to extensive settlement and increasing agricultural production, now too large to be consumed locally. A first effort was made to solve the problem of interior economic isolation (already signaled by the Whiskey Rebellion of 1794) by seeking to secure from the Spanish government the rights of passage down to the mouth of the Mississippi and of deposit of goods on the docks of New Orleans while waiting for forward transport by sailing ship thence to the eastern American market and to foreign markets then aggressively being sought. After protracted negotiations with the Spanish government, the United States signed the Treaty of San Lorenzo on October 27, 1795, finally granting to the new republic the right of free navigation on the lower Mississippi and of deposit for reloading at New Orleans. At first this seemed to assure to the American West the same potamic transportation that the East Coast enjoyed; but that

was an illusion. The Treaty of San Lorenzo granted the right of deposit for only three years, but at the end of that period the Spanish government interposed no objection to continuing deposit. In 1800, however, in the secret Treaty of San Ildefonso, Napoleon had secured the retrocession of Louisiana, although he did not immediately put that provision into effect. In 1802 the Spaniards were still in control of Louisiana, and their governor abruptly ended the Americans' right of deposit at the "island" of New Orleans.

This closing of the transportation route to the west joined with a growing concern felt by President Jefferson that the French would implement the Treaty of San Ildefonso even to the extent of stationing an army of veterans of Napoleon's most successful European campaigns in Louisiana. This latter undertaking was to be related to the effort of the French to retake Haiti from the black insurrectionists who had defeated their French slave masters. Fortunately for the Americans, the French troops were defeated in Haiti by yellow fever and the persistence of Toussaint l'Ouverture; by 1803, when Jefferson sought to buy from France the French and Spanish domains east of the Mississippi or, failing that, the Island of New Orleans— or at the very least the right of passage on the Mississippi and space for an American free port at New Orleans—the French were having second thoughts about a mercantilist empire in the Americas. Napoleon, realizing in 1803 that war with England would resume shortly, instructed Talleyrand to offer all of Louisiana to the Americans in order to keep it from the British. The only hitch was a typically Gallic argument over the price, with the Americans offering 20 million francs and the French holding out for 60 million, about $12 million.

The Louisiana Purchase most effectively carried river transport to the American West, which now extended in places as far as the crest of the Rocky Mountains. It would eventually prove difficult to reach that new western border in what had become the standard American way, by boat. Still, the earlier efforts, until around 1840, did depend on just such a traditional approach. It should not be lost on us how very exacting was the perpetuation of this practice on Lewis and Clark's exploratory expedition to the Pacific. Their struggle was up the Missouri River and its headwater streams to reach the mountain crest, then down the Columbia and its tributaries to the Pacific, with a return over similarly trying routes to inform the expanded republic in 1806 that there was no easy potamic route either to the western boundary of the nation or beyond it into the *terra nullius* of the Oregon Country. Later we shall see that, although the United States made a more exclusive use of waterways than did any European country, it was here that Europeans first had to realize that such natural provision was geographically limited. As the subhumid frontier on the Great Plains was reached, the explorers found a transportation frontier as well—one Europeans had never before seriously faced. Not until pack and wagon transport west of the Hundredth Meridian was developed could the economic frontier be pushed farther toward the mountains.

The Rise of the Canal in America: The Short Improvements

The American dependence on inland navigation quickly made the settlers aware of the places, even within the humid regions, where nature's provision was less than sufficient. Before the Revolution, while the frontier still lay to the east of the Appalachian crest save in the Mohawk-Champlain glacis of settlement beyond the mountains, the main insufficiency was encountered at the Fall Line between the Atlantic Coastal Plain and the Piedmont slope rising to the Appalachians.

Because that line assumes so much importance, it should be identified geographically. North of New York City the Fall Line disappears because the coastal plain lies off the present shoreline, exposed only where glacial deposits have been heaped on it, as in Long Island, Fisher's Island, Martha's Vineyard and Nantucket, and Cape Cod. South of New York City the Fall Line passes through Trenton; the lowest falls on the Delaware, the western parts of Philadelphia, just northwest of Wilmington, across the Susquehanna at Conowingo, through the northern and western suburbs of Baltimore, to Ellicott City, Georgetown in the District of Columbia on the Potomac; Alexandria, Fredericksburg on the Rappahannock, Richmond on the James, Petersburg on the Appomattox, all in Virginia; Roanoke Rapids on the Roanoke, Rocky Mount, and Fayetteville on the Cape Fear River, in North Carolina; Camden on the Wateree and Columbia on the Congaree in South Carolina; Augusta on the Savannah River, Milledgeville on the Oconee, Macon on the Ocmulgee, and Columbus on the Chattahoochee in Georgia; and Montgomery on the Alabama River. Anywhere along this line, which is essentially the shoreline or just inward of that alignment in New England and the inner edge of the coastal plain south of New York City, the natural navigation of streams was interrupted.

For Americans seeking during the early period of independence to improve on nature in transportation, the obvious place to begin was at the interruptions of the river navigations. Even in the seventeenth century there had been minor canal ditches cut around Ipswich, Massachusetts; but the first canal akin to those being built in Europe at the time came elsewhere in the Puritan Commonwealth, at the South Hadley Falls of the Connecticut River. That stream—the largest in New England and the entry route to central Massachusetts and western New Hampshire and eastern Vermont—was easily navigable to just above Hartford in Connecticut even by some sea-going vessels. At the Enfield rapids river boats could pass under favorable conditions, but 10 miles above Springfield in Massachusetts the Hadley Falls intervened to force a difficult portage on boatmen operating toward northern New England. The South Hadley Falls were not at the Fall Line; such does not really exist in New England, and what serves in its place—a point at the head of the often flooded or overdeepened lower courses of the streams—lay below Enfield. But because the first rapids could be passed, though with difficulty, the lowest absolute obstruction of the stream came in those Hadley Falls. In 1792 Massachusetts chartered "The Proprietors of the Locks and Canals on the Connecticut River," whose purpose it was to render navigable the entire course of the Massachusetts reach of the stream. In doing so they commenced an interregional, interurban competition that was to characterize much of the canal development in the United States, particularly that between the Appalachians and the sea.

To understand the nature of this interurban competition, which grew out of the application of mercantilist notions to the welfare of individual cities, we must look for a moment at the geography of the rivers flowing to the Atlantic. Because the original English charters or patents creating the mercantilist colonies in North America were issued well before there was any clear understanding of the detailed geography of this new land, the pattern they took was that of *entrepôts*—doorways, if you will—sited on the coast and assumed to hold easy access to the productive areas of the interior. Sometimes that was the case, as in New York with the Hudson and in Virginia with the James; sometimes the location of the entrepôt proved poor in opening up the back country, as was the case in Boston with the Charles

River and in Charleston with the Ashley and Cooper rivers. These very names suggest the hopes the founders held. The Charles River, never in a Bostonian's mind without the definite article, was named for the heir to the throne but proved as tortuous and incompetent a stream as he was a monarch, rising only 30 miles west of the port sited at its broad mouth. Similarly, the Ashley and Cooper honored the leading proprietor of the Carolina colony and were similarly broad but short. For a true entrance to the staple-producing hinterland, Boston would have been better served by the Merrimack, which reaches the sea at Newburyport 30 miles to the north, and Charleston by the Santee with its mouth some 50 miles north of the Carolina metropolis. In each case a splendid harbor was chosen by early settlers whose view could hardly be more than coastal: in New York and Virginia the harbors—Upper New York Bay and Hampton Roads, respectively—were among the world's great anchorages but also were the mouths of major streams extending well inland; in Boston and Charleston, by contrast, the harbors were certainly good for the time, and remain so, but the interior access was poor indeed.

The boundaries drawn between the English colonies were geographically arbitrary, based mainly on courtly maneuver in a climate of geographical ignorance. To cite only the most egregious examples, Massachusetts was given the lower course of the great river of New Hampshire, the Merrimack, the upper course of the rivers of Rhode Island, the Blackstone and Taunton, and the middle reach of the stream for which the Connecticut colony was named. Pennsylvania held the mouth of the Delaware, whose headwaters were in New York, but was denied the mouth of the Quaker Commonwealth's own master stream, the Susquehanna. In the South matters were handled a bit better, although the Roanoke does reach the sea in North Carolina, not in

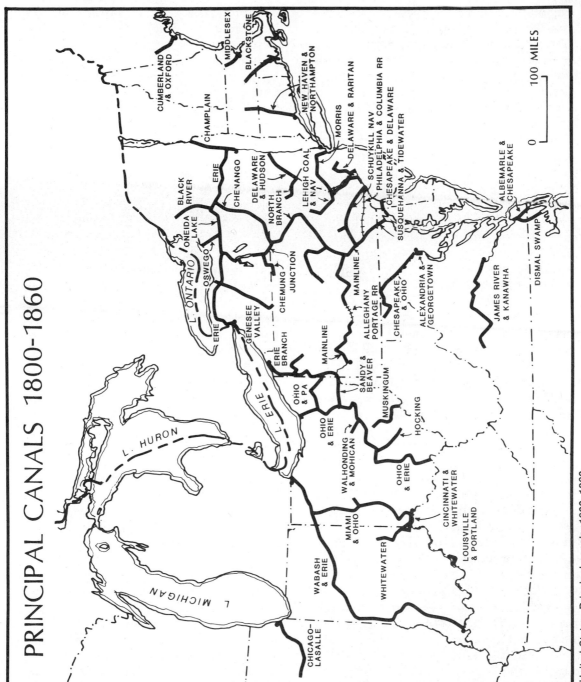

PRINCIPAL CANALS 1800-1860

100 MILES

0

L. ONTARIO

L. HURON

L. MICHIGAN

L. ERIE

CUMBERLAND & OXFORD

MIDDLESEX

BLACKSTONE

CHAMPLAIN

NEW HAVEN & NORTHAMPTON

MORRIS

DELAWARE & RARITAN

ERIE

CHENANGO

DELAWARE & HUDSON

NORTH BRANCH

LEHIGH COAL & NAV

SCHUYKILL NAV

PHILADELPHIA & COLUMBIA RR

CHESAPEAKE & DELAWARE

SUSQUEHANNA & TIDEWATER

ALBEMARLE & CHESAPEAKE

BLACK RIVER

ONEIDA LAKE

OSWEGO

ERIE

GENESEE VALLEY

CHEMUNG

JUNCTION

CHEMUNG BRANCH

MAINLINE

MAINLINE

ALLEGHANY PORTAGE RR

CHESAPEAKE & OHIO

ALEXANDRIA & GEORGETOWN

JAMES RIVER & KANAWHA

DISMAL SWAMP

ERIE

ERIE BRANCH

OHIO & PA

OHIO & ERIE

SANDY & BEAVER

MUSKINGUM

HOCKING

WALHONDING & MOHICAN

OHIO & ERIE

CINCINNATI & WHITEWATER

LOUISVILLE & PORTLAND

WABASH & ERIE

MIAMI & OHIO

WHITEWATER

CHICAGO-LASALLE

United States: Principal canals, 1800–1860.

Virginia where its main extent is found. It is probable that this better showing comes not from greater wisdom among English monarchs but, instead, from the more orderly nature of the streams crossing the southern piedmont and coastal plain.

The misfit of entrepôt to hinterland, of harbor to source of its cargoes, and of potamic transportation to the colony or state charged with developing a first effort at internal improvements accounts for most of the early canal-building efforts in the United States. The same can be said for Canada, where the Treaty of Paris in 1783 left part of the master stream, the St. Lawrence, as an internal boundary causing the colonial government to have to build canals to avoid the strategic hazard thus produced.

Returning to New England, the effort to organize American transportation and to integrate the previously separate economies of the thirteen colonies sought to build on the rivers by overcoming their geographical and political obstacles. Nature had left the lush Connecticut Valley of Massachusetts rather isolated from the coast either within the commonwealth of Massachusetts or even down river to Hartford, the port for the great valley. In the first forty years of the federal union, Boston and Hartford, and then New Haven, entered into competition to tie this, the best of New England's farming areas, to its mercantile establishment, all working with the instrument of transportation advance characteristic of their time, locks and canals. Boston was the first to discuss a solution. Early accepting a charge that has often confused observers, General Henry Knox of the Maine District of Massachusetts, who was the republic's first Secretary of War, proposed within his first year in office that a canal be built from Boston to the Connecticut River. In the summer of 1791 Knox engaged a surveyor, Captain John Hills, and lent his support to the project which, he argued, would serve "to take the trade from Hartford."[93] The central Massachusetts upland proved too much for this undertaking, which would have been carried on by a private company as was the practice in England, and nothing came of the speculations of Knox and his associates.

In the absence of an effective Boston effort, the merchants of Hartford and other Connecticut Valley towns gained the lead. At Warehouse Point just north of Hartford, the first of three "falls" within the graben is encountered. At the right conditions of water and wind, these Enfield Falls could be navigated, although it took about one poleman per ton of freight to gain headway upstream. At South Hadley, 25 miles to the north, a tough red shale associated with the traprock sill there exposed formed an absolute barrier to navigation, requiring portaging. Again, another 30 miles farther north, at Montague, the Turner's Falls again interrupted the river flow where the stream issued from its northernly reach. That reach is similar to that below Middletown, Connecticut, passing in a deeply incised valley through the metamorphic rocks of the northern Appalachians and extending almost to their northern edge just south of the Logan Fault that bounds the St. Lawrence Valley on the south. From Turner's Falls to Wells River, Vermont, some 90 miles, there were three falls that had to be overcome. All told between Barnet, Vermont, just above Wells River and Hartford, Connecticut, the river fell 420 feet, with well near half in six collected "falls."

It was at South Hadley Falls that the first canal of any importance in the United States was built. The Proprietors of the Locks and Canals on the Connecticut River had originally intended to build locks and short canals at the South Hadley and Turner's falls, but such a novel undertaking urged caution on the merchant capitalists of the valley and their Dutch foreign investors. Thus, to improve for navigation the drop of

50 feet in 2 miles, the South Hadley Falls canal was the first undertaken, beginning in 1792, and it was dealt with not by locks but rather by an inclined plane, the first facility in the United States to move boats over a vertical distance. The cradle on the plane could handle boats 40 by 20 feet and was operated by waterpower. A 2.5-mile canal served along with this inclined plane to circumvent the falls with water diverted into its inlet by a wing dam built well to the center of the river.

The success of this cut was immediate, leading to a rapid rise in the traffic on the Connecticut once it was opened in 1795. Litigation over the effect of the wing dam in flooding the meadows of Northampton, leading to an epidemic of "intermittent fever," was enough to drive off the Dutch investors, whose courage must have conformed to the stereotype. Soon American investors undertook the construction of the Turner's Falls canal, 3 miles in length and with ten locks, handling 70 feet of rise, that was opened in 1800. Fairly rapidly the lowest upper-river canal, that at Bellows Falls, was taken in hand by local residents using the capital of a single English investor, Hodgson Atkinson, and a short canal with eight locks gained 52 feet and further access to the important timber-producing areas of New Hampshire and Vermont. Two final canals, one at "Water-Queeche," now Sumner's Falls, of 12 feet at Hartland below White River Junction, Vermont, and another of 36 feet at Olcott's Falls just above, opened the final navigable reach of the river to Wells River, Vermont—some 220 miles above tidewater at Hartford.[94]

The tying of northern and western New England to Hartford rather than to Boston came through fairly modest modifications of the natural river navigations. It served as a lesson to two groups: those facing similar obstacles on other rivers, and the Bostonian merchants whose displeasure at the loss of trade from northern and western New England can easily be imagined. Elsewhere along the Atlantic-flowing rivers, short canals around interruptions in river navigation were begun. On the Merrimack River at its lowest insuperable falls, the Pawtucket Falls at what is today Lowell, work began on a similar proprietorial canal opened in 1796. On the Hudson in 1792 two private companies were incorporated to improve the connections from that stream to the west and to the north. The Northern Inland Lock Navigation Company was to improve the streams between the Hudson and Lake Champlain, with a short watershed canal at their parting. The Western Inland Lock Navigation Company was to connect the Mohawk tributary of the Hudson with some stream flowing into Lake Ontario. The companies succeeded in raising considerable capital as they would open new lands for development, affording landowners hopes for speculative profits from land sales. The first fruit came when Western built a short canal of five locks, 74 by 12 feet, at Little Falls on the Mohawk River, where that stream fell 30 feet in less than a mile.[95] At Rome on the Upper Mohawk in 1797 a 2-mile canal with two locks and a depth of 4 feet was completed to connect to Wood Creek that flowed westward into Seneca Lake. With other improvements on the Mohawk, the navigation to Seneca Lake from Albany was cheapened to $32 a ton from $100 and the transport to Niagara cut in half.[96] But still the great obstacle of the Cohoes Falls between Schenectady and the Hudson remained, beyond the financial resources of the Western Company to improve. This first effort was significant but still highly flawed. The connections westward from Seneca Lake were problematic, as were those on the Mohawk between Utica and Rome; and the portage from Albany to Schenectady remained. Neither the Western nor the Northern Locks proved a functional or a financial success. The problems faced in gaining long-distance access from such equivocal plans were too great; parts might be improved, but the whole was not adequate to the demands place on it. Those solutions came only in the next, truly canal, stage of waterway improvement.

The removal of limited obstacles was more successful on the Merrimack as an extension of America's first canal of any length, the Middlesex. We shall look at that waterway as the initiator of the American Canal Era, but first we may logically consider the short canals carried out around the falls of the Merrimack to extend its reach by using the first effort characteristic of all waterway improvement plans. Minor improvements over riffles in the river were made at Wicasee Canal just above present-day Lowell (one lock, a dam, and a short canal); at Cromwell's Falls, another lock; and in New Hampshire at four places with twenty-three locks, some 11 miles of improvements and a number of dams. By 1814 a working navigation 113 miles above the mouth of the river had been shaped by this removal of limited barriers.[97]

In the Middle Atlantic states the Susquehanna was beset by riffles but not unnavigable save in drought periods well toward northern Pennsylvania. In Maryland the Potomac was improved by the company of that name between 1785 and 1802. Of the five falls and rapids that interrupted navigation below Cumberland, the three uppermost rapids were passed by lockless canals by 1792. Lower down, the Little and then the Great Falls required locks and were much slower in being circumvented; the canal and locks at the Great Falls were completed only in 1802. At that point the Potomac was basically navigable for 220 miles, from the mouth of Savage River down to tidewater at Georgetown.[98] The improvement of Virginia rivers came mainly on the James, which could admit boats drawing 15 feet to within 3 miles of Richmond. There rapids impeded further navigation, so a canal around the obstruction was begun in 1784 and completed in 1794. In the former year George Washington urged the development of a waterway to the West "by one or both of the rivers of this state, which have their sources in the Appalachian mountains."[99] Although Washington was more interested in a canal along the Potomac, as his family had been since well before the Revolution, the actual effort by the commonwealth came along the James. At Richmond the canal was 2.5 miles long and 3 feet deep, and raised boats the 80 feet to the river above the falls in twelve locks. With another short canal with three locks, 3 miles farther upstream, the navigation to Lynchburg was opened, though with only 12 inches of water. The Appomatox from the James to Petersburg was improved, and locks around the falls there continued boat navigation another 60 miles to Farmville.[100]

THE CANAL ERA IN AMERICA

By 1800 gaps in the potamic system began to show up when efforts were made to meet the demands of the emerging national economy. Perhaps the first to appear came with respect to the nonpotamic entrepôts planted in colonial times—notably Boston, Providence, New Haven, Baltimore, and Charleston. In addition, as the early years of the nineteenth century passed, it became clear that the United States was fast changing from a coastal to a continental state: the sorts of transportation sufficient for the colonial period and the earliest phase of the staple economy of the new republic were proving inadequate in dealing with the emergence of the trans-Appalachian West, particularly that north of the Ohio River.

A third gap in the potamic system came with respect to the rise of coal mining in the United States. Little coal had been mined before independence, but the use of anthracite to heat and power the growing cities for the first time forced Americans to face the need to transport large tonnages of the sort the English faced thirty years earlier. Thus in the first phase of the American Canal Era there were essentially three different purposes for canals, each with its own geographical and financial characteristics.

The first to be met came in the canals built to repair the geographical mistakes of the English planters when they set up their entrepôts in poor accordance with the potamic system of transportation that emerged from the first effort at transportation improvement. In this undertaking canals were built to connect Boston, Providence, New Haven, Baltimore, and Charleston with rivers viewed as not what they should be in outlet. The second need came in shaping what nature could never have been expected to provide, a trans-Appalachian waterway. This effort involved a considerable amount of urban mercantilism not so different from that which brought the entrepôt-connection canals into being. The difference came in the scale of the trans-Appalachian undertakings and the ease with which these could be portrayed as benefiting more than a single port; state mercantilism came to supplement entrepôt mercantilism. Finally, with this focusing of a great deal of attention on what Jean Gottmann has called "the economic hinge" between the outside world and the burgeoning American economy, came the need for cheap and plentiful energy resources in the ports and mill towns of the Northeast. That need was met by the buildings of a number of anthracite canals from eastern Pennsylvania coalfields to Chesapeake Bay, the Delaware River, and the Hudson.

The Correction of English Mistakes:
The Entrepôt Canals

We have already noted the difficulty that faces settlers who arrive on an unknown shore in selecting the proper place for entrepôts. The record of the English settlers was none too good on this score, the French and Dutch having rather bettered their record by occupying the best entrances to the country when the French settled on the lower St. Lawrence and the lower Mississippi and the Dutch on the Hudson, the Connecticut, and the Delaware. Plymouth, Boston, Newport, Providence, New Haven, Baltimore, and Charleston showed little wit in their choice, beyond the narrow objective of securing a limited entrepôt for a timidly conceived expression of national mercantilism. What can be said for the American English is that they were fast to appreciate their ancestors' errors and certainly persistent in seeking to rectify them.

The Middlesex Canal Having bruited a canal to try to divert the trade of the Connecticut to Boston Harbor at a time when only the most initial efforts could be undertaken by the capitalists of the time, the merchants of that port, noted for its sound business sense, dug instead a narrow cut designed "to preserve the longest possible Level, in the shortest possible course, [and to] unite as many links as possible, with least possible Expence."[101] They chose their route so as to minimize the number and scale of engineering works and to concentrate the major descent on the canal in six locks at Horn Pond in Woburn. Most important, they turned in their search for an accessible tributary area away from the Connecticut, more than 100 miles distant, to the Merrimack, a mere 25.

The canal they planned in 1792 was a typical Brindley structure, though one with every possible corner cut. When construction began on September 10, 1794, its purpose was to provide a waterway from the Merrimack River above the Pawtucket Falls southeastward to the northern arm of Boston Harbor in Medford River. As designed the cut began at Chelmsford on the Merrimack, where it rose in a flight of three stone locks to the long summit level carried with two wooden aqueducts, supported on freestone abutments and intermediate piers, to the level crossing of the Concord River at Billerica. When filled with water this 5.75-mile stretch was found to have some faults but Baldwin succeeded in perfecting the fabric, and limited use of the canal began in 1798. Slowly the summit pond was pushed farther toward Boston, but only at the cost of cheapening its fabric by the substitution of wooden for masonry locks. In particular the problem came from gaining access to hydraulic cement, first used in America on this, the Middlesex Canal. Baldwin was forced to import his *trass* at a considerable cost from the Dutch West Indian island of St. Eustatius. Wood was extremely plentiful in New Hampshire and could be floated to the construction site. In addition, the local skills in Middlesex and Essex counties in northeastern Massachusetts were mostly those of house and ship carpentry, thus supportive of such a shift in material. In 1802 a raft of timber passed down the canal from Chelmsford on the Merrimack to Woburn, where the flight of six descending locks was still under construction. After exertion of every possible effort, the canal was completed to the Charles River basin at Charlestown on the last day of 1803.[102]

From 1804 until about 1815 the main traffic flow on the Middlesex Canal was downbound from the back country of New Hampshire, and heavily weighted toward timber products. With the opening of the canal and lock improvements in the Merrimack northward to Concord, a reversal of the flow was accomplished; manufactured goods and imported staples gained on timber and came to be distributed to a rapidly industrializing region in succeeding decades. The rapidity of factory construction, first at Lowell after 1823 but later at Derryfield (to become Amoskeag and then Manchester), Nashua, Souhegan, and elsewhere called inland from the port of Boston increasing quantities of baled cotton,

which became the prime staple of the burgeoning textile industry. But that industrialization also rather quickly encouraged competition for the canal. In the late 1820s teamsters were competing successfully with the waterway by using the turnpikes, which extended in a rather dense net over eastern Massachusetts and southern New Hampshire during the first two decades of the nineteenth century. In 1830 some of the main undertakers in the Lowell textile manufacture had begun to finance the building of a railroad from Boston to Lowell, which, when it opened in 1835, rapidly made the operation of the canal unprofitable. Company reports for the year 1836 noted that use of the canal "went on as usual with the exception of the amount of transportation to Lowell by the Rail Road."[103] But by 1842 a railroad was opened to Concord, and it quickly displaced the cut as the main instrument for tying the developing tributary area of Boston to that port. This substitution demonstrated without contradiction the greater ease that railroads offered to an aggressive mercantilist group in overcoming the mistakes of "nature," or of the early settlers, in their choice of entrepôt sites.

The Middlesex Canal stands as important in the transportation geography of the United States out of all proportion to its length and facilities. This cut proved a number of things and demonstrated the beneficial contribution that improved facilities could make in regional development. Loammi Baldwin cleverly built the canal and its structures with very little actual detail learned from Europe. He solved the hydraulic cement problem, he learned to puddle the canal to gain a tight seal, and he and his successors experimented and often succeeded with the operation of the canal. Passenger boats were introduced, as was the first tug to operate in the United States and one of the earliest anywhere.[104]

Once the relative success of the Middlesex

Canal was open to observation, two other unfortunately located colonial ports, New Haven and Providence, began discussing schemes. Already in the 1790s New Haven had envisaged some vague waterway to intercept the Connecticut River somewhere upstream of Hartford, diverting the river traffic from that head of sloop transport on that stream to the tidewater harbor of New Haven. Organized as the Farmington Canal in Connecticut and the New Haven and Northampton in Massachusetts, the 78-mile cut was begun in 1825, rather late in time to enjoy much of a headstart on the railroads then being discussed. But 1825, the year the phenomenally successful Erie Canal opened, was a time of sanguine views on such waterways. Built with wooden locks and not enough money, the New Haven to Northampton staggered to completion in 1835, but only at the expense of building the Massachusetts section to tighter dimensions than those in Connecticut. As finished, the canal had to rise and fall 520 feet in sixty locks to reach tidewater from Northampton, whereas the river fell only 90 feet in ten locks to gain the same end at Hartford. If that disadvantage were not sufficient, the late completion of the canal meant that it had only about a ten-year life before its right-of-way was mercifully taken up for use as the embankment of a ralroad. Yet the New Haven and Northampton Canal should not be overlooked: it was the longest and, in a way, the most audacious, of the canals built to correct the mistakes in the location of colonial entrepôts.

The Ultimate Industrial Cut: The Blackstone Canal More successful along that line was the canal that Providence projected into the back country of central Massachusetts. As soon as waterways were first seriously proposed in the 1790s, the then very active Providence merchant class eyed the upper Blackstone River Valley as the natural trib-

utary area for the Narragansett port. Unfortunately for their interests the colonial limits of Massachusetts had been drawn a scant 14 miles to the north and merely across the river to the east. The political realities totally forfended any canal strategy within the 1,200 square miles of Rhode Island; thus the merchants had to turn their attention elsewhere. This they did by financing the early episodes of the American Industrial Revolution, so much so that for the first generation of that attack on traditional technology it was the environs of Providence that were the "seat of the war," as the times would have phrased it. It was the Blackstone River Valley, a stretch of country adjacent to that stream that rose within the important county town of Worcester in Massachusetts to flow for 50 miles southeastward to enter the Seekonk River, a tidal arm of the bay just east of Providence, that saw the greatest concentration of industrialization in the United States before 1815. The result was that the mill owners in central Massachusetts came to desire an easier approach to tidewater than could be provided by the steep and rolling Boston-Worcester Turnpike, all Massachusetts offered. This conjunction of interests in Rhode Island and central Massachusetts led, in 1823, to the chartering of the Blackstone Canal by both state legislatures. Benjamin Wright, an important Erie Canal engineer, was retained to report on the topography of the line and the facilities that would be needed for the creation of slack-water navigation.

Holmes Hutchinson, Wright's assistant, reported that the distance would be 45 miles, with a descent from the Thomas Street basin in Worcester to tidewater at Providence canal basin of 451.5 feet. No very considerable facilities would be needed as this was essentially a lateral canal, save at its southern end where it passed out of the Blackstone Valley at Central Falls crossing overland for a few miles to gain a canal basin in the center of Providence. As built it was 32 feet wide at the top, 18 feet on the bottom, and 3.5 feet deep. The locks conformed to the standard on the Middlesex Canal, although there was no interconnection between the two, with chambers admitting boats of 70 by 10 feet. The upper part of the canal was rather steep: the first 11 miles would have twenty-six locks giving 175 feet of descent. In the next 17.5 miles to the Rhode Island boundary, there was a drop of 107 feet taken in fifteen locks. The remaining eight locks in Rhode Island handled the final drop taken in the river and the cross-country section of the canal to its basin in Providence. Construction was begun in 1824 and completed in October, 1828.[105] The operation of the canal was of considerable value to the valley merchants and manufacturers, though the latter were always of mixed mind toward the cut. Its effect on freight rates was highly beneficial, perhaps reducing charges by half, but it was also seen as a sharp competitor for the most vital resource of the valley industry, the water in the river passing over numerous falls that drove the spindles of the mills, already some twenty thousand when the construction began.[106]

Baltimore Stays on Land   Two other colonial entrepôts strove in similar fashion to improve their geographical situation through such diversionary canals. Baltimore was in a situation that frustrated the conditions of access to the logical headwaters of Chesapeake Bay—that is, the ramified Susquehanna Valley in Pennsylvania. That stream reached the bay not at Baltimore but some 30 miles to the northeast, and then only over the rapids at Conowingo that made upstream navigation difficult. The problem was intensified by the fact that most of the Susquehanna Valley lay in Pennsylvania, so that commonwealth had little concern for enhancing the interests of the port in the ad-

jacent state. But in the 1820s Baltimore was far more dynamic a city than Philadelphia; in this period it grew faster than the Quaker City and came to be the second in population after New York, so its merchants tried all possible entrées to the interior. This meant active support for the Baltimore and Ohio Railroad after 1828, though not for the Chesapeake and Ohio Canal that reached tidewater at Georgetown, D. C., and Alexandria, Virginia, and promotion of the attempt to canalize the lower section of the Susquehanna River. In the 1830s those Baltimore merchants secured a city investment in the Susquehanna and Tidewater Canal, 15 miles from tidewater in Maryland to the Pennsylvania line, and 30 miles above in Pennsylvania. In 1837 Baltimore made a $380,000 subscription to the shares of the Susquehanna and Tidewater, enough in combination with the state of Maryland's loan of $750,000 in 1839 to complete the canal in 1840.[107] But this effort was obviously too late. Already in 1834 a railroad between Philadelphia and the Susquehanna at Columbia had been completed, serving to reattach the interior of the commonwealth to Philadelphia in defiance of the hydrography of the region. Soon Philadelphia returned to the role of second city of the Republic.

Charleston Seeks a Hinterland: The Santee Canal   The other entrepôt that attempted a canal to the interior in defiance of the river courses was Charleston, whose site had been chosen for the good harbor there available but whose situation was poor, as neither the Ashley nor the Cooper river gave much access to the interior. While rice was the main staple the Carolinas produced, the circumstances were tolerable; but when cotton came into prominence, the better-drained soils of the sandy inner reaches of the coastal plain, and more particularly of the Piedmont, came into use for agriculture. At that time the misplacement of Charleston became apparent; it needed either the Savannah or the Santee River to gain connections with the interior. As the Savannah was farther away, and was navigable from the Fall Line to the port of Savannah, interest turned to the Santee, located almost wholly within South Carolina. This cut, completed between 1792 and 1800, was intended as stated in the words of its chief engineer "to give the Inhabitants of the Upper Country an Opportunity to receive a Reward for their [agricultural] Industry, which would at the same time benefit the Metropolis" of Charleston.[108] As built the Santee Canal extended from the head of the Cooper River (the stream on the north side of the Charleston peninsula) in a northerly direction for 22 miles across the coastal plain to the Santee opposite Black Oak Island.

Money was not plentiful in the Carolinas, where the merchant class tended to invest its earnings in buying plantation estates so as to gain the social cachet they afforded, so the Santee Canal was meanly constructed. Although it was 34 feet wide at the surface and 4 feet deep, its locks were of wood, which in this latitude and climate lasted even less well than they did on the Middlesex. The result was that the canal was never in very good working order. At first the waterway had been built by slaves rented out by the plantation owners when there was a slump in that staple farming in 1792. Needless to say, the poor slaves knew nothing about canal building and their drivers precious little more. For five years construction was mired in ignorance and the rice paddies before a rapid rise in cotton production, consequent on Whitney's perfection of his gin, placed a premium on slave labor. The rise in the cost of labor made it difficult to complete the canal even to a rather low standard of construction. Further disappointment came when the nature of the tributary area changed almost entirely during the course of that construction. When the Santee was pro-

posed in the late 1780s, the Up Country was engaged mostly in the production of grain and the raising of livestock to feed the coastal indigo and rice plantations. By the time of its completion, the indigo trade was ruined; the rice trade was greatly reduced by the embargo of American rice in the British West Indies; and cotton had come into the Up Country to replace, or to consume locally, all the meat and grain that could be grown. The result was the drying up of the provision trade with the Low Country without its replacement by cotton. Cotton was light enough, and then of sufficient value, that it could, and did, carry the cost of wagon transport over a more direct route to Charleston.[109]

Government Takes an Interest: The Gallatin Report of 1808

The concern for the integration of the American economy that was evident in the adoption of the United States Constitution in 1789 was not totally laid to rest with the creation of the federal republic. Instead, the shaping of a national government seems to have engaged most of the attention of the political elements while the merchant class was especially taken up with creation of factory industry. Any overall transportation plan must languish with these other interests paramount. Private investors did place several million dollars to the account of transportation improvement, in those canals that we have discussed and the turnpike roads built between 1790 and 1830. Still, these were local interests finding local solutions to parochial problems. Save in the cases where merchants in an entrepôt in an adjacent state took interest in a canal or a turnpike in another state (because it might divert trade to that port city), little investment seems to have come to the aid of these projects from outside their immediate regions. What investment there was seems to

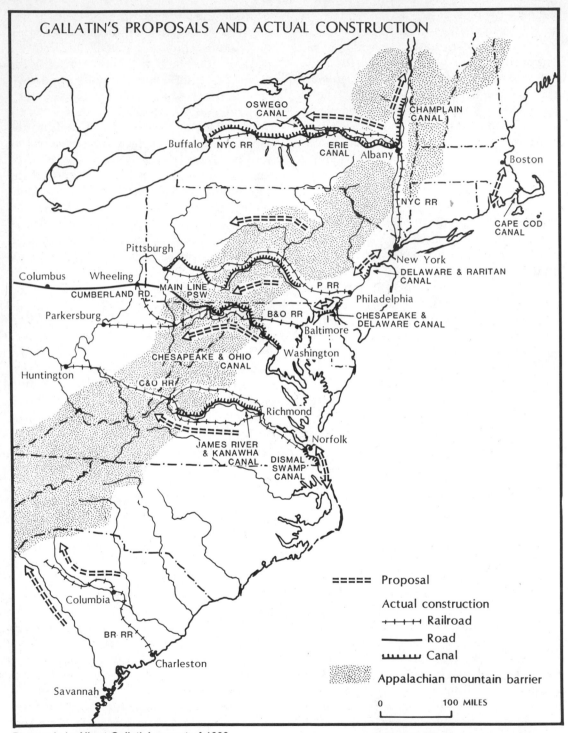

GALLATIN'S PROPOSALS AND ACTUAL CONSTRUCTION

OSWEGO CANAL

CHAMPLAIN CANAL

Buffalo

NYC RR

ERIE CANAL

Albany

Boston

NYC RR

CAPE COD CANAL

Pittsburgh

New York

DELAWARE & RARITAN CANAL

Columbus

Wheeling

MAIN LINE PSW

P RR

CUMBERLAND RD.

B&O RR

Philadelphia

CHESAPEAKE & DELAWARE CANAL

Parkersburg

CHESAPEAKE & OHIO CANAL

Baltimore

Washington

Huntington

C&O RR

Richmond

Norfolk

JAMES RIVER & KANAWHA CANAL

DISMAL SWAMP CANAL

Columbia

BR RR

Charleston

Savannah

===== Proposal

Actual construction

+++++ Railroad

——— Road

⊔⊔⊔⊔⊔ Canal

Appalachian mountain barrier

0   100 MILES

Proposals in Albert Gallatin's report of 1808.

have come from Dutch or British capitralists, not American compatriots.

Congress was eventually aware of the unarticulated quality of American transportation. What interregional transport existed in 1800 had been furnished by nature, not by human endeavor. The major rivers, particularly the larger rivers west of the Appalachians, might tie together two or more regions: human efforts up to the beginning of the nineteenth century had operated on a much more restrained geographical scale. But in 1807 the U. S. Senate directed the Secretary of the Treasury, Albert Gallatin, to have prepared "a plan for the application of such means as are within the power of Congress, to the purposes of opening roads and making canals, together with a statement of the undertakings of this nature, which, as objects of public improvement, may require and deserve the aid of Government."[110] Gallatin's response, on April 6, 1808, found the provision of roads and canals most desirable. But the work faced two unusually American problems—the shortage of capital in comparison with Europe and the vast geographical extent of the American republic. The report foresaw that only the national government could overcome those two problems. In the hope that Congress might see fit to fund such undertakings, Gallatin first described what had been accomplished, largely by private investment in canals and roads, and then what needed to be done and might be seen as the critical projects to receive "the aid of Government."

The first step proposed by the secretary of the treasury was that of taking surveys and levels of the routes outlined, having in mind the determination of the practicability of waterway or road construction. To guide that survey work, Gallatin outlined "four necks of land" that interrupted the coastal navigation on the eastern seaboard and "four pairs of rivers" that seemed to control the inter-connection of that seaboard area with the interior of the country. The call for breaching the four necks of land that interrupted continuous, protected sailing from Boston to halfway down the North Carolina coast was the reassertion of one of the fundamental purposes for the American Union, to create an "inter-state commerce" to replace that with the former home country. Between Boston and New York sloop sailing was exposed to the difficulties of voyaging in the open sea in passing around Cape Cod and through the fog and shoals of Nantucket Sound. By building a canal across the narrow neck of Cape Cod the worst of that passage would be avoided. Again, it was only a short distance across mid-Jersey, between Lower New York Bay and the Delaware River at the farthest reach of the tide below the falls at Trenton. Even shorter was the neck of the Delmarva Peninsula, which separated the heads of Delaware and Chesapeake bays. From the southern end of the latter, Hampton Roads lay separated from Albemarle and the other sounds in eastern North Carolina by the low, flooded area of Dismal Swamp. If these four necks could be opened with cuts for sloop travel, then the great Economic Hinge that tied America to the rest of the world would have available good coastal sailing protected everywhere but for a short stretch in Block Island Sound.

The vulnerability of this route to the elements was well known in passing around Cape Cod, New Jersey, and the two southern peninsulas. During the War of 1812 the young republic learned how exposed it was in time of hostilities. There are estimates that the British blockade of the Jersey coast cost the overtaxed treasury of the United States some $20 million as well as straining national resources when goods, materiel of war, and men passing from one theater of the fighting to the other were forced to pass overland across the Jersey Neck. After 1815 the federal interest in such a system of sloop-waterways was acknowledged politically and not challenged constitutionally.

Similar to the four necks of land were Gallatin's two "Northern Openings." These were essentially "Necks of Land" breaking a continuity of waterway between tidewater on the Hudson at Albany-Troy and (1) the St. Lawrence (via Lake Champlain and the Richelieu River draining it to the great river of the north just below Montréal), and (2) the Great Lakes via the Mohawk River and the Rome Portage to streams flowing into Lake Ontario. We have already noted the efforts to improve these openings and will further examine the western one in its role as a crossing of the Appalachians.

The final element in Gallatin's analysis of the broad features of American transportation came in the four pairs of rivers that held out hope for a usable crossing of the Appalachians. In these proposals there was more than a little politics, perhaps for the first time demonstrating that Congress could rise above sectionalism only when all sections were served. The northernmost pair of rivers was that comprising the Susquehanna and the Ohio—specifically the west branch of the former, the Juniata, and the north branch of the latter, the Allegheny and its Conemaugh fork. Ever since the years just before the American Revolution there had been a considerable migration of people along or near this alignment, and the Pittsburgh Pike was then being built along the route. Just to the south the Potomac matched with the southern branch of the Ohio, the Monongahela, with only Allegheny Mountain between; it was breached by a fairly low divide toward Old Redstone Fort. In Virginia the James River rose in the foothills of the Allegheny Mountains only a short distance from the Kanawha headwaters of the Ohio. Finally, it was assumed that through "geographical balance" of the sort the early Greeks were constantly pro-

posing, there must be paired rivers in the Carolinas and Tennessee. Either the Santee or the Savannah must approach some mountain headwater of the Tennessee River, though Gallatin's report was indefinite on just which pair and which gap would afford the national road or waterway of the South. For a regionally sensitive Congress, however, there must be such a pair.

Cutting the Four Necks of Land

It is not surprising that in the early years after 1815 fairly vigorous efforts were made to secure passages across the four necks of land. The first to be completed was a canal cut through the Dismal Swamp on the Virginia–North Carolina border[111] The Dismal Swamp Canal was never heavily used for intracoastal navigation, and it was not kept in good enough repair, but it was useful in shipping lumber from the swamp and agricultural products to the Norfolk market. In 1860 the Chesapeake and Albemarle Canal was built nearby with only a single lock, instead of the older canal's seven, to control the relationship of levels in Chesapeake Bay and Albemarle Sound, handling an average difference of 2 feet in a lock 220 by 40 feet. With 7.5 feet of water in a canal 80 feet wide, this replacement could far more easily handle the coastal sloops, thus taking most of the traffic from the Dismal Swamp cut.[112]

As early as 1802 interests in Philadelphia and elsewhere in Pennsylvania were promoting a canal across the narrow northern end of the Delmarva peninsula, but these were unavailing because of a shortage of capital. Benjamin H. Latrobe, the famous architect, was retained to undertake a survey, but he had to write:[113]

My business here is to meet the Directors of the Ches. and Del. Canal, which is now at a stand [still]. . . . The true reason, however, of the suspension of the internal improvements of the country, is the absorption of all our active capital by the Neutral trade. The turnpike roads which have been opened near Philadelphia, as well as the Ches. and Del. Canal were children of the peace of Amiens [1803]. They sickened, and our canal indeed has died in consequence of the abstraction of pecuniary support by the foreign trade, which revived with the new War. . . .

No further progress was gained until nearly twenty years later, when new efforts were made to secure financial support for this canal, favored by Philadelphia; tolerated by Delaware; and used as a bargaining point by Maryland, which exacted from the Pennsylvania legislature the promise to improve navigation on the lower Susquehanna (in connection with Maryland improvements at Conowingo) in return for Maryland's participation in the Chesapeake and Delaware project. Thus by 1824 Delaware subscribed $25,000 to canal shares, Maryland $50,000, and Pennsylvania $100,000.[114] At that time a letter in a newspaper observed, "And precisely in the same degree that this canal will be important and advantageous to Philadelphia, so must it take from the trade of Baltimore."[115] In such a parochial context it is easy to see that internal improvements of a broader sort would be hard to obtain.

Although heavily used from its opening in 1829, the Chesapeake and Delaware Canal had been so costly to build that it was never highly profitable. Still, it was the only truly successful opening of a cut through any of the four necks of land. With its completion, boats of moderate size, under both steam and sail, could now navigate the coast from Hampton Roads to Trenton. *Niles Register* in 1829 noted changes in the price of goods at Philadelphia with a larger hinterland now accessible to the city, and Baltimore felt itself even more at a disadvantage. That feeling

probably did as much as anything to advance the U.S. railroad system.

Two other necks remained to be cut, that between the Delaware and New York Harbor and the base of Cape Cod. The first undertaking came in mid-Jersey where the War of 1812 had proved the need and the years following it had taxed land transport. Perhaps in a sanguine frame of mind after the submission of Gallatin's Report, with its call for federal support for internal improvements, the Jerseymen sought Washington's help in building a waterway across the Jersey neck. But both Madison and Monroe adopted a strict-constructionist view, holding that internal improvements were the responsibility of the state within the organized states, and of the national government only in the unorganized territories.

The only solution lay in a constitutional amendment specifically giving the federal government responsibility for internal improvements and the authority to aid in their construction. New England, however, strongly opposed any national expenditure to open up the West and encourage westward migration away from the seaboard states. The five states there (six after 1820) were numerically sufficient to stymie the amendment process and assure to two strict-constructionist presidents the power of the veto over such federal aid. Federal aid had been forthcoming on the Chesapeake and Delaware Canal, but not on many other turnpike roads and canals. With Andrew Jackson's veto of the Maysville Turnpike (located wholly within the commonwealth of Kentucky), exercised on May 27, 1830, the issue was closed for the rest of the nineteenth century. States had to stand as the unit for most transportation planning and financing. In that context New Jersey and its citizens had to undertake the construction of the waterway from the Delaware to the Raritan River that flowed into Lower New York Bay.

By 1830 it was obvious that the route across mid-Jersey was so heavily traveled that some improvement was essential. Eighty-six thousand passengers a year crossed the isthmus according to the governor's report on the canal to the House of Assembly. Eight thousand tons were taken by wagon across this section, and 56,000 tons of freight were carried by coasting vessel between New York and Philadelphia.[116] In February, 1830, "a fourth and last general act for a waterway between the Raritan and Delaware Rivers" was passed. Even then the act had been gained only by an agreement between the supporters of the canal and those for a railroad across this neck. By this time the Canal Era was fast closing, and the railroad was being advocated when these later canals were undertaken. In the first 10 minutes of sale all the railroad stock was subscribed to, whereas the canal could gain subscribers on its books for only one-tenth that amount in some days of hard pushing of the stock. The result was curious: the legislature forced a consolidation of the Camden and Amboy Railroad and the Delaware and Raritan Canal, so the greater investor appeal of railroads that was fast emerging helped to pay for this important canal.[117]

The Delaware and Raritan, opened in 1834, though well planned and executed, was never the great success it might have been if completed before the coming of the railroad, but it did serve well to carry the heavy freight across New Jersey. Again the War of 1812 had aided its cause by cutting off the supply of bituminous coal from Britain and turning the Americans' attention to their most nearly coastal coal deposits, the anthracite fields of the Schuylkill and the Wyoming valleys of Pennsylvania. Those areas began to produce anthracite to fuel Philadelphia and New York, and the Delaware and Raritan carried millions of tons of this coal before it was finally closed to navigation in 1932 and transformed into an open aqueduct to carry

Delaware River water to communities and industries along its course.[118] There is certainly irony in the fact that the canal today earns a great deal more for the state of New Jersey, its present owner, than it ever earned for its private owners as a waterway. But it did effectively give passage by water across the third of Gallatin's four necks of land.

The last neck, Cape Cod, had to wait for over a century to gain its cut, though not for want of earnest efforts. Already in 1627 the Pilgrims had begun portaging goods from the headwaters of a stream flowing into Massachusetts Bay for 3 miles to one flowing to Buzzards Bay "to avoyd the compassing of Cape-Codd and those deangerous shoulds; and to make any vioyage to ye southward in much shorter time, and with farr less danger."[119] In 1697 the Massachusetts General Court adopted a resolution calling for a survey of the 8-mile isthmus. Nothing came of it. Again in 1777, partly to avoid the British Navy off our coast, another investigation was made, but again to no lasting result. From then until 1899 a number of efforts to promote a canal all failed for one reason or another. In 1883 some digging was done by a private company but was abandoned within a short time. Finally in 1899 the Boston, Cape Cod and New York Canal Company was organized, undertaking a careful investigation of the project. Before the panic of 1907 August Perry Belmont, who was then gaining both success and notoriety in building the Fourth Avenue subway in New York, became interested in the project and asked his chief engineer, William Barclay Parsons, to investigate the cut through the Sandwich Isthmus. So confident was Belmont on receiving Parson's report that he went ahead with the canal despite the panic. Between 1909, when construction began, and July, 1914, when the canal was opened, great problems were encountered because of the huge glacial boulders found 15 to 20 feet below the surface. In place of the dredging operation the company had in mind, there had to be much digging "in the dry" that laboriously uncovered the erratics so they could be broken in pieces by explosives and carted away for riprap.[120]

At the opening ceremonies of the Cape Cod Canal on July 29, 1914, Mayor Seth Low of New York emphasized that the canal had been built by New Yorkers who "take kindly to canal construction partly by inherited instinct and partly as a result of experience." In contrast, "The genius of New England for a century has expressed itself . . . in manufacture, and the significance of the canal to manufacture is indirect, not direct."[121] This condescension must have been particularly galling to any of the thousands of New England investors whose money had built railroads from Boston to Los Angeles well before the 8-mile New York cut of the Cape Cod neck was completed. There was no lack of appreciation for transportation improvement among the true Yankees: rather, there was in the New England money markets a very shrewd analysis of the up-to-date and profitable means of transport, with a strong adherence to railroads as early as 1830. New York, slow to enter the railroad age, gained control of rail companies late in the day and then only by dint of massive financial power rather than much understanding of the geography of transportation. I suspect the Yankees fully realized that the Cape Cod neck should have been breached a century earlier and shied away from placing too much emphasis on this undertaking past its time, both for transport and for investment. By 1914 the constitutional objections to federal support of internal improvements were diminishing at last. In 1911 the federal government had begun the construction of a 10-foot-deep canal between the Neuse River and Beaufort Inlet in North Carolina to commence the construction of the Intracoastal Waterway between Chesapeake Bay and Key West, completed only in 1936.[122]

With only 15 feet of water in this sea-level Cape Cod Canal there was some disproportion between the facility and the trade it was intended to serve. Barges drew more water than could comfortably be counted on in the canal, so the main early traffic came from yachts. By 1916 the channel had been dredged to 25 feet, and business picked up. Still, it was below expectations and tolls were not what had been anticipated. During World War I the federal government used the excuse of German submarine warfare on East Coast shipping lanes to justify buying both the Cape Cod and the Chesapeake and Delaware canals from their private owners. Thus only after ninety years from the time of Jackson's Maysville Turnpike veto had a constitutional justification been found for national ownership and improvement of the two more useful cuts through the four necks of land. In 1918 the Cape Cod became federal property. Between then and the present the Chesapeake and Delaware, the Cape Cod, and the Intracoastal canals have been improved with funds from the national treasury and without the earlier test of demonstrable economic need. It is not without significance that the most critical neck cut, that across New Jersey, was not nationalized and came to be abandoned.

The Trans-Appalachian Crossings: The Work of the Age

Enough has already been said concerning the role that the Appalachian barrier played in the colonial period of American historical geography. It may be accepted that even before the American Revolution there was a concerted reconnaissance of the barrier, discovering the main practicable routes across the mountains. The only easy crossing was that obtained along the fjorded section of the Hudson, which cuts completely the Appalachian chain, gaining tidal access to the ultramontane plateaus characteristic of the

Appalachian orogeny. In the area of Albany the Helderberg "Mountains" to the southwest of the city show the outer edge of that plateau. Between the Appalachian plateaus and the southern extension of the Laurentian Shield in the Adirondack Mountains there exists a structural depression in which the Mohawk River flows eastward to the Hudson, just above Albany. Wood Creek-Oneida Lake and the Oswego River flow first west and then north to enter Lake Ontario at what became Oswego. Nowhere does this opening across the Appalachians to the Great Lakes rise to as much as 500 feet elevation. The saddle at the traditional Rome Portage was about 420 feet.

For comparison it is noteworthy that south of that point there was no crossing of the mountain chain under 500 feet until northern Mississippi was reached, and north of Georgia the crest was consistently above 2,000 feet even in the complex opening afforded by the Potomac and James river water gaps through the Blue Ridge range and the transit of the Great Valley of Virginia southward. The main heights of the Appalachians north of North Carolina lie mostly toward the eastern edge of the plateau, commonly called Cumberland or Allegheny Mountain, so it was the crossing of this mountain that imposed a barrier to westward movement north of northern Alabama. Only there the central course of the Tennessee River opens a way between the southern end of the folded ranges and the plateau to the west. Such is also the case in upstate New York, where the Mohawk-Oneida depression furnishes a similar route around the plateau. The Appalachian Plateau has but a single river that passes completely across its width—the New River of Virginia–West Virginia, which rises in the Blue Ridge, crosses the Great Valley, and continues westward in a deep gorge across the plateau. In general the westward-flowing streams cut into the plateau to rise close to the east-

facing Allegheny Front. That fact accounts for the presence of the summits of most trans-Appalachian routes somewhere along the line of the Allegheny-Cumberland front. The main exception comes in the connections between the northern headwaters of the Susquehanna River, within the plateau of southern New York state, and the Lake Ontario basin to the north. Because of the severe valley glaciation within the plateaus in the Finger Lakes region, open glacial valleys filled with Seneca and Cayuga lakes provide trans-Appalachian routes below 1,000 feet.

Not all these routes were very difficult to cross. The Great Valley route in Virginia has a summit at about 2,000 feet but possesses long gentle ascents to its crest near the Tennessee line. For a canal, however, absolute elevation is more crucial than for any other means of transport: every foot of rise in a slackwater system has to be taken in locks, which are slow to operate and highly consumptive of water. The 420-foot summit at the Rome Portage was, any way you looked at it, only one-quarter of that required for any possible canal via the Great Valley. The argument for the upstate New York crossing of the Appalachians was geographically overpowering. As long as canals were to be the facilities to provide a connection across the mountains, that advantage was controlling. The historical geography of canal transport, however, is not all hypsometry. In the United States it is compounded of equal parts of urban and state mercantilism, and political geography.

The three states with the right political geography to participate in the trans-Appalachian race were New York and Pennsylvania, with their tidewater ports and western shores on Lake Erie, and Virginia, then extending from Chesapeake Bay to the Ohio River. To the south the Blue Ridge was a political divide as well as the highest range in the eastern United States. In such a

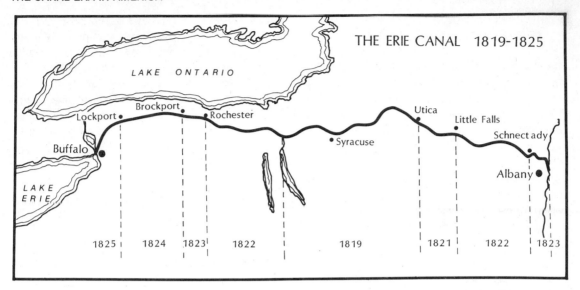

THE ERIE CANAL 1819-1825

LAKE ONTARIO

Lockport Brockport Rochester Utica Little Falls Schnect ady

Buffalo Syracuse Albany

LAKE ERIE

1825   1824   1823   1822   1819   1821   1822   1823

geographical context, we may limit our consideration of the building of a canal across the mountains to New York, Pennsylvania, and Virginia-Maryland, the three entrants in the competition. The first finished smartly, the second crawled across the line, and the third fell well out of sight of any laurels.

So much is generally known about the Erie Canal that I shall discuss it more briefly than its absolute importance might warrant. But as every school child knows its tale, and few know anything else about American canals, I wish to use my limited space to add to, rather than repeat, common knowledge.

The Erie Canal From the 1790s on there were numerous proposals for making the Mohawk route navigable. Gallatin had singled out this route less as a crossing of the Appalachians than as an opening to the St. Lawrence Valley and the Great Lakes, but the net effect was the same. Once on the lakes, the Middle West was open to the traveler and trade. With several established portages—the Maumee, the Peoria-Chicago, and the Green Bay—the low divide between the Great Lakes and the Ohio-Mississippi

was not an undue burden. Given these conditions, it was merely a matter of time and the selection of a specific route that were unfixed. If any canal was to be built across the mountains, the likelihood was that the Mohawk route would be the first and the most certain. In 1810 the New York legislature established a commission to investigate the project; it made its report in 1811. Most prominent in their thinking was that the canal should be built by a public agency. The commissioners feared a private canal, which they suspected would be used to encourage land speculation, already rife in western New York state.[123] The actual route of the canal was left vague, along with the precise form the waterway was to have; but the report definitively resolved the great geographical question raised by any Hudson–Great Lakes canal in upstate New York.

When the first proposals were made for a Mohawk waterway, it was assumed that the line to be constructed could be quite short, made of disconnected stretches of the canals around the falls on the Mohawk and the summit from Rome on the Mohawk to

Wood Creek flowing into Oneida Lake. Experience showed that the Mohawk was a difficult stream on which to operate: it was ice-clogged for four months or so, too high in its water when the ice melted, too low before the ice returned. When the thinking turned toward an entirely artificial waterway, the scale of the undertaking shifted. In the first decade of the nineteenth century, two schools of thought emerged. One held with the original proposals, calling for a cut passing from the Rome portage via Oneida Lake to the Oswego River, and then as a lateral canal down that stream to the Lake Ontario port of Oswego. This would have been the shortest and cheapest route to accomplish the basic objective of tying the Hudson to the Great Lakes. It would, however, have had several shortcomings. To reach the upper lakes, a canal around Niagara Falls would be essential. The Hudson-Ontario canal would have severe competition from the St. Lawrence and the port of Montréal, already handling a large part of the growing grain trade of western New York. This route would also force the reloading of goods several times, as the canal barges were hardly able to navigate in the open water of Lake Ontario.

Once the notion of a full canal was accepted, some proponents began looking toward a canal directly to Lake Erie. It was discovered that the terrain was very favorable. With little lost elevation a line could be run westward from the Rome summit at 420 feet to enter Lake Erie at 570 feet. In fact, on a canal considerably longer than any before undertaken there would be only three summits: that at around 420 feet near Rome, with a continuous rise from the tidewater mouth of the canal just above Albany; a second level somewhat to the west at around 400 feet, separated from the first by a slight depression; and finally a long uninterrupted rise of nearly 160 miles to the Lake Erie level. This route would avoid a Niagara canal, any

reloading between Lake Erie and New York City, and effective competition from Montréal in the absence of a canal down over the Niagara Escarpment. The 1811 commissioners' report was predicated on an *Erie* canal as opposed to an *Ontario* one, finally giving a name to a projected waterway previously known by a number of prospective names. From then on there was no question that what would be built would be an inclined-plane canal rather than one to Lake Ontario. Although the first hazy notion that a continuous plane downward from Lake Erie might be found had to be dropped, as constructed there was very little redundant lockage on the Erie Water; the total rise and fall in the canal was 675 feet to rise the 565 feet from the Hudson to Lake Erie.[124]

The 1811 report actually proposed a continuous inclined plane from Lake Erie to the Rome summit. If this had been built as envisaged, with a 4-foot depth and a grade of 6 inches per mile, the velocity of the flow would have been about 1 mile per hour, enough to make horse traction difficult and costly. In addition, to supply all the water from Lake Erie would have required greatly enlarging the western end to carry the flow.[125] Although the commissioners were not fully aware of the problems the inclined plane would have introduced, they soon began to sense the weaknesses of such a plan. A second commission was appointed in 1816, evidently to counteract some of the ridicule the inclined-plane plan had drawn. They modified the proposal to introduce locks and slackwater navigation. Their plan was the one adopted and built, so we may look at it briefly to see the nature of the original Erie Canal.

In the east the alignment along the Mohawk River almost immediately faced the Erie with passage up the Cohoes Falls. Between West Troy (Watervliet) and the top of Cohoes Falls, some 12 miles east of Schenectady, the cut rose in nineteen locks, which have remained a feature that slows down passage of the waterway. Even above the falls the route along the Mohawk was difficult, requiring two long aqueducts between Cohoes Falls and Schenectady before it took up its customary alignment on the right bank.[126] All told, twenty-seven of the canal's eighty-one lift locks were in the 30 miles from the Hudson to Schenectady. Above that town, which had been the traditional lower limit of navigation on the Mohawk, locks followed at reasonable intervals, but it was difficult to find a shelf for the canal around the repeated noses of the southern hills when the undercut section of meanders removed any alluvium from the foot of the rocky slopes. At Little Falls on the left bank an impressive aqueduct was built to serve as a feeder to replenish the water in the canal from the flow of the river and to give that growing town a branch connection to the cut still clinging to the right bank. By Rome the canal had risen 420 feet and had reached its critical summit. A Long Level followed, which was the first part of the canal constructed after work began in 1817. The 15-mile section from Utica to Rome was opened in 1819, followed by the stretch to Montezuma on the Seneca River in 1820. In this central section the greater problem was dealing with the swamplands found adjacent to the northern ends of the Finger Lakes. In part to deal with that problem, a minor raising of the level of the canal was undertaken in the Jordan Summit, which got the footings for the banks of the cut up out of the mucks (at the expense of some modest redundant lockages).

In the Montezuma Marshes west of the Seneca great difficulty was encountered in making a usable cut and maintaining a firm towpath. Still, between Rome and Rochester the canal had an undulating profile without any great rises or falls. Some twenty-six locks handled this rolling profile between the Long Level at the Rome Summit and

Rochester, where the final climb to Lake Erie commenced. At Rochester the canal was carried across the Genesee River, its local base level, on an 800-foot aqueduct. From its western abutment another long level of more than 50 miles followed to the base of the Niagara Escarpment at what became Lockport. There the need to climb up some 60 feet introduced the only staircase of locks to be found on the canal. Five in number and doubled so that boats could pass up and down simultaneously, with some conservation in water by using one lock as a side pond of its pair, the locks here reached to the maximum height feasible to operate by hand, some 12 feet. Once at the top of the Lockport staircase, the canal was taken through a deep cut, from which some 600,000 cubic yards of limestone was removed towards Lake Erie, only some 8 feet higher than the top of the Lockport staircase. After a course of 363 miles the Erie Canal issued into the lake of that name at Buffalo, providing the most impressive waterway to be built up to that time.

When the Erie Canal was being planned in 1817, there was considerable discussion of how large to make it and its locks. The proponents finally settled on a cut with a "width on the water surface, forty feet, at the bottom, twenty-eight feet, and depth of water, four feet; the length of a lock, ninety feet, width, twelve feet, in the clear. Vessels carrying one hundred tons, may navigate a canal of this size.... "[127] In an interesting recent analysis Langbein has shown that in economic terms, and using modern cost-benefit analysis, this was a most fortunate decision. Even before the canal opened in 1825, it was becoming well used. Once the through route was available, the traffic became heavy both for passengers and for freight haulage. Within ten years some 700,000 tons a year were moving during the navigation season, which was more than half the canal's ultimate capacity of about 1 million tons a year. It was decided in 1836 to enlarge the canal to assure that it could cope with a growing traffic:

> The optimal economics would have been to retain the 40 × 4-foot canal. But optimism, one may judge, led to a decision to build a canal at the upper level of solvency—not the optimal net revenue, but the largest canal for which projected revenues would defray the costs. The results [of such an analysis] . . . explain the decision to build a 70 × 7-foot canal to replace the original cut that was such a good balance between potential trade and a tolls total to pay for its facilities.[128]

It may be true that the original canal prism represented a size that would gain the greatest return for the least investment, particularly when the locks were built not to a 12 but rather to a 15-foot width; but this is the sort of economic analysis that is after the fact. At the time the Erie Canal was designed, around 1817, or rebuilt, after 1835, the total future transportation system was highly conjectural. Even though railroads had begun to appear by 1835, they were seen, particularly in upstate New York, either as a winter replacement for the canal or as a specialized facility mainly useful for carrying passengers and undertaking specific tasks (such as avoiding the time consumed by the heavy lockage between Schenectady and Albany). Any historical-geographical analysis of transportation must begin from the viewpoint of what was then perceived to be the ordering mechanism, not what by hindsight we appreciate to have been the case.

The first decade of use of the Erie Water was so prodigious that we can easily understand why the belief arose that larger facilities would shortly be required. In 1836 there were three thousand boats operating on the canal. As early as 1826 Albany saw the arrival of seven thousand boats from the west. By 1835 Buffalo was clearing 5,126 boats eastward, a figure that rose to 8,630

clearances in 1847. The pressure on the original single locks (everywhere but the staircase at Lockport) can be envisaged from the fact that at Fort Plain lock on the Mohawk River 38 miles east of Utica lockages rose to 34,940 in the navigation season of 1846.[129] It was in such a context, with very great pressure on the locks requiring that priorities be established such that packet boats could jump the queue of freighters and up- and down-bound boats had to be paired so as to conserve water, that enlargement was seen as essential. In the years after 1836 the whole canal was deepened to 7 feet (often by raising the banks), widened to 70 feet (providing much of the earth to raise the banks), and the locks were enlarged to 110 × 18 feet and doubled everywhere.[130]

The success of the Erie cut quickly led to demands for branches to complete a true waterway system, which made New York the only part of America where a comprehensive system typical of France and the Low Countries was constructed. Elsewhere in the United States and in Canada the pattern was much more limited, with a single or a couple of arterial canals, as in the Middle Atlantic and Southern states and Canada, or else a British-type industrial-urban canal system built by private investors, as in southern New England and the anthracite canals of Pennsylvania, New Jersey, and the Appalachian Valley of New York. A Champlain Canal was built contemporaneously with the Erie and proved quite successful in moving staple products from the Champlain Lowland toward New York City.

Lafayette termed the Erie Canal "an admirable work of science and patriotism." That patriotism was highly tinged with sectional interest—with securing to the state and city of New York a dominant position in the economic geography of the United States that it has not totally lost. With the extension of the network and the enlargement of the main Erie cut, completed in 1862, the system was as complete as any canal system in America would ever be. Yet, in contrast to the handsome surpluses in the Canal Fund, earned from tolls in the early years, there began to be deficits. The branches cost more than they earned, and the main canal, though still self-supporting, was declining in its earnings. In 1882, in an attempt to encourage the greater use of the waterways, tolls were abolished by state referendum. But the real problem was that with the full development of railroads then accomplished, the waterway had to change its function. No longer was it a general transporter: it had become essentially a bulk transporter wherein energy and labor could be economized to gain the cheapest possible transport costs. On the Erie this was being done by running two 110-foot barges in tandem, sometimes towing a second tandem pair. If these had to be detached at the locks and taken through separately, much time and labor was consumed. Thus in 1884 the New York Legislature began a lengthening campaign for one of the two locks at each rise, making them 220 feet long but maintaining the 18-foot width,[131] and

To New York it all meant an active fight to hold the trade that formerly came to her without any effort on her part. Other ports began actively to compete for a share of her [sic.] export trade. Western states began to assert themselves as trading centers. Canada became a formidable competitor. And, to cap it all, the railroads, pushed to the limit of their capacity by the enormous export trade of New York and by the demands of her constantly enlarging local business, sought to divert some of her heavy export traffic by establishing differential rates against her in favor of other cities, where it could be handled at less expense to themselves and with less interference with high-class freights. As a result, although New York still remains the great center of international trade, she has not made the relative gains in comparison with other ports.[132]

Thus it was to continue its practice of urban mercantilism that New York City and the state it dominated voted in the 1880s to enlarge its canal system for "thousand-ton barges."

For ten years after 1884 the lock-lengthening went ahead. Forty of the seventy-two Erie locks then existing were lengthened, and twelve of the twenty-three locks on the Oswego were changed. In the 1890s efforts were made to deepen the canal to 9 feet, or even to make it a true ship canal permitting oceangoing ships to reach the Great Lakes. Finally in 1903 a bill was enacted that called for the creation of a barge canal between Buffalo and Albany, from Syracuse to Oswego, and along the route of the Champlain Canal.

The Erie, Oswego and Champlain canals shall be improved so that the canal prism shall, in regular canal sections, have a minimum bottom width of seventy-five feet and a minimum depth of twelve feet and a minimum water cross section of eleven hundred and twenty-eight feet, except at aqueducts and through cities and villages where these dimensions . . . may be reduced. . . . In the rivers and lakes the canal shall have a minimum bottom width of twelve feet and minimum cross-section of water of twenty-four hundred square feet.[133]

Locks were to be 328 feet long, 28 feet wide, and with 11 feet over the sills. All locks were single, though often of high lift, except for a staircase of three locks just above Waterford, where the waterway joins the Hudson, and two at Lockport. Opened in 1918 these waterways transformed the purpose of the Erie Canal from a general to a highly specialized transportation system. Vessels were to be self-propelled, which allowed the New York State Barge Canal to be carried in the canalized Mohawk River, Lake Oneida, and several other rivers and lakes. Most of the route was significantly relocated with respect to terrain, but the waterway continued to serve the same general alignment of cities that the Erie had brought into existence. The branch canals, other than the Oswego, which had been of marginal economic worth, were dropped, or used as water-supply feeders for the Barge Canal.

Since 1918 there has been a slow decline in use. By 1970, at 2.5 million tons, the freight movement on the Barge Canal did not seem too impressive compared with the million tons the Erie Canal was carrying by 1845. The latter figure continued to rise until at the close of the Civil War, for the navigation season of 1866, the canal was carrying 60 percent of the freight movement across New York State.[134] In 1862 the Erie originated more than 3 million tons for the first time, and in most years to 1895 it stood above that figure, with a peak of 4,608,651 tons in 1880.[135] In comparison, the New York State railroads had come, by 1876, to carry almost 15 million tons, three times as much as the canals of the state.[136]

It was the Erie Canal that assured that there would be an American Canal Era. The Middlesex had shown that canals could be quite useful, particularly to the mercantile community in one of the colonial entrepôts: the Erie showed what a great potential existed in the American economy if only a reasonable transportation connection between the eastern seaboard and the vast fertile area of the Middle West could be opened. It seemed that New York's success was the model for other states to follow in hope of gaining the same prosperity and growth. But no other state so prospered from canals, and only one, Pennsylvania, even secured any waterway connection across the mountains, though one of little value in contrast to the New York cut.

The Pennsylvania Mainline System Philadelphia always found New York an upstart, and that feeling was not helped by the early success of the Erie Canal. When it was finished in 1825, the Keystone State was still discussing what to do. Pennsylvania's problem was exacerbated by the actual existence by that time of working railroads. In 1825 the Stockton and Darlington Railway, from the Bishop Auckland coalfield in County Durham to the sea at Stockton-on-Tees, had been completed and put to use with several steam locomotives. There was true conflict of opinion about the best course for Pennsylvania to take. In 1825 the commonwealth had what was considered the best road system of any state, with 1,807 miles of turnpike; yet these could hardly be accepted as modern and adequate in an era of canals. The Lancaster Turnpike had been the first macadamized road in America; the Pittsburgh Turnpike, finished to the Forks of the Ohio in 1817, was in this forward-looking tradition. Local wisdom was divided, however, between canals and railroads as the facilities that would permit the state to match its northern rival. In 1824 the Pennsylvania Society for the Promotion of Internal Improvements was founded. Almost immediately it sent the leading Philadelphia architect-engineer, William Strickland, to England to try to collect information on railroads and canals and to help the Society make up its mind. When Strickland returned, he was an enthusiast for railroads despite his earlier canal work; but the society and the leaders of the commonwealth came down on the side of a canal. This was no doubt in the interests of showing that Pennsylvania could have internal improvements as impressive as those of New York. Also, canals were the proven system, as opposed to the doubts that still surrounded the railroads.

It was perhaps the greatest blunder in the historical geography of American transportation that Strickland's preference for a rail solution to the problem of crossing the Pennsylvania Appalachians was not adopted. What the commonwealth gained instead was a mule mated with a unicorn: however biologically impossible that may be, its result would be more useful than was the Pennsylvania Mainline Canal as built. The trade was already in existence; by the early 1820s the Pittsburgh Pike was carrying 30,000 tons of goods annually, though in contrast to the Erie Canal the main flow was of manufactured goods westward rather than of staples eastward.[137] The success of the Erie Canal was so immediate that Pennsylvania feared not only losing its pike traffic but also the withering of its colonial entrepôt. This was not idle fear; just at this time Philadelphia did fall not only second to New York, which had happened a generation earlier, but also third to Baltimore with its somewhat easier access to the West. Urgency was great, so, "whereas New York embarked on her project after long consideration and experimentation, Pennsylvania plunged into hers under extreme duress, bitterly aware of lost marches and of the need to overtake a powerful rival."[138] The experience with the Pennsylvania Mainline system is one wherein haste and irresolution crop up repeatedly.

Although the Society for the Promotion of Internal Improvements at first seemed neutral on the rail versus canal issue, by late 1825 Mathew Carey (its most influential member) had come out on the side of canals. Strickland's letters, and subsequently his final report, admitted of some unresolved questions about railroads but strongly supported such facilities, particularly when the line was forced to cross a summit of nearly 3,000 feet. Bear in mind that the "mountainous" lines of England had their highest summit at 638 feet on the Huddersfield Canal, so British experience was not very helpful in resolving this question. Strickland could not prove all the virtues of rail transport, which was still in its infancy; but the available evidence led him to believe the

iron road was superior. "Alnus," writing to the editor of the *United States Gazette*, predicted: "Should the advocates of canals gain a victory, . . . it is one they will never boast of. An error committed at present will have the most serious consequences on the future destinies of this state."[139] But Carey and the sectional interests in the state, who could see branch canals of the sort the Erie was then spawning, joined forces to convince the state legislature to approve the first two sections (of a continuous route to be opened between Philadelphia and Pittsburgh) as canals. The sections were at either extremity or the route between the Susquehanna and the Forks of the Ohio, seemingly assuring that a waterway would be built as the basic connection.

The construction of the Mainline Canal began on July 4, 1826. Not only would this artery be built, but also 273.5 miles of lines along the North and West Branches of the Susquehanna and the 60-mile Delaware Division Canal lateral to that river. In the west a 112-mile link from Beaver on the Ohio to Lake Erie was to be undertaken. These canals were required in order to secure legislative approval of the plan for the Mainline. As authorized the eastern connection for the canal, which began at the Susquehanna, was the Schuylkill Navigation and the narrow Union Canal, which joined end-to-end provided a difficult but passable waterway between Philadelphia and Harrisburg. It was appreciated that these waterways were likely to be overtaxed once western trade in any volume began to flow eastward across Pennsylvania, so the legislature illogically authorized the building of a railroad, the Pennsylvania Railroad, from Philadelphia to Columbia on the Susquehanna, whence navigation westward would begin. This 82-mile line, put into operation in 1834 with one track but quickly double-tracked, was paradoxically the most impressive railroad opened up to that time

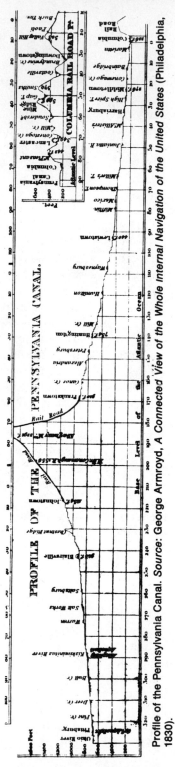

Profile of the Pennsylvania Canal. *Source: George Armroyd, A Connected View of the Whole Internal Navigation of the United States* (Philadelphia, 1830).

in America. At Columbia the canal began and ran 172 miles lateral to the Susquehanna and its Juniata branch to an elevation of 923 feet in Hollidaysburg at the base of the Allegheny Front, which formed the eastern escarpment of the Appalachian plateau.

This distinctive feature of the Pennsylvania Mainline Canal was its confrontation of this Allegheny Front that rose some 1,400 feet above Hollidaysburg, to a summit at 2,322 feet, before dropping to a second canal basin at Johnstown on the Conemaugh branch of the Allegheny, at an elevation of 1,150 feet. In the 36.7 miles between Hollidaysburg and Johnstown, all efforts to devise a waterway alternative eventually had to be abandoned. In 1826 it had been proposed that a 4.5-mile tunnel some 750 feet below the crest be bored to permit reasonable lockage in this mountain section. This project was abandoned because of its cost and the long time its construction would have required, further delaying Philadelphia's return to the lists in the seaport competition. The only practicable solution to crossing the Allegheny Front was finally seen to be just such a facility as had been found impracticable for the whole system—a railroad. Between the canal basins on either side of the mountain a portage railroad was constructed, with a total rise and fall of 2,570 feet, more than twice the lockage on the Huddersfield Canal and nearly four times that of the Erie; this in addition to the 1,141.5 feet of rise (or fall) taken in 174 locks between the Susquehanna and Hollidaysburg and Johnstown and Pittsburgh.

The portage railroad had ten straight inclined planes, five on each side of the summit, whose angle of inclination varied from 4°9′ to 5°51′.[140] Barges were placed in a cradle in the basin at one end or the other and then drawn first by horses to the foot of the lowest inclined plane on either slope. On those planes, stationary engines drew the boat on its cradle up the slope to the next reasonably level stretch. On it and succeeding planes and levels the boat was drawn to the summit at Blair's Gap. Thence it would be lowered by planes and levels to the basin at the opposite end of the Allegheny Portage Railroad. The rise in the east was much the sharper, with 1,397.7 feet taken in 10.1 miles, as opposed to the western slope of 1,171.6 feet taken in 26.6 miles. The system of horse traction on the levels provided by the owners of barges was soon found inefficient, and the state undertook to furnish locomotives on each of the ten or so levels. The problem of attaching and casting off the ropes of the winding engines at the ten planes and the drawbars of the ten locomotives at the levels was very time-consuming when added to the cradling and eventual floating of the barge at the ends of the railroad.

The portage railroad was generally disliked by shippers and boatmen alike and was thought badly constructed and operated. Finally in 1847 the state began a reconstruction of the line, which was completed in 1855 two years before the Portage Railroad was sold to the newly organized Pennsylvania Railroad Company. The Pennsy operated the reconstructed portage railroad for only three months, until the fall of 1857, when it succeeded in abandoning it.[141]

West of the portage the cut resumed at Johnstown and was carried 105 miles down the Conemaugh and Allegheny rivers as a lateral canal to reach its western terminus at Pittsburgh. As opened in 1834, the Mainline comprised the 82 miles of railroad from Philadelphia to Columbia and 278.5 miles of canal from there to Pittsburgh, separated into two sections by the 36.5-mile Allegheny Portage Railroad. The full 396-mile system between the port on the Delaware and the city growing at the Forks of the Ohio required such handling of goods and barges that its transportation charges were considerably higher for the shipment of goods from Philadelphia and the West than were charges for sloop or steamship transport from Philadelphia to Albany and shipment thence to Buffalo via the Erie Canal. For a time, express passenger service was run on the Mainline, taking five days from Philadelphia to Pittsburgh; but by 1852, when the Pennsylvania Railroad was able to provide continuous rail service between the two cities, this was given up. In 1857, with the abandonment of the portage railroad, through canal service was abandoned. The freight traffic was never large in comparison to the New York waterway; in its peak year, 1845, the Mainline carried a total of 83,972 tons in both directions. That same year the Erie rose above 1 million tons of freight for the first time, a total it and its successors

have maintained or bettered down to the present.[142]

Why did the Erie so prosper and persist, while the Pennsylvania Mainline never showed much life and earned no great longevity? They both served to open up the interior of the continent by providing a route across the mountains that would shorten the flow of staples from the farms and mines of the Middle West to their main markets on the eastern seaboard, and in western Europe. Each was promoted by an active trading port in its efforts to expand its tributary area from that assigned to it in the original English charter to a much more continental extent. Although the Erie was finished nine years before the Mainline, that should not have given it such a strong edge, because the latter

The Stecknitz Canal suggests nineteenth-century American canals. *Source*: Author's photograph.

gained direct access to the more developed part of the Middle West, the Ohio and the middle Mississippi river valleys. Certainly New York outdistanced Philadelphia in foreign trade and in population, but not to such an extent that one was bound to succeed and the other to fail.

The main conclusion we can draw is that the nature of the canals themselves determined the differential success of the two routes. The Erie required at most one transfer movement between New York and Buffalo, and that could be obviated with the introduction of steam tugboats on the Hudson. In addition, the northern canal had less than a hundred feet of redundant lockage in order to reach the western base level at Lake Erie, at some 580 feet. By contrast, the Mainline had a smaller irreducible grade (the difference in elevation between its ultimate termini), of 385 feet between Harrisburg and Pittsburgh, in contrast to the Erie's 575 feet between Albany and Buffalo. Even including passage to Philadelphia, the Mainline had only 743 feet of necessary rise. In actual operation, however, the Erie had 675 feet of lockage, whereas the Mainline had lockage of nearly 1,000 feet. In addition, the Pennsylvania route had 2,570 feet of rise and fall on the portage railroad for a total between Harrisburg and Pittsburgh of 3,711 feet, to which had to be added the passage of the Philadelphia to Columbia railroad with its grades, particularly those taken in two inclined planes—one just west of the Schuylkill in West Philadelphia and the other dropping to Columbia on the Susquehanna.

The Failure of the National Project A final trans-Appalachian canal was that seeking to connect the Potomac with the Ohio. This project merits our attention more by the scale of its failure and the aegis of its advancement than by any striking success, as in the Erie, or unusually impressive facilities, as in the Mainline.

On July 4, 1828, at the Little Falls of the Potomac in the District of Columbia, President John Quincy Adams—the last chief executive to agree to federal support of internal improvement for the remainder of the nineteenth century—turned the first sod for the Chesapeake and Ohio Canal. In Baltimore, in similar activities on that festal day, Charles Carroll of Carrollton, one of the last surviving signers of the Declaration of Independence, carried out the same office for the Baltimore and Ohio Railroad. Each company, because both were ostensibly private at that point, started construction toward the West. The canal had been aided primarily by governments; of its $3.5 million subscription up to that time, $3 million had come from the cities of the District of Columbia, the state of Maryland, and several smaller places to the west. Those governments had exercised considerable influence in shaping the projects. The Washington interests had forced the adoption of the mouth of Rock Creek in the District as the eastern terminus, which thwarted any embryonic Baltimore interests that might have grown. The national government had insisted on a larger canal prism than that of the Erie and Mainline, evidently in the hope that this would become a steamboat canal, which also led the proprietors to seek to avoid any bridges over the cut (substituting for them the oddity of a canal ferry). All the public supporters insisted that the eastern section to the Allegheny Front at Cumberland, Maryland, should be completed before the western section was begun.

The construction of the C&O Canal was slow and intermittent. For the first fourteen years work progressed continuously, if hardly rapidly. Because the eastern terminus of the canal lay on the Fall Line, in a section where there is only a narrow Appalachian Piedmont, the earliest construction was some of the hardest: "The sixty miles from Georgetown to Harper's Ferry encompassed the greatest ascent in the whole distance. In this first third of the eastern section, almost half of the locks (thirty-two out of seventy-five) and the dams (three out of seven) were located."[143] The waterway at Georgetown itself had to rise 35 feet in four locks and be supported by a heavy embankment on the river side. This Georgetown–Harper's Ferry section also introduced the greatest conflict between the canal and the railroad. At Point of Rocks, 11 miles below Harper's Ferry, the B. and O. Railroad, which was coming across the Piedmont from the Maryland entrepót, joined the Potomac and sought to use the easternmost of the watergaps, that through the Blue Ridge (here South Mountain), in gaining a low-level entrance to the Great Valley (here the Shenandoah Valley) and the junction of the Potomac and its southern branch, the Shenandoah. That gap was equally desired by the C&O Canal. In an early example of injunctive obstruction, each company enjoined the other from building west of Point of Rocks. After much litigation and the intervention of the state of Maryland—then being pressed to increase its financial support of the canal—a compromise was struck that permitted the two lines to be built simultaneously. Both reached Harper's Ferry in 1834; but west of there the railroad made more rapid progress, gaining the east face of the mountains at Cumberland in 1842 and the Ohio River at Wheeling, Virginia, on Christmas Eve, 1852. The canal limped into Cumberland in 1850 and soon thereafter gave up any real hope of constructing the western section thence to the Youghiogheny Branch of the Ohio. Between Harper's Ferry and Cumberland the canal used the repeated watergaps through the Folded Appalachians but was forced to cross the trellis drainage in the intervening valleys on heavy aqueducts. Those intervening streams, and the main stem of the Potomac, were subject to violent flooding consequent on a regional tendency toward concentrated, though often localized, rainstorms that might dump 5 to 10 inches of water in a watershed within a short period. The canal was forced in places to encroach on the Potomac bed, though divided from it by the canal bearm, in such a way that flood damage and silting therefrom could be severe. Some flood crests in the river rose 40 feet or more, overtopping the bearm and, if not breaching it, filling the cut with silt. In places the water gaps were so narrow that the canal engineers were hard pressed to find a way through. In one place they had to tunnel to gain westering. There was plenty of water in some seasons, furnished by ponds behind the rock rubble dams thrown across the river that diverted its flow into the cut, but in the summer drought both the river and the canal could become unnavigable.

The scale of the C&O Canal was both distinctive and costly. In the Georgetown Level the canal was 80 feet wide at the surface and 7 to 8 feet deep. This larger size was partly to meet the federal demands for a canal possibly usable by steamboats and partly to supply water for power purposes in factories along the lower course of the waterway in the District. West of the Little Falls the depth and width were reduced to 6 and 60 feet, respectively. Above Harper's Ferry the width dropped to 50 feet but the 6-foot depth was maintained. This large size, along with the high level of construction and the numerous dams and aqueducts, made the capitalization of the line so high that the governmental support available for its building was fully exhausted by the time the waterway to Cumberland was opened. The western section thence to the Youghiogheny was daunting indeed, particularly in the 1850s when the railroad was an accepted alternative to the canal. This Allegheny Mountain section would have had a summit level at 1,900 feet, requiring even then a four-mile tunnel as well as 246 locks.[144] That this route across the mountain was perhaps the best in the Middle Atlantic states is shown by the alacrity with which the Baltimore and Ohio Railroad adopted it when it built a line from Cumberland to Pittsburgh that opened in 1871.

The C&O Canal succeeded not as a transAppalachian route but as a coal-carrying line, in this instance transporting bituminous coal rather than anthracite. At first the trade of the canal was more typical of the westering waterways—agricultural staples eastbound, particularly wheat and its flour, with manufactures westbound. But soon after the canal reached Cumberland in 1850 the coalfield adjacent to that canal port came into wide exploitation. Coal began to move to Washington, and thence to Baltimore, in heavy tonnages. This explains why the halcyon days of the C&O came later than those of the Erie or Mainline canals. This Cumberland coal traffic was largest in the late 1860s and 1870s. Even then, however, the shadow of effective railroad competition was emerging in two ways. First, the canal could not reach to the headframes of the mines themselves, so short rail lines had to be built from those points to the Cumberland canal basin. The B. and O. Railroad refused crossing rights for these feeders wherever possible, effectively killing some of the economic roots of such a colliery canal. Second, as the Cumberland coalfield began to be exhausted, the subsequent western Maryland and then West Virginia coalfields lay farther and farther from the canal basin, with less reason to transfer the coal to the canal as that interface lay ever farther away. The C&O Canal was instrumental in organizing the Western Maryland Railroad to secure access to the coal fields independent of the B. and O., but in the end even that friendly line came to carry the coal all the way to the urban markets as the relative reduction in line costs gained on the Cumberland-Washington stretch were essentially lost in the increased terminal costs incidental to reloading at Cumberland and wagon

transport from the canal basin in Washington to that city, or schooner transport from there to Baltimore.

Canals as a Development Device: The Middle West

The arrival of the Erie and Mainline canals in the western part of New York and Pennsylvania afforded to the emerging agricultural area farther west some chance of export agriculture, and to the seaboard merchants some hope for expanding their wholesaling area. With those prospects in mind, there grew in the Middlewestern states the belief that canals would benefit their economic development as they were demonstrably enlarging the populations of the entrepôts, and there arose in the mercantile community of the ports the interest in financing this regional development of Ohio, Indiana, and Illinois to gain for themselves the profits of trade in staples eastbound and manufactures westbound.

The thin bands of settlement and cultivation along the rivers and Lake Erie left much of Ohio underdeveloped in 1825 when the Erie cut opened, and even much country still unsettled in 1834 when the Mainline was finally assembled as a single route. It was in the period of euphoria right after the Erie opened that the townspeople and farmers of Ohio began to think in terms of planning for an internal improvement policy. In the early 1820s a canal commission had been appointed by the legislature. Its first report, in January, 1824, called for the development of a grandly encompassing waterway from Portsmouth on the Ohio up the Scioto to a point just south of Columbus, where the line would be turned eastward over the low Licking divide to the Muskingum. That Ohio tributary would then be ascended to its head and a second crest, the Portage Summit, which was to be crossed to the drainage toward Lake Erie following along either the

Cuyahoga or the Black River. In addition, a more local canal was proposed down the Miami River from Dayton to Cincinnati. The canal between the lake and the river was particularly to provide a feeder from the interior of the state to the lake ports for transshipment of wheat to Buffalo. The Miami Canal had a more limited purpose—to give the rapidly growing packinghouse town of Cincinnati better access to its agricultural hinterland. Farmers still tended to drive their hogs to market rather than using the canal, but other agricultural commodities that were not self-propelling benefited from the waterway.

With these waterways Ohio would increase the area of farming capable of export. "Although statistics of crop output were not recorded [before and after the opening of the northern section of the Ohio Canal in 1827], it was well known, as a prominent contemporary economist asserted, that 'immediately after completion of the canal . . . not only greater attention but greater breadth of land was devoted to wheat' in the counties that bordered the canal. Until the canal went into operation, the price of wheat near Akron had been 20 to 30 cents a bushel. By 1833 the price was 75 cents; no longer was the farmer without cash markets, 'the produce of his farm . . . literally rotting in his yards'."[145] It was this developmental function that engendered the Ohio canal system, not any notion of connecting the Great Lakes with the Ohio River for long-distance transport objectives.

Indiana's effort to forge external links came in a "Mammoth Internal Improvement Bill" adopted in 1836. This authorized the building of the Wabash and Erie Canal to connect the center of the state with the Great Lakes east of the Michigan peninsula and the Ohio River; the Whitewater Canal; a Central Canal to serve as a spur from the Wabash and Erie at Logansport to Indianapolis, the state's brand-new capital; and several railroads or turnpikes to serve

where waterways seemed impractical.[146] This sanguine proposal led to little actual construction, as the next year saw the worst financial panic to strike the United States up to that time. Only in 1841 was the first limited segment, from Fort Wayne to Lafayette, put into operation. The next year the connection to the Maumee Canal of Ohio and Toledo was completed, giving a continuous navigation of 240 miles from that lake port to Lafayette. Now the farmers of northern Indiana were provided with a cheap and direct route toward their markets in the northeast. In 1856 the Hoosier cut was completed to Evansville, 458 miles from Toledo, making this the longest canal ever built up to that time, and certainly a work past its time. While this digging was going on in southern Indiana, the Ohio and Mississippi Railroad, the B. and O.'s extension in this area, was rapidly completing its line from the seaboard to St. Louis across the same rolling countryside. The Whitewater Canal had been abandoned by the state to private developers, who did eventually complete it, but again after railroads had entered the area seen to be connected to the outside by canals.

In Illinois the canal era began as it did in the two states to the east, as an attempt to open up land for settlement away from Lake Michigan and the main rivers by furnishing a route for agricultural export. In the 1820s Illinois appointed a board of canal commissioners to survey the state's needs. This effort was bolstered when, in 1825, Congress granted 300,000 acres along a route across the Chicago Portage to the Illinois and Michigan Canal. That portage had been used by the Indians and was well known to the French fur traders of the seventeenth century. In any effort to tie inland Illinois to Lake Michigan, there could hardly be any other route than this. Its improvement was necessitated by the configuration of the land at the south end of that lake. The glacial

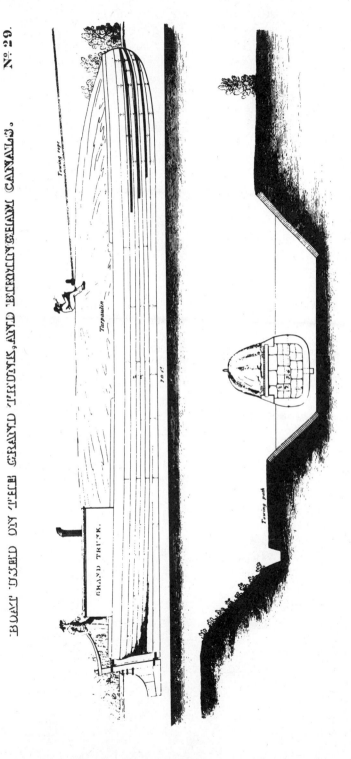

Barge used on the Grand Trunk Canal. *Source:* William Strickland, *Reports on Canals, Railways, Roads, etc. Made to the Pennsylvania Society for Internal Improvements* (Philadelphia, 1826).

moraines that surround the lake lie close to its shore and reduce the drainage area flowing to the lake to a thin band only a few miles wide. South and west of the moraines, streams flow to the Wabash or the Illinois River, so that opening up the interior of northern Illinois meant cutting a waterway across the moraine from the upper course of the short Chicago River to some stream flowing in the opposite direction toward the Illinois River. With that fact in mind, the canal commissioners began to plan a town at the mouth of the Chicago River, named for it, and another, Ottawa, at the head of navigation on the Illinois River, the largest left-bank tributary of the Mississippi north of the Ohio, and the master stream in the hydrography of Illinois. But Illinois lay too far toward the frontier to seem a very plausible place for a canal. Indian title to the land remained, except where limited by a cession in 1816 of a band of country adjacent to the Chicago River and portage. That corridor permitted a canal to be considered but it did not provide much space for agricultural settlement until further treaty negotiations in the 1820s extinguished the Indian title to most of northern Illinois and opened the way to American settlement.[147] Without the canal, however, the cost of export would be higher than the market might endure. Finally in 1836 work began on a canal from Chicago across the very low portage and then down the Des Plaines River to La Salle on the Illinois, where the river was deep enough for barge navigation.

As planned the Illinois and Michigan Canal was ambitious in two ways. It was larger than any other but the C&O, with a prism 60 feet at the surface, 36 at the bottom, and 6 feet deep. It was also cut down to the lake level so Lake Michigan could supply it with water. Thus all the six locks would be descending toward the river, whose upper reaches were for the most part lower than the lake surface. But by 1841 the credit of the

state, which along with a federal land grant was supporting the construction, was lost and serious revisions had to be introduced to save the canal. The lake-level route was abandoned and replaced by a low summit with locks rising from the east as well as the west. When the state's credit improved in 1845, this cheaper cut was financed, construction resumed, and completion secured. On Patriot's Day in 1848 the Illinois and Michigan Canal was opened for navigation the 102 miles from La Salle to Chicago. Until the Rock Island Railroad was completed paralleling the I&M route in 1854, passengers, fast package service, and freight moved along the waterway to the extent of its capacity. After that freight in fair quantity remained, but it did not pay enough to amortize the cost of the canal. Other concerns kept the canal in operation and in fact "improved" it.

The average elevation of Chicago is about 5 feet above the normal level of Lake Michigan and when heavy rain falls it inundates the city, both in the nineteenth-century city and that of today. Under those circumstances sewerage disposal was a severe problem, befouling the Chicago River and the lake adjacent to the water intakes for the city. To solve the problem, it was appreciated that the I&M Canal could serve as an outfall for Chicago's sewerage effluent if the summit were reduced to the lake level. The Des Plaines and Illinois rivers were flowing below that level, so a cut through the flat limestone beds at the summit could relatively easily secure gravity drainage of that effluent away from the city and the lake that supplied it with water. In addition, the lake could provide considerable quantities of water to flush the discharge through the cut, although it never made this tolerable to the communities beside the cut and the river or to the boat operators floating on this flood of human excrement, garbage, waste from packing houses, and the like. This open sewer was completed in 1871, but within a decade it had become appallingly clogged and malodorous. Something had to be done. In 1892 a massive cut, capable of handling steamboats and large enough not to clog up, was begun, which, when finished in 1900, finally solved Chicago's basic sewerage problem. In addition, it provided a large barge canal between the lakes and the Mississippi that remains in heavy use today for bulk products with no severe time demands.

One other canal was built in the Middle West, but it played little role in our historical geography. It lay between the south end of Green Bay and the Wisconsin River at Portage. The Fox River and Lake Winnebago provided much of the route, but artificial cutting was used at the historic portage at the great easterly bend of the Wisconsin River. The canal served to export agricultural products from central Wisconsin but was abandoned from Lake Winnebago to Portage when rail took over in the late nineteenth century. This Fox River Canal was in keeping with the state programs for internal improvements to be found in almost all western states in the last century. Like the others, it was abandoned when rail transport became the standard integrated transport system.

Rapids on the Ohio River at Louisville were a minor impedence to the rafting that opened that river to American transport, but when steamboats were introduced to the Father of Waters in 1811, they encountered considerable problems at the Falls of the Ohio. In 1825 the commonwealth of Kentucky chartered the Louisville and Portland Canal to be built around the falls on the left bank. When completed in 1830, this canal proved both convenient and profitable. By 1835 the company's earnings were in excess of 25 percent, and the canal was becoming crowded both by traffic and by an increase in the size of steamboats. The three-deckers then being launched were too big to fit in the locks, so in 1855 the federal government ordered the canal enlarged. When completed in 1872 (the Civil War had delayed construction), the waterway passed under federal government control. This facility remained the sole navigation lock on the Ohio until the 1930s, when the creation of a series of relatively still ponds behind dams transformed the Ohio from an open stream to a canalized river. By then the purpose of the work was to allow an enlargement in the size of boats that could pass along the river. These barges were long in themselves and could extend in a train for a thousand feet behind a tow boat or for hundreds of feet in front of the pushers that became more common on the Ohio and Mississippi. The Louisville and Portland, like the Illinois Waterway (the river and the Chicago Drainage and Navigation Canal), the New York barge canals, and the Chesapeake and Delaware, survived beyond the American Canal Era by being transformed into a waterway large enough to handle the large barges and strings thereof that proved so labor- and cost-efficient that, without having to pay tolls, they could hold their own against the continent-size integration that the railroads offered. But the waterways survived only as carriers of most specialized cheap bulk goods.

The Canadian Use of Canals

In this survival came also the more important Canadian waterways. The first to be undertaken can well be anticipated. The Erie Canal had, after a fashion, provided passage over the Niagara Escarpment for American boatmen. With the branch canal from Syracuse to Oswego an actual, though circuitous, waterway existed between Lake Erie and Lake Ontario. This was no consolation for the Canadians, who had become very sensitive to the threat from the American joint ownership of four of the Great Lakes when one of the few American victories during the War of 1812 was won at Put-in-Bay on Lake Erie on September 13, 1813. After the war the British government was ever anxious to shape what might be termed an all-Canadian route to and through the lakes. With that strategic purpose in mind, and with the growing flow down the lakes of grain and other staples—more considerably from the United States than from British lands—the government of Upper Canada was anxious to encourage a Canadian canal around the falls at Niagara. That this was more a commercial than a naval canal is attested by the size of the investment from New York in the canal company that began construction in 1824, and particularly in the pressure from the New York stockholders, who sought to have the canal enlarged from the dimensions of the Erie Canal, then nearing completion, to one capable of handling lake sloops and schooners.[148]

As finally built the waterway around the falls, the Welland Canal, was very much a North American affair—adequate for the initial purposes for which it was built, but neither very elaborate nor enduring. Money was short, so construction had to be painfully economical, even to the extent of using wood for the locks, of which there were to be thirty-five between the Welland River level and Lake Ontario, the stretch that carried the canal over the Niagara escarpment and down 310 feet to the lower lake. When the project was examined for the British government by a Scots engineer named Mac-Taggart, his report was properly condemnatory: this was not the way to build a canal, and this was not how he and his colleagues were building the Rideau Canal farther east in Upper Canada at the time.[149] That eastern waterway was a direct undertaking of the British government with full call on the exchequer and, no doubt, the idea of showing colonials how canals should be built. As completed the Welland Canal was capable

of handling small lake boats that drew no more than 7 feet, but it did not fit easily into an integrated transportation system between the upper lakes and Lake Ontario and the Atlantic ports. Larger boats were needed on the lakes than could pass through the canal. Meanwhile, the wooden locks on that cut were rapidly deteriorating.

In this situation the British government was asked to undertake a review of the Canadian canal system, which they did under Lieutenant Colonel Phillpotts of the Royal Engineers. In 1839 he concluded that

> unless we open an uninterrupted navigation for large freight steamers, capable of conveying a cargo of at least 300 tons, without transshipment before they arrive at Montreal or Quebec, we have no chance whatever of securing any great portion of that vast and important trade which must ere long be carried on between the Western States and the Atlantic Ocean.[150]

There can be no doubt that the Canadian canals were as much intended to tap the vast productivity of the agriculture of the American Middle West as were those of New York and Pennsylvania. Montréal was just as much an entrepôt for the American interior as were New York, Philadelphia, and Baltimore—a fact shown clearly by the British practice of permitting American shipments via the St. Lawrence to pass in bond to Montréal and Québec. To capture that trade it was necessary both to make the Welland Canal more usable and to overcome the interruptions in navigation encountered on the St. Lawrence between the foot of Lake Ontario and Montréal.

The reconstruction of the Welland Canal to a larger size, and with stone locks, came when the government of a then united Canada took essential possession of the waterway on July 5, 1841. A year later enlargement began to make the locks capable of handling ships that could easily navigate the lakes. With continuous improvement up to 1883, this canal remained the operative control on the size of shipping between Lake Ontario and the upper lakes until construction of the St. Lawrence Seaway in the 1950s.

To tap the American staple export, the Canadians needed to make the St. Lawrence navigable between Montréal and the foot of Lake Ontario. This section of the river flows across that neck of the Canadian Shield that ties the Adirondacks of New York State to the vast extent of the basically crystalline block. The effect is to produce a series of rapids, *saults*, that interrupt the smooth flow of the river in six places, the lower two east of the neck of the shield. Just west of the original city of Montréal were encountered the Lachine Rapids, which kept the early French explorers from ascending the river any farther. To the west the great river broadened as Lac St. Louis ponded behind the resistant rocks at Lachine. Beyond its western end lay another resistant stratum, creating the cascades that ponded Lac St. Francis at the western limit of the great structural valley of the lower St. Lawrence. At Cornwall, Ontario, the eastern edge of the neck of the shield (the Frontenac Axis) was reached and for some 30 miles the river upstream was repeatedly broken by saults. This stretch of the river was part of the 112-mile section that forms the boundary between the United States and Canada. Thus any large-scale improvement here would depend on international cooperation.

In the first half of the nineteenth century, in fact down to 1871, relations between Britain and the United States were not particularly amicable, leaving the poor Canadians hostage to a conflict not of their making. Only when Britain, fearing American reprisals for its open support of the Confederacy during the Civil War, granted real autonomy to Canada was the boundary with the United States made reasonably secure and river navigation adjacent to it practicable. Thus we find two phases in the opening of the St. Lawrence waterway westward from Montréal: the first, carried out soon after the War of 1812, sought to create an alternative route to the St. Lawrence in the International Section of the river; the second, as fear of the Americans waned, sought at last to use the river for its great potential as a route toward the productive Ontario and Middle western farm belt that surrounded the Great Lakes. Resistance to the improvement of navigation of the St. Lawrence did not come from the Canadians and British alone; the Americans seem to have been reluctant to see a waterway opened that might permit the passage of British war vessels from the ocean to the Great Lakes. Only when reasonably amicable relations between the United States and Britain were obtained in the 1870s did the prospects for the canalization of the river become brighter. Even then the Canadians sought an all-Canadian canal through the International Rapids section of the river and in the Welland Canal around Niagara.

In the years after the close of the Napoleonic Wars—and the close of its North American phase, what we call the War of 1812—the American invasion of Canada, unsuccessful as it was, left the British and Canadians reluctant to improve the St. Lawrence route. Merchants in Montréal were willing to take what they saw as a minor risk for a major commercial advantage that would attach from opening the more direct St. Lawrence route, but the imperial authorities were strongly for an improvement that would be routed farther from the boundary, using the Ottawa River to the foot of the Chaudière Falls. This lower section of the Ottawa flows largely at the northern edge of the St. Lawrence Lowland, which is here considerably lower in elevation than the St. Lawrence that flows towards its southern margin. To the west this last extent of the

Lowland is bordered by the narrow neck of the Canadian Shield that attaches the Adirondacks to the remainder of that vast granitic plate. Surveys showed that the lower hundred miles of the Ottawa, below the Chaudière Falls, could be navigated with only minor improvements, but not far west of those falls the river issues from the Canadian Shield and is repeatedly interrupted by rapids. Just below the Chaudière Falls the Ottawa is joined, over a 50-foot fall on the left bank, by the Rideau River that rises in the neck of the shield along the Frontenac Axis. That narrow neck is also the headwaters of a small stream, the Cataraqui, that flows to join the lower end of Lake Ontario at Kingston. In the hills formed by the Frontenac Axis there are many glacially scoured rock-basin lakes that offer natural reservoirs divided one from another by very short portages. Some of those Rideau Lakes are the source of the river of that name, others of the Cataraqui.

The plan of the Rideau Canal favored by the British engineers called for a route beginning on the Ottawa at the Rideau Falls. In a 123.5 mile waterway, only 18 miles would be in artificial canal, the rest being handled by the canalization of the Rideau and Cataraqui and in the channels through the Rideau Lakes. The route required forty-seven locks, giving a total rise and fall of 439 feet taken in thirty-three locks on the north slope, where the rise is 277 feet from the Ottawa River entrance at just above 130 feet above sea level; and fourteen locks on the lake slope, with a rise of only 162 feet from the Lake Ontario level at 246 feet. These locks are relatively concentrated in the Frontenac Axis and in an impressive flight of eight locks above the beginning of the canal in what became Ottawa, with the Canadian Parliament buildings located directly to the west. The waterway was to have locks 134 feet long, 33 feet wide, and with a depth of 8 feet—large enough to permit small naval vessels up to 110 feet in length and 30 feet across the beam to pass through. Construction was undertaken directly on the account of the Canadian government in 1826 and pursued with vigor till completion in 1832. Along the southern end military blockhouses were built along the canal and a martelo tower at Kingston to defend this strategic waterway against the potential enemy from the south. [151]

The Rideau Canal never assumed any great importance in the commercial transportation above Montréal. For a few years, until the opening of steamboat service through the St. Lawrence canals in 1851, vessels passed up the Ottawa and through the Rideau cut in a service between Montréal and Kingston, but the great flow of U.S. staples that might bring prosperity to the St. Lawrence ports stayed away: the Erie was a more direct route, leading to a much more important Atlantic harbor than those on the St. Lawrence with their winter freezing, shallow channel between Montréal and Québec, and inferior mercantile community. Only the improvement of the St. Lawrence itself held any hope of capturing a considerable part of the export trade from the U.S. Middle West that was the objective af all the early canals and railroads leading southwest out of Montréal.

The first efforts to bypass the rapids on the great river came at the Cascades between Lac St. Louis and Lac St. Francis when a small canal was opened in 1783 with a depth of 2.5 feet; it was deepened to 12 feet and otherwise improved in 1819. This still left the lowest rapids, those at Lachine, to be rendered passable for upbound boats, something that was not accomplished until 1824 when an 8.5-mile canal with six locks 100 by 20 feet and 5 feet deep was finished. Above the Cascades there were still the four rapids in the international section to deal with before boats that might shoot the rapids downbound could return to the lakes. In

1834 construction of the Long Sault Canal above Cornwall was begun, but it languished along with the other St. Lawrence canals as long as Lower Canada (Québec) and Upper Canada (Ontario) were separate colonies divided in their economic interests as well as their language and religion. After the union of the two Canadas in 1841, the St. Lawrence waterway could be treated as a single unit and be developed by a single government. Construction on the Cornwall Canal resumed in 1842 and was completed a year later as an 11.5-mile canal with six locks measuring 200 by 55 by 9 feet—a size that became the standard for the system of six canals finally constructed between Montréal and Lake Ontario. In this recontruction in the 1840s the waterway around the Cascades, then renamed Beauharnois, was shifted from the north to the south bank of the river, when commercial interests overcame the military's objection to a canal more approachable from the United States. "In the end, the decision was in favor of the southern route, the decisive factor apparently being the friendship of Lord Sydenham [the Governor-General] for Edward Gibbon Wakefield, whose company, the North American Colonial Association for Ireland, wished the canal to cross its property, the Seigniorie of Beauharnois, located on the south shore." Begun in 1842, the Beauharnois Canal was 11.25 miles long, broken by nine locks of 200 by 45 by 9 feet. In this same reconstruction the Lachine was enlarged to the same dimensions. Several new cuts around the rapids at Williamsburg, west of Cornwall, used the same dimensions and, on completion in 1847, finally opened the St. Lawrence to boats large enough to navigate the lakes as well as the river.[152]

The desire to forge a connection for seagoing vessels to reach the Great Lakes was matched by the efforts of the port of Montréal to gain reasonable access to the ocean. When the French first arrived in Canada, the river above Québec was quite shallow in places, particularly at Lac St. Pierre. By 1850 most oceanic shipping could not pass through the lake in the river, so the port of Montréal set about dredging to create a 13-foot channel immediately, an 18-foot channel by 1857, and a 20-foot channel by 1866. To match this increase in the draft of boats that might reach Montréal, the river canals had to be enlarged. In the 1890s a new canal at the Cascades was constructed on the north shore, with Sydenham and Wakefield both gone from the scene. This Soulanges Canal was completed in 1899 to a 14-foot depth, and by 1904 all the St. Lawrence canals were completed to that depth, which remained the standard until the St. Lawrence Seaway was inaugurated in 1957.

The St. Lawrence waterway finally came into its own when the farming frontier of Canada expanded into the prairies, where wheat became the main crop. Thousands, hundreds of thousands, and ultimately millions of tons of grain moved from the far interior to the east coast. The St. Lawrence–Great Lakes waterway served to handle that increasing demand for transportation when the flood became too great even for the railroads that were constructed to handle it. By the time of World War II, the Lake Superior iron ore deposits began to prove insufficient for U.S. and Canadian demands, there was greatly increasing support for a further enlargement of the St. Lawrence canals to permit ocean shipping to bring ore to the Middle West from Labrador and overseas. The Welland Canal had been increased in size in a reconstruction completed in 1932 to contain locks with 30 feet of water over the sills, a width of 80 feet, and a length of 800 feet. This took up 327 feet of the rise in the whole system but left the 230 feet between Montréal and Prescott, Ontario, whence navigation to Lake Ontario is possible, still handled in small locks. It was to overcome this constraint that the St. Lawrence Seaway was proposed directly after 1945 to provide a 114-mile waterway, largely comprising seven long pools separated by eight locks, between the lakes and tidewater. Opposition within the United States delayed congressional action, however. Only in the early 1950s, when Canada stated its willingness to build the seaway without U.S. participation, was the diverse opposition finally beaten. In 1954 Congress authorized U. S. participation, and in 1958 a canalization of the river created a channel 27 feet deep for the 112 miles west of Montréal. The locks matched those on the Welland (800 by 80 by 30 feet) so that at last reasonably large ocean shipping could reach the Great Lakes. There some of the channels, particularly those in the Detroit, St. Clair, and St. Mary's rivers, had to be improved. Once completed, however, a waterway that had been sought along several routes was finally in hand.[153]

CONCLUSIONS

The canal in America during the two hundred years it has been used as a means of transport has served basically two functions, both rather distinct from the purposes for which such waterways were constructed in Europe. During the decades before the development of an integrated rail system—that is, prior to the close of the U. S. Civil War and the creation of the Canadian Dominion—North American canals served most fundamentally as an instrument of internal development in an era when serious efforts to improve the economic growth of the two formerly British domains depended on bringing to a logical conclusion the original externally derived transportation organization of those former colonies. That is, further facilitation was needed of the great drive for the reasonable handling of export staples that had characterized all the European colonies in North America from 1607

in the United States and 1608 in Canada. In what became the United States and Canada, nearly the first two hundred years of settlement and economic effort had used very largely the natural provision of externally oriented routes in what I have termed the *potamic phase* of transportation—and thereby of waterways—development.

In serving this externally derived function, nature had been particulary generous to North America. It remained to create a comprehensive transportation system that might serve other than externally oriented demands for movement. The railroad gave North America not merely a route to the seaboard, which became the concern of the second major study of American transportation needs following on the completion of most of the proposals that Gallatin made in 1808,[154] but also the means of integrating individually the U. S. and Canadian economies. As the rail nets in the two North American democracies were advanced, the orientation of their economies could be changed and their settlement could be completed in ways that the original mercantile settlement projected outward from western Europe would not have foreseen. In place of the trans-Atlantic orientation there came an internalization of trade to North America. Canada and the United States became each other's greatest trading interest in the same way that they developed internal, more endogenic, forces to call transportation into existence. The movement, and its individualization in the road and automobile, was adopted and advanced in North America to a degree that Europe never witnessed until recently. In that adoption came the emancipation of North Americans from a system dictated from afar.

The remains of the exogenic system are all about us, but its demands were moderated already a century ago. In that moderated form the waterways continued to serve an externalized objective, still very important in the North American economy, but they no longer had a general American purpose. That role fell first to the railroad and subsequently to the highway and the airway. With the entrance to the second phase of waterway development in North America, it was never again possible to think of a single solution to the provision of modern transport.

NOTES

1. Quoted in Carlo Cipolla, *Before the Industrial Revolution: European Society and Economy, 1000–1700* (New York: W. W. Norton, 1976). p. 98.
2. Ibid., p. 99.
3. Lewis Mumford, *The City in History* (New York: Harcourt, Brace and World, 1961), p. 300.
4. Dates for the works around Milan are taken from Charles Singer et al., *A History of Technology*, vol. 2 (New York: Oxford University Press, 1958), pp. 445-448; or Roger Calvert, *Inland Waterways of Europe* (London: Allen & Unwin, 1963), pp. 202–208.
5. Singer, op. cit., p. 442.
6. Ibid., pp. 443–444.
7. Ibid., p. 446.
8. Loc. cit.
9. Jan de Vries, *Barges and Capitalism: Passenger Transportation in the Dutch Economy, 1632–1839* (Wageningen, Netherlands: Afdeling Agrarische Geschiedensis Landbouwhogeschool, A. A. G. Bijdragen 21, 1978), p. 83. Republished by H. E. S., Utrecht, as *Barges and Capitalism* (pagination in that edition is 31 pages in advance of the earlier edition cited here).
10. For a detailed discussion of this contrast between central-place theory and the mercantile model, see Vance, *The Merchant's World*.
11. de Vries, op. cit., pp. 77–78.
12. L. T. C. Rolt, *From Sea to Sea: The Canal du Midi* (Athens: Ohio University Press, 1973), p. 15.
13. Ibid., p. 17.
14. Ibid., p. 19.
15. André Maistre, *Le Canal des Deux Mers: Canal Royal du Languedoc, 1666–1810* (Toulouse: Édouard Privat, 1968), p. 34, quoting P. Pinsseau, *Le Canal Henri IV ou Canal des Briare* (Orleans, 1943).
16. Information on the canal is somewhat contradictory. Here greatest reliance has been placed on Rolt, op. cit., pp. 19-22; Singer, et al., op. cit., pp. 460–462; Maistre, op. cit., p. 34; and E. E. Benest, *Inland Waterways of France* (London: Imray, Laurie, Norie, & Wilson, 1956), pp. 59–60.
17. Rolt, op. cit., pp. 22–23.
18. Maistre, op. cit., pp. 34–35.
19. Rolt, op. cit., p. 23.
20. Quoted in ibid., p. 77.
21. Maistre, op. cit., p. 42.
22. Ibid., p. 43.
23. Ibid., p. 47.
24. The data in this paragraph are assembled from several sources, the main one being Benest, op. cit., pp. 109–111.
25. Huerne de Pommeuse, *Des Canaux Navigables* (Paris: Bachelier et Huzard, 1822), p. 265.
26. Rolt, op. cit., p. 72.
27. de Pommeuse, op. cit., p. 262.
28. Rolt, op. cit., p. 75.
29. de Pommeuse, op. cit., p. 276.
30. Ibid., pp. 289–290.
31. Rolt, op. cit., p. 94.
32. Roger Pilkington, *Small Boat in Southern France* (New York: St. Martin's Press, 1965), P. 120; de Pommeuse, op. cit., p. 276. Here I use the American canal-boater's term *pond* in place of the Briticism *pound* employed by Pilkington and Rolt as a translation of *bief*.
33. de Pommeuse, op. cit., p. 277.
34. Rolt, op. cit., p. 79.
35. Ibid., p. 81.
36. Ibid., p. 97.
37. Ibid., pp. 97-98.
38. Roger Pilkington, *Small Boat through France* (New York: St. Martin's Press, 1964), p. 174; Roger Calvert, *Inland Waterways of Europe* (London: Allen and Unwin, 1963), p. 65; Benest, op. cit., pp. 55–58; *Michelin Guide Vert, Bourgogne* (1970), p. 136.
39. Calvert, op. cit., p. 62.
40. *Michelin Guide Vert, Nord de la France,* pp. 12, 150.

41. Ibid., p. 30.

42. Ibid., p. 38.

43. Several popular books give us a clear view of how this canalized navigation worked in the past and at present. Philip Gilbert Hamerton, *The Saône: A Summer Voyage* (Boston: Roberts Brothers, 1888), furnishes an account of the problems still encountered in traversing the "canalized" Saône, much benefiting from a number of pen-and-ink drawings by Joseph Pennell. In his *Small Boat through France*, Roger Pilkington gives a graphic account of navigating the canalized Meuse at a time of flood and the passage over the sill of one of the Poirée's dams.

44. Rolt, op. cit., p. 118.

45. Calvert, op. cit., pp. 102–104.

46. Ibid., p. 104.

47. Loc. cit.

48. De Vries, op. cit., p. 56.

49. Loc. cit.

50. Ibid., p. 59.

51. De Vries, op. cit., p. 43.

52. Pirenne, op. cit., vol. 1, p. 247.

53. Singer et al., op. cit., p. 453.

54. Pirenne, op. cit., vol. 3, p. 468.

55. Calvert, op. cit., p. 117.

56. Pirenne, op. cit., p. 468.

57. J. R. Ward, *The Financing of Canal Building in Eighteenth-Century England* (New York: Oxford University Press, 1974), pp. 166–167.

58. Ibid., p. 169.

59. Ibid., pp. 173–174.

60. Singer et al., op. cit., p. 456.

61. Charles Hadfield, *British Canals, An Illustrated History* (New York: Augustus M. Kelley, 1969), p. 139. L. T. C. Rolt agrees with Hadfield about the nature of the locks on the Exeter Canal [L. T. C. Rolt, *The Inland Waterways of England* (London: George Allen and Unwin, 1950), p. 68]. The Oxford *History of Technology* refers to the locks on the Exeter Canal as having miter gates.

62. Hadfield, op. cit., pp. 21–22.

63. Ibid., pp. 86–87.

64. Charles Hadfield, *The Canal Age* (New York: Praeger, 1969), p. 22.

65. Ibid., p. 23.

66. Most of the facts contained in this account are from Frank Mullineux, *The Duke of Bridgewater's Canal* (Eccles and District Historical Society, 1959), and in the Manchester Ship Canal Company, *The Bridgewater Canal Handbook* (Cheltenham: Ed., J. Burrow, n.d., but apparently 1973). In addition, Hadfield and Rolt in their books on British canals supply odd bits of information. The data on the coal prices appear in all these works.

67. Mullineux, op. cit., p. 29.

68. Manchester Ship Canal Company, *Bridgewater Canal Handbook,* pp. 36–38, 51–61.

69. Mullineux, op. cit., p. 29.

70. Hadfield, *British Canals*, op. cit., pp. 91, 106.

71. For a discussion of these, see de Pommeuse, op. cit., pp. 427–464.

72. In Brisson's classification he argued as follows:

I will include in the first class those [canals] which lead from Paris to the most important commercial places of the realm and those which traverse France in great extent thus being of importance to a number of Departements. It is these which can be regarded as the great arteries of the kingdom, upon which will branch off the secondary communication lines . . . . In the second order I will place the canals destined specially for the outlet of productions of a province or a region [*contrée*], and to tie together a small number of Departements. The canals of this class, of secondary importance and extent, ought to be connected with those of the first class . . . . Finally, the third class will be comprised of canals of still smaller dimensions, destined for boats of 10 to 12 ten-hundredweight burden, and having as a purpose a specific exploitation [of resources] or to serve as a branch to a region of lesser extent or productivity . . . .

P. Brisson, *Essai sur le Système de Navigation Intérieure de la France* (Paris: Chez Carilian-Goeury, 1829), translated and summarized from pp. 7–8.

73. Hadfield, *British Canals,* op. cit., p. 79.

74. Data for the Trent and Mersey Canal are taken from Charles Hadfield, *Canals of the West Midlands* (Newton Abbot, Devonshire, 1966), chapter 2.

75. Ibid., p. 39.

76. H. Thorpe, "Litchfield: A Study of Its Growth and Functions," *Transactions of Staffordshire Record Society*, 1951–1952, p. 196, quoted in Hadfield, *West Midlands*, op. cit., p. 36.

77. Ibid., p. 49.

78. J. Douglas Porteous, *Canal Ports: The Urban Achievement of the Canal Age* (New York: Academic Press, 1977), pp. 86–91.

79. Ibid., p. 85.

80. Porteus, op, cit., has provided us with an interesting account of these English curiosities that are hardly in the same class with Chicago or Ottawa, or even with Sète.

81. Hadfield, *West Midlands*, op. cit., p. 64.

82. Quoted, loc. cit.

83. Ibid., p. 66.

84. Rolt, *Inland Waterways*, op. cit., p. 43.

85. Hadfield, *British Canals*, op. cit., p. 96.

86. Quoted in *Life of Thomas Telford*, edited by Rickman, 1839 [Hadfield, *West Midlands*, op. cit., p. 86].

87. Ibid., p. 88.

88. Data from *Bradshaw's Canals*, op. cit., pp. 314–319.

89. Hadfield, *The Canal Age*, op. cit., p. 150.

90. Paul Mantoux, *The Industrial Revolution in the Eighteenth Century* (New York: Macmillan, 1961), pp. 123–132.

91. Adam Smith, *The Wealth of Nations*, book 1, (New York: The Modern Library, 1937 [original edition, 1776]), chapter 3.

92. For a more extended discussion of this mercantile settlement and its origin, see Vance, *The Merchant's World*.

93. Quoted from the Knox manuscripts, in Christopher Roberts, *The Middlesex Canal, 1793–1860*, Harvard Economic Studies 61 (Cambridge, Mass.: Harvard University Press, 1938), p. 21.

94. This account of the Connecticut river canals depends heavily on Edwin M. Bacon, *The Connecticut River and the Valley of the Connecticut* (New York: G. P. Putnam's, 1906), chapter 22.

95. Ronald E. Shaw, *Erie Water West, A History of the Erie Canal, 1792–1854* (Lexington: University of Kentucky Press, 1966), P. 17.

96. Ibid., p. 18.

97. Roberts, op. cit., pp. 124–135.

98. Walter S. Sanderlin, *The Great National Project: A History of the Chesapeake and Ohio Canal* (Baltimore: Johns Hopkins Studies in Historical and Political Science, Series 64, no. 1, 1946), pp. 34–36.

99. Letter to Governor Benjamin Harrison, October 10, 1784, quoted in Carter Goodrich, *Government Promotion of American Canals and Railroads* (New York: Columbia University Press, 1960), p. 87.

100. From entry "Rail-roads and Canals, " in William Darby and Theodore Dwight, Jr., *A New Gazetteer of the United States of America, etc.* (Hartford: Edward Hopkins, 1833), p. 442.

101. Roberts, op. cit., p. 57. The quotation is from Laommi Baldwin, the superintendent of the Middlesex Canal.

102. Ibid., pp. 101–116.

103. Quoted in Roberts, op. cit., p. 170.

104. John Langdon Sullivan developed a human- and horse-powered tugboat in 1810; but by July, 1812, he was using his tug with an engine secured from Oliver Evans of Philadelphia. As Evans's high-pressure steam engines were generally superior in the early nineteenth century to the low-pressure engines of England, it is possible that this was the first economically successful steam application to canal operation. The *Charlotte Dundas* run on the Forth and Clyde Canal in 1802 was obviously earlier but not notably successful. Ibid., p. 143.

105. Edward A. Lewis, *The Blackstone Valley Line: The Story of the Blackstone Canal and the Providence & Worcester Railroad* (Seekonk, Mass.: The Baggage Car, 1973), pp. 5-12. Darby and Dwight, op. cit., p. 449.

106. Edward C. Kirkland, *Men, Cities, and Transportation: A Study in New England History, 1820–1900* (Cambridge, Mass.: Harvard University Press, 1948), vol. 1, p. 81.

107. Goodrich, op. cit., pp. 82–83; Carter Goodrich, Julius Rubin, H. Jerome Crammer, and Harvey Segal, edited by Goodrich, *Canals and American Economic Development* (New York: Columbia University Press, 1961), pp. 212–214.

108. Quoted in Goodrich, *Government Promotion*

of American Canals and Railroads, op. cit.,p. 102.

109. Caroline E. MacGill, *History of Transportation in the United States before 1860* (Washington, D. C.: The Carnegie Institution, 1917), pp. 277–279.

110. *Annals*, 9th Congress, 2nd Session, pp. 95–97.

111. Federal Writers' Project, American Guide Series, *The Intercoastal Waterway: Norfolk to Key West* (Washington, D. C.: U.S. Government Printing Office, 1937), pp. 89–92; G. D. Luetscher, "Atlantic Coastwise Canals: Their History and Present Status," *Annals of the American Academy of Political and Social Science* 31 (January, 1908): 92–93. Special number on *American Waterways*, edited by Emory Johnson.

112. Johnson, *American Waterways*, op. cit., p. 93.

113. Talbot Hamlin, *Benjamin Henry Latrobe* (New York: Oxford University Press, 1955), pp. 211–212.

114. Ralph D. Gray, *The National Waterway: A History of the Chesapeake and Delaware Canal, 1769-1965* (Urbana: University of Illinois Press, 1967), p. 137.

115. *Daily National Intelligencer*, May 30, 1823, quoted in ibid., p. 141.

116. Wheaton J. Lane, *From Indian Trail to Iron Horse: Travel and Transportation in New Jersey, 1620–1860* (Princeton, N.J.: Princeton University Press, 1939), p. 257. *Report of Committee on Delaware and Raritan Canal*, New Jersey House of Assembly, Trenton, January 15, 1829.

117. Ibid., pp. 259–260.

118. James Cawley and Margaret Cawley, *Along the Delaware and Raritan Canal* (South Brunswick, N.J.: A. S. Barnes, 1970), p. 110.

119. Governor Bradford, quoted in Robert H. Farson, *The Cape Cod Canal* (Middletown, Conn.: Wesleyan University Press, 1977), p. 9.

120. Ibid., pp. 33–48.

121. Quoted in ibid., p. 51.

122. *Guidebook to the Intracoastal Waterway*, op. cit., p. 11.

123. Ronald E. Shaw, *Erie Water West: A History of the Erie Canal, 1792-1854* (Lexington: University of Kentucky Press, 1966), p. 44.

124. Ibid., p. 87.

125. It appears that the western end would have had to be something like five times as large as the prism mentioned. W. B. Langbein, *Hydrology and Environmental Aspects of Erie Canal (1817–99)*. (Washington, D.C.: U.S. Government Printing Office, 1976), p. 14.

126. Shaw, op. cit., pp. 279–280.

127. Quoted from N.Y. Assembly Journal, 40th Session, pp. 313-314, in Langbein, op. cit., p. 22.

128. Langbein, op. cit., pp. 22–23.

129. Shaw, op. cit., p. 239.

130. Ibid., p. 241.

131. Noble E. Whitford, *History of the Barge Canal of New York State* (Albany: Supplement to the Annual Report of the State Engineer and Surveyor, for year ended June 30, 1921), published 1922, pp. 16–17.

132. Ibid., p. 18.

133. Ibid., p. 108.

134. Johnson, *American Waterways*, op. cit., p. 118.

135. *Historical Statistics of the United States*, Table Q 243-244. U.S. Bureau of the Census, 1960.

136. Johnson, op. cit., p. 118.

137. Julius Rubin, "An Imitative Public Improvement: The Pennsylvania Mainline," in Carter Goodrich et al., *Canals and American Development*, op. cit., p. 68.

138. Ibid., p. 69.

139. Letter of December 30, 1825, quoted in ibid., p. 92.

140. Ibid., pp.104–105.

141. MacGill, op. cit., pp. 388–389.

142. Pennsylvania data from Rubin, op. cit., p. 108; New York data from *Historical Statistics of the United States*, Series Q 243-244. op. cit.

143. Sanderlin, op, cit., p. 162.

144. Ibid., p. 167.

145. Harry N. Scheiber, *Ohio Canal Era: A Case Study of Government and the Economy, 1820–1861* (Athens: The Ohio University Press, 1969), p. 192.

146. Harry Sinclair Drago, *Canal Days in America* (New York: Clarkson N. Potter, 1972), p. 238.

147. Harold M. Mayer and Richard C. Wade,

Chicago: Growth of a Metropolis (Chicago: University of Chicago Press, 1969), p. 3.

148. Hugh G. J. Aitken, *The Welland Canal Company: A Study in Canadian Enterprise* (Cambridge, Mass.: Harvard University Press, 1954), p. 52.

149. Ibid., p. 61.

150. Quoted in ibid., . 75.

151. Robert Legget, *Rideau Waterway* (Toronto: University of Toronto Press, 1955), pp. 13-20.

152. Willoughby, op. cit., pp. 16–27.

153. Harold M. Mayer, *The Port of Chicago and the St. Lawrence Seaway* (Chicago: University of Chicago Press, 1957), pp. 30–53.

154. *Transportation Routes to the Seaboard*, Report of the Select Committee, Washington, D.C., 1874. 2 volumes.

TURNPIKE ROADS.

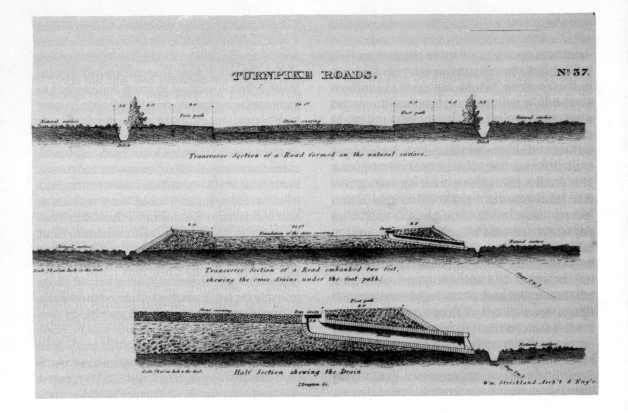

Transverse Section of a Road formed on the natural surface.

Transverse Section of a Road embanked two feet,
shewing the cross drains under the foot path.

Half Section shewing the Drain

J. Drayton Sc.

Wm. Strickland Arch't & Eng'r.

THE ROAD IN TRANSITION I: THE CANAL YEARS

By now it should be abundantly clear first that all forms of transportation play distinctive roles, and second that human society has made use of several media at the same time, even when giving pride of place to a single "advanced" medium. Thus, while the canal was engaging the most attention with its technical advances in competence and cost, the road continued to be the main facility used by people. Agriculturalists bringing their products to the local market normally went there by road, as did drovers with their flocks. Pedlars with their bags of luxuries of distant origin trudged the highways as well. Thus to understand the full significance of the canal, we must look briefly at the roads of the era.

Broadly considered, the roads of the canal years were little transformed from their medieval antecedents: local labor duties—the corvée—provided what actual construction there was. Thus it should not surprise us that lack of repair and even of routing made through travel difficult—circuitous at best if

not actually interrupted where the interest of one corvée failed to adjoin that of its neighbor. As labor was the main element of investment, the actual fabric of the road was of natural and local provenance, commonly earth that became impassable when wet. To remedy that state, corvées frequently used the most common locally available tools—the plow, scraper-board, and shovel—to remove the muddy or rutted earth in order to gain a new bearing surface. In doing so they effectively depressed the surface of the road below that of the country through which it passed, giving to the highway a trenched quality that encouraged subsequent rains to flow along that course, futher muddying the ground that was used for movement. The parochialism innate to the corvée was thus further encouraged by the frequent impassability of roads maintained in that manner. In wet climates, water courses and their extension by canals had the virtue of avoiding the problems of maintaining a firm bearing surface on land by accepting the abundance of moisture and using it for its own buoyant qualities given the right vehicles.

Still, canals were expensive to build and rivers only navigable toward their lower courses. Roads could not be foregone, so the needs that led to canal building also forced an effort to create roads of better quality and greater durability than those shaped by local corvées. Here we shall consider only two of those diverse efforts: the creation of a national system of highways in France of the *ancien régime* through the agency of the Corps des Ponts et Chausées and the more piecemeal provision of improved roads by the various quasi-public turnpike trusts of England.

THE ROAD UNITES FRANCE

Only in the seventeenth century was much accomplished in France or England. The Wars of Religion in the former and the stinginess of the Tudors in the latter made of the sixteenth century a time of awareness of the problem but little effective solution. With the respite in the sectarian conflict that came with Henry IV's ascension to the throne of France in 1594, attention could be given to improving internal conditions, notably in transportation. During the wars the various forces had degraded roads and destroyed bridges to deny movement to their enemies. Commerce was localized, and the traditional rights of passage and of the king's peace were denied. Once on the throne Henry tried to solve the problem by first making his great Huguenot minister, the Duc de Sully, the Grand Voyer de France with clear supervision of the long-distance highways known popularly as the royal roads.[1] A professional approach to construction remained in the future, but with Henry's decrees a national bureaucracy had been set in place. Using the local viewers of roads as agents, the royal office of the Grand Voyer managed to bring some semblance of national objective and

order even under the workings of the local corvées, although the Grand Voyer's greater accomplishment was in establishing the practice of hiring private contractors to undertake the more important projects, thus introducing a new level of professional skill.[2]

On the assassination of Henry in 1610 and the return of intransigent Catholicism to the throne, Sully soon fell from grace. His accomplishments were largely lost save for those durable structures such as the Pont Neuf in Paris and the bridge at Rouen. Work on the Canal de Briare, as noted in chapter 2, was soon suspended, leaving the advance of public works in France largely in abeyance until well on in the long reign of Louis XIV. The Canal du Midi was undertaken late in the seventeenth century after the successful completion of the Briare cut, but road construction was restored more promptly by Colbert when he became Louis's chief minister. By 1680 he was, in the name of the king, calling on Intendants to observe their areas in order to determine where the most populous and commercially important towns were before they began work on roads. Furthermore, the roads leading to the maritime ports should always be placed in the category of principal roads, by reason of their commerce: "One must consider the great routes from the provinces to Paris as those both principal and most important, because of the continual communication that all the provinces have with the royal capital, and that [Paris] is nearly the center of all consumption."[3]

What roads there were in this period tended to be mere adjuncts of the rivers and the earliest canals. The primacy of transport by water was shown by the orientation of the more important roads to provide direct connections to navigable streams. Between Paris and Bordeaux the road reached the nearest point of the Loire by crossing the flat plain of Beauce to Orleans. Thence the river was followed to Amboise, where Francis and

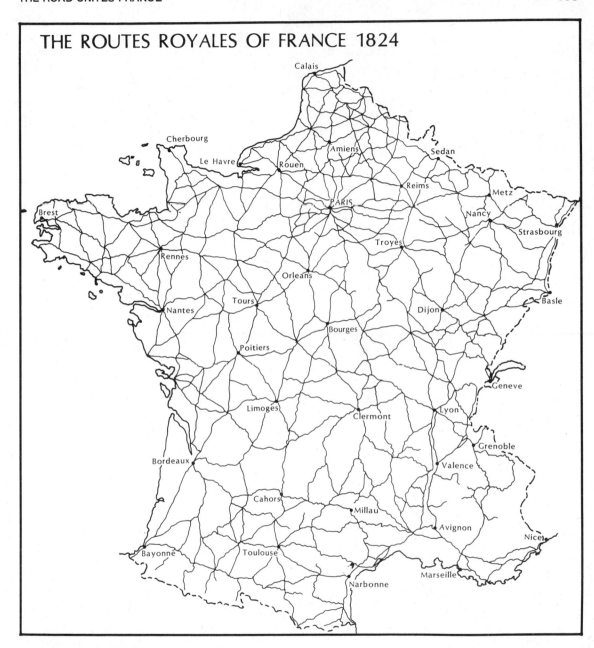

THE ROUTES ROYALES OF FRANCE 1824

Corps de Ponts et Chaussées map of 1824.

Leonardo dreamed of the canal network for France, or Tours. From there again forced overland, passing through Poitiers, the route continued through Santes and Blaye to the Gironde and then the Garonne to reach Bordeaux.[4] "The course of routes came in the end, in large measure, to be determined by the site of bridges, their strength, and the confidence that travelers had in them."[5]

This succession in routes suggests that conditions arose in the seventeenth century that led to a more orderly and sustained effort at road planning and building. Cavailles cites four main transforming forces:

1. Political reasons stemming from the rise of the nation-state of France, which are summarized in the idea that "the state ought to assume responsibility for works indispensible to communication through the improvement of roads of interconnection."
2. Technical reasons, among them the surveying and publication of the first reasonably detailed maps that made topography clear, and thereby the rational planning of a national system of routes practicable.
3. Above all, economic reasons, exemplified by the growth of production and trade after 1719, when peace was at hand, and the onset of traveling by the noble classes to visit other places and, after Rousseau, to view the wonders of nature in the fields, woods, and mountains.
4. The impact of transformed means of transport, whereby movement on horseback came to be replaced by that by carriage.

With improved roads and vehicles it became possible by the middle of the eighteenth century to travel between Paris and Lyon in five days in summer and six in winter.[6]

To accomplish the objectives of surveying needs, planning solutions, and undertaking construction, the Corps des Ponts et Chaussées was organized in 1713 and during the remainder of the *ancien régime* came to play an increasingly important role in shaping a national highway system for France. It soon became clear that training in what we now call civil engineering was needed. In 1747 the École des Ponts et Chausées was organized to provide that education.[7] No doubt one of the main reasons for that foundation was that in the earlier decades there was no plan for road improvement, "merely an order in the work." The Instructions of June 13, 1738, prescribed that national routes and great highways would be made or repaired before transverse routes were improved. Preference was to be given to the national routes departing Paris for other large cities, maritime ports, the frontiers of the realm, and interior provincial capitals.[8]

One of the more significant changes wrought by the various bureaucrats who administered French highways came first in the vigorous abolition of toll charges (*péages*) that had persisted from medieval times, when individuals and religious foundations might have gained the right to levy a toll in return for having built a bridge or improved a stretch of road, or simply been granted the privilege as a source of income without reference to any improvement in the facilities of transportation. Colbert began the abolition of *péages*, and by the close of the *ancien régime* most had been done away with under the thinking that the provision of roads and bridges was a royal responsibility backstayed by labor forced from the local corvée.

The other fundamental change was the transformation of the corvée into a tax, a trend fully in keeping with the ending of the servile dues of feudalism. The corvée was fully detested both as a feudal survival and as a most inequitably administered levy. Some cantons even within the same province might impose a schedule of up to eight times as many days of labor as did the least exacting of those local administrations, and differences between provinces were as varied. The result was grudging labor in the best of circumstances and outright wrathful participation in the worst.

Efforts to reform this initially parochial undertaking, where at least the inequities remained unknown, finally bore fruit under Turgot just before the Revolution. With a professional engineering corps, an increasing array of topographical maps that permitted clear planning of the routes, a newly professionalized construction force, and the levying of a tax to pay for the work, France was finally in a position to secure its system of national highways. This was done very much within the public framework and to a broad, national purpose. Turgot did reduce the number of trunk highways out of Paris from six to five in 1776,[9] and did adopt a somewhat lesser width than had been previously bruited, but he enforced those widths rigidly. *Grandes routes* must be 42 feet wide; lesser roads were variously 36, 30, and 24 feet. On these roads *relais* for the posts and public vehicles would be maintained.[10]

The highway development program of the ancien régime represented the first example since Roman times of a clearcut national system—with the establishment of priorities, of networks to interconnect places of military and political importance, of standards for the construction of roads, and of rationally located segments. Unlike those Romans, however, the French sought as well the provision of roads for cartage, *roulage*, to allow a strong growth of overland trade, particularly that focused on Paris, Lyon, Bordeaux, and other growing cities. It was increasingly appreciated that the flow of agricultural products from the countryside to cities, or of imported staples from the ports to those same places, had become the lifeblood of the national economy, which in turn created the national wealth more than any hoarding of gold had ever accomplished. It was accepted that most roads would be unpaved save in the wet and swampy stretches, but their surfaces must be firm—through water-bound superstructures and well-drained substructures, anticipating McAdam by several generations—to withstand the potential rutting by heavy cart wheels. Those carts and their wheels must, in turn, be controlled so as to reduce wear on the surfaces to an acceptable level.[11]

The alignment of routes changed in this period of the early application of engineering to the problem of building reasonably traversable roads for the passage of carters. Where in the Middle Ages alignments had stuck to the mid-slopes on the valley side, to avoid the potentially flooded bottoms, now with diking of stream banks roads could take up the naturally graded slope in the valley bottom. Even in crossing hills or mountains limits were placed on opposing rises with a maximum of 8 percent on the route from Paris to Lyon via the Bourbonnais (the alternative to that via Burgundy). Cuts and fills became common, both to moderate the steepest grades and to permit more direct routing, essentially matching what the Romans had accomplished in their network of roads, but in eighteenth-century France the problem was greater as the roads were intended for freight hauling to a degree the ancient highways were not.[12]

Pavement was limited to wet stretches and in villages and towns, where only some 15 feet of the total width of the road was actually paved.[13] With large state grants, major engineering works were numerous and elaborate. Multicentered arches on bridges became common, allowing a lower rise from the abutments and thus full use by carts, carriages, and wagons as well as pack animals and horsemen. Unlike medieval bridges, these bridges commonly had parapets, preventing falls from the bridge. On sloped road surfaces stone channels diagonal to the slope, called *cassis*, were used to protect the surface against sheet-wash.[14]

By the time of the Revolution France possessed a reasonably integrated network of highways, with two main lacunae: transit of the Massif Central and reasonable trans-Alpine routes between France and Italy. The pattern of this network was a creation of modern times: "The preeminence of Paris took shape with the territorial unification of the kingdom: the network of routes of communication must satisfy the new requirements of the monarchy, and above all the rapid transmission of orders."[15]

At the outbreak of the Revolution there were some forty thousand kilometers of highway in France as then constituted. Not all were in good repair, there remained some *péages* to interrupt the system, and routes other than those radiating from Paris were often problematic in their connections because of the poor state of local roads.[16] Waterways still played an important part in long-distance transportation, with barges providing part of the transit, for example, in the connection between the Languedoc and Paris. On that route boats were used up the Rhône to Lyon, where goods were transferred to wagons to be hoisted over the Col du Sauvage to Roanne on the upper Loire, whence barges could take over again passing down the Loire to Briare and the entrance to the Canal de Briare with its connection via the river Loing to the Seine and Paris.[17]

The traffic on this system was not as great as might have been expected. The French economy still had strong autarkic elements right down to the Revolution, so most of the transport was over fairly short distances, although wine and grain did move in large amounts to the Parisian market. Even under the empire active road-building was oriented mostly to strategic interests and the attempt to shape a Napoleonic Europe. In the Alps the Savoyards sought to improve connec-

tions; even before 1792 they had constructed a road tunnel under the Col de Tende on the route between Nice and Torino. Under Napoleon the French developed a route from Grenoble to Torino via the Lauteret and Genevre passes.

After 1815 the emphasis was on improving the roads for freight transport, partly because they had not been perfected for that purpose under the ancien régime and partly because they had been devastated in the last war-torn years of the Napoleonic period. An enquiry of 1811–1812 had distinguished various types of cartage: cartage over a short distance, practiced by peasants carrying goods to their local markets; cartage during slack time, conducted by those peasants who wished to supplement their incomes and occupy their leisure; the grand cartage conducted by professional carters; interregional cartage, still conducted by rural people but not peasant farmers; and finally, fast cartage carried out by professionals. The distinction between the latter two came in the speed and support structure of the operation. The rurally based slow transporters worked with a single team of horses or oxen, using them without relays and operating only during the day, making a *petite journée* of about 40 kilometers. The often town-based speedy carters used relays, operated both day and night, and managed *grandes journées* of 80 kilometers. Thus the trip from Lille to Paris in 1840 took only four days, and that to Marseille no more than fourteen.[18]

The growth in the royal routes was striking. Those from Paris to the ports and the frontier increased from 17,000 kilometers in 1815 to 35,000 in 1847. In this period two transverse routes across the Massif Central between Lyon via Clermont-Ferrand and then separately through Ussel-Tulle-Brive to Perigueux or Aubusson and Limoges to Perigueux were completed, the first with a road tunnel through the Cantal.[19] That expansion went along with an improvement in vehicles, a modification largely in terms of speed more than comfort, such that the most rapid vehicles made 10 kilometers an hour in 1815 but 15 in 1840.[20]

With the onset of industrialization, very much based on this improvement in highways, the volume of traffic grew so rapidly that an overtaxing of these roads was combined with an economic exaction of transport costs increased by poor stretches. These high costs led to discussion of the creation of a new and improved form of economic transport: "In 1822 the route from Lyon to St. Étienne, 'the most heavily traveled and the most fatiguing in the kingdom,' was not able to accommodate an intensive exploitation of coal mining" as existed in the Stephanois basin.[21] It should not surprise us that the second railroad line undertaken in France came along this taxed route, where the so-called friction of distance was made more costly by poor upkeep and major crowding.

The development of French highways before the advent of railroads reached the highest level obtained for road transportation. The system was undertaken according to a national plan, carefully reasoned to provide connections from the metropolis to provincial capitals, port cities, frontier posts, and main sources of the alimentation of that great city. The costs were borne heavily by the national treasury with the provinces providing largely the *main d'oeuvre* that physically built the roads under a generalized corvée. Interconnections among the outlying provinces were underdeveloped in this centralized, bureaucratic state, but with the onset of industrialization in the early nineteenth century regional capitalists managed to urge on the government some improvement not directly related to Paris. Whereas the system of royal routes had been initiated in the seventeenth century in the interests of governance and military operations, in the eighteenth and nineteenth the network came increasingly into economic use with a large

increase in cartage both locally oriented and nationally directed. Hauliers of a professional and national origin began to provide increasingly rapid services through the employment of continuous operation and the use of relays of draft animals. Given the objectives of speed and endurance, it is not surprising that efforts were made in the early nineteenth century to introduce early steam locomotives to the hauling trade. These were only partially successful as a result of the low efficiency ratio of these early, low-pressure engines, whose weight had to be great in relation to their tractive effort. The largely unpaved roads could not easily bear the wheel loadings without considerable depression of the flexible surface, which meant the engine had to advance up a continuous slope even on a level stretch of unpaved road. The logic of the steam locomotive was sound, but its employment on an ordinary highway—even one as improved as those in mid-nineteenth-century France—was unsound.

The most distinctive feature of the French highway system was its national scale in both provenance and geographical pattern. It shared this quality with its contemporary, the national system of canals and canalized waterways, as well as with its subsequent competitor, the national system of railroads, whose infrastructure was decreed by the state and paid for by the national treasury. From the Middle Ages on—that is, in the period of France as a geographically comprehensive nation-state—there was a fundamental acceptance of transportation facilities as a responsibility of the nation, as much as defense and national economic policy.

ENGLAND HARNESSES PRIVATE AND REGIONAL INTERESTS

Political philosophy seems to have guided French policy to the point that a centralized state necessitated a centralized administration. This caused Paris in the sixteenth century to gain a dominant place that was never again challenged within France. In England no such theoretical speculations would have been characteristic, or consistent policy politically acceptable. Instead, the monarchy in Elizabeth's Proclamation of 1580 had sought to constrain London's growth by arguing that only the port functions of the city might expand. But since it was precisely those functions that were inducing general growth in the city, the proclamation was quite futile.

> From being an economic backwater, with the opening up of the New World England found herself suddenly in the centre instead of upon the very edge of the commercial world. Her shipping and overseas trade, for a long time in competition with Holland, finally established its European supremacy in the seventeenth century.... The most remarkable result of trade was the growth of the towns, and the most striking sign of the evolution from medieval to modern England was the development, both in size and importance, of London. At the end of the fifteenth century the population of London is estimated to have been some 50,000, and by the last decade of the sixteenth that estimate had more than trebled.[22]

The seventeenth century was the time when London even more strikingly became the national metropolis. During the next two centuries, when road development remained the backstay of industrial and trading evolution, London grew from perhaps 150,000 to just over a million people. Having been considered the Great Wen in Elizabethan times, it was now the Great Metropolis. By the first British census in 1801, London was some twelve times the size of the next largest town in the United Kingdom, Edinburgh (population 83,000), and only six other towns rose above the population of London at the beginning of the fifteenth century: Liverpool

(82,000), Glasgow (77,000), Manchester (75,000), Birmingham (71,000), Bristol (61,000), and Leeds (53,000). Thus in many ways, but for very different reasons, London shared with Paris a dominant role in the shaping of a national road system. Most roads led to London and the ties to the metropolis became the first concerns of road improvers, both in a temporal and in a geographical sense.

Unquestionably, English roads were badly in need of mending and maintenance. The Romans in the first century A.D. had established a network of highways of a superior construction that had been neither matched nor even actively maintained before the seventeenth century:

> "[T]he memory of the Romans, which is so justly famous, is preserv'd in nothing more visible to common observation, than in the remains of those noble causeways and highways, which they made through all parts of the kingdom, and which were found so needful, even [in the recent past] when there was not the five hundredth part of the commerce and cartage that is now [in the early eighteenth century]: How much more valuable must . . . new works be, tho' nothing to compare with those of the Romans, for the firmness and duration of their work?[23]

Thus Daniel Defoe, when he published his *Tour through the Whole Island of Great Britain* in 1724-1726, after traveling thousands of miles about that kingdom, took note of the generally low state of British highways and the recency of any effective efforts to make improvements. He paid particular attention to two basic problems of those roads: access from the provinces to London and the crossing of the sodden clay vales extending between the Severn and the Humber that lay athwart the main road transportation of the island. The ravening growth of the metropolis made such demands on the agricultural productivity of the kingdom that food became scarce there, and consequently expensive for the burgeoning poor of the city, because wagon transportation was inefficient and costly and the driving of flocks—ranging from cattle to pigs, sheep, and even thousands of turkeys—was so taxing as a result of the miry quality of the roads that weights were reduced and the flesh was made tough and stringy. But without good, fast transportation no other means of transport would have availed to bring palatable meat to the metropolitan market. Defoe tells us:

> I might give examples where the herrings, which are not the best fish to keep neither, are, even as it is, carry'd to those towns [of the interior], and up to Warwick, Birmingham, Tamworth and Stafford, and tho' they frequently stink before they come thither, yet the people are eager of them, that they buy them, and give dear for them too; whereas were the roads good, they would come in less time, by at least two days in six, and ten-fold the quantity, nay, some say, an hundred times the quantity, be consum'd.[24]

The need to secure faster and more efficient transport came to be seen as a cost to all shippers and the consumers of their products. The produce of the farms had to be heavily discounted to bear the costs of movement to the metropolitan, or even to the provincially urban, market; the products of the artisans and the emerging factories came in return at a similar inflation. Even the carters, whose profit came from the haulage through the boggy stretches, could see that they were impoverished by a nature that did not furnish usable natural routes to the increasingly productive, and raw-material-importing, Midlands. The general interest could see the need for road works, but those grievously inept monarchs, the Stuarts, could find no solution. The absence of an English Colbert, or even a Sully, left the fish to stink in Birmingham.

The absence of a national program of road construction in seventeenth-century England forced on private capitalists the task of providing the infrastructure necessary for growth in economic activity. There was a general sense that the common wealth required an earnest and sustained effort along those lines, but that recognition could be translated into action only to the extent that Parliament granted counties the right to mobilize private capital to attempt to meet their road needs by appointing trustees empowered to borrow money or sell shares to undertake construction, and in turn to levy a toll to repay that investment.

The bars leveled across the existing roads improved by these trusts gave to the routes the name *turn-pikes*, recognizing that passage could be permitted only after payment of toll and the rotation of the "pike" to allow the user to pass on to another section of road. Even in the Middle Ages that expedient form of support for road maintenance had been attempted: in 1345 Edward III of England granted the privilege of levying a toll to those undertaking to maintain the road between St. Giles and Temple Bar in London, with other such undertakings following similar practices.

Only in the quickening economy of the seventeenth century, however, did the turnpike become the accepted, and peculiarly English, manner of securing more long-distance roads. The chaos and destruction of the Civil War period had left Restoration England badly in need of a Corps des Ponts et Chausées, but without the administrative climate to call it into existence. Thus in 1663 Charles II signed England's first turnpike act, one authorizing the justices in the counties in a band extending northward from London toward York to appoint surveyors whose job it was to secure material for rebuilding the Great North Road, gaining labor to do so under the existing highway laws, basically the medieval corvée. Once in repair, the road was to be further maintained by a toll levied on users thereof. The Great North Road remained the only turnpike for a quarter century despite its general success in accomplishing the goals set for the turnpike trustees.[25]

By the time Daniel Defoe toured Great Britain in 1724–1726, other turnpike acts had been passed and additional stretches of toll road were in existence, largely within a hundred miles of London:

> [T]urnpikes or toll-bars have been set up on the several great roads of England, beginning at London, and proceeding thro' almost all those dirt deep roads, in the midland counties especially. . . . Several of these turn-pikes and tolls have been set up of late years, and great progress has been made in mending the most difficult ways. . . .

[that make up a system of highways to interconnect the productive Midlands with the great consuming Metropolis].[26]

Defoe goes on to cite the road from London to Ipswich and Harwich as probably the best road in the kingdom and a product of the establishment of turnpike trusts. The Great North Road impressed him less well:

> [T]hese roads, which were before intollerable, are now much mended, but I cannot say, they are yet come up to the perfection of that road from London to Colchester [and on to Ipswich]. One great difficulty indeed here, is that the country is so universally made up of deep, stiff clay; that 'tis hard to find any materials to repair the ways with, that may be depended upon.[27]

Describing Britain's highways in colorful and typically caustic prose, Defoe has praise for little but the modest number of turnpikes completed by 1725.

Although only a modest number of turnpike acts had been adopted before 1760, after that crucial date—which saw England take up the canal in earnest—the spread of turnpikes was rapid:

> In the fourteen years following 1760 four hundred and fifty-three acts creating turnpikes were passed by Parliament, but a departure from the principle of Charles II was made. Instead of requiring that the designated road should first be put in thorough repair by the parish in which it lay, a turnpike trust was created with jurisdiction over such road and having authority to borrow money on the security of the tolls which it was thereafter to collect.[28]

The arrangement appeared ideal from the viewpoint of the parishes that had previously been totally responsible for the upkeep of roads. Under the turnpike trusts, once the parish had put the road in repair, it was assumed that toll collections would pay to keep it that way. Given the mismanagement of most of the trusts, the absence of well-qualified surveyors to lay out and undertake the construction work, and other unanticipated financial drains, most turnpikes did not earn enough to maintain themselves and pay interest on the borrowings made. As those bonds remained unrepaid, it became possible for the bondholders to foreclose, taking the tolls for their debt service and leaving the parish still responsible for the maintenance of the road, while the parish residents were required along with others to pay tolls for the use of a road that previously had been open to them free of charge. If the maintenance was improved, perhaps those unfortunate residents were no worse off: as it often was not, they might be so beset by this so-called improvement scheme to the point they destroyed the gates, burned the toll houses, and generally resisted the unfair impositions of the trusts.[29]

There can be no doubt that in broad terms the turnpike era in Britain was crucial to the functioning of the economy and the communications of the kingdom. Without the trusts, it is doubtful that the Industrial Revolution could have taken place, and it is for that reason that some £ 9 million of private capital were invested in the toll roads

ROADS ENGINEERED BY THOMAS TELFORD

——— Under his supervision
.... From his designs

Source: Hitzer, *Die Strasse* (Munich, 1971).

before 1839, which saw the close of that epoch as railroads became the standard for land transportation in the 1840s. Previously, British merchants and manufacturers had had to depend on two older forms for any improvement in the transportation infrastructure. The canal was used where physically practicable and economically jus-

tified by the mass of transport. When terrain or potential income ruled against the costly waterways, the turnpike road was the expedient—as, for example, in the Bishop Auckland coalfield of Durham, whence came the world's first railroad in 1825. Thus in England and Wales by 1838 there had been 1,116 turnpike trusts established to improve and maintain some 22,000 miles of road, certainly the main facility for transportation in the kingdom.[30]

The greatest problem with this solution came from its totally adventitious and incremental quality. Some 3,800 private and local acts had been adopted over nearly two hundred years, though the greater number in the last fifty years of the turnpike era, to permit the construction of this system: "There was no general arrangement or comprehensive scheme in the allotment of these trusts, but [rather] they were granted indiscriminately, forming separate units not part of a connected plan.... On the Middlesex side of London there were one hundred gates within a radius of four miles."[31] In a major study of English turnpikes, Pawson has shown that those roads were not merely an adjunct to waterways—a road where a river or canal was absent—but also

an important independent land transport system. This involved the transfer of people and information, as well as goods, over long distances without any recourse to water transport. Three factors underlay the existence of this independent system: the disadvantages of water transport, and its absence in many areas (the negative), and the better service often available by land transport (the positive).[32]

By the close of the turnpike boom in 1770, England and Wales had such an extensive system of turnpikes that all major towns were connected. In the environs of London the pattern was strongly radial, although in the Weald of Kent there was a dense local network. The western counties—Somerset, Gloucester, Worcester, Warwick, Stafford, Hereford, and Shropshire—had a particularly dense local system independent of that radiating from London. Wales had been breached to Swansea, Aberystwyth, and Holyhead. The West Riding of Yorkshire, the Durham coalfield, the Lancashire Plain, and the Kendal region all had local systems as well as through routes to and from the metropolis. An east-coast and a west-coast route to the Scottish border were in use.[33]

The basic rationale of British road construction before the nineteenth century seemed to lie along three lines: giving the road a flat level surface, raising that surface well above that of the land through which it passed in an attempt to provide drainage of the subgrade, and providing culverts and bridges in wet areas and at stream crossings. The raised grade did afford some drainage, and the bridges and culverts worked to that end, but the flat surface was on the whole a deficiency. Only in the last century, when Thomas Telford and John Loudon McAdam began to propound their proposals for the actual paving of roads with a rigid or water-repelling surface, was any real advance made in giving British roads the sort of surface that would permit the transport of heavy loads and the speeding up of both passenger and freight transports.

The organization of haulage and passenger transportation became perhaps the most successful accomplishment of British road transportation. Traditional medieval transportation in England had been by horseback, with most goods moving on pack animals along narrow paths, though these were provided with narrow, steep-crested bridges over major streams. The use of the semicircular arch suggested such a form, and the sure-footedness of unharnessed horses made it possible. By the sixteenth century, however, wagons were coming into use, making a bridge with a gentler rise toward its crest desirable. This was accomplished by building more ramped approaches, often with side arches, or by adopting the multicentered arch that might be built with far less spring from the abutments.

John Stow had noted that "long wagons" were serving London from Canterbury, Norwich, Ipswich, and Gloucester about 1564, and John Taylor's *Carriers Cosmographie* of 1637 listed over two hundred haulage services into London at that time. In addition, the *Cosmographie* listed four regular coach services into the metropolis—from St. Albans, Cambridge, Hertford, and Hatfield, all within a short distance of the city. Within a generation, wagon services had been expanded to reach to Lancashire, to the Northeast, and even to Edinburgh. By 1680 the "four towns served by stagecoach had increased to 88. In 1705, the *Travellers' and Chapmans' Instructor* listed 180 such towns, and in 1715, the *Merchant's and Trader's Necessary Companion* had increased this to 216."[34]

While the general haulage was growing and becoming regularized by the creation of established routes and frequencies of service, interest arose in providing specialized passenger services. The earlier wagons carried passengers, and it is difficult to draw a sharp line between passenger and freight transportation in this period. That line emerges only when specialized passenger transportation conducted at a higher speed and commonly associated with the transport of mail and what we would call express was introduced:

> In England the stage-coach—which did not carry and mail—still presented a rather depressing picture at the beginning of the eighteenth century. It was generally a clumsy, quadrangular structure, carrying four to eight passengers huddled together on its wooden benches. But gradually the situation improved. The jolting of the carriage was reduced by steel springs, and the seats were made somewhat more comfortable. The old vehicles which were little different from the ordinary carriers' wagons were used now only by people of small means.[35]

But the carrying of passengers by road did not gain great importance before the last years of that century:

> The first stage coach had appeared on the roads around the middle of the seventeenth century but it was not until the late eighteenth and early nineteenth century, that a real boom in coaching occurred. Then the major provincial towns could begin to measure their coach services not in so many per week but in terms of dozens or scores per day, and when road-books began appearing in annual editions, even tourism may be said to have begun to move into its popular phase.

On the London and Birmingham run there was only one coach a week in 1740, but that figure grew to thirty at the close of the American Revolution, and thirty-four a day in 1829. Other cities saw similar growth in passenger coach services.[36]

The spread of the turnpike network, particularly in the early nineteenth century when Telford and McAdam were actually improving the surfaces, allowed speed to be increased. It took ten days to go from London to Edinburgh in the early eighteenth century, but the introduction of the "flying coach" in 1754 reduced that to four days. By the close of the coaching era that run was reduced to a mere two days of hard and continuous travel, for a daily average of around two hundred miles.[37] The decrease in elapsed time for these journeys stemmed from two changes: an actual increase in the speeds of the coaches, and the substitution of continuous running for operation only during the day as had been the case in the earlier period. Jackman figured that "travel times were only one-third to one-fifth what they had been in the 1750s" by the close of the road era in the 1830s.[38] From speeds of 4 to 6 miles per hour in the beginning coaches were increased in operation to 12 or even slightly more miles per hour at the end. The Edinburgh-London service (three nights and two days in the 1830s) showed that even 10- to 12 mile-an-hour rate could place most of England within a 24-hour range of London just before the coming of the railroad, and all of Great Britain within reach of the more determined traveler.

Similar fast services were available elsewhere. In France the system of *diligences* operating on the *routes royale* accomplished similar goals, but in Germany less rapid through routes were necessitated by the political parceling out of that cultural entity. In Flanders and Holland the greater comfort of the *trekschuiten* tended to preserve those canal passenger services right down to the coming of the railroad. It was the greater pace of industrialization and trade growth in Britain that gave the island kingdom its dominant position in this coaching era. British coach builders were the leaders in the construction of sturdy, fast, and commodious vehicles.

Spared the direct disruption of the Revolutionary period in America or France and the warfare of the Napoleonic Era on the Continent, Britain continued to expand its turnpikes, to construct ever more ingenious coaches, and to shape the business organization that pitted coach operators against each other in a rapidly expanding market. All these innovations gave Britain the dominant place in the coaching era and allowed that period to stand out in the historical geography of road transport for that kingdom. The romance of the time is preserved in prints and writing, and in the strangely anachronistic terminology of automobile morphology found in the "coach work" of the British motor industry.[39]

The Industrial Revolution, particularly with its increasing demands for the consumption of heavy tonnages of raw materials and fuels, spelled the end of this coaching era. The shift was, however, rather indirect. The need to move coal shaped the so-called Newcastle railways of the Northeast of England, and the technology there evolved came to be applied to the first truly common-carrier railroad, the Stockton and Darlington Railway, which opened in 1825.

The Stockton and Darlington was intended as a substitute for the construction of a canal to serve the Auckland coalfield of County Durham in the transport of coal to the loading port at Stockton: freight carriage was its basic purpose. But it was discovered that the steam locomotives that came to be used on the line could provide faster land transportation than even the best of coaches, so rather quickly the steam railroad was seen as a potential passenger carrier. In fact, when the next railroad to be built, that between Liverpool and Manchester, opened in 1830, the design of the line was strongly shaped by anticipation of heavy passenger revenues. Thus, although the 1830s represent the epitome of coaching in England, that decade also signaled the rise of a deadly competitor, one so powerful that within a decade a decline in turnpike usage and support was commonplace: "In 1864 the systematic reduction of the trusts was commenced in England and from one thousand to eighteen hundred miles of turnpikes were made free each year, Parliament making appropriations to help in the maintenance and authorizing local borrowings to pay off the debts of the trusts." In 1864 there were 1,048 trusts controlling 20,589 miles of turnpike: "By 1886 the number of trusts had been reduced to twenty with seven hundred miles of roads, and in 1890 seventy-seven miles were controlled by five trusts. By the end of 1896 the last turnpike had vanished from English soil."[40]

ROADS IN COLONIAL AMERICA: THE PATH

When the French and the English finally established permanent settlements in North America, in 1605 and 1607, respectively, they did so as trading colonies set up under a trans-Atlantic mercantile system. Since the ties were maintained by sailing vessels, it was logical that many small anchorages would be used to tie various plantations to

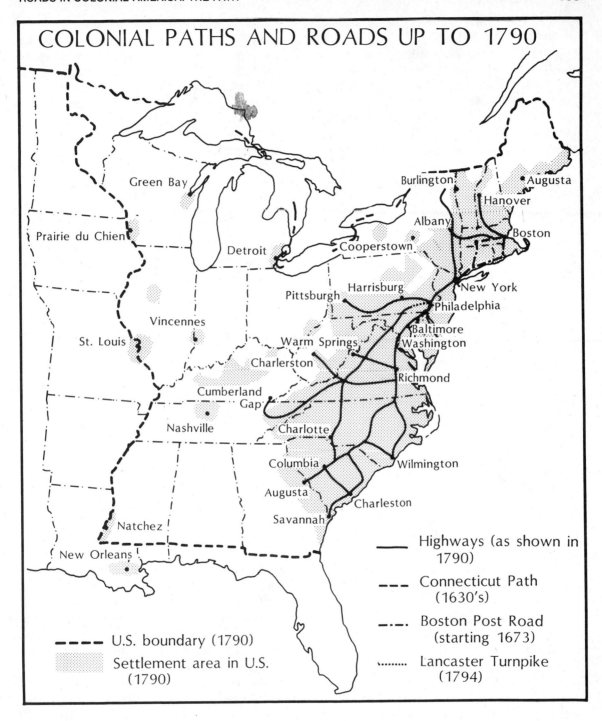

COLONIAL PATHS AND ROADS UP TO 1790

Green Bay

Prairie du Chien

Detroit

Cooperstown

Burlington

Augusta

Hanover

Albany

Boston

Pittsburgh

Harrisburg

New York

Philadelphia

Vincennes

Baltimore

St. Louis

Warm Springs

Washington

Charlerston

Richmond

Cumberland
Gap

Nashville

Charlotte

Columbia

Wilmington

Augusta

Charleston

Natchez

Savannah

New Orleans

————— Highways (as shown in
1790)

– – – Connecticut Path
(1630's)

–·–·– Boston Post Road
(starting 1673)

········· Lancaster Turnpike
(1794)

– – – U.S. boundary (1790)

Settlement area in U.S.
(1790)

the home countries. The French first settled at Port Royal on the Bay of Fundy in 1605, but the main colonizing effort came along the great estuary of the St. Lawrence when Québec City was founded three years later. There settlement came in *rangs* stretched along the river bank both below and above Québec as far as marine sediments coated the surface and boats on the river might reach the shore margin of the *arpents* (a French areal unit) of the habitants' farms. On land all that was needed were paths for animals and carts to move among adjacent farms strung along the shore. Even as late as the British-American conquest in 1763, this riverine pattern greatly dominated Canadian settlement, leaving the paths and local roads short, discontinuous, and parochial in orientation.

The English colonies were less coherent than those in French Canada. Many harbors and rivers became the site for plantations extending from the Kennebec River of Maine ultimately in the colonial period to the Altamaha River of Georgia. Ties were more with England than with neighboring colonies. Thus in gaining access to the productive interiors—where the tobacco, rice, indigo, meats, grains, minerals, and naval stores that whetted England's interest in the New World were grown, cut, or mined—the lower, navigable river courses lying below the Fall Line were used.

Before the Europeans had landed on the North American shore, the Indians had found the best way to move overland through the dense forest that clothed the St. Lawrence Valley and the Atlantic Coast was on foot. The Indian trail, in generic terms a path, averaged some 12 to 18 inches wide and was kept clear of brush by the movement of the Indians. In some places, particularly west of the Appalachian crest where buffalo were plentiful before the late eighteenth century, animal paths broke the forest fastness. In the case of the buffalo,

a veritable highway followed their tracks as their destruction of trees was in keeping with the reputation of their genus. Wagons could move along buffalo tracks, whereas east of the mountains Indian and animal trails admitted of horseback transportation at the most. Still, when the English arrived in Massachusetts and Virginia, they were quick to adopt the prior system of communication open to them. The fur traders of Plymouth and the Massachusetts Bay colonies moved over the Indian paths, as did the later traders and long hunters of the Carolinas in their approach to the mountains, where deerskins were available in a virtual blanket.

It was in New England, in the migration from Massachusetts Bay toward that soft interior area of the Connecticut Valley, that the first true road in America came into existence. In the 1630s those moving out of the original towns around Massachusetts Bay used an Indian path to reach the great valley at present-day Springfield. In doing so they fixed the alignment of the Old Connecticut Path that still wanders westward from Boston to the Connecticut, standing as America's oldest road, though in the beginning it was, as its name implies, merely a path.

Throughout the colonial period the ability to provide roads was sharply limited. The settlers brought with them the notion of the parish corvée for building and maintaining roads, and this was used to the extent any labor on such paths was consistently applied. But in a frontier society forced to clear land for farming and living in a dispersed fashion, there was little will to improve on the most basic of paths. So long as the commercially productive farms were near rivers or tidewater, as they tended to be in the plantation South, roads could be largely disregarded beyond the simple provision of riding tracks. In the North there was relatively little export agriculture, so interior settlement was predicated more on a combination of good general farming land and the ability to find naturally occurring resources—forests for lumber, naval stores, pot ashes, furs, and minerals—that might provide the staples for trans-Atlantic trade. In this potamic phase of American economic development, settlement clung to rivers. What roads there were—such as the Connecticut Path or the later Boston Post Road—were used mainly for interconnecting settlements for news, administration, and the movement of people, all of which could be accomplished using the rough paths that had been shaped from the Indian inheritance.

The first highway of any length was laid out to provide postal service to interconnect the colonies. No specific date can be given for its inception, as it shared with other colonial roads its origin as a path that only slowly evolved into a usable road for wheeled vehicles. The first definite use of the alignment came with the migration of the Oldham party to the Connecticut valley in 1633. Subsequently, small improvements in this natural alignment of the Bay Path, as it came to be known, were made to reduce the steepness of grade on intervening hills, to provide a rough bridge across an intersecting stream, or to carry a causeway across the swampy ground that tended to exist where land was flat. In fact, the original paths of New England were fine compromises in location between the steepness of the low hills that dot interior New England and the wet bottoms of the flatter areas.[41]

By the 1670s the English colonies had become continuous on the Atlantic Coast with the capture of the New Netherlands and its transformation into New York. In 1673 Francis Lovelace, governor of New York, dispatched the first post rider to operate in the colonies on a service to Boston. Although service was highly intermittent, efforts were made to improve the roads between the two northern cities. The Bay Path between Boston and Springfield

was adopted as the route of the posts, gaining thereby the name of the Boston Post Road, later the Upper Boston Post Road when another route was carried between Boston and New York via Providence and the Rhode Island colony. Throughout the early decades of the eighteenth century the Upper Boston Post Road was straightened by building causeways and bridges across swamps, cutting ramps in the sides of intervening hills that permitted crossing ridges around which movement previously had had to take place, and cutting new passages through the forest where Indian paths had not existed. By the 1750s a reasonable post road had been shaped by the incremental efforts of local corvées working over a century, although even then it was the nearly universal practice to carry mails in saddle pouches and passengers on horseback. The road between Boston and New York was, at 250 miles, perhaps the first interregional road in the British colonies, though one hardly used for freight transportation.

The father of the American road was that polymath born in Boston in 1706, Benjamin Franklin. In his early thirties Ben was appointed deputy postmaster-general for the English colonies, and in 1753 he succeeded to the full post. Franklin quickly undertook to improve the service, encourage the betterment of post roads, and even make the carrying of mail pay for itself. By 1764 he was able to inaugurate day and night postal service between Boston and New York. On this, the most important overland route in America, Jonathan and Nicholas Brown sought in 1772 to begin the first public passenger stages; but the outbreak of the Revolution forced a suspension of service, and only after the peace of 1783 did the stagecoach come into more general use. The American experience during the war, when the British navy had succeeded in blockading the coast, helped to encourage efforts at overland transport improvement. Further encouragement came from the greatly transformed pattern of trade and transportation that emerged from the Treaty of Paris in 1783. With the close of hostilities the United States became independent but was largely excluded from participation in the importing trade of Britain. In the first decades of the Republic it was crucial for Americans to shape an interstate transportation network, largely on land, in place of the trans-Atlantic system that had previously served their economic needs.

Freedom also opened the interior in a way never possible under the British administration. The hated proclamation of 1763 had decreed that the area beyond the crest of the Appalachians would forever remain a preserve of the Indians, and thereby of the fur traders who exercised such political power in London. With the proclamation swept away, the first West became the focus of a great amount of American attention and the objective of transportation projects. Before the Revolution the settlement frontier had extended only a very short distance from the coast. Two towns of some significance— Worcester in Massachusetts and Lancaster in Pennsylvania—were beyond the reach of coastal and lower riverine navigation. Each lay on one of the earlier interregional roads: Worcester on the Upper Boston Post Road and Lancaster on the eastern end of the road to the Forks of the Ohio at Pittsburgh, laid out first as Braddock's Military Road in 1755.[42] As the active area of cultivation spread inward, pressures increased to develop usable economic roads that could permit the transport of freight from points above and beyond the reach of the coastal sloop navigation that had been the prime mover of goods in the colonial period.

The interior regions not well served by navigable rivers flowing to the Atlantic lay in southwestern New Hampshire and parts of interior Massachusetts, Vermont, and Connecticut; in the Mohawk Valley; in southern and southwestern Pennsylvania and adjacent areas of Maryland; in the Shenandoah Valley of Virginia; in the trans-Appalachian settlements of Kentucky and Tennessee; and in Peidmont Carolina. It is no surprise that these were the areas where the first effective efforts at road-building in the United States took place. By the time of the Revolution, wagon roads of a sort had been pushed into all the landlocked sections where settlers had established themselves, but most of the roads were so rough, miry, and indirect as to serve only as migration routes for those seeking frontier settlement. Once located in those areas, settlers had to draw a distinction that must also be noted here between the non-economic migration route and the most definitely economic trading route. We shall see this distinction made strongly again when, in the second vignette on road transportation, we look at the creation of the trails in the western United States in the nineteenth century. The contrast became painfully evident to the interior settlers of the eighteenth century, even though they resided only a short distance beyond the limit of potamic transportation. The rough emigrants' trails, such as the Wilderness Road to Kentucky, permitted those moving to the frontier to bring with them livestock, agricultural machinery of a rudimentary sort, and a few household possessions all in the heavy wagons, such as the Conestoga from southeastern Pennsylvania, that became the "covered wagon of the emigrant trails." But most of these trails exacted too high a cost of movement, because of the necessity of very heavy teaming and passage at a crawling pace, to be used in trade connections.

Each of the interior areas of agricultural settlement had its rough, largely unmade road toward the coast and the market that existed for interior products. Most of these led to the closest navigable river whence from "Landings" boats carried the produce down toward the coastal harbors. In this way, colonial American transportation bore a striking resemblance to that in England before the turnpike era of the eighteenth century. Economic transportation had to be complex to be feasible. The natural path of the interior could be cheaply made into a barely passable way, and its rigors could be borne in economic movement as long as they were not too long and led to landings where very cheap river transportation could be employed. On a sparsely settled frontier, where for much of the distance to market there might be no settlement at all, no parish corvée could be raised to make and keep roads in repair. In that circumstance the Indian trail, the buffalo trace, and the breaks of natural grasslands all became important locating features for these minimum-cost frontier roads. But wherever such expedient routes had to be employed, they often proved the maxim that the cheapest initial solution to a transportation problem may prove extremely expensive in the long run, when all the repeating operating costs are totaled.

The truth became clear after the Revolution, when transportation internal to the United States gained in relative importance. The first self-evidently economic road was constructed to improve the access from the Valley of Virginia to its markets at the Fall Line to the east. Before independence most roads had been both tracks and laid out for migratory purposes. When Daniel Boone blazed the Wilderness Road in 1774–1775,

this was but a trace, and no vehicle of any sort passed over it until some years later, when it was converted into a wagon road. The route was, however, well located, and, recognizing the necessity for a wagon-road to Kentucky, the legislature of Virginia [of which Kentucky was then a county] in 1770 passed an act by which "commissioners were appointed to explore the country on both sides of the mountains, and trace out the most convenient site for the road, and cause it to be cleared and opened, so as to give for the present passage

for travelers and pack-horses, and report the practicability of making a wagon-road." No improvement was accomplished, however, for 12 years. In 1792, by private enterprise, money was raised and expended for the clearing and improvement of the road.[43]

This progression of facilities can serve as an example for most of the transition from noneconomic to economic roads in the period of the Revolution. First there was an Indian or animal track used by explorers. It was followed by the specific location of a continuous route by the blazing of a *trail* or *trace*, the two terms being, respectively, the more common northern and southern designations. Once these had encouraged the migration of settlers, the desire arose for a possible trade route between the *ecumene* and the emerging frontier settlements, and a call for a pack trail was made in anticipation of the subsequent provision of an actual wagon road. The construction of that wagon road posed a major constitutional problem in this period of the early Republic. The tendency of early presidents to join with the Supreme Court in a strict interpretation of the U.S. Constitution made it difficult to find the money for such construction. Since most of the states emerged from the War of Independence with empty treasuries and little credit, appeals were made to the new federal government. But the strict constructionists argued that federal money could not be used for improvements internal to a state—a view encouraged in New England, where the likelihood of any considerable grants was small. As Virginia claimed Kentucky, and North Carolina Tennessee, the securing of federal funds for construction in either area raised constitutional questions that clouded efforts until finally resolved against such appropriations in President Jackson's veto of funds for the Maysville Turnpike in 1830.[44] As we shall see presently, only in one rather particular instance were federal funds made available for building roads to the West. All other instances of trans-Appalachian roads had to be funded either by the state—as in Pennsylvania—or by private investment, as in Virginia with the modest improvements of 1792 carried out on the Wilderness Road and making it partially a toll road.

Even before the tapping of private investment came on the Wilderness Road, that source of funds was tried in securing the money to improve one of the roads across the Blue Ridge that were coming into increasing use for the transport of wheat and other agricultural products from the Valley of Virginia to tidewater at Alexandria:

> Because of the great amount of travel over the roads leading from the town of Alexandria to the northwestern parts of the state, extensive repairs have been found necessary for which the resources of the territory traversed were inadequate [to secure improvement through the use of the traditional corvée]. Hence nine commissioners were appointed [under Chapter XXX of the Virginia Acts of 1785] and instructed "to erect, or cause to be set up and erected, one or more gates or turnpikes across the roads, or any of them, leading into the town of Alexandria from Snigger's and Vesta's Gaps [in the Blue Ridge]."[45]

With this authorization and its implementation, the turnpike came to America from its earlier home in England.

THE AMERICAN TURNPIKE ERA

This American turnpike era is one of the less well known periods in the historical geography of transportation, so it requires some geographical identification. Between this first act in 1785 and the coming of the railroad in the early 1830s, turnpikes became the standard means of gaining the improvement of primitive paths to the status of wagon road in those parts of the United

States where the economy of the interior was expanding rapidly. Particularly in New England, in Pennsylvania and New Jersey, and in Maryland and Virginia, the turnpike was widely adopted as the instrument for gaining funds for road improvement in a time when state funds were inadequate and federal ones were denied on constitutional grounds. If we take the first turnpike as an example, this road to Snigger's Gap improved in 1785 remained a turnpike until May 11, 1896, when Fairfax County finally took possession of it and extinguished tolls.[46] Its life was rather longer than most, particularly those in New England where many turnpikes had ceased to support themselves even before the railroad arrived. The highly visible and distinctive Worcester Turnpike that connected that considerable interior town with its port, under a charter issued in 1806, had by 1825 sought to abandon significant parts of its route, finishing the job in 1845.[47] So we seem justified in confining our discussion to that period from 1785 to around 1830. After the latter date turnpike survivals came more from the holding of corporations to their earlier bargains than much viability in those institutions. As Wood tells us:

> Contrary to the general impression the railroads were not usually responsible for the cessation of turnpike operation. In a few cases where favorable conditions had kept old toll roads alive until the invasion of their territory by the locomotive, it was but natural that the competition should relegate the old-fashioned methods to the past; but in the majority of cases the turnpikes had given up the struggle before the appearance of the rival. It was simply a case of not enough business to make the investment pay.[48]

Perhaps the main force in bringing this turnpike era into existence was the crystallization of views on facilities and service necessary for economic transport such that the "made road" became an economic necessity. Blazing the way, clearing the trees, and making minor approaches to fords while maintaining the use of the natural surface of the ground, as had been the colonial practice, had proved adequate for the single migratory journey but inadequate for repeated trading trips. Writing in France and England had begun to popularize the idea of engineered highways, and Americans were eager to have such facilities. Two specifically geographical attributes of those made roads caught the national attention: the fact that they could moderate the steepest grades by the building of ramps on embankments and the cutting of openings below the natural crest of hills, and the fact that by making new alignments independent of the older paths they might shorten the distance between the termini of the route. In addition, the better class of made roads might also afford a much improved surface, resistent to deterioration through use or wet weather, that would permit more productive transportation in terms of fixed tractive effort. Only through access to capital and supervision absent from the traditional corvée could these advantages be anticipated.

The argument for private investment came in making these roads toll facilities to repay the investors and to sustain the maintenance necessary to keep the roads in a condition sufficient to permit cheaper transportation. Thus the tractive effort of horses could be increased sufficiently to allow the payment of tolls and still do the job more cheaply. An 1831 report by the canal commissioners of Pennsylvania recounts the assumed benefits. The greater efficiency of teams operating on a turnpike was sufficient to allow four horses that commonly drew a load of 1 ton for 12 miles on an unimproved road to pull 1.5 tons for 18 miles, for a 50 percent gain in tractive effort on both a tonnage and distance measurement. "In other words, the energy which was necessary to move one ton twelve miles on the old roads was sufficient to move the same ton twenty-seven miles on the turnpike—an increased efficiency of one hundred and twenty-five percent."[49] The argument was economically sound, but hardly operationally so. The earnings from tolls almost nowhere supplied enough money to repay the investors and maintain the road; thus maintenance tended to be delayed, and the savings through using the road were considerably reduced for the hauliers. The average toll per ton-mile seems to have been around 1.35 cents, and any attempt to increase it led to such opposition that collections might drop off sufficiently to yield a smaller total than the lower toll had done.

The made roads that encouraged the establishment of turnpike companies—commonly private in the United States in contrast to the quasi-public nature of their relatives in England—were of two basic types: those that had a considerable engineering component in the location of the road but used the local soil for a surface, and those similarly engineered but additionally surfaced with selected materials—broken rock, gravel, and sand—often introduced from outside. The contrast was clear in the minds of early-nineteenth-century observers, commonly indicated by the application of the name *natural roads* to the former and *artificial roads* to the latter. Gallatin, in his 1808 report on the status of transportation in the United States, described the natural road:

> The labor bestowed on the least expensive species consists of shortening the distance, diminishing the ascent of hills, removing rocks, levelling, raising, and giving proper shape to the bed of roads, draining them by ditches, and erecting bridges over the intervening streams. But the natural soil of the road is used, instead of covering it with a stratum of gravel or pounded stones.[50]

Either kind of made road could hope to offer much improved operating conditions in reasonably dry weather; what the artificial road accomplished was the provision of a usable surface even during wet spells and far less need to repair damage that might have been inflicted on the made surface of the natural road by those attempting to operate on it while it was wet.

In some states—Connecticut in particular but southern New England in general—the pattern of turnpikes was sufficiently comprehensive that it might be said to constitute an effective system of basic roads. In other states—New York, New Jersey, Pennsylvania, Maryland, and Virginia—turnpike companies made a major contribution to the provision of arterial roads. That contribution was especially evident where the turnpike companies created true artificial roads rather than less-enduring natural ones. In Massachusetts, where turnpikes were common, the ones with actual artificial pavements were limited in number; but the striking feature of the roads was that they were commonly new creations, even where a town might have been relieved of the responsibility for maintaining a particular stretch of preexisting highway on the same general route. The reason for the new locations of Massachusetts, and many other New England turnpikes, was that earlier roads had been Indian paths and ungraded or local roads tied together to create a makeshift regional highway. The promoters of turnpikes became obsessed with the straightness of their roads, so that in some instances their grades were actually too steep to be surmounted by ordinary teams.[51] The thinking seems to have been that making as straight a route as possible would constitute a great inducement to hauliers to use the road rather than the numerous free roads of New England. In developing this advertising point, the proprietors of the turnpikes had to abandon the circuitous older routes they might

have agreed to "improve and maintain." Not all new arrow-straight alignments were paved with broken rock and a sand-gravel surface, but many were; most had at least a gravel covering due to the near ubiquity of that material in post-glacial New England.

It is impossible here to look in detail at the thousands of miles of turnpike constructed in the area between Maine and Virginia during the American turnpike era. Three examples must serve for the group: the Newburyport Turnpike north of Boston; the Philadelphia and Lancaster Turnpike in Pennsylvania; and the road called variously the Cumberland Road, National Road, and National Turnpike in Maryland, Pennsylvania, and the states of the Old Northwest.

The Newburyport Turnpike represents the epitome of that kind of road in New England. It was authorized in 1803 to be built "as nearly in a straight line as practicable . . . in a course south twenty-four degrees west, as nearly as possible" from the top of the hill on State Street in Newburyport to the north end of the Chelsea bridge on the outskirts of Boston. Only in a short section in Lynnfield and Saugus, where this alignment passes over the low escarpment of the Boston Basin, was any deviation from the established straight line accepted. In a 1907 report of the Massachusetts Highway Commission, the turnpike alignment was criticized for its location:

> In its building no change of direction was made, either to avoid hills or to accommodate the population to the right or left of a straight line. The road from Andover Street to Newburyport is improperly laid out, the grades are excessive, the population along it is sparse, the villages on either side are provided with other roads better laid out, and there appears to be no reason why it should become a State road.[52]

This, after a hundred years of existence, attests to the appropriateness of the design

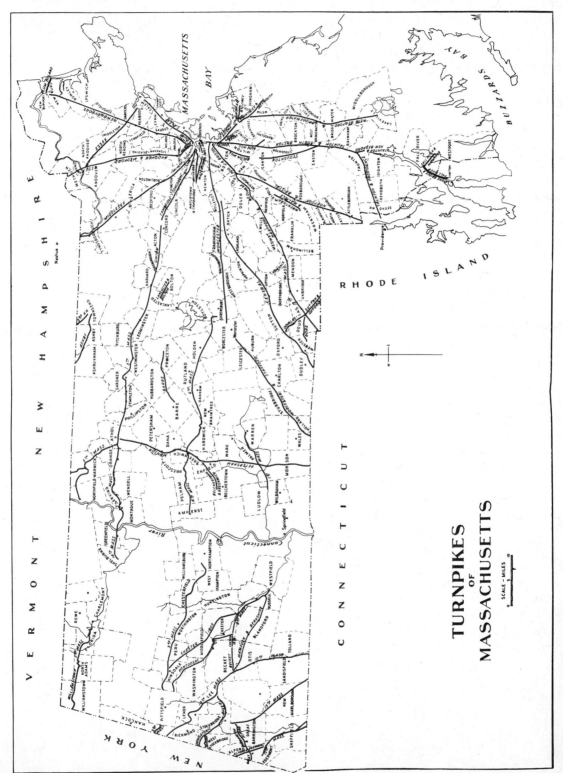

**TURNPIKES
OF
MASSACHUSETTS**

SCALE - MILES

Source: Robert J. Wood, The Turnpikes of New England (Boston: Marshall Jones, 1919).

for the basic purpose the original proprietors envisaged—to provide a true regional highway interconnecting along the most direct line between two moderately distant major terminals, in this case the state metropolis (and the third-largest city in the country) and a major colonial port (and the nation's tenth-largest city in 1790) located 35 miles to the north. Such "improper location" (in the context of the earliest automobile roads, the state's interest in 1907) came from the fact that the early automobile roads returned to the medieval road-builders' practice of laying out routes to provide the most comprehensive *coverage* rather than the most efficient long-distance *connection*. As early as 1761 a stage line was opened along this basic route between Portsmouth and Boston, but passing through the numerous ports dotting this shore between the two terminals. As one of the earliest coaching efforts the service failed after a short time, but in 1794 a successful permanent stage line was introduced. Within a decade travel between Newburyport and Boston was such that private investors organized to collect and expend some $417,000 to create a direct turnpike road between the two ports in anticipation of eventual profit from that expenditure:

> In general there must have been a great disappointment, for the heavy grades prevented the road from being much used by private travelers, most of whom preferred the old route through Rowley, Ipswich, and Salem. The stage-coach companies, however, usually shared the delusion of the preference for the straightest line, and we commonly find them adhering to the turnpikes.

From its opening at the beginning of the century, the Newburyport Turnpike earned little on its capital but remained in operation until "this turnpike received its mortal thrust from railroad competition" when the Eastern Railroad was opened from Boston to Newburyport in 1840 (running via Salem and the old coastal towns). By 1852 the Newburyport Turnpike had been freed of tolls and reverted to a slumbering existence.[53] Only when the first phase of road development for automobiles had run its course, and it was realized that there was a demand for regional movement that could be met by specifically long-distance highways, was the largely unused Newburyport Turnpike cleared of encroaching vegetation, given a sound pavement, renumbered U.S. Route 1, and made the major road connecting Down East with the rest of the United States.

The Lancaster Pike: America's First Paved Road

Although the turnpike was best developed in southern New England, its earliest application to the problem of providing economically usable roads to the interior came in the Middle Atlantic States. We have already seen the erection of toll gates on the road from the Valley of Virginia via Snigger's Gap to Alexandria that began the practice in America in 1785. Ten years later Pennsylvania adopted the practice when it sought to secure for its largest inland town, Lancaster, an improved road to the city and port of Philadelphia. As early as 1714, even before the Penn estate developed Lancaster, there had been a road from Philadelphia westward toward the Conestoga and Susquehanna valleys. That town, once established in 1730, grew rapidly and during the Revolution gained further importance as a refuge for the Patriots and their government when the British threatened Philadelphia. After peace in 1783 the general shift of interest to the interior strengthened the position of Lancaster, as demonstrated by the removal of the state capital there in 1799. With the rise of the first important commercial grain-livestock farm belt in American experience there in southeastern Pennsylvania, the need for improved road transportation was clear.

To accomplish that end it was decided that the route should be "turnpiked," as the active word then stood. The commissioners appointed in 1793 to lay out the road shared with their later New England colleagues a passion for the rule of straightness:

> Already in 1767, a survey of the old road was made and then an absolutely straight line was run from one end to the other, and studies were made as to the feasibility of constructing a new road on that direct alignment. The committee to whom this question was submitted concluded that it was not practicable to build on an absolutely straight line, on account of the steep grades which would be met on the various hills, but they recommended the location of a new road with but little variation from it.

When action was finally taken in the early 1790s, the previously agreed-on alignment was adopted. "Financing the construction of the road was the puzzle, but it was finally solved by leaving the matter to private investment by a business corporation." The stock was rapidly oversubscribed in anticipation of the favorable returns to be secured by tolls. The most striking feature of the undertaking was the proprietors' decision to "pave" the road with a broken-rock surface, the first instance of such construction in America. Thus, when the Lancaster Turnpike opened in 1794 (with final completion in 1796), it was remarked far and wide as the introductory artificial road in American experience.[54]

The pavement constructed was fairly austere by European standards—merely crushed rock with some side drainage rather than the elaborate foundations of various courses built by the Romans and later somewhat reproduced by the French Corps des Ponts et Chausées and by Thomas Telford in England. It may not be entirely coincidental that the British developer of a somewhat cheaper and more adaptable pavement, John Loudon McAdam, was serving in a Philadelphia mercantile firm during the decade of the discussion of a turnpike road to Lancaster; he returned to Britain, his fortune made, only in 1790.

The Lancaster Turnpike proved an immediate financial success to both the proprietors and the hauliers, who found it worth using the road even despite its tolls: "Robert Fulton, in a letter to [Albert] Gallatin, stated that a barrel of flour (200 pounds) on the Lancaster Turnpike, from Philadelphia to Columbia [on the Susquehanna River], 74 miles, paid $1 carriage. A broad-wheeled wagon carried 30 barrels or three tons and paid for turnpike tolls $30."[55]

The National Turnpike

The intentions that lay behind the turnpike movement reaching out from the traditional Atlantic ports that had served as the entrepôts of English colonial trade also attached to the proposals for improvements in trans-Appalachian transport. Braddock's Road, the Wilderness Road, and other traces reaching across the mountains to Kentucky, Tennessee, and Ohio—the earliest objectives for migrants—had served thier historic purposes but failed as economic routes. In the South there seemed no practical solution to the problem of improvement; there certainly was not enough potential traffic to encourage sufficient private investment beyond the very minor improvements of the sort wrought at Cumberland Gap; and the local corvée, whatever its frontier expression might have been, would have mustered too small a group to have accomplished any real improvement. Thus the southern approaches to Tennessee and Kentucky remained largely as they had first been blazed.

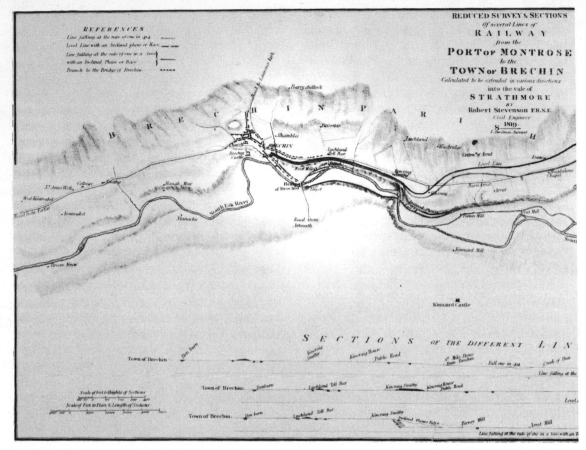

A plateway. Robert Stevenson, C. E., 1819. Author's collection.

An expedient solution was, however, possible with respect to Ohio. That territory (until 1803) had been part of the public domain yielded (by previous state claimants) to the federal government in 1783 as the Congress of the Articles of Confederation had been established. When the U.S. Constitution was adopted in 1789, it accepted a distinction that had come with this notion of a public domain—the argument went that, as directly administered by the federal government, the area was legally entitled to federal expenditure. And as the Ohio land sales had been organized, it was stipulated that 5 percent of the proceeds were reserved for road-

building, 3 percent within Ohio and 2 percent for wider uses in providing transportation developments between the East and the then Northwest Territories.[56]

With the money from the 2 percent fund of the Ohio land sales, the proponents of an improved road across the mountains finally had an ostensible source of funds. A Senate committee appointed in 1803 recommended the construction of a road "from Cumberland on the northerly bank of the Potomac, and within the State of Maryland, to the Ohio River at the most convenient place on the easterly bank of said river, opposite to Steubenville and the mouth of

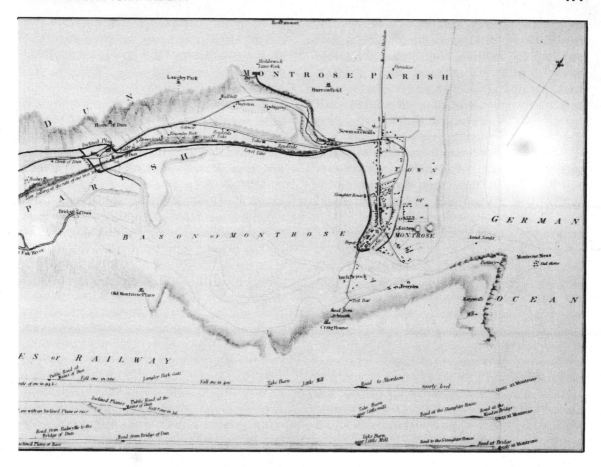

Grave Creek, which empties into said river Ohio, a little below Wheeling in Virginia.... [57] The arguments for the route were several: that it would serve both Baltimore and Washington; that it would cross the upper Monongahela near Brownsville (site of Old Redstone Fort, the traditional launching point for flatboats carrying migrants down the Ohio River system); and that from its western end several primitive roads, among them Zane's Trace, led onward into Ohio. As Pennsylvania was already undertaking the road that became the Pittsburgh Pike, and Maryland was constructing turnpikes westward from the District of Colum-

bia and Baltimore toward Cumberland, the place a national effort could best serve was seen as connecting the farthest interior reach of river navigation in the east (Cumberland) with the upper reaches of Ohio navigation in the west (Brownsville on the Monongahela and Wheeling on the main river). As a result of this report, an act of 1806 established the Cumberland Road, as it was commonly called. Eventually, when tolls were charged to provide funds for the maintenance of the road, this became the National Turnpike or National Road.

There was considerable political maneuvering about the location of the road across southwestern Pennsylvania, which need not concern us greatly here. President Jefferson showed impatience with the narrow sectional jealousies, but temporized as politicians must: "If, however, inconsiderable deflections from this [shortest] course will benefit particular places, and better accommodate travellers, these are circumstances to be taken into consideration."[58] Even so, progress was slow: construction did not begin until 1811, and Wheeling was not reached until 1818.[59] As constructed the National Road east of the Ohio was paved with crushed rock or gravel, sloped from the midline toward the edges, and drained by lateral ditches. Its right-of-way was 60 feet wide, initially rolled in the paved section to provide a firm surface. Under an act of 1822, toll houses were erected at an interval of 15 miles, and "strong iron gates hung to massive posts were established to enforce payment of toll in cases of necessity." But President Monroe vetoed the legislation on a question of jurisdiction within the organized states.[60] The legal basis for the road-building within the states seemed to remain clouded, leading to desultory results.

Still, the National Road became "one of the chief avenues to the West. . . . It enabled goods to be hauled from Baltimore to the Ohio at a considerable reduction in the cost of transportation and thus enabled that city to increase its trade in the western country, somewhat at the expense of Philadelphia. Wheeling, too, was much benefited for a time." In 1822 one of the five commission houses in Wheeling was reported to have unloaded a thousand wagons and paid $90,000 in freight charges. The line had been constructed to speed up as well as cheapen the transport across the mountains. A solid surface, low grades, and a direct route between eastern and western navigation aided that effort.[61]

With its ultimate width of 30 feet of pavement, the National Road became somewhat of a standard to attempt to match. Even in

crossing the Allegheny Mountains of the broad Appalachians, the surveyors managed to maintain a maximum grade of 554.9 feet per mile. Once at Wheeling, there was pressure to continue the road to the Mississippi, leading in 1820 to an appropriation to continue the road thence. With money limited and the country nearly as bad as in the Appalachians east of the Ohio, the National Road reached Columbus, Ohio, only in 1833. Next heading for Indianapolis on the drive for the Great River, the road crept westward, reaching the Hoosier capital and pushing onward in a semicompleted fashion into Illinois by mid-century: "Construction had always been haphazard with improved sections alternating with stretches only partially completed. Indeed it was not uncommon for the road to pass over surfaced miles and then run into a region that was not grubbed. And when the western division was new and in fairly good condition, the eastern sections were rutted and dangerous. Never at any one time was the National Road a good road all the way from Cumberland to [its final terminus] at Vandalia" in central Illinois, the territorial capital, but a terminus of exhaustion short of its objective on the left bank of the Father of Waters. "From Terre Haute . . . to Vandalia the road never was graded and in some sections not entirely clear of stumps."[63] By the time the road builders were inching across the eastern prairies, their railroad colleagues were close behind, and the heart had gone out of the effort to create a single national trunk road from the East to the Great River.

THE ROAD AT THE COMING OF THE RAILROAD

America had not gone so far toward securing a comprehensive system of roads as had western Europe before the coming of the railroad. When the railroad entered on the scene, the effect was rapid and general. As the great effort had been to shape a system of economic roads, the advance of the rails led almost immediately to the shift of long-distance travel and transport to those carriers. Roads reverted to a localized role in providing access to rails and waterways. The main exception came in the great emigrant movements that stirred America till nearly the end of the nineteenth century; these often stuck to roads because they provided the cheapest route if only out-of-pocket costs were totaled. West of the Mississippi the settlement pattern was not yet set when steam railroads reached its left bank. As much of that interior still remained in the public domain, the investment of federal funds that seemed forbidden in the states was still possible. As we shall see in the next vignette on highways, the roads remained in use as an emigrant and developmental way well through the nineteenth century. At the same time the level of improvement reached around 1830 within the more settled parts of western Europe and North America became frozen, if not actually deteriorating. The instrument of the turnpike employed to collect funds for maintenance began to decline, leaving to the parish corvée most of the small effort that was invested until late in the century, when general tax funds began to be applied.

With the exception of the emigrant and frontier wagon roads we shall examine in the second vignette, there came a hiatus in the historical geography of the road, at least in dynamic terms, between about 1830 and the end of the century or even World War I. Thus, for any discussion of the general evolution of roads, we must wait even longer, to the third vignette, when the rise of the modern automobile road will be considered.

NOTES

1. Jean Petot, *Histoire de l'Administration des Ponts et Chaussées, 1599–1815* (Paris: Librairie Marcel Riviere, 1958), pp. 44-45.

2. Ibid., p. 55.

3. Circular of May 9, 1680, quoted in Henri Cavailles, *La Route Francaise: Son Histoire, Sa Function, Étude de Geographie Humaine* (Paris: Librairie Armand Colin, 1946), p. 54.

4. Ibid., pp. 64–65.

5. Ibid., p. 66.

6. Ibid., pp. 67–68.

7. Petot, op. cit., p. 144.

8. Cavailles, op. cit., p. 72.

9. Ibid., p. 111. On the abolition of the corvée, see ibid., p. 89.

10. Ibid., pp. 111-112.

11. Pierre Fustier, *La Route: Voies, Antiques, Chemins Anciens, Chaussées Modernes* (Paris: Editions A. et J. Picard, 1968), p. 224.

12. Ibid., pp. 229-230.

13. Ibid., p. 234.

14. Ibid., pp. 235-236.

15. Georges Livet, "La Route Royale et al Civilisation Francaise de la Fin du XVe au Milieu du XVIIIe Siecle," in *Les Routes de France depuis les Origines jusqu'a nos Jours* (Paris: Association pour la Diffusion de la Pensée Française, 1959), p. 60.

16. Ibid., p. 108.

17. Ibid., p. 109.

18. Ibid., p. 119.

19. Ibid., p. 118.

20. Ibid., P. 122.

21. Ibid., p. 126.

22. R. M. C. Anderson, *The Roads of England* (London: Ernest Benn, 1932), pp. 91–92.

23. Daniel Defoe, *A Tour through the Whole Island of Great Britain [1724–1726]* (London: Everyman's Library, 1962), vol. 2, p. 119.

24. Ibid., p. 132

25. Frederic J. Wood, *The Turnpikes of New England, and the Evolution of the Same through England, Virginia, and Maryland* (Boston: Marshall Jones, 1919), pp. 4–5.

26. Defoe, op. cit., p. 119.

27. Ibid., p. 122.

28. Wood, op. cit., p. 5.

29. Ibid., pp. 5-6.

30. Ibid., p. 5.

31. Loc. cit.

32. Eric Pawson, *Transport and Economy: The Turnpike Roads of Eighteenth Century Britain* (New York: Academic Press, 1977), p. 25.

33. Op. cit., passim.

34. Ibid., pp. 31–33.

35. Laszlo Tarr, *The History of the Carriage* (New York: Arco Publishing Company, 1969), p. 256.

36. H. J. Dyos and D. H. Aldcroft, *British Transport* (Leicester: Leicester University Press, 1971), p. 74.

37. Loc. cit.

38. Pawson, op. cit., p. 287.

39. For a romantic view of the coaching era, see Anthony Burgess, *Coaching Days of England* (London: Paul Elek, 1966), which sumptuously reproduces the graphic representations of the time, as well as excerpts from authors describing the experience.

40. Wood, op. cit., p. 6.

41. James E. Vance, Jr., "The Growth of Suburbanism West of Boston: A Geographic Study of Transportation-Settlement Relationships," Ph.D. dissertation, Clark University, 1952, pp. 19–26.

42. Wood, op. cit., p. 18.

43. Caroline E. MacGill et al., *History of Transportation in the United States before 1860* (Washington, D.C.: The Carnegie Institution, 1917), pp. 8–9.

44. Carter Goodrich, *Government Promotion of American Canals and Railroads* (New York: Columbia University Press, 1960), p. 153.

45. Wood, op. cit., p. 7.

46. Ibid., p. 8.

47. Ibid., pp. 165–166.

48. Ibid., p. 35.

49. Ibid., p. 36.

50. Quoted in ibid., p. 16.

51. On the Cambridge and Concord Turnpike the road assaulted the sharp edge of the Boston Basin at Belmont straight up the face of the slope on a grade Wood figures may have reached as much as 12 percent. Ibid., p. 120.

52. Quoted in ibid., p. 124.

53. Ibid., pp. 123–127.

54. Ibid., pp. 11–12.

55. MacGill, op. cit., p. 80.

56. Ibid., p. 13.

57. Quoted in ibid., pp. 13–14.

58. Quoted in Phillip D. Jordan, *The National Road* (Indianapolis: Bobbs-Merrill, 1948), p. 80.

59. MacGill, op. cit., pp. 15–16.

60. Ibid., pp. 16–17.

61. Ibid., p. 18.

62. Jordan, op. cit., p. 87.

63. Ibid., pp. 95–96.

Coll. du P.-L.-M.   The Railway station (1860)

chapter 3

Transportation Remakes the European World

The Railroad Era

Revolutionary events often fail for some time to produce clear-cut results or obviously constructive changes. This was true of the Transportation Revolution of the sixteenth and seventeenth centuries. Canals had been built to allow large cities such as Milan to emerge; to permit the economic integration of a politically centralized nation, such as France; and to foster a vast increase in manufacturing and trade, as in England and the Low Countries, respectively. Similarly, the improvement of roads, which might have existed for millennia without providing continuous links between distant points, served to allow the expansion of the interactive system of agriculture, mining, and trading to the point an industrial revolution might be fed both at the hearth within the worker's tenement and at the hearth within the capitalist's factory.

So successful, in fact, was the Transportation Revolution in reshaping economic and social conditions that by the closing years of the eighteenth century those conditions were overtaxing the transportation that had engendered their transformation. Canals were crowded and running short of water in drier periods, roads were similarly clogged when traffic in wet periods tended to destroy the surface on which it must run, and the inexorable demand for feed to keep the necessary horses in traction was pressing both the acreage that might be used for human food and the transportation itself that must bring the fodder thence to the cities where horse traction was most densely needed.

In this situation three problems arose that were not consciously so categorized at the time, but which we may observe clearly in retrospect. The first was the simple overtaxing of existing facilities. Using our established dichotomy between facilities and technology, it is obvious that such overburdened facilities might have been relieved in two ways: by simply building more facilities of the sort that existed—doubling a canal, for example, or constructing a wider turn-pike—or by so improving the technology of transport that the same facility might carry a greater traffic without clogging up completely. Given the nature of the overburdening in various parts of western Europe, there were regional differences in the solution to this problem. The ubiquity of canals and specialization of purpose on particular lines found in the Low Countries seem to have made that area reasonably free of intolerable congestion even as late as 1815. In France the canal and road systems were so well developed and so rationally interrelated that little problem arose. Thus it was in England that the *point of stress* first became evident.

All sorts of measures convey to us the obvious basis for the overburdening of the English transportation system. Coal production rose greatly, as did the necessary transport of food to the burgeoning industrial villages and cities with their concentrations of a no longer agricultural proletariat. Iron ore must be moved to the enlarging foundries and forges. John Nef sees the basis of this classical industrial revolution of the eighteenth century two centuries before.[1]

> There are, then, grounds for speaking of an early industrial revolution in the north of Europe, and particularly in Great Britain. They do not rest on statistics of increasing output, impressive though such statistics sometimes are. They do not rest on the growth in scale of industrial enterprise, though there was a remarkable increase in the scale at this time in many industries, from mining and metallurgy to the manufacture of allum and brewing. They rest on the novel movement during the late sixteenth and early seventeenth centuries, especially in Great Britain, towards a concentration of industrial enterprise upon the production of cheap commodities in large quantities.

By the onset of the generally accepted Industrial Revolution, a change of fundamental importance to the historical geography of transportation had occurred. Accepting Nef's view that the earlier industrial revolution had come when Britain began to concentrate on "the production of cheap commodities in large quantities," we can see that two centuries later that practice would have severely taxed traditional transportation. In those two hundred years, Usher states, the population of England nearly doubled, from 4,460,000 in 1600 to 8,331,000 in 1801. In a similar period France remained remarkably stable, with 20,000,000 in 1581 and 26,000,000 in 1789.[2] In addition, there were several million Britons living in colonies when the major Industrial Revolution began in the 1760s and 1770s. Thus even with the same level of consumption that had characterized the earliest stages of industrialization, the demand for transport in the late eighteenth century would have been likely to be three times as great as it was when the Transportation Revolution of the sixteenth century took place. That increasing demand was, indeed, greatly enlarged because an increasing array of goods were being subjected to this particular expression of industrialization, traditional production but on a larger scale, that had become characteristic of England. Iron goods were coming into much more general use; bricks were becoming a rather tiresome universal in British building practice; coal was removing the most basic chill from the housing of the rich as well as the poor, or; and the vastly growing urban population.

To understand whether technology or enlarged facilities would solve this first transportation problem, we may turn again to Nef, who tells us how his earlier industrial revolution was transported. The first stress came in the transport of coals to London, particularly from the Tyneside, Wearside, and Teeside collieries in the northeast of England. Water movements were essential to this trade, with coastal sailing vessels carrying coals from the riverbank staiths adjacent to the mines to the various coal docks in London and other port cities. Even well inland, rivers were pressed into use in the coal trade. In the northeast the coal measures closest to the river bank were quickly worked out, requiring that some way of reaching farther "inland" be found. Mining practice would have automatically suggested the means to that end, the wooden trackway on which cars had been operated in mines since at least the late Middle Ages:

> Between 1597 and 1606 the first efforts were made to develop a new method of haulage. Wooden rails were fastened to the ground from collieries at Wollaton to the river Trent and from collieries at Broseley to the river Severn. These rails were apparently laid along an inclined way for a distance of some miles, so that wagons loaded with coal would, by the force of their own weight, run along them to the wharves where the river ships were loaded. Then the empty wagons were hauled back on the rails by horses to the pits.[3]

In this way we learn that the first stages of the industrial revolution had already seen the introduction of a new technology to meet the specific needs of coal transport. It is not difficult to understand why, once the overall movement of goods began to rise to the large scale that coal had first introduced to transportation, there would be efforts to apply the technology of rail-guided transportation to the general movement of goods.

Before we take up the story of the early *plateways*, as they tended to be called in England, and their transformation into the full-fledged railroad, we should return to the other two problems that faced transportation in England at the time of the eighteenth-century Industrial Revolution. The first of these has already been suggested—that the increasing number of horses needed to draw canal barges, wagons, and carts on streets

and roads, as well as carriages and coaches of various sorts, were proving both expensive to provide and support and directly competitive with human demands on British agriculture.

The search was for a form of traction economically superior to that provided by the horse, donkey, or ox. Several were already in wide use. The flow of streams had long been used to make the movement of goods and people reasonable in cost. With the wooden trackways of the sixteenth century, the same force of gravity was harnessed to land transport, though with identical problems introduced on "return journeys" where these were possible. The use of slackwater in canals had gone a long way to improve the tractive effort of the horse as a prime mover, and the pound lock had harnessed gravity (in falling water) again to move the vehicles up as well as down. Sailing on wide and gently graded rivers had proved a boon to some movements, and stood as the main interregional transportation technology in Britain and other areas where coastal shipping was used in preference to that "overland." The transportation up to the beginning of the nineteenth century had had to depend on animal muscle—people hauled canal barges nearly as much as did horses—to cover any great and continuous distances.

The solution to this problem had become evident, if not immediately possible, when in the early eighteenth century the steam engine was first successfully developed. This is not the place to discuss that development beyond a few significant events. Denis Papin and Thomas Newcomen, in experiments at the turn of the eighteenth century, succeeded in using the weight of the atmosphere and the expansive power of steam to create vertical motion in a piston, thus making possible the use of steam power. Still, the so-called fire engines built on this principle were mechanically very inefficient, heavy in relation to their power, and impractical for other than stationary prime movers. Only in 1769, when Nicholas Cugnot sought to devise a steam tractor to draw cannon for the French army, was any success obtained in building a steam engine small and light enough to move on wheels it could power. Subsequent developments turned toward steam road carriages, several of which were in use by the early nineteenth century on England's better turnpikes. These, however, had little influence on the transport of freight, our main concern here.

It was in England and Wales, on the plateways built to carry coal from pitheads to staiths, that the application of steam to heavy traction first was attempted. "Heat-economy and thermal efficiency were of the highest importance for the future development of the steam-engine. Full exploitation required the introduction of high-pressure steam."[4] Early work by Oliver Evans in the United States and Richard Trevithick in Wales increased the pressure from 1 atmosphere, as used by Papin and Newcomen, to some 3.5 atmospheres in Evans's and Trevithick's 1810 engines. Less and less coal had to be used to accomplish the same job, so obviously the thermal efficiency of the engine was increasing. Newcomen's 1718 engine was only 0.5 percent efficient, Watt's 1775 engine 2.7 percent efficient, and his 1792 engine 4.5 percent. The famous Corliss compound engine of the 1870s was 17.2 percent efficient, and the triple-expansion engine of 1906 reached to 23.0 percent thermal efficiency.[5]

Increasing thermal efficiency meant a reduction in the consumption of coal per unit of work, further reducing the cost of mechanical traction. In addition, the increased efficiency meant that smaller power plants could be built to gain the same ends, making the inclusion of such an engine in progressively smaller vehicles possible. The first low-pressure, thermally inefficient en-

gines could only be borne by boats, a fact that helps to explain why the steamship is older in general use than the steam locomotive. Only with the higher-pressure, higher-efficiency engines that Oliver Evans in Wilmington and Philadelphia and Richard Trevithick in Wales began to build at the turn of the nineteenth century was a steam locomotive on the existing plateways a possibility, one accomplished by Trevithick in South Wales in 1804. There, on the Pennydarren tramway, connecting the iron works to the Glamorgan Canal 9.75 miles away, Trevithick ran a 5-ton engine that he noted "was the first and only self-moving machine that ever was made to travel on a road with 25 tons at four miles per hour, and completely manageable by only one man."[6] As developed and improved by George Stephenson and other engineers during the next twenty-five years, the steam locomotive became the way mechanical traction might be introduced to the transportation problem, gaining thereby rapidly increasing flows without further taxing either animal muscle or the limited supply of arable land in Britain.

THE ORIGIN OF RAILROADS AND THE PLATEWAYS

The problems with existing transportation that became evident toward the end of the eighteenth century—its overburdening, its need for a mechanical supplement to animal muscle for traction, and the disruption of easy flow of trade due to the relatively low ubiquity of then employed media of transport—all may be seen to lead fairly directly (in the minds of those of us who have grown up with the steam railroad) to the creation of such a set of facilities as railroads and to the technology of the trains that came to run on them. In 1800, however, that inexorable direction of advance was far from certain.

Instead it seemed that steam vehicles on roads held as much or more hope, and the canal was matchless in the cheapness of its transportation. As yet the industrialized areas were both small and essentially conterminous with the areas possessed of these navigations. In this way it might seem that canals were characterized with all the ubiquity they needed to support *the* industrial structure. The truth was emerging, however, that there were areas even of England that were beyond the economic reach of waterways, whereas in the United States early experiences with artificial cuts suggested they were too costly to build to meet most transportation needs.

In this situation two problems existed that seemed to require something other than the highest technology then existing: first, those areas where water was becoming increasingly scarce while demands for transportation continued to grow (let us call this the basic *British problem)*, and second, those areas where potential trade or the reasonable availability of private capital for construction were too low to permit the high-cost construction that canals implied (let's call this the basic *American problem)*. Obviously the geographical division was not quite as neat as that dichotomy would suggest, but the distinction is useful in structuring the explanation of the virtually contemporaneous adoption of railroad transportation in two very different areas (from an economic geographic viewpoint). Here we shall first be concerned with the British problem and its characteristics and then with the American, and its quite distinct technical solution.

The Earliest Plateways

Knowing that the railroad was the outcome of this dichotomous search for improved transportation, we can be thrifty in our historical-geographic investigation, although we still must explain why that technology, rather than road transport, succeeded the canal. We must turn back to earlier times to see why rails were first adopted in the movement of goods. We know that in classical times there was a technology that fulfilled one of the aims accomplished by the railroad—the physical guidance of the vehicle. In Greece in particular, though Malta and other areas had some examples, there were routes and facilities that depended on ruts incised into the rock surface both to provide the running way and to control the direction of movement. We know little about these rutways, and some authorities consider them no more than the grooves worn naturally by rigid-tired wheels passing constantly in the same course across fairly friable rock. Certainly such ruts, incised deeply enough to hide a dachshund, are to be found near Ft. Laramie, Wyoming, where the Oregon Trail passed through a narrow defile during the seventy-five years of its frequent use. If such a short period could produce ruts 8 inches deep, the longer traffic of classical antiquity could be expected to show similar evidence in the landscape. What makes us believe that there was more than this wearing down through usage are the known existence of ruts deliberately cut in the *Diolkos,* the ship portage constructed across the Isthmus of Corinth in ancient times, and the elaborate pattern of such rutways to be found in Malta, neither of which seems to have been accidental in origin.[7] But there was no continuity to this technology, which seems, if ever formally adopted, to have been abandoned with the ending of the Roman Empire.

Only with the upsurge of mining in the Middle Ages do we begin to find illustrations suggesting that some sort of wooden railway came into existence to support the wheels of mine carts across rough ground within or outside the mines. The actual invention of such a surface-and-guidance system is lost in the earlier years of medieval mining.

Though the railway may perhaps have been born just before the great slump of the fourteenth century, it was not until the early sixteenth, with the peak of mining activity, that it came into its own. From the seventeenth century onwards the European railway showed little technical development, although it was widespread geographically from Brittany and England in the west to Russian Central Asia in the east.[8]

The occurrence of such wooden railways in virtually all mining areas of Europe meant that in the transport of minerals, and any equally heavy product, there was experience suggesting the facilities best proved adequate to the task. It is hardly necessary to say more when we recognize that it was in the transport of coal that railways outside the mine began to take on a very substantial fabric and a reasonably extended form. Earlier mineral productions—gold, silver, copper, iron ore, lead, and the like—all depended on a great reduction in the volume of mineral that must be handled (through the interjection of a smelting process commonly carried on near the mine entrance). Thus the underground railway length was likely to dominate over that in the open air leading to the smelter or the other concentrating facilities that provided "shipping ore." Only in coal was the mineral product little reduced in volume until it was used by the ultimate consumer. Thus it was in coal transportation that for the first time a heavy, bulky, and undiminished mineral flow must be accommodated over some distance.

In England, coal mining first took on a large scale in production and distant sale. The rise of London in Tudor times created a relatively vast market located at some remove from the mineheads. England was lucky enough to have a potential coal-mining area geographically suited to that supply. In County Durham and adjacent areas of Northumberland, a low plateau reached from the Pennines to the east coast. Underlain by fairly gently dipping coal measures, that raised area was cut into by a number of streams flowing to the North Sea over a short course. At first the coal could be produced by adit mines cut directly into the steep banks of the rivers Tyne, Wear, Wansbeck, and Blyth, from which the wooden wagonways used in the mines could be extended in the open air to connect to a staith above the river, where the coal could be dropped by gravity into small coastal sailing vessels that could take it directly to the docks in London. In this way *Newcastle*, as the area came to be known collectively from its largest town, entered our language as the self-evident source of "sea coal," which moved to the metropolis in such astounding volumes during the late sixteenth and seventeenth centuries. Those volumes, however, soon exhausted the potential extractable coal of the riverside mines (when adits dipped sufficiently to encounter water that at that time could not effectively be pumped out of the workings). Only in the early decades of the eighteenth century, with Newcomen's fire engine that was capable of more effective pumping, were deeper mine workings a possibility. Before that advent the coal mining in the Northeast had had to be carried farther away from the streams to places where additional shallow workings could be found. To bring those new mines into economic operation, the formerly short open-air wagonways had to be increased in length continuing the lading of coastal schooners at the established staiths located on the Tyne and its neighbors.

The Newcastle Railway

Even before 1700 there were a number of Newcastle railways in the Northeast. These differed one from another in the several hundred miles that were built, but their characteristics were generally established.

First, a route was sought between the mine-head and the staith that would have the most favorable characteristics for gravity working. This meant wherever possible the line should descend continuously from the tipple to the riverside dock. Where intervening valleys might be encountered, embankments (a *battery*, in local parlance) were carried across to maintain the level of the line. In extreme cases—as at Causey Burn, where an arch still stands—masonry bridges were used on a scale unknown since Roman times. Low hills were cut into, again to maintain a constantly falling line. In some instances, where hills had to be surmounted, graded ramps were employed to reduce the extremities of slope while teams were doubled in marrowing to haul the load over the barrier. It was accepted that wagonways would be somewhat circuitous in routing to gain the overriding objective of the downhill or level line that would place the minimum possible demand on traction.[9]

The graded alignment was commonly up to 20 feet wide at the top when a double wagonway was to be laid upon it. The line itself comprised two parallel timbers—often called *plates*, as in present-day wooden house construction—run some 3.5 to 4.5 feet apart. To keep this gauge, cross timbers—sleepers in British parlance to this day—2 to 3 feet apart, were attached to the rails and partially or completely buried in the earth or gravel of the substructure. It was common for these cross-ties to be completely buried so the hooves of the horses drawing the wagons would not cut up and destroy those timbers. Where they were completely buried it was necessary that the longitudinal plates be doubled, one placed on the other, in order that a guideway above the surface would be secured. The plates ranged between 6 and 7 inches in breadth, so running wheels on their surface required some contrivance to guide the wheel along the track. Two possibilities were opened. Either the plate might

have a raised section that would keep the wheel on its surface in the same way that loading ramps on car-hauling trucks keep automobile tires on their narrow width. Or the wheels themselves might have a flange, which would run somewhat below and beside the plate, as modern railroad wheels do. Both techniques were employed, but the flanged wheel soon demonstrated a great advantage over the flanged plate. As horses plodded between the plates on an earth or gravel path, they tended to throw that gravel onto the plates. With a flanged counter attached to the plate, gravel tended to collect on the flat surface, adding resistance to the rolling of the wheel or even, in severe cases, causing the wheel to rise, possibly overtopping the counter and dropping to the earth to the side in a derailment. Because the flanged wheel proved so superior in operating characteristics, it was generally adopted by the turn of the nineteenth century, the time with which we are most concerned.[10]

The wagonway of Newcastle was adopted in other areas as its efficacy in the handling of heavy goods was accepted. Lewis shows that the Newcastle wagonway was normally adopted for lines in Yorkshire, Cumberland, Northern Ireland, and Scotland, as well as increasingly in continental Europe, where such lines had become an adjunct of mining operation in the Vosges, the Hartz, the Carpathians, and in Styria.

In England a slightly variant system arose in Shropshire along the upper Severn, where coal and ironstone were produced in increasing quantities during the eighteenth century. These Salopian lines were commonly called *rail-roads* or *rail-ways*. Evidently, *rail-roads* was somewhat more widely used at first, perhaps explaining why Americans adopted it as the generic term for the resultant steam lines. The English, after accepting both as names for the railed lines, by the mid-nineteenth century had settled on the latter. To my mind this decision only im-

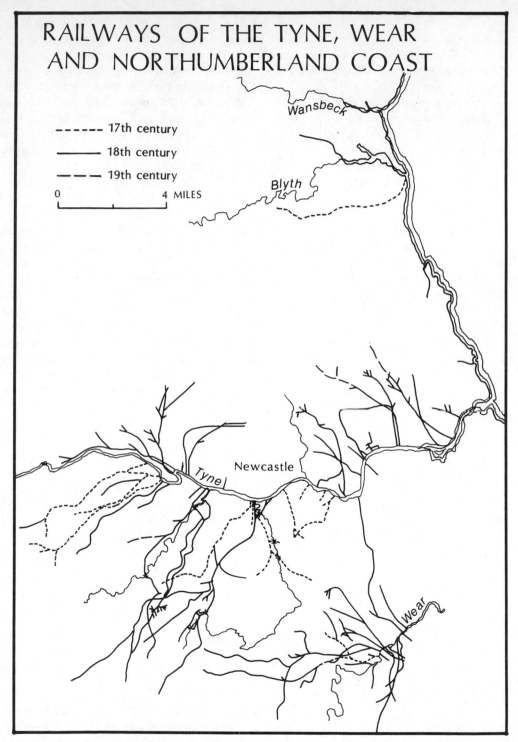

RAILWAYS OF THE TYNE, WEAR AND NORTHUMBERLAND COAST

Wansbeck

Blyth

17th century
18th century
19th century

0   4 MILES

Tyne   Newcastle

Wear

Source: M. J. T. Lewis, *Early Wooden Railways* (London: Routledge and Kegan Paul, 1970).

poverished the mother tongue. Americans can distinguish between a standard heavily built line—a *railroad*—and a light, commonly specialized line of limited extent—a *railway*, such as exists in mining, agricultural, and manufacturing operation and in street running in cities. The English lack this useful differentiation, which will always be used in this book.

The Shropshire lines were narrower in gauge, 2 to 3 feet whereas the Newcastle lines averaged around 4 feet 3 inches, and saw the wheels normally placed under rather than outside the wagon box. Because these lines were widely used in the iron-producing area around Broseley and Coalbrookdale at the gorge of the Severn, they were also the first to experience the cladding of plates by iron straps, or the full replacement of wood by iron for the running rails. Although the Newcastle lines were the most numerous, there seems to have been a stronger innovative history on the lines of the Shropshire model. The first *English railways*, as they came to be known on the Continent when introduced there in subsequent years, were around Broseley, Willey, and Benthall along the Severn Gorge starting in 1605.[11] It was in this same area that the first cast-iron strap to place on the top of the wooden plates (to guard them against excessive wear) was made at Coalbrookdale foundary in 1767, with application to local railways assumed to have been immediate.[12] Finally, it was on the Shropshire-type lines, which were also employed in North and South Wales and in Lancashire, that the first successful efforts were made to use all-iron rail, commonly called *edge rail* because its wider dimension was now vertical to the cross-ties that supported it. There are differences of view as to where the first cast-iron edge rail was founded, though again it was probably Coalbrookdale. It has long been thought that William Jessop was the first to use all-iron rail on the Loughborough railway in Leices-

tershire in 1789.[13] More recent investigation holds that the Darbys at Coalbrookdale probably first thought up the idea and that similar rails were laid as early as 1791 on the line between the Dowlais Iron-works and the Glamorgan Canal. Jessop's rails were actually ordered in 1792 and not laid until 1793–1794.[14] The first all-iron rails on the Newcastle lines date from 1797.

With the development of the primitive lines of wagonways, railways, and other specialized facilities, mainly for carrying coal, the early problems of transportation seemed to be soluble. Where canals proved inadequate, or where they could not be constructed for physical or economic reasons, the railway might be substituted. For these reasons a network of railway lines operated largely by gravity was constructed on the coast of the Northeast of England between the river Wansbeck in Northumberland and the river Wear in Durham. Most of these lines existed to carry export sea coal to staiths, from which it might be carried coastwise to London and even to more distant ports. A second cluster of lines focused on the middle course of the river Severn in southern Shropshire, where the carriage was more internalized, with a considerable transport of ironstone as well as coal to the iron foundries that were springing up in that region.

The next large concentration of lines came in South Wales where each of these previous purposes was fostered by railway lines. In some of the vales the railways descended to docks on the Bristol Channel for export of coal to England and even to America. In other valleys coal was the backstay of an emerging iron industry with the railways leading to canals or directly to iron works. In these areas, as well as the minor systems constructed in the West Riding of Yorkshire, southern Lancashire, Cumberland, and the industrial sections of Scotland and Ulster, the railways were privately financed and constructed for quite localized needs, often those of a single owner whose mines might supply the entire trade. Where the canals of the time were true common carriers serving an increasingly wide public, the earliest railways were for the most part private haulers and not articulated one with another, as the canals were by about 1800.

THE APPLICATION OF POWER

From these unpropitious beginnings, the second stage of a Transportation Revolution began. Up to 1800, answers to the other two problems facing industrial transportation—the absence of mechanical power to supplement costly animal muscle and the failure to gain any considerable level of ubiquity—were not sought by the railways. But in the next generation the first of those problems was attacked, and the second was at last being appreciated. Turning to the effort to bring mechanical power to the railway, we follow on the earlier and generally unsatisfactory efforts to bring such power to road transportation. William Murdock at the Soho Works in Birmingham and others had experimented with road steamers, with little success. Steam engines had been used to propel boats by the 1790s, and by the first decade of the nineteenth century they had come into wide-scale use on American rivers. As we have seen, it was the inefficiency of the engines that limited their employment in road vehicles; the pavements or untreated road surfaces were inadequate to bear the weight of the cumbersome engines then available. It is not surprising that thought turned to using the railways, which could generally bear heavier loads. This association was particularly probable because the early stationary steam engines, from which locomotives evolved, were developed mainly for pumping out water-drenched mines. Thus the mechanics—the *wrights* who laid out and operated the gravity

railways—were likely to have had experience with steam engines used either to pump water from the mines or to operate winding engines that ran the elevators used to reach the deeper galleries of those mines.

It was in such a geographical and historical context that Richard Trevithick first succeeded in running a steam locomotive on the rails of the Penydarren Tramroad (railway) in South Wales in 1804. Two years earlier the Cornish engineer had built an experimental pumping engine at Coalbrookdale with the then unusual pressure of 145 pounds per square inch. The reduction in the size of the engine possible when operated at this high pressure amazed those associated with this early center of iron working and railway construction.[15] Subsequently Trevithick was asked by the proprietor of the Penydarren Tramroad, his patron Samuel Homfray who sought to win a bet with Anthony Hill, to try to build a locomotive capable of drawing a 10-ton load along that 9.5-mile cast-iron-plate tramway from Penydarren mine to Abercynon Wharf. On February 25, 1804, Trevithick's engine succeeded for the first time in tying the steam locomotive to the iron railway. Unfortunately, the Penydarren line had such light iron rails that even a high-pressure engine weighed too much for use thereon. The evolution of gravity railway technology into that of a true steam railroad had to wait for nearly another generation.

There were more successful experiments toward running steam locomotives on the railways around Newcastle before that generation passed. The effort was called forth by the ever-present desire to reduce the cost of transportation in a movement that was rapidly increasing both in volume and in the median distances over which the coal must be carried to reach the staiths.

Messrs Wood and Taylor, two of the most experienced and competent men in the Northern coal-trade, calculated that previous to the introduction of tramroads [wagonways] the old pack-horse conveyed three cwt. [336 pounds] at three miles per hour, and travelled on an average about eight miles with his load. The cost of this mode of conveyance was about 1 1/2d. per cwt. per mile, or about 2s. 6d. per ton mile, so that if the coals had to be carried a distance of six miles, there would be a tax of 15s. per ton for carriage alone. This heavy cost was reduced to 8 1/2d. per ton per mile by the introduction of macadamised roads, which increased the horse-load from three to eighteen cwt. [2,016 pounds]; and on the early wooden tramroads the cost of haulage was still further reduced to 3 3/4d. per ton mile—the horse-load . . . averaging about two tons. But careful and accurate calculations made by the same gentlemen from unquestionable data show that the immediate cost of actual haulage on private railways, exclusive of interest on capital and wagons, in cases where horses, inclines, and fixed engines are intermixed as circumstances require, is no more than .07d. per ton per mile.[16]

In this way we find that the first efforts at mechanical traction came on the banks where the Newcastle railways were forced to climb over a slope that would require marrowing and thus might benefit from the substitution of fixed engines operating winding drums for the cables that were used to raise or lower cars over the bank. In such an arrangement the poor weight-to-power ratio of the Newcomen and early Watt engines could be disregarded as long as local coal provided a cheap fuel for those winding engines.

The use of bank (winding) engines was not solely the result of the poor efficiency of those early steam engines; it resulted as well from the belief that an iron-wheeled locomotive could not draw itself and its train on a smooth iron edge rail save on absolutely level track, and even then it was anticipated that some tractive effort would be lost through slippage. The result was that the

first proposals for working locomotives, as opposed to those developed by Trevithick's *Catch Me Who Can* run as an exhibition near Gower Street in London in 1808, and John Stevens' small-model exhibition in Hoboken in 1820, called for some means for the locomotive to apply its power mechanically to the track. This was done by the use of a geared wheel whose teeth meshed into a rack run alongside the rail. Such a locomotive was constructed and operated by Blenkinsop at the Middleton Colliery near Leeds in Yorkshire in 1812, with another employed at the Cox Ledge Colliery Railway in 1813.[17] These are the earliest successful applications on a sustained basis of steam traction propelling itself along an iron track.

Ultimate resolution of this adhesion question came soon thereafter on the Wylam Colliery tramroad, beside which George Stephenson was born in 1781. In 1808 Christopher Blackett, the new owner of the colliery, had the wooden plates removed to be replaced by cast-iron edge rails. It was discovered that the substitution allowed one horse and driver to draw not one chaldron car, of 53 cwt. or three short tons,[18] but two. Encouraged, Blackett then ordered a Trevithick locomotive, the engine for which was built locally at Gateshead and brought to Wylam and mounted on a frame of wood constructed there. Fired up in 1812 Jonathan Foster told Smiles, "She flew all to pieces, and it was the biggest wonder in the world that we were not all blewn to pieces."[19] Still Blackett persevered, trying an engine of his own construction, *Black Billy*, on his tramway, but to little effect as it moved little more than 1 mile an hour with rack and pinion action at work along his cast-iron track. In 1813, however, he joined with his overseer Hedley to patent a new frame on which to mount an engine:

One of the first experiments which he made with this frame was, to test the adhesion of the smooth wheels of a carriage, properly weighted, upon the smooth rails of the road. Six men were placed upon the frame, which was fitted up with windlasses attached by gearing to several wheels. When the men were set to work the windlasses, Mr. Blackett found that the adhesion of the wheels on the smooth rails was sufficient to enable them to propel the machine without slipping. Having then found the proportion which the power bore to the weight, he demonstrated, by successive experiments, that the weight of the engine would of itself produce sufficient adhesion to enable it to drag after it, on a smooth tram-road, the requisite number of wagons in all kinds of weather. Thus was the fallacy which had heretofore prevailed on this subject completely dissipated, and it was satisfactorily proved that rack-rails, toothed wheels, endless chains, and [mechanical] legs, were alike unnecessary for the efficient traction of loaded wagons upon a moderately level road.[20]

As we shall see, that last modifying adjective was taken most seriously by George Stephenson when he began to build railroads far beyond Wylam and Limington, the termini of the tramroad where he received his first impressions of what a railroad should be.

THE RISE OF THE NEWCASTLE RAILWAY

The great interest in mechanical traction for these Newcastle tramways arose during the Napoleonic Wars, when the cost of feed for horses was increased enormously. Charles Brandling, proprietor of the Middleton Colliery outside Leeds, was perhaps the first to take effective action when he authorized his agent—John Blenkinsop, whom we have already met—to construct a locomotive for drawing cars from mine tip to market in Leeds. In fact, two were built—*Prince Regent* and *Salamanca*, each with a great gear wheel at the side to engage the rack built exterior to one of the rails. Beginning regular service on

August 12, 1812, they seem to have run successfully, the first locomotives ever to do so in regular service. Several more were built and one was loaned to the Kenton and Coxlodge tramway, only 3 miles from where George Stephenson was then living as engine-wright at West Moor near Killingworth. There can be no doubt that the colliery's engine-wright would have observed its trial and have thought even more earnestly about the steam locomotive as a traction source for his tramway.

L. T. C. Rolt in his biography of Stephenson makes the point that the development of a successful steam locomotive depended on the realization that heavy enough engines could draw loads simply by adhesion even on smooth tracks and that a sufficiency of steam to gain power was largely a function of a strong enough draft in the chimney of a locomotive.[21] That draft might be secured through discharging the spent steam up that chimney. Christopher Blackett had clearly demonstrated the adhesion of iron to iron on the Wylam tramway that ran in front of Stephenson's birthplace, which he continued to visit. The success of that experiment led to the building of the four-wheeled locomotive *Wylam Dilly*, whose flangeless wheels ran on the L-shaped cast-iron plates of the tramway with no further assistance. The steam was evacuated up the chimney. This locomotive can be considered the first to possess the qualities necessary to the building of a successful steam locomotive. Its failing was that of any pioneer, in the likely mismatch of technology and facilities. The Wylam Tramway was too light of construction for so heavy an engine, requiring the rebuilding of the *Dilly* with eight wheels to spread the load, and it seems that four-wheel trucks (English "bogies") may have been first used successfully here.[22]

In 1813 the colliery-owning Grand Allies, whose engine-wright at Killingworth George Stephenson was, decided to follow the lead of Charles Brandling and Christopher Blackett. One of the owners, Thomas Liddell, ordered Stephenson to construct a locomotive for Killingworth. Its first trial came on July 25, 1814; it was christened, as topically as *Salamanca* had been, *Blücher*. There has been controversy for a century and a half over whether George Stephenson should be considered "the Father of the locomotive" as Dr. Dionysius Lardner termed him in a lecture in Newcastle in 1836. Blackett's collaborator at Wylam, William Hedley, immediately took exception, arguing his own right to the name; protagonists of others, including Trevithick through his son Francis, took up their personal causes. Certainly Stephenson was not the father of the locomotive, although he probably deserves title to the paternity of railroads as they were first built as common carriers. His main contributions at Killingworth were to build a locomotive that ran on cast-iron edge rails, in distinction to Trevithick's 1804 plateways at Pennydarren (and those at Wylam) and to show that even with the thus reduced contact between tire and rail adhesion working still obtained.

GEORGE STEPHENSON

George Stephenson combined a quick ability to build and improve locomotives with the intelligence of *necessary facilities* to make those engines function economically and effectively. His technical abilities were largely derived from others, extending back as far as Oliver Evans's pioneering work on high-pressure steam engines in 1787, which Trevithick evidently took up and perfected to the point that he can justly be termed the "true father of the locomotive," but Stephenson's skill in developing geographically appropriate facilities was truly pioneering.[23]

With the success of *Blücher*, George Stephenson was invited by the Walker Iron-works in Newcastle in 1815 to become what

we would term an engineering consultant. In that role he developed improved edge rail, better chairs for attaching it to the cross-ties (sleepers), malleable iron wheels to replace those of cast iron, a steam spring, and improvements to the actual engine. Equally significantly, he was chosen to lay down "new railways at Burraton, Mount Moor, Spring Vale and Hetton, besides relaying and improving the Killingworth, Southmoor and Derwent Brook lines and 'several others'."[24] In all this he demonstrated his mastery of the complexity of railroad development—facilities as well as transportation technology. In 1821 that advocate of railroads William James wrote what became a vastly significant letter to an unrecorded colleague of Edward Pease, the Quaker woolen merchant and banker in Darlington near the landlocked Auckland coalfield. In that letter he noted, after a visit to the Newcastle railways in 1821, "The Locomotive engine of Mr. Stephenson is superior beyond all comparison to all other Engines I have ever seen . . . ."[25]

Before looking closely at the railroad that resulted from the combined efforts of Edward Pease and George Stephenson, we should consider a development that has not received much attention from transportation historians—the advent of the common carrier. The English and Welsh plateways that were built in the seventeenth and eighteenth centuries were virtually all private undertakings for very specific local movements of heavy mineral products. In essence these were adjuncts of mining and, certainly in the beginning, open-air extensions of underground railed-ways, although some came to extend 8 or 10 miles from the mine entrance to the loading staiths. The construction of a plateway or railway was begun because a mine was in existence or under development that would require this transportation; the way could be expected to fall into disuse, as some in the Northeast clearly did, when the mineable coal deposits were worked out. The employment of the cheap flat plateway, of wood alone or merely sheathed in iron, was the result of this mining activity and the possibly ephemeral nature of the line, although the more prosperous or long-lived lines came by the end of this two-century period to use cast-iron edge rails that stood as the innovation permitting more efficient working, through the reduction in wheel friction. Once the adhesion-working question was favorably resolved, practical steam locomotives became possible, making the railroad as we know it a practical possibility.

This tale of technology leaves out one consideration that always concerns us in the geographical analysis of transportation: "Was there any transfer of this specialized technology developed for a particular narrow purpose to the general needs of transportation?" The answer is to be found in two applications of the horse railway to common-carrier transportation. There had been instances, as in a rail link between the two detached parts of the Lancaster Canal fashioned in the 1790s, of plateways becoming common carriers because canals were such. Starting in 1801, with the chartering of the Surrey Iron Railway, a plateway that was to extend from Wandsworth on the Thames to Croydon, and some proposed all the way to Portsmouth, was opened in 1803. This line was the first *public* railway in the modern sense of the term, although of course it was constructed by private capital. A similarly public line was the Oystermouth Railway, opened in 1807 between Swansea and its distant outskirts on the Mumbles. It was a short step from the creation of such essentially urban lines—to bring farm produce to growing towns and carry people to the open country at the edge of the city—to the transformation of the mining tramway into a common carrier of the sort that canals had always been. The transformation was fully accomplished in the Stockton and Darlington Railway, which Edward Pease and George Stephenson completed in 1825.

THE FIRST RAILROAD: THE STOCKTON AND DARLINGTON RAILWAY

The Auckland coalfield of southern County Durham lies 25 miles from the coast and in the Weardale, well above any possible navigation. This isolation meant considerable difficulty in marketing any coal produced there. In the first campaign for canals in the 1760s, James Brindley's son-in-law, Robert Whitworth, was retained by local merchants to examine the possibility of building a canal from the coalfield to the head of easy navigation on the Tees at Stockton. In 1768 Whitworth found such a canal feasible, a view confirmed in the field by Brindley himself the next year, but at a high cost of £64,000.[26] Deterred by that sobering news, the local investors dropped the matter until 1796 and again until 1800, when further investigations were carried out, to the same effect. Only after improvements in the lower Tees, made in 1810, had strengthened the position of Stockton as a port in this potential trade was further interest expressed. By 1818 that interest had crystallized into proposals not for a canal but rather for a horse railway to run between Whitton Park Colliery and the port of Stockton. A Welsh engineer, George Overton, was retained to survey a line for such a railway. When he accepted the appointment, he "pointed out that where the gradient was with the load, as would be the case between Auckland coalfield and Stockton, the railway would show to best advantage because on the alternative, a heavily locked canal, the boats would take just as long to lock down as to lock up."[27] From his work came a proposal that became the basis for seeking parliamentary approval for the building of a railway. After losing the first battle in Westminster—perhaps as much because Overton's line ran through one of the Duke of Cleveland's fox-covers as for any rational reason—further efforts were made and an act was secured in April, 1821.

Act in hand, Edward Pease, always the main promoter of the Stockton and Darlington Railway, had an interview with George Stephenson on April 19, 1821, the day of royal assent to the enabling legislation (though Pease had been confident enough to enter serious discussions in anticipation of that success). The myth surrounding this meeting holds that Stephenson came barefoot and uninvited to beg to be made the engineer of this considerable project. In fact, though less well known throughout Britain as a railway builder than Overton, the Northumberland engine-wright was sufficiently famous in the Northeast to be known to Pease already, and hardly one to make any barefoot supplication in any event. On April 28 Pease wrote inviting Stephenson to resurvey the line:

> In making thy survey it must be borne in mind that this is for a great public way, and to remain as long as any coal in the district remains. Its construction must be solid, and as little machinery introduced as possible—in fact, we wish thee to proceed in all thy levels, estimates, and calculations, with that care and economy which would influence thee if the work was thy own; and it would be well to let comparative estimates be formed, as to the expense of a double and single railway, and whether it be needful to have it only double in some parts, and what parts; also comparative estimates as to the expense of malleable [wrought] or cast iron.[28]

In January, 1822, Stephenson presented his plans for the railroad from the Auckland coalfield to Stockton.

Work began under the general direction of George Stephenson, though he was increasingly engaged in other rail construction that took him away from Teeside for periods of time. The line he had surveyed was typical of those he employed for the remainder of his career as a civil engineer of railroads. Grades were made as gentle as the country permitted; curves were carried wide to accommodate the fixed frame without leading trucks then, and for a very long time, typical of Stephenson and other English locomotives; and grades tended to be taken in sharp banks with haulage provided by steam winding engines operating cables. The country in southern County Durham encouraged these practices, which became the mark of most of Stephenson's future lines. One significant contribution he made was in advancing the notion of the zero-sum cut-fill operation, wherein the material taken from a cut was used to the limit to fill the batteries adjacent to it. In this way a line particularly favorable to the rather weak locomotives was constructed.

Such a shifting of investment toward facilities, rather than the vehicular technology running thereon, was to be expected in this pioneering work. For two centuries advances in transportation had been mainly in facilities—the canal and its lock, the turnpike and its Telford and macadam pavements, and the plateway and its gravity working—while the first locomotives could be expected to be lacking in power. Britain also had become the great citadel of capital accumulation, so the potential for large fixed investments was greater there than anywhere else, a fact that was abundantly demonstrated by the consistent overbuilding of early railroad lines there when compared with those constructed in less capital rich areas. It should be remembered that the Stockton and Darlington received financial support not merely from the Pease family of bankers in Darlington but also from their London relations the Richardsons, who were related by marriage to the famous Gurneys of Norwich (Barclay's Bank).

From Stephenson's assistant, Nicholas Wood, we may gain some measure of how this favoring of the locomotive came to be expressed. From experiments jointly conducted with Stephenson, he concluded:[29]

> 1st, On the level or nearly level gradients, horses or locomotive engines were proposed to be used, it being laid down as a rule that, if practicable, the gradients, ascending with the load, should not be more than 1 in 100 [1 percent].
>
> 2nd, In gradients descending with the load, when more than 1 in 30 [3.3 percent], the use of self-acting planes; and
>
> 3rd, In ascending gradients with the load, where the gradients do not admit of the use of horses or locomotive engines [that is, more than 1 percent] fixed engines and ropes should be adopted.

Thus the locomotive was seen as only a mechanical horse, rather than as a totally different animal, and as one that needed ideal conditions to be employed. This view no doubt reflected the very tentative role to be played by those engines in the planning of the Stockton line. The original act creating the railroad runs to sixty-seven pages, but nowhere does it mention either locomotive traction or steam winding engines.[30] The impression given is that the Stockton and Darlington differed from earlier railways only in being, like a canal, a common rather than a private carrier. It is implied that the line would be open to all desirous users employing their own vehicles and traction by horse—the practice adopted on the opening of the railway—so the locomotive was distinctly an afterthought, introduced by Stephenson probably from his experience with private Newcastle railway lines, where the proprietors not only provided the facilities but also the wagons and traction to draw them. As construction progressed, Stephenson succeeded, through demonstration to Pease and Richardson of his engines at work

on the Killingworth Railway, in convincing the directors that such mechanical traction was both practical and economical in a time when protective tariffs were rapidly increasing the cost of fodder in Britain. With Pease's support the company made tentative commitments to steam power by ordering two locomotives to be built by the newly organized Robert Stephenson and Company of Newcastle, a firm organized by Pease, George, and his son Robert; and Michael Longridge of the Bedlington Ironworks, which was to supply the wrought-iron rails to the line. Thomas Richardson of London also became an active investor in this firm, which went on to become the leading locomotive builder in Britain for many years and which survives to the present.

The line as laid out demonstrates the ambiguous qualities of the Stockton and Darlington. Beginning at the Phoenix Pit of the Witton Park Colliery in the Auckland coalfield, the line ran under horse traction for a mile in the upper Weardale before confronting the Etherley Bank, up which the cars were drawn by a winding engine. They were let down again on the east side of Etherley ridge, on a self-acting inclined plane using gravity to work a line with a strongly unidirectional flow. Thus the Gaunless valley was reached, across which horses drew the cars to the foot of the Brusselton West Bank. A second time winding engines pulled the cars up out of the valley and then let them down again to Shildon Lane End, 5 miles from the Phoenix pit. From Shildon, for the 20-mile run to Stockton, locomotives or horses could easily be used on a line with a generally descending grade, but in no place with a slope in either direction of more than 1 percent.[31] Stephenson adopted the track gauge then in use on the Killingworth Railway, 4 feet 8 inches (for unrecorded reasons and at an undetermined time, an extra 0.5 inch was added to this standard or Stephenson gauge) and employed wrought-iron rail for 75 percent of the line, cast iron on the rest. Rails from Bedlington Ironworks furnished the wrought iron which were then seated in cast iron chairs for attachment by bolts to granite blocks, in the western part of the line, and to oak blocks sunk in the ballast, east of Shildon.

There has always been some argument why this support structure was adopted, but the answer seems fairly obvious. As originally proposed the line was to be worked by horses, and even as it was opened horses were common in traction. Experience on the Newcastle plateways had been that cross-ties must be buried for horse haulage, but this led to rapid decay of the wood. Adopting separate blocks avoided introducing the problem of poor footing for horses or any destruction of exposed ties by the cutting action of their hooves.

Perhaps by chance, the Stockton and Darlington made a fortunate division in the kind of supporting blocks used. Those west of Shildon, where horse traction or cable operation were the order, were of rigid granite, suitable for bearing the rails and not destructive of those cast-iron supports when the force of traction worked off the rails (either in horses or cables pulling the drawbar). The blocks east of Shildon, which supported wrought-iron rails, were of much more elastic wood where the extreme pounding action of steam engine pistons was applied directly to the track and would almost certainly have caused trouble with wrought-iron rails on granite blocks, probably destroying cast-iron ones. Many early lines were badly served by such rigid granite rails or cross-ties combined with cast-iron rail.

The original rails of wrought iron were of the fish-belly pattern—that is, with a deepened web in the mid-section to give greater bearing strength between the supporting blocks where the rail itself had to carry the full weight of the locomotive and cars. They weighed 28 pounds per yard, a measure

maintained to the present (though the weight has risen five- or sixfold in main-line usage). The surface of the edge rail was 2.25 inches wide, with a 0.75 inch flange. The rails were 2 inches thick where they rested at their ends on blocks and 3.25 inches in the fish-bellied mid-section.[32] Anyone with a knowledge of modern rail will wonder at such light rail, but we should remember that Stephenson estimated the weight of his initial locomotive, *Locomotion*, (preserved today at Darlington North Road Station) at 5 to 6 tons. Chaldron cars for coal carried only about 3 tons, so the weights borne by these early rails were quite modest.

On September 27, 1825, the Stockton and Darlington Railway was opened with great celebration. Clearly its promoters appreciated that their line was not just an ordinary Newcastle railway. Its length, a 25-mile main line with several, and increasing, branches; its utilization of stationary and traveling steam power; its status as a common carrier; and its firm intention to engage in passenger transportation all gave it distinction.

> The working of the line then commenced, and the results were such as to surprise even the most sanguine of its projectors. The traffic on which they had formed their estimates of profit proved to be small in comparison with the traffic which flowed in upon them that had never been taken into account. Thus, what the company principally relied upon for their profit was the carriage of coals for land sale at the stations along the line, whereas the haulage of coals to sea ports for export to the London Market, was not contemplated as possible.[33]

That because Parliament had inserted a clause in their act at the insistence of John Lambton, the member of Parliament who owned large coal properties farther to the north in Durham and who wished to preserve his own coal export against competition. Lambton's clause required that coal carried for export by sea must be transported at a charge of no more than one halfpenny per ton per mile, whereas land-sold coal could be charged at a rate of fourpence per ton.[34] This seemingly uneconomic charge proved instead to be quite practicable, so coal for sea export began to move to Stockton in such volumes that the company profited unexpectedly and the port facilities on the Tees were greatly overtaxed. The outcome was the laying out of a new port, the world's first railroad town, at Middlesbrough on vacant land some 4 miles east of Stockton. There in 1829 the Middlesbrough Owners, led by Edward Pease, bought 500 acres and commenced the creation of a seaport town. The railroad was extended thence from Stockton in 1830, bringing into being a transshipment port for coal that began to rival Newcastle, all because Lambton tried to create an impossible situation for the newly emergent common-carrier railroad. That institution quickly showed how it could refute the seemingly fixed truths of transportation.

The railroad company also was conservative in its anticipation of passenger traffic. It decided to test the potential by authorizing Stephenson to have the world's first railroad passenger car, appropriately called *Experiment*, constructed in Newcastle. Smiles notes:

> It was, however, a very modest, and indeed a somewhat uncouth machine, more resembling a caravan such as is still to be seen at a country fair, containing the "Giante and the Dwarf" and other wonders of the world, than a passenger coach of any extant form. A row of seats ran along each side of the interior, and a long deal table was fixed in the centre; the access being by means of a door at the end, in the manner of [a horse-drawn] omnibus.[35]

Even such a peculiar clapboarded shed on wheels proved popular when drawn the 12 miles between Darlington and Stockton by horse in about 2 hours. Unfortunately, *Experiment* was too heavy for one horse to draw it back uphill to Darlington, so it came to be superseded by "passenger carriages" put on by various innkeepers in Stockton and Darlington. These were thought to be an improvement on *Experiment* both by being lighter, and thus able to be drawn by a single horse, and by being more in keeping with tradition as simply several coach bodies lined up on a flatbed frame with doors opening lateral to the car. In this way the compartmented passenger carriage, which became the standard for European passengers for well over a century, was probably determined by the innate conservatism and lack of imagination among the victuallers of the Cleveland district in 1825 and 1826. Passengers proved anxious to move on the railroad and it was seen that as locomotives picked up speed, from equivalence to horse traction in 1825 to considerably faster rates of 10 to 12 miles an hour within a decade, passenger transport could become a major economic support for the fast-developing railroad.

The immediate success of the Stockton and Darlington, and the rich body of experimental data it provided, quickly encouraged others to think in terms of common-carrier, steam railroads. And George Stephenson became, whatever his paternal role with respect to the locomotive, the true father of the railroad, viewed as a facility on the ground rather than strictly the technology that operated on the rails. The working of the Stockton and Darlington produced several surprises. Perhaps the two most significant were that there was a considerable amount of general freight traffic that might be profitably developed and that the railroad offered to passenger transportation a new dimension hardly anticipated by the promoters of this line.

THE RISE OF OVERCONSTRUCTION: THE LIVERPOOL AND MANCHESTER RAILWAY

Already while George Stephenson was fully engaged in the construction of the Stockton and Darlington, a general interest in railroad development arose in Britain. William James, a wealthy Warwickshire estate agent and colliery owner, became an ardent propagandist for railroads. During 1819 and 1820 he surveyed at his own expense a line, the putative Central Junction Railway, to carry coal directly from the West Midlands to London, though nothing came of it beyond a short line from Stratford-on-Avon, the Stratford and Moreton Railway. We have seen how his enthusiasm for the working of the Killingworth Colliery railway by steam had led him to recommend George Stephenson to the promoters at Darlington. In 1822 James visited Liverpool and was struck by the resentment of the Liverpudlian merchants occasioned by the Bridgewater monopoly of freight traffic between Manchester and its port. He set about surveying a line between the two cities, partly assisted by Robert Stephenson. The experience with this attempt to lay out a line was that of the Duke of Cleveland's fox-cover become grotesque. Surveyors were shot at, dunked in bogs, stabbed with pitchforks, and otherwise discouraged from the effort to project a railroad across what is one of the most gentrified landscapes of England. Lords Sefton and Derby were particularly scandalized at the approach of change but James completed his survey on October 4, 1822.[36]

In an episode that still is argued over by George Stephenson's protagonists William James was replaced by that Geordie brakeman-become-railroad-builder on the Stockton and Darlington. Rolt believes that George's son Robert, then only a young man of twenty but still an experienced civil and mechanical engineer, was so disturbed by his father's unthinking acceptance of a post, which probably should have been James's as chief engineer of a Liverpool and Manchester railroad project that the younger Stephenson departed from the management of their locomotive works at Newcastle taking up an appointment as the leader of a British expedition to develop gold mines in Colombia.[37] The limit to George Stephenson's abilities was subsequently demonstrated when his revisions of James's survey proved highly inaccurate and led to a mortifying embarrassment when the noble opponents of the line had that self-taught engineer examined before a parliamentary committee. In that debacle the elder Stephenson developed such an aversion to formally-trained engineers, who would not have made the mistakes he had, and said as much, that from then on there existed two approaches to railroad development in Britain: (1) the increasingly conservative dependence on overconstruction and established practice exemplified by Stephenson, and (2) the more experimental, theoretical, and variable practice as exemplified by Isambard Brunel, and in a different sense, the American engineers who were setting about devising a variant form of railroad construction to that that Stephenson was institutionalizing in Britain and for her overseas clients. From this comprehensive experience the practice of railroad development came to take two major lines, what may be called British practice and American practice. By looking at the Liverpool and Manchester Railway we may see the initial and most significant example of what came to be British practice.

There were many obvious reasons for building a railroad line from the great manufacturing metropolis of Lancashire to its seaport. The monopoly of the Bridgewater interests in canal navigation was sufficient to give immediacy to any plan to introduce

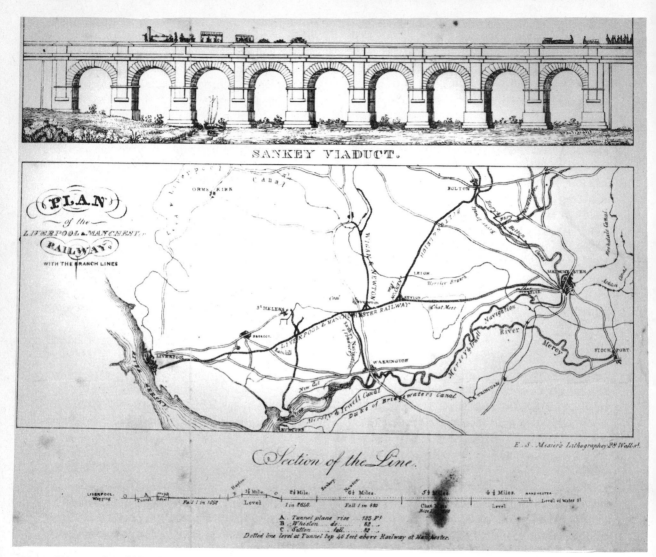

Map of Liverpool and Manchester Railway. Paterson, N.J., 1830. Author's collection.

competition. The rapid increases in the cotton textile industry in southeast Lancashire had introduced not only a greater population, requiring increasing imports of food, but also enlarged shipments of the cotton staple inland from the port of Liverpool and of finished, though often quite cheap, products outward to a worldwide market. Although there were coaches enough to carry some seven hundred people a day between the two cities, there was the confident expectation that that considerable flow could be shifted to the railroad and then possibly augmented. In a rather different sense from the situation in southern County Durham, that in southern Lancashire may be termed a specialized transportation problem or demand. Liverpool and Manchester was the closest large-city pairing in England, approached only by the somewhat unrealistic pairing of Manchester and Sheffield (40 miles) and Leeds (50 miles), where the high Pennines intervened to make intercity flow rather modest. Obviously as the Industrial Revolution had reshaped the system of cities in Britain, Manchester and Liverpool could not live without each other whereas the large towns of Yorkshire and Lancashire could exist in isolation one from the other.

As finally surveyed, in part to avoid the Sefton and Derby estates, the Liverpool and Manchester Railway was to extend 30 miles in a quite direct line between those towns. To gain such a routing only three terrain obstacles were encountered. Rising from Wapping wet-dock at Liverpool to the commencement of the railroad proper there had to be a tunnel 1.27 miles long comprised of a curved section of 270 yards basically on the level, followed by a 1,980-yard straight tunnel rising 123 feet. This was intended to be worked by cable-traction but the 2-percent grade proved well within the working ability of adhesion locomotives as time passed. But as finished this incline was operated by stationary engines. At the top of the incline a level stretch a thousand yards long reached to the top of an extremely gentle grade that began what was essentially a slightly falling line to reach the Manchester station some 46 feet lower than the upper lip of the tunnel incline at Liverpool. This first falling grade, 0.08 percent, continues "for a distance of about five miles, four feet in a mile, a descent so trifling, that it is imperceptible to the eye." To maintain this nearly level line, "The vehicles rapidly merge into a deep marl cutting, in which the surrounding country is soon lost to view.... This cutting, the largest *in stone*, on the whole line, is little short of two miles in length ... with solid rock rising almost perpendicularly on each side to a

height of seventy feet [at the deepest point]."[38] Thus the first obstacle of terrain, the low plateau rising above the Mersey at Liverpool, was crested and its eastern slope cut into a gently descending plane by a very considerable rock cutting.

In order to maintain a nearly level course, the line was then carried on a *battery*— henceforth called an *embankment*. This Broad Green

> embankment is formed of marl, moss [peaty soil], and other materials, compacted with brushwood. ... The embankment is, for some distance, elevated 45 feet above the level of the fields. Running through it are several bridges, for the passage of the field roads. The traveller is here, as it were, on a pier, running out into a sea of verdure.... [H]aving left the Broad-green battery, which is above a mile in length, he soon skims along that of Huyton.[39]

Once across this nearly level line extending some 6 miles from the upper lip of the incline at Liverpool—Edgehill, it was called— the Liverpool and Manchester Railway encountered its first bank to be climbed by locomotive working:

> The pace of the engine is now gradually reduced, by the ascent of the Whiston inclined plane, one of the greatest on the line, and which rises 82 feet in a mile and a half [just one cent in opposing grade].... Here [at the top] is placed a stationary engine, as an auxiliary to the locomotive in ascending. The Rainhill level is now traversed at a rapid rate. [After 2 miles, some in cuttings of the Sutton Excavation, an increase in] the velocity of the carriages assures the traveller that he is descending the Sutton inclined plane.[40]

This plane interposed a grade of 82 feet, similar to that at Whiston, for trains returning to Liverpool.

From the bottom of the Sutton plane the

line dropped very gently eastward at 0.03 percent over 2.5 miles to reach the Sankey valley through which flowed that brook whose improvement created, in the Sankey Navigation, the first of England's industrial-era canals. The rail line was carried across the valley

> by a battery of great height—in one part more than 70 feet above the fields—and a magnificent viaduct. The embankment is formed of marl, moss and other materials, compacted with brushwood. The Viaduct has nine arches, each fifty feet span, and varies from sixty to seventy feet in height. The St. Helen's Canal [rebuilt from the Sankey Navigation] passes under one of these noble arches; a small river under another. . . . [41]

Thence 6.5 miles the line fell eastward at 0.11 percent, passing along a number of embankments, some up to twenty feet in height, to reach the western edge of Chat Moss.

Of the three terrain obstacles—Edgehill in Liverpool, the Whiston-Sutton ridge with its 1 percent banks, and Chat Moss—it was the last that most tested George Stephenson. Four and three-quarter miles wide, this great accumulation of living peat was thought impassable. To gain a straight line—and, incidentally, to avoid the noble fox-covers that lay to the north—Stephenson was forced to attempt to cross the Moss, which was 20 to 34 feet thick with peat.

> The engineer, however, overcame every difficulty, and established upon it the incrustation of a road. The moss is higher than much of the land round it, and draining was resorted to. Where it was softest, branches, brush-wood, and hurdles (twigs and heath twisted and plaited in frames), were laid down, to form a foundation, and the whole was covered with sand and gravel two or three feet thick, as occasion required. Upon this, as it became compacted, were laid the wooden sleepers [crossties] for the rails, and

> the road over the Moss is now not inferior to that on any part of the line. [42]

East of the Moss the line was level 4.5 miles to its termination in Manchester. This easily worked line was secured by carrying the rails in a rather deep cutting as the city was approached and then on a number of arches and bridges above the river Irwell and the lower sections of the great textile town. At its termination separate freight and passenger stations were built in London Road, demonstrating the considerable expectations of the company.

BRITISH CONTRASTED WITH AMERICAN FINANCING

The purpose of this detailed look at the original fabric of the Liverpool and Manchester Railway is to bring out the very substantial construction involved during the period 1826 to 1830, clearly demonstrating that funds for that undertaking on a grand scale could be obtained. As originally proposed it was thought the project would cost around £800,000, though it actually cost half again as much, a figure that put the per mile cost at over £40,000, perhaps $200,000 a mile, which would have put a price tag of over $200 million on the Union Pacific if it had been built to the same standard. Even forty years after the Liverpool and Manchester, and the conduct of the greatest war ever fought with its inflationary effects, the construction of that frontier line cost only about a quarter that amount per mile. [43] In all it required four years and $6 million of valuable 1820s currency to construct the 30 miles of the Liverpool and Manchester, whereas it required only the same time and $54 million in much cheaper dollars to construct the thousand miles of the Union Pacific completely beyond the economic frontier of the United States.

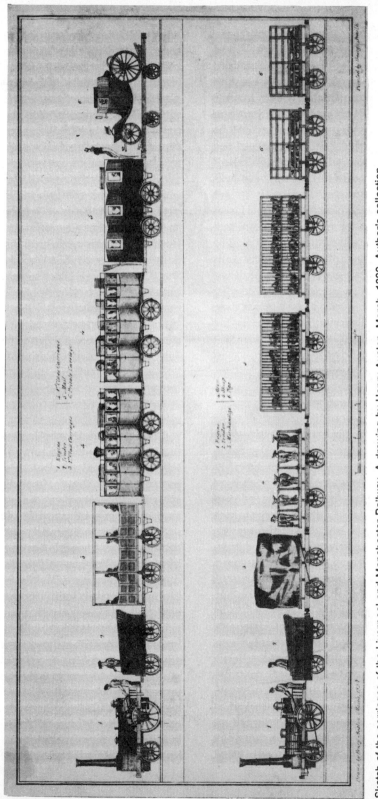

Sketch of the carriages of the Liverpool and Manchester Railway. A drawing by Henry Austen, March, 1839. Author's collection.

In this we find perhaps the most graphic evidence of the contrast between British and American practices and systems of railroad building. Stephenson and the proprietors of the Lancashire pioneer line were facing a very different frontier from the one that Grenville Dodge and his Union Pacific directors faced between 1865 and 1869. For the Lancastrians the problem and challenge was the provision of more, and with luck cheaper, transportation in an already highly developed and overtaxed movement. There were two waterways—the Mersey and Irwell Navigation and the Duke of Bridgewater's Canal—connecting the textile metropolis with its port. As Smiles notes:

> The formation of a *third* line of water conveyance . . . was also considered; but it was almost immediately dismissed as impracticable, as the two existing establishments had already possession of all the water. There was no choice left but a tram or railroad [sic], and the very necessities of the case forced on the adoption of the measure.[44]

It seems fair to say that with the undertaking of the Liverpool and Manchester it became British practice to build for an existing, demonstrated market. Thus the scale of the construction would tend to reflect directly the appraisal of the scale of that market, although clearly there would be some element of predicted incrementation as a result of new facilities. No doubt then—and it is patently the case today with very large public works—there was a tendency to increase the imputed returns in terms of the inflating costs. As originally presented in a prospectus in 1824, the Lancashire line was thought to be obtainable for £400,000. When actually begun it was priced at twice that sum, and when completed it ran at three times the first estimate of cost. Even so, when opened the Liverpool and Manchester exceeded its estimated annual earnings of £62,500 by £20,000.[45]

In this the line was typical of British railroad development: though costly to build, it was entering a market that was immediately profitable for the investors. In the case of the Union Pacific the reverse was true, which helps to explain why construction had to be so cheap. That truly pioneering line was built both temporally and geographically well beyond the market, and the company that owned it went bankrupt after trying to run it for reasonable earnings. The greatest railroad speculator of the time, Jay Gould, correctly perceived that there was little profit to be earned by these lines on the American frontier, so he bought and sold their securities, gaining and relinquishing operational control, not for the dividends they might pay. "Gould was influenced in his final decision[s] by his clear view of the possible profits from western railroads. He saw [even in the 1870s] that for the time being the only large return lay in either the manipulation of the securities or in securing a monopoly of the business of some particular territory."[46] But such regional monopolies could be made to pay only if the actual cost of the line could be reduced through bankruptcy or failure to repay money advanced by the federal or state governments.

Both the Liverpool and Manchester and the Union Pacific were constructed with money loaned by the national government, but in the first case it proved easy to repay that credit because the line had a developed market to tap immediately once it opened, whereas in the second there simply could be no sinking fund to extinguish the debt because there was hardly enough income to cover operating costs. Once the investing communities began to perceive the difference in experience, which came long before the Union Pacific in the United States, there were distinctly different levels of investment support for railroad development in the two countries. In Britain money for any likely prospect was easy to obtain; but in the United States even the more eligible lines, such as the Baltimore and Ohio of 1826, encountered great difficulty in finding even modest construction funds.

The fabric of the Liverpool and Manchester was typical of Stephenson's rapidly rigidifying notions as to what a railroad should be. His Newcastle railway gauge, then still 4 feet 8 inches, was adopted along with fish-bellied wrought-iron rails carried on blocks. There were two tracks from the beginning as well as heavy investments in buildings and loading, unloading, and freight-handling yards.

For the first time architects were employed to give to the structures the proper impression of grandeur and power. For example, the outlet for the tunnel from the Wapping dock in Liverpool was given a Moorish arch in keeping with the notion of stylishness and power exemplified by the Prince Regent's pavilion at Brighton. Again, as in the case of the provision of the actual alignment and grade of the track, money was not stinted in an undertaking that clearly displayed confidence in the ultimate profitability of operating the transportation service.

The Liverpool and Manchester was still a gamble in the sense that when its construction began it was not at all certain that it would be more than a much improved form of the horse plateway or railway. But after the Rainhill locomotive trials of 1829, which showed Stephenson's *Rocket* to be a reasonably efficient engine that was capable of hauling loaded cars up the 82 feet of the adjacent Whiston and Sutton banks through adhesion working rather than the use of winding engines, the fundamental shift in tractive power away from animal muscle was set. Because the pair of cities joined already had a considerable passenger movement by horse-drawn coaches, there was confidence that rail passenger movements could be developed. An annual total of half a million

passengers was soon reached. From the beginning the line had a beneficial effect on freight movements between the textile metropolis and its port:

> Although the bulk of heavy goods continued to go by canal, yet the opening of the railway immediately caused a large reduction in the price of coals and in the rates for the carriage of merchandise. The annual saving to the public in money, not to speak of the great saving of its equivalent—time—was about 250,000 l. a year.[17]

THE FIRST TRUNK LINES: THE LONDON AND BIRMINGHAM AND GRAND JUNCTION

The demonstrated success of the Stockton and Darlington came as the Liverpool and Manchester Railway was under construction: in the same way the next stage of railroad evolution in Britain was being shaped as the initial success of that Lancashire line was being written in its corporate ledger. There had been efforts to undertake other short lines contemporaneous with the construction on the first great Stephenson line, and the Canterbury and Whitstable in Kent was actually begun. But all of these, including the connection between the great towns of south Lancashire, were basically local facilities, even if handsomely constructed. There remained still to be accomplished any experimentation with the creation of a regional or national system of railroads. In truth, every line opened before 1837 was transitional in its geographical purposes between the long-operating plateways and what we might think of as the modern railroad. The facilities had been elaborated, the technology of traction greatly advanced, and the introduction of common-carrier service accomplished. But parochialism was still the guiding force in economic geography.

The change came with the proposals for what have ever since been known as the trunk lines, that is railroads intended to interconnect two distant and previously somewhat separated systems of towns. The proposal in the late 1820s to build a rail line from London to Birmingham was a partial evolution onward from the earliest lines. The Midland Hardware District in and around Birmingham was tied to London, as to Bristol, so it was not a totally new link that was being forged; but certainly an attempt to provide a new level of competence and speed was being envisioned. Where before the opening of rail communication the trade from the Hardware District to London was particularly in "toys"—small metal fabricates that might bear the high cost of pack or wagon transport—after 1837 the flow of goods became larger both in volume and in modular size of products. Similarly, the considerable movement of people across the belted escarpments between the metropolis and the Hardware District existed before the Stephenson line was opened, but the potential size of the movement had hardly been suspected. It was London mercantile interests that particularly saw the need for a London and Birmingham line, and as an extension of the area geographically integrated with the capital.

The situation north of the great West Midland city first captured the attention of what came to be known as the Liverpool Party, that group of merchants and investors in the great western port who had first shown interest in improved inland connections through their financial support for the Liverpool and Manchester. Its success, measured both in increased flows through the Mersey port and in handsome returns on Liverpudlian investments, was such that there was enthusiasm for further investing the burgeoning local wealth in other extensions of the effective hinterland of Liverpool. Already the Trent and Mersey Canal had

turned the trade to and from the Potteries of Staffordshire toward the northwest but Birmingham and the Black Country, though connected by the Staffordshire and Worcestershire and the Trent and Mersey cuts to Merseyside, were still effectively quite distant therefrom because of the time it took to navigate the intervening country and a shortage of lockage water that could limit transit between the two areas in certain seasons. In this economic-geographic situation the construction of the first undoubted trunk-line railroad was bruited; in recognition of that novel status, the line was called the Grand Junction Railway in the act authorizing its undertaking that received royal assent on May 6, 1833.

The Grand Junction and London and Birmingham Contrasted

A significant contrast between the London and Birmingham Railway and the Grand Junction Railway can be discerned in the matter of the level of investment per mile. To set the stage several facts should be cited. Although both lines had initially been seen as undertakings of George Stephenson, in the end neither was directly his work, though the London and Birmingham was that of his son Robert. The Grand Junction had some vague input from George in its earliest phase, but as constructed it was almost wholly the work of Joseph Locke, whose earlier apprenticeship to the Northumbrian had ended in rupture when Locke found Stephenson's alignment for the Lime Street tunnel in Liverpool so faulty that the parts would not have lined up. Thus, on the trunk line constructed without Stephenson a completely different concept of rail building was at least a possibility. The way it worked out can be simply demonstrated by comparing the per mile cost of the Liverpool and Manchester, the London and Birmingham, and the Grand Junction. Although there were contrasts in terrain that account for some of the differences, those contrasts cannot account for all the variation, and did themselves often stem from varying notions of what level of construction should be attempted. The London and Birmingham seems to have cost about £53,000 per mile, a truly immense sum in the 1830s, the Liverpool and Manchester about £35,000 per mile, and the Grand Junction between £14,000 and £15,000 per mile.[48]

It is readily apparent that Joseph Locke and the Liverpool Party that backed him in the Grand Junction had discovered that it was not totally necessary to build in the Stephenson fashion to have a satisfactory rail line. The keys to cheaper construction were several:

1. Acceptance of slopes in grade that George Stephenson had tended to argue were undesirable, if not actually impossible of operation with locomotives rather than stationary engines.
2. Acceptance of circuity in routing that the Northumbrian would rigidly have rejected as uneconomical to work, even though he had never examined the question analytically.
3. Avoidance of extremely heavy engineering and ostentatious display.
4. Experimentation with the actual fabric of the track in search of a less rigid, costly, expensive to maintain, and doctrinaire form of railed way.
5. Recognition that locomotives were likely to be improved over the years so building to cosset the weak engines of the first generation was not always the wisest course.

In the matter of the highest grades that would be accepted on a line, what we still term the *ruling grade* as it is the one that determines what the minimum of locomo-

tive power must be to transit the course, Locke and Stephenson differed most graphically, and incidentally most vocally. The difference of viewpoint emerged clearly when Locke was commissioned to survey a line to connect northward from the latitude of Liverpool and Manchester toward Scotland, to give the Grand Junction Railway a northerly connection to expand its business. His

report of 1835 . . . is the work of the newly-liberated, fresh, enthusiastic engineer, eager to develop and explain his approach and methods. It is fair to claim that no one could have done better—certainly not George Stephenson, soon to criticise Locke's boldness and to advocate a coastal line to Carlisle in this same territory [rather than Locke's bold line over Shap Fell that became the second highest summit in England, at 916 feet]; certainly not Robert Stephenson or Brunel, who, with their insistence on ruling gradients of 1 in 300 [0.33 percent], could only have engineered this route at enormous expense. The approach was uniquely Locke's, a confident conception, with its advocacy of a practicable line through wild hilly country.[49]

His line faced a 4-mile grade of 1 in 75, 1.33 percent, opposing northward movement,[50] some four times what either of the Stephensons or Brunel would have tolerated.

Locke also attacked the circuity question when he examined the several possible routes from Carlisle to Glasgow and Edinburgh:

If I were asked how far I would go round to avoid such a plane [as Beattock Summit at 1,015 feet, which was 370 feet higher than Cummock Summit on the alternative route], I should, before giving my answer, desire to know what kind of line the circuitous one was to be, whether perfectly level or otherwise, and whether the additional cost of the longer line would compensate for the practical disadvantages to be encountered on the other.

Becoming more specific, Locke propounded a differential inequality:

> A dead level on lines of abundant traffic is undoubtedly best where it can be obtained; but it ought not to be purchased when the interest on the original capital expended would exceed the cost of the increased amount of fuel necessary to surmount the incline. It is a mere matter of calculation.[51]

In accepting the Beattock Summit he laid out 10 miles at over 1-percent grade, a third of a mile at 1.44 percent, facing northbound traffic. But in doing so he avoided most of the redundant grade introduced by the existence of two summits separated by the Kilmarnock lowland on the Cummock route as later built. Also his line between Carlisle and Glasgow was 102 rather than 115 miles. So in working out actual location problems in rough country the sorts of established truths that George Stephenson tended to advance on the basis of his first two railroad projects, with their basically rather simple terrain, often lost that absolute quality. This was particularly the case when the higher line over Beattock also took the rails directly through the Clyde Valley coalfield while the other did not.

The building of the two railroads—the London and Birmingham and the Grand Junction—joining at Birmingham, provided Britain with its first trunk line. That pair serve to show not the extremes of construction practice—the cheap and the dear—but rather the range between the adequately constructed line and one that is overbuilt. The London and Birmingham and the Grand Junction were promoted at the same time so, when the royal assent was given to the two bills on May 6, 1833, construction could begin and the contrasts developed. The southern line (London and Birmingham) was to be constructed across what would seem to most persons a low rolling area, though in England it was thought quite hilly

and difficult terrain. In 112 miles between the termini of the London and Birmingham—Euston Square in the Metropolis and Moor Street in the Hardware town—any reasonably direct line must cross the low escarpments of the gently dipping strata that dropped away from the axis of the Welsh Mountains and the Pennines. London was located at the center of its own basin so the railroad had to rise for 31 miles up a gently graded slope of the Chiltern Hills to their summit at Tring. From Tring the line dropped on a fairly continuous ramp, shaped by heavy embankments and cuttings, for the 20 miles to Wolverton and the great embankment viaduct built across the river Ouse. A mile and a half long, averaging 48 feet in height, and with six elliptical arches of 60-foot span, this was the greatest battery built up to that time in Britain. Sixty miles from London the Oolite Ridge was met, through the southern edges of which the line was carried in the deep Blisworth excavation a mile and a half long, up to 55 feet deep, and out of which a million cubic yards of spoil had to be moved. The northern part of the oolitic belt again had to be pierced, though now by the Kilsby tunnel, 1.37 miles long, carried through extremely treacherous ground that made this the most costly bit of an extremely costly line, some £400,000. From Kilsby on to Birmingham the line was alternately borne on embankments and cuts to maintain gentle grades and curves with radii of a mile or more keeping the average cost per mile very high but adding no further "engineering wonders."[52]

It is noteworthy that either the Tring or Blisworth cutting represented the movement of more spoil than was required in the building of the thousand-mile Union Pacific Railroad in the 1860s. Such is the contrast between a temporally and a geographically pioneering line. With the market in hand and capital readily available for investment, Robert Stephenson was able to build the

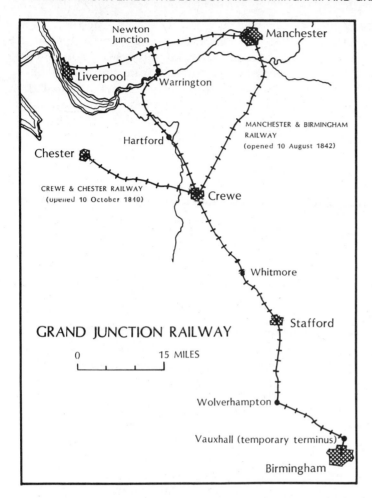

GRAND JUNCTION RAILWAY

0   15 MILES

very costly Stephenson-type line even at the dawn of railroad development, whereas in a truly geographically pioneering situation— even well after the railroad as a facility had been proven—there was not the agreed-on prospect for economic support to call forth investment sufficient in scale to allow such high-cost construction. Only as the market developed would such an investment come into existence.[53] With the creation of such a market the Union Pacific was able in 1952–1953 to spend $18 million, one-third of its original investment, on moving more rock and earth than was handled in the first construction to secure a 40-mile freight relief line over Sherman Hill in order to be able to operate with a grade of 0.81 percent (43 feet per mile) throughout its entire main line.

The London and Birmingham opened in 1838 to immediate success. Even though turnpike roads existed along its course and coaches operating thereon could maintain respectable average speeds up to 12 miles an hour, the railroad still managed to reduce the journey time to less than half, from 12.5 to 5.5 hours, over the 112 miles.[54] That running (at around 20 miles per hour) was rapidly increased, so the time advantage by rail became even greater. The coaching lines declined almost immediately, and within six years the Grand Junction Canal (connecting London and Birmingham) had lost half its trade. So long as a monopoly of rail service could be maintained, profits were handsome and self-satisfaction was great. Bury, the engine master for the London and Birmingham, early froze the design of its locomotives as four-wheelers with rigid frames when he "decided it would do henceforward to the end of time."[55] With such an extravagantly built line as the London and Birmingham, poor and weak locomotives could survive well past their time, to be replaced only when competition could prove their failings.

The Grand Junction Railway

It was the other half of the first trunk line, the Grand Junction Railway, that made such competition more likely, through its experimentation with designing and building less lavish railroads. A less costly line would mean that more problematic pairings of cities might be joined by rail and second lines be added between the most likely pairs. As constructed, the Grand Junction extended 82.75 miles to connect between the northern terminus of the London and Birmingham and Newton Junction, located halfway between Liverpool and Manchester on the railroad that had connected them since 1830. The country between the Midland Hardware District and southern Lancashire was similar to that to the south toward London, though there were fewer escarpments ranged across it. Still, the differences between the two lines were due more to the style of route location, as practiced by Robert Stephenson and Joseph Locke, than to the actual terrain. Only the crossing of the river Weaver on two sides of a loop west of Northwich in Cheshire posed any considerable engineering problem. There two high and impressive viaducts were necessary as a result of the entrenchment of the stream below the general level of the Cheshire plain. The more northerly of these viaducts, that at Dutton, became the *pièce de résistance* of the line 1,400 feet long and built of 700,000 cubic feet of stone in twenty arches of 65-foot span and a maximum height of 65 feet.[56] Although it was the most massive viaduct constructed to its time, Dutton alone could not match the array of heavy engineering its southern connection could display. From WolverHampton the Grand Junction Railway had similarities to the London and Birmingham, but always on the more modest side. A ruling gradient of 1 in 177 (0.56 percent) was accepted by the promoters and Locke, in contrast to George Stephenson's original proposal for the line of 1 in 355 (0.28 percent).[57] The 15 miles to Stafford was on a continuous downgrade dropping very gently off the Midland Plateau at between 0.21 and 0.32 percent. Continuing north for another 15 miles up an even gentler slope along the Sow tributary of the river Trent, the Grand Junction reached a local summit at Whitmore, 390 feet above sea level. From that Whitmore summit the line fell essentially continuously to Warrington, where it crossed the Mersey to enter Lancashire. This 35-mile stretch dropped the trains 331 feet, 9.5 feet per mile or 0.18 percent on average.

Within that generally very easy grade, the beginning, the Madeley Bank for 3 miles, was the steepest on the line with a gradient of 0.55 percent opposing southbound traffic. Contemporaries criticized Locke for accepting such a bank in his layout and the normally underpowered British trains have ever since encountered difficulties in drawing the southbound expresses up this bank from the stop at Crewe located just to the north. Crewe itself is perhaps the *chef d'oeuvre* of the

Grand Junction Railway. There in open fields one of the very few "railroad towns" to be created in Britain, we have already seen the first at Middlesbrough, was located. From Crewe railroad lines built in the early 1840s connected westward to Chester and Birkenhead (for Liverpool) and Bangor and Holyhead (for Dublin) and eastward to Manchester to make this the most important junction in England. Northward from the junction the main line of the Grand Junction continued across the Chester Plain, and its two great viaducts at Royal Vale and Dutton across the river Weaver. In part this line was negatively located. The citizens of the old salt towns of Sandbach, Middlewich, and Northwich that lay along the most logical route of the railroad so objected to the innovation that the alignment was carried a couple of miles farther west, and thereby to cross the eastward bend of the Weaver at Northwich.[58] For the last 10 miles to Warrington the line is rolling, even to having a short tunnel at Dutton, before crossing the Mersey to end 5 miles to the north at Newton Junction where connection was made to the Liverpool and Manchester.

From this description it is clear that Joseph Locke was willing to build an extremely well engineered line, but one conservative to the extent of not being overbuilt. The Liverpool Party that backed its building demonstrated the economic wisdom of such reasonable construction both from the handsome returns earned on their investment and from their ability to expand their system. Only a railroad investment group using Locke's reasonable standards for construction could have shaped an extensive system by 1846. The main line extended from Birmingham to Preston, with strong interests as far northward as Carlisle. Branches existed from Newton along the original Liverpool and Manchester to those two cities, from the latter to Bolton, and from Crewe to Chester (the Crewe and Chester

Railway opened in 1840) and to Manchester (the Manchester and Birmingham Railway opened in 1842). On completion of this merger in 1846, a schedule of 4 hours and 10 minutes for the 210 miles from London to Liverpool was announced—at an average of 50 miles per hour almost certainly the fastest long-distance train service available anywhere in the world at the time.[59] Thus in less than ten years the technology operating on British rails had grown rapidly, from a level permitting operation at around 20 mph to around 50 mph under the best of conditions. It is instructive to note that present-day Amtrak service from Chicago to Oakland (the *California Zephyr*) averages just over 52 mph for the 2,427 miles between those two cities, whereas the *Empire Builder* (Chicago to Seattle) averages just under 52 mph, and the *Lakeshore* (Chicago to Boston) 58 mph.[60]

THE CREATION OF THE BRITISH SYSTEM

With the completion of the Grand Junction and the London and Birmingham, railroading in Britain had taken on a completely different character from that it had possessed only eight years earlier at the opening of the Liverpool and Manchester. No longer were local potentials the overriding controls; a large part of the flow of passengers and goods between Newton Junction and Birmingham (the Grand Junction) was clearly unrelated to Birmingham; it was merely passing through the Hardware District on the way to the national metropolis in London. The emerging system of railroads was demonstrating that the whole was greater than the sum of the parts: the total potential for movement was unappreicated because the resistance to travel over long distances by previous means was such that there was little indication of how readily people, and the goods they handled, would undertake new and longer journeys under improved technological and economic conditions.

Making the large embankment at Wolverton, London and Birmingham Railway. *Source:* London: J.C. Bourne, 1839.

We should not forget that the railroad, though hardly cheap in absolute terms, was relatively less dear as a carrier than were the carriages on turnpikes it tended to replace. It is worth noting that there was a considerable distinction to be drawn between rail travel in Britain (and Europe in general) and that in North America at the same time. In Canada and the United States, river-borne transit tended to be very cheap as well as marvelously ramified, so the railroad frequently meant an increase in the cost of travel (though obviously a sharp improvement in the conditions thereof), whereas in Europe railroading commonly reduced transport costs as well as obviously improving its conditions. The fares on coaches seem to have ranged between 4 and 5 pence per mile in the 1830s, whereas the railroad companies of the 1840s charged about 3 pence per mile in first class, tuppence in second, and a penny a mile in third.[61] With such downward shifts in costs and great increases in capacity to transport passengers, human mobility was increased so radically that early predictions proved hopelessly low.

In the transportation of minerals, goods, and other commodities the railroads could work a similar revolution, particularly once the trunk lines were in place, to connect the great manufacturing districts—the Midland Hardware District, the cotton manufactory of Lancashire, and the woolen industry of the West Riding of Yorkshire—with the great consuming cities or ports whence exports could be carried around the world. In evolving freight transportation considerable innovation of thought and practice had to transpire. To begin with, railroads "had unique technical qualifications; for they combined, with the ability to transport very heavy loads at a small cost in energy, a capacity for very high speeds at a not prohibitive increase of energy." Even on a horse railway that beast could draw many times what it could on a road. "On the Surrey Iron

Railway soon after the nineteenth century opened, a horse drew a train of over fifty tons a considerable distance, whereas the former draught of a horse on a good road had been considered to be about three-quarters of a ton."[62]

Through the introduction of the locomotive, after about 1812, the loads and the speeds could be advanced strikingly, but a basic geographical constraint continued for nearly another generation. The Newcastle railways, the Surrey Iron Railway, the Stockton and Darlington, and even the Liverpool and Manchester all suffered from parochial conception: they were viewed as local solutions to local problems, some of which might be of considerable scale but none of which was of great extent. Neither speed nor ultimate volume was likely to advance radically in such a parochial frame. The result was that the various hypogeographic railway systems failed to evolve a distinctive railroad technology capable of maximizing the economic and geographical potential of the rail facilities and technology.

Much of the problem revolved around who would carry the goods and the people over the line. As we have seen, the Stockton and Darlington in its earlier years allowed independent coachmen to run its passenger service, to disastrous effect on speeds and capacities. An English judge remarked, "The notion of the railway being a highway for the common use of the public, in the same sense that the ordinary highway is so, was the starting point of English railway legislation" and practice.[63] Even the Grand Junction Railway at first allowed a trader to use his own engine on their line to draw coal. This notion of the railroad as a variant form of the highway persisted in legal minds somewhat after it began to become inoperative in the minds of railroadmen.

The legal dictum already quoted went on to lay down three possible arrangements for a railway. "The company might be merely the owners of a highway, and toll takers for the use of it by other people with their own carriages and locomotives." Or under "a second state of things . . . the railway company provided the line, and provided the engines and trucks [sic], but they were not carriers. The large warehouses and sheds wherein the goods were received, sorted, loaded, covered, checked, weighed and labelled, and trucks and carriages marshalled . . . the staff . . . necessary for these operations were all provided and maintained at the expense of the carrier, and no portion of it fell upon the [railroad] company. The third state of things . . . existed where the company themselves were the carriers of the goods."[64]

Only when that third state of things was reached could railroad transport of goods begin to expand into an effective system of distant freight handling.

In the early days in England . . . there were three systems, corresponding to the learned judge's outlined arrangements, in force on English railways. "(1) The London and Birmingham Railway did not collect or deliver goods, this work being performed by carriers such as Pickford and Co., and Chaplin and Horne, fifteen such firms acting as carriers on this system in 1840. (2) The Grand Junction Railway between Birmingham and Liverpool and Manchester, both acted as carriers and allowed carriers to use their line. (3) The Liverpool and Manchester Railway acted as carriers, performing the service of collection in Manchester."[85]

With the merger, effective in 1846, of these three lines that we have been considering at some length, the trend was toward the exclusive role of carrier for the railroad companies. Only the later Midland Railway gained absolute control of both transport and car ownership, but by the later part of the nineteenth century the control of the actual movement over their lines had fallen entirely to those operating companies.

Britain seems to have anticipated modern conditions, in that freight transportation never became the private preserve of the railroads to the extent that passenger transport did. Several factors contributed to that restraint. There was an elaborate sytem of canals fully at work in a number of the areas of the kingdom when the railroads were introduced. There was, in addition, a well-established and complex road transportation system of carters, draymen, and the like who continued to compete, often successfully, with the fledgling iron roads. Distances in Britain, particularly within the areas of heaviest freight flow of manufactures in England, were sufficiently short that the line economies of rail transport tended to be masked by the terminal diseconomies of that same medium compared with road transport. Finally, the gauge problem meant that interchanges among the rail companies were often impractical.

It would be a bad mistake to assume that the rails did not become the great hauliers; they did, and particularly for minerals, most notably coal. But they did not take over that role so completely as was the case in Canada and the United States. Data for the early years are incomplete, but those that exist suggest a much more significant role for the railroads in passenger than in freight transportation, as Table 3.1 suggests. The domination of railroad receipts and train mileage by passenger rather than freight operations is noteworthy. Only in the early 1860s do the British rail operations seem to have taken on the characteristics common to railroads in other countries, of freight's becoming the backstay of the industry. This early domination by passenger service came to be reflected in the way the lines were constructed and run, further divorcing British practice from the experience elsewhere, particularly in America.

Before looking beyond Great Britain at those contrasting conditions, we may look

The Blisworth Cutting, London and Birmingham Railway. *Source:* London: J.C. Bourne, 1839.

	Millions of Passengers Carried	Train Mileage (in millions of miles)		Receipts (in millions of pounds)	
		Passenger	Freight	Passenger	Freight
1838	5.4				
1843	21.7			3.1	1.4
1844	25.2			3.4	1.6
1845	30.4			3.9	2.2
1846	40.2			4.6	2.8
1847	47.9			5.0	3.3
1849	57.8			6.0	5.4
1850	67.4			6.5	6.2
1851	79.7			7.6	6.9
1852	82.8	33.3	24.5	7.3	7.7
1853	95.2	34.6	29.7	8.0	9.2
1854	104.3	36.0	33.3	9.6	9.7
1855	111.4	36.9	33.4	10.0	10.5
1856	121.4	38.3	35.5	10.6	11.4
1857	130.6	41.6	37.6	11.1	11.9
1858	130.7	43.7	38.7	10.9	11.9
1859	140.3	46.1	42.4	11.7	12.8
1860	153.5	48.8	48.0	12.2	14.2
1861	163.0	49.6	49.5	12.4	14.7
1862	170.0	52.8	48.8	13.0	14.7

Source: Data from Table Transport 5, B. P. Mitchell and Phyllis Deane, *Abstract of British Historical Statistics* (Cambridge: Cambridge University Press, 1962), p. 225.

within to see how a distinctive development was begun but how in the long run it failed to defeat the Stephenson system for obvious historical geographic reasons.

Misunderstanding of Ubiquity: The Great Western Railway

One of the paradoxes of English transportation history is the greater interest expressed outside than inside London for the construction of railroads. Just as Lancashire began the railroad revolution, it was in the southwest, in Bristol, that the first interest was shown in a rail connection westward from the metropolis. In the fall of 1832 a meeting drawn from the mercantile groups of Bristol—the city government, the ancient Society of Merchant Venturers, the Bristol Dock Company, and the Bristol Chamber of Commerce—met to consider the organization of a railroad to London. Ultimately a London committee was created to work with those on this Bristol Committee; but, in a fashion that is better known in the construction of the first American transcontinental railroad, these two committees of the Great Western Railway were responsible for the building of the line at their respective ends toward a junction point midway toward the other. Fortunately, however, they did agree on the same chief engineer, so at least the basic facilities of the railroad were the same throughout, though the architecture and finish of the buildings and bridges differed markedly.[66] Their choice for an engineer was rather improbable, not so much for his youth—Robert Stephenson had been no older when he undertook the London and Birmingham—but for his lack of any association with the Northeast England–Lancashire hearth of rail development. Isambard Kingdom Brunel, who was just twenty-six when the Great Western was first discussed, had aided his father in the early construction of the Wapping Tunnel in London and had designed the successful entry for a competition for a bridge across the gorge of the river Avon at Clifton in Bristol. But in 1832 work on the Thames tunnel was in suspension, with grave doubt whether it could be completed, and the Clifton Bridge was a set of plans unrealized and seriously questioned by some engineers. Brunel, however, seems to have had a most persuasive manner, as he was given the commission despite his failure to meet the requirements set by the two committees, that the line would be given to that engineer who could come up with the cheapest plan. His contention was compelling: "You are holding out a premium to the man who will make you the most flattering promises, and it is quite obvious that he who has the least reputation at stake, or the most to gain by temporary success, and the least to lose by the consequence of a disappointment, must be the winner in such a race," he told the Bristol Railway Committee.[67]

That Committee would ultimately learn the difference between Brunel's reputation and the running of a railroad. No one ever questioned the young man's integrity, ingenuity, and search for knowledge; but many over the years came to question his practicality and, as we must, his understanding of the geography of transportation. What Brunel built was a fascinating experiment in transportation, but one that a calmer analysis of how that transport is intended to serve society might have put in question at the beginning, long before its costly disappointment had run its course. Brunel was neither alone for his time nor in history. As recently as the post-World War II decades, British transportation has witnessed two similar grand but basically irrational experiments in transport—the hovercraft and the supersonic transport.

In setting about the layout of the Great Western Railway, Brunel followed the geographical, if not the technological, practice of the northerners. His 118-mile line between London and Bristol was truly exceptional in its easy grades from London to the summit of the line, if such a term is appropriate for an elevation of some 292 feet above the London terminus (and 318 above Temple Meads in Bristol). Thus in the 76.5 miles from Paddington to the "summit" at Swindon the average rise per mile was 3.8 feet, and the steepest grade 1 in 660 (0.15 percent). Brunel quite appropriately referred to this as a virtually level line. West of Swindon in the 41 miles to Temple Meads in Bristol, the line was a gentle downgrade for 8 miles to the beginning of the Wootton Bassett Incline, where the slope changed from 0.15 to 1.00 percent for 1.5 miles. From the botton of that incline, at Dauntsey, a 0.15 grade, first down and then up, continued for almost 11 miles to the east portal of the Box Tunnel. In this nearly 2-mile tunnel through the Great Oolite ridge (which we saw earlier in the Kilsby Tunnel on the London and Birmingham), the descent westward was at 1 percent on a heading such that the rising sun on Brunel's birth date, April 9, illuminated the whole tunnel. From Box, at the west portal, the 16 miles through Bath into Bristol had very heavy engineering works to carry the line alongside the river Avon and through two major towns, but at no place did the gradient exceed 1 in 1850, 0.11 percent. In essence, with the exception of two banks, the Wootton Bassett Incline and the Box Tunnel incline, Brunel had managed to run a line from England's east to west coast with grades no greater than 0.15 percent. And his banks made up no more than just under 4 miles, in 118, and even then with no grade over 1 percent.[68]

The remarkable line Brunel had engineered for the Great Western Railway certainly justified his choice as a locating engineer. Again, like the Stephensons, he might exercise his skill because the project was heavily financed from the beginning. Not only London and Bristol, England's traditional second city, but Liverpool as well were involved. There was in this western line a Liverpool Party, just as there had been on the Liverpool and Manchester and the Grand Junction. It is worth noting that it was this group of experienced railroad financiers who most questioned some of Brunel's more ingenious, but later proven to be impractical, schemes for the fabric and technology of this line. Only by being outvoted were they defeated. In that defeat there seem to have been two components—a poor choice of consulting engineers who might have shown the weaknesses in their chief engineer's arguments, and the brilliant nature of his mind, which made him as ingenious in his defense as he was in making innovative proposals for his line.[69]

The Broad Gauge: Failure to Realize Its Benefits

After shaping an outstandingly good line for the Great Western, Brunel set about determining what its track and motive power should be. Quite appropriately he examined the question of gauge as one open to experimentation and possible variation. The fortuitous nature of the adoption of the Stephenson gauge—originally 4 feet 8 inches because that was the gauge George Stephenson found when he started building locomotives for the Killingworth Colliery, and then mysteriously increased a half inch sometime in the first decade of common-carrier railroading, with the time, place, and reason lost from the record—was such that there was no reason to be bound by it if a more rational one could be proposed. It was

still early enough in the history of railroad development to think of the adoption of another gauge, although the sensitivity of George Stephenson to any change in his system of railroad building (and the money already invested in lines built to his gauge) would have meant that a compelling objection would have had to be sustained. Simply put, Brunel convinced his committees, who outvoted their Liverpool Party, but he failed to convince the potential users in most of the world. Only in Ireland and India, where he dealt with civil servants rather than those actually involved with building and running railroads, did he gain converts, leading to the Irish lines being of 5'3" gauge and those of the Indian subcontinent of full width being 5'6". South Australia, Victoria, Chile, Argentina, and Brazil all had some lines built to a wider-than-Stephenson gauge, usually under British influence. In the United States this argument was also joined, but we shall look at that situation in its own context.

The Great Western's gauge was established at 7 feet (ultimately 7'0.25") for reasons that at first seem compelling. Brunel argued that on a line as nearly level and straight as his, fast running would become one of its economic strengths. To gain that fast running he wished to have larger wheels both on the passenger cars and the locomotives, and to enlarge the wheels he reasoned that it was desirable to place the wheels outside the frame of the various vehicles so as not to make them appreciably higher than those running on the Stephenson lines. Why he was willing to accept the north-country constraints in height but not in gauge is unclear, unless it was that he viewed high cars as necessarily unstable. At least he intended that the center of gravity of the cars should be close to the track. But as London Transport later proved with respect to double-decker buses, and Amtrak with its *Superliners*, it is possible to have a low center of gravity in a tall vehicle. Brunel was too good an engineer not to have discovered that fact if he had experimented in the matter. He did nonetheless accept a low height when he would not agree to a 56-inch gauge. In that fact lies the eventual failure of his proposal.

John Hawkshaw, one of the outside engineers commissioned to examine Brunel's plans, raised questions as to the wisdom of isolating the Great Western by differences of gauge, to which Brunel responded:[70]

> The Great Western Railway . . . broke ground in an entirely new district, in which railways were unknown. . . . The Great Western was therefore free to adopt its own dimensions; and none of the difficulties which would entirely prevent such a course in the north of England had any existence in the west. Consequently all the general arguments advanced and the comparisons made, on the supposition of such difficulties occurring—all excellent in case they did—are totally inapplicable to the particular case of the Great Western Railway, to which they have no reference whatever. [He even further sought to isolate the Great Western by arguing:] Railway carriages and waggons must belong to the particular line on which they run; and, except in such cases as the Grand Junction and London and Birmingham Railways, which form in fact one line, although they happen to be made by two Companies, it will never pay to trust them in the hands of others.

Thus did perhaps the greatest, certainly the most original, engineer of the nineteenth century pronounce on the geography of transportation. It is easy now to see how egregiously wrong he was, but in 1838, when he was fighting for his ideas and their implementation in the 7-foot gauge, there was no certainty that he was wrong. Still, he (like the Stephensons) found it very hard to accept geographical relativity. In this he set the standard that died slowly and painfully among British engineers when they were

called to work elsewhere. Only Joseph Locke thought differently.

Track Gauge and Loading Gauge

In assessing the role of the Great Western— that is, really, the part played by Brunel—in the shaping of the British rail system, we find it was limited and passing. Now we can see that his great mistake was in failing to distinguish between two expressions of gauge. The first, *track gauge*, should be familiar by now; the other, *loading gauge*, needs to be defined. Loading gauge is the two-dimensional vertical prism that bounds the size of the car that may pass along a track without encountering obstructions from stationary or passing trains, from buildings alongside the track, from bridges and tunnels, the sides of excavations, signals and other railroad furniture. In essence, the loading gauge tells you how large a car in height and width can pass along the line, and at curves indirectly how long a car may be maneuvered around that curve. Taking this loading gauge, we find that Brunel's Great Western enjoyed rather little increase over the Stephenson lines—little more than a foot in width and essentially the same height. Even that extra width was taken up mainly by the placement of the wheels outside the car frame, rather than under it as in the northern lines. So it is quite problematic whether Brunel gained any essential increase in carrying capacity for all his ingenuity in widening the gauge.

What he thought he gained, though it has been largely discounted in subsequent decades, was less friction from his larger wheels. One is forced to conclude that Brunel's victory in the battle of the gauges in 1838 was Pyrrhic indeed: he gained precious little benefit technologically, and he sustained a truly excessive cost in terms of economic geography. The Great Western did push branches to the end of the Cornish peninsula, throughout South Wales, and even to Birkenhead on the Mersey across from Liverpool; but it remained quite parochial throughout its life. The company's engines were distinctive, though not necessarily better, until nationalization in 1948. For a few years even after that final merging of all British railways, the Western Region still sported the livery of the Great Western. Its cream and brown is now gone, but few of the protagonists of the GWR would admit that there ever was a greater railroad, though obviously there was in the Union Pacific, which also had its distinctive livery of bright yellow until 1971 when Amtrak made virtually all the same in the United States, as it was by then in Britain. But the American transcontinental fully understood the concept of ubiquity in rail travel as Brunel's line never did. In that greater wisdom came the Union Pacific's longevity and ultimate superiority to Britain's premier line.

The Phases of British Railroad Development

Phase 1   When we seek to determine the mature pattern of railroads in Britain, it is striking how strong the drive for ubiquity became in the face of the original notions of regionalization or even specialization of lines. If we consider the Stockton and Darlington and the Liverpool and Manchester as simply specialized rail lines, generically similar to the plateways that had been in use for nearly two hundred years, there were other lines of this sort. In the Northeast and South Wales a number of short lines from the interior to the coast had been constructed as steam railroads to carry coal to the loading docks whence it was taken to London and other cities as well as widely "overseas" to Europe and even North America. Of similar stripe were the rail lines of Furness and Cumberland, intended to take iron ore to smelters or docks. We may

logically term this the first phase of railroad development—for the meeting of a specialized local need which had a tendency to be the transportation of minerals. In Britain that phase began in 1825, with the opening of the Stockton and Darlington, and ruled for about a decade.

Phase 2   The second phase of development came with the shift toward the building of lines that in geographical terms were different in two important ways: they were intended for a general traffic, both passenger and freight, and they were constructed to interconnect distant pairs of cities. In the case of London we have already considered three such *trunk lines*—the London and Birmingham, the Grand Junction line, and the Great Western Railway—but there were a number of others. Because England is so dominated by a single city, as well as standing as a highly centralized state, the trunk lines almost always paired a provincial city with London. Bristol, Birmingham, Manchester, and Liverpool have been accounted for, but the West Riding of Yorkshire towns have not. At first they were served circuitously via the London and North Western Railway created from the joining of the Birmingham and Grand Junction companies. Ultimately direct service was offered by the Great Northern Railway constructed from King's Cross, London, via Peterborough and Doncaster to York, a 186-mile mainline with branches to be built to Sheffield, Wakefield, Lincoln, Boston, and Bedford to compose a system of 327.5 miles.[71] To the east several relatively short lines—from Cambridge, Norwich, and Ipswich to London—were built in the 1830s and 1840s and operated in small markets and with low profits. A similar though somewhat more prosperous situation obtained southeast of London in the London, Chatham and Dover Railway and the South Eastern Railway leading to the Kentish coast and the Channel ports. These lines tapped the passenger movement to the Continent and gained modest support therefrom, but they were hemmed in to the west by the London, Brighton and South Coast Railway, so each of the three had to operate in a rather narrow and shallow vector from the metropolis, providing the short-distance trunk functions similar to the lines in East Anglia.

Only to the southwest was the hinterland of London deep enough to allow a reasonably large system to grow. The Great Western had already been continued onward from its western terminus by the Bristol and Exeter and had itself spawned subsidiaries in Devon and Cornwall and South Wales, as well as alliances with other broad-gauge companies in this considerable sector. Between the Great Western country and that of the short lines of Kent, Surrey, and Sussex lay a classical city pair, the metropolis and its outport at Southampton. Organized as the London and Southampton Railway in 1834 and thus as a peer of the early trunk lines, this company reorganized as the London and South Western in 1839, giving legal evidence of its interests beyond a single trunk line. Joseph Locke was appointed chief engineer:

> The railway grew into a characteristic Locke line: straight-forward to Basingstoke and Battledown, with imposing cuttings and no tunnels. Then southwards over the Downs it went, slicing through the chalk, sweeping across the intervening hollows on embankments up to 90 ft. high, and still with only the shortest of tunnels.[72]

Only in 1840 was the Southampton line opened, but fairly soon the company looked southwestward, as it had proposed, ultimately to run lines through Salisbury to Exeter and Plymouth in direct competition with the Great Western.

Phase 3 At the time these radiating lines from London were being constructed, the north of England was still the scene of local specialized railroads. The route between the industrial areas and ports of Lancashire and Yorkshire became the scene for the first step beyond true parochialism toward trunk-line development not directly related to London. Five main routes were ultimately developed, but for the moment we need consider only the first three to be built. Promoted by the Liverpool Party and other North Country business interests, the Lancashire and Yorkshire Railway connected Manchester to Leeds via Todmorden and a summit tunnel 8,655 feet long. Laid out by George Stephenson, this line had modest grades for one carried over the so-called backbone of England, though it did have about a mile at a stiff 1.58 percent just outside Manchester; otherwise the grades in the Pennine hills stayed below 1 percent—mostly well below. Though promoted by the same general group that had pioneered the Liverpool and Manchester, this line remained independent up to the so-called Grouping of 1923 when Britain's myriad of earlier lines was reduced to four companies. Thus we seem justified in viewing the Lancashire and Yorkshire as an independent trunk.

The second trans-Pennine railroad was laid out in considerable measure by Joseph Locke and—ironically given that engineer's dislike of tunnels—utilized the Woodhead Tunnel (3 miles 22 yards), then by some measure the world's longest bore, as well as grades that would have frightened George Stephenson into his sickbed. Near Hadfield there was a 2-mile stretch at 1 percent, and for the last 5 miles up to the west portal of the Woodhead Tunnel the line was carried at 1 in 117, or 0.85 percent.[73] Again this line, soon to be the Manchester, Sheffield and Lincolnshire Railway, remained outside the realms of the southern companies until the 1890s, when on its own it projected a line southward first through Nottingham to Hitchin on the Great Northern, for access to

London, and in 1899 to its own station. Marylebone, in the metropolis using the trackage of the Metropolitan Railway from Aylesbury inward.[74]

Phase 4 The existence of regional companies located totally outside the metropolis (Phase 3) led to a fourth phase of British railroad development when those companies—the Midland Railway and the Manchester Sheffield and Lincolnshire Railway—sought to join in the London service.

The result of this hard focus on London was to leave what are still termed *cross-country services*—those that neither originate nor terminate in the metropolis—in a definitely secondary position. So secondary were these lines, and so difficult access to them, that a whole literature of the horrors incident to boarding them at Crewe, March, Didcot, Retford, Bletchley, and Newmarket became a special genre for nineteenth-century British writers. In a survey of English railroads late in that century, W. M. Acworth notes that "[t]he Midland branch from Bristol to Derby, originally the property of three separate companies, to say nothing of the Cheltenham and Gloucester Tramways, which were bought up by the Gloucester and Bristol, is undoubtedly the most important line in Great Britain not terminating in the metropolis."[75]

If we look at this line as an example of the low priority the English placed on such rounded regional development, we might well look at the segment from Birmingham to Gloucester, that part where the main terrain barriers were encountered. Bearing in mind that the developments here were being bruited at the same time as those on the London and Birmingham not far away, it is interesting that the Quaker promoters of this line in 1832 called on the then very young Isambard Brunel "to make a survey for a cheap line between Birmingham and Gloucester."[76] However, such a cheap line

was too burdensome, so the matter was delayed:

> Even when the success of railway enterprise elsewhere gave an impulse to the movement, all the arrangements of the Company, and the very route along which the line was to be taken were cramped by considerations of economy. Captain Moorson [sic] the engineer, . . . was engaged on the modest terms of "no success—no pay."

Surprisingly, it was at first proposed that the line should avoid almost all towns between Birmingham and Gloucester "in order to diminish expense," but ultimately Cheltenham was to be served:

> One disadvantage of the route finally adopted was that it passed down what is known as the Lickey Incline. To avoid this, Mr. Brunel had proposed that the line should be carried farther to the east, by which he would have secured, what was then deemed indispensable to a heavy traffic, a gradient of 1 in 300 [0.33 percent]. Such a course would, however, have been to give even wider berth to the towns and the population, and it was rejected.[77]

It also would have been much more costly in construction as a result of greater length of line. So the Lickey Incline of nearly 2 miles at 1 in 37.75 (2.68 percent), was constructed in 1836 to carry the Birmingham and Gloucester Railway over the southern edge of the Midland Plateau, where it dropped off into the Vale of Evesham. Both Stephenson and Brunel predicted that it could not be worked with locomotives, because, as Appleton points out, "At this date . . . there was a difference of nearly nine times between the maximum gradients advocated by Stephenson for the North Midland [Railway] and by Moorsom for the Birmingham and Gloucester."[78] They were proved correct in their terms of reference:

And apparently they were right, as far at least as English locomotives were concerned. For Mr. Bury, a famous engine-builder of the day, sent an engine which not only could not draw a train but actually could not take its own weight up the hill. But a set of engines built by Mr. Norris of Philadelphia . . . succeeded in performing the task successfully. Oddly enough, they were in no sense designed for this special work. The specification was for "engines of a higher power, greater durability, and less weight, than could be obtained in this country," and they were to be tested to prove their capability of "drawing up a gradient of 1 in 320 a load of 100 tons gross weight at the speed of 20 miles per hour." . . . The steam pressure was about 60 to 64 pounds.

By increasing the weight on the driving wheels, the engine *Philadelphia* "ascended the Lickey inclined plane at a speed of between 8 and 9 miles per hour" drawing 53.25 tons. As the Norris locomotives proved cheaper than most English engines in ascending banks less steep (the incline in the Box Tunnel on the Great Western, for example), "the Birmingham and Gloucester directors had certainly every reason to be satisfied with this result."[79]

It is significant that the line from Bristol to Derby was brought together and successfully operated by the Midland Company. That railroad, the first to shape an important system without direct reference to London, was joined over the course of the years by only two others—the North Eastern and the Manchester, Sheffield and Lincolnshire (later transformed into the Great Central). The demonstration that there was a large potential traffic within regions well removed from the metropolis only slowly influenced the companies focused on the capital, though it was well appreciated much earlier on the three distinctly provincial railroads. They had begun what subsequently can be seen as the fourth phase of British railroad development, the creation of regional systems and the effort to give these as complete geographical coverage as possible, and as great a domination of the intraregional traffic as Parliament and the Board of Trade would allow.

In this fourth phase, which began on the provincial lines by the 1860s and 1870s, the effort was toward a limited, regional ubiquity, under which all the important traffic within a region could be contested for by that particular company. The Midland Company sought to dominate the Midlands, southern Lancashire, and the West Riding—as the North Eastern did Northumberland and Durham—and in the process the Midland Company showed how very profitable that practice might be. The extremely costly extensions outward from that regional base—to St. Pancras in London and to junction with the Glasgow and South Western at Carlisle—could only have been built by the rich company that the Midland was when it began those efforts in the 1860s.

The transformation of the Midland Railway, from a provincial regional system to yet another of the London radials, signals for us the transformation that came in the other radial lines in the next generation. Governmental approbation, particularly at the close of World War I, supported the amalgamation of provincial with radial systems—as in the North Eastern and the Great Northern juncture and, in a different way, the merger of the Midland with the generally disliked North Western. The effect of this tying together of a trunk line to London with a dominance within a sector radiating outward from the capital advanced the notion of ubiquity a farther step: now all systems were striving to gain as complete coverage as possible of the sector they occupied. A single kind of English railroad company had emerged from evolutionary forces working over nearly a century. That company sought an oligopolistic ubiquity that permitted it to tap most of the large markets of the country (in companies north of the Thames and

Entrance portico, Euston Grove Station, London and Birmingham Railway. *Source:* London: J.C. Bourne, 1839.

Severn) or important vectors (south of that line). The Midland Company in the late 1860s built to London and the Border in order to compete on an equal basis with its northern peers; and the Manchester, Sheffield and Lincolnshire constructed its line to London, becoming the Great Central Railway in the 1890s, again to make its participation in the northern rail oligopoly practical.

Phase 5   The last phase of British rail evolution was foretold in 1923 with the grouping into four clearly regional companies, the Southern and Great Western occupying the area south of the line from Chester to London and the London, Midland and Scottish and the London and North Eastern north of that line. It was only a matter of time, and a repetition of government operation during World War II, before Grouping, which might be seen as the search for a high level of geographical ubiquity, was transformed into absolute ubiquity through nationalization of those four companies, and oddments of independent lines that had escaped capture by them in 1923. In 1947 nationalization came, proving that this trend toward ubiquity has always been a part of European railroading. The French, as we shall see in the next section, started far along the road, establishing regional monopolies by the 1830s. The Belgians started even farther along the evolutionary line by creating a national railroad system in the 1830s, leaving only very local services outside the sphere of the national railroads. France reached absolute ubiquity in 1938 with the creation of the S.N.C.F., the national system, and Britain joined fully in the European practices only a decade later.

CONTRASTING DERIVATIONS FROM BRITISH PRACTICE: EARLY RAILROAD DEVELOPMENT ON THE CONTINENT

It is important at this point to establish the timing of railroad development in several parts of the world, notably Britain, the European continent, and North America. If we adopt 1825 as the date of birth for the fully realized railroad system—of which George Stephenson does deserve the title of father—we must immediately ask where and at what delay that system spread beyond its birthplace on Teeside. Essentially all the pioneers of railroad development generously acknowledged their debt to Stephenson and British practice, although, as we shall see presently, that debt was quite variable, with some areas doing little more than copying rather slavishly the characteristics of the Stockton and Darlington or the Liverpool and Manchester while others merely took this demonstration of the practicability of railroads as encouragement for a largely independent invention of their own particular national technical details.

An interesting contradiction of the simplistic assumptions contained in the contagion theory of innovation diffusion can be seen in this spread. The earliest adoption outside Britain came not on the Continent—with one partial exception—but rather in North America, where the United States became unquestionably the second nation to experience the railroad revolution, only a year or two after Britain's transformation. From no real experience with the plateways, which nurtured the railroad idea in Britain and Europe for several centuries before 1800, the United States saw its first serious rail line in 1826, in Quincy, Massachusetts, and the creation of nearby Boston as the world's first rail hub when it opened three radiating lines in 1835, before London had any such line in operation. That tale must await our discussion of the North American development, in the next chapter, which I propose represents a nearly independent railroad revolution with a technology and pattern of geographical facilities different from that found in Britain and Europe. First, however, it is useful to examine the subsequent adherents to the

A contemporary view of a train in 1841. A pencil sketch in the author's collection, dated September, 1841.

revolutionary forces of the railroad, most of which were Britain's neighbors on the European continent.

There is some difficulty in timing that adherence to the cause of increased mobility because France was the first to begin the movement, but its efforts were small and disorganized for a decade after British and American investors had undertaken to provide extensive *systems* of railroads in their respective countries. Belgium was the pioneer on the Continent of the integrated transportation system that the term *railroad* calls to mind. Only a generation after Britain and the United States did Germany, France, and Italy gain the level of rail service available in the pioneering lands by 1845, though from the beginning those two showed different approaches to the problem. Some parts of Europe, Scandinavia in particular, were peculiarly slow in adopting rail transportation, not because of lack of population or even wealth but perhaps from tendencies toward conservatism.

Among the European countries it is unnecessary and unwise to try to examine the historical geography of railroads in the detail that has been given to Britain and subsequently will be bestowed on its main rival in establishing a *system of railroads*. Several European countries do, however, deserve modest attention, as they display distinctive features that help us understand the ways in which such rail systems were transformed with transfer across the Channel and how the railroad as a facility is expressive of the culture, economy, and terrain in which it is constructed. To these ends Belgium, as the first nation with a planned system of rail lines; France, as the epitome of the rationalist system of rail transport; and Italy, to demonstrate the way in which a developed market can provide the justification for monumental engineering works, will be considered in turn.

Belgium Uses the Railroad for Economic Survival

Throughout early modern centuries the Spanish—later Austrian—Netherlands was viewed as the "cockpit of Europe," the place where dynastic conflicts led to open warfare, where religious wars burst into battles, and where too many powerful neighbors meant that there was no liberty for the descendents of the ancient Belgae. In the attempt to return Europe to the status ante Napoleon, an Austrian governor-general was appointed in 1814 to rule over the former Austrian Netherlands, which the First Consul had captured and made integral *départements* of France. Such a revanchist course was too strong for many to stomach, so in 1815 the southern part of the Low Countries was joined to the northern in a union with Holland under William I. These Belgian provinces prospered economically during the next fifteen years but had relatively little say in the government of the united Kingdom of the Netherlands, which remained as before a Dutch government.

In 1830 the July Revolution in France, aimed at removing the surviving revanchist Bourbon monarchy given to France at the close of the Napoleonic Wars, sparked a revolt in the Belgian provinces of the Netherlands. Perhaps chiefly as a result of the ineptitude of the Dutch, the Belgians prevailed and succeeded in gaining a great-power conference in London that declared Belgium an independent kingdom on December 20, 1830. The Dutch provinces of the now sundered Netherlands refused to accept that decision. Until forced out of Antwerp the next year by French forces and the British Navy, William I hung on to that port, the only Belgian city the Dutch managed to maintain under their control in 1830. Even then the Dutch manned the forts on the lower Scheldt, thereby impeding sea access to the main Belgian port, a situation that obtained until 1858 when the last vestige of anti-Belgian acts, the levying of a toll on navigation, was extinguished by purchase.

In this situation, just at the time the Liverpool and Manchester was opened, the newly independent Belgians were in a difficult position with respect to their traditional transportation, which had passed down the Scheldt and Meuse to the Dutch ports. There is little difficulty in explaining why the Belgian mercantile interests and the new king, Leopold I, greeted the word from Britain so enthusiastically and began almost immediately to ask George Stephenson to come to Belgium to advise the government on establishing a rail system that would provide to that country, whose trade had traditionally flowed north and south, a line of communication that would flow just as well from east to west, gaining a new port that was to be built at the largely sand-girt mouth of a small stream at Oostende.

The initial decision made by the Belgian government was that the rail lines would be planned and built by the newly established central government. Although Brussels was the seat of that government, and the most important city in the new kingdom—Antwerp being effectively cut off from its traditional function as entrepôt—the undefined geographical qualities then assigned to railroads lent no usable guide to the Belgian planners. In 1831, when they began to look into the question of what a national system of railroads should be, British practice offered little guidance. The Stockton and Darlington and the Liverpool and Manchester were completely parochial affairs, technologically of great interest and example but without any demonstrable geographical perception beyond connecting the interior hinterland of a port with its docks. Only in America were there examples that might better have served the Belgians, as for example in the early thinking on the Baltimore and

Ohio; but Europeans were not then of the mind that American practice might inform Europe. Only the surprising experience with that United States rail technology in the late 1830s and 1840s opened the eyes of the Continentals to the fact that there were other than British precedents that might be followed, although in Belgium the heavy political reliance on Britain and the earlier ties—particularly by way of John Cockerill, the great Liègoise textile and iron maker—to the textile revolution of late eighteenth-century Britain, pretty well assured a dominating role for rail practices from the land across the narrow rather than the broad seas.

The plan that emerged from the earliest examination seems to have combined two elements: first, the forging of the east-west artery made necessary by the establishment of such a boundary between Belgium and the Holland, which had left the mouths of all the waterways the Austrian Netherlands had used to gain access to the sea in Dutch hands—the route to Sluis north of Bruges, the canal from Ghent to the lower Scheldt, that stream itself, and the Meuse that drained the former Prince Bishopric of Liège toward Rotterdam—and, second, the shaping of a route from Cologne westward to the North Sea Coast. "Belgium had an exceptionally favourable geographical location from the point of view of handling transit traffic between Antwerp and western Germany. Far-seeing German industrialists (such as Fritz Harcourt) and statesmen (such as Friedrich Motz) also appreciated the advantages that would be secured by building a railway between Antwerp and Cologne."[80]

Because it was possible to combine these two goals in one line, the early planners of the Belgian rail system seem to have gone from the too parochial route of Britain to the geographical absolutism of the Romans, the most recent precedent that might have been found for shaping such a long-distance system. As laid out the rail system was to be in the form of a cross, producing a north-south line tying Antwerp on the Dutch border to Mons adjacent to the French and an east-west line providing a good direct line from the German border near Aachen (for Cologne) through Liège to Ghent, Bruges, and the North Sea coast (at Oostende). Such routes crossed at Mechelen (Malines), giving that ancient cathedral town a surprising centrality, to be reflected in its adoption as the location for the Belgian railroad's main shops. Thus Brussels was left some 14 miles south from the main junction, a rather arbitrary decision that seems to have been demonstrated at the very beginning when the first segment of this national rail system to be built was that from the capital to its "junction" at Mechelen. This work was carried out under a law, of May 1, 1834, and was completed to Mechelen in 1835. On May 5, 1835, an ostentatious opening of this line was carried out, as illustrated. When Victor Hugo made this 22-kilometer journey two years after the opening he was intrigued:

> It is a magnificent journey and must be experienced to be described. The speed is extraordinary. The flowers beside the line are no longer flowers, they are spots or rather red or white rays; truly all become rays; wheat seems long golden locks while alfalfa looks to be long green tresses; cities, clock towers, and trees dance before you and become wildly mingled all the way to the horizon.[81]

The direct diffusion of British rail practice into Belgium is above question. King Leopold called George Stephenson there in 1835 and at his suggestion added a further 95 miles to the 246 miles authorized in 1834, to shape what was demonstrably the first carefully thought out national system. Even it, however, was not complete. The rapid adoption of rail travel in Europe's most densely settled area—160,000 rode the Brussels-Mechelen line during the first two months it

was opened—combined with an increasing movement of freight in the most industrialized area on the Continent, to encourage ramification of lines. It was decided in the mid-1840s that additions might be made by private companies:

> In 1845 eight such companies were founded in London (under Belgian law) to build the following lines: the Sambre-Meuse [to tie together the great industrial towns of the Sambre valley with Namur to the east]; the West Flanders; the Namur-Liège; the Charleroi-Erquilines; the Tournai-Jourbise-Landen-Hasselt; the Anglo-Belgian; the Belgian Grand Junction; and the Great Luxembourg. Over £6,000,000 was subscribed in Britain for these lines.[82]

Although these and other routes—Antwerp to Ghent, Louvain to the Sambre, Mons to Manage, in the valley of the Dendre, from Spa to Pepinster—were built by private companies, after 1870 the state sought to buy out those capitalists in which they were successful save for one main line—Givet on the French border to Liège—and a few minor lines. The Chemin de Fer Nord of France constructed the line down the Meuse from Givet, calling it the C. de F. Nord-Belge, which, with trackage in the coalfields of the Mons-Charleroi-Erquelinnes triangle, gave this French-owned Belgian railroad 170 kilometers of line until the concession came to an end on the very day (May 10) the Germans invaded Belgium in 1940.[83]

So complete was the Belgian adoption of the railroad that even its state system supplemented by British- and French-financed branches was thought insufficient. By 1875 there were 2,133 miles of railroad in Belgium, a country of 11,373 square miles, or 1 mile of railroad for every 5.3 square miles of area. No other country in the world could match that figure. In the next decade another six hundred miles of standard-gauge line were added, but after 1885 little growth took place, although considerable im-

Construction shaft, Kilsby Tunnel, London and Birmingham Railway.

provements in lines and alignments were carried out over the succeeding century. In 1968 there were only 2,588 miles of line operated, a net growth of about a fifth in mileage over the hundred-year period, yielding an area of 4.6 square miles per mile of railroad.[84] But so dependent on good rail transportation had they become that there was continuing agitation for a second-level national system that would provide local connections to the national railroads. The outcome was the formation, by Leopold II in 1884, of a local railway authority (*Société Nationale des Chemins de fer Vicinaux*) instructed to build such a supplemental system to provide rail service to most towns of any size in the kingdom. In many ways these meter-gauge lines fulfilled the same purpose as the interurban electric railways in the United States, whose construction began virtually at the same time, though using a different technology. Those interurbans were called by many contemporaries "the farmer's railroad," and we may appropriately assign the term as well to the vicinal railways of Belgium, and later of France and Germany.

The essential point is that by the 1880s the railroad system in much of western Europe and in the humid parts of the United States had gained its full stature, providing to urban populations an excellent system of freight and passenger transportation. The rural areas—even in such a country as Belgium, with its dense rural agricultural settlement—were not so well cared for by standard railroads, so the vicinal system was proposed to gain that service at a rather lower cost than that required by normal English-style rail construction. The narrowed gauge permitted sharper curves, the lighter line cheaper construction, and the slow speeds less protection of the line from the regular road system of the country.

It is clear that this sort of farmer's railway was the precursor of the automobile and

truck more than the logical amplification of the standard railroad. In Canada and the United States the interurban lines were abandoned over a twenty-year period (about 1920 to 1940) when automotive transportation became nearly universal in the farming areas: in Belgium the vicinal system did not decline until after World War II, the period of automotive substitution in rural western Europe. The apogee of the mileage operated by the S.N.C.V. in Belgium was 1934, when 3,178 miles of vicinal railway were in use. By the early 1970s only about 1,800 miles of the local system remained in operation, and the decline has probably continued.[85]

FRANCE USES THE RAILROAD FOR SPATIAL ORGANIZATION

The vigor with which the ancien régime pursued the shaping of a waterway network for France proved no indicator of the acceptance of the railroad in the early nineteenth century. Certainly that older strain was not dead—it continued during the Napoléonic years in canal building—but it did not express itself with much force in the new technology. It seems that the aggressive spirit was centered in the completion of the waterway system, which might incidentally call forth the construction of rail lines in those places where the terrain and hydrography were difficult for canal building; but it did not enter into the matter of shaping an independent, long-distance railroad system. Plans were proposed in the 1820s that would have used *chemins de fer*—presumably similar to the iron plateways of the Newcastle area—for such difficult connections. These were to be built only as exceptional segments in a comprehensive network that would have envisaged thousands of miles of artificial canals, either as laterals to large rivers or as cuts across the more practicable watersheds. It was only in units of a few tens of miles that railroads, *chemins de fer*, were to be employed

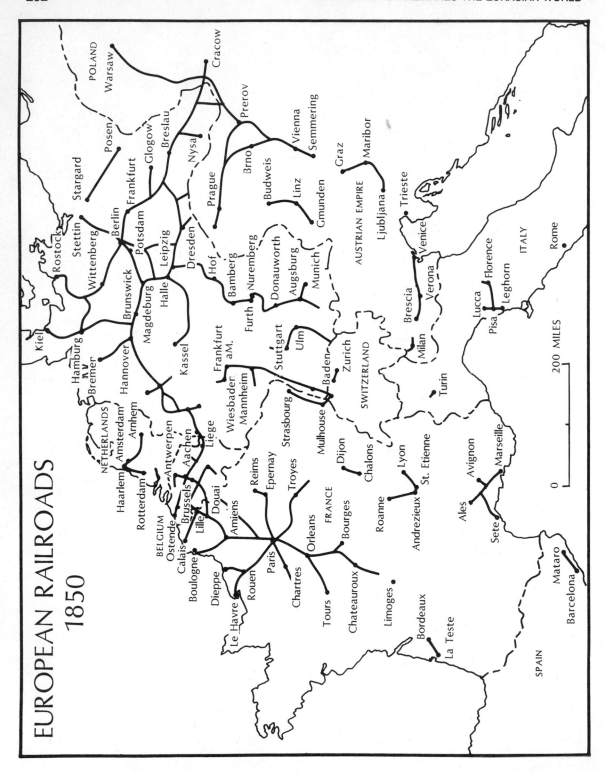

EUROPEAN RAILROADS 1850

in the plan presented by Brisson, divisional inspector of the Corps de Ponts et Chausées, in 1824.[86] The first rail line to be constructed came in just such a situation, at the water parting between the upper Loire and short right-bank tributaries of the Rhône just below Lyon. After that line was completed in 1828, save for extensions at either end, it was nearly a decade before any other rail construction took place in France.

The first French line had a characteristic location for such very early railroads. Like the Newcastle railways, the Stockton and Darlington, and the first railroad in Belgium—opened in 1830 to join the Grand-Hornu colliery at St. Ghislain with the Mons-Condé canal[87]—the horse-operated railway from the mineral basin at St. Étienne to the upper Loire at Andrézieux was intended for the transport of coal. Organized in 1824 as a private company under a charter from the monarchy of Louis XVIII, this 14-mile line was completed in 1828. It was constructed with the Stephenson gauge but not in his manner. Curves were sharp and engineering works were kept simple. In 1832 this coal carrier began to provide for passengers and one of the earliest piggyback services by offering coaches with their wheels removed placed on appropriate flatcars. These were lifted by a crane at either end for return to their own wheels.[88] Through the adoption of such a railway, the colliery owners in the Stéphanaise were able to increase the tractive effort of horses significantly, to the point that one horse could draw four *wagonnets* (tub-cars), each containing 2 tons of coals. It is hard to know at this late remove how significant the passenger service really was. The fact that it was pursued would tend to demonstrate its profitability to the company, but at least in these earliest French lines there can be little doubt that it was for the transport of heavy commodities, particularly coal, that lines were constructed.

The extension of the original Stéphanoise coal line came at both ends from Andrézieux farther down the Loire to Roanne, avoiding some rocky stretches that made navigation difficult in low water, and from St. Étienne over the low divide to the upper river Gier and down that rushing stream through its deep gorge to Rive-de-Gier, whence a canal reached to the Rhône at Givors. Subsequently the rail line was carried all the way to the Rhône and then the 12 mile upriver to Lyon. We are fortunate that the pioneer French engineer Marc Seguin the elder, who was responsible for building the St. Étienne-Lyon line—and who, by the way, greatly improved on the earlier Stephenson engines in 1825 by inventing the tubular boiler that made steam more readily available and with less consumption of coal—has left us a contemporary discussion both of the economics and the engineering of rail lines.[89] In *The Influence of Railroads and the Art of Their Laying Out and Construction*,[90] he presents a detailed analysis of the role of curvature and gradients in the efficient and economic operation of railroads. He seems to have been one of the first to understand the concept of *ruling grade*, wherein the steepest section of a line determines the power that must be given to the engine that draws the train, or else the train must be split or assisted by further engines at those steep bits. Seguin visited the Stockton and Darlington and the Liverpool and Manchester (the latter while under construction) to gain insights as to how to build his coal-carrying line in the Massif Central. It was at the behest of Stephenson, Rennie, and Brunel that he increased his radii for curves from 150 meters to 500 meters, even at the expense of additional tunneling in the Gier valley.[91] Although Seguin tended toward rational and ordered analysis, he does note in 1839 that

the rules by which the alignment and route *trace* of a railroad are established are not, and cannot be, absolute. It cannot be a route created [solely] for a special purpose or for the service of a small place as well as one which has for its purpose to move with great speed a large number of passengers or quantity of goods: in this second case, when it is a question of a line of the first order, all the most significant reasons are combined to urge upon the government that the line be constructed to a level of perfection that utilizes all the resources of the art of railroad building.[92]

Thus the notion of the railroad as something more than a supplement to the canal system, or a parochial venture, was emerging in the minds of the more introspective French observers by the mid-1830s.

To meet the needs of this higher-speed and long-distance service, Seguin believed particularly that gradient, specifically ruling gradient, was of critical importance. As he noted, "If the engineers of the Manchester to Liverpool road had been able, in 1826, to see what that railroad would be in 1838, perhaps they would have been able to find a means to obtain a better graded line, and to take more account of the actual method of working." He found particular fault with the "banks" on either side of Rainhill that forced Stephenson into running trains over a grade double that found elsewhere on the line. The excess of power needed in this small section had to be run throughout the line, where it was superfluous. A further surprise to the earlier rail developers was the shift in relative position of passenger and freight transportation. The earliest lines were almost entirely built to move commodities, particularly heavy ones, whereas by 1839 it was clear that the prosperity of companies stemmed from their passenger receipts in considerable measure.[93]

Practicing what he had been preaching, Seguin tells us, "When I made the alignment of the line from St. Étienne to Lyon, I had decided ahead of time to shy away from no

sacrifice to give to my curves all the space that the terrain would allow, and to maintain a regularity of slope between all the points the royal charter obliged it to serve."[94] With that determination expressed by the father of his nation's railroads, at the moment it is sufficient to note the truly infantile baptism of the French in heavy engineering of rail lines. The result was that they never could give quite the attention to minor detail that the English could in their gently rolling landscape.

The third division of this line extended from Rive-de-Gier to the western terminus at St. Étienne, a distance of just under 13 miles. At that city the line was 1,750 feet above the sea, 1,225 feet above its low point at Givors on the Rhône. Such a rise in less than 25 miles constituted a great challenge indeed in this period of hesitant experimentation at the very beginning of rail development. Seguin was forced to moderate some of his engineering perceptions, but he proved remarkably adept in salvaging the more important elements of his ideal line: that is, the curves were reasonable for such terrain and the grades were kept at practicable levels for the weak locomotives then available. In this third section a ruling grade of 1.38 percent had to be accepted, along with three tunnels and two high bridges.

At Rive-de-Gier Seguin reached one of the small coal basins preserved within the flanks of the Massif Central, which played such an important role in the French Industrial Revolution just then underway. For that reason it is well to note that France, until well into the nineteenth century, was basically dependent on these pockets of coal preserved in down-dropped or folded parts of the great mountain mass in the heart of southern France. As the flanks of the Pennines furnished coal to the British Industrial Revolution, the enclosed basin within the much higher Massif Central played that role in France. This necessitated the adoption of a level of engineering never called forth in Britain by its more hilly than mountainous terrain. It is enlightening to compare this first important French line, which already had to deal with mountain railroad building, with the English, where bog and buildings were the main obstacles. The result was that the French very early became the greatest constructors of bridges and viaducts, to span deep grooves eroded into a high plateau. We shall presently examine this phase of transportation geography, but for the present we must examine the Lyon-St. Étienne line, a route that was France's first significant railroad, built between June 7, 1826, when the royal ordinance was issued, and 1832, when the line was completed. Only then did France possess a line built for and operated by steam locomotives. Also, though the St. Étienne-Lyon line was intentionally a coal carrier, Marc Seguin, through his clear distinction between the locally important line and the *ligne de premier ordre* that was intended for long-distance and speedy travel, contributed to a clear adoption of a national railroad policy for France.

French Railroad Strategy   That came when the central government was faced with the problem of authorizing rail lines to improve connections from the provinces to the metropolis. So long as the question was that of authorizing a short line to tie the Stéphanoise coal basin with the purely local metropolis of Lyon, individual ordinances could suffice, but once Paris became involved some broader policy had to be devised. This was done in a somewhat different political climate from that obtaining when the St. Étienne-Lyon line was authorized under Louis XVIII. In 1830 that revanchist monarchy was overthrown, to be replaced by a more liberal July Monarchy of that year, which placed the bourgeoisie in political control. Interest in industrialization and

necessary economic improvement during Louis Philippe's reign as "king of the French" was enhanced and the authorization of railroads was removed from absolute control by royal ordinance, passing to the national legislature. In 1835 the government of Thiers was not sympathetic to railroads, but he remarked that a line to the suburb of St. Germain must be allowed: "It is necessary to give that to Paris, as a plaything, but that will never transport a passenger or a bag." In 1836 a line to Versailles was added, leaving a national rail policy still in limbo.

The French policy differed from the one that obtained in Britain—and in America, as we shall see—in two fundamental ways, one geographical and the other financial. Both in Britain and in the United States the rail system was freely evolutionary. Short, often not surpassingly significant lines, which began the railroad evolution, determined its history more than its ultimate geographical pattern. It was in the provinces in England— at Liverpool in particular but in Manchester, Bristol, York, Glasgow, and Newcastle as well—that railroading began and its first geographical decisions were made. This creation of a number of nuclei of interest was even more true in the historical geography of American railroads. Still, in Britain and America a coherent and focused system ultimately evolved, in the first instance because provincial interests fully appreciated from the beginning that the most luxuriant trade would come from establishing connections with the metropolis. Liverpudlian and Bristolian investors helped shape the private systems of Britain, and it was a fairly direct laissez-faire contest that finally determined the extent of the Great Western Railway or the London and North Western.

In France the rise of Parleament as a force in the government came just at the onset of railroad development, but it did not transform the innate Gallic preference for a strongly centralized administration. Not only was the government essentially *bureaucratic*, in the precise sense of that term, but the capital itself was also vastly dominant, as it remains to this day. When railroads were being bruited, there was no city in France of the relative importance of the provincial towns of Britain. Lyon, Marseille, and Bordeaux had people, but they lacked an economic significance equivalent to that of Birmingham or Manchester. Thus the combination of the desire to govern centrally and the dominance by Paris was such that it was entirely to be expected that the French would do what they did, establish a series of governmentally encouraged lines located in radial fashion from Paris. The government, in 1842 when the law establishing this national system was passed, assigned vectors for development to various companies, but first that government actually undertook to construct the *infrastructure* of the main lines:

> Government was to find the land, local authorities furnishing two-thirds of the cost, and to construct the road-bed (the *infra-structure*), including bridges and tunnels. Companies were to furnish the *super-structure, i.e.* rails and ballast and station equipment, rolling stock and working capital. The local authorities disliked their share of the burden, which was removed in 1845. There remained the state and the companies.[95]

The vectorial pattern assigned by the government can easily be anticipated by anyone with any knowledge of French geography. Paris lay at the center with lines projected to Rouen and Le Havre; to Nantes and Brest; to Orléans, Tours, and Bordeaux; to Lyon and Marseille; to Nancy and Strasbourg; and to Belgium and the Channel ports. Companies to operate in these sectors were soon found except in the vector via Chartres to Brittany, where the state interest remained dominant throughout the whole period while railroads were privately oper-

ated. In the 1840s there were grand plans for a *système de la Méditerranée* by which an isthmian service from Havre to Marseille would be operated, presumably for the benefit of British imperial communications.[96] But reality was more modest; the services were mainly to connect the metropolis with the provinces.

As separate endeavors of private companies, though heavily subsidized by the government construction of the *infrastructure*, each company established its own terminal in Paris, located toward the edge of the densely built-up core of the city but still well within the walls of the city then existing. The Gare de l'Ouest, more popularly known as Gare St. Lazare, was the first terminal to be opened in Paris, serving initially the line to St. Germain. When service began in 1837 the actual station was somewhat to the west of the present terminal, on Rue du Havre, at Place de l'Europe. There the line was below street level, allowing the station to be built as a bridge above the platforms. As the rails were carried westward to Rouen and then Havre, a larger terminus was required, which was obtained by clearing more space to the east of the small original station. This was not too difficult, as the Quartier de l'Europe where the yards were built had only been laid out in 1826 and was not fully developed when the railroad arrived in the 1830s. The present impressive station was constructed during the years 1886–1889, in time for Monet to paint his famous series showing the light and vapors within the high trainshed.[97] As the western suburbs of Paris became the most fashionable, the commuter traffic to St. Lazare, on both the main line and the Chemin de Fer de Ceinture (the inner belt line of the metropolis), became the heaviest in the city.

The Chemin de Fer du Nord, with its lines to Calais, Boulogne, and Valenciennes (for Brussels), was the first fairly complete system to open to its terminus, Gare du Nord, which was erected in 1846. Although that station, in some ways the most interesting in Paris, has never been totally rebuilt, it has been massively transformed to deal with increasing traffic and grander expectations. Around 1864 the original façade was removed piece by piece to Lille, where it was reassembled, while the Gare du Nord received a new front far more impressive than the original. In part this was in response to the shame Napoleon III felt when Victoria and Albert made a state visit to Paris in 1855. Normally they would have disembarked at the Gare du Nord, but Bonaparte felt it so shabby and nonimperial that he had a track laid from the throat of the station bypassing it to go on to the nearby Gare de l'Est, thought more regal. The Ceinture circumferential line also had a station at the Gare du Nord when that route fulfilled a larger intraurban transport role than it does today.

The route to the east, via Épernay, Nancy, and Strasbourg, similarly sought to approach the Grand Boulevards in the northeast so as to be within reach of the business center of Paris. Although its terminus was only a few hundred yards to the east of the Gare du Nord, the Chemin de Fer de l'Est deliberately maintained its separate identity, thus demonstrating conclusively that the lines reaching to Paris were not thought of by any company as going *through* that city. In this they shared with a number of European capitals—London, Brussels (even with the initially integrated Belgian railroad system), Vienna, Budapest, and Berlin—the notion that the capital was a place where one was going, whether for a short or a long time. As a result, even today trains seeking to pass from north or west of Paris to the Mediterranean or Central Europe normally must operate well outside, via northern and eastern France and Switzerland, save for four a day—two between Calais and Italy and two between the Low Countries and the Riviera—that enter Paris at the Gare du Nord

and then back to the outer belt line to pass around the metropolis to reach the Dijon line southeast of the city.[98] The Gare du Nord remains the main international station for Paris. Trains from the Channel ports, the Low Countries, Scandinavia, northern Germany, Poland, and Russia enter there, as does the rail connection to Charles de Gaulle Airport. Today considerable suburban traffic to the *villes nouvelles* also comes here via a line of the R.E.R. (to be discussed in chapter 6).

The Gare de l'Est was a decade later in being completed (1855), mainly because the eastern company was slow in building its line. The route as far as Nancy was opened only in 1852 and that to Strasbourg only about the time the great Parisian terminus was completed. Never so dominantly an international station, the Gare de l'Est grew rapidly only in this century, when the eastern suburbs of Paris burgeoned and their more working-class residents finally had wages high enough to permit railroad commuting.

The service to Lyon and the Mediterranean was unrewarding at first, so the company to Dijon was essentially bankrupt before it was reorganized and merged with the proposed lines from there to Lyon and Marseille. This merger came in the climate of early 1850s concentration that produced six reasonably profitable companies finally possessed of discrete and viable territories. The resulting Paris-Lyon-Marseille company in the southeast became one of the strongest. We shall examine its progress in more detail presently, but for now we should look at its metropolitan terminal. The Gare de Lyon was begun in 1847 and finished in 1852, before the line to Marseille itself was completed. Only in 1855 was the tunnel under Lyon and the Colline de Fourvières finished, for the first time permitting trains to pass through that major provincial city. Prosperity soon came to the P. L. M. company.

The Paris-Orleans and Paris-Rouen lines. Nineteenth-century lithograph in the author's collection.
Note should be taken that the Rouen line laid out by a British contractor, Thomas Brassey, ran left,
whereas the Orleans line, with a French contractor, ran right.

The left-bank stations in Paris were three in number, only two of which survive. The Chemin de Fer de l'État, which began as a line to Chartres but was ultimately carried via Tours to Bordeaux, found its metropolitan terminus at the southwestern edge of the built-up city of the years just before it was opened in 1855. The Chemin de Fer de l'Ouest used this same metropolitan access for its route passing to Brittany via Le Mans and Rennes dispatching its trains from this southwestern terminus, the Gare de Montparnasse. A later line passing along the left bank of the Seine from the west gave these two companies access to the government quarter when an in-town station was opened adjacent to the Chambre des Députés at the Gare des Invalides (which until the mid-1970s served in a transformed role as the central air terminal for the capital). Suburban services grew importantly from these two stations to the more elegant residential areas around St. Cloud and Versailles. The final initial line to be projected from the metropolis was that to Orléans, whose terminal was placed just in the fringe of the city at the Quai d'Austerlitz ultimately leading to a change of its name from Gare d'Orléans to Gare Quai d'Austerlitz (today simply Gare d'Austerlitz). The Orléans company also sought to develop its suburban service by continuing its left-bank line downriver from Austerlitz to a point on the Quai d'Orsay adjacent to the Chambre and just across the river from the financial center of Paris. The Orléans station was the first in the metropolis, built originally between 1835 and 1838, whereas the Quai d'Orsay was one of the last, in 1900.

The pattern of the Parisian stations was clearly determined by two sets of geographical facts: the edge of Paris in the late 1840s and the rather natural vectorial division of France into six sectors, each to be served from Paris. After 1837, with the opening of the Place de l'Europe station as a rather temporary arrangement at the end of the St. Germain line, a series of great terminals followed. The Gare d'Orléans came in 1838, the Gare St. Lazare just inward from the Place de l'Europe was developed in the 1840s to replace that first and soon cramped terminus. The Gare du Nord came in 1846, the Gare de Lyon in 1853, and the Gare de l'Est and Gare Montparnasse in 1855. In these twenty years Paris grew rapidly, so the later arrivals tended to be farther from the functioning heart of the metropolis. St. Lazare not only had the best location, but also had the most flourishing suburbs, to the extent that in 1869 it handled 13,254,000 passengers a year, whereas the other six Parisian termini among them saw only 21,417,000.[99] By the 1960s St. Lazare was used by a quarter of a million commuters a day, clearly demonstrating that decisions made initially in relation to the long-distance functions of a railroad could, as time passed, have profound effects both on the location of commercial activity in the city and on the siting of various types of residential areas in the suburbs. No doubt the line to St. Germain was originally a "plaything" for wealthy Parisians; but by the years before the Franco-Prussian War it had become a serious thing that was reshaping the metropolis.[100]

Subsequent Developments in French Railroads It is impossible in this short compass to discuss the evolution of the French rail system from the time of its initiation in 1842 with the governmental decision to shape five vectorial companies surrounding Paris and one regional company, the Chemin de Fer du Midi, in the south of France between Bordeaux and the lower Rhône valley. The Six, as they were called, had a great deal of evolution to accomplish before France had an encompassing network of lines. To that end both company strategy and governmental persuasion were used to restrict the companies to their sectors and to make within those gores a reasonably complete system. The initial lines from Paris to major provincial cities posed no great problem. The infrastructure was financed by the government, with the Corps des Ponts et Chaussées—the national engineering corps we saw previously at work on roads and canals—often doing the work of laying out the line and supervising its construction. At various times the government instead guaranteed the interest on construction loans and secured the infrastructure in that way. As it is not our purpose to discuss the financial base for transportation, which historians have tended to do to the exclusion of much consideration of the geography of those undertakings, we shall merely consider the geographical conditions that shaped the rail system as it came to be completed.

We discover a staged development. First the trunk lines were built, but in France they were rather slow in completion. Whereas much of the basic network in England, Belgium, and Germany was in existence by 1850, that system was still in pieces in the French Republic. Only after Prince-President Louis Napoleon's coup d'état in December, 1851, could the completion of the French trunk lines confidently be predicted. The Revolution of 1848 had found the line to Brest only just beyond Chartres, little more than 50 miles from the capital; the Orléans Company's line reached Tours, but there was a long gap towards Bordeaux and no work to speak of beyond that city. The line toward Toulouse had not yet reached the Massif Central in the Auvergne. The line that became the Paris-Lyon-Marseille company was finished to Chalons-sur-Saône and from Avignon to Marseille, but in between there was a long gap only unsatisfactorily crossed by steamer service on the Saône and Rhône or expensive road transport. The Strasburg railroad was more advanced, to Chalons-sur-Marne by 1848, to Nancy by the time of the coup d'état, and to the Rhine by the mid-

1850s. At the time of the 1848 revolution only the lines to the Channel coast at Calais and to the Belgian border north of Valenciennes some 125 miles north of Paris had been completed.

The Second Empire that saw Prince Bonaparte as Napoleon III soon witnessed much activity in railroad construction and organization. In the first five years of the empire the concentration of power into the Six companies was nearly complete:

> As part of the bargain between these great new companies and the Imperial Government, the concessions [made to the predecessors] were extended; but a point of time in the future was always contemplated at which the whole property would fall in to the state. The stronger companies, like that of the North, needed no financial help; but some of the others secured a guarantee of interest.[101]

At the time these concessions were reassigned, the government required of the companies that they undertake a system of subsidiary lines that would assure to most larger towns in France connection to a national rail network. These were not to be subsidized by the state.

The 1850s became the period of trunk-line completion and the 1860s that for building the subsidiary lines. France in 1850 had about 1,850 miles (3,000 km) of railroad when Germany had twice that mileage and Britain three and a half times as much. But by 1870 France, with nearly eleven thousand miles (17,500 km), was approaching Germany's 12,000 miles and Britain's 15,000 miles.[102] At first the six companies may have been reluctant to complete the network of subsidiary lines within their assigned sectors, especially in those areas with little prospect for earnings or with very high construction costs. The outbreak of war with Prussia in 1870 further complicated the picture because the eventual defeat of France was blamed by many on the collapse of the railroads as the Germans pushed southward in the Saône valley behind a besieged Paris. The Paris-Lyon-Marseille company was particularly badly affected. On December 19 the company was hastily called upon to move the 18th and 20th Army Corps from Bourges, Charité, and Nevers just north of the Massif Central, to the area of increasing German pressure in Burgundy—to Autun, Chagny (near Dijon), and Chalons-sur-Saône. Ninety thousand men and their supplies and guns must be moved, but one line of track was blocked for nearly ten miles by cars with provisions that could not be discharged. With temperatures hovering just above zero Fahrenheit, water tubes froze and burst:

> The situation was complicated still further when Gambetta [who escaped by balloon from Paris on October 8 and sought to organize France for defense], impatient to obtain decisive results, decided to send the 15th Corps to [aid General] Bourbaki. On the 31st of December [the politician] de Freycinet telegraphed the company "Wish you to make all arrangements to be able, as soon as you have received the order by telegraph, to transport in thirty-six hours the 15th Army Corps from Vierzon, where it is presently, to a point to be determined on the line from Vesoul to Montbeliard."[103]

This movement, to begin January 3 at 6:00 A.M. and to finish by the evening of January 4, would carry 35,000 men, twenty batteries of artillery, and all their equipment, ammunition, and stores. Even though the company strongly objected, because there were no platforms or sidings for the disembarking of horses or artillery there, the French politician-soldiers selected Clerval, the last stop accessible between Besançon on the line to Montbeliard. The movement of 275 miles began on time, but slowly the line became clogged as the trains reached the Jura only to be unable to unload. For more than six days there were trains stopped at intervals from Saincaize north of the Massif

all the way across the two hundred miles to Clerval, but the troops and horses were kept aboard, in zero-degree weather, in readiness to move when possible. The suffering was terrible, and many horses died in the four days. Furthermore, the line of stalled trains across the full width between the Morvan and Jura so impeded supply of the French troops to the north that when on January 19 the German Manteuffel broke out into Burgundy, it was nearly impossible to resupply or reinforce the French troops needed to oppose the Prussians. The French defense failed, the siege of Paris continued, and there was no escape from defeat.

In the years after the disaster of 1871 the railroads were often blamed for somehow having led to the collapse. De Freycinet became minister of public works in 1877 and premier twice in the early 1880s. It is not surprising that in those offices he began an investigation of how to improve the French railroad system, specifically by completing the system where logical components remained unbuilt. In this we again discover the Gallic passion both for central control and planning and for a seemingly rational network. The result was what has come to be known as the Freycinet plan of 1883, under which the remainder of the basic railroad network of France was obtained.

There were several financial commitments that saw the companies provide most of the capital while the state gave loan guarantees. In return for this understanding, the distinction between the old and new lines controlled by the Six companies was abolished, systems became fully integrated, and the gaps were filled. The companies had to approve of this agreement with the government, and some of the stockholders' meetings were spirited. There was a Gallic quality to the meeting held by the P.L.M. on December 24, 1883. In an interview given in 1895, Noblemaire, a director of the company, gave the following account:[104]

Voyager de 3e classe completement geles (Third-class passenger completely frozen). *Source: Hommes et Choses du P.L.M.*, N.P., P.L.M. Co., privately printed, 1911.

The stockholders, overheated for a month by the effort of several newspapers to drive down the value of the stock, were excited greatly at the meeting by a former actress, Mlle. O...., whom various circumstances and a laudable spirit of economy had made an important stockholder of the Compagnie de Lyon, when she contributed to the waivering opinion in the hall. [The directors' arguments] encountered a systematic opposition. Some demanded a public investigation. M. Blount, vice president, standing before an urn followed the commotion among the stockholders with a truly British phlegm. When it came her turn to vote, Mlle. O.... turned to the directors and fist hammering the table: "I say no, Monsieur, I say no!" Then M. Blount, in a strong voice and grim English accent that laid emphasis on each word said: "Oh! Mademoiselle, You, who have so often said 'Yes....'" 290 stockholders, representing 1,427 shares voted against and 92 stockholders representing 222 shares voted to approve the wicked contract [conventions scélérates].

The susceptibility of French audiences to former actresses rather than frosty English accents was evident. But in the end the P.L.M. and all the other companies came to an agreement with the government, accepting the new relationship that under the Freycinet plan saw the system completed, though with a revision in earlier practices that extended their concessions to expire between 1950 and 1960.[105]

Before we consider several examples of the accomplishments of this third phase of French railroad building, we should note the general changes that took place. Between 1870 and 1890 French rail mileage doubled (108 percent), whereas Britain's increased by only 34 percent. Germany grew even more than France, 120 percent, but a considerable part of that came from the conquest of Alsace and Lorraine during the 1870 war. In the next twenty years (1890–1910) the growth continued, though at a slower rate. France added 36 percent to its mileage, Germany 42 percent, but Britain only 15 percent.[106]

From 1870 onwards, the geographical history of railway construction is a localized and specialized story. It is the story of a network of ever increasing density, with now and then the completion of some specially significant line, either within the West European economic area, like the St. Gothard and, much later, the Simplon, or linking that area to eastern points—to Constantinople, Salonica or Vladivostock.[107]

Within France, Freycinet's completion of the "national equipment" included not merely railroads but also canals, harbors, and roads. As he proposed adding over five thousand miles to the then existing network, a 50-percent increase, there were some lines that gained little private interest. In particular, the line from Chartres via Tours to Bordeaux was left without a taker, so this became the first nationally operated line, the Chemin de Fer d'État. Ultimately the route from Paris to Brittany, the Chemin de Fer de l'Ouest, which could not operate without continuing government subsidies, was joined with this earlier triangle of public interest—Chartres-Nantes-Tours-Bordeaux—affording to the État system access to Paris via Gare Montparnasse, and later Gare des Invalides.

In the Massif Central the Freycinet round of construction created some of the most interesting rails to be found anywhere. These were commonly designed by the Corps des Ponts et Chaussées or a special group formed to effect the plan, the *Ingénieurs auxiliares*.[108] By standards elsewhere the construction was on a grand scale, particularly with respect to the bridging of the great valleys carved into the generally level to rolling upland surface of the Massif. The purpose of these lines was twofold: to create a system across the large upland to provide more direct routing from Lyon to Bordeaux and Nantes or from Nîmes or Béziers to Clermont-Ferrand; or to accommodate the considerable traffic in coal produced in the relatively small basins enclosed within the borders of the Massif, as at St. Étienne, Decazeville, Brassac-les-Mines, Buxières-les-Mines, St. Éloy-les-Mines, Carmaux, and Alès (La Grande Combe). The Ligne des Cévennes, as the most important of the mountainous lines in the heart of France came to be called, was an extension of the last radial to be projected from Paris, the Grand Central that was constructed jointly by the P.L.M. and the Orléans companies but came to be the second main line of the former operating as the Ligne de Bourbonnais from Paris, Gare de Lyon, to a junction in the Bourbonnais, St. Germain-des-Fossés, 225 miles to the south. There the first of the transverse lines not radiating from Paris, that from Lyon toward Nantes and Bordeaux, was encountered, while ahead any radial faced the great Massif Central. For the first hundred miles the line uses the rolling countryside of the Limagne and the broad valley of the Allier River that drains it. From Clermont-Ferrand southward the Allier still serves for half the distance to Nîmes, but only in a narrow, steeply stepped valley. The scenery is superb but the construction was very difficult. For 116 miles the line continued to ascend the valley, but at a cost of very heavy engineering. Viaducts and tunnels alternate for most of the way, some fifty tunnels north of the main intermediate town, La Bastide, and 101 to the south. These range up to a mile in length while the viaducts are both long and high, particularly in rising up out of the plain of Languedoc in the south through the great anthracite basin with its mines around La Grande Combe. La Bastide, at three thousand feet, is the summit of this route, the highest mainline in France. Thence the drop to about a hundred feet at Nîmes is taken across the grain of the terrain of the Cévennes. Viaducts cross valleys divided by ridges that must be tunneled. Only obedience to a design for a complete network of rail lines throughout France, as envisioned by the Freycinet plan and heavily subsidized by the government, could have produced such an undertaking.[109]

This Ligne de Cévennes was the main stem around which a rail network within the Massif was shaped. To the west Les Causses, a great dry limestone plateau, posed a particular problem with its extremely deep valleys cut with nearly sheer walls rising hundreds of feet. The P.L.M. and Midi companies joined forces to drive a line northward from Béziers to a junction at Arvant with the Paris-Nîmes line:

Cutting transversely the deep valleys which descend from the Massif Central toward the Garonne: the Truyére, Lot, and Tarn; and toward the Mediterranean; the Ord; its profile in sawteeth is extremely difficult. The embankments and slopes of 3.7, 3.0 and 3.3 per cent continue over long sections, but electric traction permits a supple and satisfactory working; throughout its course there are 44 tunnels of which five are over a kilometer long.[110]

More spectacular still are the viaducts involved. Most of the viaducts on French railroads, even those in the Massif, are of masonry construction, carrying the tracks at various heights up to a hundred and fifty feet above the streams or side valleys they span. In a few cases there may be several stories of arches, rather in the Roman fashion used in the aqueduct of the Pont du Gard not far away. Although there are plain viaducts that carry the various lines straight across a valley, many of these great arched structures are curving and help to maintain reasonable gradients not only on the lines but around sweeping curves as well. But in Les Causses and several other districts on the western slope of the Massif, where rainfall has its maximum for the latitude and closeness to the Aquitainian plain makes for steeply graded streams, the valleys are particularly deep and narrow. A number of great metal viaducts are found there, mostly steel and built in the late nineteenth century. The Ligne des Causses has one of the greatest,

that across the Truyére at Garabit, which stands 403 feet above the natural surface of the river (which is now dammed, reducing the apparent height somewhat), and 1,853 feet from one lip of the plateau to the other. A great parabolic arch with a span of 541.2 feet carries the line over the river; the bridge deck is borne over the full length by five tall steel towers to make Garabit one of the world's great bridges, and typical of those on railroads employing iron or steel arches or cantilevers rather than suspension cables. The latter have never been very effectively used on rail lines as the motions set up by locomotives and numerous cars moving in unison have tended to become harmonic and destructive to the suspended fabric of the structure.

With the completion of the Garabit viaduct in 1889 the second of the continuous north-south rail lines through the Massif Central was open for service, offering to Béziers and the route northward from Spain at the east end of the Pyrenees the shortest route to Paris. With the increasing speeds on well-graded main lines that came at the turn of the century, however, the expresses along the corridor of the Rhône and Saône, the main line of the P.L.M., proved able to match and then reduce the running times on the more direct Ligne de Cévennes and Ligne des Causses. The common assumptions in the 1870s and 1880s that air-lines stood as an improvement on the earlier trunk lines—which might be somewhat more circuitous because they passed through the larger cities that might be expected to furnish the first economically significant flows of goods and people—proved only partially true at best. Only intermediate cities—Clermont-Ferrand and Vichy in the case of the longitudinal lines of the Massif— really benefited from such air-line construction.

In the Massif these trunk lines also were able to serve important coal basins. The Ligne de Cévennes passed directly through the important anthracite field of La Grande Combe, and the Ligne des Causses actually employed an earlier coal-carrying line from Graissesac to Béziers at its southernmost segment that dropped through Cévennes and Garrigues down on to the Languedocian plain. Other important coal fields were dotted within the western flanks of the Massif within reach of the lines that had been carried north-south over the upland surface.

Two will suffice to show the sort of construction required to carry coals from distant and relatively small fields to the markets in the Saône and Rhône valleys, the Aquitainian Basin, and Provence. The first was the line constructed by the Compagnie du Midi as a branch between the Ligne des Causses and the Carmaux coalfield. Although the upland surface here is gently rolling, the Viaur River cut deeply across the line proposed between Rodez and Carmaux toward Albi. Fortunately this valley was narrow, about 1,350 feet, but it was very deep, about 500 feet. The Midi company and the government set up a commission to examine the question, leading in 1895 to a definite project. Cantilevered arms, in the form of an arc from each footing, were to be thrown across the gorge for a total distance of 721 feet to carry a bridge deck 380.5 feet above the river surface. Clearly at such heights, as at Garabit, falsework to support an arch until it was completed was impracticable, so the use of cantilevered construction was indicated.

As completed the Viaur viaduct stood as perhaps the most daring railroad bridge ever constructed, light in structure but buttressed against wind by a spreading of 25° from the vertical (from the deck to the footings). There is no more visibly economical structure to be found. The overengineered Forth Bridge in Scotland is clumsy and timid by comparison, obviously built to avoid another Tay Bridge disaster.

The coalfield at St. Éloy-les-Mines west of Vichy needed to be connected with the upper Allier valley and Clermont-Ferrand; there was interest as well in completing the secondary rail net between the Ligmagne plain on the Allier and the Gate of Poitiers to the west. To those ends the Sioule River had to be crossed, between Lapeyrouse and Volvic, by a viaduct 1,541 feet long, supported by three granite piers about 300 feet tall, and carrying a continuous truss of steel, the central opening of which spans 472 feet while the side spans are of 377 feet. Even more surprising, given the fact that this was in the beginning only a very secondary line of the Orléans company, is the height of this structure. The bridge deck stands 436 feet above the surface of the Sioule, making this the highest bridge in Europe when it was first put to use in 1909.[111]

To understand the high level to which railroad construction was carried in the Massif Central, we must appreciate that French policy had come to envision the railroad as the basic transportation for the republic and a service that must be furnished to a relatively high standard in all parts of the country. In Belgium such national objectives had seemed both logical and expectable because of fairly uniform terrain outside the Ardennes, and rather rolling than outright mountainous country even there. In France, with much stronger contrasts in terrain, it might at first seem that the rather special exertions required in the Massif presented a situation that would have vitiated the principle that a centralized nation needs a relatively uniform provision of transportation. That was not the way Parlement viewed it, however; adoption of the Freycinet plan was a statement by that body that public funds were to be used to encourage such a basic uniformity. Obviously the lines in the Massif Central were less dense than elsewhere, but they were to be basically available. And in those margins of the plateau where down-folding or dropping had left coal-bearing strata preserved, the railroad facilities could be both fairly dense and very heavily engineered.

Today we would never build much of this mileage in the Massif, but at the turn of the century there was an unformulated awareness of the process of ubiquity with respect to railroad pattern at work in the bureaucracy, Parlement, and electorate of France. There was the firmly held idea that railroads were the ultimate form of transportation, and no country could deny this service to any of its citizens, even those living in rough terrain.

We shall see this process of ubiquity at work again with respect to the Alps, but first it is well to try to discover why anyone would make such efforts to cross that truly imposing barrier.

THE RAILROAD AS LIBERATOR AND UNIFIER: ITALY

The three countries considered so far all were nation-states by the time the railroad became the accepted form of transportation, although Belgium had to have that new medium in order to enjoy its new-found freedom. South of the Alps, Italy had yet to gain a political extent to match its cultural realm. In the south the Kingdom of the Two Sicilies—commonly termed the Kingdom of Naples, for the Bourbon capital—was the most extensive state, though one so badly ruled that Gladstone could call its rulers "the negation of God erected into a system of government." (Of course, he did set a moral standard many mortals found beyond their reach.) In central Italy one of the worst despotisms ever contrived was in control of the Papal States in the early nineteenth century.

Even by the railroad era conditions were not much better. Certainly the Roman Curia was extremely reactionary with respect to the new medium, so much so that the Romans circulated one of those archly anticlerical

jokes they greatly enjoyed about Gregory XVI, who died in 1846 after a thoroughly unenlightened rule. The Romans had it that Gregory

> was walking up a dusty road towards heaven when he encountered St. Peter as is usual on such a journey. Gregory XVI asked St. Peter if there was yet a long way to go. "Much farther yet," said St. Peter. "But I am tired," said the Pope. "Ah," said St. Peter, "if only you had built a railway you would have been in paradise by now"—a rejoinder with a double or even triple meaning which delighted the Roman mind.[112]

In northern Italy all of the Po Basin east of the Ticino River was a vice-royalty of Austria, whereas Tuscany, Modena, and Parma were dukedoms owing respect to the Hapsburgs. The only reasonably modern state was to be found in Piedmont where Victor Emmanuel's realm, extending from Nice to La Spezia along the Riviera and to and beyond the Alps in the northwest (where what is now French Savoie was then Piedmontese), was both modern and moderately liberal. Industry had arisen that needed good transport, so the Piedmontese government had promoted a line across the Apennines to the port of Genoa, as well as two railroads east to west across the Po Valley from the foothills of the Maritime Alps in the west to the Austrian border at the Ticino west of Milan.

Victor Emmanuel's great minister, Camillo Cavour, who was premier of Piedmont through most of the 1850s, was particularly interested in railroads, perhaps because of his engineering training. As Cavour saw it, the railroad could be a great force for *Il Risorgimento* by bringing Italy together and advancing its economic growth. He wrote tracts to that effect and was, as a politician, to prove more directly the utility of railroads in that political-cultural drive. In 1859, when France under Napoleon III joined Piedmont in picking a fight with

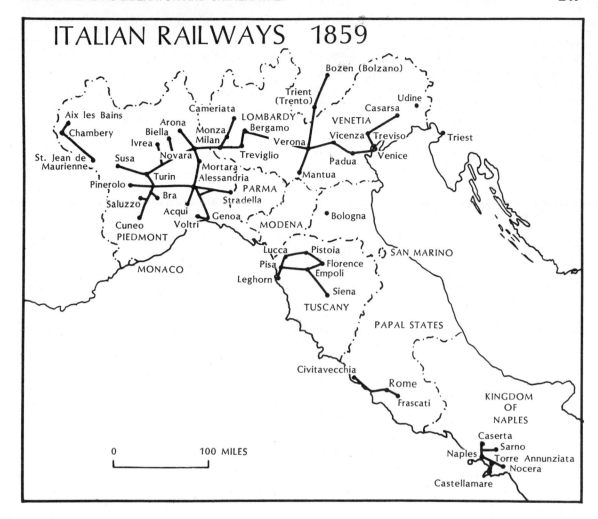

ITALIAN RAILWAYS 1859

Austria leading to warfare on the Piedmont-Lombard border, it was Cavour's well-developed rail system that allowed the Allies to shift troops to the Austrians' right flank, with such speed that they soundly defeated the Hapsburgs in the great battle of Magenta. The speed with which they pursued those Austrians along those rails in the route to the east was such that there was an early Austrian call for negotiations. From those came the conditions that led to the unification in 1860 of all of Italy save Venetia and the Papal States directly adjacent to Rome.

Clearly the victorious Piedmontese saw in the railroad the true instrument of Italian rejuvenation; they quickly set about building lines southward along both coasts of the peninsula.

It is ironic that the railroad played such a striking role in the reunification of Italy, as the building of railroads on Italian terrain was so very difficult. No doubt the key lies in the fact that the one moderately easy part for rail development was in the western Po Basin where the thickly graded depression was reasonably flat and the drainage was fairly well contained in the river courses. In the surrounding mountain girdle and in the eastern Po Basin, where poor drainage led to wide swampy areas, the initial effort would have encountered far more trouble. Even in Piedmont the early engineers met severe problems. To take two as examples, we may look at the effort to reach across the Apennines to Genoa and the Alps to the transmontane provinces of Savoy.

The industrial development of Piedmont needed a port on the Mediterranean, but all were cut off by the sharp crest of the Apeninnes, with the lowest usable pass about 2,500 feet. Genoa was the best port, though hardly a good natural harbor on this truly cliffed coast that extends from the mouth of the Arno, beyond Piedmont in Tuscany, to the French border, then west of Nice. The Romans had used the Bocchetta Pass (2,532 feet) for a road between the Po Basin and *Genua*; but when a Piedmontese engineer in government service, Luigi Ranco, was commissioned in 1844 to find the best possible line through the Ligurian Apennines, he adopted the next pass to the east, the Giovi, for his line as he, through the boring of a tunnel, was able to cross the range at 1,180 feet. Even then his route had to reach that elevation in only 14.5 miles, from dockside in Genoa to the south portal of the Giovi tunnel. "This Giovi pass was to be conquered by 4½ miles of 1 in 28½ [3.5 percent] gradient leading to a 2-mile summit tunnel at 1 in 33 [3.0 percent] throughout."[113] It had at first been proposed that Isambard Brunel be employed as a consultant on this line but it was probably fortunate for the Italians that he was too busy to leave England for the undertaking. It is highly unlikely that an English locating engineer could have been persuaded to build such a line as was laid out, though it was all that a capital-poor country like Piedmont could have afforded. It was thought that the Giovi Pass line would have to be operated by winding engines, but the

Italians—always ingenious engineers—obviated that awkward situation. Robert Stephenson passed through Genoa and was asked for advice, "but the great man merely remarked enigmatically that he would not care to be responsible for the operation of the incline and went on his way."[114] Three Italian engineers—Severino Grattoni, Germaneo Someiller, and Sebastiano Grandis—came up with a winning solution: they coupled two locomotives back to back, permitting one engineer to operate them and thereby gaining sufficient power for the line with ordinary adhesion working. In 1853 this 103-mile line, the first of any length in Italy, was opened; its midpoint, Allesandria, became the great junction of Piedmontese lines.

From that city rails were carried northward through Novara to Arona on Lake Maggiore, a distance of 68 miles. By 1859, the year of Magenta, a rail line from Cuneo in the very southwestern reaches of the Po Basin was carried almost to the border of the Duchy of Parma, to Stradella, while from Turin the Lombard border was reached by a second route somewhat north of the Po passing through Novara. A connection at the Ticino frontier was made with Austrian lines, which then passed via Milan and Bergamo to Verona whence branches extended to Bozen (Bolzano) in the South Tyrol, Mantua, and Carsara, via Venice Mestre. This integrated system contrasted sharply with railroad patterns elsewhere in Italy. In Tuscany there was a self-contained system tying Florence, Lucca, Pisa, Livorno, and Sienna together; in the Papal States a line from Frascati through Rome to the Papal port at Civitavecchia was all that had been undertaken in the years since Gregory XVI's weary journey to the Pearly Gates; and in the Kingdom of Naples a line of sorts extended from north of the city at Caserta to south thereof at Nocera. This then was the pattern of Italian railroads on the eve of the successful political integration of the peninsula.

While Piedmont was still an *á cheval* kingdom, Victor Emmanuel and Cavour encouraged the attempt to pierce the Alps with a railroad, clearly requiring a tunnel through one of the *cols* where valleys heading in the range from opposite sides came reasonably close together. The ridge selected was that at the Col de Fréjus (commonly misnamed as the Mont Cenis in recognition of that nearby *col* of 6,893 feet, over which Napoleon had a carriage road built between 1803 and 1810 and where a narrow-guage line invented by Dr. Fell was built in 1868 only to be abandoned three years later when the Col de Fréjus tunnel was completed).

A railroad had already been constructed to Susa, at the southern end of the Napoleonic road, as well as a totally detached section from Chambery to St. Jean-de-Maurienne in Savoy. The Col de Mont Cenis was at 6,893 feet with a wider summit ridge than that found 16 miles to the west at Fréjus. There it was possible, at around 4,200 feet, to pierce the ridge with a tunnel 7.5 miles long. The railroads were extended from Susa to Bardonecchia at the head of the valley on the eastern side and from St. Jean to Modane on the west.

Between those two stations, boring of the tunnel began in 1857. In the early 1850s Robert Stephenson and the English engineer Swinburne

> were called to Switzerland to lend their advice on a tunnel through the Alps. They took one look at the country and declared that it could not be done. No locomotive could climb the gradients necessary for a railway to cross the mountains. They left it to the natives to muddle through as best they could. [115]

Fortunately the Piedmontese knew from experience on the Giovi Pass line above Genoa that there were stronger engines than those used in the British Isles, so they were not daunted in planning the Fréjus line, although its tunnel might well have given them pause. In 1838 a native of Bardonecchia, G. F. Medail, who had in his youth been a shepherd in the adjacent mountains, already proposed the winding line that would carry the railroad from the open Isére valley along its tributary the Arc to Modane north of the narrowest divide in this section. To the south of the ridge, which he proposed be tunncled, he found a similarly circuitous but possible line down the Dora Ripária from Bardonnechia to Susa. In 1845, after Medail's death, King Carlo Alberto of Sardinia (Piedmont) had a Belgian engineer, Heinrich Mauss, commissioned to find an extension of the Genoa-Turin railroad to carry that line across, or through, the Alps to his Savoyard province beyond the mountains. The geology was found acceptable at Fréjus, so Mauss ultimately recommended Medail's plan.

Nothing came of it; Sandström believes it was infeasible at that time because of the great depth beneath the surface the tunnel would lie. Any long tunnel up to that time had been built as the Romans had worked, with several working shafts driven down to the tunnel level below the low hills so as to allow a number of headings for excavations as well as essential chimneys for ventilation of the completed bore. At Fréjus the rock was 3,937 feet thick at its deepest point: thus all work must be accomplished at only the two end headings, and ventilation must be gained only from those points.

The key to the successful completion of the Col de Fréjus tunnel was furnished by the Swiss physicist Collandon, who proposed a method of drilling using compressed air to drive the drill bit, thus greatly speeding up the work on the headings as well as furnishing, through the exhausted air released by the drilling, a source of ventilation for the advancing tunnel. By the use of the water

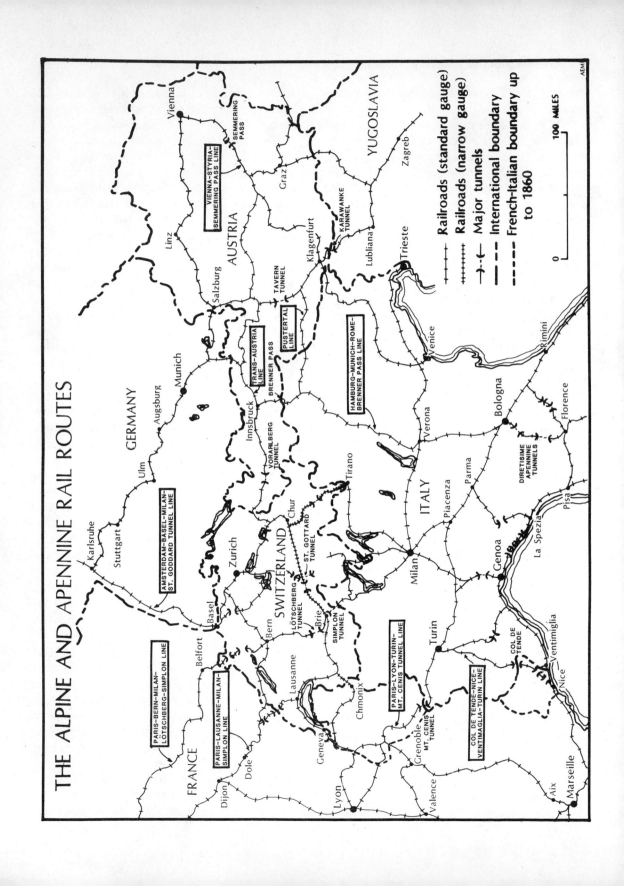

THE ALPINE AND APENNINE RAIL ROUTES

Railroads (standard gauge)
Railroads (narrow gauge)
Major tunnels
International boundary
French-Italian boundary up to 1860

0   100 MILES

AEM

YUGOSLAVIA

Zagreb

Lubliana

Trieste

Venice

Rimini

Bologna

Florence

Pisa

La Spezia

DIRETISIME APENNINE TUNNELS

Genoa

Parma

Piacenza

ITALY

Verona

Milan

Tirano

Turin

COL DE TENDE

COL DE TENDE-NICE-VENTIMIGLIA-TURIN LINE

Ventimiglia

Nice

Aix

Marseille

Valence

Lyon

Grenoble

MT. CENIS TUNNEL

PARIS-LYON-TURIN-MT. CENIS TUNNEL LINE

Chmonix

Geneva

Dole

Dijon

FRANCE

Belfort

PARIS-BERN-MILAN-LÖTSCHBERG-SIMPLON LINE

PARIS-LAUSANNE-MILAN-SIMPLON LINE

Lausanne

Bern

Brie

SIMPLON TUNNEL

LÖTSCHBERG TUNNEL

ST. GOTTARD TUNNEL

Chur

Zurich

SWITZERLAND

Basel

AMSTERDAM-BASEL-MILAN-ST. GODDARD TUNNEL LINE

Karlsruhe

Stuttgart

Ulm

Augsburg

GERMANY

Munich

Innsbruck

VORARLBERG TUNNEL

TRANS-AUSTRIA LINE

BRENNER PASS

PUSTERTAL LINE

TAVERN TUNNEL

HAMBURG-MUNICH-ROME-BRENNER PASS LINE

Klagenfurt

KARAWANKE TUNNEL

Graz

AUSTRIA

Salzburg

Linz

VIENNA-STYRIA-SEMMERING PASS LINE

SEMMERING PASS

Vienna

power available in abundance in these mountain valleys, the air itself was compressed and carried in hoses as much as 4 miles long to the advancing headings in this 7.46-mile tunnel. Prior to the adoption of compressed-air drilling—that is, from 1857 to 1860—the headings advanced only an average of 46 feet per month, whereas after the Savoyard engineer Sommaeiller—one of the three who proposed the coupled locomotives at Giovi Pass—adopted the air drill, the average rose to 243 feet per month. The tunnels were absolutely straight, that course maintained by strong lights at either portal projected down the tunnel on which bearings were taken until the two bores joined the day after Christmas in 1870. The heading from Modane had advanced 16,902 feet while that from Bardonnechia had made 23,222 feet in the thirteen years the tunnel was under construction. The quality of the surveying is evident from the fact these headings met with an error of only 14 inches.[116]

The success of the Col de Fréjus tunnel, opened to traffic in 1871, was immediate. Not only did it provide the first rail connection from France to Italy, but it also demonstrated the practicality of drilling long bores under high mountains. This had been thought impossible because of the expected high temperatures in the heart of a mountain. These were encountered—more at Simplon than at Fréjus—but they were kept to sufferable proportions by the air pumped into the workings. Today the highest temperature in the Fréjus tunnel stands at about 75° Fahrenheit.

The experience here gave the Italians and the Swiss both the technology and the confidence to undertake many other long tunnels. The Italians became the acknowledged masters of this construction, no doubt largely as a result of the fact that 5.5 percent of the Italian railroad mileage lies in some 1,850 tunnels, with the recently completed 57-mile line from Genoa to La Spezia reaching the astounding figure of 60 percent subterranean.[117]

The Piedmontese, aided by the French, pursued the Austrians eastward from Magenta to fight again at Solferino just before the Mincio. Again defeated, the Austrians sued for peace, and Lombardy was ceded to the Kingdom of Sardina (Piedmont). In the next year the Duchies of Parma and Modena and the Grand Duchy of Tuscany and the Kingdom of the two Sicilies (Naples) were extinguished, and Victor Emmanuel became the first independent King of Italy. Even the Papal States were attacked by the victorious Italians before the French troops of Napoleon III were dispatched to defend that despotic regime. At that point relations between the two Latin monarchies were somewhat strained. France demanded and was ceded the County of Nizza (Nice) and the trans-Alpine parts of Piedmont (Savoie) while the Italians were restrained from completing the conquest of the rump of the Papal States (Romagna, the Marches, and Umbria had been liberated in 1860) until after France's humiliation by Prussia in 1870.

Thus, with the exception of the environs of Rome, which languished under papal misrule for another decade, Italy was a newly unified country desperately in need of the infrastructure of modern economic life. Cavour had the chance to apply his theories of railroads as unifiers, but unfortunately he did not live to take direct action. He died in 1861 just after the unified Italian Parliament began to sit. In November of that year a line parallel to the ancient Via Aemilio between Piacenza in Lombardy and Bologna in Romagna was completed, and work began on a second crossing of the Apennines toward Florence.

That link was perhaps the most important section of railroad internal to Italy, as it tied the Po Basin system—already well developed by 1862 when the Apennine link was undertaken—to the detached systems soon to be joined that lay around Florence, Rome, and Naples. From Bologna the alignment followed the narrow and sinuous valley of the Reno River passing through great numbers of short tunnels to reach the summit at Pracchia (2,037 feet), gaining half that rise in the last quarter of the 45 miles to the north portal of a 1.7-mile tunnel carried under the ridge that separated the Po from the Arno drainage. From the south portal of that Galleria di Pracchia, the railroad headed for Pistoia only 6 miles distant but some 1,825 feet below on the Florentine plain. Using the by-then established practice, the railroad was carried down the south slope of the Appenino Tosco Emiliano in two great switchbacks, with numerous tunnels cut through minor spurs of the range, thus lengthening the route 15 miles to gain a workable gradient.[118] When completed in 1864 the Pracchia line set the stage for continuous rails to Rome, which came in 1866 with the linking of the Florentine and Roman systems via Foligno.[119] Earlier, in 1863, the Roman and Neopolitan systems had been linked: "This Rome-Naples railway was heavily graded, for it avoided the malarial and deserted coastal plain and ran through the foothills of the Apennines, serving the towns of Frosinone, Roccasecca and Cassino."[120]

A start was made on the line down the Adriatic coast when the private Societá Generale delle Strade Ferrate Romane, the company operating in the Papal States, began a railroad from Bologna still in the alignment of the Via Aemilia southeastward around the curve of the Apennines through Rimini to Ancona, which was reached in 1861. Thence the Rothschilds, who had been significant investors in the private lines of France and Austria as well as Italy, promoted a line along the coast, but nationalism demanded that it be an Italian company

when it was organized as the Strade Ferrate Meridionali (Southern Railroads) in 1862. Brindisi was reached in 1865, introducing that peculiarity of Victorian travel, the approach to India by way of a fast run from the Channel ports to Brindisi—later much speeded up in 1871 with the opening of the Fréjus tunnel. The Southern Railroad came to Taranto in 1868, thus completing the Adriatic line, which waited only for the route along the deserted malarial coast of the Gulf of Taranto to the toe of Italy to join with the west-coast route in creating the basic trunk lines of peninsular Italy.

All this railway building was aided by the government of the new Kingdom of Italy from 1862—railways were to unite the new nation. The government granted concessions to the railway companies that provided for the cost of building the railway to be returned to the company concerned after it was open to traffic.[121]

"Normally, the period [for repayment] was anything from fifty to ninety-nine years and the subsidy was paid as to 60 per cent by the national government and 40 per cent by the provincial government concerned." Under such an arrangement a number of secondary lines were constructed that filled out the network the Italian Railroads possess today.

Two aspects of that completion of the system at public expense deserve mention even in a short summary: the completion of a number of direct lines (*direttissime*) and the construction of the links between Italy and its neighbors. Although those links antedated the *direttissimi*, it is more practical to consider the evolution of the Italian railroads internally before looking at their international connections.

There had been government participation in rail development in Italy from the very beginning. Even in Piedmont before unification there were government lines, and we have seen that the reimbursement of construction expenses for private companies came early on, just after unification began. There was always implicit, as in France, the assumption that the actual infrastructure of the railroads was a national responsibility and, in ultimate legal terms, a national possession. Thus, as the basic trunk network was completed by about 1870, attention turned to filling the gaps—tying all large towns to the network, creating several crossings of the spine of the Roman and Neopolitan Apennines, and improving the alignment of the more important sectors of the system. As we have seen, in the 1870s the governments, for the kingdom and for its provinces, assumed the responsibility for the repayment of private construction costs. Even with these generous provisions—necessitated in considerable measure by the excessively high cost of even the most economical construction given the Italian terrain outside the few lowlands—the railroad companies proved unprofitable. In that position the private companies had been unable to maintain a sufficient rolling stock to cope with the rise in traffic that began about the turn of the century, laying themselves open to the always popular argument that the lines should be taken over by the state, which was done in 1905. The Ferrovie dello Stato, or F.S., was organized with 6,672 miles of line. This figure had risen to somewhat over ten thousand miles with new construction.[122] Important lines were double-tracked, as the earliest routes often had not been to save precious construction capital. The line from Florence to Rome was finished only in 1933, and the spectacularly engineered line from Genoa to La Spezia only in 1970[123] More unusual was the development of the *direttissime*, fundamental improvements in the alignment and grading of important segments of the F.S. The first to be undertaken was between Statione Piazza Principe in Genoa and the opening of the Scrivia valley toward the Po Basin in the north. This

Giovi Pass section had both the very steep grades already noted and a 2-mile summit tunnel (Upper Giovi Tunnel), as well as only two tracks. The funnel of traffic this represented was severely hampering access to and from the main Italian port so a plan to add two tracks was advanced for the 22 miles to Arquata-Scrivia. By boring a 5.14-mile Lower Giovi Tunnel beneath the original gallery a better gradient was obtained, though still not an easy one. Finished in 1923, this solution sufficed for a time but was further improved in the 1950s and 1960s by a third bore that added still more tracks to this critical bottleneck for the Italian railroads. In addition, there is nearby a separate line from Genoa to Turin, passing through the 4-mile long, double-tracked Turchino Tunnel. Probably no other restricted area has such a wealth of mountain railroading as is found in the environs of Genoa. The La Spezia line lacks stiff grades but holds the record for tunneling over such a distance (60 percent). The four tunnels through the Ligurian Apennines, with eight tracks, present a remarkably staged evolution of one of the great industrial lifelines to be found anywhere.

The *direttissime* normally involved particularly mountainous sections of the original lines, which had been more modestly engineered than mature traffic conditions suggested wise. The ex post facto quality of the linkage of the Neapolitan and Roman railroads meant that the tie between those two great cities was awkward and roundabout. The other great barrier was that over the Apennines between Bologna and Florence, where the main flow from northern to peninsular Italy took place. These projects were begun in 1907 and 1914, respectively, though obviously not to great effect until after 1918. The original line from Rome to Naples passed, as noted, in the foothills of the Apennines—through Frosinone, Roccasecca, Cassino, Capua, and Caserta—introducing stiff grades and considerable curvature. Yet this route did pass through the larger towns lying between the two cities, thus providing the maximum possible conformity to settlement in a region where the coast remained sparsely settled because of the malarial swamps found there. But as the traffic between the main termini increased, it was clear that there was plenty of trade to support a more direct route across those very deserted stretches. To avail themselves of that route, the F.S. had to undertake several major tunneling projects through the spurs of the mountains that reached to the Tyrrhenian Sea. Finished in 1927, this route permitted high-speed operation between major cities. The fastest trains today make the 133 miles between Rome and Naples in 106 minutes, or at a speed of 75 miles an hour.[124]

The Bologna-Florence *direttissima*, begun in 1914, is an even more spectacularly engineered line with 45 percent of the distance to Prato, 50 miles, taken in tunnels. Using the Savena valley, rather than the Reno employed in the earlier line, the rise out of Bologna is somewhat steeper but still within the limits of fast working through the boring of the 4.42-mile Adone tunnel through the divide to the Brasinone valley to the west. Passing up that stream on a well-graded line, with several short tunnels and a major bore of 1.89 miles at Galleria di Piandisetta, the *direttissima* reaches San Benedetto and the north portal of the world's third longest tunnel, the Galleria dell' Appennino, 11.47 miles of double track, in some ways more impressive than the longer Simplon with its two single-track bores. With a summit level of 1,040 feet, as opposed to the older route's 2,020 feet, broad cruves, and absence of a rolling grade, this direct route of only 50 miles from Bologna to the common junction at Prato outside Florence, 72.5 miles by the older route, made it possible to institute fast working when it was opened in 1933.[125]

Today the fastest services along this new line operate over the 72 miles from Bologna to Florence in 66 minutes (68 minutes northbound) or 65.4 miles per hour.

ALPINE ROUTES

The same spirit that led to the building of the *direttissime* was to be found in the effort made by the Italians and their neighbors to open passages through the Alpine barrier that rimmed the kingdom to the north and west. After the completion of the Fréjus tunnel in 1871 further major projects were proposed. The earliest juncture with the Australian rail system came rather easily even before the Fréjus, when in 1860 junction was made with the Vienna-Trieste line near Udine. This trans-Alpine route was actually the first to be developed, merely the extension of the Südbahn that passed southward from Vienna over the Semmering Pass. Begun in 1848 it took six years to complete. When grades of 2.5 percent were found necessary to cross the eastern Alps special trials were conducted in 1851 to find a locomotive capable of operating over such a line. Already George Stephenson had been consulted, rendering the expected conclusion that such a line was impossible.[126] Karl Ritter von Ghega did not think so, no doubt in part because in the 1840s he was studying the characteristics of some thirty railroad routes in the United States.

> [I]n the workshops he became convinced that a locomotive could tackle a gradient of 1 in 30 [3.33 percent] on an adhesion line without the assistance of a rope. So he ordered his first locomotive, not from Robert Stephenson & Co., but from America, and the machine was sent over in packing-cases from Philadelphia.[127]

By the mid-1840s the Nordbahn had already been completed from Vienna to the northern foot of the Semmering at Gloggnitz, while by 1848 the Südbahn was gaining Mürzzuschlag on the southern end of the same pass. "The line crossed Alpine ravines, ran along boulder-strewn ledges, often at dizzy heights, where avalanche sheds and walls had to be built to protect the track. Single- and double-tiered bridges, galleries, and tunnels followed one after the other. Nothing of this sort had every been attempted before.... During the building of the summit tunnel, nine working shafts were sunk into the mountain, although there was still no explosive other than gunpowder, no other drills than hand drills, and no locomotives for use in the tunnels—only horses. The 900-yard tunnel was already under construction, and here and there the first gradients were taking shape." In this tense situation engine trials were proposed with a prize of 20,000 imperial ducats for the locomotive best able to overcome the rigors of the Semmering line. "On a specially chosen, steeply inclined section near Eichberg (1 in 40 [2.5 percent]) four locomotives presented themselves for the heavyweight contest"—one from Bavaria, one from Belgium, and two from Austria. It speaks well for the great advances in en- the Rainhill trails twenty-two years before that all four succeeded in the basic task, with all four succeeded in the basic task, with *Bavaria* gaining the first prize. She opened the line, the first across the Alps, in 1854. Among the visitors to the trials was the Counsellor of the Prussian Embassy in Vienna, Otto von Bismarck, who nearly fell to his death while walking through an unfinished tunnel where a temporary bridge over a 45-foot chasm gave way under him, leaving him clinging to the edge until he was helped to climb to safety.[128]

By 1857 the line was completed all the way to Trieste, for the first time affording a through route, albeit a highly circuitous one, from the North Sea to the Adriatic and from northern to southern Europe. There were ob- vious advantages to applying the *direttissime* approach to these external connections of Italy. The next crossing of the Alps was that through the high but open Brenner Pass at 4,500 feet. This, the highest of trans-Alpine routes, depends not on great borings but rather on very heavily engineered and graded lines on either flank of the crest. When completed in 1867 the line was still internal to the Austrian system, as the South Tyrol did not pass to Italy until 1919. Both in rising to the pass from the north and in descending to the south the Brenner route makes diversions into side valleys to extend the length of the line and lighten the grade.

The great appeal that such glacial valleys, as at the Brenner, had for the locating engineers was their fairly gentle profile, save at the head of the valley; their broad width compared with river-eroded valleys; and the possibility that the great glacial grooves on one side of a crest may come close to those on the opposite side—or, as in the Canadian Rockies, that they may actually join one with the other to produce a low open saddle, as at Kicking Horse Pass in Alberta–British Columbia. In the Alps there were no such good fortunes, but there were the reasonable proximations of valleys being eroded in opposite directions along basically the same access. At Brenner the glacial grooves were still wet separated, sufficiently so that no summit tunnel could be envisioned, as its length would have been far beyond the technical abilities of heavy engineering in the 1860s, but sufficiently proximate that the summit was notched well below the general crest line of the range. A further aspect of the Brenner line was that at the foot of the north slope, at Innsbruck, the route entered the structural Inn Valley with its easy access downstream through the northernmost range of the Alps to open onto the Bavarian plateau. Thus a single crest divided Germany from Italy, making this the most likely route between the two countries, a fact abundantly demonstrated during World War II.

The next trans-Alpine route to be developed for rail was dependent on a different expression of the single crest from that found at Brenner Pass. By the early 1870s "direct" routes had been opened between France and Italy, particularly with the completion of the difficult line along the Riviera between Marseille and Genoa, which was accomplished just five months after the first service through Fréjus tunnel—that is, in March, 1872—and Austria and Italy, via Udine and the Semmering line in 1860, and the South Tyrol with the rest of Austria and Germany via Brenner in 1867. With four such Alpine routes the connection of northern and southern Europe was clearly in hand, but—particularly between Italy and Switzerland, the Rhine valley, the Low Countries, and even Paris and London—the routing was rather indirect. It is not surprising that plans were soon underway to breach the highest crest of the Alps, that directly north of Milan.

The first proposal came where the open valleys—the Ticino, leading from the St. Gotthard Massif through Lago Maggiore to enter the Po Plain northwest of Milan, and the Reuss, which drains from the northern slope of that same massif passing across the northern range of the Alps in Switzerland (the Berner and Glarner Alpen) to flow directly northward across the Swiss plateau to the Rhine just north of Baden—reach a close proximation. In fact, the single crest between the two was less than 10 miles wide. Because the St. Gotthard Massif lay entirely within Switzerland—there being yet a third political glacis here (similar to the Piedmontese one in Savoy and the Austrian in the South Tyrol)—any plans for its breaching had to be basically Swiss. Certainly part of that interest was in opening an easy access to the trans-Alpine canton of Ticino, but the real basis for such an engineering feat was in

providing a *direttissima* from Milan to Switzerland, the Rhine valley, Paris, and London. It is not surprising that the Swiss turned to the Germans and the Italians to contribute to the cost of constructing a St. Gotthard tunnel. Germany and Switzerland were to contribute 20 million francs each while Italy contributed 45 million. It was, after all, a *direttissima* for Milan and north Italy.[129]

Because the Gottardo Line, as the Italians viewed it, was still a Swiss undertaking, its Milanese connection traversed the full extent of the Canton Ticino, from Chiasso on the Italian border through Lugano and Bellinzona to gain the head of the Ticino Valley at Airolo. In the upper part of Ticino the slope increases rapidly after the fashion of glacially eroded valleys, forcing considerable problems on the prime contractor for this project, Louis Favre of Genoa, before he reached the actual summit tunnel. The three countries mentioned signed a convention in 1871 to undertake the Gotthard railroad, and work was begun on September 13, 1872—an inauspicious day for Favre, as it turned out.

In outline, the Favre contract involved advancing a tunnel 9 miles 452 yds. long from a point with an elevation of 3,460 ft. at Göschenen on the northern slope of the massif to a point with an elevation of 3,760 ft. on the southern slope near Airolo. The tunnel was to accommodate a double-track railway and had a width of 24 ft. 11 in. and a height of 26 ft. 3 in. From the northern portal the incline was 7:1000 to a point 25,586 ft. inside the tunnel with a summit elevation of 3,818 ft., from which it descended towards Airolo with a gradient of 1:1000.[130]

Even to reach the north and south portals of this tunnel, Favre and the other contractors confronted the stepped nature of glacial valleys. A reasonable grade could be obtained for several miles, but ultimately they would reach a step that was beyond the ability of rail operation to surmount directly.

The Brenner route showed us one experiment used in such a case, the diversion of the line along a side valley to gain more mileage in a great loop to rise above the step. In the Ticino Valley and the Reuss to the north, no such side valleys were available. Instead the contractors came up with an ingenious circular tunnel that lengthened the line by boring through the rock of the slope of the mountains bordering the valley. With portals closely adjacent to each other in location, but one well above the other, engineers managed to leap over steps of terrain through use of this spiral internal to the mountainside.

First devised on the Gotthard line in the mid-1870s, this helicoidal solution had been used earlier in the Colorado Rockies, and contemporaneously in the Tehachapi Mountains of California, in such contrivances as the Georgetown and Tehachapi Loops carried on embankments in the open air. In the Ticino Valley the narrow width pushed any such spiral into a tunnel within the adjacent mountain. Between Giornico at 1,328 feet and Lavorgo some three miles farther up the valley, a rise of some seven hundred feet had to be made, roughly a 4.4-percent grade if the valley floor in its natural gradient were used. Although such grades exist on some minor lines (for example, at Saluda Hill in North Carolina, the steepest mainline grade in the United States), no important European line with 100 million gold Swiss francs to spend was likely to tolerate it. The spiral tunnel—two circles in this case—kept the grade to a more manageable figure. Farther up the Ticino, between Faido and Rodi-Fiesso, another step was encountered with a rise of 650 feet in 2.5 miles, again introducing a natural grade of over 4 percent. As built the Gotthard line maintained a ruling grade of 2.6 percent throughout its mountain section, no more there than in crossing the divide between Lake Lugano and the Ticino below Bellinzona in the Alpine foothills.

At Airolo the real challenge lay directly ahead in the Gotthard Massif itself. The Ticino Valley pinched out, leaving only the pack trail that had existed since the Middle Ages across the 6,927-foot pass. Airolo lay over three thousand feet below that pass (though only a couple of miles away from it in a direct line), so any normal railroad must be carried beneath it. Favre undertook to build that tunnel and in the process lost both his fortune and his life, because he accepted both a fixed figure and a fixed time. Sandström finds his great misfortune in his choice of the Belgian method of tunneling, opening the original cut from the top rather than the bottom of the finished cross-section, as was done in the Fréjus tunnel. For reasons we need not go into here, it is more difficult to complete the cross-section from the top down than from the bottom up, so Favre was constantly held up in his work, time ran out, and the penalties he had accepted for delays in completion began to run as a hemorrhage of his own blood. Great amounts of water entered the workings, particularly in the south. Temperatures in the heart of the mountain rose to 124°F, which combined with the endless jets of water spurting from the rock walls to create truly tropical rain-forest climates in the darkness of the bore. Disease became chronic, and the original funds were used up.

In 1876 further contributions from the three countries permitted the work to progress in its painful way. At last, at 11:00 A.M. on February 29, 1880—a mercifully extra day that made the task seem a mite less long—the wall between the headings was finally broken and the rough tunnel was complete. The error in alignment was 12.87 inches, in level 1.95 inches; the bore proved to be 25 feet shorter than computed in the original surveying. Although Favre's company (he had died of exhaustion and a heart attack the year before) finished the rough bore seven months ahead of schedule, his choice of the Belgian system of heading now struck them with disaster. It took so long to complete the cross-section, twenty-one months, because of the section of highly pressurized rock under Andermatt (which lay above the level of the tunnel) along the great structural valley that extends all the way from Grenoble in France to beyond Innsbruck in Austria.

The other "direct" route from Italy represented an even greater refinement of this concept. Although the north portals of the St. Gotthard and Simplon tunnels are less than 40 miles apart, and their south portals are separated by only 28 miles as the crow flies, the orientation of those northern valleys differs considerably. The Reuss on the St. Gotthard route flows due north, leading the railroad to Zürich, the Rhine valley, and the Low Countries and north Germany. London and Paris could be reached, but only fractionally more easily this way than via the first trans-Alpine route at Fréjus. To gain the most direct practicable route, another single-crest tunnel seemed desirable—that under the bulk of Monte Leone in the western section of the Lepontine Alps. There 12 miles separated the glacially eroded upper part of a branch valley of the Toce in the south from the largely structural valley of the upper Rhône in the north. A railroad already existed to Domodossola, 12 miles from Iselle at the south of the 6,563-foot Simplon Pass and at approximately the same elevation as a railhead at Brigue in the flat and moderately wide structural valley to the north. As planned this Simplon tunnel was to connect two existing lines not greatly separated in distance, though walled off from one another by a great mountain. The valley on the Italian side could have been ascended somewhat higher, as the road does, before the grades became impossible; but at Iselle the elevation of the valley floor to the north of the mountains had been attained, so this great work offered the chance to

avoid the redundant grade introduced by climbing up on both sides of a ridge to reach the bore through it. At Simplon the relatively level line to Brigue from Geneva, Lausanne, and Bern could be projected by tunnel through the mountain to come out on the Italian slope at an elevation of about 2,100 feet. The only mountain railroading on this line would then be between Iselle (2,060 feet) and Domodossola (886 feet). Some 1,300 feet of rise was taken in the 12 miles of line built between Domodossola and Iselle up the branch valley Diveria, where heavy tunneling, viaducts, and a spiral tunnel at Varzo combined with a general gradient of 2.5 percent to reach the south portal of the second-longest tunnel ever constructed.

Between 1898 and 1905 work on this bore progressed with great difficulty. The rock was poor in much of the distance, creating severe pressures that had to be met with extremely strong steel cages cantilevered out from more stable rock at either end. At first only one of two working tunnels was finished to full dimensions, the second bore and track being added only in 1921. These were joined in the middle to allow switching from one to the other.

Because this undertaking, though under the boundary ridge between Switzerland and Italy, was mostly carried out by the Swiss, the road that Napoleon had constructed across the summit in 1805 was heavily used to bring machines and supplies from Switzerland to the south portal workings. When completed and put into operation in 1905, the whole project from Brigue to Domodossola was operated by Swiss Federal Railroads, with the change of engines and the location of Italian customs to be found at Domodossola. At 12.06 miles the limit of tunneling seemed to be reached. The tunnel under the Apennines on the *Direttissima* Bologna-Florence is less than a mile shorter and with double-track width is actually greater in size. Only in our time with the opening of a 30-

mile subaqueous tunnel to interconnect the rail systems of Honshu and Hokkaido in Japan has a longer rail tunnel been bored.

THE ENDURING ROLE OF THE RAILROAD IN EUROPE

Were space unlimited, it would be interesting to look in similar detail at railroad evolution in Switzerland, Germany, Iberia, and eastern Europe. This brief survey of four of the more significant, and I believe representative, of European rail systems should help us to establish the more signal features of that British, and subsequently European, system of railroad development and evolution. Germany's historical geography of railroads does not serve us so well, as it grew in the militaristic objectives of the Prussian State Railroads and exists today in an awkward transformation to deal with the realities of the Cold War.

At first the Prussians used private companies, carefully guided, to secure their rail system; but as other kingdoms that had engaged in public construction, such as Hanover and Hesse-Kassel were annexed in 1866, the public component of the Prussian railroads grew rapidly. Clapham believed,

> In a country whose road system was still new and very imperfect [at the time the railroad was developing] and whose towns were almost without exception small and half rural, [the railroad's] revolutionary influence was far more conspicuous than in older developed and more urbanised lands. There was something American about it, just as there was a technical likeness between German and American railway methods. Like America, Germany had got her railways quickly and cheap. Land was cheap in the first place.

Lardner wrote in 1850:

> The vast expenditure for earth work and costly works of art, such as viaducts, bridges, and tunnels, by which vallies [sic] are bestridden and mountains pierced to gain a straight and level line in the English system have not been attempted. The railways have been carried more nearly along the natural level of the country. [They] have been constructed on principles and analogous to those which have been found to answer so well in America.[131]

The average cost of a mile of line opened in Germany up to 1850 was estimated at less than £11,000, while in Belgium the figure was £16,000 and in England £30,000-40,000 per mile.[132]

Germany certainly does not fit with the essentially British-West European pattern of rail development, nor did Austria-Hungary and the rest of eastern Europe. As we shall see in the next chapter, there was an essentially American pattern as well, and Russia looked to it perhaps as much as to Stephensons' insular model. The first long Russian line, that from St. Petersburg to Moscow, was heavily the work of George Whistler, the engineer of America's first well-constructed line, the Boston and Lowell.

Clearly, western European railroads have had a complex and continuously active history, its geographical pattern established very early but its functions evolving over a period of one hundred and fifty years. The high level of construction at the beginning, or the massive reconstruction to that high standard—made possible mainly by easy availability of capital either from private investors, as in Britain, or governmental support, as in most parts of the Continent—has meant that the rail systems could continue right down to the present to perform the basic transportation service for the nations involved. The institution of high-speed passenger service in recent years has demonstrated how well rail technology can serve even modern demands if sufficient capital is available to provide the facilities necessary to make that technology work.

No doubt western Europe was fortunate in

the level to which its railroads were constructed originally—they were bought at a cheap price compared with the present—but a constant infusion of capital over the decades has been necessary to keep those lines abreast of technological improvements and to give them the capacity necessary for increased freight and passenger flows. The high-speed line on a new alignment constructed by the French between Paris and Lyon, opened in the fall of 1983 throughout its full length, seems a probable model for a further improvement of facilities in the next generation. The *Trains á Grande Vitesse* (TGV) that pass over this line cover the 275 miles from Paris to Lyon in just 2 hours, operating at maximum speeds of just under 180 miles an hour. A notable feature of this line is its exclusive use for passenger transportation, leaving the traditional trunk line of the P.L.M., constantly improved over more than a century, to the service of an ever-enlarging freight flow.

NOTES

1. John U. Nef, *Cultural Foundations of Industrial Civilization* (New York: Harper & Row, 1960), p. 59
2. Abbott Payson Usher, *An Introduction to the Industrial History of England* (Boston: Houghton Mifflin, 1920), p. 89.
3. Nef, op. cit., p. 58.
4. Charles Singer et al., eds., *A History of Technology* (New York: Oxford University Press, 1958), vol. 4, p. 165.
5. Ibid., p. 164.
6. This description is sufficiently complex and specific that it is undoubtedly "true." If self-propulsion of a heavy vehicle is the issue, it badly slights Oliver Evans, whose plans for high-pressure engines were sent to England in 1787 and 1794-1795 and are thought to have been seen by Trevithick, and who constructed a large dredge mounted on a scow and proceeded, in 1804, to have it propel itself from the workyard where it was built to the

Schuylkill River, where the wheels were removed and paddles added to make it one of the earliest steamboats. Thus not only did Evans probably contribute significantly to Trevithick's success, but he also seems to have built a heavy self-propelled road vehicle that operated at exactly the time the Pennydarren trial was made. *Encyclopaedia Britannica*, 11th ed., 1910, vol. 10, p. 2, for Trevithick's observation of Evans's plans; Singer et. al., op. cit., p. 189, for Trevithick quotation; John H. Morrison, *History of American Steam Navigation* (New York: Stephen Daye Press, 1958), pp. 13-15, for Oliver Evans.
7. M. J. T. Lewis, *Early Wooden Railways* (London: Routledge & Kegan Paul, 1970), p. 2.
8. Ibid., p. 7.
9. A detailed account of these "wagonways" of Newcastle's environs is presented in ibid., pp. 137-162.
10. A detailed discussion of wagonway track, plates, flanges, and similar topics is contained in ibid., pp. 163-183.
11. Ibid., p. 233.
12. Ibid., p. 170.
13. J. Elfreth Watkins, "The Development of American Rail and Track, as Illustrated by the Collection in the U.S. National Museum," *Report of the National Museum, Smithsonian Institution* (Washington, D.C., 1891), p. 657.
14. Lewis, op. cit., p. 293.
15. Singer et al., op. cit., p. 189.
16. J. S. Jeans, *Jubilee Memorial of the Railway System: A History of the Stockton and Darlington Railway, and a Record of Its Results* (London: Longmans, Green, 1875), pp. 6-7.
17. Ibid., p. 9. Samuel Smiles tells us the Middleton line extended 3.5 miles from that colliery to Leeds and was used for many years to draw up to thirty coal-wagons at a speed of 3 miles an hour. Smiles, *Life of George Stephenson* (Chicago: Belford Clark, 1883), p. 78.
18. B. R. Mitchell and Phyllis Deane, *Abstract of British Historical Statistics* (Cambridge: Cambridge University Press, 1962), p. 108, give the weight of a chaldron, after 1686, as 53 cwt. These cars ran until the early 1960s, when I saw some of the last being dismantled by British Railways at their very early

artificial port at Seaham Harbour, County Durham, in the spring of 1961.

19. Smiles, op. cit., p. 80.
20. Ibid., p. 82.
21. L. T. C. Rolt, *The Railway Revolution: George and Robert Stephenson* (New York: St. Martin's Press, 1962), p. 38.
22. Ibid., p. 48.
23. L. T. C. Rolt, an engineer, presents a detailed and balanced critique of the "father of the steam locomotive" argument (taken in a literal sense) in his distinguished biographies of Trevithick, George and Robert Stephenson, and Isambard Kingdom Brunel. But he does not advance the claim made here that George Stephenson's great genius was his understanding of how to build a system of facilities to show his locomotives to best advantage.
24. Ibid., p. 57.
25. Ibid., p. 57.
26. Ibid., p. 59.
27. Ibid., p. 63.
28. Quoted in Jeans, op. cit., pp. 38–39.
29. Quoted in Jeans, op. cit., p. 48.
30. Ibid., p. 43.
31. Rolt, op. cit., pp. 59–86; Jeans, op. cit., pp. 57–64; Smiles, op. cit., pp. 172–186; P. J. Holmes, *Stockton and Darlington Railway: 1825–1975* (Ayr, Scotland: First Avenue Publishing Company, n.d.), pp. 6–11; K. Hoole, *The Stockton & Darlington Railway* (Newton Abbot, Devon: David & Charles, 1975), pp. 9–15.
32. Smiles, op. cit., p. 175.
33. Ibid., p. 179.
34. Loc. cit.
35. Ibid., p. 180.
36. Rolt, op. cit., pp. 87–92.
37. Ibid., pp. 87–118.
38. James Scott Walker, *An Accurate Description of the Liverpool and Manchester Rail-way, the Tunnel, the Bridges, and Other Works throughout the Line; with a Sketch of the Objects Which It Presents Interesting to the Traveller or Tourist* (Paterson, N.J.: D. Burney, printer, 1830), pp. 24–25.
39. Ibid., p. 26.
40. Ibid., p. 27.
41. Ibid., pp. 27–28.
42. Ibid., pp. 29–30.
43. Grenville M. Dodge, chief engineer for the construction of the Union Pacific Railroad during its effective construction, computed the cash cost for building the line at $54 million. Grenville M. Dodge, *How We Built the Union Pacific* (n.p., n.d.), p. 45.
44. Smiles, op. cit., pp. 187–188.
45. Ibid., p. 266.
46. Robert Riegel, *The Story of the Western Railroads* (New York: Macmillan, 1926), p. 164.
47. Smiles, op. cit., p. 266.
48. Norman W. Webster, *Britain's First Trunk Line* (Bath, Somerset: Adams & Dart, 1972), pp. 67–68.
49. Ibid., pp. 139–140.
50. In English railroad practice grades are always rendered as ratios, in this example 1 in 75, whereas American practice renders them as percentages, which are easier to compare one with the other. For data on British railroads, see *British Rail–Main Line: Gradient Profiles* (London: Ian Allan, n.d., ca. 1971).
51. Ibid., pp. 144–145.
52. Details of the line are from John S. Bourne, *Drawings of the London and Birmingham Railway ...* (London, 1838; reprinted by David and Charles, 1970), and Thomas Roscoe, *The London and Birmingham Railway* (London: Charles Tilt, n.d., ca. 1838).
53. This matter of the role that economic support plays in transportation location and development, with special reference to the Union Pacific Railroad, is discussed in detail in James E. Vance, Jr., "The Oregon Trail and Union Pacific Railroad: A Contrast in Purpose," *Annals of the Association of American Geographers* 51 (1961): 357–379.
54. Roscoe, op. cit., p. 194.
55. Hamilton Ellis, *British Railway History: 1830–1876* (London: George Allen & Unwin, 1954), p. 60.
56. Webster, op. cit., pp. 41, 86.
57. Ibid., p. 37.
58. Ibid., p. 85.
59. Ibid., p. 167.
60. The speeds of Amtrak trains are computed from their *National Train Timetables*, effective October 30, 1983.

61. H. J. Dyos and D. H. Aldcroft, *British Transport: An Economic Survey from the Seventeenth Century to the Twentieth* (Leicester: Leicester University Press, 1971), pp. 210-211.

62. M. R. Bonavia, *The Economics of Transport* (Cambridge: Cambridge University Press, 1946), pp. 35-36.

63. Ibid., p. 37.

64. Ibid., pp. 38-39.

65. Ibid., p. 39.

66. E. T. McDermot, revised by C. R. Clinker, *History of the Great Western Railway* (London: Ian Allan, 1964 [original edition, 1927]), vol. 1, pp. 2-5.

67. Ellis, op. cit., vol. 1, p. 64.

68. These data are secured from a letter from Daniel Gooch to Brunel, quoted in McDermot, op. cit., p. 61; various places in chapter 4 of that same work; and profiles W1 and W6 in *British Rail–Mainline Gradient Profiles.* Reference to the sun's lighting of the tunnel on April 9 is from Ellis, op. cit., p. 76. Such lighting of tunnels was practiced by the ancient Egyptians, as in the case of King Tut's tomb, which was lighted on his birth date.

69. McDermot, op. cit., chapter 3.

70. Brunel, quoted in ibid., p. 42.

71. Ellis, op. cit., vol. 1, p. 169.

72. Ibid., p. 79.

73. J. H. Appleton, *The Geography of Communications in Great Britain* (Oxford: Oxford University Press, 1962), p. 11.

74. Ellis, op. cit., vol. 2, pp. 78-81.

75. W. M. Acworth, *The Railways of England,* 4th ed. (London: John Murray, 1890), p. 154.

76. Frederick Williams, *The Midland Railway: Its Rise and Progress: A Narrative of Modern Enterprise* (London: Stratham and Company, 1876), p. 73.

77. Ibid., p. 74.

78. Appleton, op. cit., p. 13.

79. Acworth, op. cit., pp. 155-157.

80. W.O. Henderson, *Britain and Industrial Europe, 1750–1870* (Leicester: Leicester University Press, 1965), p. 136.

81. Quoted in J. Pecheux, *La Naissance du Rail Européen* (Paris: Berger-Levrault, 1970), p. 76. The free translation is the author's.

82. Henderson, op. cit., p. 137.

83. H. Lartilleux, *Géographie des Chemins de Fer d'Europe,* (Paris: Lib. Chaix, n.d., ca. 1955), vol. 11, pp. 7-8.

84. Statistical sources: ibid., p. 57, and *Jane's World Railways, 1971–72,* p. 194. The area of Belgium was increased by 401 square miles by German cessions at the end of World War I.

85. Lartilleux, op. cit., p. 75.

86. B. Brisson, *Essai sur le Système Général de Navigation Intérieure de la France* (Paris: Chez Carillan-Goeury, 1829). The plan is presented on a "Carte des Routes Royale de la France," prepared by order of the director-general of the Corps de Ponts et Chaussees in 1824. Interestingly enough, only three short rail lines are suggested, one of which, extending between Lyon and St. Etienne and Roanne, was the first railroad to be built in France.

87. Henderson, op. cit., p. 136.

88. Pecheux, op. cit., pp. 47-48.

89. Louis Pouget, *Du Transport par Eau et par Terre* (Paris: Napoléon Chaix, 1859), vol. 2, p. 270.

90. Seguin Afné, *De l'influence des Chemins de Fer et de l'Art de les Tracer et de les Construire* (Paris: Lib. des Corps Royoux des Ponts et Chaussées et des Mines, 1839).

91. Ibid., p. 75.

92. Ibid., pp. 89-90.

93. Ibid., pp. 97-99.

94. Ibid., p 100.

95. J. H. Clapham, *Economic Development of France and Germany: 1815–1914* (Cambridge: Cambridge University Press, 1961), p. 145.

96. Rene Clozier, *Géographie de la Circulation,* vol. 1: *L'Economie des Transports Terrestres* (Paris: Editions Genin, 1963), p. 111.

97. Harold P. Clunn, *The Face of Paris* (London: Spring Books, n.d.), p. 154.

98. As shown in *Thomas Cook Continental Timetable,* January, 1984.

99. Anthony Sutcliffe, *The Autumn of Central Paris: The Defeat of Town Planning, 1850–1970* (Montreal: McGill-Queen's University Press, 1971), p. 155.

100. Ibid., p. 284.

101. Clapham, op. cit., pp. 147-148.

102. Ibid., p. 339.

103. Quoted in a volume privately published by the Chemin de Fer Paris-Lyon-Marseille, *Hommes et Choses du P. L. M.*

104. *Hommes et Choses du P. L. M.,* op. cit., p. 115.

105. Clapham, op. cit., p. 343.

106. Ibid., p. 339.

107. Loc. cit.

108. *Hommes et Choses du   P. L. M.,* op. cit., p. 111.

109. A detailed discussion of this line is contained in H. Lartilleux, *Géographie des Chemins de Fer Francais,* vol. 1: *La S.N.C.F.* (Paris: Lib. Chaix, 1950), pp. 292–309.

110. Ibid., p. 310.

111. Information on the railroads of the Massif Central is taken from Lartilleux, op. cit., vol. 1, pp. 291–320, and *Autour des Chemins de Fer Francais,* op. cit., pp. 31–32, 36–40.

112. P. M. Kalla-Bishop, *Italian Railroads* (New York: Drake Publishers, 1972), p. 27.

113. Ibid., p. 25.

114. Loc. cit.

115. Gösta E. Sandström, *Tunnels* (New York: Holt, Rinehart and Winston, 1963), pp. 132–133.

116. Lartilleux, op. cit., p. 78. The tunnel was later extended at the French end to its current 8.6-mile length.

117. Kalla-Bishop, op. cit., pp. 13, 62.

118. Data from H. Lartilleux, *Géographie des Chemins de Fer d'Europe,* vol. 1: *Suisse-Italie* (Paris: Lib. Chaix, 1951), pp. 206–208.

119. Kalla-Bishop, op. cit., p. 38.

120. Loc. cit.

121. Ibid., p. 39.

122. Lartilleux, *Géographie des Chemins de Fer d'Europe,* vol. 1, p. 152; Kalla-Bishop, op. cit., p. 59.

123. Kalla-Bishop, op. cit., p. 62.

124. Lartilleux, *Géographie des Chemins de Fer d'Europe,* vol. 2:2, pp. 221–222.

125. Ibid., pp. 204–208.

126. Erwin Berhaus, *The History of Railways* (London: Barrie and Rockliff, 1964), p. 68.

127. Ibid., pp. 68–69.

128. Ibid., pp. 69–70.

129. Sandström, op. cit., p. 162.

130. Ibid., p. 164.

131. Clapham, op. cit., pp. 155–156.

132. Loc. cit.

STEAM CONVEYANCE
ON A
GENERAL IRON-RAIL-WAY.

No Speed with this, can fleetest Horse compare;
No weight like this, canal or Vessel bear;
As this, will Commerce every way promote!
To this, let Sons of Commerce grant their vote.

If the conveyance of Mails across the Channels by Royal Mail Steam-Packets prove so highly important; how much more so, the early distribution of the Foreign & Inland Mails, in all our commercial and manufacturing Districts, by Royal Mail Steam-carriages; the safe and expeditious conveyance of Passengers by Steam-coaches; & the rapid transport of Merchandise, of every description, by Steam-caravans and Waggons.

By the Author of Observations on a General Iron-Rail-way.
Published by Ibbitson, Cradock & Joy, London.

chapter 4

The American Railroad

Instrument of National Development

Even the less-developed regions of Europe were long settled, with well-defined settlement patterns and economies, when the railroad was introduced in the first half of the nineteenth century. In North America railroads were created nearly simultaneously, though only the eastern fringe of the continent was really settled, and the economy was not at all mature. Though the elements of rail technology were shared, the railroad was not a single thing, but a form of transportation adaptable enough to serve the heart of industrializing Europe as well as the advancing frontier in North America. All railroads shared the use of rail guideways, of coupled strings of locomotive and cars, of steam power, and of unidirectional movement (though it might alternate direction on a protected basis). But the specific nature of the facilities, of the locomotives, of the geographical alignment of routes, and of the relationship to settlement showed a striking Atlantic split.

In chapter 3 we saw both the absolute origin of the railroad and its English-European expression. Here we shall consider its largely separate American origin and North American expression. Almost from the first morning two distinct rail systems were emerging, with perhaps less shared evolution than is thought by those who accept the notion that Britain was both the fountainhead and the reservoir from which knowledge and practice were carried to distant lands. Geography made such a single source of innovation unlikely, however much historians may have missed that point in focusing on the organization and financing of railroad companies. True, business practices were jointly those of free-enterprise capitalism; but it is a remarkably adaptable economic system. The market available to repay investment, the geography on which the earlier lines must be sketched, and the scale of the geographical canvas on which that sketch must be drawn were so different on the opposite sides of the Atlantic that there could not have been a single school of railroad building. Here I intend to show how different the two undertakings were throughout much of the evolution of the historical geography of railroads.

At the beginning of the nineteenth century the United States suffered a problem peculiar to its specific economic origin and the recency of its political union. England's interest in New World settlement had come within the strongly mercantilist economic frame of mind that characterized early seventeenth-century northwestern Europe. The colonists might have come for reasons of political, religious, and personal freedom—but the Mother Country saw in the colonies almost entirely an expansion of its realm of commerce. Such a system had its particular geography, which meant establishing a string of proprietorial colonies little related to one another and tied together mainly through the homeland. Each had its port whence staples could be dispatched to England and retributive manufactures received on return journeys of English ships. The result was the shaping of what in chapter 3 we called the *potamic* phase of domestic transport, linked with an extensive set of trans-Atlantic routes for British ships. There was little interprovincial travel in British America before the Revolution; what there was had resulted to a considerable degree from Benjamin Franklin's recent efforts at shaping a post road from Boston to Virginia when he was appointed the first Postmaster General for all the British colonies after the capture of Canada in 1763. In little more than a decade not much was accomplished; in 1783 the newly independent United States found itself a political but hardly an economic or transportation union. The ensuing efforts at turnpike and canal constructon sought such a union. But in the first instance the "friction of distance"—the per-mile cost of wagon transport—restricted the road ties

mostly to urgent passenger services, whereas in the second instance the great shortage of capital, typical of a staple-producing land, made canal construction practicable only in response to demands for improvement in fairly well settled areas.

There is no need here to review the development of American canals covered in chapter 2, but before turning to the eventual substitution of rails for canals it is well to look at the technological underpinnings that existed in the United States toward the creation of the complete system that was to become the steam railroad. Those underpinnings were scant by comparison with Britain, but still important. In mining Britain had a long and complex history compared with the United States. Virtually no coal was mined in America until the time of railroads, and other minerals produced in colonial times—copper and iron particularly—were of such small scale as not to require the tramways or pumping engines that had given Britain a steam-engine school for railroad development. America did have an independent and vigorous steamboat industry that began earlier, in practical terms, than Britain's and probably was as vigorous—indeed, even more advanced in the matter of boiler pressures. Even before 1800 Oliver Evans had been working on steam engines with considerably higher pressures than those characteristic of their English peers and the diverse efforts to create a practical steamboat during the first decade of the last century gave Americans a practical equivalence to Britain in technology, if not in the scale of production, with respect to steam engines. Whatever claim is asserted for the invention of the steam engine, there is little question that by 1825 Americans had developed that essential element of early railroading to a state adequate that the United States proved fully able to outfit its earliest railroads with locomotives of domestic make. English locomotives were imported for a very few years around 1830, fixing the Stephenson gauge in America. British locomotives failed in most other regards, to the point the net export flow of these pioneer engines of the early railroad years was strongly eastbound across the Atlantic.

Probably the major British contribution to the birth of the American railroad era was its demonstration of the viability of the form rather than any direct contribution of genetic material. There was obviously an early investigation by Americans of the very earliest English practices and experiences, such as William Strickland's report to the Pennsylvania Society for the Promotion of Internal Improvements in 1826; but these were neither numerous nor terribly important beyond seeking to resolve the question whether or not Americans should build railroads as a cheaper substitute for canal construction. Once this was answered in the affirmative, American railroad development was remarkably independent in a technical sense, though much less so in the financial terms that historians tend to look at so earnestly. In appraising nineteenth-century technical capabilities we should not forget that in that great technical adjunct of the railroad, the telegraph, it was the Americans who replaced the awkward British experiments with the successful form ultimately used throughout the world.

For the important knowledge that railroads could be used successfully and could earn their keep, Americans owe thanks to Britain. But to argue the debt further is unjustified and obscures the fact that the American railroad is a distinct medium of transportation living under different environmental conditions and having its own historical cycle independent of Britain.

The first planting of that American root stock came in the environs of Boston at just the time the Stockton and Darlington was being opened in the northeast of England. Seeking to commemorate the Battle of Bunker Hill (1775) on its fiftieth anniversary, a group in Boston set out to build a granite obelisk on an enlarged scale. To secure the granite they turned to Great Blue Hill in Quincy whence the stone could be brought by water to the foot of the hill on which it was to be erected, save for the 3 miles from the quarry, where Gridley Bryant built a "rail-way" that was well financed (by Thomas Handasyd Perkins) and ingeniously devised. He was the first to use the eight-wheel freight car (the Europeans still use many with only four wheels) and to mount the wheels in four-wheel trucks capable of swiveling (most Europeans used fixed axles until very recently). Bryant devised his own switches, turntables, and cranes. The one element of a pioneering steam railroad he did not shape was, of course, a locomotive, because his heavy loads were strictly downbound from the hillside quarry to the wharf on the Neponse estuary. But his rail line proved very workable, even taking on some common-carrier functions and showing that in 1826, when the line was built, Americans were fully capable of shaping their own railroad to their special needs. The Granite Railway was given the power to condemn land for its use because it was perceived to have general utility, thus further establishing the means by which a privately financed project could be carried out for the public good.[1]

THE ROLE OF THE MISPLACED CITY IN AMERICAN RAILROAD DEVELOPMENT

The period after the War of 1812 witnessed a number of efforts to revive the national economy from the slump occasioned by that conflict. The decline in the American merchant marine had freed capital in a number of ports for investment in emergent industry and internal improvements. The earliest efforts toward the latter goal were found in the building of turnpike roads, for the use of

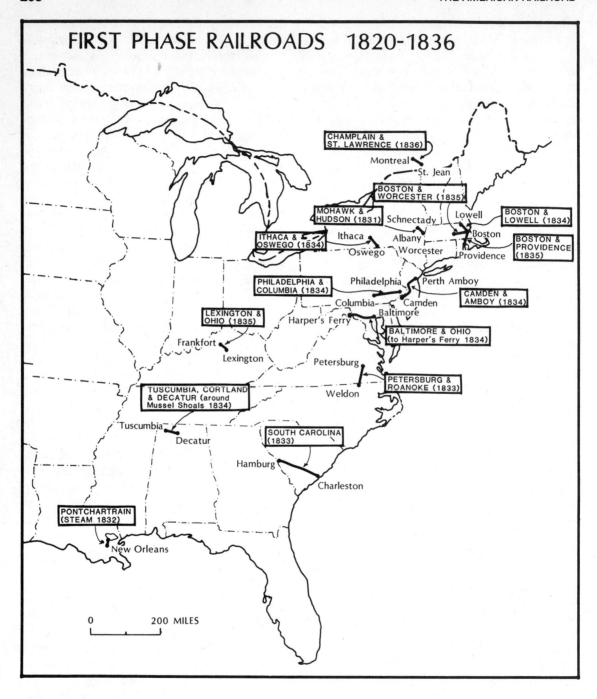

FIRST PHASE RAILROADS 1820-1836

CHAMPLAIN &
ST. LAWRENCE (1836)

Montreal

St. Jean

BOSTON &
WORCESTER (1835)

MOHAWK &
HUDSON (1831)

Schnectady

Lowell

BOSTON &
LOWELL (1834)

ITHACA &
OSWEGO (1834)

Ithaca

Albany

Boston

Oswego

Worcester

BOSTON &
PROVIDENCE
(1835)

Providence

PHILADELPHIA &
COLUMBIA (1834)

Philadelphia

Perth Amboy

Columbia

Camden

CAMDEN &
AMBOY (1834)

LEXINGTON &
OHIO (1835)

Harper's Ferry

Baltimore

BALTIMORE & OHIO
(to Harper's Ferry 1834)

Frankfort

Lexington

Petersburg

Weldon

PETERSBURG &
ROANOKE (1833)

TUSCUMBIA, CORTLAND
& DECATUR (around
Mussel Shoals 1834)

Tuscumbia

Decatur

SOUTH CAROLINA
(1833)

Hamburg

Charleston

PONTCHARTRAIN
(STEAM 1832)

New Orleans

0   200 MILES

which tolls would be charged to repay investors. These roads, however, did not provide the low operating costs for wagon hauliers that canals afforded to their bargees, so there was continuing pressure for further improvement, raising the question of canal construction or rail building. In 1826 Pennsylvania chose the former course but few followed its lead, particularly those whose vision was confined to a private undertaking. Among the private groups thinking along the lines of transportation development were the merchant communities in a specific type of port, those places that had been badly sited (in the colonial period) to deal with the rapidly expanding hinterlands of the early nineteenth century.

The ports so sited were those not located at the mouth of a major river offering access to the developing interior in this period of principal reliance on potamic transport. Boston had a splendid harbor, as did Baltimore and Charleston, cities that had become the dominant points of attachment (entrepôts) of the prerevolutionary English and American mercantile systems. But when the focus shifted the creation of mercantile ties toward the developing American interior—the replacement for the British trade lost after 1783—the absence of good river connections inland from Boston, Baltimore, and Charleston became a critical gap in the development of an American trading system. There were cities at the mouths of the master streams of their respective areas: Newburyport on the Merrimack for eastern Massachusetts, Alexandria on the Potomac for the northern part of Chesapeake Bay, and Savannah on the river of that name for the south Atlantic states. But Boston, Baltimore, and Charleston were not about to yield to these smaller rivals a free exercise of urban mercantilism in the regions they viewed as their own economic fief. To avoid such a distasteful outcome, each sought to adopt the railroad, signaled as a practical alternative to the waterway by the building of the Stockton and Darlington. In this very rapid adoption of a railroad, attended by none of the timid dithering encountered in Philadelphia's search for access to the interior, these three cities became the first anywhere to appreciate the superb developmental properties of the railroad, and to shape in turn a form of railroad that could benefit from their continued prosperity. These first-phase but short-distance railroads leading inland from the colonial entrepôts gave the initial evidence of the power of the iron road as a development route.

The first to act was Baltimore, then becoming the second city of the Republic and even outdistancing Philadelphia for a couple of decades. Its merchant group promoted the building of a rail line over a distance totally different from that envisaged in Britain. The line from the Monument City to the great river route of the Middle West, the Ohio at Wheeling (where Baltimore hoped to gain equal footing with those coastal points of attachment—New York, Philadelphia, Alexandria, and Richmond—that it viewed as its rivals in developing "the West") was nearly three times as long as the most ambitious line to be proposed in the first phase of English rail promotion. In addition, it required crossing a major mountainous area in western Virginia (later West Virginia) like none to be found in the British Isles. The audacity of such a proposal, on a frontier where the earliest European settlement had been planted only forty years before the first sod was cut on the Baltimore and Ohio Railroad, was equal to that of the most pretentious English line. In England overweening confidence attached to railroad engineering, whereas in the United States it came in the geographical scope of railroad construction. It took only two generations, forty-three years, to progress from the first rail line, the Granite Railroad of 1826, to the transcontinental connection of 1869.

The Baltimore and Ohio: The University of Railroad Engineering

On February 2, 1827, a group of merchants met in Baltimore on a call to "take under consideration the best means of restoring to the city of Baltimore that portion of the western trade which [had] recently been diverted from it by the introduction of steam navigation and other causes."[2] From that meeting came the successful effort to secure a charter from the state of Maryland, extended to Virginia, to permit the construction of a railroad from Baltimore harbor to some point on the Ohio River. Charter in hand, in 1827 the promoters set about raising money, largely in the local mercantile community, to begin construction. First, however, something more than the vague descriptions of the railroads being undertaken in Britain was needed. Fortunately, the report made by William Strickland to the Pennsylvania Society for the Promotion of Internal Improvement had recently been published, so the established British practice of railroad construction could be ascertained.[3] The B. and O. company initially attempted to copy that British practice precisely, even to the extent of laying out an absolutely level line and seeking to concentrate the grades in banks that might be operated by winding engines, as on the Stockton and Darlington. Quickly, however, they discovered that the costs became prohibitive, and the results in certain cases dubious. Construction was inaugurated on July 4, 1828, and almost immediately the company faced several bridge projects that they accomplished in the proper British manner, with stone arches of considerable span. This section was followed by a rise onto the Piedmont accomplished in an English-style deep cut so costly and slow to complete that it came as a pleasant surprise when one of the Baltimore merchant investors, Alexander Brown, convinced the engineers that to make the line so

flat was undesirable, as it caused water to collect within the cut.[4]

The rigid doctrinal quality of English engineering began to be questioned, both from an innate American pragmatism and from the increasing realization that America would be slow indeed in being spanned by railroads if that practice were followed very widely. By the time the B. and O. reached to the Potomac River at Point of Rocks in 1832, the British handbook for railroad construction had been almost entirely rejected and an American replacement largely formulated.

The construction engineers for the B. and O. had at first been interested in that British practice. Captain William McNeill, Major George Whistler, and Jonathan Knight were sent to England to examine the Stockton and Darlington and the Liverpool and Manchester. They returned aware of the Stephenson practice of using fish-belly cast-iron rails borne on stone blocks but quickly devised a necessarily cheaper expedient, wooden stringers kept parallel by wooden cross-ties and clad on the weight-bearing edge with a thin strap of iron to reduce friction on the wheels and wear on the wooden (stringer) rails. Problems were introduced by this fabric, however, so eventually the iron fish-belly was settled on, though wooden cross-ties were most fortunately substituted for the stone blocks.

When enough line had been laid for service to begin, one of the great pioneers of American railroading, Ross Winans—then just beginning his railroad career—was asked to fit up a passenger car. He did so by turning to basic principles rather than simply copying earlier stagecoach operations. Winans devised an open car, exceedingly plain but far more practical of operation than the compartmented cars with which European lines were burdened for more than a century (because the coach operators between Stockton and Darlington had been allowed to mount their coach bodies on flatcars in the first years of the running of that line).

The first B. and O. passenger car also worked a significant change over wagon practice: in place of the four separate wheels turning on fixed axles, with four separate bearings to be kept in working order, Winans introduced two rotating axles, borne in journal boxes, with wheels fixed permanently to them. In that way what came to be nearly universal railroad procedure was first employed, further demonstrating the distinctive quality of the railroad as it sprang up and evolved in America. Winans further simplified rail technology by moving the flange from the outer to inner edge of the wheel and assembling axles into two-wheel trucks that were made to swivel. Ultimately most of these practices were adopted on European railroads, although the four-wheel swivel-truck took nearly a century to be widely used there. Less chauvinist was the Russian government, which called Ross Winans to St. Petersburg to help supervise the early technical installations on the line to Moscow, which George Whistler had laid out for them.

Certainly the clearest evidence of the distinctive nature of the American railroad was furnished by the early experience of locomotive provision in the Great Republic. By 1831 the B. and O. had been completed to Frederick and was being operated by horse-traction. Wishing to adopt steam locomotives instead, the company looked into securing several engines. The very earliest lines—short ones from Albany to Schenectady; from the end of the Delaware and Hudson Canal at Honesdale, Pennsylvania, over Moosic Mountain to the mines around Carbondale; a line promoted by Colonel John Stevens between Perth Amboy and Camden, New Jersey; and from Charleston to Hamburg in South Carolina—had in several instances bought locomotives from the Stephensons, but most of these proved both feeble and fussy, failing to draw loads very effectively and running off the track at the slightest opportunity. The doctrinaire practices of building very level and very expensively engineered lines seemed essential to the working of these gelded Iron Horses. The Baltimore and Ohio and other early railroad companies in the United States could not afford the quality of lines necessary to make a Stephenson engine perform satisfactorily.

That Maryland company's decision was likely to have great effect, as in 1832 45 percent of all America's 136 miles of rail were on the B. and O., a greater distance than the Stockton and Darlington and the Liverpool and Manchester combined. The B. and O. decided that an American locomotive could serve their purposes better than an English one, and they set about building it. Wellington in his classic book on American railroad engineering tells of the particular qualities of these American locomotives as they developed.[5]

The distinctive peculiarities of the running gear of American locomotives, as compared with foreign, are two: the swivelling TRUCK in front (in England called "bogie"), and the EQUALIZING LEVERS by which the load is kept uniformly distributed on the four or more drivers, and the effect of any chance irregularities in the track reduced to a minimum. The first was invented by John B. Jervis in 1830 soon after the trial of the Rocket took place; the second was invented by Ross M. Winans, who also invented the double-truck railway car which has become all but universal in this century, only a few years later.

Both of these inventions, with much else that was novel and meritorious, had their origin in the necessities of the earlier years of American railways, which required that the locomotives should be adapted to ready passage over sharp curves and imperfectly surfaced track and road-bed. Both of them are now gradually making their way into England and throughout the world; and both of them, beyond doubt, will eventually become universal, since they are almost equally advantageous on good roads and on poor roads, the only difference being that on poor track they are absolutely indispensable, while on good track they are not indispensable, but merely advantageous. In great part, we owe to them two advantages which experience appears to indicate that the American locomotive possesses: It can (at least it unquestionably does) haul greater loads in proportion to weight on drivers, and it is less readily disorganized, so that it can run in practice (at least it does) a great many more miles in a day and a year.... [T]he cost per ton hauled is enormously in favor of American engines.... [I]t remains true, that whenever American locomotives have fairly come in competition with those without their distinctive features, as in Canada, Mexico, South America, and the Australasian colonies (in nearly all of which the right of decision has rested in English officials), they have invariably obtained the preference, with exceptions that prove the rule.

Many of these distinctive features that made American engines both strong and durable were developed within these machines during their first decade of evolution, a significant precedent set while locomotives were being worked out for the B. and O. in the early 1830s.

The strength of these early American locomotives quickly influenced the engineering of the pioneer lines, obviating the practice that both Stephenson and Brunel had followed of massing the grade on a line so that it might be overcome through the use of winding engines if necessary. Between Baltimore and Frederick the surface of the Appalachian Piedmont was relatively flat, save for a single ridge, Parrs Spring Ridge, where the grades surveyed ranged between 170 and 264 feet per mile (3.2 and 5.0 percent). At the beginning, when the B. and O. was still slavishly following British practice, it was assumed that winding engines would be

used. But the locomotive engineers saw the ridge as a challenge and soon were successfully assaulting it, drawing the short trains of the time over the rise without helper or winding engines. When the line reached its next great grade—that west of Cumberland when construction was underway in 1850—it was found that the continuing improvement of American locomotives was such that the civil engineers could confidently lay out a grade of 116 feet per mile (2.2 percent), which was to become the *ruling grade* for most subsequent constructions (including the Union Pacific and even the Canadian Pacific). Such a grade "rules" because, as the steepest climb facing a locomotive on the specific line, it determines how much engine power must be used to pass over that route. As American railroads usually possessed stronger engines than those used on most British lines (the exception being found in the most egregious English example at Lickey Incline south of Birmingham, with its employment of an American locomotive), it became possible to engineer the lines with heavier grades, thereby reducing construction costs and making developmental railroads more feasible. For that reason the separate and spectacular locomotive evolution in the United States goes far toward explaining the existence of two railroad technologies, developing in parallel rather than diffusion.

As laid out, the Baltimore and Ohio demonstrated that American system of railroad construction in one of its earlier expressions. To avoid excessive tunneling or grades, the B. and O. headed fairly directly westward from Baltimore to gain the valley of the Potomac at Point of Rocks. Thence upriver the water gaps cut by that stream through the repeating ridges of the Folded Appalachians gave a graded line westward as far as the front of the Appalachian Plateau at Cumberland in western Maryland. We have already seen that once west of

Cumberland (reached in 1842) there was no way to avoid climbing onto the Plateau, and this was done in the 2.2-percent grade that came to be known as the sandpatch because in wintertime and wet weather so much sand had to be used to gain adhesion working of the line that the environs of the track were perceived as being sandy in soil conditions, much as that was not actually the case. Once over the lip of the Plateau, the alignment facing the locating engineers was straight but exceedingly rolling as the track had to dip down into the valleys cut by tributaries of the Monongahela that lay across its chosen westerly course. With the strong engines available, those long and repeating hills were accepted, if regretted. On Christmas Eve, 1852, the track was completed to the Ohio River, at Wheeling in western Virginia (later West Virginia), gaining the original objective of the company organized to open the developing interior to the mercantile interests of Baltimore.

Boston Seeks a New Northwest Passage

The same concern to reorient the geography of trade after the colonial period gripped Boston, more so because the Hub had been the leading colonial entrepôt for English trade in America. Almost immediately after 1783 the seaborne trade of the great Yankee port became worldwide, gaining particular importance in its connection with China. It was natural that Boston's merchants also thought in terms of gaining access to the interior, but nature had served the city badly. No river of any extent reached to the splendid harbor that made Boston a port of world importance and home to one of the largest mercantile fleets afloat. Turnpike roads were thrust outward from the Yankee metropolis to much of New England even before the War of 1812, but these provided limited economic links as the cost of wagon transport soon restricted the potential hinterland

of the port. A canal was called for but preliminary surveys indicated that even to reach the Hudson River in the west meant crossing two summits—one nearly a thousand feet above sea level and the second nearly fifteen hundred feet high—before even that limited goal was reached. The shrewd investors of Boston could see no private support for such a project, and the General Court of the Commonwealth would not legislate any such economically doubtful undertaking.

We should keep in mind that building a canal across Massachusetts would have been a considerably heavier task than was the crossing of upstate New York with the Erie Canal. If Boston were to gain access to the interior, (1) it must come through private investment, and (2) no private investor would seriously consider a canal. There was grave doubt that they would even consider financing a railroad, although if anything were to be provided, it would have to have the prospectively developmental qualities of the "American railroad."

It was both typically Yankee and fortunate that the New England approach to railroad promotion was cautious but forthright; not too much was hazarded at first, but when it was begun it was executed promptly and practically. With the opening of the Liverpool and Manchester in 1830, Boston, then in frequent contact with the Mersey port, knew much about it and set out to introduce the railroad to America. That effort was so successful that by 1835 Boston became the world's first railroad hub, though its sobriquet came from a more cultural pretension, its status at that time as the "hub of the universe" of learning and literature.

In 1835 there were three railroads in operation between Boston and its most important neighboring cities, Lowell, Worcester, and Providence. Of these, the Lowell Road was the first to be finished and the most impressive in its fabric. That latter quality could be justified by the fact that the earliest true canal to be completed in America, the Middlesex Canal of 1803, ran between those two cities and was a very sound business proposition encouraging further investment in a privately built railroad to run along the same route, tapping the trade in the winter while the canal was frozen and that in the summer that could be won from the canal either by greater speed of movement over the railroad or more reliable transport in times of summer drought.

The Boston and Lowell, some 26 miles long, passed over fairly level country, though it did have to rise out of the Boston Basin. It was planned as a double-track line from the beginning, though only the right-hand track heading out of each city was laid at first (forcing on the somewhat startled contractors an S-curve at midpoint where the two right-hand tracks were found to occupy opposite sides of the embankment wide enough for two lines). Track was to be fish-belly in form and be carried on granite blocks located at the end of track segments.[6] The Boston and Lowell passed through few settlements, apparently to keep down land-acquisition costs on a route that was seen as having sufficient through traffic to disregard any small change of on-line support. Although shares were set a startlingly high value, $500, the sale was accomplished rapidly. With the necessary $1.2 million subscribed, constructon was carried out to completion of the line in May, 1835. A Stephenson locomotive, the *Choctaw*, was bought but proved unsatisfactory. Quickly the machine shops of the Proprietors of the Locks and Canals at Lowell became an important American locomotive builder. Having disposed of the Stephenson engine, the railroad proprietors soon got rid of the granite blocks, replacing them with wooden cross-ties, and the railroad began to operate both efficiently and prosperously. It was overbuilt by American standards, but it was one of the few early lines that could follow the British practice of creating a new medium of transportation on a largely developed, and possibly overtaxed, route where prospective earnings could justify such heavy construction.

The other two trunk lines radiating from Boston had no such sanguine prospects, and their construction showed a proper accordance between financial expectations and expenditures. The Boston and Providence Railroad was undertaken not to divert the trade of a river but rather to cut one of the major necks of land that interrupted the coastal navigation along the Atlantic coast. By building a railroad between those major ports, as was proposed in 1832, a land passage around Cape Cod was secured, avoiding perhaps the worst coastal sailing conditions on the American Atlantic coast. William Gibbs McNeill, whom we met on the Baltimore and Ohio, was given the task of selecting a route between the two cities, little more than forty miles apart. McNeill examined a number of possible alignments. We know from his analysis that his choice represented a compromise of length of line and efficiency of grades. His detailed account describes the particular attention he paid to what we might call redundant grade—that is, rising grades that are introduced not by the single summit elevation that most routes must overcome but rather by repeating summits, gained only to be partially lost in succeeding valleys intervening before the final, ultimately irreducible summit is reached. Even on the worn-down surface of eastern New England, a string of hills to cross could introduce fairly considerable totals of opposing grade—that is, hills that must be climbed in the direction of movement. If the absolutely necessary summit could be reached without such a rolling grade, the efficient route available would be secured. Only a tunnel under that ultimate summit could further improve the alignment.

In his search McNeill examined eleven

The Canton Viaduct. Author's photograph.

possible routes, with redundant grades ranging between an astonishing 6.90 feet and 122.50 feet, and a length between 52.82 and 63.75 miles. He selected a combination of redundant grade of only 16.50 feet and a mileage of 53.82 miles, one mile over the shortest, to secure the sort of line that Americans were seeking in this pioneering railroad phase when there was little money for heavy engineering works. Even then the great engineer had to plan for a stone viaduct across Canton Vale, which was primitive by our standards but hardly mean: it is still carrying Amtrak's line a full century and a half after it was built.[7] This line proved a reasonable financial success when it was opened in 1835. The need to transit those necks of land, which Albert Gallatin had perceived a generation before, had continued to grow to the extent that a reasonable market was already in existence for an

economically constructed line. That was what McNeill found and developed for his Board of Directors.

The third line, which made Boston the rail hub, differed from the other two in its obviously longer probable extent. The Merrimack River was reached within less than thirty miles, and Narragansett Bay in just over fifty, but the great American west lay far away, and even the waystops on the route were considerably removed from the Hub. The first practicable objective was Worcester, some forty-five miles to the west, but it was merely a temporary terminus that allowed for the promotion of a railroad company of a conservatively modest scale. Boston mercantile interests could not think in terms of a line extending at least to the eastern end of Erie Canal at Albany. The country west of Worcester toward the Hudson was very hilly and was stagnant or even shrinking in its agricultural accomplishments. The first promoters therefore settled for building the Boston and Worcester Railroad.

The Boston and Worcester Railroad was built within an area that possessed a reasonably developed market, though its expectations were more problematic than on the first two lines projected outward by Boston mercantile capitalists, having neither the capture of the Merrimack traffic nor the shortening of the dangerous journey outside the Cape to count on for success. When the western line out of Boston was begun, the existing trade with Worcester was only moderate because of the existence of the Blackstone Canal, which diverted the flow of goods away from Boston and toward Providence. The experience of the B. and O. lent hope to the proceedings as in 1832 the Maryland Line had carried 41,000 tons of freight and 9,000 passengers in a situation similar to that of the Boston and Worcester.[8] With some prerail flow between the two cities demonstrated by the Boston and Worcester Turnpike, which had been operating for nearly a quarter of a century, and the developmental potential of the railroad shown by the B. and O. in its first five years, the B. and W. was well if thriftily constructed. Despite the fact that there was no master stream connecting the two termini, there was only a hundred feet of redundant grade (westbound) in reaching to the inland center located at 456 feet and 43.5 miles away by the rail alignment. The steepest ascent was only 30 feet per mile (0.56 percent) in quite rolling country, and the curves were no tighter than a radius of at least 1,150 feet, a figure even George Stephenson could have faced.[9]

As soon as it opened in 1835, the Boston and Worcester proved profitable. Using a common measure of rail performance, the company had an operating ratio of 47 percent, meaning that it managed to retain as profit 47 percent of its gross receipts. That same year, 1837, the Belgian railroads had

an operating ratio of "little more than a half per cent per annum income."[10] The explanation for the greater profitability of the American line was its far cheaper construction cost more than its rates, only modestly higher than found in Belgium—rates that were actually considerably lower than those in England. Such profitability was crucial to the working of the American system of railroad building, which had as a critical component the idea that the early earnings by the various pioneer lines would provide the capital necessary for the "completion" of the line, through reconstruction and enhancement of the physical fabric of the route by the building of branches and extensions.

The success of the Boston and Worcester gave necessary strength to its companion company, the Western Railroad of Massachusetts, planned from the beginning as an extension from Worcester to the Hudson River. When this railroad was completed in 1841, it was the longest in the country and one of the highest in the world, though it was still able to keep its ruling grade to 87 feet per mile (1.5 percent). But it had 107 miles of track with grades steeper than any on the Boston and Worcester, and its summit section (only 1.8 miles long) had cost $241, 311.[11] Despite the relatively high cost of construction, the Western Railroad adopted a most logical policy for a truly developmental line: it held out for relatively low fares when it met with its cousin the Worcester Railroad to establish a through Boston-Albany fare. The directors of this first American railroad to cross the Appalachians argued: "The true principle, all must admit, is to obtain the largest *net* income. . . . The circumstances to govern the sagacious director, will not so much be looked for in Belgium, or France, or Austria, as much nearer to home."[12] Nearer home it was obvious that the long-run profitability of the Western Railroad would be advanced by the encouragement of on-line

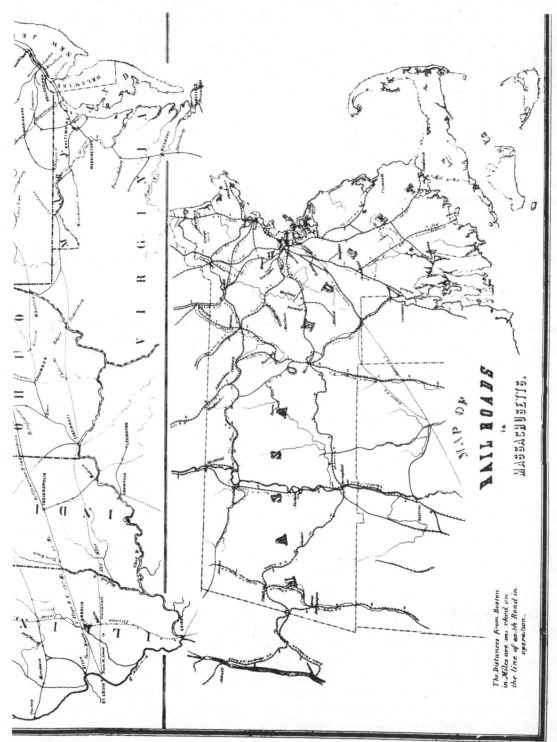

Map of railroads in Massachusetts, 1851. Skeleton map. *Source:* Armroyd, Map of Rail Routes from Cape Canso to St. Louis, 1851.

development through reasonable fares. The principle was sound, but the opening of the line to Albany in 1841 did not bring the heavy traffic the developmental line hoped to secure. The fault was Boston's, not the railroad's.

Just as this first truly developmental line was finished, Boston began to lose to New York much of its seaborne trade, particularly that from the west beyond the Hudson, which still arrived at Albany by canal, finding it cheaper to continue thence down the Hudson rather than over the sharp grades of the Berkshire Hills to Boston on the newly arrived steam cars. As one of the greatest of nineteenth-century American railroaders wrote in 1868, there was at first a "fallacy that steam could run up hill cheaper than water could run down."[13] To that observation must be added another—that terrain was to prove an ultimate, if not an initial, barrier to the flow of freight once a fairly ubiquitous network of rail lines had been shaped. Furthermore, in the shaping of that network competitive urban mercantilism was to play more of a role than is commonly recognized. Boston was the first American city to adopt the railroad as a general solution to land transportation, and its mercantile class played the largest role of any such group in America in shaping the American rail system, but its political geography made certain that Boston would become a first-class center of railroad finance but not of railroad operation. The early confidence of Bostonians in railroads could shape much of the American pattern of rails, but it could not tie the interior as a hinterland to Boston over those rails.

Boston tried harder than most cities but lost out in the end to the Middle Atlantic ports. Its most determined effort came in the search for a "new Northwest Passage"—one by rail. Even the line to Albany proved a disappointment in opening a route to the west, for two major reasons: first, that New York

State saw no reason to encourage railroads in competition with the Erie Canal and, second, that any railroad competition that might be tolerated should advance the mercantile interests of the great entrepôt of the Empire State, not those of the Bay State.

Railroads were built in sections to connect adjacent pairs of cities in upstate New York—the first completed in 1831 from Albany to Schenectady to avoid the troublesome eastern end of the canal, where heavy lockage made passage very slow—until in 1842 there was a continuous if poorly integrated string of lines between Albany and Buffalo. This loose string was not consolidated and made fairly usable until 1853, when the New York Central Railroad was formed. Even then there were restrictions on the transport of freight during the season the canal was in use, and the equivalent of canal tolls was levied on rail freight. In this complicated situation the Massachusetts railroad was left without any very useful western connection, encouraging the Boston investors in railroads to look along a different vector.

The way for Boston to reach toward the frontier seemed to lie through northern New England and New York State north of the Adirondacks. Once the Boston and Lowell was in operation, in 1835, that prosperous first-phase company looked northward, promoting lines farther up the Merrimack Valley into central New Hampshire and then westward across the rolling upland to the deeply trenched Connecticut River valley at the mouth of the White River where the archetypal American rail junction, White River Junction, Vermont, came into existence. This was a "new town," something becoming uncommon in New England by that time because most rail interchanges took place in established towns, which were the termini of the relatively short lines connecting adjacently paired cities that formed the second phase of American railroad building. Boston, as we have seen, was the first hub, and enlarged its conflux during the decade after 1835 by promoting further lines tying adjacent cities together.

In 1842 a charter was issued to a group of merchants and manufacturers in Fitchburg, to the northwest of Boston, to construct a second-phase line between that pair of cities. Completed to its namesake in 1845, the Fitchburg Railroad became a striking instance of the dynamic qualities that attached to some of these smaller New England cities. The company continued to expand northwestward from its base in the Nashua valley manufacturing town, adding a line to the Connecticut Valley at Greenfield, Massachusetts, and a second farther up that master stream of New England to Brattleboro and Bellows Falls, Vermont. Each of these was seen as an approach not only to the rail frontier of America but also to the forging of a tie to the potential hinterland of New England's coastal entrepôts and mill towns.

Once on the Connecticut in 1850, the Fitchburg faced the most tantalizing railroad terrain within the Appalachians. By carrying a rail alignment up the Deerfield River Valley, which joins the Connecticut just south of Greenfield (at pioneering Deerfield), a well-graded route could be secured nearly across the backbone of the Appalachians in New England, here called the Berkshire Hills. From the upper Deerfield Valley only a 5-mile summit ridge separated the Connecticut and Hudson drainage, with approaches to that ridge at fairly low elevations. The investors of Fitchburg saw this as the last barrier to the West and one that might be pierced by a tunnel—in fact the only place in the Appalachians where such an opportunity availed. Elsewhere the summit was made up of the broad Appalachian Plateau, which could be several hundred miles wide, a situation totally impracticable for tunneling. Only where the New River, rising in the Great Valley of Virginia, flowed

totally across that Appalachian plateau to the Ohio River was a similar low crossing to be found, though it was not brought into the American rail network as a developed route until the 1870s, when Collis Huntington, fresh from his leading role in building the western end of the first transcontinental railroad, organized the Chesapeake and Ohio Railway to use that low-level route of the Middle Atlantic area.

The financial interests joined in the Fitchburg Railroad even before that line reached Greenfield secured a charter in 1848 for the Troy and Greenfield, which could practicably be built only if the 5-mile Hoosac Mountain were to be breached by a tunnel. In 1851 the directors of the Troy and Greenfield received a sobering engineers' report. It pointed out that a tunnel 4 miles long had been completed in France and "had been constructed on an average cost of less than five dollars per cubic yard of excavation, including the expense of erecting the required masonry; hence it was supposed that the 350,000 cubic yards of excavation requisite to bore through Hoosac Mountain would at a maximum not exceed $1,750,000."[14] But that sum seemed large to the Fitchburg capitalists, a modest if brave group. They secured a state loan to begin construction in 1855. For the next twenty years the heroic struggle typical of the early long tunnels confronted first the Fitchburg Company and then the state engineers who took over construction in 1863. The contemporaneous development of the compressed-air drill (first used on the Mont Cenis Tunnel) and of nitroglycerin as an explosive advanced the pace of boring, but the hard rocks of Hoosac Mountain were a match for the considerable engineering skill evolved over the twenty-four-year period between the first contracts for construction and the completion of the Western Hemisphere's first long tunnel. Hoosac was 25,081 feet long—four and three-quarters miles—but its portals were only some 760 feet above sea level, cutting essentially in half the summit on the older Western Railroad of Massachusetts and thereby affording fairly easy grades across the Appalachians. There was, however, an ironic outcome to this whole project: it had not been the stiff summit climb on the Western Railroad that had limited its success but rather the barrier erected by New York State to any Massachusetts railroad seeking to reach the west along that vector. The Troy and Greenfield (leased by the Fitchburg), though possessed of a much better route, still faced the too-powerful opposition of the Empire State. If a way to the west were to be found for Boston, this again was not that way.

The search continued toward the northwest, rather than the west, using the extensions of the Boston and Lowell to White River Junction and the Fitchburg to Bellows Falls. From each of those river towns a valley led toward the crest of the Green Mountains whence westerly flowing streams gave access to the structural Champlain Lowland lying to the west, with its direct continuation in the lowlands of the St. Lawrence Valley. The Rutland Railroad was carried over the mountains to its eponymous town and thence along the shore of Lake Champlain to a bridge at its lower end, just within the United States, giving further access through St. Lawrence County, New York, to Ogdensburg at the foot of navigation on Lake Ontario, and thereby to steamships on the Great Lakes. From White River Junction another pair of valleys, made easy by the fact that the Winooski River flowing westward actually rises well east of the main chain of the Green Mountains permitting a railroad to pass the Green Mountain crest by a watergap. The rail line from White River Junction, originally the Vermont Central, later the Central Vermont of the Canadian National Railway, continued on through St. Albans, Vermont, where the initial project was begun. That tiny town gained a most unlikely importance

in the historical geography of the United States, as it was also the first home of the Northern Pacific project. Once across the border, Canadian affiliates carried the Vermont Central line to the south bank of the St. Lawrence opposite Montréal. With one Boston line at Ogdensburg and another at Montréal, there was some hope that the barrier of New York interests in the Mohawk Valley might have been circumvented by a "new Northwest Passage." That hope, however, was never well realized. The necessary shift to water transport at Ogdensburg limited the use of that gateway as a link between Boston and the Middle West. The competition of Portland, Maine, as a winter port, and Saint John, New Brunswick, as a summer port (served via the Grand Trunk branch to the first and the later Canadian Pacific branch to the second) ultimately restricted the use of the Vermont Central route. For a hundred years Boston tried to forge a directly controlled link to the great market of the Middle West, but it never succeeded in accomplishing that goal.

The New York and Erie Railroad: The American Appian Way

The necessity to choose between a canal and a railroad was spared the New Yorkers by their adoption of the canal option in 1817, before even England saw these iron roads as a logically alternative solution in the provision of heavy transportation. The Empire State, however, brought on itself a different but equally tortured choice once railroads were gaining acceptance: were the regions of the state not amenable to canal construction to be denied transportation more competent than the wagon road? This question arose particularly with respect to the southern tier of counties, those clearly within the Appalachian Plateau, that had been an active settlement frontier right after the Revolution. In 1792, while wagon roads were thought the ultimate practicable accomplishment in transportation development, it was proposed that an American "Appian Way," giving access to this frontier and that likely to grow beyond it in the Old Northwest, be built across the southern tier as a national project. That project gained no serious acceptance at the time so once the Erie Canal had been dug, by the state and with the political support of the plateau counties, there was a new call for a railroad to open up this country. In a book published in 1829, William C. Redfield of New York proposed a *Sketch of the Geographical Rout* [sic] *of a Great Rail way* . . . across the southern counties to Lake Erie that was the initiating proposal for what became the New York and Erie Railroad.[15] When chartered in 1832, the Erie Railroad, as it came to be known, was required first to be built entirely within New York State and, second, to avoid interconnecting with any railroad in an adjacent state. Under those conditions the line could not have its terminus on the west bank of the Hudson opposite New York City, as would have been logical, because that shore was in New Jersey. Instead, the Erie had to commence at Piermont farther north, where the west shore was also part of New York State. Thence westward the line had an unusual alignment, forced to cross repeating ridges between major valleys drained by rivers flowing transversely north or south. Here it is impossible to sketch the complexities of that route beyond noting that some steep grades and sizable viaducts were required before a practicable way across the plateau could be found all within New York.

When the railroad company came into existence in 1833, it undertook to observe the requirement that no external connections be made, adopting a different gauge from most of the other American railroads then being built: 6 feet instead of the Stephenson gauge of 4 feet 8½ inches most common on the other lines. Also it experimented with the underpinnings of the track, substituting wooden piles with stringers carried thereon in a parallel alignment and capped with a thin strip of iron on which the wheels would run in place of the gravel base with wooden cross-ties and cast-iron fish-belly rail that were becoming the American standard of track. It was thought that this pile-supported track would be cheaper to construct—obviating the need for grading—and would allow surface water and snow to pass easily beneath the stringers on which the trains ran. Experience was different from expectations: the piles rotted, the stringers sagged and leaned out of gauge, repairs were more complicated than on the typical American track, and operations were complicated by the absence of a base on which to alight from the locomotives and cars. Soon the trial was abandoned with reversion to the standard American practice of gravel base and iron rail kept in gauge as well as supported on wooden cross-ties.

The grades on the Erie Railroad were held well below the ruling grade of the B. and O., with the steepest ranging between 1 and 2 percent and any even that stiff were not too frequently encountered in the 445 miles over which the railroad passed between Piermont on the Hudson and the port of Dunkirk on Lake Erie in western New York.

This feat was accomplished by making adept use of the hydrography of the region in what might be thought a second expression of the potamic phase of American transportation. By clinging to river valleys as much as possible, reasonable gradients could commonly be secured, though at the cost of excessively curving track on occasion. Of course, curves did reduce operating speeds as well as increasing the cost of traction (because of the increased friction encountered on curving as opposed to straight track), but the tractive effort for drawing a train around curves was far less than that required to surmount stiff up grades. If the locating engineers faced a choice between curves and grades to climb, they almost always accepted the former unless an extreme lengthening of the line resulted. The B. and O. used the Potomac River to gain a reasonable route across the Folded Appalachians, accepting grades only to rise upon and pass across the Appalachian Plateau. The Erie Railroad had less freedom; it had to accept grades throughout its course because the streams flowed basically across its course. To the extent possible, however, stretches of river and tributary valleys leading thence were incorporated in the alignment of the Erie to keep down both the total rise and fall of the line and the ruling grades encountered.

The complexity of the building of the line was sufficient to assure both a slow construction and repeated calls for funds, which were raised only with considerable effort and expenditure of time, such that the original route was not completed until 1851. Soon it was found that the two termini were awkward to work: the Hudson end had eventually to be carried southward to Jersey City opposite New York City, through a relaxation of the embargo against out-of-state extensions, while the Lake Erie end was shifted when a line was completed to Buffalo in 1852. Even with those improvements much more seemed required as the Erie Railroad still was isolated from a wider market by its choice of gauge. Only by pushing for extensions on the 6-foot gauge could trade be greatly enlarged. The Atlantic and Great Western (A. and G.W.) Railroad branched off the Erie at Salamanca, New York, reaching Dayton, Ohio, in June, 1864, adding 369 miles of broad gauge. The A. and G.W. was leased by the Erie in 1871 to serve as the base for further extension of the 6-foot lines to Chicago from Marion, Ohio, a further distance of 250 miles, in 1880.[16]

The building of the Erie Railroad demonstrated clearly the failure found in trying for a regional monopoly. In the end it could not be maintained, while with the passage of time it was found the adoption of a distinct gauge tended to make acquisition of branches difficult. While the New York Central and the Pennsylvania railroads could assemble most of their extensions from the originally independent second-phase lines promoted to tie adjacent pairs of cities together, and thus burdening small local investors with the usual failures encountered in the early years of railroading, the Erie could grow mainly only by direct intervention. The result was both a limitation of the lines and a tendency to avoid major cities. This was the result of the later development of the 6-foot lines, which meant that the obvious city pairs had already been served by standard-gauge lines when the 6-foot gauge promoters arrived on the scene, forcing them to try to find a new way through on less obvious routes. But in the end such successor routes proved less developable, and the Erie had to gain a late and only partial improvement by accepting the existence of an American standard gauge. The Erie as completed extended 985 miles from Jersey City to Chicago, but the largest city en route between the two was Youngstown, Ohio, with only some 33,220 people even in 1890. The shift to standard gauge, beginning in the mid-1870s, finally integrated the Erie into the national rail system, while its original broad track gauge endowed it with the roomiest loading gauge of any of the eastern lines—a Pyrrhic victory but still a source of moderate freight earnings over the years when oversized loads had to be moved.

The South Carolina Railroad Shapes the South

The effort by the colonial entrepôts to tie an enlarged hinterland to their docks and wholesale houses, though fiercest in the North, was not restricted to that area. The leading southern trading port, Charleston, by 1828 was perceived to be not merely less vital than other entrepôts but in actual decline.[17]

> The trade of Charleston . . . had for several years past retrograded with a rapidity unprecedented. Her landed estate has, within eight years, depreciated in value one-half. Industry and business talent, driven by necessity, have sought employment elsewhere. Many of her houses are tenantless, and the grass grows uninterrupted in some of her chief business streets.

But Charleston had strong, direct ties with England and with eastern New England, both areas of active railroad promotion at this time. Thus it is not surprising that Charleston merchants should see in the railroad some relief for their plight of operating in a city that had been sited on the finest port of the South Atlantic states, but one without any appreciable potamic connections. In 1827 Alexander Black, a state representative from Charleston, introduced a bill calling for the construction of a railroad from Charleston to Hamburg, across the Savannah River from Augusta, Georgia, the trading town of the western Piedmont. Augusta, though inland, did not see itself as terribly isolated because it had the Savannah River that reached the sea at its own port of Savannah. The Carolinians, however, believed Charleston must grow in its tributary region; that expansion would require the early and eager adoption of a form of transportation not fundamentally tied to hydrography, which served it badly.

A preliminary survey of the line to Hamburg at the falls of the Savannah River demonstrated

> that the summit between the two places was 375 feet above Hamburg and 545 feet above Charleston Neck at the Lines [the city boundary]. This summit was 123 miles from Charleston by public road and 17 miles from Hamburg. Obviously, the grade on the Hamburg side presented serious difficulties. How-

ever, [the surveyor] Colonel Blanding thought this could be overcome in several ways, depending upon the type of power adopted. In case the locomotive was used, an inclined plane with a stationary engine would be necessary; in case of horse power, these could be dispensed with.[18]

Steam power was adopted very early in the construction phase, so it seemed that the inclined planes would be a basic feature of the line. As the railroad was laid out, the engineers pioneered the notion of carrying the tracks—iron strap on wooden stringers—on piles rather than a gravel substructure with the fate that later affected the Erie Railroad, though in the warm, moist Carolinas the rate of decay was even more rapid. In time a grade, easily obtained on the seemingly flat coastal plain of the Carolinas, was shaped to carry rails on cross-ties, and at a gentle rise of only 30 feet per mile (0.56 percent) at the extreme. Horatio Allen of the Delaware and Hudson (D. and H.) Canal, operators of the first steam locomotive to run in full scale in North America, was appointed chief engineer of this line, called the South Carolina Railroad. He quickly adopted steam traction and accepted a design for an engine, *The Best Friend of Charleston*, that he had built at the West Point Foundry in New York City. Allen, a strong-minded and independent man (with the courage to operate the D. and H. Canal's pioneer engine, the *Stourbridge Lion*, on its first and only run in 1829), felt it desirable not only to adopt steam from the beginning but also, given his control over the details of the engine built in America, to specify a wider track gauge for that locomotive. An axle length of 5 feet between the flanges, the basis of a track gauge, was adopted for *The Best Friend of Charleston* and thereby for the South Carolina Railroad. This established the standard track gauge for most southern railroads until these were adapted to the national standard in 1886.[19] Allen was proud to report to his directors that their decision to adopt steam traction and "The resolution then passed, and placed on the record, was the first act by a corporate body in the world to adopt the locomotive as the tractive power on a railroad for general passenger and freight transportation."[20] It should be emphasized that the South Carolina Railroad used independently designed American locomotives from the very beginning.

The line to Hamburg, open in 1833, was the longest railroad in the world but only a moderate business success. The city of Augusta forbade any physical connection between the South Carolina Railroad and the Georgia Railroad soon undertaken between that Georgia city and what became Atlanta. As Phillips points out, once cotton had been loaded on a dray to cross the city, it was as easy to deposit it on the riverbank for loading on the cheaper steamboats for passage to the port of Savannah as it was to take it across the river bridge to Hamburg for reloading on a rail car and further transit to the port of Charleston.[21] The South Carolina Railroad needed more ramified connections if it was to become profitable. At the urging of the South Carolina legislature, the route westward across the Blue Ridge (here the Great Smoky Mountains) was investigated but was found daunting and well beyond the financial capabilities of a poorly financed southern railroad. That line, when constructed in the 1880s, resulted in the steepest stretch of mainline railroad accepted permanently into the American rail network. Saluda Hill, as it was called, began with 6 miles of 1.5-percent grade followed by 3.1 miles at a very rugged 4.7 percent, making this the most trying line still operated in general service in this country. It was overcome mainly by the superbly strong engines that were available by the 1880s, which obviated the use of any inclined planes or very sophisticated civil engineering. But this western exit from South Carolina had to wait for half a century, and the South Carolina Railroad never enjoyed the success its pioneering deserved. As in New England, South Carolina could gain the West only by securing passage through a neighboring state that sought to advance the interests of its own port to the exclusion of others.

Georgia quickly adopted the railroad as an instrument to advance internal development. The Central of Georgia Railroad was encouraged to build inland from the port of Savannah, eventually gaining the Piedmont in two places and there collecting cotton, the great staple of local agriculture and trade. From Augusta (at the head of navigation on the Savannah River) the Georgia Railroad was contructed along the Piedmont toward the western boundary of the state. The Central of Georgia was begun in 1836 and within seven years was carried 190 miles to Macon. This line cost only $13,000 per mile, or $2.5 million for the whole undertaking, certainly a classic developmental route. Between 1833 and 1845 the 170-mile line from Augusta reached to the foreseeable limit of private railroad development in interior Georgia, a place designated as Terminus.

In 1845 the state undertook to carry on further railroad building at its own expense providing a connection for the Central of Georgia (which also reached Terminus in 1845) and the Georgia railroad. This state line, the Western and Atlantic Railroad, was carried through the low outliers of the Appalachians that make up the hills of north Georgia to reach the Great Valley, here drained by the Tennessee River, at a new railroad town—Chattanooga, Tennessee. Once this southernmost of the trans-Appalachian crossings was completed and opened for service in 1851, it was decided to rename Terminus for the state railroad, calling it Atlanta and creating what would become the largest railroad town created in the United States. The success of the Western and Atlantic in opening a hinterland for the

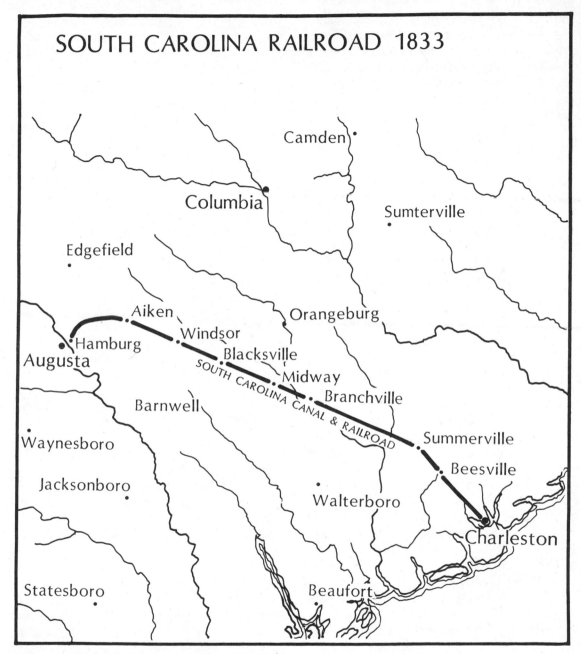

SOUTH CAROLINA RAILROAD 1833

Camden

Columbia

Sumterville

Edgefield

Aiken

Windsor

Orangeburg

Hamburg

Blacksville

Augusta

SOUTH CAROLINA CANAL & RAILROAD

Midway

Branchville

Barnwell

Summerville

Waynesboro

Beesville

Jacksonboro

Walterboro

Charleston

Statesboro

Beaufort

The South Carolina Railroad as orginally constructed.

southern colonial entrepôts—Charleston and Savannah—in the interior south and even the Middle West made Atlanta a great junction city. Unfortunately, neither Charleston nor Savannah managed to become the general cargo port that would have assured their growth as did the northern entrepôts when their rail lines reached across the Appalachians at this very same period.

In one of those striking coincidences of historical geography, five trans-Appalachian railroads were completed in the United States in 1851–1852 (with the first in Canada, the St. Lawrence and Atlantic–Atlantic and St. Lawrence between Montréal and Portland coming only a year later). Starting in the north, these were the consolidation into a practically working company, the New York Central, of the second-phase short lines across upstate New York (1852) and the completion of the New York and Erie to Dunkirk on Lake Erie in 1851; the opening of the Pennsylvania Railroad to Pittsburgh (using the Portage Railway across the top of the plateau until 1854) and the completion of the Baltimore and Ohio to Wheeling on the Ohio River, both in 1852; and finally the completion of the Western and Atlantic to Chattanooga the previous year.

With these crossings of the great mountain barrier that shut the Middle West off from the Atlantic, the great ports of the Atlantic Coast—Portland, Boston, New York, Philadelphia, Baltimore, Charleston, and Savannah—were ready to enter a new phase of American railroad construction, the laying down of clearly developmental lines throughout the interior South and the Middle West. The three earlier phases of American railroad evolution had seen, first the building of short, almost experimental lines out of the entrepôts (phase 1); second, the construction of many short lines connecting closely adjacent pairs of cities (phase 2); and, third, the assault on the Appalachian Barrier (phase 3) which had to be won before the larger contest of American urban mercantilism, the so-called winning of the West, could begin.

THE FOURTH PHASE: THE CREATION OF SUBCONTINENTAL SYSTEMS

Crossing the Appalachians could not be an ultimate goal—that would be like opening a door without entering. Each of the companies had fought hard first to find a way through and then to accomplish the construction necessary to reach the inviting economic frontier of the Middle West—then still often called the Northwest. By 1853 six vigorous companies were looking onward from what might at first have seemed their prime objective. They had subsequently discovered it was simply their immediate one. In crossing the Appalachians each had tended to have a band of territory to itself, a pairing of entrepôt and inland articulation point. For the Atlantic and St. Lawrence–St. Lawrence and Atlantic, these were Portland (whence came the first impetus) and Montréal; for the New York Central, Albany (later New York City) and Buffalo; for the Erie, New York City and Dunkirk (later Buffalo); for the Pennsylvania, Philadelphia, and Pittsburgh; for the Baltimore and Ohio, Baltimore and Wheeling; and for the South Carolina Railroad–Georgia Railroad, extended by the Western and Atlantic, the pairing was Savannah and Charleston on the sea and Chattanooga on the Tennessee River. The rationale behind these pairings was traditional in North American transportation: the supplementing by other means of the natural waterways that had furnished the pioneering phase of American transportation development. Secretary Gallatin had first signaled this prosthetic phase in his proposals for cuts across the four necks of land and for the inland openings by the interconnections of Atlantic and Mississipian streams.

The railroad, after the costly experiment of the Pennsylvania Mainline Canal system, seemed the ideal prosthesis to integrate the Atlantic and interior rivers. From that conclusion followed the trans-Appalachian epoch of railroad building, but once these lines were completed it was quickly apparent that to use the costly mountain lines required a collection and distribution network west of the mountains. Even the Canadian line—the British-owned Grand Trunk that took over the St. Lawrence and Atlantic–Atlantic and St. Lawrence—quickly adopted the North American strategy of searching for justification of the trans-Appalachian line through extending and ramifying connections in the American Middle West. In fact it was the preference that the Grand Trunk had for lines in Michigan and Illinois over lines across the Canadian shield to western Canada that forced the Canadian government to seek a new company to undertake the building of a Canadian Pacific railroad.

Only in the South was the field a bit different. Again it seems that the first trans-Appalachian railroad (the South Carolina Railroad and extensions) and subsequent mountain crossings had the Middle West within their sights, but to reach that region required crossing the interior South of Tennessee and Kentucky. Only then would you reach the articulation points at the edge of the railroad bonanza that was the vast staple-agriculture-producing Middle West. The length of time it took the southern lines to build across the interior South was sufficient to assure that when they arrived on the Ohio River, the locus of their articulation points with the mid-western railroads, the Middle West had been effectively occupied by the northeastern railroads. They had started closer to the finishing line through their attainment by 1853 of an alignment of intermediate articulation points extending from Montréal through Buffalo to Pittsburgh and Wheeling (later Parkersburg, West Virginia). Only in the 1970s has the South largely won the battle for equal access to the Middle West through the bankruptcy of many of the northern railroads and the merger of formerly northern lines into vast subcontinental systems based largely on southern roots—the Southern Railway and the Chesapeake and Ohio Railway.

The Middle West did not wait for the arrival of the trans-Appalachians lines to introduce railroads; the region had its own second phase, which was also true of the interior South, Canada's Maritime area, and even California.

In the early period of railroads the passenger business was of greater relative importance than freight, in Ohio as well as on the Atlantic coast. Passenger routes were more flexible, and, moreover, the roads were not built substantially enough to transport large amounts of merchandise. The long use of the water routes to New Orleans formed a powerful factor in retarding the development of freight traffic, while the novelty and rapidity of travel by railroad as compared with other modes quickly attracted many passengers.[23]

Only with the arrival of the trans-Appalachian lines did it make sense to ship all the way by rail, thus efficiently reducing terminal time and costs as goods loaded either at the ocean port or the farm-town siding could reach the other without significant rehandling. The locally promoted (first-phase) lines in Ohio were proposed earliest in the environs of Cincinnati, Cleveland, and Sandusky as adjuncts to the waterways and thus mainly tapping the hinterlands of these river and lake ports through north-south lines. By the onset of the fourth phase (the trans-Appalachian railroad invasion of the Middle West), which began in 1853, there were twenty-two railroads in operation in Ohio, with the longest extending 234 miles from Cleveland to Cincinnati and 216 miles from Cincinnati through Dayton to San- dusky on Lake Erie. These represented somewhat ad hoc alignments as they were end-to-end consolidations of second-phase (city-to-city) routes in a number of cases. This consolidation, either by means of "through-running" agreements or by out- right corporate merger, produced somewhat circuitous routings but increasingly useful operations that obviated the awkward trans- fers that had characterized intermediate- distance travel by rail under the full control of the second phase of development.

It was this tentative enlargement of the second phase in the Middle West, with its consolidation but absence of truly wide- ranging objectives, that set the stage for the eastern conquest of that burgeoning region. The Baltimore and Ohio, Pennsylvania, and New York Central each encouraged the crea- tion of extensive second-phase lines, as a means to the end of furthering even more ex- tensive consolidations, before gaining out- right control through purchase or very long term lease.

Here we cannot do more than allude to this fourth phase with respect to the four eastern lines. In addition to the three that arrived physically on the doorstep—the Erie, New York Central, and Pennsylvania—two others deserve brief notice—the Grand Trunk arriving on the Ste. Claire River fron- tier in 1859 and the detached but highly significant efforts by Boston capitalists to gain a foothold in the Middle West, using first the Michigan Central Railroad in the late 1840s.

The first to arrive on the doorstep, the Erie, was slow in having great impact on the mid- western rail network because of its broad and unstandard gauge. As we have already seen, 6-foot gauge lines were eventually driven as far west as Cincinnati (whence a broad gauge line was carried all the way to East St. Louis, Illinois, but control thereof was early gained by the Baltimore and Ohio) and Chicago. As already noted the largest city on the directly controlled line was Youngstown so it is clear that the Erie managed merely to carry its line to the great junction of the Middle West in Chicago rather than to tap a large part of the market in the region. The New York Central and the Pennsylvania, though the latter had a track gauge of 4 feet 9 inches (rather than 8.5 inches), could interchange with most of the shorter lines in the northeastern quadrant of the country, as well as with other major com- panies, so their westward progress was finan- cially far more rewarding, a fact reflected in the rapid ramification of lines either fi- nanced or encouraged by the northeastern giants.

The Pennsylvania, using the Pittsburgh and Fort Wayne Railroad as an instrument, secured a line from the Forks of the Ohio to Chicago only six years after first crossing the Appalachians in Pennsylvania. The New York Central reached the Great Junction not through promoting a company to build across the Middle West but instead by gain- ing control of the Lakeshore and Michigan Southern Railroad, which was the first to reach Chicago from the east, in February, 1852. Subsequently the Central also wrested the Michigan Central, which reached Chi- cago six months after the Southern, from the Forbes group and obtained thereby a se- cond route into the junction, using the Canada Southern and Michigan Central to pass north around Lake Erie between Buf- falo and Detroit and Chicago, and the Lakeshore and Michigan Southern from Buffalo via Cleveland and Toledo south around the lake to Chicago.

The Baltimore and Ohio, starting from a more southerly gateway, headed for Cincin- nati and St. Louis before Chicago. The B.

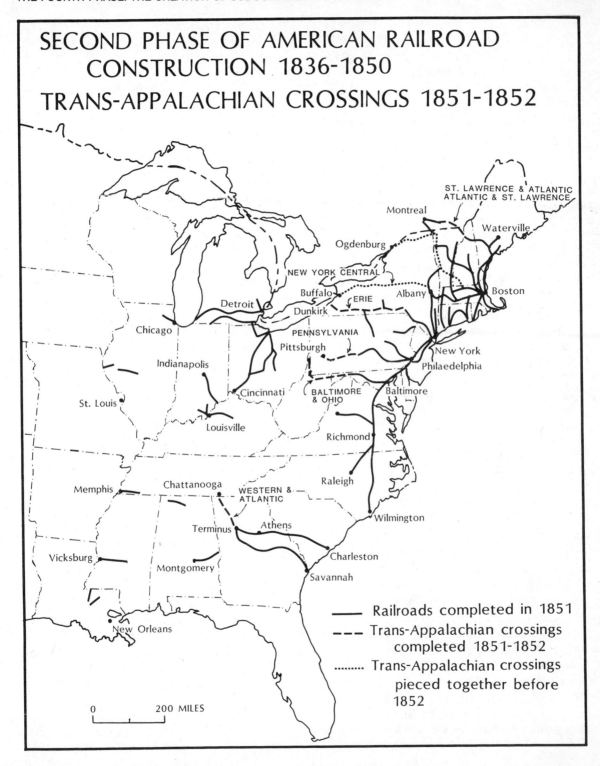

SECOND PHASE OF AMERICAN RAILROAD
CONSTRUCTION 1836-1850
TRANS-APPALACHIAN CROSSINGS 1851-1852

ST. LAWRENCE & ATLANTIC
ATLANTIC & ST. LAWRENCE

Montreal

Waterville

Ogdenburg

NEW YORK CENTRAL

Buffalo   Albany   Boston
Detroit   ERIE

Dunkirk

Chicago   PENNSYLVANIA

Pittsburgh   New York
Indianapolis   Philaedelphia

St. Louis   Cincinnati   BALTIMORE   Baltimore
                                  & OHIO

Louisville   Richmond

Memphis   Chattanooga   Raleigh
                    WESTERN &
                    ATLANTIC

Terminus   Athens   Wilmington

Vicksburg   Charleston
          Montgomery   Savannah

New Orleans

⎯⎯⎯ Railroads completed in 1851
- - - Trans-Appalachian crossings
        completed 1851-1852
.... Trans-Appalachian crossings
        pieced together before
        1852

0   200 MILES

and O. reached Cincinnati by consolidation with lines it had encouraged and continued westward to East St. Louis, creating in 1857 the first easterly connection from what was then the metropolis of the Mississippi Valley. The branch that had been projected from Cumberland to Pittsburgh was completed in 1871 and extended to Chicago in 1874. In this way the B. and O. reached the two western articulation points—Chicago and St. Louis—which it shared with the New York Central and Pennsylvania, each of which reached St. Louis after the Civil War.

To gain further access to the lavish interior market, the northeastern trunk lines—New York Central, Pennsylvania, and Baltimore and Ohio—also pushed branches southward toward the southern boundary of what came to be known as the Trunk Line Territory, to Cincinnati and Louisville, which were established as the doorsteps to and from the South. As matters matured, the Mississippi River, Chicago in the northwest, and the Ohio River defined this great interior market supported by both agriculture and industry. The southern region ended at the Ohio in the north and similarly at the Mississippi in the west. Articulation of the southern railroads with those pushed beyond the Mississippi came at Memphis, Vicksburg, and New Orleans, so that in neither the North nor the South did the original trans-Appalachian railroads manage to push their junctions beyond the Mississippi.

At that first American western political frontier, the fourth phase of railroad development reached its termination, leaving two blocks of subcontinental railroading east of the Mississippi, divided one from the other by the Ohio River. To the west of the great river (first bridged at Rock Island in 1857) lay both a railroad and a settlement frontier, to such an extent that by 1859 the head of iron had nearly overtaken the outermost line of the pioneers' cabins. Indeed,

after the Civil War the railroads became literal pioneers—the first to plow the Plains, even if only for the embankment on which to lay their rails, and the architects of the settlement pattern through the location of their

THE EVOLUTION OF THE SOUTHERN RAIL NET

Before we turn to that trans-Mississippi pioneering, we should summarize the spread of the rail net across the South, both coastal and interior. The first of those expansive efforts was shared with the North, as once railroads came into widespread use it was appreciated that north-south lines interconnecting the colonial ports were desirable even in an era of considerable coastwise shipping. The progress in the Northeast was surprisingly slow until we note that any line near the coast had to ferry or bridge a number of estuaries. Between Boston and New York there was no coastal plain, and the rolling country away from the actual seashore encouraged the construction of the components of what became the New York, New Haven and Hartford Railroad Shore Line, close to salt water. To make that route deeply reentrant estuaries had to be traversed with either bridges or ferries. Ferries remained on the Thames and Connecticut rivers in Connecticut until after the Civil War, and even an otherwise continuous rail line from Boston to New York was not completed until after Chicago was joined with the east (1852). South of New York (or, rather, the Jersey shore of the Hudson, where all through railroads stopped until 1910) the Delaware and the Susquehanna forced gaps for many years, although the Camden and Amboy had been completed in 1834 and Philadelphia and Washington had been joined—other than at the Susquehanna ferry at Perryville, Maryland—in 1838. By then the stretch between Philadelphia and Baltimore had been completed, joining the Baltimore and Washington section opened in 1835.

Longitudinal railroads demonstrated the most diversity south of the Potomac. The first, the Richmond and Danville, was extended incrementally from a pairing of its eponymous cities southwestward along the Piedmont until it reached Atlanta, elevating several cities on its route to the status of major railroad towns, notably Charlotte in North Carolina and Atlanta itself. As agriculture expanded in the Piedmont, the Richmond and Danville became the backbone of the Cotton Belt of that time with all the demands for wholesale trading it introduced. Richmond, Danville, Winston-Salem, Charlotte, Spartanburg, Greenville, and Atlanta became an alignment of wholesaling-retailing towns based on the collection of staples grown in the great agricultural belt and the retributive distribution of seed, fertilizer, wagons, machinery, and a great variety of manufactures (and even food) necessary to the conduct of such a striking monoculture. Eventually this Piedmont Line became the base on which a further extension of the trunk line skirting the southern Appalachians could be carried all the way to New Orleans. When the R. and D. joined twenty-four other southern railroads in financial difficulties in the 1890s, J. P. Morgan forced an amalgamation that began with a system of two thousand miles in 1894 but expanded to nearly eight thousand by 1900.

At the boundary of the Piedmont and the Coastal Plain—that is, the Fall Line—a second South Atlantic rail line was pieced together in the 1890s, starting at Richmond but continuing southwesterly halfway between the mountains and the actual coast through Raleigh and Athens to Atlanta, underpinning an alignment of towns of greater age along the Fall Line. These thereby became a second string of trading centers originally sited at the head of navigation on

rivers, but now mainly supported by the efflux and influx of trade by rail between the most agriculturally productive part of the South and the manufacturing North. This Seaboard Airline Railway was bifurcated beyond Hamlet, North Carolina, sending a major branch through Columbia and Savannah to Jacksonville and southward into Florida when that state witnessed economic development in the first quarter of this century.

The final longitudinal railroad in the South was begun as a relatively modest route between the port of Wilmington, North Carolina, and Richmond; but by sending a much longer branch from Wilson in North Carolina through Fayetteville, Florence, and Charleston to Savannah and then onward to Jacksonville and Florida, this Atlantic Coast Line became an interregional connection between the North and Florida. These longitudinal railroads of the South began in the traditional context of Cotton Belt agriculture, and the monoculture it implied; but in the last quarter of the nineteenth century and the first of the twentieth, the interaction between North and South changed fundamentally. With railroads available, or projected, the subtropical climate of the South became its greatest resource, both as an area of agricultural production of fresh food—fruits and vegetables for the burgeoning urban markets of the North and Middle West—and a potential winter resort for people from those same consuming areas. In the 1870s and 1880s those ties were with resorts in North Carolina—Southern Pines and Pinehurst, for example—and with fields in the Carolinas and Georgia—for early peaches, for example. In this century, as the railroad developments and consolidations projected lines into northern and then peninsular Florida, the resorts moved southward—to coastal Georgia and then into Florida at St. Augustine and Daytona—and new truly subtropical crops, such as citrus fruit, could be produced and sent northward. The railroad was crucial to this development, and subtropical agriculture and resorts in turn to the prospects for railroad construction and operation. Coastal shipping might have sufficed for cotton but had little appeal for the transport of perishable fruit or, initially, wealthy tourists. The longitudinal railroads of the South have relied on the area's subtropical climate ever since as the backstay of their support.

West of the Appalachians a similar pattern of regional connection evolved, though the flows were somewhat different from those in the coastal South. Within the interior South the drive was to tie articulation points on the Ohio River with the Gulf Coast and its ports. Those entrepôts—New Orleans and Mobile in particular—were motivated in much the same way as their peers between Portland and Savannah; they wished to open a hinterland to provide enlarged support for the merchants' port. With the Western and Atlantic Railroad at Chattanooga, the question of further advance arose. Thus there were two main objectives that operated in the area we now call the East South Central United States, which began as "the Southwest" and seems to be best called the interior South, even if it did have a Gulf Coastline. In Alabama, Mississippi, Tennessee, and Kentucky, the region under discussion, the objectives for rail construction were either to tie the Ohio River articulation points with potential markets farther south, or to tie the southern trans-Appalachian crossings with the Middle West. The purpose of the latter alignment of railroads was to interconnect the wonderfully diverse agricultural region of the Middle West with a potential consuming area, mainly for food, in the Cotton Belt. That monocultural region then skirted the Appalachians from South Carolina to the point those mountains gave out in central Alabama, continuing westward to the Mississippi around Memphis.

Cincinnati saw the commercial appeal of this market so clearly that the city government promoted and accomplished the building of a railroad thence to Chattanooga, one that remains in the city's possession though it has been leased to the Southern Railway. The Queen City's rival on the Ohio, Louisville, was equally motivated, though it used a private company to accomplish its drive toward southern markets. The Louisville and Nashville Railroad first joined those cities before continuing its line both southeastward toward that emerging junction at Chattanooga and southwestward toward New Orleans. With a further branching to the other Ohio articulation point, the long famous "Queen and Crescent Route" provided an interior tie between the Northeast (at Cincinnati) and New Orleans to compete with the Piedmont Route from Washington via Charlotte, Atlanta, and Birmingham to the Cresent City.

In the western interior South a different set of objectives shaped the railroad pattern. In the early 1850s there was strong agitation in Illinois for a north-south route to tie the earlier-settled southern part of the state with its emerging north. The Illinois Central (I.C.) Railroad was organized in 1850 and quickly succeeded in constructing a line from Cairo, at the confluence of the Ohio and Mississippi rivers, to the northern part of the state, where two branches carried the railroad to the canal port of Chicago and the lead-mining Fever River district in the northwest. To accomplish such an ambitious project in a pioneering area, it was essential to secure governmental assistance—in this case through an indirect instrument, the land-grant, rather than public funding. The I.C. was the first railroad given a federal land grant; to secure it there obviously had to be the sort of sectional balancing essential to legislation before the Civil War. If Illinois was to receive a land grant, so must some southern state's railroad. In this instance it was the entry of Mobile that profited. That port had promoted the Mobile and Ohio (M. and O.) Railroad, projected inland and perfectly willing to make juncture with the Illinois Central if that produced federal assistance. In 1850 the M. and O. started building northward while the I.C. laid track southward. Just before the outbreak of the Civil War they approached each other on the two sides of the Ohio at Cairo, and a practicable through—though not continuous—route between Chicago and New Orleans was in hand.

The I.C. never particularly enjoyed sharing this route. After the war, and with the increasing domination of the national economy by the North and Middle West, that company assembled a number of short lines in Mississippi and western Tennessee to create a continuous trackage between Chicago and New Orleans, leaving the Mobile and Ohio mainly as a regional line of the interior South. Only in the 1930s did the latter change its role through merger with the Chicago and Alton Railroad, which afforded it an entry to Chicago, Kansas City, and St. Louis. This merged company, the Gulf, Mobile, and Ohio, prospered with the economic awakening of the interior South in the 1930s during the Tennessee Valley Authority developments, gaining thereby greater equivalence with the I.C. By the 1970s they became rational partners, formally joined as the Illinois Central Gulf Railroad, which finally brought a major interregional system to that interior South and, incidentally, the two components of the 1850 land-grant experiment into a single rail system.

The merging of the Louisville and Nashville Railroad with its commonly owned family members—the Seaboard Airline Railroad and the Atlantic Coast Line (formally joined just prior to the ultimate creation of the so-called Family Lines)—created a second trunk carrier in the South to pair with the Southern Railway shaped three-quarters of a century earlier by Morgan. Further amalgamation in the 1970s joined the Family Lines with the Chesapeake and Ohio (already merged with the Baltimore and Ohio) and the Southern Railway with the Norfolk and Western, a prosperous coal-carrying line shaped in the coalfields of West Virginia and western Virginia. In the early 1980s the south, coastal and interior, became the workplace of two major companies, CSX transportation (Family Lines and Chesapeake and Ohio–Baltimore and Ohio) and the Norfolk Southern (Southern and Norfolk and Western). Over the years several midwestern railroads had managed to project a route or two into the South. For example, the St. Louis and San Francisco Railway was merged into the Burlington Northern to provide a line from the Middle West to the weakest of the three Gulf entrepôts, Pensacola.

The Railroad Pattern West of Chicago

Returning to the decade just before the Civil War, we must ask how the railroad net of the United States expanded westward? In less than thirty years the nation had gone from a few timid developments adjacent to the more active but unfavorably located ports of the Atlantic Coast—the railroads of Boston, the Baltimore and Ohio, the Pennsylvania railroad from Philadelphia to Columbia on the Susquehanna (as part of the larger Mainline Canal System), and the South Carolina Railroad from Charleston to Hamburg opposite Augusta, Georgia—to considerably the largest system of railroads in the world, nearly half the world total, extending westward in separate lines from most of the major ports to the Mississippi River. It seems that the level of confidence for private investment could not carry such development much farther west than St. Louis or Chicago, which became the common objectives of virtually all the eastern companies, even if we realize that the southern ones were long in reaching such goals (the Southern Railway successor to the South Carolina Railroad did not make it to Chicago until the 1960s, as did the Louisville and Nashville). West of Chicago and St. Louis the market seemed too small and undeveloped to capture the attention of the eastern trunk lines before the Civil War. Instead, those companies showed only vague interest in promotions heading west out of the Great Junction City. It seems highly significant that the first railroad into Chicago from the west (and the first railroad to reach the canal port) was the Galena and Chicago Union Railroad, which entered the city in 1848. The railroad was locally promoted, as were several of the lines seeking specifically to create a hinterland particularly for Chicago, and necessarily thus lying to the west of it.

The main exception to this generalization that the lines "beyond Chicago" were locally sponsored came with respect to the rather exceptional interests of Boston in railroad promotion. Having failed to break through the barriers to Boston mercantile advance interposed by New York State, the Yankee capitalists had divorced ownership of western lines from direct connection with the Hub. Instead, the Forbes Group had invested heavily in the Michigan Central, using it as a springboard toward western railroad promotion lying beyond the Empire State. When in 1852 those Bostonians secured access to Chicago for the Michigan Central, though they eventually lost control of that company to the Vanderbilts, the now somewhat abstracted interest of the mercantile community in the Hub in western railroads meant that they were not seeking further extensions of a direct Boston line but instead the financial health of an investment in internal improvements detached from their local mercantile concerns. Still, the health of

the Michigan Central seemed to dictate caring for its western connections and to secure that end the Forbes Group took up one of the western feeders reaching Chicago from the prairie of central Illinois. Those interests crystallized in the promotion of the Chicago, Burlington and Quincy Railroad, constructing lines between Chicago and two river ports on the Mississippi. From the southern one of these, Quincy, Illinois, it seemed that a further push to the west could be rationally entertained toward the great bend of the Missouri River where several truly frontier towns—Independence and St. Joseph—had taken on the role of jumping-off place for the long trek to Oregon and then California. In a line completed in 1859, the Hannibal and St. Joseph Railroad, the Boston interests joined with local promoters to construct the most westerly of American railroads at the outbreak of the Civil War. Possibly local confidence would have gained that end unaided, but certainly Boston was the one eastern mercantile community that evinced much interest in rail developments west of Chicago before 1860.

Beyond Chicago that last decade of peace witnessed the introduction of a new form of American railroad, what came subsequently to be known as the granger road, a line built to transport agricultural products, most notably grain and livestock to Chicago and thence to eastern and European markets. We have already seen that the general development of urban mercantilism in the colonial entrepôts was harnessed to providing lines as far west as Chicago and St. Louis: it remained for these granger roads to carry rail transport virtually to the fields where the grain was planted. Just before and just after the Civil War, the Chicago and Rock Island Railroad, which was the first to bridge the Mississippi, in 1857; the Chicago, Burlington and Quincy; the Chicago and Northwestern (the transformation of the Galena and Chicago Union); and the Illinois Central, which turned its vector of development from north-south to east-west extending from its northwestern terminus at Dunleith (East Dubuque, Illinois) in this period—all took on the role of creating an agriculturally based rail net in Illinois, eastern Iowa, and northern Missouri. There the outbreak of the Civil War overtook the evolution of the American railroad network.

THE TRANSCONTINENTAL RAILROAD PROJECT

While the market, observable or rationally to be anticipated, was ruling the spread of the American railroad network between its origin adjacent to the Atlantic ports and its most distant market frontier, on the Mississippi with a further salient reaching westward to the great bend of the Missouri River, there was also the assertion of another phase of railroad planning based almost entirely on geographical abstractions without any rational market justifications. This was the effort to secure a transcontinental railroad. Before 1846 such a call was even more abstract in the sense that the boundary of the United States remained where it had been for forty years as a result of the Louisiana Purchase. The crest of the Rockies and the Mexican and later republican boundaries of Texas defined the west for the United States. No line might be projected to the Pacific in totally American territory, even in the Oregon Country that remained *terra nullius* under joint American and British occupation until 1846. But if an American line were to be built, it must of necessity follow a northern route to take advantage of that equivocal "sovereignty" in Oregon. Such was the conclusion of the first public meeting held to discuss and promote the subject. A letter writer to the *Emigrant* in 1832 had already proposed such a grand project by way of the Great Lakes and the Platte Valley and onward to Oregon.[23] Before the opening

of any railroad of consequence and any serious application of steam power, such a proposal was truly chimerical.

A more serious proposal came in 1844, when Asa Whitney, a New York merchant born in Groton, Massachusetts, organized a convention in that city to promote a transcontinental line. The year had seen the negotiation of the first Sino-American trade treaty, raising mercantile expectations for a large increase in the American Pacific and East Asian trade. Again the railroad was to be built, under a vast land grant, from Lake Michigan to the Pacific in the Oregon Country. This involvement of Congress in the promotion immediately enmeshed the project in the sectionalism rampant in this period. Nothing was done until the political geography of western North America became more fixed and more favorable to the United States. In 1846 the joint occupation of the Oregon Country was replaced by American sovereignty of that part south of the 49th parallel (and by British to the north thereof). In 1848, at the conclusion of the Mexican War, what is now the American Southwest was added to the union giving the United States its current Pacific coastline (save for the addition of its Alaska component in 1867). Thus, in the early 1850s with the great Gold Rush to California, there was a bit more economic plausibility behind any Pacific railroad proposal.

There was a sufficient modicum of expectable market to allow proponents to memorialize Congress to authorize such a project, using the device of railroad land grants introduced in 1850 as an increment of economic subsidy required by prospective investors to amplify the small and distant market of California. Again with federal involvement the sectional issue arose, particularly after the Gadsden Purchase of 1853, which established a seemingly practical southern alternative to the long-standing proposal for a route between the Great

Lakes and the Oregon Country. In that situation Congress took a typically nineteenth-century approach to this significant conflict: they called on "scientific opinion" to resolve what was essentially a political problem. Congress authorized the Pacific Railroad Survey of 1854 to be carried out by the Bureau of Topographical Engineers, a branch of the War Department already engaged in extensive mapping of the vast and little-known American West.

The Pacific Railroad Survey, as this effort came to be known, set out to examine some six routes that appeared likely prospects for a transcontinental railroad extending from the settlement frontier of the time to the several possible ports on the Pacific Coast.

Considering the traditional northern route, surveys were to be run along the general latitude of the 49th and 47th parallels. Instead of establishing an independent party for this investigation, the Secretary of War, charged with the survey, asked Isaac Stevens, who had just been appointed governor of the Washington Territory, to carry out these closely parallel surveys as part of his crossing of the continent to take up his post. Next to be considered was a route from the mouth of the Platte River, basically along the 41st parallel to Salt Lake City and northern California. This route was never systematically investigated; substituting for such a survey was the report of the previous expedition of Captain Howard Stansbury looking for a wagon road to the Mormon settlements, as well as bits and pieces of survey conducted in 1854 as adjuncts to the next survey to the south, that along the 38th parallel. That investigation came almost entirely at the urging of Senator Thomas Hart Benton of Missouri, who believed that there was, there must be, a route from western Missouri across the southern Rockies near the upper Arkansas River and then onward to California. Farther south two other possible routes had been suggested: one on an alignment from Memphis via the upper Red River and the upper Pecos River in New Mexico to the Colorado Plateau and southern California—that is, basically along the 35th parallel—and another from Shreveport across Texas to El Paso and then through the Gadsden Purchase made to facilitate railroad building in that latitude. The 32nd parallel route continued on to Fort Yuma on the Colorado River and San Diego.

The first of these surveys to be completed was that of Isaac Stevens, though its publication came only in the twelfth of the thirteen quarto volumes of the Survey.[24] The governor sought to answer two basic questions: (1) whether the winter climate of this northern region was too severe to permit the operation of a railroad and (2) whether there were passes through the Northern Rockies that would permit the building and operation of a practicable line. The report was perhaps a bit sanguine with respect to the winter in reporting that "all who traversed the Rocky Mountains, during almost every winter month [have found that] the snow there would not present the slightest impediment to the constant passage of railroad trains."[25] It also held out hope for the discovery of a usable pass, although the exploring party did not actually discover it. They considered Cadotte's Pass and Lewis and Clark Pass, but both would take considerably more engineering than a truly developmental line could afford. The question of which pass to use remained open after the Survey, even though the general conclusion was that one usable on a pioneering line could be found.

The 38th Parallel Survey began at Fort Leavenworth, Kansas Territory, in June, 1853, led by Lt. John Gunnison. Its primary objective was to find and explore a reputed "Cochetopa Pass" leading westward out of the San Luis Valley of southern Colorado and reported to provide a practicable rail crossing of the wide cordillera in that lat-

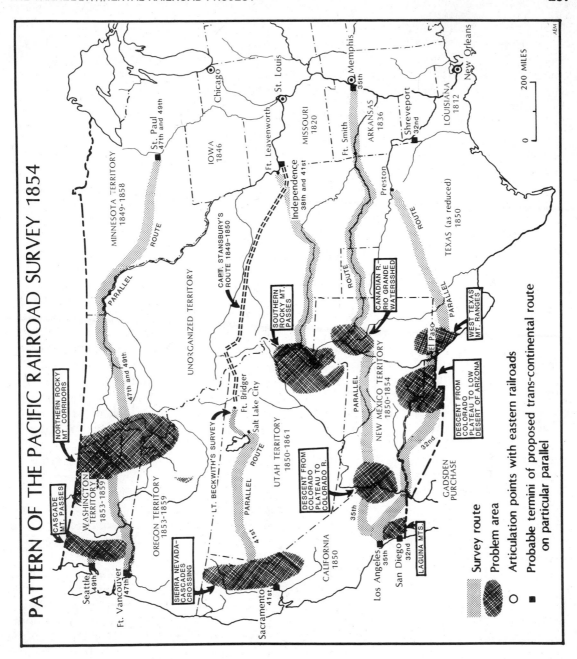

PATTERN OF THE PACIFIC RAILROAD SURVEY 1854

200 MILES

Survey route

Problem area

○ Articulation points with eastern railroads

■ Probable termini of proposed trans-continental route on particular parallel

itude. Senator Benton was convinced of its existence, so it must be sought. The Arkansas River was used to cross the Plains and approach the mountains. There a usable pass (Sangre de Cristo) was found through the front range of the Rockies in that latitude, the Sangre de Cristo Mountains. But in the San Luis Valley, west of those mountains, no easily traversed Cochetopa Pass was found extending farther westward. Instead, the pass that best suited the description furnished by Old Bullion proved to require tunneling and very heavy grades, something an initial transcontinental line probably could not afford. All these routes—the 49th, 47th, and 38th—were eventually traversed by railroads, but the level of tunneling and of general construction was too costly for any truly developmental railroad. Such lines had to be constructed quickly in order to begin earning revenue to help bear the cost of construction in a territory without markets and to begin to pile up surpluses that might be employed on improvement of the railroad. In some cases these early lines beyond the settlement frontier were barely operable when opened, so this improvement was often so fundamental that continued use of the route would require it. The fact the 38th parallel route could eventually be developed as a narrow-gauge mining line does not belie the early judgment that it was not the alignment for a pioneering transcontinental route.

The 35th Parallel Survey was early seen as a compromise between northern and southern interests. As proposed, the exploration began at Fort Smith on the Indian frontier of Arkansas. Thence a party led by Lt. A. W. Whipple set off, ascending the Arkansas River as far as its confluence with the Canadian, and then up that stream to a low interfluve between it and the Pecos River of eastern New Mexico. Over the watershed of that major left-bank tributary of the Rio Grande, the line could be carried with fairly easy grades to the next divide to the west, that between the Pecos and upper Rio Grande just to the southeast of Santa Fe. Stiff grades were encountered there in ascending the Canyon Blanco tributary of the Pecos and passing into the valley of the Galisteo branch of the Rio Grande, but these could be handled with what was heavy pioneering engineering rather than truly impressive tunneling and bridge-building. West of Albuquerque the Rio Puerco tributary of the Rio Grande provided an approach to the actual continental divide—here a gentle parting—before reaching the high Colorado Plateau across which the line could progress on the fairly unbroken surface south of Grand Canyon before facing the long descent to the Colorado River. No very satisfactory route down from the plateau was discovered, but it was fairly clear that a line could be built that would not introduce extreme grades or excessive engineering. Across the Colorado the grades within the Mojave Desert were reasonable, and Cajon Pass provided a possible route down from that high desert of southeastern California into the Los Angeles Basin, with its graded approach to that pueblo or several possible roadsteads in southern California. The judgment of an assistant railroad engineer who accompanied the Whipple party was that there were only three difficult stretches along the 35th parallel route—the Galisteo crossing of the spurs of the Southern Rockies between the Pecos and the Rio Grande, the drop from the Colorado Plateau down to the Colorado River—each of which would require grades of up to 1.5 percent—and the drop down Cajon Pass from the Mojave Desert to the Los Angeles Basin, which would have grades of 2 percent.[26]

The 35th parallel route was seen as a possible sectional compromise because its eastern terminus at Fort Smith could quite efficiently be approached from three points of articulation located on the Mississippi.

From St. Louis, then the dominant city of the western part of the Middle West, and thus a commonly assumed northern gateway, a line could be built east of the Ozarks to the vicinity of Little Rock whence it might join a similar approach line from Memphis, the gateway of the interior South, in passing westward up the Arkansas Valley of Arkansas to Ft. Smith. The Deep South could also have its approaching line from Vicksburg or even New Orleans passing on either the eastern or western sides of the Ouachita Mountains to gain the Arkansas Valley of that state.

The southernmost survey, that along the 32nd parallel, was not as formal as the three already mentioned. There had been several previous partial explorations along an alignment from northeast Texas to El Paso and San Diego, leading, as we have noted, to the Gadsden Purchase of 1853. What remained were questions about three sections of this long route: passage through the Guadalupe Mountains of west Texas, from the high desert of southern New Mexico down the plateau escarpment to the low desert of the Gila Valley of Arizona, and across the mountains east of San Diego. The Guadalupe Mountains proved a true barrier, but only in the climate of geographical abstractions so typical of the last century. By abandoning the most direct route between northeast Texas, where the survey began, and El Paso, a line entirely across plains could be secured around the southern ends of the three Basin Ranges lying athwart the direct passage to El Paso from the east. West of that El Paso del Norte through the Basin Ranges cut by the Rio Grande, the route would continue over the elevated surface of southern New Mexico until it must drop into the low desert of southern Arizona. Here much difficulty was encountered in finding a good route, but the exploration of several possible alignments led to the general conclusion that with further, even more detailed exploration a practicable alignment (with grades of no more than 2 percent) might be secured within the territory of the Purchase. On the matter of the final barrier, the Laguna Mountains east of San Diego, no practicable route could be found across these within American territory, so the 32nd Parallel Survey proposed acceptance of a more northerly pass, San Gorgonio, leading directly into the Los Angeles Basin from the east with the understanding that a coastal route between the Basin and San Diego could be developed.

The final route to be considered, that along the Platte River, through the Wyoming Basin to Great Salt Lake and thence to California, received even less attention than the 32nd parallel route. The reconnaissance up the Platte, referred to at the time as the survey along the 41st and 42nd parallels, may best be termed the 41st Parallel Survey as it lay closer to that latitude and more commonly to the south of it. It was the Secretary of War's decision to depend on an earlier survey of a wagon road to Salt Lake City, undertaken by Captain Howard Stansbury, to cover the eastern half of the possible route along that latitude. West of Great Salt Lake a supplemental survey was undertaken that looked in some detail at the crossing of the desert east of the Sierra Nevada and at possible crossings of those mountains themselves.

We may best begin by summarizing Stansbury's findings. Although he was writing about a wagon road, he did in at least one place comment on the building of a railroad on the route he surveyed. There was no problem with the route as far as the eastern foot of the Rockies. The Platte and its northern branch provided a well-graded approach to those mountains, then known as the Black Hills and today as the Laramie Range. The Oregon Trail had passed around the northern end of the Laramie Range using a great sag in the mountains to gain

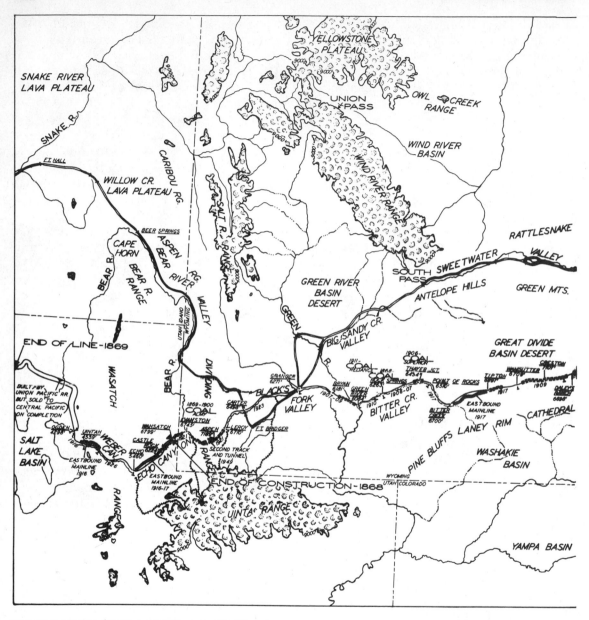

Map of the Union Pacific and Oregon Trail in Wyoming.

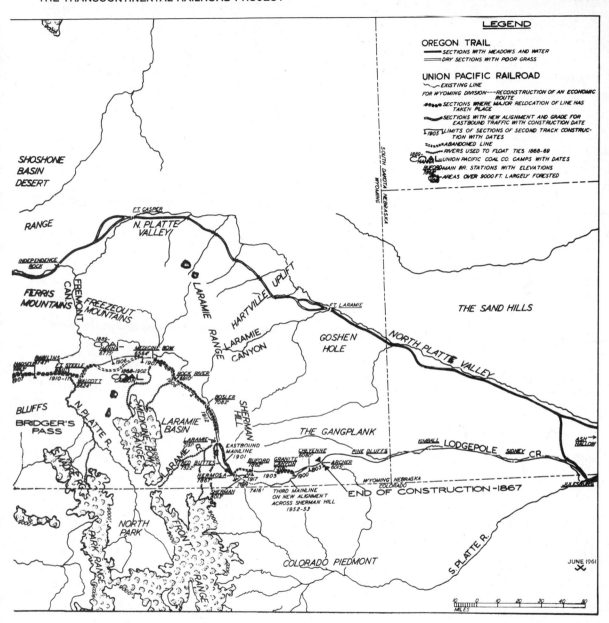

LEGEND

OREGON TRAIL
— SECTIONS WITH MEADOWS AND WATER
= DRY SECTIONS WITH POOR GRASS

UNION PACIFIC RAILROAD
~ EXISTING LINE
FOR WYOMING DIVISION --- RECONSTRUCTION OF AN ECONOMIC ROUTE
███ SECTIONS WHERE MAJOR RELOCATION OF LINE HAS TAKEN PLACE
SECTIONS WITH NEW ALIGNMENT AND GRADE FOR EASTBOUND TRAFFIC WITH CONSTRUCTION DATE
1905 LIMITS OF SECTIONS OF SECOND TRACK CONSTRUCTION WITH DATES
ABANDONED LINE
1889 RIVERS USED TO FLOAT TIES 1868-69
COAL UNION PACIFIC COAL CO. CAMPS WITH DATES
BUFORD MAIN RR. STATIONS WITH ELEVATIONS
AREAS OVER 9000 FT. LARGELY FORESTED

the Wyoming Basin that lay to the west. But both the wagon road and a potential railroad were seen as seeking a more direct routing by crossing the Laramie Range at a point essentially west of the forks of the Platte. Using Crow and Lodgepole creeks, a graded approach from the South Platte just to the west of the forks to the foot of the mountains could be secured. Stansbury found that the crest at the head of Lodgepole Creek was broad and rolling and suggested in his report that grades adequate for a railroad could be found over what came to be known as Sherman Hill. Over that crest the possible rail alignment continued across the rolling Laramie Basin to a low but broken divide dropping on the west to the North Platte River. Westward from a crossing of that stream Stansbury's party, led by the famous mountain man, Jim Bridger, discovered an easy approach to the low lip of the Great Divide Basin perched on the crest of the continent in an area of enclosed basins and low escarpments. This passage of the great structural basin lying between the Southern and Northern Rockies gave to the railroad a high but no more than rolling transit of the continental cordillera leading to the Green River in its center. West of the Green River the country rose gently toward the Wasatch Range that shuts off the Salt Lake Basin to the east. Approaching the Wasatch at an elevation of over 7,000 feet there was little rise to its summit but a long descent to the Great Salt Lake at an elevation just over 4,000 feet.

Stansbury demonstrated that there were three stretches of critical terrain between the Missouri River and Great Salt Lake: the crossing of the Laramie Range (Black Hills), the rise westward from the North Platte to the center of the Wyoming Basin, and the crossing and the western descent of the Wasatch. The reading of Stansbury satisfied most of the topographical engineers with respect to the first two of those. Bridger's

Pass, as the rise into the Wyoming Basin from the east came to be known, was specifically cited by Stansbury as a possibility for a railroad. And the Lodgepole Creek approach to the Laramie Range crest seemed favorable enough to leave a more detailed location survey for the future. The route east of Salt Lake City was in doubt in the transit of the Wasatch, particularly the way to get down from the high country east of that range to its western piedmont.

The further elucidation of the 41st Parallel Survey came mainly at the hands of a party led by Lt. Beckwith, deputy leader of Gunnison's party on the 38th parallel, and his successor when the latter was killed by Indians in eastern Utah. Both Gunnison and Beckwith found the 38th Parallel route impracticable, so when Beckwith and his party reached Salt Lake City it was proposed that instead of further investigation along that latitude their attention be turned to filling gaps in the 41st Parallel Survey. Somewhat reluctantly, it seems, the Secretary of War permitted them to do so. Beckwith first moved eastward out of Salt Lake City, searching the Wasatch Front for a route toward the high plateaus beyond the range. In Weber Canyon such a route was found, and Beckwith carried his reconnaissance as far as Fort Bridger in the Green River Basin to assure the connection, one that permitted a line to be built with no grades over 2.2 percent. Returning to Great Salt Lake, Beckwith then turned toward California, seeking a way to cross the repeating ranges of the Great Basin and a route through the Sierra Nevada.

Moving out of Salt Lake City on May 5, 1854, Beckwith's party found the main problem one of discovering firm ground in the great bolson in which the vast saline lake occupied the very bottom. Near what is today the Utah-Nevada boundary, the first basin range lying across the route was encountered. No firm alignment was adopted, but

have used the last century's panacea, science, to come to his decision.

The result was that even after the Survey was completed and published, Congress was as paralyzed by sectional conflict as it had been before. Davis's judgement was so obviously partisan that no Pacific Railroad Bill could hope for passage along the lines he proposed, but none favoring any other route could be approved in the face of the scientism he invoked. Only when the sectional conflict evaporated with the secession of the southern states and the departure of the southern senators could such a bill be successfully adopted. At that time the 41st parallel route won hands down for reasons of both political and economic geography. It was the North's line, and it was the most rational economic route in a situation where economic justification was so dubious as to require the most plausible, if still improbable, market support for any rational action.

The Construction of the Transcontinental Railroad

The departure of southern representation in Congress in 1861 did not wholly remove disagreement about the desirable alignment of a Pacific railroad. Chicago had grown in importance since the collapse of the effort signaled by the Pacific Railroad Survey, now challenging St. Louis as the premier articulation point in the western part of the Middle West. But that departure assured a resolution of any disagreements, if for no other reason than it now became urgent national policy to construct such a transcontinental railroad. The fairly clean division of loyalties that characterized the heart of the North and the South was missing in two parts of the former United States—in the Border States of Mary-

land, Kentucky, and Missouri, and in the western territories and states, particularly California. That state assumed great importance as its gold was viewed in the North as an important resource for the Union in successfully concluding the Civil War. Senator Gwinn of California, who had been a strong proponent of the 35th parallel route after 1854, was perceived to be attempting to tie the Golden State to the Confederacy. Lincoln and Congress believed it was critical to tie California to the Union through the building of a Pacific railroad that would quickly accomplish a connection—and with the northern states. On July 1, 1862, Lincoln signed into law the Pacific Railroad Act calling for federal aid for such a railroad and seeking a different decision-making device to resolve the question of the eastern terminus. There was general agreement that Sacramento must be the western terminus but the one in the east was still worried by the rivalries of various articulation points, notably St. Louis and Chicago. In the end Congress left to the president the choice of the eastern starting point.

There have been several theories concerning Lincoln's motivation, but only the overly suspicious mind need look beyond fairly direct geographical logic. The terminus obviously had to be within territory fully loyal to the Union. That effectively ruled out St. Louis, not so much because of the sympathies of the city as of the country lying west of it, which was appropriately called Little Dixie with cotton cultivation, slave holding, and evident southern sympathies. Once St. Louis was out of the running, Chicago took over as the unchallenged articulation point. But Lincoln, himself once a lawyer for the Chicago and Rock Island Railroad, knew a lot about corporate rivalries in this region. It was inconceivable that

there seemed reasonable evidence that a railroad could be carried across that boundary range and into the uppermost part of the valley of the Humboldt River near what was then known as Humboldt Wells (today's Wells, Nevada). Once on the Humboldt, Beckwith saw the use of that stream as a graded route across the Great Basin until the river disappeared in its own bolson at Humboldt Sink. What ceased was river flow rather than the generally flat surface on which it had descended. West of Humboldt Sink there was another sink, of the Carson River rising in the Sierra Nevada, so the same river valley alignment could be carried westward toward the foot of the great range of the west.

It is impossible here to describe the several routes across the Sierra Nevada investigated by Beckwith's party. Suffice it to say that they demonstrated that there were several possible, though difficult, crossings of the range. Needed was a long enough run on the hill to handle the 6,000-foot ascent from the Sacramento Valley to the west. In the north, along the Pitt River, such a run was found, though it passed far north of Sacramento and the gold fields that were the logical western terminus of a transcontinental railroad in this latitude. But Beckwith seemed as gripped by geographical abstraction as Old Bullion and his Cochetopa Pass. The 41st parallel route should follow the latitude so numbered, which brought the line over the Sierra Nevada—actually the Cascades—at or near Fort Redding in considerable defiance of any economic logic.

The Secretary of War's Decision

With the five separate latitudinal alignments investigated by the Pacific Railroad Survey, and the results submitted, some decision must be made by the Secretary of War, the cabinet officer bearing responsibility for the Corps of Topographical Engineers. The survey had concluded that a transcontinental line might rationally and economically be built along three of the alignments—the 32nd, 35th, and 41st parallels—with a possible development along the 47th and 49th parallels, though there the terrain seemed less favorable. Only the 38th parallel line was rejected outright. Clearly the 41st parallel route was the leading northern contender, whereas the 32nd held that role in the South. The 35th parallel route was the only one that might logically be viewed as a compromise treating both sections equally. In due course the Secretary made his decision, calling strongly for the adoption of the 32nd parallel route as capable of year-round operation, cheapest to construct, and probably of the easiest grades. These conclusions, though probably true, were hardly appealing on political or economic grounds. The 32nd parallel route was most eccentric with respect to the likely markets on either coast. In the settled part of the country east of the Mississippi, it was the Northeast and Middle West that were likely to generate the major agricultural as well as manufacturing trade. In the West it was northern California that must stand as the self-evidently dominant market for goods, and the source of return freights and passengers. San Diego was rather an abstraction as a port, just as the peripheral location of a railroad along the 32nd parallel was an abstraction as to profitable operation, however low its actual line costs. The 35th parallel line would have been circuitous but plausible; the 32nd parallel line was not. Thus it is not surprising that the Pacific Railroad Survey was a failure as an instrument of policy formulation, however massively important it was as an exploration and survey of the American western territories. There was an immediate belief among most northerners that the Secretary, former Senator Jefferson Davis of Mississippi, decided along lines of sectional prejudice—however much he claimed

The Union Pacific Bridge across the Platte at Gannett, Nebraska Territory. Union Pacific Railroad photograph.

the Pacific railroad would build its own line all the way from Chicago; this meant it must be attached to one of the granger roads that already existed west of the Great Junction City. If the Rock Island was chosen, then the Burlington, the Illinois Central, and the Chicago and Alton would be highly peeved. Lincoln displayed Mosaic judgment by selecting Council Bluffs, Iowa, as the eastern terminus, thereby setting a point sufficiently

beyond the head of iron of all the granger roads that each might build to meet that through a location on the left bank of the Missouri River, the Pacific railroad must provide the largest bridge on its route, that across the master stream of the plains. This was not the legal "initial point" of the railroad; it was, according to the act, to be set on a north-south line extending along the starting point, and share in its use. Also,

100th meridian between the southern margin of the valley of the Republican River in the Kansas Territory and the northern margin of the valley of the Platte in the Nebraska Territory, and branches were to be built to that point from Sioux City in Iowa, Council Bluffs, Leavenworth in Kansas, and Kansas City in Missouri. Lincoln favored the Council Bluffs branch as the one to be directly undertaken by the company—logically called the Union Pacific Railroad—leaving the other three branches to be built by other companies. During the construction phase of the transcontinental, only one other branch was begun, the Leavenworth, Pawnee and Western Railway Company, later called the Union Pacific Railroad Company Eastern Division, which began building westward from Kansas City. That project failed to head toward the 100th meridian in the Platte Valley, which was the initial point in the legal sense of the act, constructing instead parallel to the Union Pacific as far west as the longitude of Denver. This line, further renamed the Kansas Pacific Railroad, served less as a branch than as a competitor for the original transcontinental. Thus we may disregard it and the stillborn "branches" in our discussion of the true Pacific railroad.

When a Pacific railroad was authorized, it was split into two projects in the belief that the line across the Sierra Nevada would be so difficult and slow to build that it needed both separate and concentrated attention. Thus the Pacific railroad was begun at both ends by separate companies, the Union Pacific from Council Bluffs and the Central Pacific Railroad from Sacramento. The early assumption was that they would be likely to meet in their construction somewhere near the eastern boundary of California. That was not the case. To understand why, we should first consider the construction of the Union Pacific, certainly the more interesting of the two undertakings.

In 1862 the closest railhead to Council Bluffs—or Omaha, which became the effective base of construction across the river in the Nebraska Territory—was St. Joseph, Missouri, 125 miles downstream. All construction material had to be taken by steamboat that distance, or even farther if goods were carried by boats from eastern factories and rolling mills. In addition, there was no source of local labor anywhere near the base of operations, let alone the head of construction. This meant that labor had to be recruited, a major task in the midst of the first modern war with its demand for millions of men under arms. The simple truth was that although construction ostensibly began in 1863, little was accomplished until after the war was over. Iron was the most essential item the Union used in winning the war, and manpower was scarce because of the fighting. This was not the case on the Central Pacific. Calfornia was then so isolated and so detached from the reality of the war that manpower was in relatively more plentiful supply on the distant than on the adjacent frontier, and iron probably no less so.

The financial arrangements made with respect to the two Pacific railroad companies took on a wider importance in North American railroad promotion: these provisions tended to appear, at least in a general fashion, in many of the subsequent lines built in the western United States and in Canada. The two companies were given a loan of government bonds for a twenty-year period to aid them in raising construction money for the lines. These bonds were at the rate of $16,000 per mile of construction until each company reached the foot of its respective mountain barrier, the Rockies for the U.P. and the Sierra Nevada for the C.P. Within the mountains, for a distance of 150 miles, each was to receive a bond subsidy at a rate of $48,000 per mile. All remaining mileage either built was to be subsidized at a rate of $32,000 per mile. These bonds had to be repaid in thirty years, principal and interest, which became a fatal requirement in the case of the Union Pacific. As the U.P. was constructed at an average cost of $26,222 per mile, it would have seemed that this was an adequate subvention when combined with a generous land grant, but several things made it less than adequate. First, the money had to be repaid, and investors in the late 1860s seemed to have so little confidence in the ultimate profitability of the transcontinental railroad that the status of this debt as a first mortgage on the line built dampened the ardor of investors. Another problem was that railroad building in the period seems to have engaged the attention of investors more for the collateral profits they made in controlling construction companies employed than for the long-term earnings expectations of the railroad. With government directors of the company, and considerable public notice of its activities, there may well have been a doubt about the chances of the rapid recovery of investment that railroad investors were accustomed to at that period. Again, it was the doubt about long-term profitability that seems to have driven away investors.

Not only were the returns dubious, but also the exactions of quality in construction were disturbing. The line constructed could have no grades steeper than 116 feet per mile, the 2.2 percent that had been established a dozen years before on the B. and O. as it climbed the Allegheny Front. Curves also had to have a radius of 400 feet or larger (14°), and only American iron might be used. The next year Congress established that the gauge of the transcontinental railroad would conform to the most common, but far from universal, gauge of American railroads. With the South departed from the Union, there was no question of adopting the gauge of the South—that is, 5 feet.

The land grant made to the two companies was at first 6,400 acres per mile built, or ten sections per mile. But in 1864 a sup-

plemental act raised that figure to twenty sections per mile, or 12,800 acres. This act also made absolute the grant (giving the mineral as well as the surface rights to the companies), moved the junction of the two companies to no more than 150 miles east of the California-Nevada boundary, reduced the branches east of the Initial Point on the Union Pacific to one (the Iowa or Omaha branch), and made the repayment of the bonds loaned the companies a second rather than a first mortgage. Finally, this act rescinded a peculiar provision of the original Pacific Railroad Act of 1862 that had restricted any single stock ownership to twenty shares. There had been no rush to invest; in fact, there was a chronic shortage of funds for the undertakings. It finally fell to a few men to place their private funds at the call of the two railroads, making it plain that there was no great rush to purchase the securities of the companies.

The chronic problem of both companies was that so little stock sold that it was a continuing battle to secure working funds for construction. In this matter the Central Pacific was more fortunate. Because it was constructed directly from a reasonably developed city, Sacramento, and toward an important mining area—both the Mother Lode of California and the Comstock Lode of Nevada—the C.P. could begin to earn income after little more than a year of construction. The U.P. could earn nothing until it joined the C.P. and was reached by one of the midwestern railroads building toward Council Bluffs to provide a connection with the developed railroads of the eastern half of the country.

The failure of the stock sales left the Union Pacific particularly disadvantaged, so its promoters sought some expedient to secure funds for construction. This was found in copying current French practice, which had devised investment companies that sought to combine the funds of small in-

END OF UNION PACIFIC TRACK - 1867
NEAR ARCHER, WYOMING

End of construction, Union Pacific, December, 1867. Union Pacific Railroad photograph.

vestors into companies with the capital to undertake major works. This became the *Crédit Mobilier de France*, for capital to undertake rail development, and the *Crédit Foncier*, for capital for the construction of large apartment-house schemes in Paris. George Francis Train, whom we shall meet again in the construction of horsecar lines in London, had suggested to the officers of the U.P. the adoption of the *Crédit Mobilier* organiza-

tion, which in due course was done with expectations of profit derived not from the long-term ownership of the Union Pacific Railroad but instead from the rapid returns to be gained from the construction contracts let by the company. In this way the contractors financed the building of the railroad from which they were the main group to profit. A similar situation obtained on the Central Pacific where "the Big Four"—

Crocker, Huntington, Hopkins, and Stanford—provided much of the capital while profiting from their construction contracts.

Actual construction of the Union Pacific did not begin until 1865, when the Civil War ended in April. Work began at Omaha, where an awkwardly located line rose out of the Missouri Valley onto the rolling loess hills that bordered the river to the west. This section of the railroad was so badly chosen that it subsequently had to be relocated. Improvement came when General Grenville M. Dodge, who had been an engineer for several granger roads before entering the Union Army and there building further railroads, was appointed chief engineer of the U.P. in the summer of 1865. Dodge was honest and intelligent, as well as professionally qualified as an engineer, so the quality of the location work of the U.P. rose markedly.

Once across the low divide that here separated the Platte tributary from the Missouri, Dodge followed the Platte for some 400 miles as a well-graded ramp on which to rise slowly toward the front range of the Rockies some 500 miles to the west. Only as his line approached the Rockies, where the Platte was formed from two tributaries that lay too far north and south of west to serve his purposes, was different country encountered and overcome. Leaving the South Platte Valley some 75 miles west of the Forks of the Platte, the Union Pacific resolved a problem that had lain in wait as construction proceeded on a clearly determined course across the lower plains. That problem was how and where to cross the Rockies, as any transcontinental railroad must do north of El Paso. The U.P. had hoped to profit by the C.P.'s example, carrying its rails through Denver and near the Central City gold mines in order to secure existing on-line support that would begin to provide earnings for the company. But west of Denver the crest of the Rockies lay at 11,000 feet elevation or above, and with grades that could not possibly be held to the required maximum of 2.2 percent without massive—and delaying—engineering works. As a result, General Dodge reluctantly abandoned the only town on the 41st parallel route between the Missouri and Salt Lake City and sought a practical crossing of the Rockies at the expense of any on-line support.

That mountain crossing became the key to the successful prosecution of the Union Pacific construction project. Dodge himself had found the key, one that may earlier have been discovered by James Evans, a locating engineer for the U.P. It was clear to Dodge how crucial this precise mountain route became by 1865. He told an Omaha audience many years later:

I wish to say here that while my surveys and my conclusions may have been of great benefit to you, still they were made because there was no question, from an engineering point of view, where the line crossing Iowa and going west from this river, should cross the Missouri River, and it was also my conclusion that it was the commercial line. The Lord has so constructed the country that any engineer who failed to take advantage of the great open road from here [Omaha] west to Salt Lake would not have been fit to belong to the profession; 600 miles of it up a single valley without a grade to exceed fifteen feet; the natural pass over the Rocky Mountains, the lowest in all the range, and the divide of the continent, instead of being a mountain summit, has a basin 500 feet below the general level.[27]

The line Dodge projected, having continued up Crow and Lodgepole creeks to the foot of the Laramie Range, there had to be located in a fine detail unnecessary throughout most of its nearly 600-mile course from Omaha. There were two specific problems: the actual summit to be crossed and a practicable railroad route to reach it from the highest part of the plains.

At the conclusion of the war in 1865 Dodge had been appointed army commander in the Great Plains and adjacent mountainous areas. Returning from an expedition to the Yellowstone country, he took his command along the east base of the Laramie Range in order to investigate possible railroad crossings of that chain. One day, while carrying out such a reconnaissance along the crest of the range, he discovered he was being followed by an Indian party that had inserted itself between Dodge's group and his main forces. In seeking to avoid the Indians, the general continued to move southward.

> It was getting along in the afternoon as we worked down this ridge, that I began to discover we were on an apparently very fine approach to Black Hills [Laramie Range], and one of the guides has stated that I said: "If we saved our scalps I believed we had found a railroad line over the mountains." About 4 o'clock, the Indians were preparing to take the ridge on our front, the cavalry now saw our signals and soon came to our rescue, and when we reached the valley [to the east of the range] I was satisfied that the ridge we had followed was one which we could climb with a maximum grade within our charter and with comparatively light work.[28]

What Dodge had found was an exceptional physiographic feature, a place where the highest strata of the Great Plains structures lapped onto the granite core of the Laramie Range. In most places the front range of the Rockies—the Laramie Range in this latitude—is separated from those strata by a broad longitudinal valley eroded into the plains structures at the contact of these

two different morphological units, adding up to 500 feet to the length of slope that must be surmounted to reach the summit of the range. West of what was to become Cheyenne, Wyoming, however, that contact of the highest plains stratum with the granite occurred over a distance of only several tens of feet. But with such a Gangplank, as it came to be termed by geomorphologists, the perfect ramp up onto the mountain slope was obtained. This site—called Granite Canyon as the railroad was being constructed because this was the first place on the line that good igneous rock ballast could be secured—was at over 7,000 feet elevation, reached entirely on the gentle slope of the High Plains. The summit of the range, in a pass discovered by James Evans and subsequently found to be the easiest crossing of the heights (though not the lowest, as Dodge alleged) was at 8,200 feet, so in surmounting the Rockies the U.P. had to climb only some 1,000 feet, and that on a fairly rolling slope. The rolling nature of this slope meant that, with the Gangplank from which to spring, the grade could be kept to that magic 2.2 percent decreed for the transcontinental. In the deprecatory speech of western railroaders, though with some nugget of truth, this crossing became Sherman Hill, named for the station at its summit and the plausible description of its slopes.

Construction on the Union Pacific began in earnest in the summer of 1865, though most of the progress that summer came in organizing the effort, ordering the necessary material, and recruiting a labor force (facilitated by the large number of discharges from the Union armies). On October 6, 1866, the track crossed the 100th meridian in central Nebraska, its legal initiation point, and continued on westward. When winter weather finally stopped construction, the line was at O'Fallons Bluffs in western Nebraska, 305 miles from Omaha. The next year, 1867, construction was uninterrupted by the

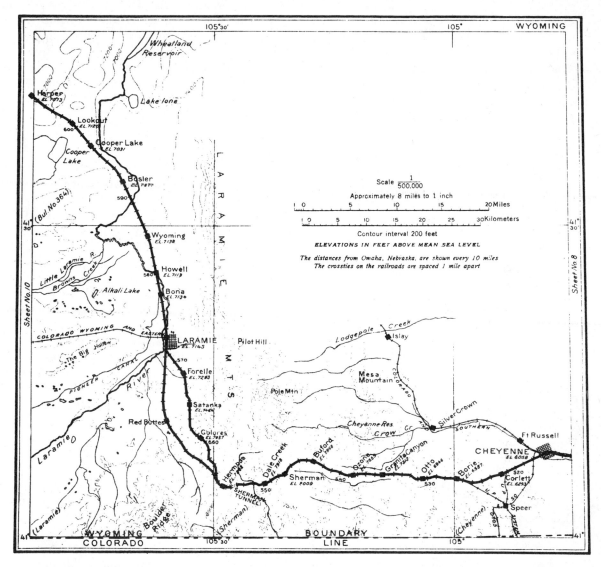

Map of the Union Pacific crossing of the Black Hills (Laramie Range). U.S. Geological Survey map.

winter; the end of the year found the head of iron at Granite Canyon ready to assault the Laramie Range. As surveyed Granite Canyon was at 7,298 feet, less than 1,000 feet below the summit at Sherman (8,242 feet). That crest was reached on April 5, 1868, and construction was in full stride. The largest bridge on the route—other than the Missouri River bridge at its eastern terminus—had to be built across Dale Creek, where a high spindly viaduct was constructed of pine cut on site. Soon thereafter the line began to drop down into the Laramie Basin over fairly stiff grades, which were later improved against upcoming traffic when an upbound mainline with better grades was constructed.

Throughout 1868 the Union Pacific was

under construction across Wyoming, first over the rolling floor of the Laramie Basin and then dropping through the sharply sloping but low hills dividing it from the valley of the North Platte. Rising out of the open valley of that westernmost water flowing to the Gulf of Mexico in this latitude, the U.P. was carried over the lip of the Great Divide Basin just north of the low pass that Jim Bridger had found while guiding Captain Stansbury fifteen years before. Moving steadily westward, the tracks were laid quickly across the Great Divide Basin to its western lip and then on down a gently sloping valley of Bitter Creek that eventually joined the Green River at the point where the railroad town of Green River grew up. This passage across the Red Desert was trying not for its terrain but rather for the poor quality of the water encountered on its course. West of the Green River, however, conditions improved. Streams flowing northward out of the Uinta Mountains to the south gave repeating sources of the good boiler water steam locomotives required. In addition the U.P. had found reasonably good coal in two places on its route: just east of the North Platte at the northern edge of the Laramie Basin and again just east of the Green River where extensive mines led to the founding of Rock Springs, Wyoming. Throughout this stretch water was made available, if not very desirable, by the drilling of wells.

The construction continued without stop to the end of 1868, which found the head of iron at Wasatch Station, just at the headwaters of the Weber River that was to provide a relatively steep but graded course down the 2,500 feet between the crest of the Wasatch Range and the floor of the Great Salt Lake Basin where the railroad town of Ogden grew up. Down Weber Canyon it was found possible to carry the line at a stiff but manageable grade of 90 feet per mile (1.7

percent). While this construction was underway, the locating engineers were ranging far ahead, setting their stakes around the north end of Great Salt Lake, over the Promontory Range that jutted into the lake from the north, and westward over the desert floor toward the low basin ranges that formed the head of the watershed of the Humboldt River that was to furnish a route across Nevada. While all that survey work was going on, the locating engineers for the Central Pacific were laying out a similar, parallel course. The construction gangs of either company were building as quickly as they could toward each other in the hope of capturing as much of the route—and of the construction subsidy—for their company as possible. By early May, when it was clear that the iron would be joined near the crest of the Promontory Range, it was arranged that a junction be made there, as was done on May 10, 1869, 1,108 miles west of Omaha. The most significant single act of the historical geography of American transportation was accomplished there and on that day.

When first proposed the Central Pacific Railroad could have been no more than the 142 miles from Sacramento to the California-Nevada line. As events turned out, it was more than four times that distance—691 miles to Promontory, Utah. The problems facing construction were quite different from those opposing the U.P., with engineering rather than absolute distance as the major difficulty. The greatest challenge to the California road was the vast mountain block of the Sierra Nevada, which began not far from Sacramento and rose steadily for most of the 106 miles to the summit on the railroad, gaining in the process over 6,000 feet. The Pacific Railroad Survey had found definitive locations for many of the lines built during the next fifty years in the West, but its equivocal findings with respect to the Sierra Nevada crossing were little actual guide to the construction of the transcontinental railroad. The Beckwith survey had concluded that the best route over the California mountains was to pass across the high Modoc lava plateau in northeastern California so there would be little rise from the east, and then to drop down toward the Sacramento River on a left-bank tributary that would join the main stream somewhere within the Sacramento River Canyon south of Mt. Shasta. Such a line was actually built by the Pitt River Railroad, so we know that it could have been done. But to have attempted such a line as a pioneer route was undesirable, as the line constructed was extremely curving and very indirect in attaining the economically important part of California that lay in the mother Lode east of Sacramento and the Northern Diggings just to the northeast. Also, such a route across the mountains in extreme northern California would have taken the Pacific railroad far from the then highly productive Comstock (silver) lode in Nevada.

Even before the Pacific Railroad Act was adopted, there had been interest within California in the building of a trans-Sierra, transcontinental rail line. Theodore Judah, the chief engineer of the first railroad to be built in California, the 12-mile Sacramento Valley Railroad leading from Sacramento eastward to Folsom, had proposed such a project, and with such fervor that many looked upon him as irrational. The promoters of the Folsom line saw it as the beginning of such a route, continuing on to Placerville and then over the mountains to the East, asserting that view with such force that the *Alta California*, San Francisco's main newspaper, commented "We shall next hear that the best way to Heaven is through Placerville."[29]

Judah believed otherwise. He understood that the critical locational problem facing any railroad across the Sierra centered on the question of avoiding redundant grades, something the Placerville route would not have accomplished. To understand the nature of the problem, it is necessary to appreciate that the Sierra Nevada is a great block, with its highest uplift toward its eastern edge and with a series of streams cutting deep erosional valleys into the block surface dipping gently toward the west over a distance of 75 to 100 miles. Theoretically the best possible route would be one starting at the beginning of the foothills in the west and rising evenly (with the uplift of the block) toward its eastern crest. But in most places the complexity of the stream-cut valleys is such that no clear ramp toward the east exists, forcing any alignments of road or railroad to pass over a number of repeating, thereby redundant, grades. If a perfect ramp could be found, given the height of the crest and the width of the block, the rise eastward would be at a rate of 70 feet per mile (1.3 percent), a considerable but not an insuperable climb for a railroad. The main distinction of this section, which in the deprecating parlance of western railroaders became Sacramento Hill, was its length, essentially 100 miles, not its absolute steepness.

Judah's great contribution to the engineering of the Sierra line was in finding that nearly perfect ramp. It passed through Dutch Flat, rather than Placerville, so this was referred to by contemporaries as the Dutch Flat Route (as it will be so designated here). By leaving from the Dutch Flat mining camp in the lower foothills it was possible to pass northeastward along an interfluve between the Yuba River on the north and the American River on the south, each flowing through a canyon that tended to deepen as one progressed eastward until somewhat below the crest where the river valleys shallowed, though widened due to replacement of river erosion by glacial action. In places the interfluve narrowed to a

Thousand-mile Point on the Union Pacific at Devil's Slide, Utah. Union Pacific Railroad photograph.

few hundred feet at its crest, but it did not disappear, so an alignment could progress upward without loss of height or redundant grade. At Cape Horn the route was moved from the south slope of the ridge, dropping to the American River, to the north, overlooking the Yuba.

A second problem in surmounting the Sierra Nevada in an efficient fashion was to avoid the transverse structural valleys that furrowed the crest of the block, as, for example, in the mountain-girt valley in which stood Lake Tahoe (Mark Twain's Lake Bigler of less romantic but more historical appropriateness). The Dutch Flat Route indirectly helped to solve that problem in that the ramp beginning at that gold camp reached to a crest at Donner Summit, where on the east side of the range a glacial valley collected water, ponded in Donner Lake, and then flowing across the transverse Sierra Valley and through a canyon in the Carson Range spread itself in a sink within the Great Basin to the east. That river, the Truckee, rising in the eastward drainage from Donner Summit, provided a narrow but graded course across the transverse valley and its easterly bounding range again to avoid the redundant grade so costly in railroad operation. Even though the Truckee River eventually ended in the enclosed basin of Pyramid Lake to the east, it did the necessary work of cutting a canyon through the parallel Basin Ranges that were strewn in a north-south alignment across the high floor that became Nevada. In dropping down the east side of the Sierra from Donner Summit to Truckee Meadows (Reno), 2,500 feet of elevation had to be dealt with in 50 miles. Even though the grade here was not as uniform as on the west, it could be held to the statutory required maximum of 2.2 percent through lengthening the line by constructing a great loop into a side valley near the summit, which gave more run to gain the height.

The Central Pacific Railroad had been incorporated under state law in 1861 before the congressional action on the Pacific railroad; but that national legislation, through the active lobbying of Theodore Judah, named the C.P. as the recipient of the federal subsidy to build eastward from Sacramento. On January 8, 1863, Leland Stanford—a Sacramento grocer whose locally large fortune was the earliest backing for the trans-Sierra railroad—turned the first sod, and construction began on the floor of the Sacramento Valley. Collis Huntington—then a Sacramento hardware dealer but later to be-

come the real force behind both the Central Pacific and its larger successor—the Southern Pacific (as well as of the last great trans-Appalachian railroad, the Chesapeake and Ohio built in the 1870s), stayed away, telling his associates, "If you want to jubilee in laying the first spike here, go ahead and do it. I don't. These mountains look too ugly and I see too much work ahead. We may fail, and I want to have as few people know it as we can."[30]

A schooner, *Artful Dodger*, had brought the first locomotive to the C.P. by midsummer so the company could run trains over its first 18 miles to Grider's Ranch, renamed Roseville when iron reached there in November. Public service began in the spring of 1864 when Newcastle, 31 miles from Sacramento, was reached. The local funds were nearly exhausted and the federal money could not be obtained until another 9 miles was laid. Collis Huntington, for whom we might assume the schooner that brought the first locomotive was named (if we did not recall Charles Dickens), took matters in hand deciding that the "foothills of the mountains," where the subsidy in bonds went from $16,000 per mile to $48,000, lay only 7 miles east of Sacramento, in a place where the ground was so flat the water that fell there in winter collected in puddles that had to evaporate to disappear. This provided an infusion of capital, making the money problems of the C.P. less exigent, though hardly solved. In fact, it was only access to eastern capital—first introduced by Oakes Ames who was to become the primary backer of the Union Pacific and its president—that kept the Central Pacific construction going. That $800,000 from Ames permitted the assault on the Sierra, when its true foothills were reached at Rocklin (23 miles out), to proceed fairly consistently.

The construction on Sacramento Hill was slow and painful, requiring a great deal of blasting—of side-hill embankments and cuts and of tunnels through spurs jutting out from the canyon side across the course of the alignment. But progress came and the track went forward and upward. Newcastle, 31 miles from and 920 feet above Sacramento, was reached at the end of 1864. Construction became more difficult in the hard rocks of the Sierra, so progress slowed. Clipper Gap, 43 miles from and 1,750 feet above Sacramento, was reached in June, 1865. Construction that year had to stop at Colfax (53 miles and 2,422 feet) because at that elevation the ground froze in winter. During the year the Central Pacific had had gross revenues from service to freight and passengers on the section already constructed of $405,592, while construction expenses had been $3.2 million. That same year the Union Pacific had had no income, so the California company was able to apply the traditional American principle of using earnings to build or improve the line in a way the eastern company was unable to do.

Starting again in the early spring of 1866 the construction became much heavier but also better organized. Fifteen tunnels had to be bored with the longest carried under the crest at Donner Summit to avoid further climb when tunneling became practicable. Also at these elevations above 5,000 feet the winter snows were so heavy that not only were tunnels desirable but also snowsheds had to be constructed. Eventually some 40 miles of continuous snowsheds were built from near Emigrant Gap on the west to Strong's Canyon 5 miles east of the crest.

On December 13, 1867, the iron reached the California-Nevada boundary, the point originally assumed as the juncture of the Central and Union Pacific. The latter was still constructing in eastern Wyoming, so Congress authorized the C.P. to advance into the state of Nevada and each company to build until it met the other. The race was on. As much as 10 miles of track a day, not certainly every day, was laid. East of Truckee Meadows, where that river turned toward the north, the railroad locating engineers found a possible route in the structural opening between the Trinity and Carson (block-faulted) ranges giving access to the Carson River valley near the sink where that river disappears. That bolson also serves as the sink for the Humboldt River coming from the east as it cuts its way among and through the block-faulted ranges that stud this part of Nevada. In places short tunnels were cut through river-meander ridges, but in general the stream provided the direct and graded course the Central Pacific was seeking until the headwaters of the exotic stream were reached just east of Humboldt Wells. At that point further mountainous terrain was encountered in crossing a last range that separated the Humboldt Valley from the much larger basin in which Great Salt Lake collected and evaporated. These rather open slopes, surmounted at 6,611 feet in the Independence Mountains, could be handled with moderate grades and fairly easy construction, giving access to the largest of all the basins in the area.

The presence of Great Salt Lake in that basin forced upon the Central Pacific the decision as to which side of the interior sea to use in continuing eastward. The north shore was chosen so the alignment was faced with yet another basin range, the Promontory, and it was on the summit of that ridge that the Central Pacific and the Union Pacific construction crews met on Monday, May 10, 1869. Because Promontory seemed an awkward place to maintain a junction, it was decided that the Union Pacific would sell 53 miles of its construction to the California company, shifting the permanent junction to Ogden at the mouth of Weber Canyon. There the interchange was maintained, but since 1983 (when the Union Pacific merged the western end of the last American transcontinental railroad, the Western Pacific finished from Salt Lake City

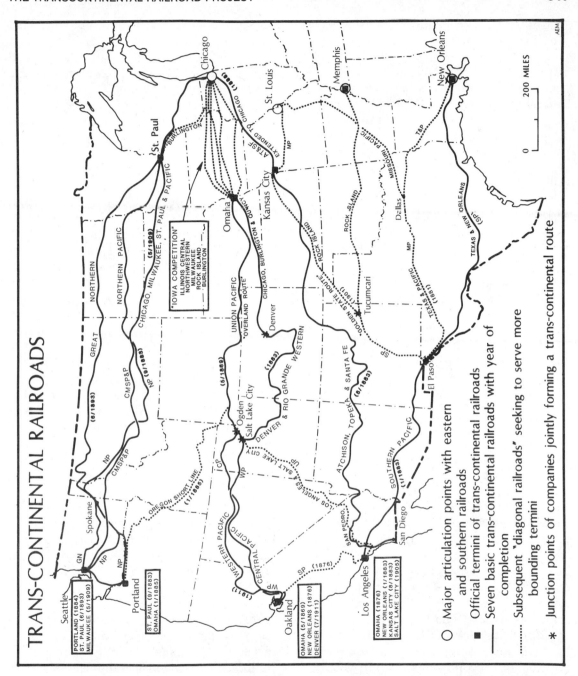

TRANS-CONTINENTAL RAILROADS

"IOWA COMPETITION"
ILLINOIS CENTRAL
CHICAGO & NORTHWESTERN
CHICAGO, MILWAUKEE
ROCK ISLAND
BURLINGTON

Seattle
PORTLAND (1884)
ST. PAUL (6/1893)
MILWAUKEE (5/1909)

ST. PAUL (9/1883)
OMAHA (1/1885)

OMAHA (5/1869)
NEW ORLEANS (1876)
DENVER (7/1911)

OMAHA (1876)
NEW ORLEANS (1/1883)
KANSAS CITY (8/1883)
SALT LAKE CITY (1905)

○ Major articulation points with eastern
    and southern railroads

■ Official termini of trans-continental railroads

── Seven basic trans-continental railroads with year of
     completion

┈┈ Subsequent "diagonal railroads" seeking to serve more
     bounding termini

✳ Junction points of companies jointly forming a trans-continental route

to Oakland in 1911, into its expanded system) the significance of the two parts that for over a century formed the Overland Route has changed. Obviously the Union Pacific interchanges traffic with the Southern Pacific (successors to the Central Pacific) only to the extent legal commitments require. And, of course, Promontory no longer has tracks anywhere near it. The difficulty of climbing yet another range and the circuitous nature of the line around the north end of Great Salt Lake led the Southern Pacific Company in 1904 to open a 103-mile relocation of the line east of Lucin, Utah, which carried the railroad directly across the northwest arm of the lake on a 40-mile trestle. As that structure began to show its age, the company replaced it with a causeway in the years after World War II, though recent rises in the level of Great Salt Lake have forced a further heightening of that fill to keep the tracks above the water level.

UBIQUITY AND THE NATURAL TERRITORY: TWO GEOGRAPHICAL CONCEPTS

By the time the Union Pacific–Central Pacific had been joined, the American railroad development process began to be clearly discernible, at least among the major regional companies. There was a sharp distinction between the process employed east of the Mississippi and that used to the west. In the East the major companies—the New York Central, Erie, Pennsylvania, Baltimore and Ohio, Southern Railway and Louisville and Nashville (and the other Family Lines joined to the last)—had developed a strategy of railroad assembly, frequently of lines for much more geographical purposes during the first and second phases of rail development. That assembly was guided, though often only roughly, by the notion of gaining a fairly ubiquitous coverage of a major region, such as the area to the north of the Ohio and Potomac rivers and east of

Chicago and St. Louis (the New York Central, Erie, Pennsylvania, and Baltimore and Ohio) or the area to the south thereof and east of the Mississippi (the Southern and Louisville and Nashville).

In the West a different strategy guided construction, as grouping of previously constructed lines was seldom possible and therefore quite uncommon. The first phase was generally missing in the West except for the Sacramento to Folsom and San Francisco to San Jose railroads. The second phase found in the east—the interconnection of two fairly adjacent cities by locally promoted railroads—was also very uncommon in the West for two reasons: there were relatively few such proximate pairings of cities in a thin urban geography, and the longer, regional railroads arrived about as quickly as the towns were large enough to think about railroads. Around Portland there were a couple of local lines, notably the Oregon and California, though it hoped eventually to be a major regional carrier that might fall within the second phase as found in the Middle West. But before we take up the concept of the *natural territory* as it evolved among western railroad companies, some brief comments on the concept of ubiquity are in order.

When eastern railroads gained their first comprehensive geographical stature as a result of the assault on the Appalachians—a drive that came before the construction of any lines running parallel with the Atlantic coast—it should not surprise us that it was those successful trans-Appalachian companies that took the next step toward occupying the whole regional market as it developed. Because the first purpose of railroads of any considerable length was to tie the interior to respective entrepôts on the coast, such city linkages were normally latitudinally constrained. The Northeast was tied to the Middle West, the Old South to a western interior South. There were modest interchanges of traffic between these linked pairs, particularly between the Old South and the Middle West, the Cotton Belt furnishing the second-largest market for the food that became the midwestern staple. Links also existed between both the Northeast and Middle West and both parts of the South with respect to manufactured items. Despite these interregional exchanges of goods, there was an almost complete divide on the Potomac and the Ohio in terms of railroad operations; until 1886 there were actually two different gauges characterizing lines north and south of that corporate and river divide.

In the South, the South Carolina Railroad's 5-foot gauge had become very widespread, though not universal. The standard-gauge lines that did exist in the South seem to have resulted not from the intrusion of northern interests but rather as a defensive distinction sought by southern companies not wishing to interchange traffic with their 5-foot neighbors or to be easily consolidated into their companies. In the North gauge distinctions had existed in the early years—the Erie (6 feet) and the Atlantic and St. Lawrence (5 feet 6 inches)—but by the years right after the Civil War most lines were being narrowed to the standard Stephenson gauge (4 feet 8½ inches). That standard, however, was not in fact so very uniform. As late as 1893 the *Official Railway Guide* contained 149 companies that used a 4-foot 9-inch "standard" in place of the more widely accepted 4-foot 8.5-inch one.[31]

It is impossible to determine definitively why the Ohio and Potomac became such crucial divides that only in the last ten years has there been any significant crossing of that corporate frontier, which even now remains largely in force. Of course, from the last decades of the nineteenth century through passenger trains existed, as did the interchange of freight cars, so some of the potential problems of operation by a diver-

sity of companies were mitigated. What does stand out, however, is the working of a force for ubiquity within these two parts of the eastern section of the country. A northern trunk carrier either reached to the borders of that northern region—to Chicago, St. Louis, Louisville, Cincinnati, and Washington—or was seen as a potential route for subsequent merger into a carrier company that did. The integrity of that northern trunk-line territory no doubt arose in part because the trans-Appalachian lines became its leaders, and they would have an interest in being as completely competitive one with another as possible. Even on the East Coast, companies that began as the servants of particular entrepôts, as was the B. and O. of Baltimore and the Pennsylvania of Philadelphia, sought to enter the port headquarters of their competitors. The B. and O. built and leased northward to the west bank of the Hudson, reaching Philadelphia and New York City, as the Pennsylvania spread both northward to New York and southward through Baltimore to the banks of the Potomac. Only the Erie and the New York Central came to depend primarily on New York, with the latter gaining access to Boston at the turn of the century when it leased the Boston and Albany, the merger of the Boston and Worcester and the Western Railroad of Massachusetts. Certainly the historical origin of these northern trunk lines showed right to the end. The distinction was most apparent at their eastern end, where the B. and O. and Pennsylvania showed their Middle Atlantic origins by having nothing to do with New England, whereas the New York Central and Erie demonstrated a much closer tie with that Yankee region but not much association with Chesapeake Bay.

The search for ubiquity was equally strong among the southern lines. The Richmond and Danville, which became the base on which the Southern Railway System was erected, had reached Atlanta, with ties west-

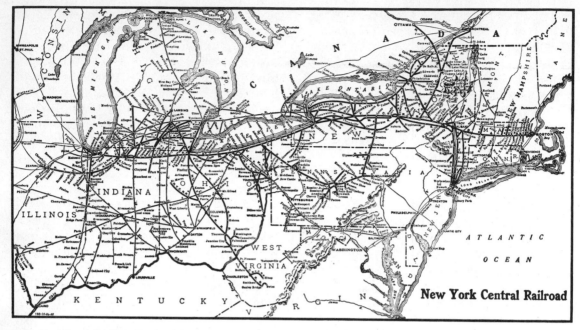

New York Central Railroad

Report of the Joint New England Railroad Committee, June, 1923.

ward toward the Mississippi, before it was formally transformed into a regional system by J. P. Morgan. Thus it and the Louisville and Nashville, through its control of the Seaboard Air Line and the Atlantic Coast Line, by the early twentieth century had spread to occupy most of the entrepôts on the coast—sharing Norfolk, Charleston, Jacksonville, Mobile, and New Orleans—and several of the interior articulation points—Cincinnati, Louisville, St. Louis, and Memphis. There were obviously distinctions of the same sort we saw among the northern trunks. The Southern, as a result of its origins, clearly dominated the Piedmont; the L. and N. had its corporate fiefs in the western interior South and in Florida.

Is there an answer to the related questions of railroad strategy that dominated the historical geography of the United States east of the Mississippi? Why was there a structural divide on the Ohio-Potomac, and why did

the main companies within each of those two regions extend their lines fairly effectively to the edges of their region, with the main restriction being that each company tended to be most dominant (that is, least sharing) of its place of origin? The answer probably lies in the distinctive characteristics of these two regions. The Northeast–Middle West was the dominant center of urbanization and industrialization in the United States while the South, coastal and interior, remained rural and agricultural. These different conditions would seem to have called for contrasting railroad operations: the Northeast–Middle West for heavily built, often multiple trackage; for extensive and complex yards; for large capital investments of the order of the $400 million the Pennsylvania Railroad spent to cross the river to New York City when it opened Pennsylvania Station there in 1910; and for an emphasis on speed in passenger transportation and volume in freight. In contrast, southern lines were almost universally lightly engineered; mostly single-track; characterized by small, simple yards; and with passenger trains that chugged slowly across what was easy terrain (the Florida trains of the Seaboard and the Atlantic Coast lines in the 1930s and 1940s standing as the exception that substantiated the speed generalization); and capital used sparingly in an area where the objective seems to have been to extend the tracks beyond as many horizons as possible. The lightness of southern construction has proved devastating in the last decade, when that region's railroads have sought to accept the much enlarged freight cars of the present on lines constructed for small, light cars built to transport agricultural products.

No detailed study has been made to answer the related question—why the divide and why the regional difference—but there is ample evidence that it was ubiquity, expressed in these contrasting regional frames, that guided the corporate strategies east of the Mississippi. There could be northern investment in southern railroads—less the other way around given the capital poverty of the South—but there was no effective operation of significant stretches of railroad by one in the other's region. The Southern Railway did have a line across southern Illinois to St. Louis, and the Pennsylvania did own a major part of the Richmond, Fredericksburg, and Potomac; but these were fairly minor restrictions of the validity of the generalization. The fact that the Pennsylvania, though the major owner of the Norfolk and Western Railway, never sought effectively to merge the two would seem to bear out the argument that the nature of the region in which it operated influenced corporate decisions and strategy in a way that is not fully understood.

Ubiquity within a region well defined for its time was the objective. Only the preemptive quality of a company that was first on the scene—the Richmond and Danville (later Southern Railway) dominance of the Piedmont and the New York Central dominance of the wider connections of Boston and New England—show this quality. So the principal generalizations may be stated simply: east of the Mississippi there were two significant railroad regions—that north of the general latitudinal line of the Ohio and Potomac rivers and that to the south thereof; within each of those two regions there was a small number of regional trunk lines, each of which sought to accomplish a pattern of regional ubiquity with lines reaching to most of the bounding coastal entrepôts and interior articulation points; and the main exceptions to that ubiquity came in access to the peripheral entrepôts and articulation points, wherein trunk lines tended to be strongest in that entrepôt or articulation point where they originated and weakest in the cities where other trunk carriers were first organized.

NATURAL TERRITORY IN EVOLUTION TOWARD UBIQUITY IN THE WEST

West of the Mississippi another strategic principle seems to have guided corporate decisions. In the West there was the effort to occupy what came to be seen as the *natural territory* of a particular corporation. Again the place of origin plays an important role, emphasizing the significant contribution that historical geography can make to an understanding of the North American rail system. The first transcontinental, and several of the half-dozen that followed it in the United States, were in the earliest period natural monopolies. Obviously when the Union Pacific-Central Pacific was completed in 1869, that line had a complete monopoly on rail transportation between the Mississippi frontier and California. When further interest in the opening of the West by railroads became active during the 1870s, there was a similar notion of occupying and dominating a territory. In 1876 the Central Pacific interests, under a holding company they organized as the Southern Pacific Railroad, completed a line from Sacramento to Los Angeles and began an eastward push to the two possible crossings of the Colorado River from the Arizona Territory—The Needles and Yuma. The Southern Pacific is the classic expression of the notion of natural territory and the regional monopoly it implies. By the early 1880s the S.P. lines to Yuma and The Needles were under construction and staking out that *company territory.*

In this same period other railroads were thinking along similar lines. The Union Pacific saw the Great Plains as their natural territory. In this the Omaha company was not nearly as successful as was the Sacramento (later San Francisco) one. The placement of the eastern terminus at Council Bluffs had drawn five granger lines—the Burlington and Missouri River (C. B. & Q.), the Rock Island, the Chicago and Milwaukee, the Chicago and Northwestern, the Illinois Central—to that vicinity and to the Missouri River frontier. Although they came to interchange traffic with the Union Pacific, the granger lines soon began to question whether the Missouri frontier was divinely ordained or merely historically determined. In the end the Rock Island (to Tucumcari, New Mexico); the Burlington (to Denver and thence to Billings, Montana); the Chicago and Northwestern (to Lander, Wyoming); and the Chicago and Milwaukee (to Tacoma, Washington, over a branch leading from southern Minnesota) all sought to reach the Pacific Coast. Only the Illinois Central accepted the division of territories initially implicit in the establishment of the original junction at Council Bluffs. However much it sought to assert control over its first natural territory, the Union Pacific was un-

able to do so. When the Missouri Pacific Railroad reached Kansas City, it began construction of a further competitor to Denver, where it subsequently encouraged the building of the Denver and Rio Grande Western (to Salt Lake City) and the Western Pacific (from Salt Lake City to Oakland) to shape an effective transcontinental, the last to be added when it opened in 1911.

Apparently because the U.P. was unable to occupy the Great Plains as its natural territory, the company turned its attention to the Great Basin. There the Union Pacific either built railroads on its own account, or encouraged others to build lines that might later be merged with the U.P. to dominate that vast, if underpopulated, area. The company itself promoted and accomplished the Oregon Short Line from Granger, Wyoming, on the original line, to Portland, Oregon—the first link from the main net of American railroads with phase 2 lines that had come into existence in the Pacific Northwest. By carrying a branch to Butte, Montana, from Utah, and effectively gaining control of the San Pedro, Los Angeles, and Salt Lake City Railroad—begun by Senator Clark of Montana but kept out of Utah by the Union Pacific's occupation of the only practical access from the southwest—the Omaha company occupied the southern part of the Great Basin. Only west of Ogden was there competition strong enough to keep the Omaha Road out—that is, until 1983, when the Union Pacific merged the Western Pacific into the larger company, along with the Missouri Pacific. By controlling the route from Los Angeles and Portland to Salt Lake City and Ogden, the Union Pacific managed to hold at bay all other western railroads, even the Southern Pacific, which gained no further foothold in the Great Basin. With the merger of the Western Pacific into the U.P., that monopoly has been increased. It will be interesting to see how it consolidates or expands in the future.

With the Southern Pacific encountering a barrier at Ogden, that company sought to push its corporate frontiers outward along easier lines. Trying to occupy both the Yuma and Needles gateways to California was more than it could pull off, but (by yielding the latter to the Santa Fe) it did manage to control the former. Building rapidly and illegally across the Yuma Indian Reservation, the San Francisco company succeeded in occupying the two usable routes for a railroad from the Gila River to the high plateaus of southern New Mexico, thereby gaining control of the economic purpose of the Gadsden Purchase. It had been the hope of the Texas and Pacific Railroad to occupy that territory, in which they were being aided by Pennsylvania money; but they lost out to Collis Huntington, who managed to occupy the Gadsden Purchase and to push his line east of El Paso before the T. and P. reached that longitude, forcing on the latter a junction at Sierra Blanca, 92 miles east of what would have been a logical articulation point at the pass city. With that further advance in hand, Huntington went on to push' his territory across south central Texas to Houston and on to New Orleans. There the different nature and operational practices east of the Great River finally brought the expansion from San Francisco to a close, although later the California company gained control of the St. Louis Southwestern, leading from Texas to its eponymous city and further defending an oligarchical, if not a monopolistic, control of the Southwest by the Southern Pacific. Adding Rock Island trackage from Tucumcari, New Mexico, to Kansas City to the S.P. has further defended that "natural territory".

While the original partners in the first transcontinental were slashing out territories vastly larger than originally foreseen for either of these two companies, other corporations sought to identify and occupy similarly exclusive regions. The clearest case of this activity was the shaping of the domain of the Northern Pacific. That company had begun as a New England promotion (first in Maine and then in Vermont) of a line of similar form to the original transcontinental, though not to be shared between two companies. Promoted effectively by the Smith group in St. Albans, Vermont, who had succeeded in building the Vermont Central (present-day Central Vermont), the Northern Pacific Railroad was to begin at St. Paul and to use the 47th parallel route thence to the Pacific. The Panic of 1873, considerably induced by investments in the Northern Pacific, caught the company at its topically named head of construction on the Missouri River in the central Dakota Territory. For most of the rest of the decade the N.P. remained at the Bismarck bridgehead. Its revival came not there but in Oregon, where the N.P. project was seen as the instrument of staking out a new natural territory—one for the Oregon Railway and Navigation Company.

That corporation had been heavily backed by German investors who, to guard their interests, had hired Henry Villard as their agent. He became a territorial monarch in his thinking, wishing not only to keep out intruders, as he sought to do against the Union Pacific's entry via the Oregon Short Line, but also to push the Oregon Navigation's frontier far to the south and east. Villard promoted the Oregon and California to build across the Siskiyous toward the Golden State, and he took up the dormant Northern Pacific as an instrument for securing an easterly and controlled connection. He was a clear and outspoken protagonist of the natural territory he believed to have been bestowed on a pioneering railroad at its birth. His double push outward of "his" boundaries proved too much, however; by the early 1880s Villard and his investors were losing control of their promotions. The Southern Pacific took over the Oregon and

California to gain a frontier on the Columbia in the structural valleys of the West Coast. The Union Pacific managed to take over the approach to Portland from the southeast. Only the Northern Pacific was not taken up by the earlier western companies. It essentially gained independence through Villard's collapse, managing to complete a line to Portland from the northeast down the Columbia Gorge in 1882, thus connecting that area with the East without being involved with either of the two pioneer lines.

Assertion of the idea of the natural territory recurs in the statements of western railroad presidents in the last century. The intrusion of a line from a different quarter was viewed with an anger seldom found east of the Mississippi. There was more than just pique in this; the markets in the West were little developed, and to share them might mean too little support for either company. This idea undoubtedly lay behind the Central Pacific–Union Pacific effort to maintain geographical monopolies, with the high freight charges and fares that became possible under such absolute control.

In the beginning the growth of the western market was so problematic that such a policy seemed economically rational, if unpopular. Certainly during the 1870s there was little support for these two pioneers. The owners of the Central Pacific—the Big Four—were extremely successful in asserting and maintaining a monopoly in California up to the early 1880s, when the Atchison, Topeka, and Santa Fe Railway reached the Needles gateway. There the Southern Pacific (as successor to the C.P.) seemed to block the way, but a temporary economic setback for that monopoly—combined with the Santa Fe's threat to make an end run around the S.P. by building a line to the Gulf of California and operating ships thence to San Diego and San Francisco—forced open the door. The S.P. agreed to sell its line between Mojave in the desert of that name and Needles

to the Santa Fe. In addition, the Santa Fe gained trackage rights to operate over the S.P. line, which crossed the Tehachapi Mountains, to gain access to the southern part of the Central Valley of California. Using that entrée, the Santa Fe built from a new station, Barstow, on the Needles-Mojave line southwestward through the Cajon Pass into the Los Angeles Basin, thereby removing absolute control of that natural territory from the Southern Pacific. The result was a rapid and massive drop in freight and passenger charges, demonstrating how profitable these regional monopolies could be to a company like the Southern Pacific, which seems to have refined if not invented the idea of charging "what the traffic would bear," as opposed to gaining a fair return on their investment.

The Southern Pacific succeeded in maintaining several extensive but more limited monopolies for the rest of the nineteenth century. Northern California remained their fief. Possessing the only connections from the area north of the Tehachapis to the rest of the United States, the company that Frank Norris called "the Octopus" grew wealthy and arrogant. (Though time has limited its wealth, it has not noticeably changed its demeanor, as any passenger riding on its lines can attest.) The arrogance of the Southern Pacific eventually earned its reward. In 1900 California interests promoted a line from Richmond on San Francisco Bay to the Central Valley and southward toward Bakersfield. Those promoters succeeded in interesting the Santa Fe in purchasing and completing that line to tie it to their trackage rights over the Tehachapis to create a second railroad operating in the Southern Pacific's territory. Still, the routes to the east and north were tightly held by the Octopus.

In the first decade of this century this last of the territorial monopolies of any appreciable market size began to give way. George Gould—successor to his father Jay and the controller of a string of railroads beginning in the east with the Erie and continuing via the Wabash, the Missouri Pacific, and the Denver and Rio Grande Western to Salt Lake City—set out to make an obvious invasion parallel to the initial route of the Central Pacific (Southern Pacific). Thus the Western Pacific was built between Salt Lake City and Oakland. After 1911 the S.P. was left with no more than its monopoly of the Oregon-to-California connection. In due course, in the 1930s, the last mainline railroad to be built in the United States was constructed as "an inland gateway" between the Pacific Northwest and northern California. This was accomplished by stringing together branches of the Union Pacific and Great Northern Railway in Oregon, adding a bit of trackage rights over the Southern Pacific, and building a line east of the Sierra-Cascades in northern California to reach Keddie on the main line of the Western Pacific.

The recent merger of the Western Pacific and the Union Pacifc has finally put this line in the hands of what has become the Southern Pacific's great competitor, the Union Pacific, which has effectively introduced the eastern notion of ubiquity of access to bounding entrepôts and articulation points as a strategy of western railroading. In the aftermath of that successful introduction, the Southern Pacific and Santa Fe have consolidated to attain their own practice of ubiquity. In reaching a ubiquitous system the Union Pacific has been much more successful, as they have now occupied all the entrepôts of the Pacific Coast—Seattle, Portland, Oakland, and Los Angeles—leaving only the cul-de-sac of San Diego to their rivals, and Seattle as their individual and more significant possession. In addition, the U.P. has gained access to most of the points of articulation on the Mississippi—New Orleans, Memphis, St. Louis, and Chicago.

The death of the natural-territory strategy is due. The West has gained a degree of development that can no longer economically or legally justify the toleration of regional monopolies. The markets there are large enough to be shared, and the evolution of corporate strategy has come to reflect that development. In the beginning, private operation of American railroads (which meant that they must be at least marginally profitable) permitted the assertion of the existence of natural territories, but economic realities no longer justify what pioneering conditions would have condoned.

The Pacific Railroad Survey Determines the Route

The location of western railroads does not stem from this concept of natural territory; the Pacific Railroad Survey of 1854 plotted most of the alignments that were ultimately built on. The Union Pacific–Central Pacific line followed the 41st parallel route save at its western end, where the Dutch Flat route between Sacramento and Reno was adopted both for terrain reasons and for its direct approach to the most rational economic objective of a transcontinental railroad. The second deliberate undertaking of a transcontinental, the Northern Pacific along the 47th parallel route, managed to stick fairly close to that alignment, though it dipped south of it to Portland before the line directly across the Cascades to Tacoma was opened.

The 35th parallel route was occupied in a peculiar manner. As originally surveyed, that alignment would have led from Memphis via the Arkansas Valley to the Indian Territory and thence across the Texas Panhandle to northern New Mexico and Arizona before entering California near Needles. So much trouble was encountered in promoting a line that its ostensible eastern terminus was shifted northward to St.

Louis with the Atlantic and Pacific Railroad that was to undertake the construction. This later became the more precisely (but not more accurately) named St. Louis and San Francisco Railway, the only project that ever claimed to be heading directly for San Francisco, though it soon became stalled in the Indian Territory, after which its transcontinental charter and land grant were taken up by the Atchison, Topeka, and Santa Fe Railway. That railroad itself had been diverted away from the Royal Gorge of the Arkansas when it lost the race to occupy that critical route west, more or less along the 38th parallel, and was forced southward through Raton Pass into the latitude of the 35th parallel route. Thus the western end of the 35th parallel route was attached to what might have become the 38th to reach California in that alignment, had such a route been practicable for other than a local railroad. Parts of the 38th parallel route in Colorado were later occupied by a narrow-gauge line built near Cochetopa Pass, but only to tap local mining camps.

The 32nd parallel route was built on the alignment much as expected, save for the failure to find a usable crossing of the mountains east of San Diego, forcing the western terminus to Los Angeles rather than the older natural port to the south. The final survey alignment, that along the 49th parallel, was the last of the six to be built along. Only in the 1890s was the Great Northern Railway completed to Seattle, basically along that route and obviously just to the south of the 49th parallel, the Canadian–United States boundary. The two remaining transcontinental lines—the Chicago, Milwaukee, St. Paul and Pacific, opened to Seattle in 1909, and the Western Pacific that reached Oakland in the winter of 1910–1911—occupied parts of the Pacific Railroad Survey routes. The Milwaukee line followed fairly closely the 47th parallel route, diverging as much to distinguish its railroad alignment

from that of the older Northern Pacific along that same general parallel as to find a truly different geographical alignment. The Western Pacific, as a completion of the Gould Lines to the Pacific Coast, ran near to the Central Pacific route but diverged from it in two fairly minor ways, running south rather than north of Great Salt Lake and using the canyon of the Feather River to cross the Sierra Nevada rather than the Dutch Flat Route.

Even in the building of the north-south line through the interior valleys of California and Oregon, a route studied under the Pacific Railroad Survey was used. And the eastern end of the 35th parallel route, unused in the initial construction of the Santa Fe, was eventually occupied by a branch transcontinental, that of the Rock Island Railroad in its junction with the Southern Pacific at Tucumcari, New Mexico. This junction, forged after the turn of the century, tied the 32nd parallel route from Los Angeles to El Paso to the 35th from Tucumcari to Memphis, as well as using a diagonal line of the Rock Island from Tucumcari to Chicago to give the Southern Pacific access to that articulation point along what they called the Golden State Route, one that freed the S.P. of its dependence on the Union Pacific.

Corporate Strategy Determines the Systems

The location of railroads in the West was largely determined by the results of the Pacific Railroad Survey more than a century ago. What was not established was the apportionment of these specific routes among the various private companies that sought to enter the contest. At first the breakdown was by vectors leading from the settlement frontier into and across the unsettled interior to the Pacific Coast. With the exception of the

35th and 38th parallel routes, each vector was taken up by a specific company (or two companies in the original transcontinental)—the Great Northern Railway on the 49th parallel, the Northern Pacific on the 47th, the Union Pacific–Central Pacific on the 41st, and the Southern Pacific on the 32nd. Eventually the Santa Fe occupied the western half of the 35th parallel route, and the Rock Island occupied its eastern end; but each was part of a different, no longer fully latitudinal transcontinental alignment. The 38th parallel route was passed over save for small stretches in Colorado taken up by local lines to serve mining areas.

On the completion of the transcontinental lines along the Pacific Railroad Survey routes, the companies then sought to gain the total market available in that vector by asserting the notion of their natural territory and striving to push further lines that would occupy it to the extent of either the natural or the corporate boundaries. At this point the strategic objective of the railroad corporations was to create a regional monopoly as absolute as could be maintained. Only since the turn of the century has that strategy perforce been changed. As the last of the transcontinentals—the Milwaukee (1909) and Western Pacific (1911) and the joining of the Southern Pacific-Rock Island Golden State Route (1902)—reached completion, there was competition closely parallel with the older transcontinentals—the Milwaukee with the Northern Pacific, the Denver and Rio Grande Western-Western Pacific with the Union Pacific-Central Pacific, and the Golden State Route with the Santa Fe. Only the two boundary railroads, the Great Northern and the Southern Pacific Sunset Route (Los Angeles to New Orleans) were free of closely parallel competition, though in both cases there was active competition between their terminal regions by, respectively, the Northern Pacific and the Santa Fe.

Once this competition had destroyed the rational assertion of a natural territory, corporate strategy changed to the effort to introduce the older (eastern) strategy of creating subcontinental ubiquity for the company's lines. The Santa Fe had moved into the Bay Area in 1900; the next year Edward Harriman, who earlier had come to control the Union Pacific, gained control of the Southern Pacific, extending the connections of the Union Pacific to southern California and the Bay Area. Soon thereafter Harriman lost out in his attempt to dominate the Chicago, Burlington, and Quincy; and that company, offering access to Kansas City, St. Louis, and Chicago, joined Hill's Northern Lines in ownership if not operation. Although Harriman's ownership of both the Southern Pacific and the Union Pacific was thrown down by the U.S. Supreme Court, the U.P. came out of the separation with broader connections—notably a line from Ogden to San Pedro, the port for Los Angeles. In turn, the S.P. gained a new articulation point, St. Louis, which it reached over the wholly controlled St. Louis Southwestern (Cottonbelt) Railroad. In this same period the Santa Fe and the Northern Lines were seeking to reach new gateways—the Northern Lines, through the Burlington ownership, reached to the Gulf of Mexico at Galveston, as did the Santa Fe, through construction. The patterns were fairly well established by the time the U.P. and S.P. were spilt under the court order of 1913. The U.P., S.P., and Northern Lines had access to the Pacific Northwest; the U.P., S.P., and Santa Fe to Los Angeles; the Northern Lines, S.P., and Santa Fe to Texas; the Northern Lines, U.P., and Santa Fe to Kansas City; and the Santa Fe, S.P., and Northern Lines (through the Western Pacific) to the Bay Area. There were still entrepôts or articulation points that were not shared: the U.P. was not in the Bay Area, St. Louis, or Chicago; the S.P. was not in Seattle, Kansas City, or Chicago; the Santa Fe was not in the Northwest; and the Northern Lines were not in the Southwest.

THE EMERGENCE OF SUPERSYSTEMS

Since the 1960s ubiquity has been advanced west of the Mississippi. With the formal consolidation of the Northern Lines and the Burlington into the Burlington Northern, their wide reach has been made apparent. The completed merger of the Union Pacific with the Western Pacific and Missouri Pacific has taken that pioneer line into the Bay Area, Texas, New Orleans, Memphis, St. Louis, and Chicago. The prospective merger of the Santa Fe and Southern Pacific will add the Northwest to the former and Kansas City and Chicago to the latter. This merging seems to have completed the adoption of ubiquity by the western railroad corporations, creating a single operative strategy among these private companies, now both east and west of the Mississippi. In both subcontinental regions there are shards of the nineteenth-century railroad structure that have not been swept into one of the six consolidations. In the East the Boston and Maine, the Delaware and Hudson, and some phase 2 lines in the South—the Florida East Coast, for example—remain unaligned, whereas in the West the Denver and Rio Grande Western and a number of nearly bankrupt granger roads (the Chicago and Northwestern, the Milwaukee, and the Rock Island) remain out in the cold. The seemingly greater neatness in the East is attributable to the debacle of the 1960s when the failed merger of the New York Central, New Haven, and Pennsylvania was matched by the financial collapse of many of its neighbors—the Jersey Central, the Erie, and others. Organized as Conrail in an emergency corporation with federal subsidies, these collapsed roads have been brought to the margin of profitability, with current arguments that they should now be "privatized." As they stand, they represent the third of the major eastern consolidations, alongside the Norfolk Southern (Norfolk and Western and Southern) and the CSX (Chesapeake and Ohio–Baltimore and Ohio and Family Lines).

Other than what seems a probable joining of the shards to one of the six major consolidations, with considerable abandonment of now-excess track, the final question is where corporate strategy will ultimately lead. Ubiquity up to this time has had a subcontinental frame. Will it now take on a continental one? The probability appears strong that it will. The Santa Fe has already expressed interest in considering Conrail for purchase and merger. In that event, it is highly unlikely that the other two western consolidations would shy from the post. It is hard to select the ultimate partners, but such a pairing seems most probable. With it would come the final corporate strategy to be brought to bear on the world's largest rail network, a quarter of the total at the height of American railroading around the time of World War I.

It should be appreciated that the actual pattern of railroads was strongly set by geography and the evolutionary history of the development of lines, with the Pacific Railroad Survey providing the grandest pandect for railroad development ever prepared. But the way those geographically determined lines have been sorted out, with many discards as well as adoptions in the present pattern of six major systems, has been the product of the evolving strategy adopted by private corporations in a clearly staged progression of phases from the first short lines around entrepôts to the subcontinental systems of today. At most one stage remains undetermined.

THE CANADIAN RAIL NETWORK

The same shortage of space that forces us to consider much of the evolution of American

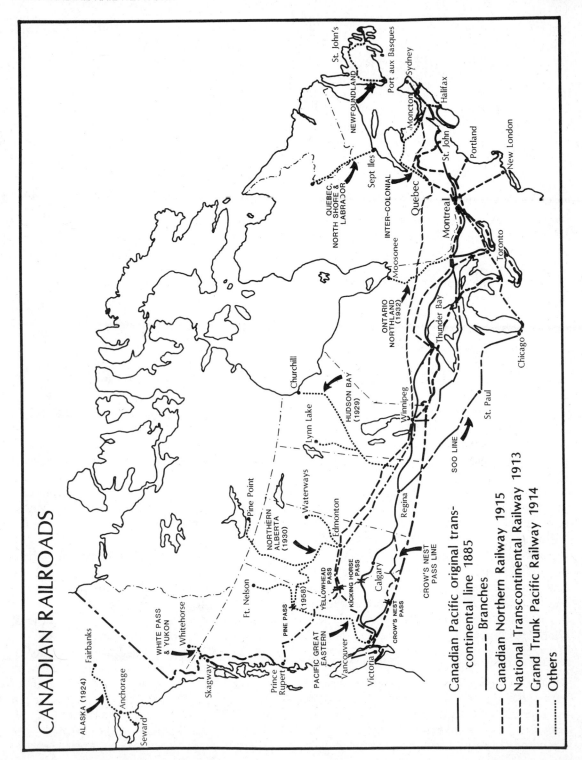

CANADIAN RAILROADS

Canadian Pacific original transcontinental line 1885
-- Branches
Canadian Northern Railway 1915
National Transcontinental Railway 1913
Grand Trunk Pacific Railway 1914
Others

ALASKA (1924)
Fairbanks
Anchorage
Seward
WHITE PASS & YUKON
Whitehorse
Skagway
Prince Rupert
PACIFIC GREAT EASTERN
Ft. Nelson
Pine Point
PINE PASS
PINE PASS (1958)
NORTHERN ALBERTA (1930)
Waterways
Edmonton
YELLOWHEAD PASS
KICKING HORSE PASS
Vancouver
Victoria
CROW'S NEST PASS
CROW'S NEST PASS LINE
Calgary
Regina
Lynn Lake
Churchill
HUDSON BAY (1929)
Winnipeg
SOO LINE
St. Paul
Chicago
Thunder Bay
Moosonee
ONTARIO NORTHLAND (1932)
Toronto
Montreal
Quebec
INTER-COLONIAL
Sept Iles
QUEBEC, NORTH SHORE & LABRADOR
NEWFOUNDLAND
St. John's
Port aux Basques
Sydney
Moncton
Halifax
St. John
Portland
New London

railroads in tight summary also affects our consideration of Canadian railroads. From the very beginning the Canadian and American experiences have been nearly parallel, but not quite. When their courses veered away from each other, it was usually caused by the fairly deliberate decision on the part of the Canadians to adopt a British precedent or practice. Because the North Americans had far more in common, the Canadians as a matter of course generally came up with the same solutions to problems that their Yankee cousins had taken slightly before them, the precedence in time due almost entirely to the more developed state of the American economy. But the northerners did not wish either to be slavish disciples of Brother Jonathan or disregardful sons of the Mother Country, so the notion was always present of showing both independence and loyalty—the first of America and the second to Britain—through veering briefly toward the way a thing was done "at home."

The first experiments toward railroad construction in Canada were startlingly similar to those in the United States, except that the Canadians took the first three steps virtually at once. In the northern Dominion there had been no extended experiment with inclined planes or horse railways, so the first Canadian "railway" came in 1830 as part of the building of the Citadel at Québec, where a steam-operated incline was used in construction.[32] The earliest common-carrier railroad came in a typical place for the New World, to carry the traffic from the Richelieu River across the narrow intervening plain to the south bank of the St. Lawrence opposite Montréal, avoiding the long detour necessary for water transport because the Richelieu flowed into the St. Lawrence well below the site of the emerging Canadian metropolis. Begun in 1835, the Champlain and St. Lawrence Railroad was at first equipped by an engine from Robert Stephenson, Ltd., only to follow continental American practice of buying North American locomotives.

There were short lines in the Maritimes by the late 1830s and soon thereafter the first international line was proposed in the joint construction of a railroad from Portland, Maine, to Montréal already referred to in the context of New England. The first mainline railroad was proposed by British capitalists as an extension of the line to the Maine port, opened in 1853, even to the extent it adopted that carrier's 5-foot 6-inch track gauge. With the nature of settlement in Canada, a generally thin band close to the United States border, any main line in Canada was likely to be a single trunk line. Between 1853 and 1856 the Grand Trunk Railway, promoted by the British firm of Thomas Brassey, was constructed between Montréal and Toronto, and at the end of that decade extended to the St. Clair River at Sarnia, Ontario. Branches were built in Ontario and eastward from Montréal to Rivière du Loup below Québec on the St. Lawrence, but the Grand Trunk remained an elongated system, one aimed at extending into the American Middle West more than westward within Canada. The British promoters insisted on costly construction, which could be supported only by tapping the partially developed American market rather than the undeveloped Canadian one.

As a result, Canadian railroads remained restricted to the more developed parts of Canada until the 1870s, with separate systems in the Maritime colonies and in Canada, Upper and Lower. The building of the American transcontinental railroad in the late 1860s contributed a new dimension to the railroad problem of Canada. The Grand Trunk Railway had, in the hands of its British owners and managers, been turned increasingly into yet another rail link from the American Middle West to the Atlantic coast, this time at Montréal and

Portland, Maine. When in 1871 the fledgling Dominion of Canada sought to join the western possessions of Britain in North America to those making up Canada—Nova Scotia, New Brunswick, Québec, and Ontario—the colony of British Columbia was the key to continental success. The government of that distant spot of European settlement on the Pacific Coast wished to secure from Canada the building of a wagon road, much in the fashion of pioneering connections to the American West in the 1850s, to tie the two coasts together. Responding to that request in an oddly exuberant vein, Prime Minister John A. Macdonald (Canada's rather gray version of George Washington) promised instead the building of a transcontinental railroad within ten years of British Columbia's joining the Dominion. That union was entered in 1871 so Canada found itself burdened with a monumental project expected to be carried out in a true wilderness within a short period of time.

The Canadian Pacific Project

Despite the obvious problems of construction by a small country of such a vast project, Canada was perhaps emboldened by the recent success of the United States in barely managing to complete the Union Pacific–Central Pacific. There was yet another problem: along what route to build to the Pacific. The Grand Trunk when approached stated determined unwillingness to build to the west except by extending its line across the American Upper Middle West, thus avoiding the sterile country, in economic terms, of the Canadian Shield that intervened between the distant environs of Ottawa and Toronto and the edge of the Prairies in eastern Manitoba. As the Dominion of Canada had been shaped in 1867 considerably in defense of British territory against the rightful resentment of the victorious Union at Britain's

support of the Confederacy, no Canadian government could undertake a national railroad that had to cross American territory and thus be subject to possible interruption in times of conflicting policies. This meant that the Grand Trunk divorced itself from the national railroad project of the Dominion and that the government was committed to crossing the Shield. In that transit there were several possible routes—along the shore of Lake Superior, along the watershed between the Great Lakes and Hudson Bay, or combinations of the two—but the basic route to the west was evident in gross terms as far as the Red River.

Beyond that crossing the field was far more open, with the two constraints established by the Canadian-American boundaries of the Pacific Coast of Canada—the 49th parallel to the south and 54° 40′ to the north. All of that 5° of longitude was walled with the Coast Ranges, to the point that some gap in the crest practicable for rails must be found. As several rivers drained from east of the Coast Ranges, it was logical to expect that there would be such openings. But between the western edge of the Prairies and the interior of British Columbia lay the continental cordillera, the Rockies. Here no river crossed in the appropriate latitudes, the Rockies being the Continental Divide, so the question was more open. To answer these problems of railroad geography, Canada turned to the device that had been employed seventeen years earlier in the United States. A Pacific Railway Survey was established, under the command of Sandford Fleming, which in the 1870s examined possible routes from the upper Ottawa valley to the Pacific.

It is unfortunately impossible here to examine the Fleming surveys in any detail, doubly unfortunate because they are even less well known than the American railroad surveys. The Fleming surveys did find most of the potential routes that were to be used in

Canada west of the edge of eastern settlement as it existed in 1870. In the Prairies these reconnaissance surveys found little terrain control of railroad alignments, beyond that of heading fairly directly from the Red River Valley to possible openings through the Rockies. Those gaps were few, and Fleming believed that by far the best was the Yellow Head Pass west of Fort Edmonton at 53° north latitude, with an elevation that turned out to be only 3,717 feet. In the Coast Ranges the problem of a passable gap was compounded by the fact that the use of Yellowhead Pass (as it came to be spelled) was paralleled to the west by an intervening block range that forced possible alignments either to the north or south, thus assuring that the whole 5° of the Canadian Pacific Coast would be under consideration. Briefly, the crossings of the coastal rampart fell finally into five basic areas—the Skeena River valley far to the north just below the Alaska boundary; some approach to Butte Inlet on the central British Columbia coast; use of Howe Sound just north of present-day Vancouver; and two passages of the Fraser River Canyon and valley to reach the mouth of the river near New Westminster. The combination of Yellowhead Pass and one of these gaps in the Coast Ranges suggested that a transcontinental railroad was feasible.

With the Grand Trunk off the scene, a new company had to be created. This became the Canadian Pacific Railway. Starting first as a government construction, the project in the early 1880s was taken in hand by a private company and brought to completion in 1885. As located, the railroad crossed from Callender in eastern Ontario over the Shield to the northern shore of Lake Superior, around it to Thunder Bay, and thence north of Lake of the Woods to reach the Red River at Fort Garry (Winnipeg). In the Prairies the company rejected Flemings's advice, passing instead much farther south across the Prairies

(in the interest of forfending incursions of American railroads onto the Prairies) to reach the Rockies at Kicking Horse Pass. At 5,339 feet this was altogether a more difficult crossing than would have been Fleming's choice. West of the crest very awkward slopes forced upon the Canadian Pacific a grade of 4.4 percent, even though it had been specified that grades could be no more than the now traditional 2.2 percent that the B. and O. had introduced. Farther west two more ranges lay across the chosen alignment of the transcontinental. Eventually one of these, the Selkirks, required a 5-mile tunnel for practical working. Use was made of the gorge of the Fraser River as that stream cut into the plateau surface between the Rockies and the Coast and the broad valley of the lower Fraser. Having reached that point, the company rejected the existing river-mouth port, New Westminster, replacing it with one on Burrard Inlet just to the north, which could be free of silting, where in 1885 the C.P.R. began shaping the new city of Vancouver.

The Canadian Northern and Grand Trunk Pacific

The completion of the Canadian Pacific "solved the western railroad problem for some fifteen years," but just at the turn of the century the farmers and merchants on the Prairies became restive under the Canadian Pacific monopoly and its claim to the region as its natural territory. The Canadian Northern Railway was organized in Manitoba to build granger lines in the wheat belt, and in 1901 it gained a Lakehead terminus at Port Arthur. Soon thereafter the promoters of this line, Donald Mann and William Mackenzie, envisioned a transcontinental extension from this Prairie road, building eastward to Montréal and Toronto and westward to Vancouver, at last using Fleming's Yellowhead alignment now extended via the Thompson River, the Fraser Gorge, and the Lower Mainland to Vancouver, reached in 1915.[33]

This same surge of railroad building belatedly gripped the proprietors of the Grand Trunk. Just after the turn of the century they began reexamining the notion of a transcontinental line and came up with a characteristic but truly ill-starred scheme. In conjunction with the Canadian government they floated another transcontinental project. The British company still could not bring itself to undertake construction on the Shield, so as part of a scheme to provide an "immigrant railway" from the Atlantic to the Prairies, the government undertook to build the National Transcontinental Railway from Moncton, New Brunswick, via Québec City to Winnipeg. This saddled the taxpayers with building directly westward from Québec to Winnipeg across absolutely unsettled country and with the cost of the longest railroad bridge span ever constructed in the Québec Bridge across the St. Lawrence just above the provincial capital.

West of Winnipeg the private Grand Trunk Pacific was carried basically along Fleming's alignment to Edmonton, Yellowhead Pass, and then fairly directly westward down the Skeena River Valley to its mouth where nearby a new port, Prince Rupert, was laid out to be connected by rail to eastern Canada in 1914. Thus, just as World War I began, Canada had not one but three transcontinental railroads. The latter two, partly as a result of the rise in costs due to the war, found themselves in bankruptcy as their final spikes were driven.

By the time the Canadian Northern opened to Vancouver in 1915, many of the routes that Sandford Fleming had discussed as possible had been occupied. There were three crossings of the Canadian Shield in Québec and Ontario, as well as two crossings of the Coast Ranges of British Columbia and the Rockies. By then the Canadian

Pacific had constructed a second line from Vancouver toward the Prairies, via the Kettle Valley and Crow's Nest Pass. Soon after World War I a railroad from the coast at Howe Sound to Prince George was begun, though it was completed only after World War II. As the British Columbia Railway it was continued northward in the province along two alignments that took it almost to the 60th parallel and the Yukon Territory. With its crossing of Pine Pass at 2,856 feet, this was the lowest passage of the Rockies in either the United States or Canada, as well as a new longitudinal route toward the northern territories of Canada and Alaska. At Dawson Creek it made juncture with the Northern Alberta Railway that had been carried from Edmonton into the Peace River Country, to be extended in the 1950s by the Great Slave Lake Railway to Pine Point in the Northwest Territories. After World War I such northern lines were driven through the brush and tundra to Churchill on Hudson Bay and Moosonee on James Bay, Ontario. After 1945 the development of iron ore deposits in Labrador led to the building of the Québec, Northshore, and Labrador Railway to Wabush and Schefferville and a separate ore road from Baie Comeau northward to the Québec Cartier mines. With the shift toward coal in the 1970s, the Alberta government undertook "railways to resources" reaching northward from Edison on the Canadian National along the foothills of the Rockies toward the Peace River Country and tapping the coal resources of the foothills for export to Japan. This shipping of coal combines with the export of the wheat of the Prairies to bring about at last the growth of Prince Rupert as a major port, half a century after the Grand Trunk Pacific unsuccessfully sought that goal.

The collapse of the Canadian Northern Railway and the Grand Trunk Pacific forced on the Canadian government a rescue that led in 1922 to the creation of a nationalized railroad equivalent in size to the older Canadian Pacific. The new Canadian National Railway absorbed most of the bits of government railroad—the National Transcontinental and the Intercolonial Railways in the Maritimes—as well as the Canadian Northern, the Grand Trunk, the Grand Trunk Western (in the American Middle West), the Central Vermont Railway, and the Grand Trunk in New England. Thus the merger movement that affected American railroads in the 1960s and 1970s came nearly fifty years earlier in Canada, leading to the existence of no more than two major railroads—the Canadian Pacific, still privately owned and operated, and the Canadian National, the public competitor thereto. The result has been the existence for a half a century of two nationwide systems that have provided effective competition one with the other—in other words, ubiquity. Only in the late 1970s was any significant change introduced when, a decade after the United States, the Dominion assumed responsibility for the running of passenger trains, in VIA— the northern equivalent to Amtrak. As south of the 49th parallel, many trains were dropped and transcontinental operations combined, leaving separate operation only in the Prairies and interior British Columbia, where the Canadian Pacific's adoption of a route other than that recommended by Sandford Fleming had created a necessarily permanent division of service between the Yellowhead route in the north and the Kicking Horse route to the south of it.

NOTES

1. Granite Railway Company, *The First Railroad in America: A History of the Origin and Development of the Granite Railway at Quincy, Massachusetts*, privately printed, 1926.
2. Quoted in Edward Hungerford, *The Story of the Baltimore and Ohio Railroad, 1827–1927* (New York: G. P. Putnam's Sons, 1928), vol. 1, p. 19.
3. William Strickland, architect and engineer, *Reports on Canals, Railways, Roads, and Other Subjects, Made to "The Pennsylvania Society for the Promotion of Internal Improvement"* (Philadelphia: H. C. Carey & I. Lea, Chestnut Street, 1826).
4. Ibid., p. 53.
5. A.M. Wellington, *The Economic Theory of the Location of Railways*, 6th ed. (New York: John Wiley, 1902), pp. 421–422.
6. Francis B. C. Bradlee, *The Boston and Lowell Railroad, the Nashua and Lowell Railroad and the Salem and Lowell Railroad* (Salem: The Essex Institute, 1918), pp. 3–4; Alvin F. Harlow, *Steelways of New England* (New York: Creative Age Press, 1946), pp. 73–93; Edward C. Kirkland, *Men, Cities and Transportation* (Cambridge, Mass.: Harvard University Press, 1948), vol. 1, pp. 111–112.
7. [William Gibbs McNeill], *Report of the Board of Directors to the Stockholders of The Boston and Providence Rail-Road Company, Submitting the Report of Their Engineer . . .* (Boston: J. E. Hinckley and Company, 1832).
8. *Report of the Directors of the Boston and Worcester Rail-Road,* (Boston: Stimpson & Clapp, January, 1833), p. 23.
9. *Report of Boston and Worcester Directors to General Court of Massachusetts*, 1833, pp. 2–3.
10. *Report of the Boston Worcester Railroad*, 1840, p. 7.
11. Kirkland, op. cit., pp. 136–137.
12. *Proceedings of the Western Railroad Corporation, with a Report of the Committee of Investigation* (Boston, 1843), pp. 28–30.
13. Charles Francis Adams, Jr., "Boston," *North American Review* 106 (1868).
14. Reported in a paper by Henry A. Willis read before the Fitchburg Historical Society, in April, 1892. Quoted in William Bond Wheelright, *Life and Times of Alvah Crocker* (Boston: Privately printed, 1923), p. 46.
15. Caroline E. MacGill, *History of Transportation in the United States before 1860* (Washington, D.C.: The Carnegie Institution of Washington, 1917), p. 367.
16. Edward Hungerford, *Men of Erie* (New York: Random House, 1946), pp. 180–199.

17. Quoted in U. B. Phillips, *A History of Transportation in the Eastern Cotton Belt to 1860* (New York: Columbia University Press, 1908 [reprinted by Octagon Books, 1968]), p. 136.

18. Quoted in Samuel Malanchton Dierrick, *Centennial History of South Carolina Railroad* (Columbia, S.C.: The State Company, 1930), p. 27.

19. Ibid., p. 148. Phillips makes the mistake of locating the West Point Foundry at the site of the United States Military Academy rather than in New York City, where it stood.

20. Quoted in ibid., p. 43.

21. Ibid., pp. 162–163.

22. MacGill, op. cit., pp. 494–495.

23. Stewart Holbrook, *The Story of American Railroads* (New York: Crown Publishers, 1947), p. 163.

24. I. I. Stevens, *Narrative and Final Report of Explorations for a Route for a Pacific Railroad near the Forty-seventh and Forty-ninth Parallels of North Latitude from St. Paul to Puget Sound: Reports of Explorations and Surveys, to Ascertain the Most Practicable and Economical Route for a Railroad from the Mississippi River to the Pacific Ocean . . . 1853–1855*, vol. 12, book 1 (Washington, D.C., 1855).

25. Ibid., p. 331.

26. *Extracts from the [Preliminary] Report of Lieutenant A. W. Whipple, Corps of Geographical Engineers, upon the Route Near the Thirty-fifth Parallel, with an Explanatory Note by Captain A. A. Humphreys, Corps of Topographical Engineers,* in *Reports of Explorations and Surveys to Ascertain the Most Practicable and Economical Route from the Mississippi River to the Pacific Ocean, 1853–1854,* vol. 8 (Washington, D.C., 1856), pp. 23–37.

27. Major-General Grenville M. Dodge, *How We Built the Union Pacific Railway [sic.]* (Privately published, n.p., n.d.), pp. 142–143.

28. Ibid., pp. 108–109.

29. Quoted in Ward McAfee, *California's Railroad Era: 1850-1911* (San Marino, Calif: Golden West Books, 1973), p. 36.

30. Quoted in Neill C. Wilson and Frank J. Taylor, *Southern Pacific . . .* (New York: McGraw-Hill, 1952), pp. 13–14.

31. John W. Riegel, "Foreword" to reprint of the *Traveler's Official Railway Guide,* June, 1893 (National Railway Publication Company, 1972).

32. G. R. Stevens, *Canadian National Railways* (Toronto: Clarke, Irwin and Company, 1960), vol. 1, p. 23.

33. T. D. Regehr, *The Canadian Northern Railway: Pioneer Road of the Northern Prairies, 1895–1918* (Toronto: Macmillan of Canada, 1976).

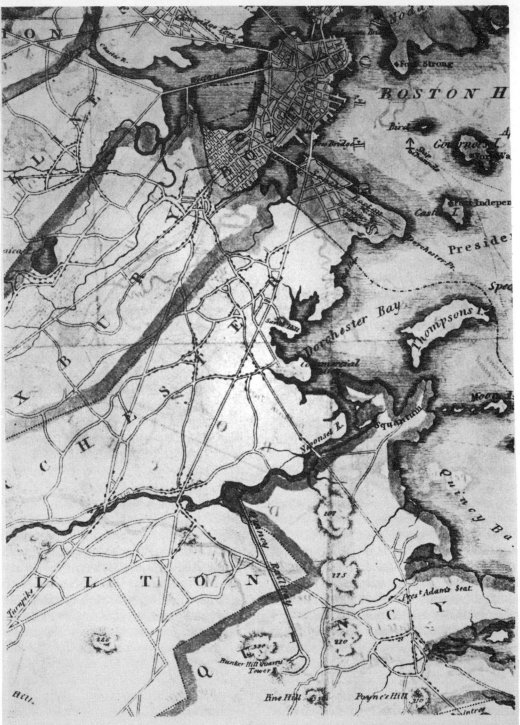

SECTION OF THE FIRST MAP TO SHOW THE FIRST RAILWAY IN AMERICA,
THE GRANITE RAILWAY (QUINCY RAILWAY)

This map was published in 1830

THE ROAD IN TRANSITION II:
THE RAILROAD YEARS

When we last considered the fate of road developments, the railroad was in prospect and a general suspension of interest in road improvements had begun. The traditional route of land transport had been relegated to a supporting role: to provide access from rural areas to canal docks or railroad platforms and to facilitate circulation within towns. Long-distance movements were made at first by waterways but ultimately by rail. In Britain, and later on the Continent, the railroad literally replaced waterway and road ties, using the already developed market as an economic justification for the investment of substantial sums of capital in a fundamental improvement of past facilities. Because the market was so densely developed in England, Wales and Scotland (decreasingly in that order), there was no difficulty in securing private investment for the construction of the new facilities, even when built to a very high engineering standard.

On the Continent the Industrial Revolu-

tion was still in prospect outside Belgium and northern and eastern France, so the Continental approach to railroad development was either of the state's provision of the infrastructure (as in France) or of that as well as the actual service to be run on the lines (as in Belgium, Prussia, and Austria-Hungary). In any of these European solutions the road played its important supporting role and was maintained at the level it had reached around the time of the advent of rails—seldom fundamentally improved but equally seldom neglected.

In North America the railroad took on quite different roles. Starting with the South Carolina Railroad of the early 1830s, the steam lines assumed an important function in developing economic activity within areas just then entering the ecumene of the United States. Elsewhere, where economies were relatively established—as in New England, for instance—the railroad became a substitute for the maintenance of long connecting turnpikes not earning their keep from tolls and of little interest to the town corvées. Unlike Europe, where governments were financially concerned in rail development (as on the Continent) and therefore interested in maintaining the tributary road system, or where road connections to rail platforms were short and essentially part of the parish circulation system (as in Britain) and thus maintained by the corvée or local rates, in the United States the coming of the iron rails tended to deteriorate the previous, rather primitive road network.

Two exceptions should be made to that generalization: roads continued to stand as a device for migration into new frontier areas, and they became the initial developmental device in those areas where the economic potential was either dubious or unfathomable. In this transitional section I wish to examine these two aspects of road development in North America during the railroad era. There is little new to be found in western Europe and little advance to be seen in the established ecumene of the United States. It was in the frontier West that the road continued to play a significant role in the period between 1830 and 1880—the halcyon days of the steam railroad, when it ruled not only grandly but nearly autocratically.

The two aspects of roads in the American West that must engage our attention are the emigrant trails, those direct descendents of the tracks and paths of colonial times, and the wagon roads constructed on the account of the federal treasury and constitutionally sanctioned because they crossed the Territories rather than any significant distances in the organized states. To accomplish this brief survey I shall depend primarily on my own much earlier work on the Oregon Trail and W. Turrentine Jackson's classic study of wagon roads in the American West.[1] As here we seek to understand only quite specialized aspects of road development in this period,

no wider survey of American or European transportation will be undertaken.

We have already seen that in colonial America a sharp distinction had to be drawn between economic and noneconomic travel; the paths and traces became well worn, but not by the oxen of hauliers as much as by the many different hooves of the migrants' teams. When those migrants had crossed the Appalachians and settled in Kentucky, Tennessee, and Ohio, they, of course, had had to establish economic routes to eastern and European markets, engendering the building of canals and artificial roads, such as the National Turnpike. Still, the sons of those frontiersmen were gripped by the same urge to move on, first perhaps to Indiana and Illinois; then to Missouri, Arkansas, and Iowa; but ultimately to the areas that came to be known farther west. The eastern Great Plains in Kansas and Nebraska at first repelled settlers—there was only grass, and the sort of agriculture Americans had known since Jamestown and Plymouth did not seem to exist once the trees gave out. The notion grew up that there was a Great American Desert, inhospitable to fixed agricultural settlement, lying to the west of the Great Bend of the Missouri River at Independence in western Missouri. When the most distant frontier reached that bend in the mid-1820s, hesitation among emigrants sent them from their westward course both north and south, into Iowa and Arkansas, respectively, in the 1830s. But in the early 1840s national awareness grew of the existence of a potential New Eden in the Oregon Country of the far northwestern coast of America, and the urge to push on to that lush green land gripped a number of American families, particularly on the Missouri frontier.

For the first time, potential American pioneers had a very different natural road before them. In the colonial period their ancestors had pushed up the coastal streams to the Fall Line and beyond, creating that potamic phase of American transportation already discussed. When the rivers narrowed to their founding springs, migrants had blazed traces through the forest to reach Kentucky; they had developed the Wilderness Road and its cousins as the characteristic emigrant trail. West of the Appalachians younger pioneers could return to the earliest phase of migrations, using the interconnected rivers of the Ohio-Mississippi-Missouri river system. At the Great Bend of the Missouri, however, none of these precedents seemed to serve: the river came down from the north heading in the wrong direction and having earned from Lewis and Clark the reputation as an exhausting way, probably hard to use by steamboats; and the country directly to the west of Independence didn't seem right—with no trees, it was thought so parched as to make the characteristic wagon journies impossible. In the 1830s more came to be known of those Great Plains; it was appreciated that in spring and early summer the grass on the plains could support wagon parties largely because the natural road was so broad—in some ways from the horizon on the left to that on the right—so that a new band of forage could be found simply by shifting over a hundred yards. Experimental journey by missionaries going to the Oregon Country in the late 1830s and early 1840s showed that a true natural road could be found that would carry a party to the Pacific if luck and guts were in good supply.

The movement to Oregon began with determination with respect to both time and the will of the migrants. In the early 1840s a few parties pushed west, but 1843 marked the beginning of the Great Migration that extended up to the time of World War I, though with few wagon parties after the 1880s, causing some 300,000 persons to pass by wagon over the trail that was marked out westward from Independence. To understand why so many passed this way, we must examine the location of the Oregon Trail and the conditions that determined that siting. First we must be aware that this road was a trace, not a trade route, even if it began as such. When we seek the origin of the Trail, we find it in unexpected directions and events. Fully in keeping with the potamic phase of American transportation, the first Americans to settle in Oregon came by sea—the Columbia River having been discovered at its mouth by a Boston ship captain, Robert Gray, possibly in 1788, certainly in 1792. Soon thereafter John Jacob Astor had established (just inside the bounding capes at its mouth) a fur-trading fort, Astoria, that managed to survive, though none too prosperously, until the outbreak of war between America and Britain in 1812. At that eventuality the nearby servants of the Northwest Company of Montréal attacked Fort Astoria, then—unaware of the hostilities—captured the post and sent the Astor employees literally packing eastward, there being no boat handy to take them home as they had come.

Passing up the Columbia, with some difficulty in its gorge where the river cuts the crest of the Cascade Mountains, the "returning Astorians" abandoned the river short of the vastly deep canyon and tormented stretch of the stream (in its tributary now called the Snake) in what came to be known as Hell's Canyon. Using a fur-trader's path across the rolling Blue Mountains of northeastern Oregon, their course returned to the Snake where that stream flows deeply entrenched in canyons cut into the surface of the vast lava plateaus of southern Idaho. With pack animals alone they managed to cross this rough, dry surface until they encountered the western spurs of the Rocky Mountain system in what is now the westernmost part of Wyoming. Luck was with them as far as terrain was concerned. The

Snake gave out at this point, reaching its origins in the Teton Range just to the north. But the other ranges of western Wyoming were discontinuous here, allowing the returners to lead their horses through the open and fairly broad valleys that form the divide between the Columbia (Snake) drainage and that to the northern tributary of the Colorado that is the Green. Once in the Green River Basin the Astorians faced the critical problem that any transcontinental migrants would have to solve—how to get through the Rockies with horses and other stock, even with wagons.

That problem had two aspects: how to crest the mountains and how to sustain the draft animals needed to do so. The Green River Basin was true desert or at least such stingy steppe that sustaining draft animals away from the exotic streams crossing it became difficult. One basic truth in the evolution of the western trails may not be widely understood: that neither distance nor elevation was a real barrier to the development of traces through the arid lands; those barriers, rather, were any stretches of true desert too wide to be crossed in a day by wagons (because of the absence of grass and water). A wagon team averaged some 25 to 30 miles a day if drawing a heavy load. To reach beyond that distance proved very difficult without rest for the animals, and grazing and water to restore them. The returning Astorians were not quite so narrowly restricted because they used only pack animals rather than wagons and thus their daily journeys could be lengthened. That advantage was partially lost in the fact that they were using horses, rather than the oxen, more commonly drawing heavy wagons, which could get by better without water.

The Astorians succeeded in finding a minimally practicable trace from the Green River crossing to the first of the eastward-flowing streams heading toward the Platte River and its confluence with the Missouri and then the Mississippi. That thin tendril of the Gulf of Mexico drainage was appropriately named the Sweetwater, because in a land of alkaline ponds its source in the snows and miniature glaciers of the Wind River Range lying 50 miles northeast of the Green River crossing, and its brisk flow, kept the stream sweet and usable for people and stock.

Once they were on the Sweetwater, the Astorians could begin to think of using the traditional pioneering transport of America, the canoe. As they moved eastward down the stream, it did not increase in size as most streams in the East did. Instead, its role was that of an exotic river, carrying water from a distant source across a parched and diminishing land. The fur traders had to continue eastward on horses, skirting narrow canyons on the stream and always looking for the expected growth of flow sufficient on which to launch skin boats. Even when the main stream of the Platte was met, the river did not truly avail them, causing the trekkers to chide the river as being one "flowing upside down," with the sand of the bedload seeming to move at its surface. Still, there was plenty of water and grass for the stock, and, after painfully trudging weeks, they reached the Missouri, a river that acted normally allowing the traders to regain the use of inland waterways that had advanced the American frontier during most of the transportation in colonial America.

The route the returning Astorians had laid out, mostly with their sweat in 1812, slowly came to be known on the Missouri frontier. During the next thirty years fur traders used it frequently to gain access to their annual *rendezvous* with the Indians in the central and northern Rockies, at which trade goods were exchanged for the prized beaver pelts. That trade, which might comprehend and overcome the maddening insufficiencies of the Platte, wore a discernible path. To locate it, the federal government sought to map the

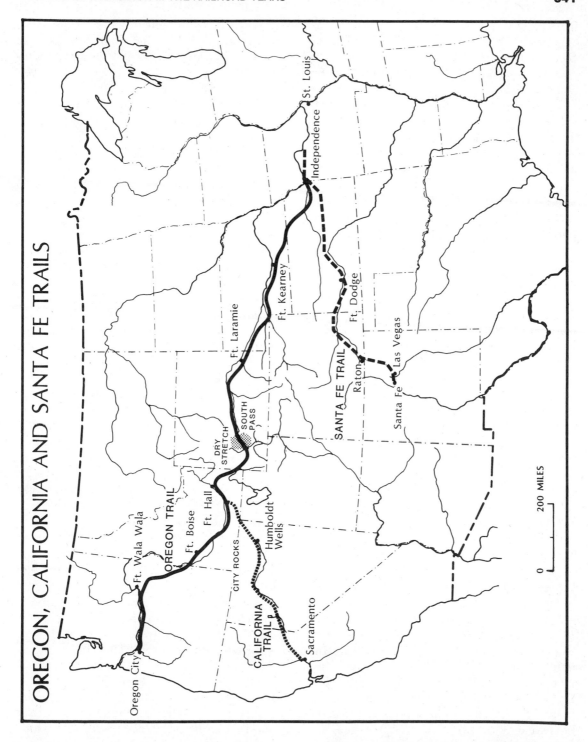

OREGON, CALIFORNIA AND SANTA FE TRAILS

trail in 1843 (at the hands of that peculiar "Pathfinder," John Charles Fremont, who could have followed the fur traders' path nearly blindfolded), making the trail to the frontier widely cited in the geographical lore of a country then terribly curious about such knowledge. When the phalanxes of emigrants began to reach the inhospitable Plains without having found a place to settle, the Oregon Trail was confidently accepted as "the way across" to a New Eden in the Pacific Northwest. By the early 1840s, when this state of emigration was reached, wagons had operated for some years over parts of the route, and the missionaries to Walla Walla had shown they might be taken all the way.

The Oregon Trail was far from the only migrant route—the track that branched from it in southern Idaho at "City Rocks" leading to the California gold fields had even heavier travel for a few years—but it was the classic example for modern times. As the emigrants organized the trek, they waited for the grass to spring up on the eastern plains, usually by mid-May, before setting off westward. Because of the considerable threat from the Indians of the plains, who tended to harry those on the Trail, the organized party became the normal unit to pass along the way. Conestoga wagons, or prairie schooners, were the most common vehicle, in which household and farm goods were carried along with those too young or too old to walk, as all adults tended to do. Cows and horses might be driven and chickens moved in cages; dogs, along with the boys, joined in a ceaseless investigation of the open ground that formed their path. For it was continuously open from the departure from Independence to the parklike groves and glades of the Blue Mountains of eastern Oregon. The animals could feed on the grass carpet of the eastern plains as far west as Fort Kearny in central Nebraska, where the

trail reached the valley of the Platte. Westward the plains became more sere, but the valley was wide and verdant in almost continuous meadows to the forks of the river. Using the northern branch, the Oregonians continued in grass both on a graded course and one heading generally westward to the foothills of the front range of the Rockies, the Laramie Range, which they skirted as it bent westward before lowering its crest to the level of the Wyoming Basin that separated the southern from the northern Rockies, leaving a high broad saddle easily passable by wagons so long as feed and water for the animals could be found. West of the northern arc of the Laramie Range the river continued to flow, but often in deep and narrow canyons without river meadows, so the going became harder.

By the Fourth of July the parties commonly reached a great rock tor in central Wyoming, which they named for that reason Independence Rock. Nearby they entered the shallow valley of the Sweetwater and gained better access to grass and water so their final climb on a gentle upgrade to the crest of the continent at South Pass was normally pleasurable and sustaining. Once on the crest, however, the greatest barrier lay directly ahead, in the 40-mile desert gap dividing the westernmost stream flowing toward the Gulf of Mexico from the northernmost affluent flowing to the Gulf of California. As already noted, by leaving in the evening and traveling for 24 hours, they managed to reach the Green River fatigued almost beyond endurance, but successful in continuing the westward migration. From the Green River toward Oregon the route was generally less hospitable, but nowhere was there the awful trial of the stretch west of South Pass. In the western Green River Basin the migrants had to shift from one thin stream of water to another, passing from one broad structural valley to its neighbor across dry sagebrush-covered divides, but none of these was as long as the South Pass-Green River stretch. Finally, in what is now southeastern Idaho, the master stream they had been following, the Bear River, turned southward to lose itself in the brine of Great Salt Lake, forcing the people on the trail to turn northward, again across a dry divide, to the Snake River near Fort Hall.

The passage along the Snake was always exhausting because the upland was a dusty, lava-broken surface with the water flowing far below in steep-sided canyons, not too deep but commonly unapproachable. In several places the argonauts were forced to cross the Snake or its major tributaries by using the wagons as makeshift boats in dangerous ferrying operations. Eventually the parties passed the lava plateau and confronted the Blue Mountains. Those mountains were reasonably rounded and clothed with open forest that might be traversed without too much difficulty to reach the Columbia river, the portal of their final objective in humid western Oregon. Passing along the southern bank of the great river to the gorge of the Cascade Mountains the trekkers were afforded reasonable grass and water despite the general aridity of the land. At that cleft in the mountains a real quandary faced them: the river was the only way through, but it was turbulent in the cascades that gave the range its name, and the mountain slopes were steep and densely covered with huge trees. At first there was rafting through the Cascades, but after a few years the need to facilitate the transit of the last barrier encouraged the opening of a toll road in a cut made through the forest to the south of Mount Hood. Increasing this, Barlow's Road, became the final approach to the New Eden, that logical continuation of the forested frontier that had attracted American pioneers since Jamestown and Plymouth.

The Oregon Trail led immigrants to the West but, in economic terms, it did not lead back to the East. When agriculture grew in the Willamette Valley, there was no possibility of using the trace to gain access to a market; it was no economic route. Only the Gold Rush in California at the end of the 1840s provided that, and then because the traditional water-borne transport could be resorted to anew. Grain, vegetables, potatoes, and similar staples, as well as livestock driven over the mountains to the Central Valley of California, began to support Oregon farming. But that agriculture remained isolated from the national market until the railroad arrived in the Pacific Northwest in the early 1880s. No economic highway across the country ever developed beyond the very specialized expression of road transport of precious minerals by wagon roads leading to the closest railhead. As the railroads were pushed westward those railheads grew closer, starting in the late 1860s with Sydney, Nebraska; Cheyenne and Green River, Wyoming; Corrinne, Utah; and Humboldt Wells and Elko, Nevada. Branch railroads could be pushed closer to productive mineral regions, such as the Utah Northern heading from Corinne toward the bonanza at Butte in Montana Territory. In opening up the interior to outside economic connection the wagon road played an important role but strictly a supporting one: the major artery was always the rail line leading over the vastness of the American interior.

Only in one case did the trail fulfill a primarily economic role. That came in the 1820s with the crossing of the southern plains, from Independence or even farther east in Missouri to Santa Fe in the northernmost part of the Mexican territories in the upper Rio Grande Valley. Because first the Spanish and then the Mexican authorities had decreed that European goods must reach this vastly distant Hispanic frontier via the port of Vera Cruz, a contraband trade with the nearer American frontier at the Great Bend of the Missouri River was a practicable alternative, as well as being largely overlooked by the local officials in New Mexico.

At first it might have been assumed that the trading trail to Santa Fe would depart from the Arkansas frontier, several days closer to the New Mexican capital and better served by early-spring and late-fall grass for the support of traders' animals. But we should not forget that in trade it is the established flow of goods that may matter most. By the 1820s when the Santa Fe trade opened, there was a continuous economic route extending from New England and the Middle Atlantic states—the hearth of American industry and mercantile effort— via the Erie and Pennsylvania canals, the National Road, and the Pittsburgh Pike to the Ohio River. Thence that tributary of the great Mississippi provided uninterrupted access to its right-bank tributary, the Missouri, that headed in the west and provided a direct route to its Great Bend at Independence. In economic terms,

> the preponderance of advantages was along the line of the Ohio, the city of St. Louis, the Missouri, and the upper Arkansas [River], which therefore determined the route of the Santa Fe Trail. This road, eight hundred miles in length from the last outfitting-point at the southern elbow of the Missouri, rising by such imperceptible degrees for three fourths of this distance as to seem quite level, guided straight across the thirsty stretches of the Great Plains by the eastward-flowing streams, bending then slightly southward to the gate in the mountain wall which opened upon the old Spanish city, made this the simplest and most direct connection between the emporium of the middle Mississippi [St. Louis] and the distribution-center of the upper Rio Grande valley. The sudden northward bend of the Arkansas between the ninety-seventh and ninety-eighth meridians brings the upper

course of this river parallel with the Kansas [River] and almost directly west of Independence, making its valley the natural supplement by land of the Ohio and Missouri route to New Mexico.[2]

Again, as for the Oregon Trail of later date, the Santa Fe route depended very heavily on the trail of grass:

> The Santa Fe Trail, after crossing the well-watered country [from Independence] to the Arkansas, followed the river westward as far as Bent's Fort in the early days, turned southwest up Timpas Creek and the Purgatory River into the Raton Hills, and over this ridge to the interlocking head streams of the Canadian and Pecos, which led to Las Vegas and San Miguel [New Mexico]. Fifty miles northwest across the mountains lay Santa Fe in its hill-locked valley. To the west of San Miguel the outer range of the Rockies is broken up into detached plateaus and ridges, between which the Apache Cañon, a pass three miles long and wide enough for only one wagon, carried the road over the watershed [into the upper Rio Grande drainage]. Thence with a slight dip it dropped to the elevated valley of Santa Fe (7,000 feet).[3]

That canyon forced the traders for the first few years to use pack horses to carry their goods, but eventually a wagon road was opened. Also the Santa Fe Trail had another diversion, symptomatic of the critical needs of an economic route. Although at first the line had lain along the Arkansas as far as Bent's Fort, that track was circuitous and thereby costly in time and the use of animals. To shorten the Trail to approximate a straight line from Independence to Santa Fe, it was necessary to make the Cimarron Cutoff passing directly from the vicinity of what became Dodge City, Kansas Territory, over the 50-mile-wide Cimarron Desert to the northern bend of the Canadian River that heads in the Sangre de Cristo Range just west of Las Vegas, New Mexico. In this way a direct line was carried to Las Vegas, avoiding the broken country on the Raton Hills, shortening the route, and giving a better approach to the Rockies. But it had a grievous fault of the same sort that attached to the South Pass–Green River stretch of the Oregon Trail: this 50 miles was too long to be crossed with ease without water and forage. "But the effort of the pioneer caravan to cross the desert to the Cimarron proved almost disastrous, and this stretch was always the scene of suffering for man and beast."[4] That suffering was borne because of the economic nature of this route, because there could be a considerable monetary return secured from the faster passage to Santa Fe and the larger loads that might be hauled along this "cutoff," particularly when it facilitated the substitution of wagons, with their higher competence, for the original pack horses.

THE WAGON ROAD OPENS THE WEST

The natural route, of the Oregon and Santa Fe trail sort, was obviously both the earliest and the most common way to the West. Given the open countryside, even in considerably mountainous areas, passage by pack horses, in many cases even by wagons, was entirely feasible without any works of man. The main problems were caused by two kinds of terrain: river valley crossings where the stream was cut down well below the surface in a narrow, if not always very deep, valley; and in crossing mountainous areas where no graded-valley approach to the crest could be found, leaving the slopes too steep to find footing along a practicable trail. At over 8,000 feet South Pass was high in the absolute sense, but it could be approached on either side by gently graded slopes, its crest was open and rounded, and there were no trees to interrupt even the pioneer movement. Glorietta Pass on the Santa Fe Trail just east of its western objec-

tive was similarly approachable and, though wooded, was clothed in a piñon-juniper stand open enough to allow wagons to pass. That trail in rising out of the Arkansas River Valley into the Raton Hills faced steep and difficult bits, though they were much lower in absolute elevation than its approaches to Santa Fe, so it was these that the Cimarron Cutoff sought to bypass, even at the expense of some dry and difficult desert teaming. In the Rockies, passage through became a complex problem. In the far south, aridity—really the absence of grass—became the barrier; but as the route was sought farther north, terrain assumed the adversary role in most of Colorado, with a return to aridity as the barrier in the break in the ranges that is the Wyoming Basin. In the far north, in Montana and northern Wyoming, terrain often opposed movement, and where it did not the increasingly dense forest cover impeded travel. Bernard DeVoto noted that in those northern reaches there were only three passes sufficiently free of tangled forest to permit wagons to move in a state of nature— South Pass, already discussed; Union Pass at the northern end of the Wind River Range, which was blocked by snow for much of the year; and Marias Pass in northern Montana, absolutely denied to the migrants by the fierce opposition of the Blackfeet Indians living at its eastern portal. The multiplicity of possible forces in opposition to movement meant that relatively few natural routes to the West existed, the Oregon and Santa Fe trails being the self-evidently better ones.

Although the federal treasury had been denied to the states for internal improvements through Jackson's 1830 veto of the Maysville Turnpike Act, no such constitutional restriction existed in the Territories. As the settlement frontier was pushed into those areas, federal monies were used to construct wagon roads—in Michigan, Wisconsin, Arkansas, Iowa, and Minnesota— often ostensibly to provide access to military posts and potential threats from the British in the north and the Indians in the Plains and Southwest. The sort of construction undertaken was small: routes were laid out, often to avoid swampy or excessively broken terrain, banks of streams were ramped to allow wagons to approach fords or ferrying sites, the crests of sharp intervening ridges might be notched to secure a more practicable grade for wagons. In Arkansas the crossing of the Mississippi floodplain for 30 miles west of Memphis was greatly impeded by the prevalence of standing water for much of the year. To overcome that, the Congress authorized the Army to construct an embanked road across these swamps starting in 1833.[5] A military justification was made for this construction, but it was argued as well that the route would be necessary to encourage migration to the public lands in western and southwestern Arkansas, where settlers might soon be numerous enough to seek statehood and thereby relieve the federal government of the considerable cost of territorial administration. This idea appears to have been sound; in "September 1836, 1,127 emigrants passed the working crews on the road."[6] Military roads in Iowa and Minnesota were undertaken particularly in response to the perceived menace of the Sioux and other Indians who threatened northern settlements. By 1840 it was possible to travel on roads paralleling the advancing frontier between the Louisiana-Arkansas boundary and the Great Lakes in Wisconsin.

The roads of this settling frontier must be distinguished from those pushed well beyond the most distant homesteader's cabin. Once the United States gained control of the Oregon Territory, in 1846, and of New Mexico, Arizona, Nevada, Utah, and California, in 1848, the responsibilities for administering and defending this vast territory required the most elemental road development without regard to migration and local settlement.

Army posts had to be established to try to protect those passing across this aboriginal interior to distant settlement areas—the Oregon Country after 1843, the Mormon settlements in Utah after 1847, and the Gold Rush towns of California after 1848. Given the still strongly aboriginal nature of the interior, there was no question that whatever development took place must be undertaken directly by the federal authorities and paid for by their funds. The main responsibility fell to the United States Army, either under its Corps of Engineers, organized in 1802, or a separate group, the Corps of Topographical Engineers, set up in 1830 specifically to make surveys of the West.[7]

By the 1850s it was clear that the Army system of roads in the West must be supplemented by one intended more for civilian and economic uses. Certainly the original and clearly arterial traces across the vast interior had been located and refined by the two Army Corps. In the absence of a settled population able to provide labor for road work, work parties of soldiers had done most of the construction in a sort of federal corvée. The Army was, however, increasingly engaged in trying to contain the Indians and force them onto reservations as the ever more numerous migrants passing through the Indian lands were producing conflict. In 1857 the government created a second agency to provide roads in the West, the Pacific Wagon Road Office, and placed it under the Department of the Interior rather than the War Department.[8] The intention was to create a system of wagon roads geared to civilian needs, to be located and actively advanced by "practical men" interested in neither military goals nor the scientific exploration that made the frontiersmen impatient.

The Pacific Wagon Roads Act grew directly out of the same political promotion that had created the Pacific Railroad Surveys of 1854, discussed in chapter 4. That signal work had established the probable routing for a railroad when it would be undertaken, but two factors vitiated its early construction: the fierce sectional conflict within the United States during the 1850s and the distinctly premature nature of transcontinental railroad promotions. The Congress could never have agreed on a single line to the West, of necessity favoring the South, St. Louis, or Chicago; and it could never, on the most sanguine appraisals of market support, justify the three lines that seemed the minimum of political practicality.

California was greatly disappointed at the impasse that resulted when the reports of the Railroad Survey were submitted. Agitation was undertaken in the Golden State to accomplish at least a partial improvement of the basic conditions of the pioneer track that was at best a natural road for some 2,000 miles. The argumentation clearly accepted a specialization of transport, acknowledging that the main purpose of the transcontinental road would be for emigrants—particularly the wives and children of earlier argonauts coming to the West to join them—more than for economic traffic. The latter was apparently accepted as an undertaking for shipping passing on the slow and greatly elongated route around the Horn. People, mail, and communications in general were the office of the transcontinental road as viewed by the California petitioners who memorialized Congress through the agency of Senator Weller of their state in May, 1856. The legislature in a resolution asked Congress to undertake "construction of a wagon road connecting that state with the Mississippi Valley, and the establishment of military posts and *watering stations* along the route to protect emigrants and mail carriers."[9] It was in response to that petition, after a considerable political compromise, that the Pacific Wagon Road Office was established and given a construction budget by Congress.

The 1857 act authorized the construction of (1) a central-route wagon road basically along the alignment of the Oregon Trail-California Trail from the Platte Valley of Nebraska to Honey Lake in northeastern California; (2) the location and improvement of a southern wagon road from somewhere in southwestern Arkansas (already reached by previously improved War Department roads) generally westward across the plains to El Paso, and through the newly acquired Gadsden Purchase to Yuma on the Colorado River; and (3) a road from Fort Defiance in western New Mexico to the Colorado River well north of Yuma. The last of the three found its "importance in extending westward into California a commercial route already established from Independence, Missouri, to Fort Defiance," to wit, the Santa Fe Trail begun in the 1820s by the traders of the Missouri frontier.[10]

The routes adopted can easily be anticipated by anyone with even the most basic understanding of where travel had flowed before 1857. Fort Kearny, where the Oregon Trail reached the Platte from the east, was adopted as the Mississippi Valley terminus of the central route, apparently because the natural conditions for a road east of there toward the Great Bend of the Missouri were adequate for emigrant travel. Toward the Pacific from Fort Kearny the Army had already begun improving the route over the Laramie Range at what later came to be known as Sherman Hill (Stansbury's Lodgepole Creek–Cheyenne Pass route on his returning from the Great Salt Lake) and via the Laramie Basin, Bridger Pass, and Bitter Creek to the Green River at their confluence. This, however, was still not a very practical emigrant route—because of aridity—so the Pacific Wagon Road Office set about improvement of the proven Oregon Trail route as far as Fort Hall and City Rocks in southeastern Idaho, where they continued their central wagon road westward on the California Trail to Humboldt Wells, along

Wagon parties passed over the Oregon Trail, even as late as the 1880s, as shown here. Union Pacific Railroad photograph.

the river of that name flowing westward there-from across northern Nevada, before abandoning that fast diminishing water course to head directly across the Smoke Creek Desert to the eastern boundary of California east of Honey Lake. That desert section proved difficult, so the more established emigrant routes southwestward to Carson Valley was improved and remained the more im-

portant approach to the Golden State.[11]

Perhaps the major shift away from the Oregon Trail came in Landers Cutoff west of South Pass, where Frederick Lander, superintendent of the building of this central wagon road, established a much more direct cross of the difficult Green River Basin by passing closer to the Wind River Range to gain access to the streams flowing therefrom, then across the narrower northern part of the structural basin and through passes in the Salt River and Wyoming ranges to reach Fort Hall on the Snake. Between South Pass and City Rocks Lander measured his route as 345.54 miles, shorter than the Trail, and he believed easier to pass over with ox-drawn wagons.[12] The clear intention of this wagon-road improvement as primarily an aid to emigrants is shown by the instructions of the Secretary of the Interior to Lander on his fourth and final season of work on the central route: "This being the last portion of the road over which the emigrants to California and Oregon have to pass after a long and toilsome march across the continent it is the desire of the Department to render its passage as comfortable and easy as the nature of the country and the means at its disposal will admit of."[13] In that season Lander's party turned their attention to the section of the road between the Humboldt River and Honey Lake, where water was the great problem. They began the construction of wells that were intended to make this direct but very dry passage less "toilsome," though those efforts were only partially availing. We cannot truly know because that fall Lincoln was elected president and the Civil War soon interrupted most migration across the continent.

The southern route to California was equally the expedient adaptation of wagon-road technology to fill the gap left by the political and economic impracticality of the 32nd parallel railroad plan. Proposed by Senator Rusk of Texas, advanced by Jacob Thompson, Secretary of the Interior, and Jefferson Davis, then Secretary of War, this was the pork barrel necessary to gain passage of the act creating the Pacific Wagon Road Office. As enacted the plan called for a road to extend from El Paso to Yuma, leaving the development of a route east of the western

Texas frontier to that state. The poor condition of roads in Texas can be determined by the fact that it took the construction parties all summer to pass from Memphis to El Paso, before they attempted any actual work. Once on the Rio Grande they set about making the provision of nature traversable by wagon through removing boulders in the relatively infrequent stretches so impeded, cutting mesquite brush where it stood for 60 miles along the course of the San Pedro River, easing the slope of washes, and particularly improving the facilities along the way for stock and human water. The route to be taken was basically that of the Railroad Survey, except west of the Rio Grande where the water supplies were too small and separated. The gentle upswell toward the almost imperceptible continental divide posed no problem other than water supply, but west of the divide some steep terrain was encountered before entering first the San Pedro Valley and then that of its master stream, the Gila, which led in a circuitous fashion to Fort Yuma on the Colorado River. It was decided through improving possible wells in the Gila Bend to cut off that arc, shortening the overall distance.

> The road was opened 18 feet wide on the straight stretches and 25 feet at curves. Timber, brush, and rocks were cleared from the right-of-way along the entire distance to facilitate passage of wagons. In making side-[hill] cuts or building up the roadbed, more than 50,000 cubic yards of earth and stone were excavated . . . . A major effort was made to reduce grades and to smooth the road surface, particularly in the Gila valley."[14]

As completed in 1859, the work on this road was of course very small in relation to its length, but it did make it possible to utilize what was truly a natural road to reach the southeastern border of California from Texas with wagons.

THE ROAD AS A DEVELOPMENTAL DEVICE

The period of wagon road construction in the West, 1846–1869 in Jackson's thinking, came as an effort to develop the West in a time when railroad construction would have been wildly premature. As we have seen in the previous chapter, it was the combination of increasing economic activity, with its enhancement of the demand for more efficient transit over the interior distances, and political motives that brought additional transportation facilities to the West, in the form of railroads. The California Gold Rush in itself was not sufficient: the response to it was California's petition to Congress for safer roads, leading to the formation of the Pacific Wagon Road Office in 1857. What finally forced railroad building in the West was the political objective of holding California in the Union during the Civil War. The Pacific Railroad Act of 1862 was aimed directly at maintaining the tie with the Union, thus the name adopted for its premier line. The very large subsidy needed to gain private construction of the transcontinental railroad speaks to the political motivation of the effort. Once the Union Pacific–Central Pacific line opened in 1869, it was a similar political pressure on the part of the other regions that had been examined in the Railroad Survey that brought succeeding lines, on the 47th parallel, the 35th parallel, and the 32nd parallel all in the 1880s. In a significant way we may argue that in 1854 much of the regionalization of the vast West of the United States was signaled and set by that survey. The pattern was clearly that of nature's shaping of terrain, but the multiplicity of lines was determined by a political parity firmly expressed in the call for the Survey and in its reported findings. Once those

"facts" had been established, the West expected them to be accepted in legislative action. That was done in the building of wagon roads in the first development phase of American transportation west of the Mississippi; that was also done with the creation of a federally subsidized railroad system between 1865 and 1885; it has been done in a similar regional transfer of funds in the Interstate Highway development since 1954.

The central fact to be drawn from all of this is that in a developmental operation, that is one wherein there is interregional transfer of capital from the rich and developed areas to the poor and undeveloped areas, through governmental intervention, there will be a strong geographical proportionality instilled largely by political philosophy, and the pressure of history. That weighty influence, shaped in 1854, exerted great influence on the geography of transportation in the United States ever since.

NOTES

1. James E. Vance, Jr., "The Oregon Trail and the Union Pacific Railroad: A Contrast in Purpose," *Annals of the Association of American Geographers* 51 (1961): 357–379; W. Turrentine Jackson, *Wagon Roads West* (Berkeley: University of California Press, 1952).
2. Ellen Churchill Semple, *American History and Its Geographic Conditions* (Boston: Houghton Mifflin, 1903), pp. 187–188.
3. Ibid., pp. 188–189.
4. Ibid., p. 189.
5. Jackson, op. cit., p. 7.
6. Ibid., p. 8.
7. Ibid., p. 2.
8. Ibid., pp. 173–174.
9. Ibid., p. 161; emphasis added.
10. Ibid., p. 173.
11. Ibid., pp. 201–206.
12. Ibid., p. 208.
13. Quoted in ibid., p. 216.
14. Ibid., pp. 226–227.

chapter 5

Dealing with Space within the City

The study of transportation is to a considerable degree the study of human history from its recognizable beginnings. At first the technology was truly innate: the ability of human beings to move about the earth's surface. Only after the passage of centuries, probably millennia, was there any assistance for human muscle in transporting goods and moving people. Rafts or primitive boats probably were the easiest addition to reduce arduous labor. Eventually horses and other animals were domesticated to the point they might be ridden or harnessed to aid in the eternal effort to overcome the constraint of movement imposed by muscle fatigue. It is surprising how long it took men to improve on these first assistants in extending the boundaries of "economical" movement. Despite some advances, in scalar terms it was not until the dawn of our Transportation Revolution—say, the last decades of the fifteenth century—that radical changes were wrought. Even then the improvements came almost exclusively in the matter of transportation over considerable distances—from the hinterland of the city to its gates, from one city to another, and after the Age of Discovery from one continent to another. Space within the city was still handled in a primitive—that is, innate—fashion. Men, and some women, carried goods on their backs and the wealthy in sedan chairs in much the same way. The streets of the medieval city were so narrow and tortuous that the traditional form of transportation—the one in use when the ground plan of the city was devised—had to continue until something happened to create a new and more commodious plan. Only in those cities so expanded by population growth as to make space within the city a trial to men's muscles—and then perhaps only in those few places sufficiently favored by reasonable safety from attack to allow the city to spread—was an alternative form of transportation used: boats. In Constantinople, Venice, and London, enclosed waterways were used. In Milan, the largest city of the West in the late Middle Ages, an internal canal system was devised at the dawn of the Transportation Revolution to gain this similar assistance to the straining muscles. But in most places space within the city had to be dealt with as all of space had been treated in earlier periods of human history.

Only when safety became more assured— or at least protected by defense of the frontiers of the national realm rather than the city's gates—and economic activity had burgeoned through the onset of the Mercantile and then the Industrial Revolution did space within the city become a pressing problem. No longer could goods be effectively transported on human backs or in the barrows that had served to accomplish the task for so long. This change came not merely from the increased spatial extent of the city but also from the enlarged scale of material that had to be moved. Particularly as that extent expanded, factories tended to be moved to the edge of the city where larger sites were to be had, reflecting the enlarged scale of manufacture and the improving extraurban transportation that could be used to handle the greater flood of goods. In Birmingham factory sites along the canal, navigation came into considerable use by the early nineteenth century, encouraging brass works, screw factories, and other modernized production facilities to be located there. By this time the provision of housing for the workers in these newer plants had become divorced from the offer of employment there; but workers continued to find part of their housing provision in the older part of the city, where tenements were shaped from buildings built at an earlier period. Those buildings had originally housed not merely the working class but the city's merchant and leisure class as well. For this transformation of the structures to working-class housing, not only the buildings but also the residential geography

of the city had to be reshaped. The middle class now sought housing toward the edge of the city, admittedly away from the factory sites found there, but still at some remove from the offices and shops where many were employed.

If the peripheral location of factories helped to solve the transportation problem of the manufacturers, it did nothing to aid the daily movement of people; rather, it aggravated that problem. Workers now had to engage in a specific journey-to-work, often a protracted one, in addition to their exhaustingly long working hours. Even the more fortunate classes shared with the workers the new experience of a wide spatial separation of their home from their workplace, something virtually unknown in the Middle Ages. That movement carried the potential for some aid to the human muscle. At first everyone walked to work, but as the middle class moved away from the city center their demand for assistance became exigent. Since they were possessed of sufficient income to expend a part on transportation in the daily journey-to-work, it is not surprising that the first developments in the intraurban transport of people took place in this activity. It was in the mercantile cities that the first efforts were made, probably because those places were both earlier in the onset of major growth than factory towns and possessed of a larger proportion of middle-class people working in the city center but living at its edge.

By the seventeenth century London had its boats moving on the Thames to carry this middle-class patronage, as Pepys's *Diary*, 1660–1669, makes clear. In the newer parts of the metropolis, where wider streets made wheeled vehicles usable, private carriages had increased in numbers with considerable rapidity in the late sixteenth century. In 1617 Fynes Morison wrote, "Sixty or seventy years ago coaches were very rare in England, but at this day pride is so increased, as there be few gentlemen of any account who have not their coaches, so as the streets of London are almost stopped up with them."[1] According to one estimate there were some 6,000 coaches in the metropolis in the 1630s, but their use was still restricted to a small part of the population. Most people walked wherever their business took them in the rapidly expanding body of London. To provide some aid for the group just below the possessors of private coaches, the hackney carriage was introduced by 1634, and Blaise Pascal put into service "public coaches on the model of stagecoaches" within they city of Paris in 1662.[2] All these efforts created costly conveyances that could not be used with any frequency except by the rich, leaving the basic problem unsolved as cities grew in the eighteenth century. For the well-to-do, who tended to move away from the heart of the city as places grew in size, the stagecoaches that came into wide use during that same century may have provided a reasonable way of moving from their houses in the Home Counties to business or social engagements in London. But for most people living and working within the metropolises there was no alternative to daily, sometimes considerable journeys on foot.

The solution to the passenger transportation problem in cities came in stages, each determined by an innovation that served the next lower economic stratum than that already served. The rich had gained coaches in the late sixteenth and seventeenth centuries; the upper middle class came to be served by hackney carriages certainly by the eighteenth century; but the broad middle class had to wait for the advent of the omnibus in the early nineteenth century for their need to be met. Only much later in the last century was anything done for the working class, as we shall see in the course of this chapter. The coaches and hackneys began passenger transport in cities, as wider streets allowed wagons to come into use to permit the horse-drawn movement of goods; but the first two centuries of change witnessed such a slow transformation that we may, in practical terms, begin our discussion of dealing with space in the city with the early nineteenth century and the introduction of the omnibus.

THE OMNIBUS AND THE FRENCH URBAN EXPERIENCE

France was the giant of the West, possessed of a population several times that of Britain, wealthy by comparison with most of its neighbors, and given to technical and administrative innovation. In the late Middle Ages Paris overtook Milan as the metropolis of the West so it should not surprise us that some of the earliest efforts toward solving the intraurban transportation problem were mounted there. France was the first western state to undertake a rational national transportation plan with the creation on November 28, 1713, of the Corps des Ponts et Chaussées—an organization charged not only with caring for roads and bridges but also with creating a corps of trained engineers to accomplish the task effectively.

Under the guidance of the Corps the communication among cities was rapidly improved. Geographers and engineers were to examine all plans and maps of routes and grand highways of the realm to assure they were properly designed, constructed, and located.[3] Highways were to be built to connect Paris with the frontiers of the realm and its ports seeking both the protection of the national state and the advance of its economy. In this way the kingdom was to find a solution to its large-scale transportation problem. Even in the metropolis the Corps was to work with local officials to find ways to improve movement about the city of increasing extent. Perhaps relatively little was accomplished, but some streets were widened, straightened, and made more usable by wheeled vehicles than they had been in medieval times. At least the stage was set for improvement when a strong central government could assert its will. This came with Napoleon, who shared with all dictators a passion for ceremonial avenues and with a few others the power to accomplish many such designs. Particularly important had been the adoption in 1787, just before the Revolution, of a new and far more powerful method of financing and constructing public works than the ancient corvée that had served France, and other countries, up to that time. This medieval requisition of labor from adjacent landowners and serfs, used to build and maintain roads, had never been particularly effective. Its abandonment in favor of the imposition of taxes on abutters and wider political units (to be used to hire workers, engineers, and teams to carry out the construction in a professional manner) was strikingly effective in gaining improved highways.[4] Under the Empire labor became even more plentiful when the numerous prisoners of war captured during Napoleon's aggressions on his neighbors were used on construction projects in Paris and the provinces. Canals and roads were actively under construction until just before 1814, using troops not needed in the interludes of peace or prisoners of war during the times of conflict.[5] This program took on such a scale that the provinces regretted the loss of the corvée, and some even reintroduced it with the approval of the imperial government.[6]

Much as the fall of Napoleon brought a great part of this earnest activity to a halt, the experience of improved communication, the persistence of the Corps des Ponts et Chausées, the successful replacement of the corvée by tax-supported construction in most areas, and the beginning of the democratization of French society all contributed to a climate of experience and opinion that encouraged further efforts to solve transportation problems. It was fortuitous that the first marked improvement came in the small provincial city of Nantes in 1825. There a former general, Stanislas Baudry, in 1823 purchased a steam-operated flour mill in the suburb of Richebourg and set about its economical operation. In doing so he found he had considerably more steam than was required to operate its milling machinery so he turned his thought to running a steam-bath, a facility for which there was a current fad as part of the rise of hydropathic medicine in the early nineteenth century. But his bath was rather removed from its potential customers residing in Nantes itself so he sought to devise a form of genteel public transit to bring sufferers to his baths.[7]

Baudry's solution followed on earlier French experiments at such genteel transport starting perhaps with the creation in 1464 of the royal postal carriages, vehicles large enough so that occasional passengers of social or political prominence might be transported between French cities. By 1690 these ad hoc arrangements were succeeded by the introduction of the diligence, more speedy and comfortable than the postal coaches, which united Paris with most provincial cities. At the same period that the postal service was being introduced over long distances, the urban carriage came into use by the royal family and the most powerful members of the nobility. The Course la Reine was laid out west of the walls of Paris for such carriage driving, and the newer parts of the metropolis had streets wide enough to permit the small number of carriages to pass. But the lesser nobility and grand bourgeois could not afford carriages and were not encouraged to seek them as the crowding consequent thereon would be considerable. At this pass the thinker Blaise Pascal came up with an ingenious proposal for the operation of public carriages carrying a few passengers. In 1661 he, the duc de Roannes, the marquis de Crenan, and the marquis de Souche applied to the king for permission to operate carriages "which will follow the same route in Paris from one quarter to another; ... for a fixed five sols and departing at regular hours ...." Such a service followed on the introduction in 1623 of carriages for rent, which came to be called *fiacres* because their first stand was opposite an *hôtel privé* bearing the arms of St. Fiacre. Under Pascal's scheme more than one party would be carried and thus the cost would be somewhat reduced. But since soldiers and other persons in livery or from the working class could not be transported, the service was very unpopular with the great body of Parisians. The life of these *Carrosses à Cinq Sols* was short despite the fact that five routes across Paris had been inaugurated in 1662. The last carriages were abandoned in 1677.[8]

During the eighteenth century Parisian passenger transport was restricted mainly to private *carrosses bourgeois*. With the Revolution, however, these were suppressed and the stage was set for a renewal of a Pascalian scheme, but with a less restrictive clientele. General Baudry's experiment at Nantes in 1825 filled that need. He had not sought to devise a public transit scheme as we commonly define the practice, though he did permit those to ride who paid his modest fare even if they did not resort to his steambath, as most seemed not to do. Realizing that his transport service was more profitable than his baths, he began to introduce a wider service of these vehicles, which, in a play on words, he called *omnibus* because their city terminus was adjacent to a hatter by the name of Omnes whose sign read "Omnes Omnibus"—a sentiment that seemed appropriate to this first transport for persons without reference to class.[9]

Baudry expanded his omnibus routes in Nantes and sought to begin such a service in Paris. In 1828 a network was laid out in the capital, and vehicles carrying fourteen passengers at a fare of 25 centimes were introduced. This was not yet proletarian transport, but it did lie within the reach of middle-class Parisians, who came to use it with enthusiasm. Soon other operators began to run omnibuses on the streets of the capital—buses called variously "Dames Blanches" (for an opera currently a favorite), Favorites, Carolines, Diligentes, Béarnaises, Citadiens, Ecossaises, and Batignollaises. Chaos took control of the streets and the authorities had to intervene. But first Baudry, fearing bankruptcy, committed suicide in 1830 by throwing himself into the Canal Saint-Martin. In 1836, the Compagnie des Algériennes introduced zonal fares, to permit lesser charges for short journeys. That year there were sixteen omnibus companies in Paris, with a total of thirty-five lines. By 1855 the number of companies had shrunk to ten and the lines to thirty, but there were three hundred omnibuses on the streets of Paris. That was the year of the first great Parisian exhibition, which drew throngs to the city. Baron Haussmann, prefect of Paris, succeeded in bringing the ten companies together as the Compagnie Générale des Omnibus, given a monopoly for thirty years. Cars were enlarged to twenty-four seats, routes were reorganized into twenty-five lines represented by letters of the alphabet, and service to the suburbs was offered in smaller vehicles of a *"service accessoires d'omnibus"* and *Messageries des Environs de Paris*. By 1860 there were 503 omnibuses circulating, drawn by a stable of 6,700 horses. The provinces followed suit with omnibus service introduced in Le Havre in 1832, Lyon in 1837, Rouen in 1856, and Toulouse in 1863. London began its service when George Shillibeer introduced the French innovation in 1829, and started in Vienna in 1872.[10] The United States was quick to adopt this partially democratic conveyance, with omnibuses operating in Philadelphia and New York in 1831—more than a hundred were operating in the latter in 1836—while Boston had the 'buses in 1835 and Baltimore 1844.[11] The American experience was far less enduring than the French but generally more rapid than among the Continentals.

London proved as fertile ground for omnibus development as Paris. Within a decade of opening, the service was heavy and lines widely ramified. Along sixteen radials from central London, ominbuses and "short stages" reached to some thirty-four exterior destinations with each radial licensed for at least ten vehicles and the most heavily traveled, that toward Paddington, certified for more than two hundred omnibuses.[12]

> It is most significant that the main drive in London's suburban development continued to be to the north-west, to the district then known as Tyburnia (which was largely built between the later 1830s and the 1850s) and beyond, and it was from that direction that the omnibus [even after the coming of the steam railroads] still derived its main support. While effective railway competition was held off by difficulty of getting railways into central London, omnibuses continued to gain traffic.[13]

It is hard to tell just how many Londoners used the omnibus. Barker and Robbins cite an 1854 inquiry that seemed to show about 200,000 persons coming into the City of London on foot, 15,000 by steamboat, 6,000 by steam railroad, and possibly 26,000 by omnibus. In other words, the omnibus was used by more passengers than the other two forms of public transportation combined. But those vehicles could hardly have been of much use to the working class, as they did not commence running until 8:00 A.M., and we know from the timing of the parliamentary Workingmen's Trains that that hour was too late for those in the laboring class.[14] Still, the popularity of the vehicle meant that numbers grew rapidly, capacity was increased from 15 to 22 passengers, charges levied by the government for use of the

streets were reduced, and seats were standardized at 16 inches—a figure that would make even the economy airline passenger groan in contemplation. In 1846 fares were reduced to 2 d. for short journeys, but such a figure was woefully beyond the command of workers, who might earn no more than 2/6 per week. To cross London the fare was standardized at 6 d. in 1851, and shorter journeys were raised to 3 d., thus assuring that this remained basically middle-class transportation.[15] Fares might drop when trade was slack, but they never remained long at a level that would permit the use of the omnibuses to become truly popular. Instead efforts were made to create a monopoly, which would rationalize the services in a desirable way but could be expected to keep fares high enough for handsome profits.

In 1855 a French company, Compagnie Générale des Omnibus de Londres, was organized. During the next year it bought out most of the London operators and created the monopoly that many reformers, including Edwin Chadwick, considered desirable. One assumed benefit was the introduction of transfers at points of correspondence among the individual lines—a system that had been pioneered in Paris and found to work well there. In London, however, it did not seem to function so effectively. It was argued plausibly, that this was due to the greater size of London and other peculiarities of British practice. There was constant friction between the company's French board of directors and its British operatives, often over the wisdom of introducing Parisian practices in London. The chauvinism on both sides was considerable—expressed as "rationalism" from the south and as "Britain is different" from the north of the Channel. Finally, the only solution was to relocate the headquarters of the L.G.O.C. which came in 1859, creating a British monopoly where previously there had been a French one. The effect was not

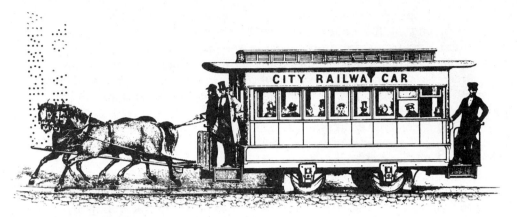

Horse-car on city railway, Philadelphia. *Source*: Alexander Easton, *A Practical Treatise on Street and Horse-power Railways* (Philadelphia, 1859).

conducive to innovation at a time when George Francis Train and some French promoters sought to introduce horse-car lines to London as they had existed for a generation in the United States and for many years in Paris.

The available data do not provide a detailed picture of the use of the omnibus even in London, where social surveys were not unknown even at the middle of the last century. We do know that the numbers of riders on the L.G.O.C. omnibuses continued to rise before the advent of the underground railway—from 38,899,247 in 1859 to 42,768, 248, the year before the underground opened.[16] Judging from the level of fares and the information we have on vehicles passing along various routes, it seems that the well-to-do suburbs provided the greatest market for the omnibus. To the extent the middle classes continued to move farther away from the City and other business areas, use of these vehicles would have become ever more essential. Certainly the problem with their congesting of the streets of the metropolitan core was constantly raised; it became obvious that were this secular increase to continue, conditions in the City and its immediate environs would become intolerable.

Still, it was not for the great body of city people that the 'bus services were undertaken. When there were approximately 26,000 omnibus riders a day—of whom Robbins and Barker figure perhaps 20,000 were commuters—there were fully 200,000 Londoners who reached work in the City on foot. To adapt Disraeli's image of the two nations of Britain, we may say there were two cities—that of a small middle and upper class served by public transportation and increasingly resident in Tyburnia and other accepted suburban areas and that of perhaps ten times as many persons forced to live close to the center, or to outlying mass employers, and reaching their work on foot.

Paris seems to have made better and greater use of the omnibus at this time. After the merger of the competing companies in 1855, passenger totals rose from 40 million that year to 74 million five years later, 107 million ten years later, and 115 million in 1873[17] Service was carried throughout the much more compact city and well into its suburbs and industrial satellites, such as Nanterre, St. Denis, and Vincennes. With a population perhaps only half as large as London's (in 1841 Paris had 935,261 inhabitants, whereas London had 1,825,714), the French metropolis seems to have run consistently ahead in the number of omnibus riders. Evidently the local authorities were better able to make use of this conveyance there. No doubt the wider streets of Haussmann's Paris encouraged the adoption of the omnibus, and the stability of fares throughout the nineteenth century made the service progressively cheaper as wages rose as a result of labor organization. The result was a sixfold growth in public transit passengers between 1855 and 1890 to 250 million per year (of whom 187 million, or 74.4 percent, still moved by omnibus despite the introduction of streetcar lines operated both by horse and mechanically), and the perpetuation of the "omnibus boats" that had plied on the Seine since the early nineteenth century.[18]

An appraisal of the overall role of the omnibus in the nineteenth-century city must be based on only partially surviving evidence. What we do know, however, suggests that this medium served particularly the middle class, perhaps with a somewhat higher income orientation in London than in Paris. Historians have become convinced that for the working class the first two-thirds of the last century witnessed little assistance by public transit to the main body of urban population, those whose incomes were simply not sufficient to cover the cost of more than very infrequent use of omnibuses or horsecars. To the extent the bourgeoisie grew with the rise of trade and manufacture, there was an increasing market for these transit systems. We do know that city streets came to be increasingly crowded with their vehicles. The existence of transit also encouraged the fortunate groups that might afford to use it to move their residence outward from the city cores, which were becoming increasingly crowded, and thereby unhealthful as a result of the need to bring people together for economic purposes coupled with the inability of the earlier transit systems to provide economically transportation for the mass of the population. There seems to have been some difference between the Continent, where the apartment house was the norm for all but the most elevated levels of society, and Britain, where row housing served as widely, though producing much more spread-out cities. Because the distances were shorter in Continental cities, walking for ordinary journeys and autobus riding for more exceptional trips must have provided a more efficient transportation system across a manageable space than was to be found in British cities. Most British and American cities fell within reasonable pedestrian limits, but London and New York were too large. That was why the mitigation of the narrow utility of omnibus travel came first in those cities: in the American case in the effort to produce a more widely available and therefore cheaper transit, and in the English in the extension of the avowedly middle-class steam railroad farther in toward the core of the city in order to improve the journey of the prosperous and the spread of their housing ever farther out in Tyburnia or other suburban realms.

AMERICANS SEEK A DEMOCRATIC SOLUTION: THE HORSE-CAR

An interesting argument has been joined as to how the Americans invented the horse-car line, what they sought, and why it took so long to bring the technology to a reasonable state of development. But first the facts. In the early 1830s, at the onset of railroad development in the major cities of the northeastern United States, New York City (then comprising what is now the borough of Manhattan alone) faced a particularly awkward problem. The city was founded at the very southern tip of the elongated Manhattan Island and by the early nineteenth century growth in scale and specialization in land use within the city had made Lower

Manhattan the site for business activities, shipping, and manufacture more than residence, which was being moved northward along the long axis of this narrow island, thus exaggerating the distance of the necessary journey-to-work. When railroads were introduced in 1832, it was decided to build the New York and Harlaem Railroad from Prince and Fourteenth streets northward to its eponymous terminus through open country of farms and a few country houses. Even Fourteenth Street was well removed from the business core of the city, so some means was sought of traversing that distance, which was too great to walk easily. The method devised has been viewed either as the introduction of a new form of transportation or merely as a specialized version of the railroad.[19] The former view seems more justified by the facts: that the horse-car line was first constructed from Prince to Fourteenth Street well before the construction began on the railroad line from Twenty-fourth Street northward;[20] that an effort, aborted by protests, was made to carry the horse-car line even farther south to Bowling Green, well beyond any possible railroad terminus; that the street guideway laid down was an attempt, though unsuccessful because of poor street maintenance, to create a nearly flush guide by using a "track" with a groove an inch deep and 2 inches wide on the upper surface of granite stringers 8 feet long and 13 inches square, further clad with a strip of iron an inch thick to bear the running wheels;[21] that this horse-car route was always run as a separate operation from the N.Y. & H. Railroad; and that the successor New York Central System continued to operate horse-cars independent of its mainline operations in New York City until after 1900, when it finally yielded its franchises to electric traction companies. All this evidence seems amply to justify the view that the New York City horse-car operation may have begun because a railroad was under consideration; but that, as is so often the case with innovations, it took on a life of its own with distinctive cars, traction, track, and a continuous life down to the time of the abandonment of streetcar lines in Manhattan in the 1930s.

This then was the origin of the horse-car, which continued to operate in Manhattan until the coming of electric traction. Merlin's notion that the service was interrupted and only restored when a French engineer improved the track seems unsupported. There is no question that the basic form of the street-running light railway with horse traction came into existence in 1832, not merely in New York City but also in New Orleans, where in 1835 a line was laid down to Carrollton, a suburb four and a half miles to the west.[22]

After this dual start—which demonstrated the utility of rail-guided and supported transportation in American cities where the streets were largely unpaved yet the distances of city journeys were often quite long— little more seems to have been accomplished for twenty years. In 1852 a French engineer, Alphonse Loubat, who was working in the United States, designed a grooved rail that might be installed with its top surface flush with the street pavement, thus avoiding the obstruction to crossing traffic that had been posed by the slightly elevated strap rail of the original New York line on Fourth Avenue and a later L-shaped rail used in Philadelphia shortly thereafter (on a street extension of what was essentially a steam railroad). As laid down on Broadway in New York in 1853, Loubat's rail was essentially an ordinary edge rail of the sort used on standard railroads, with a U-shaped trough several inches wide and deep attached to its inner side in such a way that the pavement might be butted against it and still leave a depression in which the wheel flange might advance. This invention certainly made the street railway more acceptable to other users of the street.

In 1856 Boston followed on the earlier experience in New York and New Orleans with a line from the Hub to Cambridge, Brooklyn entered the ranks of horse-car cities, and New York City expanded its routes markedly at this time. In 1858 Philadelphia gained a regular street railway, which apparently used the L-shaped rail; rather quickly thereafter most large American cities became equipped with such horse-car lines. The result was that when Loubat returned to Paris in 1853, he acquired a franchise to allow him to operate such a *"chemin de fer Américain,"* as the French seem always to have designated horse-car lines, in the capital. At first the doubtful public-works authorities demanded that a demonstration line be built. One was laid out in the broader streets in the western part of the city, along with Quai de la Conférence (the Cours la Reine of the previous century) and the Quai de Billy (the present Quai New York). The trial with the groove rail on November 21, 1853, proved highly successful. An imperial decree was issued on February 18, 1854, authorizing the building of a horse-car line from Sèvres and Boulogne in the western outskirts to the Place de la Concorde. Thence tracks could not be used, as they were thought obstructive of ceremonial traffic entering and leaving the adjacent Louvre and Tuileries. Even west of the Place de la Concorde the cars ran with flanges on only the right wheels, so that they might be derailed easily to pass around possible obstructions on the tracks. This awkward arrangement persisted until 1867, when a second Exhibition was held in Paris, necessitating an improvement in city transit. To accomplish that the *Américain*, as it had come to be called, was equipped with two sets of wheels, those with flanges to operate on the rails and flat broad wheels to operate from Concorde into the heart of Paris. It is interesting that when this substitution was made, an additional horse had to be harnessed to the car

to overcome the increased friction of the broader wheels running on a rougher pavement.[23]

While Paris was adopting the *Américain* at a very deliberate pace—only three lines, all in Paris, were built before the Franco-Prussian War—the rest of Europe was examining the form. Again the American influence was direct: George Francis Train (son of Enoch Train, who was one of the great American shipowners during America's age of sail), his father's agent in Liverpool and one of the more interesting men of the nineteenth century as a promoter, developer, politician, and civil libertarian, sought to introduce horse-car lines to Britain. At least that was his view of the matter. In 1859, at the age of thirty, Train went to Britain with the avowed purpose of "introducing" what had become a common American conveyance to a much more urban milieu than that in which it had developed. By the last five years of the 1850s horse-car lines had been opened in Boston, Philadelphia, Baltimore, Pittsburgh, Cincinnati, and Chicago. By then New York had its original route on the Bowery and Fourth Avenue, and a second line opened on Sixth Avenue in 1851.[24] Although Train refused to acknowledge it, there was a quasi-streetcar line even then in existence, operating along the Mersey docks in Liverpool, though he had some justice on his side in disparaging that as more an industrial than a true street-railway line. In any event, on his arrival he sought to interest the authorities in the larger English cities in the form of street railway he had in mind, including a "step-rail" of L-shaped cross-section similar to what had been introduced into Philadelphia in 1857 (he held a patent on an improved form of step-rail). The notion behind this was that gravel would not collect along the rail, as it would in a grooved rail—a problem much greater in America with its largely unpaved streets than it was in Europe with its paving blocks. English authors tend tediously to portray Train as "visionary," eccentric, uninformed, and generally "unsound," that most scathing of British epithets. In some measure this was because of his step-rail. Yet in the context in which Train had had to operate in America, where he was a major figure in the promotion of the Erie Railroad extension (known as the Atlantic and Great Western), it was not so unsound to support a form of street-railway track that showed its utility on an urban frontier. Also, Train attempted his promotion of street railways in Britain just at the time the powerful classes there were openly supporting the Southern side in the Civil War while Train, a New Englander in birth and spirit, was a staunch and vocal supporter of the North. Flamboyant and boastful though Train was, there were greater strengths in his efforts than his British critics care to grant.

Train attempted to demonstrate the utility of a true street railway by constructing and operating one. To do that he had to secure permission from some local authority to lay down his track. After a number of failures he finally received permission from the city of Birkenhead to lay a line 1.25 miles long from Woodside Ferry to Birkenhead Park with loop terminals, at a gauge of 4 feet 8.5 inches (though Train referred to this as a 5-foot 2-inch gauge because he measured from the outside of his step-rails rather than their inside separation, as is the standard practice). Once permission was given, he acted with great dispatch, and the line was opened in six weeks, on August 30, 1860.[25] The undertaking was immediately successful, and the step-rail did not prove an insurmountable problem, though it was subsequently replaced by groove-rail. No doubt part of the reason for this success was that Birkenhead was a fairly typical industrial and port town, one where the working class was dominant

and their interests tended to be regarded (as was shown by the opening there in 1847 of one of the first public garden parks, itself the terminus of Train's horse-car line). In this more proletarian context the virtues of the horse-car line were manifest, and there was not the selfish elite found in many British cities whose transit was assured by carriage and whose concern for those without carriages was undiscernible.

The success at Birkenhead did not herald wide adoption of the horse-car in Britain. Even before the northern line was opened, Train succeeded in having his proposal for a line between Westminster Abbey and the new station under construction that became Victoria considered and approved. Shortly afterward a second line on the Bayswater Road was agreed to, as well as a route from Westminster Bridge to Kensington Gate. The first to be laid down was that of the Marble Arch Rail Road, completed in March, 1861, over a route from the Edgeware Road westward along the Bayswater Road a mile to Porchester Terrace. Constructed to the standard railroad gauge, only a single track on the south side was finished, leaving the eastbound cars to operate against the flow of traffic, an awkward and dangerous practice.

No doubt such innovations failed to increase the popularity of Train's street-railway lines with those operating carriages and wagons. Benjamin Hall, a member of Parliament and first commissioner of works in the Palmerston government, was an implacable foe of street railways because earlier in his life he had twice seen his carriage upset while crossing the tracks of Welsh plateways. His opposition meant that none of these London experiments was either sufficiently extended or long-lived enough to present a fair trial of the medium, so we cannot be too certain whether powerful opposition or technical faults brought the tests to a quick and unfavorable end. Until Hall, who was subsequently rusticated in the House of Lords, died in 1867, the street railway had little chance to show its merits in Britain.[26] Klapper notes:

> Train's tramway managed to arouse an enormous amount of opposition on the pattern set by Sir Benjamin Hall. This was stirred up by Train's grandiloquence, the fact that his first line was not in a workaday neighbourhood but ran to nowhere in particular in a district stiff with the carriage folk most likely to be adversely affected by it, and by a series of accidents arising from the step rail and from working eastbound against the normal direction of traffic.[27]

It seems that a poor understanding of the critical social geography of London on Train's part combined with a considerable element of chauvinism and selfishness among the denizens of Bayswater to make this no fair trial. Train was forced to remove the rails from Bayswater Road at his own expense by October 4, 1861; his other two experimental stretches of horse-car lines were ordered abandoned by June of 1862.

The American also was instrumental in building short lines in Darlington, the hearth of the steam railroad, and in the Potteries of North Straffordshire. The first line was soon abandoned, but the Potteries route survived, though sold by Train in 1864 when his interests called him back to the United States. It began directly at the White Cross Street jail, where Train had been imprisoned for refusing to pay judgments against him that he considered unjust. While behind bars he had engaged in a very strenuous support of the Union cause in the Civil War, with a torrent of criticism of British favor for the Confederacy such that the authorities finally decided it would be best to allow him to depart for America, debts unresolved, rather than have more sermons on the downfall of England. In turn the Boston

Daily Evening Traveler reported shortly thereafter: "We observe that it is announced that this irrepressible Union orator and embodiment of Young America is now en route for Boston and will arrive on Friday. The Prince of Wales' suite of rooms are reserved for his reception at the Revere House." On arrival he took the platform in Tremont Temple on September 14, 1862, voicing appreciation of his departure from street-railway promotion in England with its dangers:

> Thank God I am again in a civilized country; thank God I am again in a Christian land! . . . . [He argued that England was no longer the] mother country . . . there is not more than one-tenth English blood among us. Let us think for ourselves, for we are a superior race.

Calling for a boycott of English goods and for an emancipation from cultural dependence on England, Train set about other tasks.[29]

England was certainly relieved to be rid of the "irrepressible Union orator" and irritating horse-car promoter. The effort for transportation improvement could now take a more acceptable course, that of caring for the needs of the middle and upper classes through the development of the underground extensions of the suburban railroads. Only in 1870 were any horse-car lines built, now fully under British aegis and control, as was the London General Omnibus Company as well by this time, so disturbing and unsound foreign practices might be avoided. In the remainder of the last century lines were laid out in most larger British towns, and in those where the working class tended to play a dominant role—Birmingham, Leeds, Manchester, and Liverpool as well as the Scottish cities—the horse-car lines gained great importance and ramification. But only with electrification of the traction did the streetcar finally come into its own as the great democratic transporter.

In summing up the role the horse-car lines played in the evolution of urban transportation, it is important to make several points, the most important of which is that these services were still so relatively costly that the tendency was for them to serve only the very best paid workers and the petite bourgeoisie rather than the great mass of daily commuters. Horse-car services were instrumental in allowing fairly extensive middle-class suburbs to grow around most cities, areas whence in the middle of the day cars came to the city-center shopping areas bringing women to make purchases there, whereas during the commuting hours cars transported the upper echelons of office workers to their jobs. Also at this time the functional linkage between such horse-car services and public parks and recreation areas began to be established. The first effective line in Britain led from the ferry dock to the park in Birkenhead. A similar situation existed with respect to The Fenway in Boston, Central Park in New York, Prospect Park in Brooklyn, and cemeteries in those cities, including the first of the great park cemeteries, Mt. Auburn Cemetery in Cambridge. The horse-car did permit space to be built into the urban structure, not merely in more extensive and somewhat more spacious housing areas but also in the sense of public open space of the sort that was scarce in most cities, though present in a few striking exceptions such as Hyde Park in London and The Common in Boston. The average city had to wait until the horse-car and, even more, the trolleycar lines were laid down to gain access to public recreational space on any appreciable scale.

No doubt one of the major influences of the horse-car lines was the simple familiarization with the advantages of urban transportation it provided for those who had previously had to walk. Even though housing might be shifted outward by the availability of horse-car service, at least at first the increments to the housing supply were still practicable for a pedestrian journey. Once the workers had become accustomed to riding, it is unlikely that they would revert to foot travel save in an emergency. Eventually, however, the distances involved would become sufficient that walking would be both taxing and time-consuming. At that point the true horse-car suburb would come into existence. Under the influence of horse-car service American cities expanded their built-up limits some 2 to 2.5 miles from the business district, thus considerably enlarging the space available for housing, lowering the density at which it was built, and improving the public health of the residents (in a time when partial isolation was the best available defense against diseases the etiology of which was not well understood). This contribution was important because the introduction of commuter-railroad service, which began at the middle of the last century, had been of relatively restricted value to the larger mass of city population. Railroads were so constrained by the operating characteristics of the steam locomotive that to stop at a very short interval was impractical. Thus the railroad suburbs that were growing up contemporaneously with the horse-car ones were pushed farther out, perhaps 5 miles from the core for the inner ring, and were discontinuous in extent, forming a string of beads of settlement along the railroad lines rather than the band produced by the horse-car with its ability to stop frequently and to use existing roads or streets for its right-of-way.

The suburban expansion encouraged by the horse-car was then continuous rather than interrupted; was possessed of an extremely high density of service, with stops possible and normally practiced at every street intersection; and could be expanded rapidly, as the street-railway lines were relatively cheap and quick to construct. The same sort of developmental symbiosis that had led General Baudry to commence his omnibus line in Nantes in 1825 characterized a number of horse-car operations. Real-estate developers might encourage, finance, or even operate such a line to provide access to open land they sought to have included in the functioning fabric of the city. In this way the spread of the city led almost automatically to the ramification of the street-railway system.

In most large cities in western and central Europe and in North America the final three decades of the last century witnessed a great multiplication of lines and an increasing dependence by city people on the horse-car. In the larger cities, particularly where there was a focus of many routes, the traffic congestion was becoming intolerable well before 1900. In London, with its relatively narrow streets, this problem was perhaps most severely felt; the downtown sections of New York, Boston, Glasgow, and Paris also found their streets clogged with traffic well before the arrival of automobiles and trucks. It was obvious that the street-railway, though a valuable form of urban transit, could not be infinitely expanded.

The problem was twofold: in the heart of the city the converging lines operated with relatively small cars—most carried between twenty-five and fifty riders—at relatively slow speeds—probably between 5 and 7 miles an hour; were drawn by horses that took time to accelerate the vehicle; and remained confined to streets built long before the advent of the railway, thus normally permissive of no more than two tracks. In the outlying residential areas the horse-car lines rapidly approached the outer limit of tolerable daily journeys-to-work as a result of their relatively slow speeds when stops were included over considerable distances. As we have seen, the boundary of normal horse-car service was reached 2 to 2.5 miles away from the core. To extend beyond that point, some form of mechanical traction

capable of faster operation was needed. It was in this context that the next innovation in urban transportation was introduced.

MECHANICAL TRACTION IN THE CITY: NECESSARY GRADE SEPARATION

A complexity of forces led to the next change—the introduction of mechanical traction in place of the horse. It was the desire to use steam power that started the transformation, but many other forces came into play in the completion of that shift. Steam and other types of mechanical power were seen as ways of increasing the competence of urban transit, permitting larger vehicles or longer trains, and speeding up the service. The expectation of these benefits came from the experience with the running of steam trains in the environs of cities where there was pressure for starting up a service that could furnish transport in the daily journey-to-work. Boston already had such service by the early 1850s.[30] London developed it at about the same time, when the London and North Western Railway began to establish "halts" at appropriate points in Tyburnia for service to Euston Station in London.[31] Such early services demonstrated the utility of steam traction, with its greater strength and speed that permitted the suburbs to be built well beyond the practical limit of horse-car operation. In European cities, however, the steam railroads had been forced to locate their city stations toward the edge of the built-up area of the 1830s and 1840s, often a considerable distance from the office and shopping core of the places. London and Paris experienced a particular separation of the rail terminus from the center of affairs. Not only was distance a problem, but also the numbers of commuters and shoppers that the railroads could bring from burgeoning suburbs began to tax the horse-car lines leading from the stations to the heart of the city. Particularly in London, where the stations of the railroads leading east, north, and west out of the city were all ranged along the so-called New Road of the eighteenth century, the congestion was extreme. The first and most important omnibus route had run along that alignment, and the greatest accumulation of potential horse-car passengers took place there, so both demand and congestion indicated that it was there that some relief for the omnibus was required. Commuters who were moving farther and farther out of the central city found the slow journey from Paddington, Euston, and Kings Cross railroad stations to the City an onerous addition to their increasingly longer rail journey. The answer seemed to lie in securing terminals for the steam railroads closer to the main destination of commuters in the offices of the City of London.

In other cities the situation was somewhat different. In New York, for example, the configuration of Manhattan Island—long and very narrow—aggravated a problem that would have existed in any case: the business district of the growing city was located at the very southern tip of the island, so residential expansion could only come by moving up the long axis of the island, with the insular position exaggerating the distance necessary to be traveled. Partly to overcome that amplification of intra-urban travel, the original street railway of 1832 had been laid down when the city first decreed that steam engines could not operate south of Fourteenth Street (later to be made south of Forty-second Street), thus establishing permanently the location of the main suburban railroad station at that distant remove from the heart of the city as it existed in the mid-nineteenth century.

Boston had not forbidden stations near the center as had London, Paris, and New York; rather, its problem was the very early and energetic adoption of the suburban way of life there. Because such a sizable part of the metropolitan population lived in Cambridge, Brookline, Roxbury, and even Newton, while continuing to work or at least shop in Boston, the street railway was particularly highly developed in the Hub. The result was a great crowding of Tremont and Washington streets, the two western entrances to the downtown area. Complaints were voiced that there were so many cars on the tracks that it was often virtually impossible to cross the streets involved. And certainly no great incrementation of the capacity of the system could be envisaged.

The Grade-Separation Problem

By the middle of the last century the two pressing needs for the further development of urban transit—mechanization and increased capacity at the center—indicated very much the same solution: to devise a way to apply steam to this operation. Several cities had tried steam engines in their street-working of rails, but with unsatisfactory results. The mass of the steam dummy engines was such that they could not be stopped quickly enough to deal with any opposing pedestrian or wagon traffic. Horses were frightened, steam was ejected over pedestrians, cinders burned holes in ladies' veils, and the opposition was too strong to be silenced and controlled. It became clear that if steam was to be used in the internal transportation of cities, it must be done by procuring a separate right-of-way. This the steam railroads already had done, to the extent they entered deeply into the city or crossed its built-up area. Thus American cities tended to have the benefits of steam traction even within their limits. Boston, Philadelphia, Pittsburgh, and Chicago could use the standard railroads for some level of intraurban transport. New York, London, Paris, Berlin, and Vienna were less well served, as their extent was sufficient at the inception of rail transport to mean that the mainline stations were at some remove from the part of the city that workers and shoppers sought in large numbers. It was in these cities of great size for their time that what might be termed "the grade-separation problem" was most acute.

Commuters arriving at the mainline stations still had a sufficient distance to travel that an additional transportation link was indicated. In Boston or Chicago the walk from a South or North, LaSalle Street, or Union station was acceptable to travelers; but in New York or London the hike from Forty-second Street (Grand Central Station) to Wall or Eighth street, or from Paddington to the City or Holborn, was not. The omnibus lines of London were most heavily traveled from Paddington via Euston Square and Kings Cross to the City, a route that tapped the arrivals at three mainline stations. Similarly, it was the extension of the New York and Harlaem Railroad, successively from Twenty-third and then Forty-second streets, by horse-car line to downtown Manhattan that dominated intra-urban transit. By 1860 each of these routes was badly overcrowded and there was no readily apparent way that more omnibuses might be put on the New Road in London or horse-cars on the street railway along Fourth Avenue in New York.

The solution to the grade-separation problem was patent: one might seek to construct a line elevated above the street level or a line carried underground beneath it. But the obviousness of the solution did not mean it would be easy. The cost of either solution was considerable given that ideas on urban transit were geared to the public provision of the right-of-way, with the undertaker of transportation merely providing any specialized facilities required for operation. To take an analogy from the present, it was as if Greyhound or Trailways suddenly faced the necessity of not only buying buses and hiring drivers, but also building the highways over which they traveled. In the city, how-

ever, the potential passenger traffic seemed so great that the ebullient nineteenth-century investors seemed ready to make the necessary contribution. It fell to the lot of city authorities to resolve which of the solutions would be adopted, with the investors' preference usually falling in favor of the elevated way because it would require less capital while potentially serving exactly the same market. In this way either a smaller market could be serviced, a larger market could be provided for at a lesser cost, or a higher income could be won. In America it was the first two of those advantages that tended to determine the choice of the elevated railway, whereas in Britain the market was so vast and so definite that it was practicable to require the more costly solution and still anticipate a quite acceptable return on investment. In America probably only New York could foresee a sufficient market to make the discussion of a subway reasonable.

London's Metropolitan Railway

Technically speaking, the elevated was the easier choice because its open-air operation obviated any real problem with disposing of the smoke and steam produced by the engines. Until electric traction was adopted at the end of the last century, there was no satisfactory solution to the use of steam in underground working. Yet in London the demands of aesthetics and the preservation of existing property forced that underground solution. English law required that anyone tunneling under even a part of a building must buy the whole building to do so. Robert Stephenson, when he was laying out the London and Birmingham Railway in the 1830s, had wished to continue it from Euston Square, where it reached the edge of built-up London of its time, as a tunnel under Gower Street and other thoroughfares to the north end of the Waterloo Bridge to reach the bank of the Thames. The possible cost of damage to adjacent buildings ultimately dissuaded him, and he settled for a station site on the north edge of Euston Square.[32]

This fear of city tunneling continued for another generation; only where and when the pressure for an intraurban extension of the steam railroads became overpowering was the proposition reexamined. That new look came when the City of London sought an improvement scheme for the Fleet River Valley, essentially improving the river's drainage and opening a new street, Farringdon Road, northward from Farringdon Street where it intersected High Holborn, at Holborn Hill. To the north lay an area of narrow streets and "insanitary property." In the 1850s, when the Great Northern Railway was completing its project at King's Cross, there had been a strenuous effort made by City interests led by Charles Pearson, the city solicitor, to continue this line southward down the Fleet Valley to the bank of the Thames. Nothing came of this because of the high costs involved, and the Fleet River improvement scheme largely languished in the wake of this failure. The catalyst seems to have been a proposal for an underground railway carried under the New Road as the Bayswater, Paddington & Holborn Bridge Railway. At Holborn Bridge (later called Viaduct), junction would be made with the Fleet River scheme, where a City Terminus Railway was thought an integral part.

The Bayswater, Paddington and Holborn Bridge faced few problems; the New Road was wide enough to permit cut-and-cover construction with only minimal purchases of buildings. But the Fleet area would require considerable investment as clearance and the construction of the new wide road was envisioned. In 1853 the Bayswater company, now renamed the North Metropolitan Railway, was given its parliamentary authorization and began to take over the rail aspects of the Fleet Valley scheme, reducing the size of the proposed terminus, withdrawing its location to a point north of Cheapside, and generally cheapening the costs of the project. When the question of steam operation underground was raised in parliamentary testimony, both the chief engineer of the project, John Fowler, and Isambard Brunel expressed great confidence that the problem was easily handled.

In this context of great mid-Victorian technical confidence, efforts were made to begin construction of an underground line between Paddington in the northwest and some point in or near the City of London. The Crimean War delayed action, but at its close in 1856 new activity was in evidence. Under the influence of Charles Pearson, the North Metropolitan decided to make its City terminus in the Fleet Valley at Farringdon Street, thus advancing the city corporation's effort to redevelop that area. To all intents the Metropolitan Line, as it soon became known, became a connection from Paddington in the west, where it made physical junction with the Great Western Railway, along the New Road close to Euston Station, but having no physical tie with the London and North Western whose own North London Railway gave it an independent connection to the City at Broad Street Station, thence east to King's Cross Station, with three connecting tracks to the Great Northern Railway, and then down the Fleet Valley on a totally new alignment in the redevelopment scheme to its own terminus station at Farringdon Street.[33]

Construction on this City connection carried below the surface began in 1859, when favorable bank rates and a sizable investment by the Great Western Railway finally provided enough money for the letting of contracts. The section along the New Road was fairly straightforward, passing through gravel and crossed only by a single sewer, that of the enclosed Tybourne at Baker Street; that along the Fleet Valley was in sharp contrast, with passage through clay, a tunneling of over 2,100 feet, and three crossings of the notorious Fleet Sewer that had brought up the notion of redevelopment to begin with. It was thought that all this work could be accomplished in twenty-one months, but delays due to the rupture of the Fleet Sewer slowed progress so that the first trains ran (for the directors only) in August, 1862. Formal opening of the line waited until January 10, 1863.[34]

The problems faced in the building of the Metropolitan Railway were sufficient to dampen the ardor for such construction just below the level of the city streets. It was found that blasting was almost impossible without severe damage to adjacent property with foundations on the clay and gravel surface of London. Clearance of buildings proved slow and costly, and the exactions of various governmental agencies (vestries in the Metropolis at this time) could be difficult to comprehend in any economical plan. When we note that the Metropolitan was an immediate financial success, we should not assume that there was as a result an immediate drive for many more underground lines. No doubt much of the success came from the fact that the original Metropolitan Railway underground line served an existing middle-class commutation flow of very large scale. The omnibus had developed Tyburnia; the Metropolitan further enlarged that suburban vector to the point John Betjeman and others could give it the sobriquet "Metroland" in our time. It is doubtful that such a costly facility as the underground could have been built and operated economically in the 1860s save where there was a large middle-class commuter flow.

Charles Pearson, whose greatest interest was in the provision of "Workingmen's Trains" running early in the morning and late at night at low fares between the city workplaces and new outlying working-class suburbs, had prevailed on the Great Western Railway—and through it on the underground extension thereof—to introduce such a cheap train. Because these were required by a parliamentary act of 1860, they came to be known as Parliamentary Trains. The first of these was introduced on the underground Metropolitan Railway in May, 1864. Two trains began, one at 5:30 A.M. and a second ten minutes later, running to the City, with return runs well into the evening and a round-trip fare of 3 d.[35] The underground continued to run such working-class trains as well as third-class carriages on its other trains, but its great economic strength came from its solid bourgeois underpinnings.

The greatest problem with the Underground, as the facility came to be known generically, was the disposal of the smoke and steam from the locomotives. Efforts to build locomotives that consumed their own smoke were never successful. It should be borne in mind that the original purpose of the line was as an extension City-ward of the mainline railroads so the cars were reasonably heavy and large (in the relative terms that the British loading gauge is far smaller than the American), requiring sizable engines to pull them. As the years passed, the smoke blackened the tunnels and stations and sulfured the air even when no trains were present. It was at least in part the unpleasant ambience of the Underground that led Frank Sprague to invent the successful traction motor.

Brave words are continually quoted concerning the wonders of the Underground, but honesty requires that two criticisms be noted. These lines were unpleasant—increasingly so as the years passed; and the cost of construction was such that they could not be widely duplicated so as to provide the world's largest city with an adequate urban transit system, one that could provide working-class transportation of the sort needed as London became one of the world's great industrial and mercantile workshops.

Efforts were made to improve the ventilation—by removing the glass roofs from some of the stations and in 1871–1872 cutting "blow-holes" surfaced with gratings in the New Road section, where the worst ventilation problem existed—but little could be done to relieve the source of the problem.[36] And the cost of construction and running was innate to the view that this was an extension of the mainline roads, even though the operation of the Underground directly by the Great Western ceased almost immediately after the opening of the line. The tunnel had been laid with a mixed gauge of broad- and standard-gauge tracks, first used only by broad-gauge G.W.R. trains. But when in August, 1863, that company refused to operate longer, the Great Northern, whose station at King's Cross was nearing completion (with its tie to the Underground), came to fill the breach with standard-gauge trains and locomotives.

Some extension did take place as Farringdon Street proved an awkward City terminus. The Metropolitan company had taken the precaution of securing a parliamentary act to extend its line farther into the City, to Moorgate Street, so work was well underway before the first line was opened, allowing the extension to be brought into service in late 1865.[37] By using surface lines (built as steam railroads and a short connector link) the Paddington end of the Metropolitan Railway was extended in a great curve around the outer parts of the West London suburbs to Hammersmith west of Kensington on a route opened in July, 1864. Thus, even in its earliest years the Underground stood as a mixed system, partially on the surface, and at the most a transitional technology from the steam railroad that spawned it.

In the mid-1860s further suburban connections in Tyburnia were sought with the creation of the Metropolitan and St. John's Wood, which was a true underground but

completed with only a single track when it opened in 1868. The next year service had grown sufficiently that a 10-minute headway was proposed on St. John's Wood trains, a frequency that seemed to suggest a crowding of the original Underground. To obviate that outcome, it was established that trains on this St. John's Wood line would stop at Baker Street and passengers would pass to the main Metropolitan line through "communicating galleries." In this way that strange and awkward junction at Baker Street that still characterizes London Underground working was established, to be elaborated as further suburban extensions came in Tyburnia, or Metroland.[38]

While Tyburnia was expanding, the Great Northern Railway sought to encourage suburban development in northeast London out from King's Cross. Quickly these services overtaxed the original Underground between King's Cross and Farringdon Street and Moorgate, so in the late 1860s two more tracks were added between King's Cross and Moorgate, to make this the "widened lines" that then, as now, carried so much railroad commuter traffic directly into the City—specifically today through King's Cross, but in the last century from the Midland Railway at St. Pancras as well.

Even before the Metropolitan line was opened in January, 1863, there were proposals to apply the logic that had brought it into being to all the edges of the center of London and to the other railroad stations located there. At the same time there was a proposal to improve traffic flow in the heart of the city by carrying a new arterial road along the bank of the Thames to bypass the narrow streets that served most of the core and to relieve the much overtaxed east-west arterial along the Strand. With the emerging awareness that sewerage outfalls were offensive to civic pride and a polite society, there was also a proposal for a main collector sewer to be carried beneath this proposed embankment. With such a scheme afloat, it was almost automatic that the notion of including an underground railway to serve the southern stations and the parts of the city near the river was added. At the urging of Parliament the tentative plan, advanced for extending the Underground from Farringdon Street to the bank of the Thames and thence westward along the new embankment to Westminster, was enlarged to carry the line around the eastern edge of the City from Moorgate via Liverpool Street (where a new mainline terminal was under construction) and Aldgate to the Thames at the Tower of London and then westward to Westminster. To the east and south of the City there was no improvement scheme of the sort involved in the Embankment, so such an enlargment of the plan made it much more expensive for the backers of the Metropolitan. Still the company applied for and received an act authorizing an eastern extension from Moorgate to Tower Hill and a western one from Paddington to Brompton (South Kensington).[39] The gap between these termini was to be filled by a line constructed by the Metropolitan District Railway Company, chartered in 1864 for that purpose. When all lines were completed, an Inner Circle would exist largely underground around the heart of the city, with dimensions drawn on a grand scale—some 2 miles across north-south, but 6 miles wide from east to west. All mainline stations located north of the Thames were on or very near this circle, which is really an ellipse. The extension to South Kensington was completed in 1868 and that to Liverpool Street from Moorgate in 1875. There the eastern extension hung fire for some time. Meanwhile, the District line was underway, reaching Westminster from the west in 1870 and Mansion House in the City in 1871.[40] The gap persisted; it was not until 1884 that the Inner Circle was finally closed and the design for an un-

derground railway around central London was completed.[41]

The geographical pattern of London's underground railways reveals a great deal about the service they might render. As constructed the Inner Circle was inner only in the sense that there were parts of two other circular rail lines within the metropolis. It was actually a peripheral line, carried almost entirely outside the important heart of the city. Only between Tower Hill and the Victoria Embankment could it be viewed as a mass-transit line within the core. We should not forget that this section was not completed until twenty years after the first section, and more than a decade after most of the line. The problem of mass transit within the core area remained largely unsolved by the original cut-and-cover underground lines. Construction by this technology was so difficult and so costly within the core area that it could not be applied at all widely. Instead, pedestrian movement or omnibus journeys had to suffice for two generations after the opening of the first Underground. The only significant change came when streetcar lines were opened, replacing some of the suburban omnibuses, in the early 1870s; but the core of London remained inviolate for many years after a parliamentary hassle that was lost by the horse-car proponents in 1872.[42] Throughout the last century the heart of London was reached by the sort of transportation that was already in use by 1829, and by no other.

The cut-and-cover Underground is essentially a specialized form of the steam railroad, built to handle mainline equipment and drawn by steam engines. Within its first decades the system had become an instrument for the suburbanization of the middle-class population of the metropolis. Services were introduced, such as that from the City to Windsor, that might not pay; they were then dropped and another experiment undertaken. But the field of trial was always from the Inner Circle outward, seeking to find where bourgeois society wished to travel outward from the inner edge of the suburbs. There were Workingmen's Trains and third-class carriages on other trains, but the true role of the Metropolitan and District lines was to move prosperous and polite society in the northwest, west, and southwest suburbs of the world's largest city, with only incidental service to the East End, and even there only to its more prosperous sections. As a solution to the transportation problems of the financially fortunate, the shallow Underground shaped in the 1860s and 1870s was of extreme significance; but it left two pressing metropolitan transportation problems largely unsolved: the transport of persons of any class within the urban core and the transport of the working class within most parts of the metropolis.

New York Finds A More Democratic Solution

At first it would seem that Europe and North America had strikingly different histories of urbanization. Europe had a strong tradition of cities extending back to Classical times, but in North America cities began only with the advent of the last century. Yet on closer examination one of the strikingly urban facts of the nineteenth century was the rapidity with which large cities came into existence not only in Europe (where the change was mainly in the scale of urbanization) but also in North America, southern South America, and Australia (where the settlements progressed from founding to first-rank status within a few generations). Chicago had outdistanced many of the historic cities of Europe in population by the end of the nineteenth century. The need for urban transit is largely a function of city size—both in area and in population—

rather than of longevity or political ascendency. Amsterdam could put off building rapid transit long after that luxury was denied to New York, Chicago, or Buenos Aires.

For reasons already cited, New York was the place that the grade-separation problem first became critical in the New Lands. At the same time that London was experimenting with cut-and-cover subway construction, Manhattan was the site of equally innovative attempts. As early as 1852 a rough traffic count had found 230 omnibuses an hour northbound and 240 southbound on Broadway at Chambers Street.[43] By 1864 over 61 million passengers were being transported annually on the twelve lines of street railway operating in Manhattan and The Bronx, and some streets were choked with both horsecars and omnibuses as well as other traffic.[44] All this was at a time when New York was still a large but not a giant city. In 1865

Above Forty-second street it could scarcely be said to exist, being only a dreary waste of unpaved and ungraded streets diversified by rocky eminences crowned with squatters' shanties. Railway passengers from the North still left their trains at Twenty-seventh and Thirtieth streets. Street railways were comparatively few, and there was no speedy and comfortable way of getting from one end of the city to the other. Below Eighty-sixth street there were in 1865 25,261 vacant lots. The grading of Madison avenue was still in progress.... Unable to get anywhere on Manhattan Island, people sought the suburbs and rapidly built up Southern Connecticut and Eastern New Jersey, with Long Island and Staten Island.[45]

The forces that had caused New York to grow so rapidly in the first two-thirds of the last century did not abate in the last third. That fact was already perceived by the 1860s,

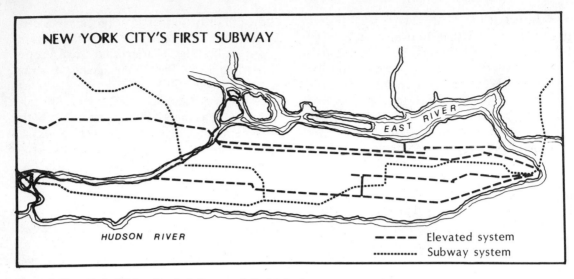

NEW YORK CITY'S FIRST SUBWAY

EAST RIVER

HUDSON RIVER

- - - - Elevated system
.... Subway system

Map of New York City's elevated lines and first subway.

when efforts were begun to provide some sort of clear right-of-way for transit in the most densely developed parts of the city. The suburban railroads might afford commutation to the residential suburbs of the upper middle class; but they availed little for the journey-to-work of the clerks, laborers, and great bulk of the population. Looking to the world's largest city of the time, the New Yorkers proposed a subway in 1864. As only a short stretch was constructed at that time, there is no need to give details of its engineering other than to point out that it seems to have been nearly as costly as that in London, which was at that time stated to cost $1.67 million per mile, while the assumed figure for New York was $1.55 million.[46] Such a sum seems to have been daunting but not totally discouraging, allowing a group of capitalists, including Henry Varnum Poor, confidently to promise $5 million to the undertaking. In 1864 the state legislature passed a bill authorizing the construction of a subway under Broadway, but the governor vetoed it—ostensibly on the argument that no time limit had been set for completion of

the line and the city had offered the company free use of public land, but apparently in response to pressure from the horse-car operators.[47]

With the subway proposal stymied, New York City's streets remained as clogged as ever. A legislative committee appointed to examine the problem submitted a report calling for an underground line from the Battery northward to City Hall and thence two lines, one on the East Side and the other on the West Side, to the Harlem River.[48] For reasons that are no longer clear, nothing came of the proposals. Instead, a minor recommendation of the report—that Charles Harvey be permitted to construct a trial stretch of his "patent" elevated railway—was adopted. The legislature of 1867 finally authorized that experiment, which was duly undertaken, on a half-mile line constructed in Greenwich Street northward from Battery Place, by the West Side and Yonkers Patent Railway.[49] Propelled by cable traction, the experimental section went into operation after acceptance by the state engineers on July 1, 1868. As built a single line of track was carried at the curb on each side of the street, raised at least 14 feet above the surface of the pavement and carried on vertical columns placed no closer than 20 feet apart. Though the trial was deemed a success, Harvey lacked the money to continue the construction northward from Cortlandt Street, where the experimental stretch ended, to Thirtieth Street and Ninth Avenue, where the New York Central Railroad terminal presented an immediate objective before the grander scheme of reaching to the Harlem River, and even to Yonkers, could be accomplished. Harvey was forced out of the company by a Wall Street group seeking large profits from the extension scheme, and in due course the structure was completed to Thirtieth Street. When the lengthened line proved less amenable to cable traction, a provision of the original charter permitting steam traction was invoked and that method of operation was introduced on April 20, 1871.[50] For a quarter of a century thereafter the standard technology of elevated-railway operation remained fixed in the form of steam dummy engines drawing trains of several cars on elevated structures carried either at the side or in the center of public streets. Only in 1902 were the New York Elevated Railways, as the reorganized company was named in 1871, electrified, retiring the dummy engines that had been a continuing trial to city residents for nearly a third of a century.[51]

It is impractical to follow the course of elevated railway construction in New York beyond noting that ultimately lines were constructed from the south end of Manhattan Island on separate routes operating on Second, Third, Sixth, and Ninth avenues. Fifty-ninth Street on the Ninth Avenue line was reached in 1876, Forty-second Street on the Third Avenue line in 1878, and Harlem in 1880.[52] The construction cost was considerably less than might have been anticipated for the building of subways: "According to testimony the original elevated roads cost about $700,000 to $8000,000 per mile of double tracked structure and the cars about $3,100 to $3,500 apiece."[53] When the elevated roads reached the Harlem River, their traffic increased impressively. For example, the Third Avenue line carried over 45 million passengers in 1879.[54] In part this growth came from the final rationalization of the railroad station problem in New York City. As originally built the three railroads reaching to the island (before the Pennsylvania Railroad and Long Island Railroad gained entry in 1910) had separate stations: the Hudson River Railroad at Thirtieth Street and Ninth Avenue, the New York and Harlaem River Railroad at Fourth Avenue and Twenty-seventh Street, and the New York, New Haven, and Hartford at Madison Avenue and Twenty-sixth Street. In 1871 the first Grand Central Station, opened at Fourth Avenue and Forty-second Street, combined the terminal facilities for all three companies and created a distant and then uptown station whence service to the business district must be provided by intraurban transit—at the time by the Third Avenue El.[55] It was over a period of less than fifteen years that most of the elevated lines in Manhattan were completed and the first rapid-transit system for the city was worked out. As the frontier of urban settlement expanded in The Bronx and Queens, as well as from a separate nucleus in Brooklyn, these relatively cheaply constructed facilities were carried into what at the close of the century became three of the four outlying boroughs of the amalgamated city. Only Staten Island lacked extensive elevated lines. There the grain of settlement was sufficiently thin to permit the Staten Island Rapid Transit to be essentially a commuter railroad of the standard sort.

THE ELEVATED IN AMERICA

The elevated railway became the late-nineteenth-century solution to the grade-separation problem in American cities in particular. As urbanization and industrialization went hand in hand in the larger cities of the Manufacturing Belt of the United States—Boston, New York, Philadelphia, Baltimore, Pittsburgh, Cleveland, Cincinnati, St. Louis, and Chicago—the more densely developed of those places had to turn to grade separation as a means of continuing the focus on the heart of the city that had allowed them to become great. In 1879 Boston began to show interest in what until then had been a distinctively New York solution. But the legislative committee investigating the proposal concluded that the ten-year trial in Gotham had yet to prove satisfactorily the safety of the elevated. Instead, the Massachusetts General Court authorized the construction of a line based on a local design by Joe V. Meigs of what we now would call a supporting monorail to extend from some place in Cambridge to Bowdoin Square in Boston.[56] Using a steam engine (with cab forward) and a tubular "Fireproof Circular Car," upholstered in quilted velour with seventy-two seats, a test section was constructed in East Cambridge and successfully operated in 1886. Like many technical achievements of the last century, however, this one was not advanced beyond the demonstration phase. The construction of an actual elevated railway in the Hub had to wait until 1898, when the Boston Elevated Railway was begun on the less advanced New York pattern.

Chicago took up the elevated in anticipation of the World's Columbian Exposition. Crowds were foreseen for which the street operations by horse- and cable-drawn railcars would not be adequate. The El managed to open as the South Side Elevated Railway in June of the quadricentennial year—unlike the Fair, which missed its ostensible anniversary by a year.

Once committed to the El, Chicago worked with characteristic determination to create an extensive system with feeders from ten suburban termini to the central-area Loop, finished in 1897, that ties it all together. Given the extremely flat site, the uniform grid pattern of streets, and the rather low density of most outlying development in the Garden City of the late nineteenth century, it is not surprising that Chicago became the most committed of elevated railway partisans. Also, it was there that some of the earliest efforts at the application of electric traction to heavy rapid-transit vehicles were made. In 1895, when the Metropolitan West Side Elevated Railway was opened with electric trains, its South Side neighbor soon followed in the transformation. On this latter installation in 1897 one of the great advances in electric traction was accomplished with the introduction—by Frank Sprague, whom we shall see in an even more pioneering role presently—of "multiple-unit" (M-U) train operation. Under that system the tractive effort was transferred from a locomotive, as had been used on the earlier West Side electrification and all earlier electric-train workings, to a series of "traction motors" mounted on each car, geared to a driving axle in each and controlled from a single master speed switch operated from the leading car. M-U operation gave transit systems a great flexibility, whereby the addition of another car brought with it the requisite power to move that vehicle, that was highly desirable in dealing with the very differential loadings of passengers experienced in intra-urban transit.

The only other American city to adopt the elevated railway over an extensive system was Philadelphia, where a major east-west system was constructed beginning in 1903. In the heart of the city the service was in a tunnel, but the outlying sections were constructed as elevated lines and remain as such even today. The same pattern held in Boston when its elevated system was begun in 1898, using the streetcar tunnel completed by the

The Loop elevated railway in Chicago. Chicago Transit Authority photograph.

city in 1897 under Tremont Street to cross the most congested section of the Hub between 1901 and 1908, when the Elevated Company finished its own tunnel under Washington Street to accomplish the same grade separation.[57] There were bits and pieces of elevated track on interurban systems that might be thought of as quasi-elevated railways, but the form was fully utilized in only four cities—New York, Chicago, Boston, and Philadelphia (with construction begun in that order). These were the American cities with the most fully developed and densely built-up city cores at the turn of the century. Elsewhere the elevated line served very limited purposes—as it did in Sioux City, for example—so we may look upon the form as one associated with massive urbanization already choked at its center even in 1900.

Europe adopted this American technology only infrequently. Liverpool had a line along the Mersey docks. Paris used above-ground sections for a third of the length of its second Metropolitan line (Dauphine-Nation) built between 1901 and 1903.[58] That semicircular line was made full circle with the completion in 1909 of Line No. 6 of the Métro, which in crossing the Seine twice, and elsewhere, was carried on a viaduct that is essentially an El. Hamburg used a similar subway-elevated construction for its first line of rapid transit built between 1906 and 1912; Berlin had a separate elevated system, the S-Bahn, to provide for much of its transit needs. But there is no doubt that the elevated remained an American form of transportation throughout its entire existence, with only incidental use in the few large Continental cities that had rapid-transit systems before World War I.

THE CABLE-CAR INTERLUDE

The grade-separation problem was not fully resolved through the building of the Metropolitan Railway in London and the various elevated railways in large American cities. There remained the need for a true subway, one where the line was totally covered rather than two-thirds so as in the case of the first London Underground. Before that could be accomplished, some cleaner substitute for the steam locomotive had to be found. On the first New York El in 1869–1871, cable traction had been employed, though not successfully. Similarly, the Parisian Chemins de Fer Américain tried compressed air, steam tanks, and other "improvements" on the steam engine, but without any overriding success. Thus in the 1870s the only practicable traction was seen as the steam locomotive, and the Els and the Underground stuck to it till the end of the century. Only a line fully or considerably open to the sky could operate with steam technology, and technical advance seemed to be stymied in these heavy-traction workings.

It was on more modest undertakings that improvements were worked out through continuous operation. The first reasonably successful application of a traction other than the steam locomotive came through a rather minor adjustment in the technology:

the substitution of a stationary for a moving steam engine. As the noise, smoke, cinders, and great mass that was hard to brake to a stop came, in train operation, from the locomotive alone, a logical improvement was seen in separating the prime mover from the train itself. If some way could be found to transmit the mechanical output of the steam engine to the moving car, this would be accomplished while leaving the bad features of the prime mover at some remove from the crowded streets on which the cars passed. There had been repeated efforts based on the technology of power transmission in American factories (waterwheels or steam engines moving belts, pulleys, and cables that powered the looms and other machines) to create this separation of the prime mover from the vehicle. The Portage Railway on the Pennsylvania Mainline Canal System had been so powered, as was Harvey's first New York El. Only in San Francisco, in 1873, were most of the inadequacies improved on and a reasonably practical system devised. This was in no sense the invention of the cable car: its technical necessities had been invented by various men in America and Britain over the previous half century. The continuous wire cable, the conduit in which it would run, and the caliper grip to attach the vehicle to it were all worked out well before 1873; there had been an actual cable-hauled rail line, though not with all the features of the San Francisco system, at work in the Blackwall Tunnel in East London starting in 1840. This 3.75-mile line was further extended to Fenchurch Street in the City in 1841.[59] Even earlier cable haulage had been used in the tunnel leading to Lime Street Station in Liverpool and in the initial line from Camden Town to Euston Square in London, as of course it was on the several banks on the Stockton and Darlington Railway. Thus cables had been employed from the very earliest years of steam power (on railroads). But all these operations were on private rights-of-way and were for the most part incidental to the conduct of mainline railroads.

The rise of the urban cable-car line came as a consequence of the deficiencies of the horse-car railways. As George Hilton points out, horse-car lines were slow (at 4 to 6 miles an hour, little faster than a brisk walker); very expensive to operate, as horses were costly; and subject to decimation with epidemic equine diseases, as in the Great Epizootic of 1872.

> Horses dropped over ten pounds of fecal material a day on the street and periodically drenched the pavement with urine. Not only was this offensive *per se*, but the feces contained the virus of tetanus, such that any skin abrasion on the streets entailed the risk of a [then] absolutely fatal disease. Urination was so frequent that smooth pavements such as asphalt were not practical; either dirt or cobble-stones had to be provided to assure traction between the horse's hooves and the street. All forms of economic activity yield external benefits and involve social costs, but the social costs of horse traction were the most offensive in the history of transportation.[60]

Applying steam prime movers to the street-car operations in cities was very much of an advance on horse traction, if it could only be worked out.

It is important to appreciate that the cable car was not a particularly desirable system of urban transit.

> The most that can be said for the cable car is that it was the best of a collection, all the rest of which were also unsatisfactory. Battery cars and compressed-air motors were limited in speed and range; both suffered from very rapid dissipation of their power supply with increase in speed. Various motors that generated heat through chemical processes using ammonia, caustic soda or other compounds never became more than curiosities.[61]

The cable railway dealt with terrain obstacles in a way that no horse-car line could. When we recall that horses had trouble gaining traction even on level stretches, it is not difficult to imagine how hard it was for them to operate on hills—oddly enough, more of a trial downslope than upslope in many cases because the horse-cars had a poor braking mechanism. Attaching the vehicle to a moving cable would permit the car to be drawn to the top of a grade evenly and with no literal traction problem: by that same attachment the course down a steep hill could be controlled by the speed of the cable. It was particularly in San Francisco that hills posed a real problem, mainly because the early promoters of real estate sales there had adopted rigid rectangular grid patterns for streets, leading those thoroughfares up the sides of hills almost too steep to be breasted even on foot. It was in this geographical context that a wire-cable manufacturer, Andrew Hallidie, sought to construct a cable-car line up the east slope of Nob Hill in San Francisco in 1872–1873.

The Clay Street Hill Railway of 1873 served to open the top of Nob Hill to housing development. It became an immediate success. Rather quickly a number of other lines were built in San Francisco, so that by 1880 there were 11.2 miles of cable route in the city, a total encouraged by the fact that with grid-pattern streets there were few curves on the lines, and those there were could often be navigated as "let-go curves" where the gripman released the cable only to pick it up after floating free around the curve using the car's momentum to carry it forward.

The second city to try out cable traction, Dunedin, New Zealand, could not use this system; there, the mechanism to permit a "pull-curve" was first employed in 1881, removing the last remaining obstacle to widespread adoption of the cable railway.[62] Another doubt about the technology was removed when cable railways were built in

Chicago, opening on State Street in January, 1882, to successful operation despite the severe winter weather. The Chicago City Railway operated by cable demonstrated that it could move passengers half again as fast as the horse-car lines, at half the cost. In the fastest portions of the system, speeds of 14 miles per hour were reached.[63] In the 1880s systems were set up in New York, Brooklyn (then a separate city), Kansas City, Cincinnati, Cleveland, St. Louis, Oakland, Los Angeles, Omaha, and overseas in London. In the end most large cities in the United States adopted cable traction for their more important routes. Mileage in use in American cities reached its peak at 305.1 miles in 1893, but even then the technology was out of date in most installations.[64]

After Frank Sprague's successful demonstration of his electric streetcar in 1887, cable technology was seen to be both far more costly and far less adaptable. Within a decade many cable lines were abandoned, and virtually no new mileage was added. "Beginning in 1891 cable installations were special cases, justified either by excessive gradients or hostility of municipal governments to electric wires over the streets."[65] The last cable-traction street-railway system built seems to have been the Elgin Road line in Dunedin, opened in 1906. It is appropriate that the only major American cities not to adopt cable traction were Boston and Detroit. It was in the former that the electric railway had its first full trial and acceptance. The role of the latter in the evolution of urban transport need not be stated.[66]

From our viewpoint the significance of the cable-car lines comes in their signaling a great desire for a removal of the prime mover from the street to some point where steam, smoke, noise, and other nuisances could be masked, or at least tolerated. At first that accomplishment came through the use of mechanical transfer of power, the standard method employed until the very end of the

nineteenth century. Once a more advanced form of transfer—electricity—was known, as it was by the 1840s, every effort was applied to try to secure its practical application to this general problem.

THE ARRIVAL OF THE TROLLEY

The first efforts at electric traction were not specifically applied to urban transport. As early as 1835 Thomas Davenport had set up the world's first electric railway, in miniature, in Brandon, Vermont. In 1842 Robert Davidson carried out trials on the Edinburgh and Glasgow Railway in an effort to utilize a battery-powered locomotive; he gained a modest success when it operated at a speed of four miles an hour. At mid-century Moses Farmer, working in New Hampshire, gained greater success; but until 1879 no truly practical installation had been accomplished. In that year, at the Berlin Trades Exhibition held in the German capital, Werner von Siemens set up the first truly satisfactory system—though again rather in miniature, as the locomotive driver had to ride astride the electric engine. This third-rail operation was powered by a dynamo that could move three small cars along the 350-yard track at a consistent speed of 8 miles per hour.[67] In the course of the exhibition some 80,000 passengers were introduced to the most rudimentary form of electric traction, but one that showed a much more reliable service than had previously been possible because for the first time an external power source had been introduced that overcame the fatal flaws that had attached to battery power.

There were several flaws in the Siemens operation. Perhaps the most important was that the dynamo was at best a makeshift motor. Its use depended on a discovery by Zenobie Theophile Gramme (in 1870) of the reversibility of function, wherein it was shown that if a dynamo's shaft was rotated, it produced electric current, whereas if electric current was fed to the shaft, it produced a rotation thereof that might be used to power a rotative movement. This was not a particularly good electric motor, but it was the first practical one. Siemen's third-rail operation, at 150 volts, also posed a considerable shock problem if attempted on a public street. The mounting of the dynamo geared rigidly and directly to the wheels also made it essential that the track be well laid and maintained if the power drive was to be kept in repair. Finally, since only eighteen persons could be drawn in the three small cars, this was a novelty rather than the final solution to the problem of separating the prime mover from the vehicle it propelled. Still, in physically separating the two for the first time, the Siemens exhibition line of 1879 stands as one of the fundamental steps in the creation of a practicable electric-traction system.

The early 1880s saw several efforts toward such a system. Other exhibition lines were laid out for brief periods at Frankfurt, Dusseldorf, and Brussels. On May 16, 1881, permanent installation came into use at Lichterfelde near Berlin where, over a 2.5-kilometer line between the Anhalt railroad station and the officer's school, there was the replacement of horse-cars with Siemens electric cars. Because the installation depended on the use of the running rails to supply the necessary electric circuit, there was a considerable problem with shocks to passersby.[68] Elsewhere in Europe, particularly in English seaside resorts, similar specialized undertakings were made, often on private rights-of-way, that provided short stretches of electric line. Another Siemens installation was made on a new tramway being laid out near the Giant's Causeway in Northern Ireland. Opened in 1883, this 250-volt, third-rail line, the Giant's Causeway, Portrush and Bush Valley Railway and Tramway Company, is claimed by some to have had the

true character of the electric-traction line. But like the line that Magnus Volk laid down on the Front at Brighton, as a third-rail system on a gauge of 2 feet 8.5 inches, this was rather an idiographic solution to a general problem. Both these 1883 lines survived for decades—the Volk line to the present—but neither broke any new ground in solving the problem of mass urban transport.[69]

The need for a general solution was most pressing in the United States. The horse-car had become an essential form of transportation in the thirty years after 1850 when the use of those carriers became widespread. The American suburb had become the main form of middle-class housing, and the solid working class was beginning to look outward in the hope of gaining more healthy accommodation. Factories were being located toward the edge of the city, while building land was in plentiful supply, encouraging a general spread of urban areas. No longer would a couple of miles encompass even rather large cities, so walking to work, to shop, and to visit was becoming ever more taxing. But the horse-car lines were both slow in speed and relatively costly. At a rate of 5 or 6 miles an hour, even under the most favorable circumstances, long intra-urban journeys were unpleasant. The steam railroads offered a relief for the well-to-do, or to the solid working class, where commutation tickets lowered the cost to frequent travelers; but for single journeys, for the average worker, and for areas unserved by railroads, there was a definite gap in the pattern of city transportation. With the higher general level of disposable income among American workers and the less dense nature of American cities, the market there for any accomplished improvement seemed immediate and sanguine.

In the early 1880s a number of Americans began to search earnestly for a general solution. In 1884 John C. Henry conducted a trial of his electric car in Kansas City wherein he sought to make for safer operation by placing his power supply in overhead wires, two for a complete circuit independent of the tracks or the ground. On those two he placed a small four-wheel pickup device that was trolled behind the car on a cable that brought the electricity to the motor in the vehicle. Thus came the popular name for the electric car in America, the "troller" that picked up the current gave to the car it powered the name *trolley*, a far more precise term than the European tramcar or tram, which may easily be confused with the primordial coal-carrying railways of the Tyne and South Wales. For this reason I will use the American term even when I take up the European form of the trolley. Beyond this verbal contribution, Henry's operation also introduced the notion of the overhead circuit, free of a track or ground return. Otherwise, however, his system was not very successful.

Again motivated by a desire to shape a system safer to operate and more compatible with street-running than were the European pioneering lines, Bentley and Knight set up a line in Cleveland in 1884 that used an underground conduit, nearly identical with that employed in the cable-car technology, in which the energized wire or pipe, as the case might be, was shielded from other traffic on the street and was contacted by the electric car through a plow that passed along the slot adjacent to one of the running rails. Problems were encountered in working this system, but eventually it became reasonably practical and continued to be used in installations in cities that opposed overhead wires for aesthetic reasons—specifically in Manhattan and Washington, D.C.—where conduit power feed was used until electric service was abandoned in the 1940s. But conduit-fed power was more expensive as the construction costs were much higher than for overhead feed and upkeep was considerable. A general solution needed further advances.

Those came in the work of three men whose contribution jointly removed most of the remaining hitches to successful electric-railway development. Leo Daft had come to the United States from England just after the American Civil War. After experimenting successfully with photography, he turned his attention to electricity and became the proprietor of an electric company in a small New Jersey town. He became interested in applying electricity to traction and began building a small electric locomotive that could pull streetcars. He tried this out on the Saratoga and Mt. McGregor Railway near that New York resort with modest success until, at 15 miles per hour, he went too fast around a curve and put his locomotive, *Ampère*, in the grass along with his load of "distinguished guests." Undaunted, and perhaps in reflection of his English heritage, Daft constructed a demonstration line in Boston and one at Coney Island. The latter was visited by Thomas Robbins, the general manager of the horse-car lines in Baltimore, whose interest was whetted by the excellent traction that electric locomotives seemed to gain for use on a particularly difficult line he had to operate at home. Daft was invited to undertake its electrification in a 3-mile trial section opened for service on August 9, 1885. This was the first American electric line that kept going for any considerable length of time.[70] Unfortunately, Daft also followed European practice by adopting a third-rail power feed, a mistake prompted by his original assumption that he could power the line with current at only 20 or 25 volts. As the feed had to be raised to 120 volts, the shock hazard was greatly increased, to the considerable discomfort of all involved in the line or living near it. Given that disappointment, it is not surprising that Daft is not remembered more for his efforts, ultimately successful, to electrify the Ninth Avenue Elevated in New York, which he accomplished in 1888.[71]

One of the great failings of the Daft system

of electric traction came from its adherence to the troller riding on the two overhead wires. This contrivance kept falling off, dropping with force on the car roof or even on the unlucky passengers as they climbed aboard. The ultimate solution to that problem came at the hands of another trolley pioneer, Charles J. Van Depoele, born in Belgium but in the 1870s a wood-carving manufacturer in Chicago. There he started an electric-arc lighting company that naturally turned his attention to the related question of the best technology for electric traction. In thinking along those lines he came up with the notion of a rigid pole extending from the roof of the vehicle to make a contact with the underside of the overhead wire, along which it would run with a channeled wheel. This trolley pole was first envisaged by Van Depoele in 1882, but he did not actually make use of it at that time. To popularize his system, he began setting up demonstration lines at the Toronto Exhibition, where, in 1884 and 1885, he gained considerable attention. Like the Lichterfelde line, Van Depoele's ran from the railroad station into the exposition grounds. In contrast to Daft, he called for very high voltages, some 1,400 volts, and he gained a speed of 30 miles per hour. In one five-day period he carried 30,000 passengers, so this was at least a realistic test of what mass transit would be when successfully developed. That same year, 1885, he had the chance to make an actual street installation in South Bend, but unfortunately he continued the use of the troller rather than the trolley pole he had envisaged. Soon lines in Scranton and Appleton, Wisconsin, were equipped with Van Depoele technology. His real chance came in 1886, when Van Depoele was given the contract to convert an entire city system of horse-car lines, that in Montgomery, Alabama, to electric traction. This system proved reasonably satisfactory—though not to buried gas and water mains, which tended to be rotted out by elec-

trolysis as a result of his use of the ground as a return in his electric circuitry. By 1888 seven of the eleven electric systems working in the United States had been equipped with Van Depoele equipment, using twenty-eight cars and 30 miles of track.[72] That same year there were only about 60 miles in all electric railway installations with less than one hundred electric cars.[73]

Occasionally events assume in fact the definitive quality that later historians tend to assign them. Such was the case with Frank Sprague's contribution to the evolution of powered transport in cities. No one man, with the possible exception of George Stephenson, worked such a rapid and complete change in the transportation he found and sought to improve. Unlike Stephenson, Sprague was a mechanical genius given to evolving ideas and wide-ranging efforts at improving all sorts of technologies. He seems to have been so full of ideas that he left to others their commercial development, not needing the jealous denigration of others that sustained the Father of the Railways. Yet Sprague was more unquestionably the sire of the trolley system than the Geordie ever was of the railroads.

Educated at Annapolis—then one of the few engineering schools in the United States—Sprague was an outstanding student in mathematics and particularly gifted in science. Graduated from the Naval Academy in 1878, he set off on a cruise on the U.S.S. *Richmond*, returning therefrom to apply for some sixty patents covering various aspects of electrical apparatus he had thought up in his spare time abroad. As a bright engineer he was assigned to the Naval Torpedo Station at Newport, where he met the "government electrician," Professor Moses Farmer, the same man we have already seen experimenting with electric traction in Dover, New Hampshire, almost forty years before his encounter with the young naval lieutenant. Pursuing his great

Steam-operated elevated line in New York City, Chatham Square Station. *Source*: Louis Figuier,
Les Chemins de Fer Métropolitains (Paris, c. 1900).

interest in electricity, the twenty-five-year-old officer requested an unpaid leave of three months to visit the Crystal Palace Electrical Exhibition of 1882 in London, and he succeeded in having himself appointed as the secretary to the award jury.[74] While in London Sprague rode daily on the Metropolitan Railway and became graphically aware of the failings of the existing system of rapid transit, notably the befouled atmosphere of the tunnels that had to admit the prime mover along with the train it propelled.[75] Returning to the United States in May, 1883, Sprague was scheduled for court martial for overstaying his leave but the 169-page technical report on the Exhibition that

he submitted convinced the Navy that he was pursuing work useful to the service, so the court was withdrawn and his report was published. Still the Navy was not as interested in electricity as its lieutenant was. To resolve that conflict, Sprague soon resigned in order to go to Menlo Park, New Jersey, to work with Thomas Edison.

At this time Edison was frenetically engaged in trying to improve his incandescent light bulb and secure city electric systems to illuminate those globes. Sprague seems to have wished to work on the electric locomotive that Edison was having rebuilt for the third time, but, "having little if any novelty," it offered no great advance on knowledge he already had. Instead, Edison assigned him to install city light systems, perhaps because the Menlo Park group had a great suspicion of theoretical work, and preferred to conduct great numbers of empirical trials to gain ends that might have been reached more quickly and easily by general analysis. In his work installing lighting systems, Sprague wished to solve problems mathematically that the "practical men" sought to answer with scale models using yards of wire to reproduce the actual system. In the spring of 1884 the unsatisfactory association was ended when Sprague quit and decided to set up his own firm, the Sprague Electric Railway & Motor Company.

The company prospered quickly because the engineer developed an excellent electric motor that was distinguished from many of its time by being designed from scratch as a motor rather than merely applying the notion of reversibility through using dynamos to do a motor's job. With the funds that came to the company, the proprietor could indulge his fascination with electric railways, whose primacy in his mind is suggested by the order of functions contained in his company's title. Using a 200-foot length of track squeezed between two buildings at the Durant Sugar Refining Company on East Twenty-fourth Street in Manhattan, Sprague began to try out his theories intended to improve on the failings of existing electric street railways. A great fault in cars then in use was in the transfer of power from the electric motor to the wheels. Most employed chain drives that were noisy, subject to breaking, and always in need of cleaning. Direct gearing had proven impossible as the poor condition of American city streets, and the track laid thereon, meant that the teeth were repeatedly being stripped from expensive gears. To solve this problem, Sprague devised the *wheelbarrow mount* whereby the motor was actually mounted on the axle of the wheels (to which the armature was at-

tached by gears) with only a spring connection to the body of the car, which could absorb the shock of the rough track. This was the first of the improvements that would make electric traction practicable.

A second problem enountered on existing systems was that of the power feed. We have already seen how Van Depoele had thought out the trolley pole, though he had failed to use it in his working systems. Sprague evidently had worked out the nature of this connection while he was at the Crystal Palace Electrical Exhibition in 1882. When he sought to have it patented, however, Sprague's application was denied in favor of Van Depoele's because the latter was resident in the United States at that time whereas the American naval officer was not. Finally a sharing agreement was worked out that left the power feed sufficiently improved to permit reasonable working of an electric railway.

Other improvements worked by Sprague were in the controller that advanced the speed of the car, handling the problem electrically rather than mechanically through brakes, as had been done by several of the trolley pioneers. By the spring of 1887 he was in a position to think in terms of actually setting up a line so he was delighted when opportunities were offered in St. Joseph, Missouri, and in Richmond, Virginia. The first system was opened successfully before the end of the year in the Missouri River port, but it was in the port on the James that true transportation history was made. There the company seeking to develop a street-railway system offered Sprague the chance to electrify an entire city system at the time of its construction. In May, 1887, his company signed a contract with the Union Passenger Railway at Richmond. As he told it later, this contract

called for the completion in ninety days of the equipment of a road having about twelve miles of track, at that time unlaid, and with a route only provisionally determined; the construction of a complete steam and electric central-station plant of 375-hp. capacity; and the furnishing of forty cars with eighty motors and all appurtenances necessary to their operation. This was nearly as many motors as there were in use on all the cars throughout the rest of the world. Thirty cars were to be operated at one time, and grades as steep as 8 percent were to be mounted. Finally, the payment was to be $110,000, "if safisfactory."[76]

There is no need to go into detail about the construction of the Richmond system beyond noting that the track laid by a separate contractor was, in Sprague's words, "simply execrable, built for profit, not for permanence." As a result, the grade that was thought to be limited to 8 percent was not so. "One grade, nearly a mile long, was in places nearly 10 percent." In general, "The rail was of antiquated shape, poorly jointed, unevenly laid, insecurely tied; the foundation was red clay. Many curves were sharp, and the rail spread easily." It was on this shaky base that Frank Sprague accomplished one of the outstanding successes in the evolution of transportation, a victory particularly impressive for that reason. The historical geography of American transportation has running through it this thread of gaining great goals despite low investment and often poor infrastructure, and thereby offering to a popular culture a democratic solution to their needs for movement. The Richmond trolley system was fully in that tradition.

The steep grades on the tracks he was provided led Sprague to think in terms of cable assistance on the sharpest rises. The two 7-horsepower motors with which he had equipped his cars seemed inadequate, and the engineers began to discuss double-reduction gears to replace the single-reduction ones provided. E. H. Johnson, the businessman who had invested consistently from its

founding in Sprague Electric, could see expensive new modifications. "Guess the first thing is to find out if the car can get up the grade by itself," he argued. Sprague later described the trial to find that out.

If we succeeded in climbing the hill I knew what would probably happen to the machines; but it was vital to learn whether a self-propelled car could be made to go up that grade at all. We went steadily up that and another hill, around several curves, and finally reached the highest point of the line in the heart of the city. I knew that the motors must be pretty hot.

An enthusiastic crowd soon gathered and in the delay I was in hopes that the motors would cool down sufficiently to permit us to continue the journey. No sooner, however, had we started than I felt a peculiar bucking movement, and knew that we were disabled. The trouble was due to a crossed [short-circuited] armature, then a little known difficulty.

Unwilling to admit serious trouble, I told Greene, in a tone that could be overheard, that there was some slight trouble in the circuits, and he would better go for the instruments so that we could locate it. Then turning out the lights, I lay down on a seat to wait, while the crowd gradually dispersed. After waiting a long time for Greene's return with those "instruments," inwardly praying that he would be late, he came in sight with four of them, big, powerful mules, the most effective aids which could be found in Richmond under the circumstances.[77]

Obviously the hills could be surmounted, but at the cost of an overload of the motors. To guard against that, double-reduction gears were added, and the trolley gained one of its most valuable characteristics, that of climbing hills of a steepness that still taxes gasoline or diesel engines. As developed in Québec City, Pittsburgh, Berkeley, and San Francisco, trolley systems climbed grades of 10 to 15 percent, more than three times the gradients practicable for steam or other standard rail systems.

At last in the winter of 1888 the Richmond system was nearly complete, but the Union Passenger Railway was facing bankruptcy. In an attempt—unsuccessful, as it turned out—to avoid that pass, the opening was rushed forward. Sprague's cars and their technology went into operation on February 2, 1888. There was trouble with the brushes in the motors, but the later adoption of carbon rather than brass solved this problem. At last a full system of some 12 miles was electrified successfully and was running with only modest problems. The tracks were poorly constructed, but the trolleys did run and great numbers of passengers stood waiting to ride the cars.

It was in this context that perhaps the most significant convert to the electric railway was made on a warm June night in 1888. Sprague had learned that Henry M. Whitney, president of the West End Street Railway in Boston, was in town to look over the Richmond operation before finally determining to mechanize what was one of the larger, and certainly one of the more profitable, horse-car lines in America. The Boston company had tentatively decided on cable traction, although the Hub's winding streets would have made such an installation a problem; but Yankee conservatism had demanded a rapid check of how electric traction was faring at that time. In particular, Whitney was concerned whether the trolleys could provide the frequency of service on their lines that the West End was already operating behind their teams. Aware of that concern, Sprague determined on a graphic demonstration for the doubting Bostonians. Longstreet, the general manager of the West End, was the stumbling block, holding that "because an inevitable traffic snarl [in big cities] would bunch a string of cars together on a single line" and thus overtax the supply of current, cables were a more reliable

source of power.[78] To demonstrate the falsity of this view, Sprague set about carrying out a demonstration of "somewhat dramatic character." On the June night in question he collected twenty-two cars, more than half his fleet, on one stretch of track after service was closed for the night. The cars were bumper to bumper when he wakened Whitney and Longstreet to come for a demonstration. They started serially, with the second and successive cars getting underway as soon as there was headway enough to follow on the car ahead. The powerhouse had been warned to carry full steam and as much voltage as could be put out, so the fleet did start out in series, albeit with a dimming of the lights. But once the cars were well underway, the lights brightened and no trouble was encountered in moving the fleet to its destination. The engineer had taken the precaution of wiring extra fuses in parallel on the circuits, and at the height of the strain the trolley voltage had dropped from 500 to less than 200, but Whitney was convinced. Back in Boston, Whitney enthusiastically adopted electric traction, specifying Sprague equipment. So the first large city adopted the trolley. Within little more than a year there were two hundred systems either finished or underway in American cities, half with Sprague equipment, and over 90 percent operated with facilities built under his patents.[79]

The rapidity with which the trolley was adopted in both Canada and the United States was startling. Unquestionably a great potential market was waiting to be tapped. Since the Civil War, street-railway operators in the United States had been searching earnestly for a source of mechanical power, but none had proved truly satisfactory. Dummy engines worked badly on streets and were not ideal even below or above that level. Cable-car lines were costly to construct, expensive to keep in repair, slow, and subject to simple breakages that would stop an entire line. The compressed air, chemically heated, and other experimental cars that the French in particular attempted to employ never proved very satisfactory. It remained for the application of electricity to provide a relatively cheap, fairly easily installed, and ultimately quite reliable intraurban transit system.

Although Werner von Siemens built the first line, and there were the tourist lines in Britain soon thereafter, there can be no question that it was the work in the United States that really solved the problem in an economically satisfactory manner. The adoption of the overhead wire (in contrast to Siemens's cumbersome elevated gas pipe), of the trolley pole, of the wheelbarrow mount for the traction motors—and the development of those motors themselves, most of which were either the work of Frank Sprague or brought to perfection by him—made the trolley work. All that remained in the creation of the techology was to devise a way in which trains of trolleys could be assembled and run by a single *motorman*, as the drivers of these vehicles came logically to be called. Again Sprague did the job. When he was asked to electrify the South Side Elevated Railway in Chicago in 1897, it was clear that single-car operation, with the requisite headways between cars, would not serve adequately on a major arterial line in a great city highly dependent on mass transit. To handle the situation, which could hardly have been dealt with by stationing separate motormen in the individual cars of a "train" (how could they possibly have coordinated their acceleration in multiple cars?), he devised a control operated in the cab of the head car that would activate the separate traction motors not merely in each car but, in most cases, on several axles of a single car. This *multiple-unit operation* made possible the electric mass-transit system that was to flower so quickly—within a decade in New York, in Paris, and in the tubes of London as well as

in most other large cities—and so work critically for the growth in urban morphology.

THE FIVE-CENT FARE AND THE REDUCTION OF DISTANCE

The West End Railway of Boston plays an important role in the evolution of American urban transportation because it was that company that brought together the flat-rate fares of the horse-car era with the expanding limits of service of the trolley times. "Where the fare on the horse roads was [commonly] 5 cents, it was rarely altered during the rapid extension of fare limits which followed the introduction of electricity."[80] The reasoning was quite direct; it was fairly clear even in the earlier years of electrification in the late 1880s that it cost less to move passengers by electricity than by horse traction, so in order to increase business it was sensible to keep the existing flat fare where it was. Electric companies tended to expand for several reasons: the speed for the vehicles was increased to three to five times that of horse-cars, so a greater distance might be covered for the same duration of journey; cars and equipment were more expensive to buy than in the past (being larger and now motor-powered), so there was a desire to try to expand the length of lines to make better use of those vehicles; the cost of generating power was high in investment terms, so there was the wish to spread the cost of powerhouse construction over a larger system; and there were a number of assumptions that the administrative and operating costs on electric traction lines could be kept down by enlarging the size of the system.

But at the same time that the companies were lengthening their lines, regulatory agencies, the public, and even the management of the traction companies shared the view that the 5-cent flat fare was a foundation of the industry. "When the [Boston El-

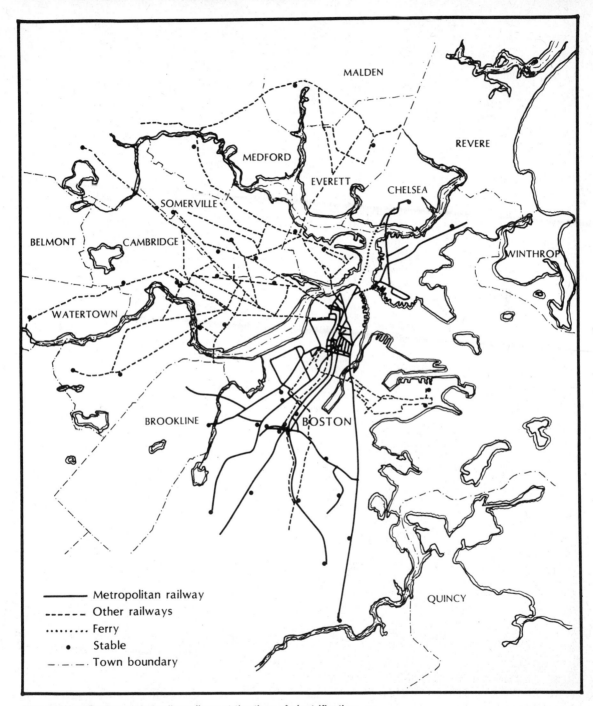

Map of West Boston street railway lines at the time of electrification.

evated Railway] was chartered in 1897 not only the state but the company insisted upon writing the 5 cent fare into the provisions."[81] Henry Whitney had held that view in 1888 when he ordered the electrification of the West End Railway and when that company was reorganized as the Boston Elevated Railway the doctrine was still strongly held.

> Both the Board of Railroad Commissioners and the Public Service Commission [of Massachusetts] considered it an institution of great social value which helped to prevent the congestion of population in the cities and all the social and moral evils caused by congestion. "A sound transportation policy," said the Commission, "requires consideration of the relations between transportation facilities and living conditions. The tenement house and the *three-decker* with all that they involve of undesirable living conditions and fire risk are closely related to the problem of adequate transportation facilities."[82]

In the social and economic view of the time, the 5-cent flat fare was the measure of "adequate transportation facilities," just as much as the existence of electric trolleys and later on of elevateds and subways. New York City, when it was shaped from the five metropolitan counties in 1899, had as a charter provision that it must be possible to move freely among the five resulting boroughs for that same 5-cent fare.

The significance of this low flat fare is evident: it meant that for the first time the economic cost of distance in the city was standardized to the extent that city people might live and shop, work, or go to school in any part of the city for a single unit fare. It cost no more to move from Cambridge to South Boston than it did within Cambridge itself. Particularly for lower-income groups, that impact was powerful: for the first time, factory workers could live well away from the factories without bearing a high eco-

nomic burden thereby, and the more menial office employees could suddenly think in terms of suburban living if those suburbs lay within the fare limits of the Boston E1 or its peers in other metropolises. When Sam Warner wrote about Streetcar Suburbs, he was dealing with just that situation—not, in fact, the more definitive suburbs that lay 10 to 20 miles from the Hub. These latter were the purlieus of the middle class, and had been so well before the stringing of the trolley wires.[83] Somewhat disregarding this earlier suburbia, Warner draws perhaps too sharp a contrast. Still, his picture is worth quoting to show the nature of the trolley's impact on the city that perhaps earliest experienced it in full force. Warner holds,

> Two qualities mark off the Boston of 1900 from all preceding eras: its great size and its new suburban arrangement. In 1850 the metropolitan region of Boston encompassed a radius of but two or three miles, a population of two hundred thousand; in 1900 the region extended over a ten-mile radius and contained a population of more than a million. A change in structure accompanied this change in scale. Once a dense merchant city clustered about an ocean port, Boston became a sprawling industrial metropolis. In 1850 it was a fairly small and unified area, by 1900 it had split into two functional parts: an industrial, commercial, and communications center packed tight against the port, and an enormous outer suburban ring of residences and industrial and commercial subcenters.[84]

The greatest weakness of this analysis is its failure to distinguish between the suburbia of the steam railroads, which already existed in the 1850 metropolis that Warner too narrowly defines as the older mercantile city, and the one that grew around the trolley lines. As I have shown elsewhere, the Boston suburbs began as stopping places on the regional rail network. Some of these were simply older New England towns that began to house some city workers once steam railroads were providing a service that could be used for commutation, as was the case by the early 1850s; others were more complex New England towns, frequently newly incorporated portions of older towns, in which industry grew up to create a satellite with employment as well as housing. Only by drawing this contrast can we begin to understand the morphogenic impact of the trolley. In *Streetcar Suburbs*, Warner is talking about the filling in of the interstices among the beads of suburban and satellitic settlement that had already come into existence along the railroads.

David Ward has shown that the growth of Boston, as with other cities, left a band some 4 or 5 miles from the heart of the city that was underdeveloped in the railroad era. This body of land could not easily be approached by steam train—either the stops of those cumbersome assemblages could not be frequent enough, or the generally radiating railroad lines left sectoral gaps—so it had to wait for inclusion in the city on the development of a much more finely grained transit, the trolley. With frequent stops and the easy construction on existing arterial roads, the electric-traction companies could serve this band too distant from the city for easy access through horse-cars and yet not far enough away effectively to be served by steam trains. These were the true streetcar suburbs, as Ward has shown.[85]

In addition, there was nearly as significant a second use made of the trolley in the morphogenesis of the modern metropolis. This was in the encouragement of industrial satellites in the penumbra of major metropolitan cities. Before the coming of the trolley, these factory towns had had to depend on local housing for their workers. With the stringing of the overhead wires, satellites could grow easily, depending on a labor force drawn from neighboring outlying towns, sometimes factory towns themselves but often just residential suburbs. The ease with which trolley lines could be built meant that not all had to focus on the heart of the core city; others could center on outlying points of lesser focus, at first largely centers of major employment likely to be in factories. For the first time it was possible to think in terms of large numbers of people moving about the metropolis, but with no geographical reference to the city core; both workplace and residence would lie within a sector, an urban realm, of the larger metropolis and might be divorced from the older mercantile city, at least on a daily basis.[86]

The joining of two distinctive daily movements—that focusing on the older mercantile core of the metropolis and that on a set of industrial satellites—meant that the volume of use of the trolley was massive even by comparison with a fully developed railroad and horse-car system. Taking Boston again, because it had one of the most fully developed of railroad commuting systems—for example, South Station in Boston was the world's busiest railroad station just before World War I—and one of the most elaborate horse-car layouts—the system of the West End Railway—we may draw some useful statistical comparisons. Mason has shown that Massachusetts—which effectively contains virtually all the suburban and satellitic trolley services around Boston, as well as being heavily dominated by that metropolis to the point we may use state figures as a rough measure of metropolitan growth—had the highest development of electric traction of any American state. Although possessing only 0.25 percent of the land area of the United States, the Commonwealth in 1902 had 10.9 percent of all electric railway trackage, 40 times the national average of miles of track per thousand square miles (287.64 to 7.16), and 2.9 times the national average mileage per 100,000 population. Massachusetts had no near rivals among the other states in these measures, so we may justly argue that by looking at the Bay State we can, at the turn of the century, see what trolley development did before there was any effective automotive competition.[87]

The emerging picture is that of a democratic society finally possessed of the daily mobility it had sought throughout the life of the Republic. Although it was not one of the stated liberties of 1776, there can be no doubt from the consideration of American history that *mobility* was an innate goal of the national drive that so characterized Americans in the nineteenth century. The settling of a vast continent that lay between the crest of the Appalachians and the Pacific in little more than the first half of the last century, the creation of a distinctively new urban morphology in the American suburb at the middle of that period, and the strongest record of invention and development in mass transit in cities all bear witness to that drive for mobility. The nature of the trolley systems in Massachusetts at the close of the last century served to show the objective of that national drive.

By 1904 more than half a billion passengers a year were being carried by Massachusetts street railways, a figure that grew to 625 million by the close of the decade,[88] this in a state with a population of only 2.8 million in 1900. "Before about 1910 the street railway industry extended fare limits, granted transfer privileges and favored consolidation,... with almost a sublime indifference as to the length of the profitable ride."[89] The result was an increase in absolute mobility greater than even the considerable growth in passenger numbers would suggest. Already before the first decade of this century the average round-trip length had considerably increased in the commonwealth, from 7.04 miles in 1890 to 10.45 miles in 1900, so the citizen's call on the trolley to get him around at a low cost was actually increasing even before the greatest period of consolidation and of fare limit extension had been reached.[90] The

results of this enhancement of the 5-cent flat fare were highly differential: for the passenger the benefits were astounding as for the first time any regularly employed persons in the cities probably had command of transportation throughout their home town and even in many cases well into the countryside around it. For the traction companies the effects were just as startlingly the reverse: their earnings failed to reimburse the stockholders for their investment in a great number of cases, and the costs of upkeep were put off.

The network of street railway lines ... spread over the countryside before the economic principles of operation were clearly understood. Fifteen years after the introduction of electric traction street railways were heavily overbuilt. Too great a reliance on the experience of the horse-car period coupled with an enormously rapid change in techniques resulted in inadequate and over-optimistic estimation of the cost of maintaining and replacing street railway property.[91]

Much has been made of the electric-traction industry.

Taking the history of the industry as a whole it should be obvious that the general public, and this is by no means exclusively composed of car riders, has received for long periods from the street railway a service whose full cost has not been paid. This means, of course, that at the termination of the life of those parts of the property whose cost does not justify replacement, street railway service must be discontinued.[92]

Here we have a case wherein throughout almost the entire life of a private and very capitalistic industry there was a subvention of major proportions from investors to the general public of the city. As a result of that subsidy, the urban morphology was fundamentally reshaped in a single generation.

Chicago elevated at Lake Street and Oakley Boulevard in 1893. Chicago Transit Authority photograph.

The electrically operated street railway introduced a new epoch in urban transportation. It made possible the continuance and acceleration of growth of metropolitan areas, one of the most striking facts in the history of the 19th century. It not only connected city and country, but, in a sense, created suburbs.[95]

The latter point was certainly true for blue-collar workers, who for the first time could take up suburban residence, either in that band 4 to 6 miles outside the core city where Warner's *Streetcar Suburbs* were located or in subsidiary suburbs adjacent to the industrial satellites that came to make up the complex urbanization of the trolley-car metropolis, as in Natick west of Boston.[94]

In 1901 the electric railway had been extended to over 15,000 miles in the United States, and not all of that in cities. In fact, as we shall see later in the chapter, the electric interurban was an outgrowth of the city street railway and hard to differentiate from it. In New England, however, the distinction is not too important, as most of the electric traction can be considered as applied to the street railway *sensu strictu*. Still, it is hard to disaggregate the census data on passengers because that agency's definition of interurbans was peculiar and changing. If we look at the industry as a whole, we find that mileages of electric railway increased from 21,682 in 1902 to 41,447, nearly twice that figure, at its peak in 1917. At that time electric railway mileage was about 16 percent of the length of the standard railroad mileage of the country. In the next decade some 5,000 miles of electric railway were abandoned, a decline that continued even more rapidly in the 1930s—to 28,500 in 1934, 19,600 in 1940, and—in a period of very rapid abandonment after the World War II period—to 10,800 in 1950 and 5,000 in 1957.[95] Passengers totals followed a similar course, reaching a peak of 15.65 billion in 1923 before beginning a rapid decline to just under 10 billion in 1932, when conditional stability was reached with a range between 8.3 and 12.1 billion until 1949 before the postwar debacle set in. Massive abandonments brought ridership down to 2.5 billion in 1957, less than one-sixth that of the peak year, 1923.[96] At the height of their success during and just before World War I, the interurban railways so well developed in the Northeast, Middle West, and populous parts of the Pacific Coast appear to have captured "about 75 percent of the local traffic from a parallel railroad line, and to have generated a considerable amount of additional short-haul traffic."[97]

In summing up the financial experience of the electric-traction industry, Hilton and Due draw a grim picture: "Most of what can be said of the rise of the automobile industry is true in reverse of the interurbans [and electric traction in general]. Those who had faith in them paid dearly. Few industries have risen so rapidly or declined so quickly, and no industry of its size has had a worse financial record."[98] Yet I would argue that no other form of transportation within cities has had so great an impact on the physical—that is, the geographic—build of the places. The American city as we know it reached its outer limits in most metropolitan areas in the time of the trolley, and it was those vehicles that made the American suburb a democratic institution—one that no legion of aesthetes grimacing in disapproval has ever been able to convince most Americans

was badly conceived or undesirably constructed. When electric traction permitted the worker's family to move to the suburbs, there was joy in their hearts, and for most it has not proved ephemeral. When trolley lines had to be abandoned as basically uneconomic, considerable problems were introduced that we will examine in a later chapter. But the trolley suburb was an interesting case of a capitalist subsidization of what most saw as a highly desirable transformation of American urban morphology, and thereby of its social geography. Those minds generally still hold to that view.

CITY EXPERIENCE IN THE COUNTRY: THE FARMER'S RAILROAD

In a chapter on transportation in the city it may, at first, seem odd to consider, even briefly, what is essentially a form of rural transport. Such was the interurban, whose existence we have already noted. But those facilities were an outgrowth of electric traction in cities, and this seems the logical place to give them at least passing notice. As Edward Mason argued, these were merely extensions into the countryside surrounding the city of the electric-traction lines that were being advanced so rapidly along city streets toward the limits of their home towns. In the general enthusiasm that gripped the trolley expansion, promoters often could see no reason to stop where the streetlights did. Because many street-railway promotions were as much real-estate undertakings as transportation developments (which helps to explain at least in part why these speculations were continued despite disappointing financial returns), their impact on urban morphology seemed to hold as much hope as threat. Once into the countryside, there was no logical termination short of the inability to find investors to pay for another yard of track. The booms in interurban construction in the first decade of the twentieth century always seemed to find money for yet another stretch, until the line began to approach another city and to gain confidence as tall buildings again rose over the horizon. In that way electric traction came to extend not merely *outside* a city but rather *between* such places. Viewed as a distinct technology meeting a new and still untapped rural market (much like the one the trolley lines had been built to serve for city populations), the interurban came soon to have its own rationale independent of many of the assumptions of the trolley companies. The interurban has been called the Farmer's Railroad, implying that the standard steam railroads failed to provide the farmer the high level of transportation that was offered to city people—with stops on every corner and relatively frequent and fast passenger service to the heart of the city—and that he should have access to it.

The interurban was actually two things: first, it was an electric-traction line intended to provide a high density of service to rural areas; second, it was a small-unit-of-service railway to provide frequent service between major towns and cities. In many ways it was the effort to combine these two, often conflicting, services that posed financial problems for the operating companies. If the interurban was to compete with the steam railroads in interurban markets, it must do so by maintaining fast schedules and keeping down the fares it charged. If it was to provide service as the Farmer's Railroad, it must stop at the entrance to any farm whose occupants sought to use the line, thus slowing down the journey and probably increasing the costs of operating the service (because of increments of passengers of extremely small size). But since a quandary is not a precise definition, we may wisely borrow one from the magisterial study of interurbans. Hilton and Due tell us: "the term interurban may be applied to railways that shared most or all of the four following characteristics: electric power, primary emphasis on passenger service, equipment that was heavier and faster than city streetcars, and operation on streets in cities but at the side of highways or on private rights-of-way in rural areas."[99] The distinction between a city system and an interurban was often clouded by the street-running in towns, which meant it had to be either merged with a city traction company or operated there in similar fashion.

The first interurban is hard to determine. Hilton and Due advance claims for the Newark and Granville Street Railway in Ohio in 1890, with runners-up in the Fidalgo City and Anacortes Railway, an 11-mile real-estate speculator's line opened in Washington in 1891, or the Canton and Massillon in Ohio the next year. But each of these represented a somewhat incomplete evolution of street-car technology. Probably the first incontestable interurban was the East Side Railway between Portland and Oregon City, opened in 1893, or the 19.5-mile Sandusky, Milan and Norwalk of Ohio, completed at the same time. Ohio became the true hearth of interurbans, much as Massachusetts was of trolleys:

> Ohio, apart from its southeastern quarter, is an area of many medium-sized towns at no great distance from one another. The rural area is fairly densely populated, and farm income relatively high. Much of the terrain is flat, and there are few impediments to railway construction. In the 1890s local railroad service in the Midwest was generally inferior to that of New England railroads. For these reasons Ohio and central Indiana (which shared Ohio's characteristics) were the most promising areas for developments of intercity electric lines.[100]

Once the first lines had been pioneered in the early 1890s, the ostensible virtues of the form appealed to promoters in many areas with fairly proximate cities and a reasonably dense rural population. Two building booms occurred between 1900 and 1908, leaving little time for the accumulation of balance sheets that might have given a full idea of the financial characteristics of these promotions. Between 1898 and 1901, 144 electric railway companies were chartered in Ohio. Hilton and Due figure that 54 percent of the electric-track mileage built in Ohio during the 1900–1908 booms came in interurbans, with 185 companies of this sort incorporated between 1901 and 1903.[101]

> Riding habits varied from one area to another [in the United States], and a promoter might anticipate receipts anywhere from about five dollars to more than nine dollars a year per person from his tributary area.... The interurban promotor could reasonably expect to attract about 75 per cent of the local traffic from a parallel railroad line, and to generate a considerable amount of additional short-haul traffic.[102]

But that traffic won from the railroads was the least profitable those companies possessed, and there was no great sadness on their part for the loss of local service that tended to overtax their lines while filling only rather small pockets in their conductors' money pouches.

The interurban fulfilled many of the service objectives of its potential customers, providing access from villages and farms to county-seat towns and larger cities. It probably also improved the frequency of service among the medium-sized cities in those regions where the form was well developed.

Because these interurban lines served places not reached by the standard railroads, a number conducted freight service. This was mostly package freight; but some more extensive systems, such as the Illinois Traction Company, had purpose-built cars, even refrigerators for the handling of meat and

other perishables. That same company offered sleeping-car service to passengers. This adaptability to local circumstance was the essence of interurban survival. These were, after all, basically parochial operations to serve specialized markets. To maximize what would never be a vast market, it was necessary to think in terms of gaining an intensity of use, as much as was available locally.

The interurbans were not big moneymakers. As for trolley companies in general, the interurbans were ultimately bankrupt by the rise in expenses that began during World War I. This rise went along with a sharp decline in passengers. If we take the Ohio interurbans as an example, we find they had reached their maximum passenger totals in 1919, at 256,963,473. By 1928 they had been reduced to 100 million passengers a year, and in 1933 ridership had declined to less than 40 million.[103] This situation is summarized by Hilton and Due in austere terms:

> The decline of the industry began very slowly in the period immediately preceding World War I, gained momentum during the war despite the good record of many lines in this period, continued at a steady pace until 1924, and then burst forth in full strength in the late twenties, culminating in complete collapse in the early thirties. There followed the gradual disappearance of the remnants (a process interrupted by World War II), which culminated in the years between 1947 and 1953. But the typical interurban, as such, had disappeared by 1953.[104]

By the early 1980s only one interurban was left, the Chicago, South Shore and South Bend, and that mainly because of its role as a feeder of freight to the Chessie System, its owner.

The fortunes of the interurban traction in the United States tell us several things that we should acknowledge: that in modern

Early electric elevated railway in Berlin.

transportation there is a sharp structural distinction between urban and rural transport not in any way obliterated by the wide adoption of personal mechanical transportation through the nearly universal ownership of automobiles in Western countries.

THE ORIGIN OF MASS TRANSIT

By the turn of the century a number of cities faced the need to evolve city transportation to the point that it might cope successfully with the movement of literally hundreds of thousands or even millions of people per day. In cities where the population was approaching half a million or more, the conflux of people in the conduct of their various daily journeys could produce truly daunting crowds that must be dealt with if the city were to survive. London and New York had already dealt with the problem in, respectively, the 1860s, with the Underground, and the 1870s, with the Elevated. But by the last decade of the nineteenth century more cities were experiencing the daily crush. Paris, Boston, Philadelphia, Chicago, Glasgow, Budapest, Hamburg, Berlin, Vienna, and a few others were so affected. Within this group there were the supercities of the time—Paris, Chicago, Berlin, and Vienna, for example—as well as very large but more traditional cities—Glasgow, Boston, and Budapest. The supercities tended to make the first efforts, from obviously more pressing need, but to do so within the technology of the standard steam railroad. If the elevated technology was associated initially with very large cities in America—New York and Chicago—and with steam traction, that practice soon changed, both in the size of the city involved and in the motive power used. In 1893 two elevated railway systems were opened with electric traction, thus heralding the arrival of the electric rapid transit that would so transform urban transport. For the World's Columbian Exposition held in Chicago in that year, an Intramural Railway was designed by H. M. Brinckerhoff and carried on a six-mile elevated structure that was "the first commercial third-rail road of the present type."[105] In Liverpool the need for transport of workers along the Mersey docks brought into existence again in 1893 the Liverpool Overhead Railway, similarly drawn by electric motors. Once these demonstrations of the practicality of those motors were in hand, other viaduct lines were electrified. In 1895 the Metropolitan West Side Elevated in Chicago and the Brooklyn Rapid Transit in New York began electrification, followed the next year by the Chicago and Oak Park El, and in 1897 by the Berlin Overhead, the beginning of the extensive system of electrified elevated lines in the German capital. Boston's elevated lines were opened with third-rail operation in 1901, the El lines in Manhattan were shifted to electric working in 1902 and 1903, and viaduct sections of the Paris Metro were completed, with electric traction, at about this time.[106]

The elevated served as a useful but rather transitional technology, one that was practicable with steam working as subways never really were despite the longevity of steam locomotives on London's Metropolitan Railway, but far from ideal from the city's viewpoint. Clearly the Underground was the more desirable form for the separation of grade; but the high cost of constructing it close to the surface, and with the requisite blowholes to permit some of the smoke and steam to escape, was such that only Lon-

don's market seemed large enough to bear the burden. The elevated had been the expedient of London's poorer relations. Again, it was the imperial capital that was to forge the next link in the evolutionary chain. Because the Thames was then still an important part of London's port, local authorities resisted any bridging of the river below London Bridge; yet the growth of the City as the business center of the metropolis made the absence of fixed crossings awkward. To overcome that barrier, only a tunnel would seem to serve. Much earlier in the century Marc Brunel, with the assistance of his son Isambard, had struggled for years to bring the Blackwall Tunnel to completion in 1843, being the first to use a drilling shield to force a way through the clays and other sediments in the river bed. To meet the need for a crossing southward from the eastern part of the City, a 1,430-foot tunnel was driven using an improved drilling shield, with the idea that it would be operated by cable traction. But when completed in 1870 the traction proved infeasible, so it was left as an awkward pedestrian tunnel crudely lighted by open gas jets and reached only by rough wooden staircases.[107] The cheapness of this method of tunneling was well proved, if the cable traction was not, so there were subsequent calls for applying deep-shield tunneling to the solution to London's transportation problems.

That solution had to wait, however, for the perfection of some form of traction that could be used in tunnels of considerable depth and very limited ventilation. The work with electric traction in Germany and America had demonstrated the utility of that form by the mid-1880s, when another proposal for a Thames tunnel was advanced. Still, its backers stated that they intended to equip their proposed 1.75-mile tunnel with cable traction between William Street in the City and the Elephant and Castle in south London. Only the failure of the company intended to provide the cables, and the extension of the tunnel railway to twice its original length to reach suburban Stockwell, changed the plan. The great success of trolley systems in the United States and the practical results of the Giant's Causeway tourist line built by the Siemens in Northern Ireland caused the promoters of the City and South London Railway to reexamine their plans. It was decided to substitute third-rail-fed electric traction for the original cable plan; when the railway opened in November, 1890, it became the world's first underground electric railway.[108]

But the City and South London was not a complete success. Its engineers had not successfully worked out its power feed so that it could operate will a full complement of cars; its King William Street station in London was on an awkward curve at the top of a sharp upgrade and with inadequate platforms; and its tunnel was somewhat too small for efficient train design. Still, the line proved that deep tunneling could be undertaken fairly easily in the specific case of London (with its deep underlying bed of clay) and the electric traction could hope to serve.

Two events finally made electric subways practical: one was the City and South London and the other was the multiple-unit control and motor-mounting that made train control practicable. Once Sprague's multiple-unit installation was made and had proved its worth in Chicago, the subway became a practical objective.

That subway, however, tended to have two expressions that still remain. One, found in large cities, was a direct outgrowth of the heavier technology employed on the earliest underground and elevated rapid transit lines first operated by steam. The other, found in somewhat smaller cities, stemmed from the lighter technology of the trolley car. As might be expected of the pioneering line, the City and South London does not fit easily into either of these categories. It was built to a small size because of the restrictions of the tunnel in which it operated, and its poor motors kept it seriously underpowered. Successor lines did, however, fall generally into the two categories. The first few to follow on the London line did so mostly in the manner of undergrounding the trolley scale of operation. This was not surprising: until Frank Sprague perfected traction motors and multiple-unit controls in the mid to late 1890s, it was his technical improvement of the street railway as a trolley line that stood as an adequate technology for city running, on the ground, in a viaduct, or in a tunnel.

We have already seen that Boston was the first large American city to adopt the trolley system, specifically the one that Sprague had improved on to the point of successful operation in Richmond in 1888. In the Hub the earlier success of the West End Street Railway as a horse-car system—one of the largest in existence—meant that very quickly the company as a trolley operator was building up impressive totals of cars running and passengers riding. We should not forget that Whitney had been greatly concerned to see how many trolley cars could run on a line in close succession, and it was Sprague's success in starting and moving at reasonable speed a fleet of twenty-two cars that sold Whitney on electric traction. Within a few yards the streets of downtown Boston laid with trolley lines were becoming so crowded with the early sparkers that other traffic was finding it hard to cross their course or proceed along their axis. Tremont Street was particularly clogged, so the city decided to force a separation of grade—one that must be underground for the electric traction, as those sacred spots the Boston Common, the State House, and Park Street Church were adjacent to this public-transit axis and could not be disfigured by a viaduct.

Before we take up the Boston subway, for historical accuracy we must account for the

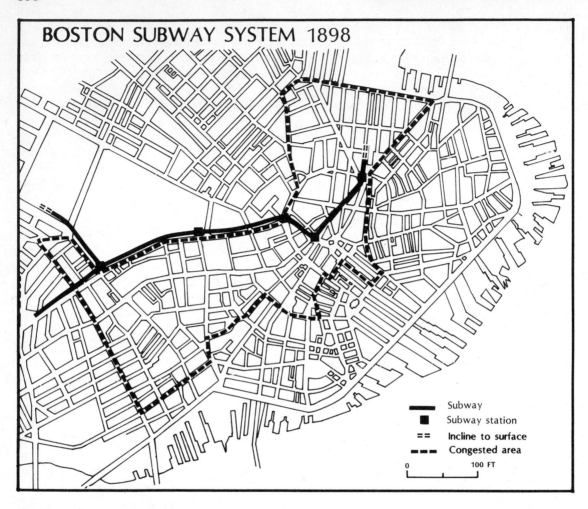

Map of rapid transit lines in central Boston.

first line to follow on London's efforts, even though it does not fit structurally into our picture. In 1896 the Hungarian kingdom was to celebrate its millennium with the exhibition that was de rigueur in the nineteenth century, and a large park with exhibition buildings was constructed near the outskirts of Pest, the capital. As was commonly true of these great fairs, there was a real-estate development associated with it. Andrassy Street, a great ceremonial avenue some 2 miles long, was laid out to connect to the park and serve as the axis for public transit to care for the fair crowds. To maintain the grand quality of the street, it was decided to carry the transit underground in a cut-and-cover tunnel in which trolley-car-like vehicles would run. These single cars were of relatively small size and served for over sixty years, in part because after the fair this subway was never as severely overcrowded as many others were. Like the Chicago Fair's

Intramural Railway three years before, it was a special facility for an ephemeral purpose—but in this case, because it passed through an emerging upper-middle-class residential area, it was continued in operation after the close of the fair in the fall of 1896. Thus, after London, the Hungarian capital has the oldest subway in existence.

Boston, however, played a much more significant role in the arrival of the subway as an instrument of enlarging urban transportation. The success of the electrification of the West End Railway was such that in the early 1890s as many as 200 trolleys an hour were passing along Tremont Street at the northern edge of the central business district of downtown Boston, leading to a severe overcrowding of that and all intersecting streets, and in turn clogging much of the downtown area.[109] The Massachusetts General Court, the Commonwealth's legislature, called for a commission to deal with this problem literally in its front yard. In 1894 a Boston Transit Commission was appointed to find a solution to the success of the trolley in its first large-scale American installation. At the end of the year that commission proposed that Boston adopt elements of what one local newspaper called the "European transit system"—that is a grade separation, with transit carried out underground. Elevated railways had been considered; but a composite photograph showing an elevated line passing along in front of "Brimstone Corner," Park Street Church, so scandalized the Brahmins that a referendum for a subway carried, 15,369 to 14,298, and construction began in 1895. The design used was based in part on English experience, but considerably modified. As electric traction was envisaged from the beginning, a complete tunnel with no open stretches or blowholes in streets would be built.

Ventilation was a matter of serious concern to the early subway builders. Their concern may seem exaggerated to us today, but it should be remembered that at the turn of the century pulmonary disease was man's most dreaded killer, so the worry about the quality of air in the tunnels was a manifestation of the human survival. After the Boston subway opened, most granted it very high marks. Ventilation shafts at several points along the route provided air of a quality much better than London's, for example, as rated by no less an authority than The New York Times.[110]

Even today the original Tremont Street Subway is perhaps the sweetest smelling subway on which one can ride.

The project called for access to the tunnel from three points, two in the south and one in the north, where ramps would lead the trolley cars down from street level. Four tracks were available over the length of two and two-thirds miles of the tunnel, so that after the opening in September, 1897, the route easily handled up to 285 cars an hour without excessive crowding. In part that success was due to the adoption of multiple-unit controls (first used earlier in that year by Frank Sprague on the South Side Railway in Chicago), permitting the operation of trains of cars, yet allowing individual units to operate on their own once out of the heart of the city. This use of trains of electric cars in a subway was first employed here in the Boston Subway, making it in some ways the earliest of the modern underground workings. The experiences in the Hub made it possible to envision what the ultimate technology of such subsurface lines would be. Vienna copied the Metropolitan Railway to some degree; but Paris, New York, and most subsequent subways systems owed more to Boston.

The success with the Tremont Street Subway, as it came to be known even though it extended over a greater distance, led the Boston Transit Commission to think in terms of additional rapid-transit lines. The Boston Elevated Company had been formed under the same act that created the subway, with the notion of carrying out grade separation above ground. But in the heart of the city it was still the firm intention to avoid elevated structures. Thus, when in the spring of 1901 the Maine Line El opened, its trains (of what we now think of as standard el-subway cars) dove down the Tremont-Broadway ramp at the south end of the original subway and passed, over the inner set of tracks, to the Haymarket ramp in the north, where the elevated structure took over again, carrying the rapid-transit trains around the North Union Station and off toward the northern outskirts of the city at Sullivan Square. Placing the elevated trains in the subway meant that trolley runs had to be turned around at Park Street and Scollay Square stations, as there were only two available tracks between the two. This cut the number of trolley runs through the subway by 1,500 a day, so there was immediate pressure to restore the subway to its original purpose of handling the "sparkers." That purpose was restored in 1908, when a parallel tunnel under Washington Street carried the elevated from Dudley Street for two and a half miles through the downtown to emerge on its own just before the North Union Station, picking up its northerly elevated structure as before. At this time another all-elevated line was carried around the waterfront, on Atlantic Avenue, providing a second route around the edge of the business district and an efficient transit connection between Boston's two stations, North and South—the latter the busiest in the world at this time.

Heavy rapid-transit cars were introduced to the Tremont Street Subway in 1901, the first time that had been done in the United States. Soon thereafter the Boston Elevated Company made a further important innovation. In 1894, when the act setting up the Boston Elevated Company and calling for the building of the subway was passed, it was

also determined that some rail connection across the harbor to East Boston must be undertaken. To carry out that mandate, a subaqueous tunnel—the second in the United States following on the Grand Trunk tunnel under the Ste. Clair River at Sarnia, Ontario–Port Huron, Michigan; and the first on any transit system—was begun under Boston Harbor. The bore of a mile in length, of which 2,700 feet were under water, was opened in December, 1904, using trolley cars as vehicles as had the original subway.[111] In 1924 this line was changed to standard rapid-transit cars, although they had to be shaved in size a bit (with smaller wheels) to pass through the tunnel.

Most outsiders, particularly New Yorkers, have tended to look on the Boston subway system with condescension on the grounds that it is run under a strangely assorted set of practices. The trolley in a tunnel has been seen as quaint and old-fashioned instead of what it really is—the pioneer that led to what ultimately became standard practice, but could hardly be so in the first years of electric traction. Boston's system was the first to integrate the subway in a more extensive transport network run by electric traction. Neither the City and South London nor the Budapest subways functioned as more than an isolated and specialized component of the city transport of their respective metropolises. It was in Boston that multiple-unit control was first introduced to subway operation. It was there that heavy rapid-transit vehicles were first run underground. And the East Boston Tunnel stood as the earliest of the subaqueous bores that were to make subways integrated systems later in New York, Paris, London, and Montréal. Only the City and South London was earlier in this regard, and it was on a much smaller scale as well as standing isolated in its route and awkward in its technology. The Boston subway system remains unusual, but no one should dismiss

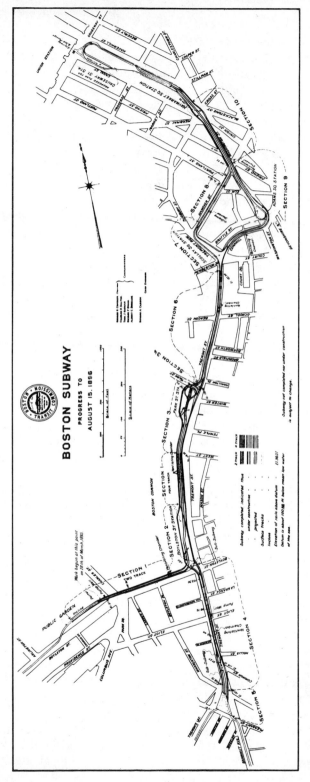

The Tremont Street subway. Author's photograph.

it as having only antiquarian interest. It was there that some of the truly significant elements necessary to the creation of what became standard technology for subways were added to the foundation laid in London. When the Main Line El Route opened in Boston in the spring of 1901, a modern rapid transit system can be said to have run for the first time.

Evolution was a necessary component of these early transit systems: the standard form for urban transportation was still in doubt. The Boston trolley subway was one approach, which, as we shall see, tended to be rejected in the early decades of this century but has returned ever more vigorously in the last several decades. The other widely proposed approach involved applying what had grown up as the elevated-railway technology—heavier cars, commonly assembled into trains, and (after Sprague's development of multiple-unit controls) run by a single motorman, all operating on a totally private right-of-way normally with a third-rail power feed—to underground operations. Boston took this route when it opened the Washington Street Tunnel in 1908. Before that, however, Paris and New York had begun this type of transit.

New York had tried to build a subway in the 1860s but had failed to gain the official and financial-community support necessary to accomplish the job. That effort had been predicated on the notion of steam traction, which certainly contributed to its failure to gain popular support.[112] In the 1890s further efforts were made to create a subway, but legal objections of property owners seemed to stymie any successful project. Finally, in 1900 the courts were resorted to, and the way was cleared for construction of the first of the three systems that ultimately were built in New York. In the first contract to be let, the city would provide $35 million for construction of the subway and would grant to the contractors who undertook the

work a fifty-year lease on the property, subject to renewal for a further twenty-five years at an adjusted rental. In addition to providing the use of the space below city streets to the subway, the city must purchase and provide free to the contractors any building space outside the street lines that was required for stations or yards, up to a total of $1 million.[113] This then was a mixed enterprise, with the actual facilities built by the contractor but paid for by the city—the system that Boston pioneered in the previous decade. New York was not yet certain about traction; the contract specified that it must be either by compressed air or by electricity. August Belmont, as banker, and John McDonald, as contractor, set about building the line that would ultimately become the world's longest rapid-transit system.

The New York subway system is too long and complex to be followed in detail here. It is sufficient to our purpose to take note of its original project. This was a subway to begin at City Hall in Manhattan and be carried northward therefrom, using Park Row, Centre Street, Elm Street, and Lafayette Place to Fourth Avenue. The subway passed northward on that straight, wide street as far as Forty-second Street at Grand Central Station (soon to be rebuilt). There a sharp curve carried the line along Forty-second Street to Times Square, where it resumed its northward course on Broadway as far north as 125th Street. In some complex trackage on a high viaduct the rapid transit continued to 133rd Street and then along Eleventh Avenue and on several local streets to Kingsbridge at the northern end of Manhattan Island. This route was 13.5 miles in length, with about 2 miles on viaduct rather than underground. A branch was carried from Broadway and 103rd Street to Central Park, under that open space to and under Lenox Avenue to 140th Street, in a curve to a tunnel crossing of the Harlem River, at about 145th Street, and then on a number of local streets in The Bronx to

Bronx Park. This branch was 6.97 miles long, of which 3 miles were carried on a viaduct, a nice term for an elevated. At City Hall this original route was given a turn-around loop, with a short platform station.[114] It was at August Belmont's suggestion that a Brooklyn Branch was added to this scheme, particularly in response to the inclusion of that large city in the Greater New York that was shaped just before subway construction was undertaken. The increased bonding capacity afforded by the amalgamation of the five boroughs is thought to have made the first subway project possible, so it was appropriate that it seek to include as many of the five boroughs as possible. The Brooklyn Branch began at City Hall; progressed to the Battery at the lower end of Manhattan along several streets in the financial district; passed under the mouth of the East River in a tunnel; and then went along Joralemon Street, Fulton Street, and Flatbush Avenue to Atlantic Avenue in Brooklyn, a distance of 3 miles.[115]

This system, of 23.5 miles, was four tracks wide on its main stem and three tracks on major parts of its branches, allowing express working in midtown and Lower Manhattan. It was by far the most extensive and elaborate system undertaken up to the time it opened in 1904. Only the link under the Harlem River delayed the completion of the original Interborough Rapid Transit until March, 1906. As soon as the subway was opened, the I.R.T. Company leased the existing elevated lines in Manhattan (on Second, Third, Sixth, and Ninth avenues) and thereby gained control of all rapid transit in Manhattan.[116] At that juncture the electric street-railway company, the Metropolitan Railway, realized that its business was likely to suffer, so its promoters backed a second subway company calling on the city to undertake such construction for lease to them. Before the engineers came forward with a plan, merger took place between the Metropolitan and I.R.T. companies, the prob-

able purpose of the former's call for a second subway; but the city decided to go ahead with a second line, one on Lexington Avenue. This began at 138th Street and Park Avenue in The Bronx, passed under the Harlem River to Lexington Avenue, down its length in a double-deck structure to permit four tracks on that narrower roadway to 15th Street, and then by various streets in Lower Manhattan to the Battery.[117] The progress of this proposal was too complicated for discussion here. Suffice it to say, in the end a second company was introduced into Manhattan subway construction and operation, the Brooklyn Rapid Transit Company, which took over the Centre Street Loop already built by the city and a new subway up Broadway as far as 59th Street as well as considerable subway mileage in Brooklyn. The Interborough Company then constructed a new line northward from 42nd Street on Lexington Avenue and a Seventh Avenue subway leading downtown from Times Square. In this way there were two separate I.R.T. lines north-south in Manhattan, with the previous dogleg between Grand Central Station and Times Square now run as a self-contained shuttle, as well as a Brooklyn (B.M.T.) line in Manhattan. Over successive years many loops and additions were added and in the 1920s and 1930s the city-owned and -operated Independent system was constructed to provide a subway from Brooklyn through Lower Manhattan and up Ninth Avenue to 207th Street. In all, thirty-two lines and branches were completed, for a length of 237.23 miles (1971), with 137.05 miles in tunnel and 77.28 miles on elevated structures.[118] Starting in 1940 the city gained control of all subways and elevateds, so that by the close of World War II a single integrated system was in hand. This giant carried over 1.3 billion passengers in 1969–1970 and with a service density reaching to thirty-four trains an hour in both directions on some of the busier trackage. This system is exceptional in its long stretches of three-and four-track line that permit parallel express and local working over considerable distances.

Other American cities took up the subway to a varying degree, though none to the extent that New York did. In 1909 Philadelphia completed an elevated-subway line on Market Street, a route extended northeastward mainly as an elevated in 1922. In 1928 a north-south subway on Broad Street was added by a different company, using a different gauge. Other stretches have been added over the years, such as the line from 16th Street parallel to Market Street Subway and then over the Benjamin Franklin Bridge to Camden, which was completed in 1936. This route has been considerably lengthened in the post–World War II years by the construction of the Lindenwald Line reaching to outer suburban Camden, where junction is made with electric train service to Atlantic City. Chicago opened two lines under the Loop during and just after that war. And in the late 1960s the Bay Area undertook to build the first extensive American system begun since Philadelphia's. But we will come to that story in the concluding section of this chapter. Pittsburgh, Cleveland, Newark, Los Angeles, and San Francisco all had short underground lines in the prewar years, but none of these was more than a specialized section of a basic street-railway system.

SUBWAY DEVELOPMENT IN EUROPE

The complexity of subway development permits only a brief summary here of undertakings in Europe. By looking at London and Paris, we may gain a view of the general practices and effects while looking at two of the more interesting systems to result from the first subway era—that is, construction completed before World War I. Taking up London first because its initial efforts came somewhat earlier, it may be noted that with the opening of the City and South London Railway in 1890 interest in expanding the underground network of the great metropolis became more focused and more immediately practical. The notion of driving deep tubes through the thick band of London clay underlying most of the heart of the conurbation immediately seemed the solution to the problem of securing a grade separation for transit in a city with narrow and winding streets. The first of these tubes (after the specialized and only partially successful City and South London) was one that cut through the middle of the city, interior to the Circle Line made up of the Metropolitan and District railways. Even this critical Central Line was slow in coming because private investors were shy of the abysmal returns to be earned. It took seven years for the City and South London Railway to pay anything on stock, so investors

knew from hard experience that such ventures, built where land and property values were very high, devoured so much capital that a good return was rarely to be had, particularly since these undertakings were relatively lightly used outside the daily rush hours . . . . It was not urban railways but horse-drawn vehicles on the roads which still made money, despite the strong competition in that branch of the industry.[119]

Britain seemed to face a quandary as there

The larger electric locomotive and, particularly, multiple-unit techniques were not available until after 1897. Until then any tube line was involved in the heavier costs of a [standard] railway [technology], and yet, for technical reasons, could hope only for the smaller returns of a tramway [trolley]."[120]

Americans and American technology were to play a major role in facilitating the eventual development of the London subways in their expression as bored deep tubes.

Before that intervention, however, a start was made by local capital and technology in the chartering of the Central London Railway in 1891.

The route secured for that company extended from Shepherd's Bush in the northwestern outskirts of the city across the metropolis via Holland Park, Bayswater Road, Marble Arch, Oxford Street, High Holborn, and Cheapside to the Bank. It had already been shown that this was the main east-west traffic artery of the city, as in 1889 it carried 5,950,000 passengers in 239 omnibuses between Bayswater and the City.[121] Thus, if any stock flotation were to gain takers, this was the most sanguine. But the proposal met a great deal of chauvinistic skepticism. William Bourn Lewis, a civil engineer who testified before the parliamentary committee considering the bill to authorize the line, showed what Barker and Robbins in an exceptionalistic frame of mind called "a realistic technical grasp of the situation." He held;

> I have noticed that we seem to need a little time to digest American ideas and to adapt them to our own use.... If we hastily adopt what is said to have succeeded in America without knowing what really we are doing, we shall only hinder the progress of electric traction.[122]

That caution perhaps caused the syndicate that finally pushed construction of the Central London line to be composed primarily of German-born financiers in London (Ernest Cassel and Henry Oppenheim), the English Rothschilds, and Darius Ogden Mills of the Bank of California. The "realism" of the English could not see the effective substitution of the electric motor for the steam engine at this time, or for some time to come, arguing before the parliamentary committee as the Metropolitan Railway did that steam was "the only efficient form of railway motive power."[123] Only the Prince of Wales's circle of financial acquaintances seem to have had faith in the project.

Although there were problems encountered in the tunneling, by that time the Greathead Shield was well developed and the London clay was an unusually favorable medium in which to employ it, so progress was steady and without any major hitch. The real problem lay in finding an electrical system better than the primitive one used in the City and South London. The General Electric Company (G.E.) in the United States, by then an amalgamation of the Edison and Sprague electric-traction interests, was contractor for the line's electrical equipment. As they had built the first really powerful electric locomotive ever constructed, for use on the Baltimore and Ohio's tunnel under its eponymous city, a new prospective was offered by the decision to adopt G.E. locomotives. It is still hard to explain, however, why locomotives rather than traction motors on individual cars were adopted. The record shows that Frank Sprague, no longer directly associated with G.E., was in London during the construction period, serving as an advisor on the motors for the elevators that were to be used in several stations. By that time, 1897, his work for the Chicago South Side Railway on multiple-unit operation had proved successful, so it is hard to explain why that more efficient and versatile traction motor system was not initially adopted by the Central London Railway.[124]

As the line neared completion in 1900, final plans for operation had to be made. It was decided to adopt a uniform fare for the line, two pence (its sobriquet, the Tuppenny Tube, persisted long after that fare had to be increased). Perhaps the general American influence in the undertaking also caused the vehicles to be termed *cars* rather than *carriages* as on the standard railroads.[125] Those cars were, in fact, modeled after cars on American elevated lines and were considerably larger than the vehicles on the City

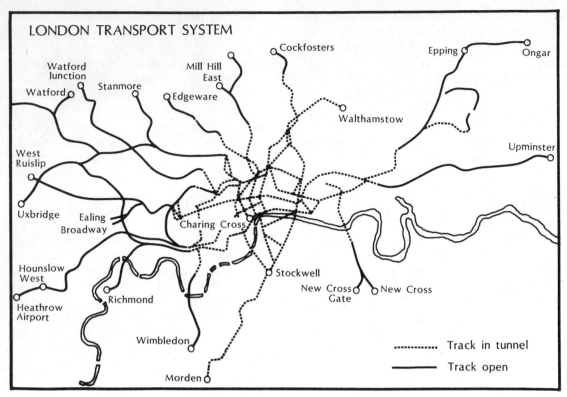

LONGON TRANSPORT SYSTEM

Map of London Transport rapid-transit lines today.

and South London. They first appeared in London on the underground connection built by the London and South Western Railway from Waterloo Station to the Bank, which opened in 1898 over its 1.5-mile line.[126] The official opening of the Central London Railway line took place on June 27, 1900, with the Prince of Wales appropriately doing the deed and Mark Twain attending as an honored guest, along with the various German-born bankers who had had faith in the line.[127] The success was immediate, though somewhat reduced after the Metropolitan Railway belatedly discovered that there was another "efficient form of motive" traction and began electrification in 1903. The 5.75-mile Central Line was entirely underground save at its westernmost end. The

heavy locomotives never proved entirely satisfactory because their great vibration was transferred to the surface buildings. An inquiry was undertaken, and it was decided to adopt the multiple-unit operation then widely used in the United States. Frank Sprague offered to equip several cars with his system free of charge as an experiment, but the General Electric Company had by that time developed their own M-U system, so this piece of American traction technology came to supplant the less practical earlier locomotives that had been exported to Britain, perhaps justifying the exercise of caution in the adoption of "American ideas."[128]

The completion of the Central Line, as the Central London Railway came to be known when it was brought into the general Underground System, was the most important event in London transportation history after the opening of the original Metropolitan Railway in 1863. The demonstration of the practicality not only of deep-tube construction but also of electric traction—if you will, the combining of the great advance in British civil engineering with the equally striking progress in American electrical engineering—was necessary before a generally applicable system of rapid transit for London could be established. Within the next decade most of the fundamental elements of the London Transport of today had been created.

The first element in that development was the arrival of yet another American seeking to play a role in intraurban transport in Britain and London. George Francis Train had sought that end in the early 1860s but had failed because of his own stubbornness and that of the British upper classes. In 1900 Charles Tyson Yerkes, who in the 1880s and 1890s had secured a controlling interest in the Chicago street railways and later trolleys, led a group of investors, mostly Americans, to enter the London scene by buying the powers conferred by a parliamentary act of 1893 on the Charing Cross, Euston & Hampstead Railway. This underground project led them directly to formulating a strategy for an integrated system of such lines in the great metropolis. As part of that strategy, the Yerkes Tubes, as they were then called, gained control of the much older and shallow District Railway, which formed half of the Inner Circle Line now being hard pressed by the successful opening of the electrified Central Railway. Yerkes immediately set about the electrification of the District Line, as part of which he had the massive Battersea Power Station constructed on a scale adequate to provide power for a much larger system.

By 1902 the strategy was fairly worked out. The District was to be electrified; its partner the Metropolitan Railway was to be forced to adopt the same system of low-voltage direct-current power feed; and a number of initially independent tube projects were to be bought out, constructed, and integrated into a workable system of rapid transit. In 1902

> the Yerkes group formed the Underground Electric Railways Company of London, Ltd., which took over the Metropolitan District Electric Traction Co., Ltd. and arranged to take in hand the building and equipment of the Brompton & Picadilly Circus, the Charing Cross, Euston & Hampstead, and the Baker Street & Waterloo underground lines . . . and also the Great Northern & Strand. Yerkes became the chairman and remained so until his death in 1905. The underground railways had become the Underground.[129]

With this management it is not surprising that such a large element of the electrical technology and rolling stock came from America. The District Line's rolling stock "was of American design," and its partner the Metropolitan Railway also adopted "American-style cars for its inner services."[130] It is impossible to follow through the further construction history of the London Underground.

Transportation for the Constrained City: The Paris Métro

The first subway in France was not to be found in the capital but rather in its main Mediterranean port. At Marseille in 1893 a steam-operated line, le Tramway de l'Est Marseille, faced a problem in reaching the port, so for some 800 meters it was carried in a tunnel beneath the narrow streets of the older city and a steep hill found there. Since electrification came only in 1905, this can hardly be counted as a true urban subway.[131] France did participate very enthusiastically in the adoption of the trolley for urban transportation, particularly in the industrial cities—St. Étienne, Lyon, and the towns of the north and east where most of the heavy industry was found. Eventually most large towns had trolleys, and the problem of clogging on narrow streets became acute. In Paris in particular the need for improvement in transport was somewhat delayed by considerations of aesthetics. The overhead wire was resisted but in 1898 the Chemin de Fer Amèricain between the Bastille and Charenton finally was electrified, demonstrating to public authorities that it was possible to establish "le trolley" in Paris. The Thomson-Houston Company of Lynn, Massachusetts, had been instrumental in this introduction.[132] The success of electric traction and the experience in Budapest and Boston with underground working quickly brought Parisian interest in a subway to the fore.

Plans had been proposed for many years that in one way or another would have given the city an enlarged transit capacity, but only in 1898 was a final scheme adopted. Traditionally in France the government provided the infrastructure while the concessionaire would undertake to furnish the stations and the rolling stock, often even the track, but never the civil engineering works that lay below it. The Chemin de Fer Métropolitain de Paris was no exception to this procedure; the city paid for the tunnels or viaducts and platforms; the Métropolitain company furnished the access to the surface and the rolling stock. Given this strong involvement of the city government and even of the national government, whose authorization of the project was essential, it is not surprising that the Métro system, as it soon became known, was viewed from the beginning as a unified project, a fully integrated network. The law of March 30, 1898, which created the Métro, designated six lines that were to be built, the order in which construction was to be undertaken, the fairly specific route of each, the gauge to be used

(which the national government required to be the standard of 4 feet 8.5 inches), the maximum sharpness of the curves permitted (a radius of not less than 75 meters), and a number of other features.

In the 1890s a general geographical conception of Parisian rapid transit had emerged, calling for an east-west, a north-south, and a circular peripheral route, with the first two intersecting each other in the heart of the city and the circular route at four points in the area of nineteenth-century housing still built within the traditional gates of the city. The east-west route, initially called Line A but subsequently designated Line 1, was to be built from the Porte de Vincennes at the eastern edge of the city across its heart to the Porte Dauphine near the Bois de Boulogne. Second in order of priority was the circular line to be carried along the *anciens boulevards extérieurs* through the nineteenth-century housing and industrial areas adjacent to the termini of the mainline railroads. Third priority was to be given to a second east-west line across the heart of the city somewhat farther north of the Seine than Line 1 that would serve the shopping areas on the Rue Lafayette, the Gare St. Lazare, the Opéra, and the financial district around the Bourse. The north-south main line, Line 4, was projected from the Porte de Clignancourt to the Porte d'Orleans, crossing Line 1 originally near the Louvre. Fifth in order of building was to be a second north-south route passing from the Gare de l'Est to the Place d'Italie via the Rue de Strasbourg, via the mainline railroad stations at the Gare de Vincennes (Place de la Bastille) and Gare Quai d'Orléans (Austerlitz). Finally, a sixth line was to pass from the Cours de Vincennes to the Place d'Italie.[133] This last route was ultimately extended from the Place d'Italie westward and across the Seine in the completion of the circular line at the Trocadéro and l'Etoile.

It is impossible and unnecessary to follow

in detail the construction of the Métro. The vigor with which that work was undertaken must startle us when we compare it with the slow pace of most recent subway construction. Line 1, passing through the heart of the city between the Bois de Vincennes and the Bois de Boulogne (to a slightly readjusted western terminus at Porte Maillot rather than Porte Dauphine), a distance of some 6 miles, nearly all of which was in subway, was completed in just seventeen months of construction, to open in July, 1900.[134] The reason for this speed was partly the hope of completing the line in time to serve the Paris Exposition of 1900. That goal was reached only belatedly, but this was the first instance of several in which the Métro system was developed to facilitate the holding of a great exposition in Paris. In that role these fairs had already been significant in bringing about rapid-transit development—in Chicago in 1893; in Budapest in 1896; and subsequently in Barcelona, Rome, Montréal, and Munich (the Olympics).

In the operation of the Métro the Parisian authorities faced a peculiar problem of how to run the trains. Because the Paris-Rouen railroad line had been constructed and equipped by British engineers, that line had run on the left since completion (though the Paris-Orleans railroad, constructed by French engineers, ran on the right). Many French railroads continued that British practice. Some saw the Métro as merely an extension of the mainline railroads—hence the central government's insistence that it be built to a standard gauge—and wanted the trains thereon to run to the left. But the city authorities viewed this as basically infeasible because Parisians were accustomed to trolley lines that ran, as did the general traffic on the streets, to the right.

The second line, the northern circular from the Place d'Etoile along the grand exterior boulevards to the Place de la Nation, was handled quite differently from the first.

As these streets were wider or less prestigious, it was decided to carry much of this line on viaducts—in Paris given a somewhat more elegant treatment with stone and concrete abutments, rather than steel posts as in the American elevateds, but still basically an el where the terrain permitted, or required. Because the central part of this line passed through an area of old plaster of Paris (gypsum) quarries, special problems of construction were encountered, necessitating heavy foundation work.[135] But in 1903 this second line was opened, furnishing the prosperous denizens of Passy and Ternes with an improved access to the gares de Nord and de l'Est; and to the rather contrasting working-class population of Pantin and Ménilmontant better travel to their places of work in the northeast of Paris, to the railyards and the abattoirs of La Villette.

In quick succession other lines were driven through the great city. From the beginning the integration of the system, sharply in contrast to the subways then being developed in London and New York, led to direct and intentional interchanges, *correspondances*, in Paris. At Nation at the eastern end of the northern circular route, interchange with the first east-west transverse was easily accomplished. There as well, a Circular Sud to pair with the Circular Nord (Line 2) was to take off and pass around the outer reaches of the city on the Left Bank, before rejoining the original half of the Circular at Trocadéro, the initial western terminus rushed to completion in time to serve the adjacent Exposition of 1900. At first it had been assumed that several lines would use some of the tunnel stretches in order to save construction costs, but quickly it was realized that desirable headways between trains on a single line could not be maintained if the busier lines were run over a single pair of tracks (as was the universal construction practice in the Métro). The Circular Sud then was carried directly in its own tunnel and viaduct between the Place d'Italie and Trocadéro (later being numbered Line 6 by the sometimes obsessive French logic because it used the original route between Cours de Vincennes and Place d'Italie that have been ranked sixth, as project F, under the law of 1898).[136] But that stretch was actually the last component of the Circular to be finished. The part originally called Line 2 Sud, between Trocadéro and Place d'Italie, was opened in 1906, whereas the final bit, Line 6, was not added until 1906, although the Compagnie du Métropolitain did not agree to operate it until 1909 because of the sparse population along the route.[137]

There is no need to follow the construction of all the Métro routes, but two deserve some mention. The Line 3—through the busier part of the Right Bank, passing from Villiers on the Circular Nord via the Gare St. Lazare, the shopping district near the Opéra, and the financial district around the Bourse, to rejoin the Circular Nord at Père Lachaise—was certainly the most important line constructed. Not only did it connect the more well-to-do residential districts in Passy and Ternes with the center of affairs, but also it provided the onward connection to the shopping and financial quarters from the most heavily used commuter station in Paris, St. Lazare. From Villiers to Père Lachaise the route was opened in 1904, leaving the last bit thence to Place Gambetta to open in its time in 1905.[138] This 7-kilometer line began immediately to carry huge crowds throughout the day, demonstrating at once the instant utility of the Métro system in a city that was both large for its time and densely built up for housing.

The other route needing some mention is the main north-south line between the northern gates of the city at Porte de Clignancourt and its southern gates at Porte d'Orléans, via the Gare du Nord, the Gare de l'Est, the great produce market at Les Halles, the Île de Cité, and the great western terminus at Gare Montparnasse. Probably the most difficult engineering was encountered in building this line. It not only had to find a reasonable access to three of the six mainline stations of the city, but it also had to pass beneath the Seine and close to the most historical buildings in the capital. This was also a very long route, some 11.4 kilometers with twenty-six stations, which gave it the shortest interstation distance of any of the segments of the system as it was developed. Finally, at Châtelet it made the fundamental junction between east-west and north-south routes that had been envisaged from the beginning. As anticipated, this proved to be Paris's busiest subway station. For all these reasons Line 4 was slow in getting underway and long in completion. The greatest problem came in the tunnel under the two arms of the Seine and the intervening island. Prefabricated tunnel sections in steel were sunk in trenches cut into the bed of the river, and the Île de Cité was crossed by similar prefabricated tunnel sections assembled on the surface and then sunk in prepared trenches. The right-bank section of Line 4 was opened from Place de Clignancourt to Châtelet in April, 1908; the southern end from Porte d'Orléans to Boulevard Raspail in October, 1909; and the gap between Raspail and Châtelet in early 1910.[139] With that opening the major part of the original plan devised and legislated in 1898 was completed.

Metropolitan Transit in Paris

Despite its name the Métro evolved as a central-city system, probably the best of its genre but limited in early decades to the legal gates of the city. In the 1950s and 1960s most of the lines were carried for several stations beyond the *octroi* boundary to reach to the centers of the first ring of suburban towns that grew up in what had been until the late nineteenth century the glacis of open land around the city where large fixed forts were intended to protect the capital. As those bastions in the end failed to protect the city in the Prussian siege of 1870, they were eventually abandoned; in the 1920s most were demolished, making room for the first suburban band. The metropolis continued to grow, and soon there were villas and housing tracts extending farther into the rolling plain of the Île de France. After World War II a massive public housing program was undertaken that further populated those environs to the point some form of truly metropolitan transit was required. The need had long before been felt. Between 1855 and 1895 several plans were advanced for carrying the mainline railroads through the metropolis, presumably in tunnels and on viaducts, but the city had effectively blocked such proposals save for the Chemin de Fer de Ceinture. In the late 1890s the city succeeded in advancing the cause of purely urban transport to the extent the Law of 1898 establishing the Chemin de Fer Métropolitain set up a distinctively urban form for that undertaking.[140] The post–World War I growth of the metropolis had been such that the Métro solution was seen to require more than a specialized answer to urban transportation in the initial heart of the metropolis. In 1929 a Métro Régional was proposed with a main north-south and a main east-west route crossing in the heart of the city but serving the full metropolitan district in the way that the Métro had come to serve the original city. It was seen that the trains on these new lines would be the same as served the suburban railroads carrying commuters to the city. The first fruit of this plan was the electrification and modernization of a previously steam-operated commuter railroad, the Ligne de Sceaux, extending from the Luxembourg southward into the distant suburbs to the south of Paris. The operation of this line was taken over by the Métropolitain, although, because of the outbreak of

war soon after the completion of its electrification in 1938, it remained a detached and specialized segment of the Métro.[141]

The postwar reconstruction of the French National Railroads and other urgent projects for housing and modernization of the Métro delayed resumption of work on the regional network until 1960. At that time the French government greatly increased the financial resources of the capital for transit development and a Réseau Express Régional was proposed as a network of avowedly metropolitanwide lines. The R.E.R., as it came to be known, was to serve a metropolis that had grown from 5 million when the Ligne de Sceaux was opened to 8 million twenty years later. To begin with it was appreciated that the standard Métro lines were so saturated with traffic that no reasonable expansion of trains was possible. Additionally, it was clearly understood that with the increasing peripheral extent of the metropolis an express system was needed that could increase the rather deliberate speeds of the original Métro, adequate for central-city transportation but taxing for distant suburban commuting. The conclusion was reached that a separate network must be built, presumably carried much deeper below the surface than the Métro had been in order to find an additional route through the city and, incidentally, a much more direct alignment.

The original Métro had been very lucky in working within a street plan that had been vastly straightened and widened by Baron Haussmann's reconstruction of Paris under Napoleon III. But that system of boulevards forced upon the first subway some awkward alignments in seeking transverse routes where the mid-nineteenth-century reconstruction had favored radial avenues. The Haussmann plan did offer streets sufficiently wide to permit cut-and-cover construction without appreciable property demolition in virtually all its stretches. The R.E.R., however, was not so fortunate. Since most of the usable avenues had already been occupied by the Métro, it had to tunnel.

It was decided that the east-west tunnel would be the first constructed. Using French National Railroads lines to Saint-Germain in the dense suburbs to the west and to Boissy-Saint-Leger to the east, respectively, to create the extensions of the tunnel, that facility was carried from the newly developing office complex at La Défense eastward under the Seine and Neuilly to the first Parisian station deep beneath the Étiole. With wide spacing of stops, the next was at Boulevard Haussmann, with successive distant stops at Auber, for the shopping district around the Opéra, Châtelet, Place de la Nation, Gare de Lyon, and then to the surface east of the heart of the metropolis. This 43-kilometer line had 14 kilometers of tunnel that paralleled the first of the Métro lines to be built, relieving some of the press it had come to experience.

Serving much of the territory previously approachable only by the railroad lines from Gare St. Lazare, the R.E.R. helped to relieve some of the crowding that forced over 70,000 passengers an hour through that elderly station in the evening rush hour.[142] With speeds of 60 miles an hour and wide spacing of stations the express line quickly reduced the travel time from the heart of Paris to many of its western and eastern suburbs when its first section opened to Boissy-Saint Leger in December, 1969, to be followed several weeks later by the La Défense-Étoile section. The final link, opened in the mid-1970s, created the first of the great lines that will eventually intersect at Châtelet, making that point even more the hub of Parisian transportation. While the east-west R.E.R. line was well underway, the north-south line was taken up with an extension of the Ligne de Sceaux from Luxembourg to Châtelet, opened in the late 1970s. Thence this express route will be carried in a new tunnel bored

well below the surface toward the Gare du Nord, where it will emerge to the surface, picking up the already reconstructed railroad line to the northern suburbs with a new extension now in use to Charles de Gaulle airport.

When this network is completed, Paris will have the rudiments of an express network distinct from the Métro and providing rapid connections from the major vectors of suburban development to the very heart of the city. In this way the French have resolved the seemingly certain conflict between the needs of central cities for a dense net of stops that force slow running and much lost time at stations, on the one hand, and the requirements of distant suburbs for widely spaced stops and fast speeds, on the other. New York City, aware of this problem, sought a reasonable solution of it in the four-track tunnels of the heart of Manhattan. Unfortunately, the cut-and-cover construction of most of the New York subways meant that long-distance routings tended to become very circuitous in many cases. Also, because the New York subway was the creation of the city government as well, it became a regional system only to the extent that New York City became in its legal limits a regional metropolis. In London that tying of the Underground to the legal limits of London was avoided; but the absence of express trackage in the heart of the metropolis and the close spacing of stations with low ruling speeds means that the great extension of routes into the distant suburbs has been only partially successful because of the long journey times introduced by a severe compromise forced by using an out-of-date concept beyond its time.

In Paris, by a characteristic practice of highly logical analysis and great central authority and financing, the French have gained what must be the ultimate solution to this problem. The Métro is an ideal central-city system and the R.E.R. a similarly vir-

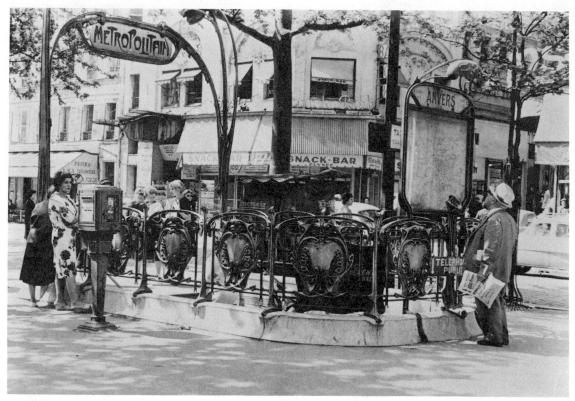

One of the entrance kiosks (by Guimard) of the original Paris *Métro*. Picture courtesy of the French Embassy, Washington.

tuous regional network. By accepting the staged nature of urban growth and adapting to it a staged development of urban transit, they have literally made the best of both times and the urban morphologies that have accompanied them.

SPECIALIZATION OF TRANSIT IN THE BAY AREA CITY

The transformation of urban society and morphology in the years after World War II, reflected in the creation of the R.E.R. in Paris, was even more extreme in the United States. Already in the nineteenth century the growth of the American suburb, the most innovative of the morphological transfor-

mations of the last hundred years, had forced the United States to create new transportation technologies in the electrified street railways and rapid-transit systems that found their first developments in the larger cities of the Great Republic. We have seen how pervasive was that American technology in bringing about the rise of the subway in western Europe. The continuing evolution of the suburb in this country, however, posed what seemed at the time to be impossible conditions for the further evolution of electric-traction technology so trolley lines and segments of transit systems, particularly those that we called interurban lines, were rapidly abandoned after World War II. By the 1950s it seemed the future held no useful

The BART Trans-Bay Tunnel. Bay Area Rapid Transit photograph.

role for electric traction save in a few densely built-up cities with a nineteenth-century morphology—Boston, New York, Philadelphia, Chicago, and possibly San Francisco. In Cleveland, Pittsburgh, Newark, and New Orleans short stretches of trolley working were preserved without those cities having any real electric-traction system. Toronto stuck with such a system but elsewhere in Canada the trolley pole was lowered for the last time. The suburb seemed to have evolved beyond the utility of electric traction, so it was assumed that a successor now ruled in the automobile. Again there was the notion of ubiquity—that one medium of transportation could, and certainly should, serve for all demands. Only in the sections of nineteenth-century morphology found in huge cities did anyone question the notion that there should be a single general transportation form.

The reversal of this thinking came in a most unlikely place, and in a form that ultimately proved highly equivocal as a test of a renaissance of electric traction. The Bay Area City, Oakland and San Francisco, had preserved a reasonably complete intermediate-distance traction system up to 1958. This so-called Key System served particularly the East Bay cities of Oakland and Berkeley with their immediate neighbors, as well as utilizing the San Francisco–Oakland Bay Bridge, opened in 1936, to gain access to the financial district and shopping area of downtown San Francisco. Within that West Bay city an extensive trolley system on the strictly central-city plan was preserved using street running for most of its network but tunnels under the spine of hills that lay to the west of the downtown for access to the residential districts along the Pacific shore. In addition, three of the nineteenth-century cable-car lines operated near the business district. Thus in the late 1950s the Bay Area had a much more extensive traction system surviving than was to be found elsewhere

west of Chicago. By that time Los Angeles had begun very rapidly to tear up its once extremely comprehensive interurban system.

One might have assumed that the San Francisco Bay Area Rapid Transit (BART) District created by the California legislature in 1957 would have intervened to prevent this abandonment of the preexisting Key System while it had time to seek modification of the existing system dedicated to its stated purpose. It did not. Instead, it seems from the beginning to have made the assumption that preexisting technology was no longer valid. By 1961 that rapid-transit district commission was actively promoting a *regional* transit system as opposed to older urban transit systems. "The recommended system is designed to serve regional needs and primarily to carry inter-county and intercommunity passengers."[143] To that end it was established that it was necessary to secure

Average operating speeds up to 50 mph, including station stops, requiring maximum speeds of at least 70 mph between stations, [with] Service during peak hours of travel governed by demand, with headways between trains of as little as 90 seconds, permitting movement of 30,000 seated passengers per hour in one direction; Off-peak service, except late at night, at least as frequent as every 15 minutes . . . [and with] routes to penetrate major centers of business and commerce and stations to be close to ultimate destination of travelers.[144]

The conscious decision to build a system primarily for commuters to serve the downtown districts of the three cities—Berkeley, Oakland, and San Francisco—had a number of important geographical consequences. The BART design placed the stations at such a long interval that it was hard, save in downtown San Francisco, to find any local use for the trains. The desire to encourage the previous auto commuter to shift to rapid transit forced the engineers who designed the system to attempt very high speed operation. As constructed, trains were capable initially of speeds up to 80 miles per hour.

Perhaps most important geographically was the focusing of the planners' attention on a few long arterial routes analagous to, and often in the medians of, freeways or preexisting railroad lines. Unlike most previous transit designs, BART paid relatively little attention to "desire lines" of travel and noncentral generators of traffic. The result was a system that required frequent and costly ancillary facilities, that at times and in places showed poor accordance to the residential pattern of its most likely customers, and was excessively dependent on intermodel shifts of public transit. Quintessentially, BART was a specialized high-speed transit system to serve office workers in downtown San Francisco and, to a much lesser degree, in downtown Oakland.

When this "first modern transit system"— as its promoters consistently and erroneously referred to it—was opened in the 1970s, several rather startling deductions could be drawn. There was certainly a demand for its specialized service, but not on the scale that its promoters, mainly as an act of faith, had assumed. In fact, the 1975 ridership of the system was only little more than half what had been predicted. San Francisco office workers did flock to the system, to the point it was heavily overloaded during the commuter rush hours on the line serving that district. But elsewhere this specialized commuter system failed to justify its high cost of construction because the system's narrow technological capabilities worked against other uses.

If any conclusion can be drawn from this episode, it is that there is truly a distinction between metropolitanwide transit and that of a more intimate urban nature. As the technology has evolved, neither serves the other well. No doubt each technology has its justification, but in determining the scale of any construction this split between services must be understood. In the Bay Area case, the promoters of BART, either unanalytically or perhaps dishonestly, argued that the two could be combined. The plan was considerably overengineered and overbuilt for the purpose it does serve because of undue credulity concerning its utility for general urban transit. Technologically the system proved wasteful because in actual operation it was impossible to maintain the high speeds built in; in the end, the average speed of BART turned out to be nearly identical with that of its Key System predecessor, 35 miles per hour. And unlike that rather too casually dispatched system, BART provided little local service to justify such deliberate running, and none of the collection-distribution network that made the Key System and other traditional transit systems so useful to so many parts of the core.

THE GROWTH OF HEAVY RAPID TRANSIT

Certain subway and elevated railway systems have been discussed for their intrinsic historical-geographic significance. Yet there are far more systems exist than can be covered in this summary chapter. It seems desirable to conclude with a survey of the spread in the application of grade-separated transit over the last century and a quarter. Most of the early systems have been mentioned, so we need only recall their timing. The first by any standard was the Metropolitan Railway of London, whose initial stretch opened in 1863, to be followed within a decade by the completion of the Inner Circle route comprising the Metropolitan and its adjoining Metropolitan District Railway. In the 1870s only one rapid-transit project was brought into use—the early lines of the New York Elevated Railway network that would ultimately become the nucleus of the world's most extensive rapid transit when it was joined, in the first decade of this century, to the earlier lines of the New York subway.

The 1880s saw the extension of existing systems in London and New York, but no new undertakings, probably because the specific technologies used in London—steam railroad underground working—and New York—steam railway elevated working—posed sufficient problems to make wider application less than enthusiastic. With the coming of electric traction in the late 1880s, mainly in the United States and Canada, the interest in heavy construction revived. In 1890 the City and South London bored-tube passing under the Thames was opened, to only partial success, as the electric traction was not very well worked out. That limitation showed up clearly in the slow pace London took in further construction. Although several other deep-tube lines were authorized, little was accomplished toward their actual building until the end of the decade.

Instead, the innovation in rapid transit moved to two surprising cities, Budapest and Boston. In the Hungarian capital a national exhibition in 1896 brought forth the first modern subway using the shallow cut-and-cover technology that was to become by far the most widespread. Boston the next year employed the tunnel technique to relieve excessive crowding in the downtown where great numbers of trolley cars converged, creating the trolley-subway that again would become a widely adapted form in our time. This Boston subway system as it expanded during the following decade became a virtual laboratory of technical innovation that was to be applied to the more extensive systems to be constructed just after the turn of the century. The only other rapid transit built in the 1890s was Glasgow's 6.6-mile circle route around the downtown, not even connected with the surface save by an elevator to lift cars that needed repair, and operated as a cable-drawn line until 1936.

This was a miniaturized technology that remained unique to the Glaswegian service. Chicago in the 1890s began its ultimately vast system of elevated lines and completed the core-area Loop that would make the whole thing work.

The great decade of rapid-transit development was the first of the twentieth century, when Paris, London, Berlin, New York, and Philadelphia joined the ranks of subway metropolises. The superb Paris Métro opened its first line in 1900 and during the decade completed its more important routes. Also in that year London received its first successful electric tube line, the Central Railway, using American traction technology in a successful pairing with British tunneling practice. During that decade Charles Tyson Yerkes managed to bring to initial completion most of the tube lines authorized in the 1890s (but seemingly held up both by the poor electric technology of the City and South London and the resistance to investment in subways occasioned by the poor performance of the first line). With German and American capital and American traction, the London Underground was completed in substantial form in the heart of London during the first decade of this century. Berlin joined the ranks, mainly with elevated lines but ultimately with subway sections, in 1902, and New York completed the first subway of its vast system in 1904, with many other lines finished before the close of the decade. In 1908 Manhattan was connected by the Hudson and Manhattan Tubes subway to the New Jersey bank of the Hudson, and ultimately to Newark, while Philadelphia opened its subway-elevated lines that pretty much followed the pattern pioneered by the Boston Elevated Railway.

The second decade of this century was largely taken up with the World War, but some transit projects were completed before its outbreak. Hamburg with its elevated-subway system on the Boston model first opened in 1912; and a subway system in Buenos Aires, initiated in 1914, became the first in the Southern Hemisphere or outside western Europe and eastern North America. Only the subway in Madrid in neutral Spain was under construction and completed a year after the close of World War I. Even the resumption of peace did not lead to a vast upsurge of construction. Extensions were made in cities with existing lines, but in the 1920s only three cities created new facilities. Barcelona completed the first of its ultimately very extensive lines in 1926, followed a year later by the first line of an even more elaborate network, that of Tokyo. The next year Oslo completed its rock tunnel to carry the suburban heavy-traction trains that extended to the west of the city into its heart at the National Theater.

The decade of the Great Depression saw relatively little construction. Athens opened its line to the Piraeus in 1930; Osaka followed Tokyo's lead in 1933; and Moscow received the first of its many lines in 1935, developing a dependence on subways that became fundamental to large Soviet cities. It was during this time of economic trial that Chicago sought, as a WPA measure, to construct a subway in the Loop, the State Street Subway; but its completion did not come until 1943, making it the only subway system initiated in that decade of war and critical reconstruction.

If the 1900s were the great decade of rapid transit, it was because the great cities of the world began their systems at that time and the technology that was to become standard was mainly worked out then. But the 1950s and 1960s saw far more individual metropolises take up that technology. Toronto began the rush, completing its first line in 1954. Stockholm went underground at the same time. Rome and Leningrad followed the next year, with Nogoya entering the lists in 1957 and Lisbon in 1959. The 1960s added nearly twice as many rapid-transit cities as the previous decade, with the obvious shar-

ing of benefits among rival cities in several countries. Kiev became Russia's third subway city in 1960, Milan Italy's second in 1964, and Montréal Canada's second in 1966. Tbilisi spread the benefits of state planning by becoming a subway town in 1966. The long hiatus in German construction, since 1912, was broken in 1968 when Köln and Frankfurt both opened trolley subways, a technology that was to be widely adopted in Germany, in part as a transition to what might ultimately, but not certainly, be heavier undertakings. That same year Rotterdam brought the first subway to Benelux, although Brussels followed two years later with a trolley subway that was avowedly a transition to heavy electric traction, and Antwerp is just finishing such a facility. Kobe in 1969 further expanded the use of grade-separated facilities in large Japanese cities.

There were thirty-two rapid-transit systems opened before 1970; there have been more than a score completed since then, the speed of adoption of the form has clearly increased. There is no point in trying to follow all of these. The 1970s witnessed the opening of the full BART system, as discussed earlier. The first year of the decade saw Mexico City's already vastly overtaxed subway system put into operation. Munich's complex transit, with a true subway and a meshing system of tunnels for suburban electrified commuter lines to pass through the center of the city, was opened in 1971. Other major systems of the 1970s were France's second subway (if the very early tunnel in Marseille is noted but not given full status), which was put in service in Lyon. The Soviet Union added Baku and Tashkent to its list, Japan Sapporo and Yokahama, Germany trolley tunnels in Stuttgart and Nürnberg, Chile Santiago, and Brazil the first first lines in São Paulo and Rio. The Washington subway opened its first lines during the 1970s. In the 1980s subway lines have been opened or are under construction in Vienna, Antwerp,

Helsinki, Prague, Caracas, Hong Kong, and Melbourne.

It is obvious that the subway, with elevated structures often in sections outside the heart of the city, has become the standard technology for any massive metropolitan area that seeks to become modern. Not all these systems are very extensive, though some extend over great distances. In the early 1970s the rapid-transit systems ranged between New York, with 237 miles of route, much of it four-track, and Tbilisi, with a modest 3.9 miles. In 1970 there were 1,711 miles of rapid transit in the world, up from just 1,000 miles ten years before.[145] The other major systems were in London, with a claimed 254 miles; but some of that was essentially standard railroad trackage integrated into the Underground network, so New York City is generally accorded the first rank in rapid transit. Paris follows with 144 miles, Moscow with 91, Chicago with 89, the Bay Area City with 75 miles, Hamburg with 54 miles, and West Berlin with 51 miles. Other systems with more than 25 miles of rapid transit were Osaka, Tokyo, Philadelphia, Madrid, Boston, Mexico City, and Washington. In addition to the more than fifty true rapid-transit systems there are quasi-subway systems in a number of other places, among them Cleveland, Naples, Sydney, Copenhagen, Warsaw, Liverpool, and Pittsburgh.

The essential doubling of heavy rapid-transit mileage, from 1,000 to 2,000 miles, in the twenty years after 1960 has demonstrated both the maturing of the technology and the wide acceptance of grade separation as a necessary transportation development in any major metropolitan area. The rise of the trolley subway—sometimes using a pantograph rather than the traditional trolley pole, but with the same notion of operating both underground and at street level on the public right-of-way—has signaled the acceptance of the existence of a need for contrasting solutions to transit in the several different morphological components of the metropolis. Such trolley subways usually have complex feeder networks in outlying sections while using concentrated and grade-separated facilities in the center. Another expression of this morphological specialization appears in the combination of subway and elevated elements in systems in Boston, Chicago, New York, the Bay Area City, Hamburg, and several other places.

There has been a renewed interest in the basic technology of the trolley during the last decade, under the disguise of a newer term, *light-rail transit* (LRT). The elaboration of the trolley subway in several German cities, in Vienna, and in Brussels undoubtedly contributed to that renaissance; but the creation of fully new systems has been particularly a North American phenomenon, with San Diego and Calgary serving as pioneers. The LRT, and the modernized version of the trolley that is the LRT vehicle, appears to offer considerable advantages over the heavy rapid transit that emerged at the turn of the century, as well as certain clear limitations. The LRT is considerably cheaper to build, perhaps $2 million to $5 million per mile, whereas the more complicated heavy transit facilities may cost between $50 million and $100 million per mile to construct. The LRT also fits in particularly well as an integration with freeway construction while at the same time allowing fairly inexpensive access to the core of the city on pedestrian malls or other restricted-access streets. The ease of ramifying the outer ends of these LRT lines to provide excellent collection systems where people live at rather moderate density recommends their wider use in North America in contrast to heavy rapid transit, which needs Eurasian city morphology to render it efficient and worth the cost.

NOTES

1. Quoted by John P. McKay, *Tramways and Trolleys: The Rise of Urban Mass Transport in*

Europe (Princeton, N.J.: Princeton University Press, 1976), p. 4.

2. Ibid., p. 5.
3. Jean Perot, *Histoire de l'Administration des Ponts et Chausées, 1599–1815* (Paris: Librairie Marcel Rivière, 1958), p. 140.
4. Ibid., p. 15. This shift has on occasion been assigned to the revolutionary government, but it was in fact adopted by the *ancien régime.*
5. Ibid., p. 440.
6. Ibid., p. 445.
7. Jean Robert, *Histoire de Transports dans les Villes de France* (Paris: Published by the author, 1974), p. 21.
8. Ibid., p. 19.
9. Ibid., p. 21.
10. Ibid., pp. 21–24.
11. John A. Miller, *Fares Please: A Popular History of Trolleys, Horsecars, Streetcars, Buses, Elevateds, and Subways* (New York: Dover Publications, 1960), pp. 5–12.
12. Data from a map presented in T. C. Barker and Michael Robbins, *A History of London Transport,* vol. 1: *The Nineteenth Century* (London: George Allen & Unwin, 1963), p. 33.
13. Ibid., p. 57.
14. Ibid., pp. 57–58.
15. Ibid., pp. 59–61.
16. Ibid., p. 98.
17. Pierre Merlin, *Les Transports Parisiens: Étude de Géographie Économique et Sociale* (Paris: Masson & Cie., 1967), p. 40.
18. Ibid., p. 44.
19. Seymour Dunbar, *A History of Travel in America* (New York: Tudor Publishing Company, 1937), p. 988, argues that this was just the southern end of an ordinary railroad that was operated by horses because it passed along city streets, whereas Pierre Merlin, Jean Robert, and other French transportation historians view it as the advent of a new form, a view shared by John Miller in *Fares Please.*
20. The line from Prince Street to Fourteenth was opened in November, 1832 (Miller, op. cit., p. 18), that between Fourteenth and Thirty-second Street on June 10, 1833; from Thirty-second Street to Eighty-fifth Street,

Yorkville, a distance of 2.75 miles on May 9, 1834; thence to Harlaem village on October 26, 1837. Dunbar, op. cit., p. 124; Alvin F. Harlow, *The Road of the Century* (New York: Creative Age Press, 1947), p. 125. The southern limit of steam locomotive operation came to rest in 1837 at the large new station built between Twenty-sixth and Twenty-seventh streets at that time (Harlow, op. cit., p. 126).
21. Harlow, op. cit., p. 118.
22. Miller, op. cit., p. 20.
23. Robert, op. cit., p. 27.
24. Charles Klapper, *The Golden Age of Tramways* (London: Routledge & Kegan Paul, 1961), p. 12.
25. Ibid., p. 16.
26. Ibid., p. 15.
27. Ibid., p. 21.
28. Ibid., pp. 22–23.
29. Willis Thornton, *The Nine Lives of Citizen Train* (New York: Greenburg Publisher, 1948), pp. 125–129.
30. Commuter service can be shown to have existed from Natick, 17 miles west of Boston, by the early 1850s. See James E. Vance, Jr., "Labor-shed, Employment Field, and Dynamic Analysis in Urban Geography," *Economic Geography* 36 (1960): 210.
31. Hugh Prince presents us with a detailed analysis of the evolution of suburban residence in northwest London in two chapters in Coppock and Prince, *Greater London,* the guidebook published for the 1964 congress of the International Geographical Union held in London (London: Faber, 1964).
32. Barker and Robbins, op. cit., p. 100.
33. Ibid., pp. 111–113.
34. Ibid., p. 15.
35. Ibid., vol. 1, pp. 54–55.
36. Ibid., p. 125.
37. Ibid., p. 126.
38. Ibid., p. 128.
39. John R. Day, *The Story of London's Underground* (London: London Transport, 1974), pp. 15–16.
40. Barker and Robbins, op. cit., p. 137.
41. Day, op. cit., p. 21.
42. Barker and Robbins, op. cit., p. 195.
43. James Blaine Walker, *Fifty Years of Rapid*

Transit: 1864–1917 (New York: The Arno Press, 1970 [reprint of 1918 edition published by Law Printing Company, New York], p. 6.

44. Ibid., p. 5.
45. James Grant Wilson, *History of New York*, quoted in ibid., p. 4.
46. Ibid., p. 28.
47. Ibid., pp. 30–39.
48. Ibid., p. 64.
49. Ibid., p. 72.
50. Ibid., p. 80.
51. Ibid., p. 81.
52. Ibid., p. 111.
53. Ibid., p. 113.
54. Ibid., p. 114.
55. Ibid., p. 121.
56. Miller, op. cit., pp. 76–77.
57. *Jane's World Railways*, 11th ed. (London: Sampson, Low Marston, n.d.), p. 503.
58. Jean Robert, *Notre Métro* (Paris: R.A.T.P., 1967), p. 8.
59. George Hilton, *The Cable Car in America* (Berkeley, Calif.: Howell-North Books, 1971), p. 14.
60. Ibid., p. 15.
61. Loc. cit.
62. Ibid., pp. 21–29.
63. Ibid., p. 31.
64. Ibid., p. 44.
65. Loc. cit.
66. Ibid., p. 47.
67. Frank Rawson, Jr., *Trolley Car Treasury: A Century of American Streetcars—Horsecars, Cable Cars, Interurbans, and Trolleys* (New York: Bonanza Books, 1956), p. 67.
68. John P. McKay, *Tramways and Trolleys: The Rise of Urban Mass Transport in Europe* (Princeton, N.J.: Princeton University Press, 1976), p. 38.
69. Charles Klapper, *The Golden Age of Tramways* (London: Routledge & Kegan Paul, 1961), pp. 56–57.
70. Rawson, op. cit., p. 74.
71. Loc. cit.
72. McKay, op. cit., p. 46.
73. Rawson, op. cit., p. 80.
74. McKay, op. cit., p. 47.
75. Rawson, op. cit., p. 81.
76. Quoted in ibid., p. 84.

77. Quoted in ibid., pp. 85–86.
78. Ibid., p. 89.
79. Loc. cit.
80. Edward S. Mason, *The Street Railway in Massachusetts: The Rise and Decline of an Industry*, Harvard Economic Studies No. 37 (Cambridge, Mass.: Harvard University Press, 1932), p. 5.
81. Ibid., p. 119.
82. The quotation is from the P.U.C. reports of 1914, p. 117.
83. Sam B. Warner, Jr., *Streetcar Suburbs: The Process of Growth in Boston, 1870–1900* (Cambridge, Mass.: Harvard-MIT Press, 1962). For a contrast with the older suburbia, see James E. Vance, Jr., "Labor-shed, Employment Field, and Dynamic Analysis in Urban Geography," *Economic Geography* 36 (1960): 189–220.
84. Warner, op. cit., p. 153.
85. David. Ward, "A Comparative Historical Geography of the Streetcar Suburbs in Boston, Massachusetts, and Leeds, England: 1850–1920," *Annals of the Association of American Geographers* 54 (1964): 477–489.
86. For a more detailed discussion of this morphogenesis and its relation to the trolley and the journey-to-work, see Vance, op. cit., pp. 400–416.
87. Mason, op. cit., p. 13.
88. Ibid., p. 117.
89. Ibid., p. 119.
90. Ibid., p. 72.
91. Ibid., p. 185.
92. Ibid., p. 186.
93. Ibid., p. 185.
94. See Vance, op. cit.
95. Ibid., p. 12; U.S. Bureau of the Census, *Historical Statistics of the United States, Colonial Times to 1957* (Washington, D.C.: U.S. Government Printing Office, 1960), p. 464.
96. *Historical Statistics of the United States*, p. 464.
97. George W. Hilton and John F. Due, *The Electric Interurban Railways in America* (Stanford, Calif.: Stanford University Press, 1960), p. 15.
98. Hilton and Due, op. cit., p. 3.
99. Ibid., p. 9.
100. Ibid., p. 9.

101. Ibid., p. 12.

102. Ibid., pp. 114–115.

103. Ibid., p. 106.

104. Ibid., p. 209.

105. Edward P. Burch, *Electric Traction for Railway Trains* (New York: McGraw-Hill, 1911), p. 26.

106. Ibid., p. 28.

107. Barker and Robbins, op. cit., vol. 1, p. 302.

108. Ibid., p. 310.

109. Brian J. Cudahy, *Change at Park Street Under* (Brattleboro, Vt.: Stephen Greene Press, 1972), p. 17.

110. Ibid., p. 14.

111. Ibid., pp. 30–31.

112. Walker, op. cit., p. 15. Another effort was made to employ atmospheric traction, which proved technically satisfactory, but as in Brunel's work in England, posed sufficient problems to make exploitation impractical.

113. Ibid., p. 165.

114. Interborough Rapid Transit Company, *Interborough Rapid Transit: The New York Subway* (New York: IRT, 1904) [reprinted Arno Press, 1971], pp. 23–24.

115. Ibid., p. 25.

116. Walker, op. cit., p. 192.

117. Ibid., p. 194.

118. *World Railways*, 1971–1972, p. 576.

119. T. C. Barker and Michael Robbins, *A History of London Transport*, vol. 2: *The Twentieth Century to 1970* (London: George Allen and Unwin, 1974), p. 35.

120. Ibid., p. 36.

121. Ibid., p. 38.

122. Quoted in ibid., p. 39.

123. Quoted in John R. Day, *The Story of London's Underground* (London: London Transport, 1974), p. 50.

124. Barker and Robbins, vol. 2, op. cit., p. 43.

125. Ibid., p. 44.

126. Day, op. cit., pp. 49–50.

127. Barker and Robbins, op. cit., p. 44.

128. Ibid., p. 47.

129. Day, op. cit., pp. 60–61.

130. Ibid., pp. 66–67.

131. Jean Robert, *Histoire des Transports dans les Villes de France* (Paris: Privately published by the author, 1974), p. 67.

132. Ibid., p. 86.

133. The detail on the construction of the Métro is taken from Jean Robert, *Notre Métro* (Paris: Musée des Transports Urbains [Neuilly-sur-Seine], 1967); Jean Robert, *Histoire des Transports dans les Villes de France*, op. cit. The section on the law of 1898 is derived from *Notre Métro*, pp. 25–26.

134. Robert, *Histoire des Transports*, op. cit., p. 253.

135. *Notre Métro*, op. cit., p. 41.

136. Ibid., p. 47.

137. Ibid., p. 62.

138. Ibid., p. 49.

139. Ibid., pp. 64–66.

140. Robert, *Histoire des Transports*, op. cit., p. 222.

141. Loc. cit.

142. Ibid., p. 223.

143. *Rapid Transit for the Bay Area: The Four-County System, A Summary of Engineering, Financial and Economic Reports Submitted to the San Francisco Bay Area Rapid Transit District*, prepared by Stone & Youngberg, October, 1961, p. 12.

144. Ibid., p. 13.

145. *World Railways*, 1971–1972, p. 548.

chapter 6

Nature's Gift to Mankind

The Evolution of the Merchant Marine and Steam Navigation in General

Our course through the historical geography of transportation should have made clear the role that water transport has played as the seedbed for the earliest crop of distant ties among peoples and areas. The ancient empires depended both for their creation and for their survival on the ease and rapidity with which sea lanes might be developed. The technology of vessels had to be shaped by men, but nature furnished the route largely in a finished state when even primitive ships were devised. The result was that the spread of a civilization, and of the economic activities that must support it, came in a strongly coastal pattern as much in the Roman Empire as in the city-states of its Greek predecessor.

Rome, though an extensive state, depended for its economic flows primarily on the sea it could justly call Mare Nostrum not only by ultimately controlling it but as well because it dominated Rome's survival. If it were not theirs, they could not survive, as was learned when the coasting barbarians swept through the Strait of Gibraltar seeking to share in the use of Their Sea. The navigators of the classic times deserve more credit than we are likely to give them because their marine architecture was little improved on for more than a thousand years. Only in the late Middle Ages, just the period when our tale in this book begins, was any radical improvement on Greek and Roman shipping secured. Thus, when we seek a brief survey of the role of marine transportation, we may, as in movement on land, cite a long period of technical stability reaching from Classical Greece to the dawn of the modern era. We must sketch not so much the geography of that ancient navigation as its technical accomplishments, that we may understand how transportation revolution came by water in its earliest skirmishes.

THE TECHNOLOGY OF GREEK
AND ROMAN NAVIGATION

The critical nature of movement by sea assured that the ancient states would look on that activity from two perspectives: that of trade that was essential to the survival of the confederation of Greek city-states or of the more extensive Carthaginian and Roman empires, and that of naval offense and defense that sought to assure the free passage of those merchant vessels. Often the two roles were combined in single vessels, as in the heavily manned rowed galleys of the Greeks and Romans that transported high-value cargoes, in the galleys of the much later Venetians on similar errands, and culminating in the East Indiamen that sailed in England's imperial trade well into the nineteenth century. More common, however, was the specialization of vessels either to mercantile or naval uses, the reason being that trade placed a premium on capacity and labor efficiency, whereas naval actions emphasized speed and maneuverability. "The warship and the merchantman, the fishing vessel and the carrier for long voyages—to name but some of the most obvious contrasts—presented separate problems to any group of shipwrights who might be called on to meet the needs of a maritime people."[1] Much of the early development of such specialized ships came in the Mediterranean, possessor of the eldest European tradition in shipbuilding. "The northern tradition may be traced back only to the long ships of the Vikings, the southern to the war craft and merchantmen of the Romans and their predecessors."[2] Borrowings from one of these traditions to the other seem to have taken place only at the time of the Crusades, when the northerners, as the troops of that effort, came into contact with Mediterranean ships and seamanship because they had to rely on Venetian and other southern vessels to carry them to Tunis, Constantinople, and the Holy Land. As Lane has it, "only in the late fifteenth century did they produce a common progeny greater than themselves, the Atlantic tradition" that was to carry Europeans across the greater outer oceans and bring to human history the first instance of full utilization of nature's path, the sea.

In the Mediterranean of Classical times we find already the two types of ships that were to characterize European marine architecture for nearly two millennia: the long ship and the round ship. The first was the naval vessel of the time as well as the packet boat for high-value and light commodities and important passengers. The large crew required to row such long boats in periods of calm or opposing winds was found useful as well in fending off pirates and political enemies who might intercept the flow of valuable trade and powerful personages. "These Homeric ships were fitted with a mast, which apparently was lowered by a forestay and had its foot in some kind of tabernacle. The square-sail set on this mast was apparently used only for running before the wind, and the high poop was designed as a protection against following seas."[3] Because these ships depended so strongly on rowing, they were low in the waist, with somewhat elevated forecastle and sterncastle to provide a fighting platform for the troops carried as a matter of course. There is considerable disagreement as to how many oarsmen and in what arrangement were used in these rowed galleys of Greece and Rome. Here it is sufficient merely to note the necessity that such power imposed on these ships to be long in the stem and rather low in the water, restricting them to relatively calm seas and no more than the coasts of the world's oceans. The cost of maintaining a galley was such that they had to be used for matters of state and of urgent communication. Over the centuries the sides were somewhat raised, mainly to allow for several banks of oars and of oarsmen, somewhat increasing the capacity and seaworthiness of the galley (as the oar ports were sealed with leather); but the very large crew and the need for great rowing benches still severely restricted the cargo hold of such vessels.

In contrast was the round ship. By Homer's time the heavy galleon had emerged with an actual deck and a main reliance on sail to move the somewhat less elongated hull of these merchantmen. "From this time onward the merchantman relied on sail and the warship on oars."[4] Over the centuries those sails on trading vessels tended to be kept to a moderate size to avoid the massive crews that the huge sails of fighting vessels required when those naval ships began to adopt sail in the late Middle Ages. Even though mariners in Classical times could not sail very effectively into the wind, they managed long trading journeys—the full length of the Mediterranean in Solomon's time, for example—and there are Carthaginian coins found in the Azores that suggest that these truly ancient mariners had ships capable of ocean sailing and an understanding of navigation sufficient to reach those distant isles.[5] The round ship, with its greater cargo capacity, its economical crewing procedures, and its higher and more seaworthy sides, seems to have reached a development by Roman times that would not be much advanced on for a thousand years thereafter. Lethbridge believes that as early as 2000 B.C. navigation had reached the state that voyages encompassed the full Mediterranean and extended thence north to the far tip of Scotland. By 300 B.C. Pytheas, a Greek from what is now Marseille, is thought to have reached Iceland, using practices developed earlier in the Mediterranean on the route between Crete and Egypt, which had witnessed dead-reckoning navigation out of sight of land since at least 1500 B.C.[6] Perhaps the greatest problem of navigation in Classical times, viewed from a geographical perspective, was its inability to beat against an op-

posing wind. The low bow and high stern shown in illustrations of Greco-Roman vessels are thought to have been imposed by the need to deal with a following sea, whereas the low sides show that the heavy swells encountered abeam in sailing into the wind would have swamped the ships.[7] But this constructional fault persisted in ship design well into Elizabethan times. Only the rigors of ocean navigation, when combined with the capability to sail into the wind, finally brought the high bow and full sides we associate with sailing vessels pictured in the last century.

The size of vessels built by the Romans is in no way inferior to that of most of the warships launched even in the mid-nineteenth century.

> The important fact for our purpose is that shipbuilding had reached so high a level by A.D. 30–40 that vessels could be built larger than any wooden ship of the line at the time of the Crimean War. H.M.S. *Duke of Wellington* (131 guns), launched in 1852, was about 240 ft on the gun deck and 202 feet on the keel, with a beam of 60 ft and a depth of 24 ft. Her tonnage was 3771.[8]

The vessels of the last century were far taller and stronger than those of the Romans, because, with cannonfire both to launch the balls and resist their impact, strong sides and frames were required; but vessels with between 100 and 200 oarsmen as well as numerous bowmen, boarders, and other functionaries had hulls essentially as large at the beginning of the Christian era. The *Roccaforte*, a buss that participated in Louis IX's crusade against Tunis in the thirteenth century, is thought to have been of about 500 tons with fighting platforms, raised bow and stern 39.5 feet about the keel.[9] Admittedly this was the largest ship offered to St. Louis—the other twelve were of about 190 tons each—but ships of up to 1,000 tons seem to have been built periodically throughout the Middle Ages. What kept most ships far smaller was not the state of the art in marine architecture but, rather, the relatively modest scale of distant trade during the Middle Ages. There was no point in sending a vessel so large that trade could only be carried on at a most interruptedly periodic interval.

This was particularly the case when, during medieval times, navigators learned to sail closer to the wind and could, as a result, accomplish two journeys a year between the western Mediterranean and Syria (while previously the winds had held the round journeys to a single one in that period).

Sailing into the wind was probably the greatest technical achievement of navigation in the late Middle Ages. The form and elevation of the sails was the key to this accomplishment. Whereas the square sail had been the characteristic Roman form, one that held navigation largely to times of a following wind, the extension of trade increasingly beyond the Mediterranean made a greater independence of wind shifts crucial. Even in Classical times some advances had been made with the development of the lateen sail, triangular with a foreshortened leading edge raised well above the horizontal, a rig that allowed an easier shift in the sail with changes of wind or direction.

> It is almost certainly incorrect to think that ships of this Roman age could do nothing more than run before a following wind, but it is clear that they could never beat to windward in anything but the most limited sense. Most vessels therefore waited for favourable winds before starting on their voyage, in the same way that traders in the Indian Ocean used to wait for the monsoon.[10]

The evolution of the medieval carack and other oceangoing ships shifted the focus of marine activity in an important way: during the Middle Ages the nations of the narrow seas, particularly the small but important trading states of the Baltic and the Medi-

terranean, had effectively ruled the seas of commerce. Just as in Classical times it is quite probable that the Carthaginian merchant sailors reached the Azores, it is now unquestioned that the economically less advanced Norsemen reached North America, at least in Newfoundland. But neither of these groups seems to have had the ships to engage in consistent pelagic navigation. Nor does either seem to have found the resident commercial partner that trade so required: the Azores, as far as we know, were unpopulated before the Carthaginians and later the Portuguese arrived; and the Indians of Newfoundland were so few in numbers and basal in material culture that even after the voyages of the Cabots they proved little more than a shadow in the forest, ultimately to be fully extinguished during the nineteenth century. In the fifteenth century the emergence of a round vessel capable of ocean navigation changed the situation. In the hands of the states fronting on the Atlantic—Portugal, Spain, France, England, and Holland—not only did the focus of the European merchant navigation shift, from the narrow to the broad seas, but as well the lands of potential trading connection were expanded.

Much has been made of the closing of the Levant as the portal of Asiatic-European trade, signalized by, but not restricted to, the fall of Constantinople in 1453. Yet this is only part of the story. The intervention of a new middleman in the trade, the Turks, need not have changed matters so very much, except that profits had to be shared a bit more widely, and except that it occurred just as the Atlantic ship was being evolved to an effective form. With those vessels available to the Portuguese, the trading route around Africa could be pioneered in the fifteenth century leading to an East where potential trading partners were numerous.

Mercantilist economic policy's encouragement of gaining the largest piece of the cake of commerce led first to the effort to take over the carrying trade in international commerce, and soon thereafter to the effort to control the sources of supply and of sale of the goods that reciprocated this trade. Already in the seventeenth century, Atlantic Europe had had to evolve its mercantilist thinking from that of controlling the nation's trade at home—in conjunction with the campaign to push the mercantile frontier far toward the trading partner's coast or frontier—to actual political control of any such distant staple-producing area. While the sixteenth-century pioneers of trade had sailed from home ports in Atlantic Europe to the coasts of India, the East Indies, and Cathay, trading there with the natives for staples and goods, the seventeenth-century commercial exploration toward North America had encountered a less developed system of trade. There was no difficulty in navigating to the North American coast, but there were no potentially very useful trading partners to be found with that landfall. The American Indians were few in number and possessed of a material culture so basic that few staples and no manufactured goods were to be found. Only in the areas of Spanish exploration was that generalization to be limited. The Europeans in the West Indies found nothing on their first voyages that constituted an established trading item in European experience. They did encounter tobacco, but it took a generation to train Europeans to use and crave that staple, and a century to do so with any mass demand.

Thus the Spaniards in 1493, and immediately thereafter, found it necessary to introduce a staple from the Old World to the New, sugar from cane, before a mercantile justification for continued voyaging thence could be found. Only in the second decade of the sixteenth century did the Americas finally yield a staple, ready to hand, that could support a rapid and vastly profitable extension of trading frontiers ultimately to encompass most of what we now think of as Hispanic America. That staple was precious metals, gold and silver, already accumulated in fair quantities by several pre-Columbian American societies because gold and silver's mineralogy included the occurrence of native ores that required merely physical separation rather than actual smelting.

With the staple of precious metals in hand, the Spaniards began in the sixteenth century to pioneer a new expression of European mercantilism, the planting of colonies of Europeans to undertake the enlarged production of gold and silver. In this they were building on the earlier tentative efforts at establishing sugar production in the island of Hispaniola, where they also had had to plant some colonists to initiate and advance the sugar trade.

When the French, English, Dutch, and Swedes sought actively to shape a system of staple production in the Americas as close as possible to the one the Spanish had evolved, those northern Europeans faced the necessity of planting people on an even greater scale than had the Spaniards or their Portuguese neighbors (who followed quickly in their footsteps to Brazil.) Both Iberian imperialists did find significant gold deposits as well as fairly large native populations, so they might create mestizo societies in their colonies that required only moderate European migration. The northerners, however, found no gold and few natives, so any New World colonization had to be based on direct plantation of Europeans and the direct extension of Old World staple production through the introduction of European products to America. From North America, furs, fish, timber, and tobacco were the only New World staples Europeans wanted, so the economic development of these colonies required not only much more effort than that asked of the Iberians, but also a much longer time lapse for completion. It was only in the nineteenth century that the European

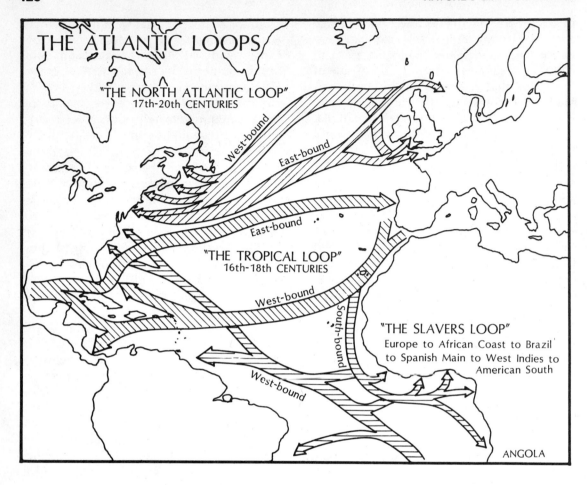

THE ATLANTIC LOOPS

"THE NORTH ATLANTIC LOOP"
17th-20th CENTURIES

West-bound

East-bound

East-bound

"THE TROPICAL LOOP"
16th-18th CENTURIES

West-bound

South-bound

"THE SLAVERS LOOP"
Europe to African Coast to Brazil
to Spanish Main to West Indies to
American South

West-bound

ANGOLA

plantation in North America can be thought to have reached maturity, in contrast to the peak for Latin America, several centuries before. Thus, in the matter of ocean shipping, we must distinguish in the Atlantic crossing between the earlier dominance of the effort in the lower latitudes by the Spanish galleons, and the nineteenth-century dominance by northern navigation using the sailing and steaming packets of the Americans, English, and French. There were then two stages in the "Atlantic Ferry," that of the period 1500–1750, centering in the Trade Wind belt, and that between 1750 and

the present, centering in the belt of Westerlies in the North Atlantic.

Because there were these two stages in pelagic navigation in the Atlantic, it serves our purpose to use this historical division as a basis for organizing our survey of the topic. The world's oceans are so vast that we must also use this look at the Atlantic navigation as the basis for the generalizations we will draw. Most of the technical advances in navigation that came after the emergence of the first Atlantic ships were to be found on that ocean, so it is there that we can discover the joined answers as to why changes came about and how they shaped a new geography of pelagic shipping.

THE FIRST STAGE IN THE ATLANTIC CROSSING

Europe in the Age of Discovery looked in all directions via the oceans, with efforts made to find southerly, westerly, and northerly passages to the Orient. The first to be delineated, though only as far as the American shores that surprised the Spaniards as a barrier to their navigation, came to the west with the voyages of Columbus in 1492 and 1493. In 1498 Vasco da Gama accomplished the circumnavigation of Africa to reach Calicut in India, commencing the first sea connection with the East, one that was rapidly pushed by the Portuguese as far as China and Japan and the easterly reaches of the Spice Islands. There trading "factories" were established whence came rich cargoes in a quantity Europeans had never known while trade remained overland. In the seventeenth century Sir William Petty figured the cost of sea transport to be only one-fifteenth to one-twentieth that of land carriage.[11] Certainly in the previous century, when the roads were even more primitive, the favor toward the sea would have been even greater. Yet so relatively underdeveloped was international trade that Portugal managed its monopoly of oriental trade with the passage to India on the average of no more than seven small ships a year.[12] Thus the southerly approach to the Orient was opened soon after Prince Henry of Portugal established a school to train sailors in the arts of navigation at sea. That activity was enhanced by the development of the compass, beginning in the Mediterranean among the Italians in the twelfth century but long resisted—as Dante's tutor, Brunette Latini, noted—because "no master-mariner dares to use it, lest he should fall under a supposition of his

being a magician."[13] By the mid-fifteenth century the compass had shown sufficient limitations to be taken as a mundane tool, soon to be joined by the astrolabe, a primitive instrument for the measurement of latitude by reference to celestial bodies. As yet no effective means of measuring longitude beyond the rough and unreliable dead reckoning was available. Only much later, in 1759, was the reliable chronometer produced by John Harrison, though again its adoption was slow because of its high cost. Even well into the nineteenth century many navigators used sightings on the moon—first devised by the British Astronomer Royal Nevil Maskelyne in 1767 but much improved by Nathaniel Bowditch in his *New American Practical Navigator*, published in 1802—to place themselves in longitude.[14]

With the southerly approach to the Indies dominated by the Portuguese and the first westerly drive, using the easterly Trade Winds, viewed by the Spaniards as their King's Highway, the northwest Europeans were forced to seek to reach their goal via the northeast and northwest. The Dutch and English dominated this effort and each nation sent expeditions to the north of Europe and North America. As ice choked either route, the main product of this effort came in the considerable commercial intelligence it afforded—notably with respect to the seal and whale fisheries, only then beginning to be developed. But no fairway to the East was found to the north, so the English, Dutch, and French—the main entrants into pelagic navigation on the heels of the Iberians— were forced to contest the Spaniards to the west and the Portuguese to the south. Taking the second of those competitions to begin with, a significant item in the development of the Dutch interest in the East Indies was the publication in 1595 of the *Itinerio* of John Huyghen van Linschoten of Haarlem, in which he gave the sailing directions for the "Indian Voyage" as he had learned them while a servant of the Portuguese. It is thought that this volume, published in English in 1598, engendered such interest in England that the English East India Company was founded in 1600, and at home a United East India Company of Holland was organized in 1602.[15]

The creation of these monopolies among the English and the Dutch effectively limited direct trade with Asia, turning the attention of the great numbers of independent ship-owners not part of the chartered companies toward the Atlantic trade. Portugal conducted its mercantile voyages as a royal monopoly, but Spain did not, controlling these ventures instead with elaborate regulations that forced participants to sail in convoys; a *flota* to New Spain left in late spring or early summer for San Juan d'Ullua (later to Vera Cruz) serving Mexico and the Greater Antilles, and a *dlora* to the Terra Firme or the Spanish Main left in August or September for Cartagena in New Grenada and Nombre de Dios on the Isthmus of Panama. The royal concern arose from the king's share, normally one-fifth, of the product of New World mines, and a very considerable duty on the rest of the trade. To assure these collections, "the entire traffic was confined to the single port of Seville, the definition of which was reluctantly extended to include Cadiz and San Lucar."[16] Between the New World and Seville the Spaniards were particularly concerned with the safety of these ships because they returned laden with the bullion that made the whole venture appealing to the Most Catholic King and his subjects. Attempting to protect the flow, eastbound ships met at Havana, after wintering in the Caribbean, and sailed in convoy, first through the Florida Strait and then northward along the southeast coast of what is now the United States to seek the current of the Gulf Stream to reach a latitude where the Westerlies would give them a fast journey to a landfall on the Iberian coast. Outbound,

having fallen down the coast of Africa to the Canaries and Cape Verde islands (in order to pick up the Trades that would carry them in similar expeditious fashion to the West Indies), the Spanish convoys made the most of terrestial circulations to move their heavy ships that could not sail very close to the wind, shaping both directions of an emerging Atlantic Ferry.

The geography of European interest in the Atlantic was determined largely by the Iberian origin of the trade and its Caribbean objective, spread in a great loop across the southern Atlantic so as to employ the westward-blowing Trades on the outward journey and the eastward returning Westerlies on the homeward leg. The Spaniards took these courses because the trade was theirs; the French, English, and Dutch because they intended to gain by force part of the profits so easily harvested by their Iberian neighbors. Until Holland gained functional independence from Spain in the first decade of the seventeenth century, Dutch ships had directly participated in the *flotas*; after that independence they frequently sailed alongside the French and English at the edges of these great lumbering convoys, ready to capture any ships that might be torn from the pack. Thus all of Atlantic Europe gave its most urgent attention to the great sailing loop fashioned by the circulation of winds over the tropical and subtropical parts of that ocean.

Only in the northerly, subpolar stretches of the ocean was there any different navigation, one of perhaps greater frequency but comprising small fishing vessels entirely. The sail from northwestern Iberia, the small Atlantic ports of France, England, and Holland to the Grand Banks of the Newfoundland Fishery, seems to have been basically hazardous, but from the elements rather than other Europeans, and conducted in a fashion so modest that little detail has come down to us. All we know is that great numbers of men were involved and that Europe came increasingly to depend on North American fish for its diet. While all this almost unremarked effort was underway, those obscure navigators were learning critical lessons in sailing close to the wind in a band of great circulating storms (the Westerlies) very different from the semipermanent wind conditions (Trade Wind, Easterlies) to be found under the first phase of the Atlantic Ferry in the voyage to the Caribbean. Only much later, when plantations of people and staples (largely) from Europe had grown vast in North America, was this northern crossing to come into dominant importance.

Toward the close of the sixteenth century we may judge the impact of the oceanic navigation on the various European participants. As early as 1532 the last Venetian galleon (the great trading ships of the Middle Ages between the Mediterranean and northern Europe) returned to the maritime republic on the Adriatic, never to be sent north again.[17] In 1598 the Hansa was finally expelled from England, bringing to a similar close the period when the Baltic merchants managed to keep the northern trading frontier on English shores. The English had turned the tables along several lanes of trade, importantly that to Italy, where the new port of Livorno (Leghorn) was established largely to continue the Florentine trade with England, when English ships began to arrive directly on the coast of the Ligurian Sea. English navigators also commenced in the time of Henry VIII to sail to the Canaries, the Azores, and the other Atlantic islands when Spain failed to restrict their trade, as it did European contacts with the New World. The Dutch and French similarly entered where they might legally, and elsewhere by stealth. The result was that toward the end of the sixteenth century the northern nations had considerably larger merchant fleets than did the Iberians, how-

ever much the latter nations sought to monopolize the trade with the East and West Indies.

> Even in 1586, when the new routes had been exploited for more than three-quarters of a century, there were only 104 ships in Spain of 100 tons and upwards, and only 92 in Portugal, while an incomplete return of 1582 shows 177 belonging to English ports. Despite laws prohibiting the employment of foreign ships, Flemish , German, French, and Italian vessels had often to be used in order to make up the Spanish fleets.[18]

The key to the emergence of the northwest European countries as the dominant powers in the mercantile marine seems to have lain in the Atlantic. The eastern trade, rich in its rewards, was apparently always possessed of two characteristics that restricted its size: it was conducted as a monopoly in the countries that participated in the trade, and it tended to deal in high-priced luxury items that did not call for many bottoms. It was in the Atlantic that contrasting conditions were to be found: there the flow was massive and participation was open to all entrants, in practice if not in law. Thus, when the northern fleets gained large numbers of ships, it is likely that they were built to be sailed on the Atlantic.

The domination of European shipping by the Dutch in the early seventeenth century undoubtedly lent to the English colonies in North America and the Caribbean a particular attraction to the Mother Country, as restrictive Navigation Acts could be given a force there that was hard to enforce in trade with the Continent. This may help to explain why the English showed so very much more interest in their North American colonies than did the Dutch, who in 1664 yielded up the New Netherlands in the Hudson Valley with far less concern than one might have expected. For the Dutch with their much greater interests in the carrying trade, in marine insurance, and in licit and illicit participation in Spain's trade with the Americas, the New Netherlands had been a minor and badly pursued interest; for England, with fewer ships, less capital available for their construction, and a greater concern for the North American than the Baltic fishery, those colonies assumed an importance that meant that before the American Revolution the lion's share of European immigration came to the British plantations there.

For the Dutch the great loop of trade that circulated from Spain southward along the African coast to the Canaries, then westward to the Antilles, with a return flow first northward through the Florida Strait and toward Bermuda and then eastward across the Atlantic to the Iberian coast, was the fundamental interest, just as it was for the Spaniards. In seeking to interlope on the American trade pioneered by Spain, Holland could not enter directly into the conquest and continental exploitation. Instead, it was largely in the role of middlemen and shipowners that the Dutch went about establishing their rather specialized empire. In the eastern Atlantic the East and West Indian interests of the Dutch somewhat overlapped; the voyage to the East Indies had to pass southward along the African coast, but it is significant that only at the Cape of Good Hope did the Dutch East India Company establish a way-station, having moved it there from an earlier attempt on St. Helena. Farther north on the African coast, in the Bight of Guinea, what Dutch forts and factories there were, particularly Elmina in present-day Ghana, were establishments of the Dutch West India Company and a crucial part of the Atlantic Loop trade. It was in these African forts that the Dutch, along with the English, French, Portuguese, Danes, and Brandenburghers, sought first gold but soon thereafter slaves. Those wretched souls became the instrument for Dutch and English interloping in the Span-

ish American trade. Ships with basic trader's goods were sent to the forts on the Guinea Coast, and items were there exchanged with local black kings for captives they had enslaved who might be sent to the New World to provide a geographically fixed source of labor in a society where most efforts to introduce European serfdom had failed. The black slaves were then transported across the narrow extent of the equatorial Atlantic to entrepôts established by the Dutch specifically for the introduction of slaves into the Spanish colonial empire. Curaçao after 1633 and St. Eustatius served respectively the entrepôt function for the Spanish Main and the non–Spanish Leeward Islands.

The Dutch did attempt to create mainland colonies, first in Brazil at Recife (an effort that ended in 1654 when the Portuguese evicted their government) and then in the Hudson Valley, whence they were driven out by the New Englanders and the English navy in 1664. The Dutch continued these efforts on the Wild Coast, now known as the Guianas, where eventually they succeeded modestly in setting out a tropical plantation colony. But to the end of slave trading it was that activity and the general carrying trade that interested the Dutch rather than the more generally popular sugar cultivation. The maritime interests of the Hollanders seem to have determined their role in the Atlantic navigation, making them the first masters of the Atlantic Ferry.

The English, the French, the Danes, and the Swedes all took up the Loop trade in the seventeenth and eighteenth centuries, leading for each of these groups to the existence on the Guinea Coast of forts and of disposing entrepôts in the Leeward Islands of the West Indies. In the seventeenth century France and England, like the Dutch, were largely interlopers on the Spanish trade; but they passed beyond that stage by shaping considerable plantation colonies on the larger islands and on the American mainland. The main distinction comes in the fact that with those producing colonies they were in the position to introduce navigation acts restricting the carrying trade to their own ships, as was done by the middle of the seventeenth century. For England the effective defeat of the Dutch after the three Anglo-Dutch Wars of the seventeenth century—perhaps the first examples of modern wars for mercantile rather than dynastic advantage—meant that Britain's navy was predominant in the world and its carrying trade had been domesticated. Colonial expansion was rapid, and the growth of the British merchant marine was equally spectacular. The Dutch continued as important shipowners, but never again could they dominate ocean shipping as they had for two centuries between 1500 and 1700.

THE SECOND STAGE
IN THE ATLANTIC CROSSING

The relative calm with which the Dutch accepted the loss of the New Netherlands in 1664 shows us how little anticipation most Europeans had of the ultimate pattern of American economic development. The Hollanders seemed fairly cheerfully resigned to their continued participation in the trade of the Tropical Loop, with a home base in the Netherlands whence came the capital, ships, and hands that conducted the operation, a "staple" base on the Guinea Coast furnishing the slaves that were the original trade good, and a pair of entrepôts—Curaçao and St. Eustatius—in the West Indies where the frightful cargo could be sold to the Spaniards and the sugar islands, respectively. For the Dutch it was the carrying and slave trades that allowed them entry in what had begun as a Spanish monopoly.

The Spanish government, it is true, also tried to preserve a monopoly in trade relations with its overseas territories, but the spirit of enterprise in the mother country was so inadequate that it could not be maintained effectively. Moreover Spain had no access to the African market in human beings and could not possibly therefore herself satisfy the need for slaves in her American colonies. The companies to which the Spanish government granted the right to import—by the means of contracts that they called *asientos*—had after 1648 inevitably had to go to the Dutch supplier, that is to say that through their agents they bought at the depots to which the West India Company transported its cargoes of slaves straight from St. George d'Elaina on the African coast, mainly at Curaçao.[19]

The earliest voyages to North America, those of the Cabots in the 1490s and the fishing vessels that came in their wake, did not follow the Spanish route using the Trade Winds from the Cape Verde Islands to the Antilles. But the English attempts to plant a colony on the Virginia shore, first at Roanoke Island in the Carolina sounds in the 1580s and then at Jamestown on the James River in 1607, followed the Tropical Loop, risking capture by the Spaniards, who claimed all the Americas as theirs. Soon the English navigators gained confidence in sailing into the face of the Westerlies and set out directly westward from Land's End. The Gorges expedition to Sagadahoc in 1607, the Pilgrims in 1620, and even the voyagers to Virginia after Captain Samuel Argall was dispatched thence in 1609 by the Virginia Company (in search of a shorter route than that of the Spanish path from the Cape Verde Islands to the Antilles) all crossed the North Atlantic. Argall in 1609 had demonstrated that by keeping just south of the easterly flowing Gulf Stream a much quicker crossing could be made.[20] Thus, by the middle of the seventeenth century the northern crossing of the Atlantic was accepted and used.

What was missing in making that route

equal in importance to the Tropical Loop was not technology—sailing had been improved sufficiently to allow the Europeans to buck directly the easterly blowing winds found in their latitudes—but rather the reciprocating trade that would make this an important route of navigation. Only as the English American colonies developed in population and produce would the northern route gain equality and then dominance over the tropical one.

The crucial concern for North American development was, as Harold Innis saw a generation ago, the creation of a large staple trade. In the seventeenth century the northern staple remained mainly fish, dried and salted so it might be kept and collected for shipment (at the close of the fishing season) to European and insular markets in the Spanish and Portuguese possessions in the Atlantic. The Portuguese, in whose half of the world as envisaged by the pope the great bank fishery lay, carried on their own fishing using the actual fishing vessels for trans-Atlantic transportation. Fishermen from the Atlantic coasts of France worked in similar fashion. Only the English had to operate differently, going on shore first to dry their fish in order to reduce the consumption of salt, with which they were far less plentifully supplied than were the Mediterranean lands. This creation of "rooms" on the shore led in due course to a more definite plantation of settlements and, from our point of view, a separation of the fishing from the transporting function. Particularly in New England the arrival of the Pilgrims, but even more that of the Puritans at Salem and other ports on Cape Ann after the mid-1620s, led to the creation of an American-based fishing fleet. That fleet, in turn, called forth an effort at shipbuilding.

> For the most part the men who came to New England in the seventeenth century had little to do with the sea until their crossing. The beginnings of maritime New England were the result of acquired skills rather than of long tradition brought over from the Old World, although a handful of trained shipwrights could be found among the early settlers. Needless to say, not even the most ingenious Yankees could have established a maritime economy except under favorable circumstances. Without timber Yankees could not have built the vessels that became the foundation of New England's maritime enterprise.[21]

Turning again to Innis's staple hypothesis concerning the historical geography of North America, New England abounded in timber from forests that were relatively easily tapped along the many rivers reaching the coast. A number of studies have shown that this resource of excellent softwood, cheaply cut, available in large timbers, and transformable into ships along a hundred ways on the same number of rivers was what made the vessels of New England a bargain by comparison with those of Britain or any other part of maritime Europe:

> Because of the abundance of timber, colonial shipyards turned out vessels at least 30 percent cheaper than English builders could match. A good many New England vessels were therefore sold abroad, both in the mother country and in continental ports, often after their thrifty owners had sailed them over with a profitable cargo.

Most New England ships, the better built at least, remained in local hands plying the various trading routes that the Yankees developed:

> Such a vessel might have a useful life of ten or fifteen years. By then, if the shifting sands off Cape Cod or the sunken ledges of the Maine coast had not already claimed her as a victim, rot would probably have worked into her timbers. At some point the cost of repair came to exceed the economy of purchasing a new

vessel, and if the owner could not palm his craft off upon an unsuspecting West Indiaman, she was consigned to the flats of a back cove, where the bones of countless vessels came to final rest.[22]

It was the exigent search for a staple to create the proper mercantilist pairing of the new with the old England that made of Massachusetts and its neighbors more of a mirror image than the homeland desired. The first staple that could be developed, after an initial transient dependence on furs, was fish—notably the superb cod that swarmed the various banks off the northeast coast of North America. A European taste could be taken for granted as the cod swims on both sides of the North Atlantic, and the European fishermen who had come to the Newfoundland banks already in the sixteenth century had devised a technique, drying and salting, that preserved the fish for the long return journey to Europe. It waited for Massachusetts, mainly in the small fishing ports on Cape Ann, to use those practices to support settlement in North America. The earliest ships built after the very first, the *Virginia*, that was launched into the Kennebec River of Maine in 1607, were for fishing on the New England coast. As experience was gained in both fishing and navigation, New England came to enjoy not one staple but rather two. The first, the cod itself, led Samuel Eliot Morison to note that "Puritan Massachusetts derived her ideals from a sacred book, her wealth and power from the sacred cod."[23] But the fact that the cod swims on both sides of the Atlantic meant that there was far less market in Britain for New England's sacred staple than there was in New England for Britain's increasing staple of manufactured goods. If a proper mercantilist trade circuit was to be established, the cod had to be used in a more complex exchange. What in colonial times were referred to as *returns*—items of trade

that might ultimately be exchanged in Britain for the manufactures America craved—had to be found elsewhere if New England's staple would not serve.

Britons wanted tropical or semitropical products blighted by the chill climate of the British Isles. New Englanders, who had learned their economic doctrine well before crossing the Atlantic the first time, rapidly devised a second staple that would make of their first the basis for gaining the returns needed for completion of their trade with the mother country. Fortunately, Cromwell's Navigation Act of 1651 had established certain principles beneficial in the creation of such a staple, earnings from a mercantile marine that would help in completing a North Atlantic mercantile circuit to match the one already in existence along the tropical loop. As Lawrence Harper in his classic study of the navigation acts makes clear, the act of 1651 was fairly simple:

> It paid little attention to exportations [from Britain] and emphasized importations. It applied to aliens and Englishmen alike. It proclaimed the doctrine that merchandise should be brought directly from the country of production or from the port where usually first shipped, and announced that goods must be carried either in ships of the country of origin or of usual first shipment or in English ships. Salted fish of the sort "usually fished for and caught" by the English, and all fish oil, whale fins, and whalebones, had to be caught in English vessels and prepared by the people of the Commonwealth, and no goods or commodities whatsoever of Asia, Africa, or America could be imported in foreign vessels.[24]

And American ships classed as English were permitted to deal directly either with other English colonies or with England itself.

This is not the place for detailed attention to the Navigation Act of 1651 or the revisions made after the unfortunate Restoration. It is sufficient to note the general impact of the several navigation acts on the development of New England's second staple. With trade internal to the increasingly dispersed realm of the English state restricted to English bottoms, the New Englanders could conduct their search for useful returns both in the fishing colonies to the north—mainly Newfoundland in the seventeenth century—and in the sugar, rice, and tobacco colonies to the south. They were more successful in the latter direction. The planters of the Middle Colonies and the Carolinas had neither the capital nor the inclination to enter the carrying trade: what money they had they sought to apply to the purchase of land and slaves to work it. This left the Yankees—who from that time looked on land as a fruitless commodity and slaves as an economic and moral ambiguity—as the main group in America interested in following the path to the sea. As fishing began to accumulate some capital in New England ports, investors there bought the region's cheap ships and started sending them along the coast to Virginia, Maryland, and the Carolinas in search of returns to England. Timber from the splendid forests of New England, pot and pearl ashes, fish, and forwarded manufactures (which had been imported from England) were traded in the more southerly colonies for goods the English wanted: tobacco in particular but later some rice and a lot more indigo, as well as grain from Pennsylvania and the Chesapeake region. In addition, the rise of grain production, particularly wheat, made available to the Yankees a source of a food their climate and stingy soils largely denied them but their culture could not forget.

Much as the West India trade was the generator of colonial New England's mercantile activity, it was the coastal trade that employed most hands: "With only occasional fluctuations throughout the eighteenth century, nearly half the vessels entering Boston

and an even greater proportion of the clearances made passages from one of the other twelve continental colonies." Adding the Maritime Provinces, 594 out of 879 entrances at Boston were coastal.[25] When at last in the decade before 1775 parliament, at the urging of the British merchants, managed to harry their Yankee competition more effectively, rebellion took place leading to the independence of the thirteen colonies and the removal of two conditions that had largely guided prerevolutionary trade and marine transportation: the first was, of course, the ending of the application of British navigation acts and trading monopolies, such as the East India Company's of the eastern trade, whereas the second was the access afforded American ships to participate in British navigation and trade. The first release was of great potential importance to the Yankee captains, but the second exclusion was of even greater immediate detriment. In 1783 a policy of excluding many American products from the British West Indies was introduced; even the livestock, grain, and lumber that might be sold had to be carried in British bottoms. The result was that the returns that had paid for the manufactured goods Americans wished to import from Britain were denied them. "American produce such as fish, whale oil, tobacco, and rice was either banned outright or subjected to prohibitive duties" in Britain.[26] The newly independent republic clearly had to start largely from scratch in becoming an important maritime nation. Even the coastal navigation that had been the backstay of early sailing no longer had its base intact; with the prohibition of tobacco and other staple shipments from the more southerly states to Britain, there was much less on which to base the sloop and schooner journeys.

The Far East became the place of opportunity when New England had to pick up the shards of its previous trade and attempt to shape a new vessel therefrom. John Ledyard from Connecticut accompanied Captain James Cook on one of his voyages, and on his return he published a report of the sea-otter trade on the northwest coast of North America. This encouraged Captain Robert Gray to sail his ship *Columbia* to that coast in 1788–1789, discovering the mouth of the Columbia River and pioneering the sea-otter trade for Yankee merchants. The northwest Indians gave Americans the name "Boston men," reflecting the *Columbia's* home port.[27] The place of sale of these sea-otter furs was China, where they were greatly prized for adornment of clothing.

> By 1792 the trade route Boston-Northwest Coast-Canton-Boston was fairly established. Not only the merchantmen of Massachusetts, but the whalers, ... balked of their accustomed traffic by the European exclusiveness, were swarming around the Horn in search of new markets and sources of supply. [Thus] on her first voyage, the *Columbia* had solved the riddle of the China trade

for American merchants and captains.[28] Subsequently pelagic whalers, seal-skinners, and those engaged in the modest trade of the Pacific islands followed in Gray's wake.

> The Northwest trade, the Hawaiian trade, and the fur-seal fisheries were only a means to an end: the procuring of Chinese teas and textiles, to sell again at home and abroad. China was the only market for sea otters, and Canton the only Chinese port where foreigners were allowed to exchange it.... Boston traders, in contrast to the arrogant officals of Honourable John Bull, were welcomed by the Chinese; and on their part acquired an esteem for the Chinese character that has endured to this day.[29]

The Chinese trade was to play an extremely significant role in New England shipping through most of the nineteenth century. From this brief view we must learn that Yankee skippers and traders began to turn wherever they might to continue the profits of that New England staple shaped of its splendid timber, its innovative shipbuilders, and its large and ingenious population of sailors. In the 1780s and 1790s European ports were not places of great opportunity for Yankees. Neither Britain nor the Continental countries would buy many American goods or New England ships. The China trade came as the salvation of mercantile New England. In the process both capital and technical experience were accumulated that allowed Yankee ships and sailors to be the leaders in their respective field during the earlier decades of the last century. While Britain and Holland were still maintaining company monopolies in the East, with all the bureaucratic superstructure they carried and the technical stagnation in ship design and construction they engendered, the Yankees were constantly improving business organization and ship design. Not only were American ships faster in the first decades of the nineteenth century, they also were cheaper to build and were captained by far better educated men than the East India Company sent to the East. The adaptability of those captains, and the supercargoes they commonly carried to conduct the actual trade, was a key to their success. Americans gained a strong position with the Hong at Canton, and they made of the island of Mauritius in the Indian Ocean a general entrepôt whence trade could be carried on, as the opportunity arose, with India, Ceylon, Zanzibar, or the East Indies. The French island of Mauritius was declared a free port, one that welcomed American ships. In 1787 the great Salem eastern merchant Elias Haskett Derby established his Asiatic base there. "Throughout the 1790s American shipmasters calling at Mauritius either sold their cargoes there for coffee and sugar or, more often, fanned out to other ports around the Indian Ocean, including Mocha for coffee, Muscat for gum arabic, Bombay for cotton and textiles, and Java for sugar and coffee. Others continued to Canton for tea and other standard China trade items."[30]

Only slowly after independence did the European component of the trading circuit regain, and then exceed, its previous significance. Britain's punitive embargoes (after the Treaty of Paris closing the American Revolution) left Britain unapproachable, a situation that became geographically more extensive in the 1790s when Britain and revolutionary France began nearly a generation of warfare. The outbreak of war between England and France in 1793 gave the Americans their chance, especially after hostilities reached worldwide dimensions before the end of the decade. Because Britannia ruled the waves, neither the French nor their continental allies could bring in the produce of their overseas possessions. As the French conquests spread, the British extended their blockade to cover all European ports from the Mediterranean to the Baltic Sea. From this situation Yankee merchants saw an opportunity to obtain their desperately needed returns. Although the West Indian possessions of the French were subject to the Rule of 1756, which reserved the carrying trade toward metropolitan France to French vessels, during the British blockade of the Continent France was glad to allow the New England skippers to undertake the voyage. To overcome the legal constraints of the blockade, the so-called broken voyage was resorted to under which goods were carried from the French West Indies to New England, unloaded and a duty paid, and then reloaded and a "drawback" of the duty given before the Yankee ships sailed for Europe. "American commercial profits soared, and the merchants of New England were in the thick of the traffic, sharing the bounty with colleagues at New York, Philadelphia, and the Chesapeake ports."[31]

Such prosperity could not last. The British began to intercept Yankee ships, to impress deserters and some Americans, and generally to threaten American merchant shipping to the point that in December, 1807, President Jefferson secured an Embargo Act that ended the participation of American vessels in foreign trade. Most of the gains since the voyages of Captain Gray and other American pioneers in the 1780s were lost. By 1815, after the close of the war with Britain that followed, much of the American merchant marine was destroyed and most of the markets lost to the enemy. Moreover, "so completely did embargo and British [blockade] stop coasting that wagon traffic began between maritime Massachusetts and the South. Federalist wits expended their energy on this new form of commerce. Pungs and wagons were christened the *Jefferson's Pride* of Salem, and *Mud-clipper* of Boston."[32]

In 1815, when peace returned to Europe and America, and thereby to the Atlantic, a virtual tabula rasa existed in the Atlantic Ferry. For six years the Yankee captains had had to wait impatiently onshore while the British were unquestioned monarchs of the seas, in a naval sense. But the war had neither destroyed the American's innovativeness nor fundamentally reformed many of the rigidities of the British merchant marine. The result was a considerable recasting of the patterns of trade and the routes of commerce. For New England the War of 1812 had been disastrous, to the extent that the region never regained its dominant position in maritime activity. New York rose as the leading American port, not because it owned the ships or raised the sailors—they still for a generation came from New England—but because Gotham had far greater access to returns that were the measure of profitability in the Ferry. The staples that England and Europe wanted came from the West and South—via coastal shipping from the latter and canal boats from the former—so New York was the fastest place to turn a ship around, earning for its owners their best profit. "New Englanders captured New York port around 1820 and dominated its business until after the Civil War."[33]

The rise of the clipper ships in the mid-1840s signaled what has remained ever since the epitome of sailing technology. Those specially designed craft could gain considerable speed but only at the expense of large crews, vast stands of canvas, and a hull design that reduced cargo capacity by about a third over conventional ships. From the mid-1840s to 1853, however, conditions of world trade—the opening of the China trade throughout the world to Americans—and of migrations—the Gold Rush to California—meant that there was a market for such extravagance in shipping. "In 1853, at the height of the clipper-ship boom, the tonnage of the American merchant fleet was about 15 percent greater than Great Britain's. . . ."[34] But even then the seeds of change were planted, with the aggravation of sectional conflict in the United States that was to lead in less than a decade to a Civil War and with the increasing shift of British maritime interests toward steam. By 1866 Britain had gained a 30 percent lead over the United States in maritime tonnage.

The Civil War had greater direct influence on the decline of the American merchant marine than did any other event. At the time of the Southern insurrection and secession in the spring of 1861, Lincoln and his government sought to create an effective blockade of Southern ports, including the Mexican port of Matamoros on the south side of the mouth of the Rio Grande, through which the Confederates sought to secure goods that were transported from one neutral port to another.[35] A considerable number of British shipowners sought to earn high profits by attempting to run the Union blockade of the South: "Before the war the captain of a merchantman might make a salary of $150 per month; in 1864 he could make $5,000 per month as a blockade-runner . . . . Lord Russell, the English foreign secretary, reported that Englishmen would, 'if money were to be made by it, send supplies even to hell at the risk of burning their sails.'"[36] There is no question that the blockade was essential to the Union strategy for the defeat of the Rebellion, but it was hardly an iron grip.

Blockade-runners violated the blockade an estimated 8,250 times, which could well mean that it was only a paper blockade—one that was ineffective and therefore interpreted as illegal under generally accepted rules of international law . . . . It was fortunate that England chose not to insist that the Union blockade was a paper one. No Anglo-American war resulted from the blockade question and the Union war effort was not distracted. England was not moved by altruism in her decision; the American precedent of the loose blockade would reinforce Britain's major naval weapon, blockade, if it should be needed in the future. In addition, the very inefficiency of the blockade assisted British commerce.[37]

The discomfiture of the previously dominant Yankee merchant marine by the loss of Southern returns in the trans-Atlantic route combined with the very high profits of running the Union blockade to give a distinct edge to the British. That edge was further enlarged when Britain—from the Union viewpoint in an unneutral and unfriendly act—fitted out several Confederate raiders; the *Alabama* was the most famous, partly for its familiar and fatal encounter with the Kittery-built *Kearsarge* and for having contributed its name to the claims the United States lodged against Britain after 1865. Those raiders destroyed impressive tonnages of Northern shipping in all the world's oceans and caused many Yankee owners to shift registry of their vessels to other flags, perhaps most commonly to the Red Ensign.

In that way a Boston owner could register a ship "Down East" in Halifax and thus avoid destruction by the *Florida*.

> There were only a few [Confederate] raiders—never more than four at sea at a time—but they left a trail of burning northern vessels from Cape Ann to the Straits of Sunda in one direction and the Bering Sea in the other. Altogether, some two hundred northern vessels were captured, . . . about two-thirds of those vessels hailed from New England ports, with Boston and New Bedford suffering the heaviest losses, each with nearly forty victims.[38]

The most dangerous seas were those between Brazil and Africa, with the Brazilian ports serving as bases for the Rebels. Thus when, on October 7, 1864, the Union ship *Wachusett* discovered the *Florida* in Bahia, the *Wachusett* entered the harbor, rammed the *Florida*, seized the ship, and took her out to sea. The storm among neutral powers was considerable, with the Tory press in Britain repeatedly calling for war against Abe and his insults; but the lasting destruction of the time arose in the American merchant marine, which came out of the war reduced in numbers and replaced in the trade that had existed before 1861. By the end of the war somewhat less than a million tons of American shipping, some thousand ships, had shifted to so-called flags of convenience, much of it never to return to the American flag. Boston's tonnage dropped during the war from 414,000 in 1860 to 54,000 in 1865. And the quintessential Yankee port never recovered its maritime role, any more than the United States regained its dominance in numbers and technology in the oceanic carrying trade.[39]

STEAM COMES TO THE OCEANS THROUGH PIONEERING ON RIVERS

The eighteenth century saw the birth of steam as a natural force harnessed to human command, at first largely for pumping and other simple, fixed jobs that were tedious or beyond human capacity. But almost from the beginning of the period when mechanical efficiency was sufficiently advanced to provide a reasonable relationship of weight to effort produced, attempts were made to use that power for traction on roads and later on railroads. It is not surprising that there should be the attempt to use steam power to propel water-borne craft of one sort or another, particularly because the heavy dead load the early steam engines forced on inventors could more readily be borne by a vessel's displacement than by a wagon's wheels. As is commonly the case with the more basic developments of the mechanical revolution of the eighteenth and nineteenth centuries, there is considerable national competition in the claim to the first efforts, successful or otherwise.

Today it is generally conceded that the first

> successful pioneer in the application of steam power to boats was the Marquis Claude de Jouffroy d'Abbans, who in June, 1778, on the river Doubs in eastern France made an unsuccessful effort to power "two flapped paddles working like duck's feet" to power a boat. Success came to him five years later in 1783 when his second boat, *Pyroscaphe*, operated against the current of the Saône for fifteen minutes on the fifteenth of July.[40]

The French Revolution ended Jouffray d'Abbans' efforts before they earned any continuing success. It remained for others to make steam truly effective in ship propulsion. In 1785 John Fitch presented a plan to the American Philosophical Society in Philadelphia calling for a primitive steamboat driven by an endless paddle-chain on the starboard side, but no experimental vessel was constructed. Two years later, however, in August, 1787, Fitch tried another system on the Delaware River vessel, which was propelled by an awkward arrangement of six overhead paddles on each side at the stern, given a reciprocating motion by a single-cylinder, double-acting, condensing steam engine. Further refinements were made, and in 1790 an infrequent but repeating service by the ship *Experiment* from Philadelphia to Trenton was carried on covering a total distance of some 2,000 miles under steam. There is no question but that this was the first successful and practical application of steam to ship propulsion.[41] Sometime in the early 1790s Samuel Morey put a small steamboat on the upper Connecticut River, and in 1797 he placed a vessel on the Delaware River that was propelled by side paddlewheels, introducing what would become the standard propulsion for steam vessels for more than half a century. Thus by the turn of the nineteenth century there were several mechanically successful experiments at steam-powered vessels, mostly in the United States, where poor overland transportation combined with broad estuarine rivers to encourage this turn to the water. Unfortunately for these efforts, there was seldom the money to continue the experiments until all the economic problems were solved.

Wealthy New Yorkers gained the first continuing service. Earlier, many Americans had attempted to create such an economic success. James Rumsey of Maryland, a contemporary of Fitch, joined in the search for a satisfactory technology to apply steam to navigation. In 1784 he experimented with a boat moved by cranks and a series of "setting poles." Three years later he devised what we now know as a system of jet propulsion, gained "by admitting water through a trunk on the keels of the vessel, and by means of a steam pump discharging it at the stern."[42] Oliver Evans built an experimental boat with a high-pressure steam engine; the first applied to navigation was one of his engines installed two years before, in 1802, at New Orleans. In 1798 Robert Livingston, Nicholas Roosevelt, and John Stevens joined in an effort to develop steam navigation on the

Hudson and New York Harbor launching a boat with an engine built by Roosevelt. Since only 3 miles per hour could be secured, further efforts were undertaken, though they ended when Livingston was appointed by Jefferson as American minister to Paris in 1800.

Livingston, while in France, met Robert Fulton, who had been engaged in experiments of steam navigation, among other things, while there; and in 1802–3 carried on several experiments on the River Seine, and in the summer of the latter year, made a trial with a boat propelled by paddle-wheels, which showed, with improvement in the engine, they might look for much better results, although they had not succeeded in obtaining as high a rate of speed as was anticipated on this trial.

As a result Livingston sought to have his monopoly on steam navigation in the waters of New York State, first obtained in 1798, extended for twenty years. This was granted with the understanding he and his associates would construct and operate a successful steamboat by 1805. Though that deadline was not met, by 1807 the partners were ready to conduct an experiment with a boat they first registered as "the *North River Steamboat of Clermont* [Livingston's home]." The boat was 140 feet long and 16 feet in the beam; it had a hold 7 feet deep; but it drew only 28 inches of water. Its engine, manufactured by Boulton and Watt, was only the third of their engines allowed to be exported from Britain. Too long in relation to its beam, the *Clermont*, as it came to be called, was not a particularly safe vessel, nor of a particularly advanced design. Though Boulton and Watt were known for sturdiness, Watt's phobia about high-pressure steam assured that the engine, though safe, was weak in relation to its weight.[43] Thus, at the trial run of this 182-ton vessel, in August, 1807, its performance was adequate but not up to the contemporary possibilities.

The key to effective working of steamboats lay in securing the greatest propulsive effort in relation to the consumption of fuel: otherwise most of the carrying capacity of the boat would be taken up with fuel (save on journeys of short duration). In the 1780s Oliver Evans had found the solution by turning his attention to high-pressure steam boilers, and these were employed in 1802 by Colonel John Stevens, who, though associated on occasion with Livingston and Fulton, set about his own independent experiments with steam for both ships and railroads. That year

> he produced a "rotary" steam engine consisting of vanes on a shaft which were enclosed in a cylindrical casing [thus a primitive turbine]; it drove a screw-propelled flat-bottomed boat at about 4 miles per hour. A believer in high pressure steam and screw propulsion, he built in 1803-04 the launch *Little Juliana*. The engine consisted of a single vertical cylinder, 4½ in. diameter by 9 in. stroke, with an overhead crosshead from which two connecting rods drove gearing attached to twin propeller shafts. This launch also made a speed of about 4 miles an hour.[44]

Thus Fulton's *Clermont* was of a rather timid design when it commenced running on the Hudson River three years later. The main thing that could be said in its favor was that it managed to run consistently and its operation represents the beginning of steam navigation as a practical undertaking. To Fitch, Evans, and Stevens—even to Miller and Symington, who in 1788 developed an experimental steamboat in Scotland that was tried out on the Forth and Clyde Canal the next year—belongs credit for the actual *invention* of the steamboat; to Fulton we owe instead respect for his ability to assemble the most practical of the works of others and, especially, to turn it into an economically productive vessel. We must regret that his mind worked along the monopolist lines typical of earlier times, so that his assembled technology hardly represented the state of the art and yet was imposed on large components of American steam navigation until the Supreme Court decision in *Gibbons vs. Ogden* effectively ended his monopoly in February, 1824. That major decision established in American law the predominance of federal control over commerce at the expense of the states and, in transportation, the open entry into the business that assured that technical innovations would be encouraged by the competitive entrants.

The greatest problem facing American promoters of steam navigation was that of fuel consumption. Coal production was small, and was largely in anthracite at this period. This meant that American marine engineering followed two lines of advance: the energetic effort to raise steam pressures and the coincident constraint of the geographical pattern of navigation to waterways and coastal waters where limited tonnages of fuel might be carried so as to allow the transportation of the heavy and not particularly valuable freights that were the core of the American demand for steam navigation.

The problem of transportation internal to the United States was so pressing that its existence goes far toward explaining one of the seeming paradoxes in the historical geography of transportation: that the United States, which increasingly came to dominate world maritime activities between the time of the Congress of Vienna and the outbreak of the American Civil War, played an amazingly small role in the early experiments with trans-Atlantic *steam* navigation, and a much decreasing role in general maritime activities once steam gained a major part of that undertaking. Because the growth of the Great Republic had to be based on the geographical expansion of settlement and extensive economic development, internal transportation became almost the first clearly accepted national responsibility. With Gallatin's report and plan for internal transportation in 1810, the greatest and most immediate call on the capital available for various innovative activities went to domestic development in the United States. During the period up to the Civil War, states beggared themselves on several occasions to provide an infrastructure of transportation before there could be the productivity to repay these investments through taxes. The inventive genius, which was not in short supply in nineteenth-century America, still could not be spread to cover all the nation's growing needs. Instead we find clear evidence, cited in our consideration of railroad development and in the previous section on the birth of the steamboat, that American ingenuity turned toward the most pressing needs as seen by contemporary Americans. Three of those needs are easily observed in transportation:

1. To make the potamic system of early nineteenth-century America work as a two-way street through the introduction of steam-powered navigation on the North American rivers (and lakes).
2. To shape a railroad system that could be secured in a country short of capital but vast in extent.
3. To cheapen the cost of American oceanic shipping, both in initial construction and in operation, in order to gain a competitive edge in a trade that was still heavily influenced by surviving mercantilist notions.

That third need led to the concentration of technical experimentation in marine navigation to sail-driven craft. In each of these three undertakings, and in the context set by domestic requirements, the American technology was by some measure the most advanced. As we have already seen, the American steam locomotive was the most powerful and adaptive of those prime movers, and for inland navigation the American steamboat was without peer elsewhere. To support this argument further, it was in the period between the close of the Napoleonic Wars and the outbreak of the Civil War that America ran away with technical dominance in sailing, gained thereby the title of the world's greatest merchant marine, in numbers as well as technology. Only when the finite abilities of the Americans (even in an ingenious period) combined with the fighting of the first modern, total war did the British manage to reassert the merchant-marine dominance they had enjoyed in the eighteenth century. Even then it was probably as much a case of greater internal opportunities in the United States that kept American effort off the seas. While Britain was regaining dominion over the world's maritime trade, the United States was actively constructing what came to be 40 percent of the world's railroad mileage.

In 1808, steamboat service began on both the Hudson and the Delaware (from Philadelphia to Trenton). Soon thereafter builders and owners excluded from New York waters by the Livingston and Fulton monopoly began to look toward navigation in more distant waters. Gaining a compromise with Fulton, Aaron Ogden in 1811 started a steam ferry service from New York City to New Brunswick, New Jersey, while the Fulton interests began service to New Haven with the *Fulton* in 1815. During succeeding years service was progressively advanced eastward on Long Island Sound, to New London, to Stonington, and finally to Providence in 1822.[45] The great spread of this navigation from New York City came after 1824, when the Supreme Court's *Gibbons vs. Ogden* decision opened the waters of New York State and, incidentally, of all other states, to the free and competitive development of steamboat lines. Long Island Sound services quickly became both numerous and highly competitive, leading to racing between the steamers of rival companies, which too often brought on explosions and fires that were very costly in the loss of life. Perhaps the most famous of all the companies using the Sound was the Fall River Line, organized in 1846 to tie the southern end of the Old Colony Railroad at the river port of Fall River, Massachusetts, with New York City. This service, which continued until just before World War II, endured longer than any other route focused on New York other than the Hudson River line.

"Steam navigation on the [Great] Lakes dates from the year 1818, when the steamboat 'Walk-in-the-Water' was built to ply on Lake Erie." Subsequently Buffalo became the greatest port on the Lakes and the terminus of what became an extensive service tying together the use of the canal for a large flow of goods eastbound and of settlers westbound to reasonable transport on the Lakes. A number of ports grew up adjacent to the areas being settled, from which an increasing flood of grain and other agricultural products was coming as a particular expression of returns. Cleveland, Sandusky, Toledo, and Detroit were tied to Black Rock by the very first steamboat service. Pushing the service farther up the Lakes created Port Huron, enlarged the earlier importance of St. Ignace at the Straits of Mackinac and Sault Ste. Marie at the rapids in the St. Mary's River, and created a string of rising ports on the west shore of Lake Michigan—Green Bay, Milwaukee, and Chicago—each of which had been pioneered in the early seventeenth century by the French. When in the 1830s Chicago became a town at the terminus of the Illinois and Michigan Canal, the major extent of Great Lakes steamboating was basically determined. Only the opening of a canal around the rapids at Sault Ste. Marie in 1855 extended continuous service into Lake Superior, where several

iron-ore exporting harbors were established and where the general port of Duluth grew apace.

Navigation on the Lakes was further advanced by the completion of the Welland Canal between Lake Erie and Lake Ontario, finished in its first form in 1832. Until then the Great Lakes service had been considerably restricted, particularly as Lake Erie had rather poor harbors, but by 1836 there were 45 passenger steam vessels on the lakes, a figure that grew quickly to 61 in 1839.[46] The screw propeller and the high-pressure engine became common on the Great Lakes by the 1840s, well ahead of their adoption by British shipbuilders for the Atlantic. "In 1836, there were on all the Northern lakes 107 side-wheel steamboats and 135 propellers, and 1,006 sailing vessels."[47]

The same rapidly evolving conditions obtained on the other great inland waterway network of North America, the system of the Mississippi and its various headwaters. As early as 1811 Fulton and his associates had caused to be built in Pittsburgh the *New Orleans*, a low-pressure steamboat of 116 feet length, 20 feet in the beam, and with a hold of 7-foot depth. At the end of September that year the *New Orleans* began the downstream voyage with Nicholas Roosevelt and his wife as the only passengers. After collaborating with John Stevens on his early steamboat ventures Roosevelt was well experienced and greatly interested in the development of the trade, because he had been engaged in engine manufacture at Belleville on the Passaic River in New Jersey. This voyage, the first on the Mississippi, must also have been one of the more exciting ones. Two years earlier Roosevelt had conducted a reconnaissance down the Ohio and Mississippi in an effort to determine the feasibility of steam navigation. His conclusion had been favorable, and in 1811 he began the actual trial. The run from Pittsburgh to Cincinnati took two days, exciting observers on the river bank but not having other incidents of note. A contemporary account tells us, "The stay at Cincinnati was brief, only long enough to take in a supply of wood for the voyage to Louisville, which was reached on the night of the fourth day after leaving Pittsburg." There the vessel had to lay idle waiting for the desired rise in the river level to permit the *New Orleans* to shoot the rapids at the Falls of the Ohio. In that interval Mrs. Roosevelt became a mother. The last week in November the level was up, so the dangerous crossing was begun. Realizing that a ship can be steered only if its speed is greater than that of the current in which it is advancing, full steam was gotten up. "The safety valve shrieked, the [paddle] wheels revolved faster than they had ever done before, and the vessel, speaking figuratively, fairly flew away from the crowds collected to witness her departure from Louisville." With that burst of speed the boat was held in the Indiana Channel through the rocks, and it successfully reached the river below the Falls, which was free of further obstruction all the way to the Gulf. But nature intervened. Already the voyagers had witnessed the passage of Haley's Comet, which frightened most who saw it as its periodicity was then not generally understood. Because the *New Orleans* began just before Christmas, its passage down the Ohio to its confluence with the Mississippi occurred while that region was being visited by a long series of earth tremors culminating in what is still believed to have been the most severe earthquake historically recorded in the United States, the one centering at New Madrid in the bootheel of Missouri adjacent to the junction of those two rivers. So severe was the New Madrid earthquake that it threw much of the water out of the rivers nearby, flooding the low-lying ground along their course and, in a number of places, creating entirely new courses as a result of tectonic action and the return flow of the water

thrown out of the riverbed. Pilots became lost, trees in great number fell or were washed into the stream, and generally the unstable, transitory geography of the Mississippi Delta was made even more dynamic. Through all this the *New Orleans* sought to continue using local cordwood for its fuel. The natives, who had been counted on to provide that fuel, were busy escaping from the quaking surface of alluvium still experiencing aftershocks. Only those on board were unaware of the instability that surrounded them. It was when they were forced to tie up and go to cut their own wood in the gallery forests along the great river that they first became conscious of the world gone wrong through which they were passing. Still they kept on, searching for the new channel, cutting wood as needed, and ultimately reaching a section of the river where the temblor had merely shaken rather than remolded its course. Thence, making better speed, they reached the steamboat's namesake on January 12, 1812, able to claim title to the first passage of the Great River by steamboat and to establish service between New Orleans and Natchez.[49]

Here we should note some of the characteristics of navigation on the Mississippi that bear on the evolution of the Atlantic Ferry. The effort was considerable and was attended with considerable success; any notion that the Americans were uninterested in steam navigation is controverted by history. From his travels in 1840 the Baron de Gerstner prepared a detailed account of western steamboating in which he sought to present a comprehensive economic analysis. He found that before steam the charge for a pound of freight from New Orleans to Louisville was "seven to eight cents" in 1817, whereas in 1840 he believed the average charge per hundred-weight was 62.5 cents, or 86 cents per ton-mile. In addition the speed was greatly increased, from a number of weeks upbound to less than a week from

New Orleans to Louisville. The improvement of steamboats had also cut the consumption of cordwood significantly at the same time the cost of building boats had been kept low. "Well-informed individuals, who are very much interested in the subject of steam navigation, estimate the average cost of a steamboat, upon the western waters, after a special calculation, at $23,400." Certainly in the mind of this contemporary, Americans had not missed the importance of the steamboat:

> It is to be regretted that steam navigation was carried on in America five years before it was successfully tried in Europe. It would be still more to be regretted, if, at present, when 20 years, with an expenditure of $45,000,000, the Americans have acquired such a mass of experience, and brought steam navigation to such a high degree of perfection, we were still to hesitate in Europe to adopt the American plan of construction. The steam navigation companies in Europe ought to compare the data given in this letter, with the rate of wages and other prices in Europe, calculate the prices of transportation of passengers and goods, compare the same with their actual prices, and they will see the advantage which would result to them by the adoption of the American system.[49]

Steamboat service on the western rivers brought cheap, fairly reliable, frequent, and rather fast transportation to the great developing interior of the country. Only the decline in navigability of streams as settlement spread to the edge of the Great Plains set a frontier to this service. Even there herculean efforts were made to carry this modernized river transport all the way to the Rockies. On the Missouri River these efforts bore modest fruit when every summer some boats reached upward as far as Fort Benton just below the Great Falls of that river in Montana.[50] West of that great cordillera such pioneer steam navigation picked up on the then Lewis Fork of the Columbia (Snake River) at Lewiston, at the foot of Hell's Canyon of that great river, to reach the Pacific.[51] The objective of opening a new and vast country to mechanized transport as quickly and cheaply as possible dominated the "American system" of steamboating, turning much of the attention inward rather than across the Atlantic.

THE ERA OF THE SAILING PACKETS

On the Atlantic we find a similar drive, but one that had such complex outcomes that some misunderstand its objectives. Again there could be no doubt that the Americans wished to bring the steam engine to bear on navigation as quickly as possible and to gain the greatest economy in the pursuit of the carrying trade. But it proved impractical to accomplish both those objectives at once during the first phase of activity, the period before 1820. It is in this context that we may reconcile several apparently conflicting conditions in the Atlantic Ferry during the first half of the last century.

The first of these to develop was the high level of perfection of sailing-ship construction and operation that came out of New England in the years after the close of the War of 1812. "The first few years of world peace were the severest test that maritime Massachusetts had ever met.... Europe at peace was recovering her own carrying trade. Only gradually did England open her colonial ports to Yankee ships, and a generation elapsed before new markets were found in California, Australia, and South Africa."[52]But meet that test the New Englanders did, by trying all ports and carrying all cargoes at low rates and as quickly as possible. To keep these costs down it had been necessary to design efficient hulls and great spreads of sail that could still be lofted by a crew of a reasonable size, a feat accomplished with excellent blocks and many small rather than a few very large sails.

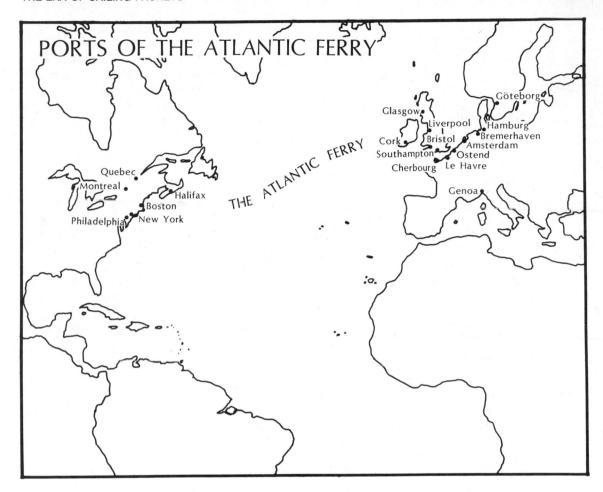

PORTS OF THE ATLANTIC FERRY

THE ATLANTIC FERRY

Quebec
Montreal
Halifax
Boston
Philadelphia New York

Glasgow
Liverpool
Cork Bristol
Southampton
Cherbourg Le Havre
Göteborg
Hamburg
Bremerhaven
Amsterdam
Ostend
Genoa

It appears that the basis of the American contribution to sailing in the Atlantic and elsewhere was a fresh and analytical look at the whole practice of propulsion through the water by wind. This meant a careful consideration of hull design and of the placing and manipulation of the sails. An English marine historian presents the case succinctly:

The Americans, spurred on by their recently won political independence, had everything in their favour; a high level of intelligence and initiative, as befitted the children and grandchildren of a generation of settlers, complete freedom from the complex of prejudice and tradition which governed the thoughts and activities of the Old World, a parliament unencumbered by a tangled mass of obsolete laws, a continent to themselves and unbounded natural resources. They made good use of them. Their softwood ships were cheap to build, but not only that. They were cleverly built as well. More profoundly than any others, the American shipbuilders studied the basic principles of ship propulsion by the aid of sails, and in fifty years they contributed as much to the development of the sailing ship as the whole maritime world had contributed in three hundred. And their ships were not only well built but they were well handled.[53]

These comments perhaps overlook that the resources of the North American continent, though vast, were at the time considered largely undeveloped and hard to utilize because capital was in short supply. Particularly pertinent to the discussion of the eventual failure of the Americans to gain a permanent possession of the Atlantic Ferry is the fact that coal, though vast in the American ground, was hardly touched in the era of the sailing ship. Only the cutoff (as a result of the War of 1812), of the supplies of Welsh coals imported into eastern American ports gave much impetus to coal mining in the United States. Even then the first mining was of anthracite, costly to produce and not particularly easy to use as steam coal. So during the period of the great domination of Atlantic navigation by the Americans, all the advantages enjoyed by Yankee shipbuilders urged on them the attempt to perfect propulsion by sail rather than by steam.

> In the twenty-five years from the end of the Napoleonic wars to 1840 they built for the Atlantic a fleet of packet ships of a size steadily increasing from 500 up to 1200 tons register. And they revolutionized the accepted theories of proportion by increasing the ratio of length to beam. In contrast to the standard figure of four to one in the case of the East Indiamen, they lengthened their hulls to a figure of 5½ times the beam. Their greater length gave them not only better lines but a greater spread of sail, and in consequence a turn of speed which European shipowners had not only never achieved but never attempted.[54]

The American sailing vessel was economical in construction, ingenious in design, and very efficient in operation—all characteristics that kept line costs of transportation within strict limits of Yankee thrift, at the same time they could outsail any competitor. The speed they gained under sail was sufficient so the 14-day eastbound voyage from

New York to Liverpool became a possibility, and even more surprisingly, the 18- or 20-day westbound homeward journey was within reach. It is important to appreciate the speeds that were obtained from the best sailing ships that came down the ways in East Boston or on the East River, because we might otherwise think that steam was introduced mainly to secure faster voyages. It took a decade of trial and improvement of the early steamers before they gained any consistent edge over the best packets. One should not forget that Dickens sailed westbound to Boston in 1840 on an early Cunarder, but he turned his ticket in and headed home by American sailing packet.

The ability to sail against the wind, as evidenced by the reasonably fast westbound voyages, meant that shipowners could schedule their vessels with somewhat greater assurance than had previously been possible with the awkward, unreliable ships that Europeans had been using on the North Atlantic. In fact, before the close of the Napoleonic Wars there had been no regularly scheduled service across the Atlantic or, for that matter, on most runs. Captains held their ships in a port awaiting cargo and passengers and sailed only when their manifest was full. Passengers and shippers of goods had to go to the port, search out a potential ship, and then wait until it was full to depart. The usage of vessels was low under these conditions: the owners might gain from their investment perhaps two round journeys a year across the Atlantic. But with the technical improvement in ships, with better navigation and sailing, and with the innately thrifty instincts of the Yankees, a more intense utilization of vessels could be tied to a selling point for the particular service, its dispatch on a scheduled day. In 1816 the Black Ball Line of sailing packets was established in New York to sail on the first day of every month, "fair weather or foul, full or empty" for Liverpool. In its first nine years it averaged 23 days for the New York–Liverpool run and 40 days on the homeward journey.[55] As the years passed and the American packet boats gained sleeker lines and more sail, the speeds increased to the point that the voyage to Liverpool could be kept to two weeks or even, with great luck, to slightly less. The larger size of the ships, their vast spreads of canvas, and their being built for hard driving meant that to make claims on the attention of customers they had to boast at least one such two-week crossing.

The Black Ball Line was followed by the Boston and Liverpool Packet Company in 1822. In 1824 the Boston packet *Emerald* astounded the trade by making a west-bound run from the Mersey Bar to Boston Light in just 17 days.[56] Although this company soon failed, the trade was established, so a number of packet companies came into being. "These new lines had come into existence around 1820.... The packets went everywhere, continuing their runs down through the decades at least to the Civil War.... From Boston alone there were more than a thousand [packets] between the 1820s and the 1860s. And those were simply the aristocrats of the packet trade; there were even more on shorter runs."[57]

The climax of the American sailing ship came with the clippers, whose sole purpose was to add still further speed to long services. By designing ships with hulls of great sophistication, which permitted faster passage through the water with the same propulsive force (though with a loss of about one-third the carrying capacity of a similarly large nonclipper hull), speed was enhanced. Between the mid-1840s and the mid-1850s these ocean racers dominated the nautical mind if not all trades. The first inducement for their construction was the China Trade with the recently opened Treaty Ports. The purpose was, "whether practical or emotional—to be the first in with tea cargoes from Canton or Shanghai." The *Rainbow* and the *Sea Witch*,

large streamlined vessels, were constructed for that trade. "They were already on hand, to their great profit, in time for the gold rush to San Francisco." For less than five years after 1849 this dash to California became the greatest trade for the clippers, but by 1853 the market was declining and the ships built after that year began to suffer from "diminishing returns." The repeal of the British Navigation Acts in 1849 meant that those Yankee ships, built largely in East Boston or on the East River, could be sold to Britain, as a number were, as well as being employed in the Australia-England run under the Red Ensign.[58] But by the mid-1850s the economic cost of this burst of speed was becoming telling: most trades could benefit more by lowering carrying costs, and those that need not economize in that way could gain more certain schedules by the growing number of steamer services.

STEAM IN THE ATLANTIC FERRY

The initial introduction of steam that came in the inland navigation of the United States clearly indicated the technical limitations of this form of propulsion in its earlier years. Steam engines were heavy and inefficient, meaning that considerable tonnages of fuel had to be burned for each hour of steaming. Hence the ability to carry profitable cargoes depended on short stages in the journeys to be undertaken: long stages would require that virtually all the hold space be taken up with the coal or wood needed to stoke the boilers. The bays and sounds of the northeastern coast of the United States proved ideal for the economical application of this pioneering technology, but longer journeys could not be envisioned. For another decade that coastwise voyaging remained almost entirely in sailing vessels. Only in 1819 did that pattern begin to change when a steam service was established between New Orleans and Mobile, followed in 1822 by steamer service from New York to Norfolk.[59] The earliest steam vessel constructed specifically for deep-sea navigation was the *Robert Fulton*, launched in 1819 and placed the next year on a New York to Havana run with stops at Charleston and New Orleans.[60] These were coastal services, where the bunkering of coal could be accomplished frequently enough to allow reasonable cargo capacity in the ships. In the 1820s such coastal service became more common, although throughout this period the sailing packet remained the workhorse of the trade as steam vessels were always expensive to run over the considerable distances of American coastal navigation.

It is surprising that just at the time the first steps were being taken to use steam along the Atlantic coast of the United States, a project was begun to build an Atlantic steamship to enter the trade then dominated by American sailing packets. Within three years of the establishment of that sailing packet service, which startled European shipping interests, the Americans gave them an even greater jolt when they sent a steamship across the stormy Atlantic. At the time, British thinking saw the steamship as useful on the Irish Sea, where it was already being employed in ferry services to Ireland, or on the narrow seas to the Continent, but not on longer journeys without bunkering ports along the way. The American pioneers of steam propulsion had greater faith in their invention. Moses Rogers, who had captained the Stevens boat on the Delaware, became convinced that an oceangoing steam-powered ship could be built and operated, and he set about becoming the projector for such an undertaking.

In 1803 Benjamin H. Latrobe, the famous architect and mechanical observer, told the American Philosophical Society of Philadelphia why a steamship was an unlikely creation:

First: the weight of the engine and of the fuel. *Second*: the large space it occupies. *Third*: the tendency of its action to rock the vessel. *Fourth*: the expense of maintenance. *Fifth*: the irregularity of its motion, and the motion of the water in the boiler and cistern, and of the fuel vessel in rough water. *Sixth*: the difficulty arising from the liability of the paddles and oars to break, if light, and from weight, if made strong.[61]

Fifteen years later most of those problems still seemed to exist, particularly when an ocean crossing was envisaged. The paddles had proved themselves in calm water, but what hope had they against a North Atlantic swell? The boxy, nearly flatbottomed riverboats might be strong enough to stand the vibration and wracking, but there remained doubt as to the sturdiness of the advanced hulls that American shipbuilders were fashioning. Certainly, the possible movement of boiler water and fuel in rough seas remained an open question. There was no arguing against the fact that engines had been improved in their efficiency, thus somewhat reduced in size for their power and made somewhat less voracious of fuel. But had enough technical improvement been gained to make oceanic steamships economical?

A master who had been associated with both Robert Fulton and John Stevens, Moses Rogers from New London, came to believe that a point in technical evolution had been reached that would permit oceanic steam navigation. As he was the first man ever to command such a voyage, that of the *Phoenix* in 1809 from New York to Philadelphia, his opinion could not be disregarded. In this he was following on the thinking of the true father of the steamboat, John Fitch, who had held of the steamboat that its "grand and principal object must be on the Atlantick." In this he held "I ... am strongly inclined to believe that it will answer for sea voyages."[62] Few had that confidence, as we

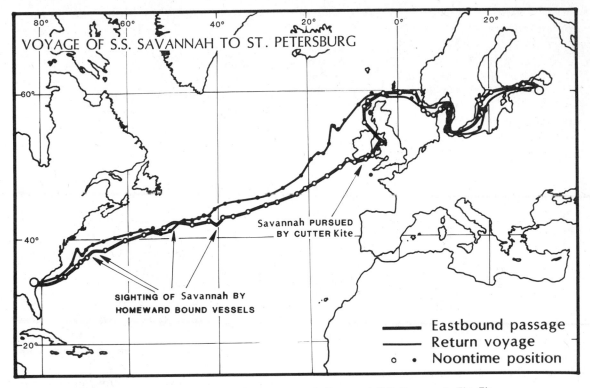

Map of the *S.S. Savannah*'s Atlantic passage. *Source:* Frank O. Braynard, *S.S. Savannah: The Elegant Steam Ship* (Athens: University of Georgia Press, 1963).

shall see, so Rogers had a difficult course to plot in making an Atlantic test. Before he could set about the task, he was to serve as master of the *New Jersey*, a steamboat constructed at Whitehill, New Jersey, in 1814 and used in the Chesapeake Bay service, where she proved the effective qualities of the high-pressure steam engine that Oliver Evans had built for her. By 1817 Rogers was thus further experienced in the rapid evolution of the steamboat. On that basis he was hired away to a new service offered by the steamboat *Charleston* that was being introduced between its eponymous port and Savannah, using the sounds and rivers that lie along the South Caroline coast. Again Rogers and the steamboat rendered effective

service, and the merchants of the quickly expanding Georgia port were greatly impressed by each of them. Savannah had experienced great prosperity with the expansion of cotton production, which became possible in 1794 once Eli Whitney, a northern visitor on the plantation of the widow of General Nathaniel Greene, invented a gin for seeding raw cotton. Much of Georgia's cotton was being sent to the British market, so there existed a substantial interest in trans-Atlantic shipping in the otherwise somewhat leisurely port. Rogers, on his frequent visits as master of the *Charleston*, was able to encourage and focus that concern into practical channels that allowed the Savannah Steam Ship Company to be formed, which, according to its printed prospectus,

> proposed . . . the purchase of a suitable ship of the first class, completely fitted and equiped in the ordinary manner—on board of which shall be placed a steam engine with the necessary other apparatus, upon the plan suggested by Captain Rogers, who will take an interest in the concern,—see that it is carried into effect in the best possible manner, and will afterwards take the charge of navigating the ship across the Atlantic.[63]

With that stated purpose, shares sufficient to the job were quickly subscribed and Captain Rogers was sent northward to New York in search of a sailing vessel that might have a steam engine added to its equipment.

On the East River he found a ship under construction that pleased him in its design and its partial construction, which would permit the necessary modification for the installation of the engine. Though unnamed, this hull soon was completed and, as the *New York Evening Post* had it on August 21, 1818,

> To-morrow, at 1 o'clock, will be launched from the shipyard of Messrs. Ficket & Crocket, the elegant steamship *Savannah*, to be commanded by Captain Moses Rogers, and intended as a regular trader between Savannah and Liverpool, principally for the accommodation of passengers.[64]

The *Savannah* seems small by present standards with an overall length of 151 feet, 109 feet from figurehead to taffrail; a beam of 25 feet 10 inches, with 5 feet on either side added for the axle on which her paddlewheels turned; a depth of 14 feet when loaded; and a register tonnage of 319 and 70/95 tons.[65]

After sailing south to Savannah, some of the way under steam power, the "elegant steam-ship *Savannah*" as she was commonly called, was shown to her backers and given trials, among them a 200-mile journey to Charleston partly to invite President Monroe (who was on a local visit) to inspect the

ship. Back in the Georgia port, preparations were completed for the critical trial, an ocean crossing to Liverpool. Somewhere between 50 and 75 tons of British coal were loaded, and cargoes and passengers for the port on the Mersey were solicited in the press and in person, but to no avail. Thus at 5 A.M. on May 24, 1819, the brave little ship lifted its anchor where it had been waiting at the mouth of the Savannah River near Tybee Light and set off to prove the capacity of American shipbuilders, engine-builders, and mariners to undertake ocean navigation by steamship.[66] Many natural hazards faced them, but perhaps even more vexing were those of an economic nature. Despite earnest efforts, no paying trade could be found, apparently because steam propulsion was thought foolhardy and dangerous; so the projectors with Moses Rogers at their head had to subsidize the whole undertaking. The ship was obviously one that could not steam all the way—the daily consumption of coal proved about 8 tons under continuous firing, and the capacity to carry coal was probably limited to around 75 tons. As the maximum speed that could be obtained from the paddle wheels was perhaps 8 knots, there was not enough fuel on board to steam the whole 3,620 miles to Liverpool.[67] In the 29 elapsed days taken for the voyage—some of which were virtually becalmed as it took 16 days from the sighting of Ireland, at Mizen Head off Fastnet, to the docking at Liverpool—steam could only be used sparingly. In the elapsed 29 days, some 700 hours, steam was used on 18 days. The vessel was underway for some 582 hours with steam used for 16 percent of the time.[68]

In crossing the Atlantic the *Savannah* made use of nature as much as possible. Sails were aloft for the majority of the time, though on occasion both steam and sail were employed. The course taken was the typical one for American captains. The French naval officer Marestier, who had come to America in 1819 to examine steamboats, which seemed to have their greatest use there, noted that Americans were much more likely to make use of the Gulf Stream to add speed to their easterly journeys than were the British. He continued that in Benjamin Franklin's time American masters "generally took fifteen days less for their trip than the English captains."[69]

The thought behind this earliest steam crossing of the Atlantic was that current, wind, and steam power would combine to produce a continuous and reasonably economical journey. When the direction and strength of the wind was favorable, it would provide the driving force; when winds dropped or turned directly to oppose the course, steam would be employed. This combination of propulsive forces, it was hoped, would provide a direct and continuous voyage, avoiding the swings that tacking made necessary in sailing or the becalming that sailing usually involved. Because no ship at that time could hope to carry enough fuel to steam all the way across the Atlantic, such mixed propulsion was essential. It might even prove to be reasonably economical, as the shorter time might combine with smaller crews (when less dependence had to be made on sails) to lead to lower labor costs. Such costs seemed to impinge more on American shipowners than their British peers. American ships tended to avoid large single sails, or difficult riggings that required large crews to operate. The *Savannah*, for example, seems to have omitted high royals—sails that required a larger crew than the nineteen she carried.

Once the *Savannah* was tied up at the Liverpool wharves, the English were intensely interested in her, perhaps even suspicious. On the whole they were generous in their praise of her accomplishments on the Atlantic, but there seems to have been some vague suspicion that the ship would be used in an expedition to aid in Napoleon's escape from St. Helena. They watched her movements carefully and used warships to keep track of her location until she finally headed northeastward to Norway on the way to her ultimate destination, St. Petersburg. No doubt part of the suspicion arose from her arrival in ballast with no apparent economic justification for the voyage. Much as the projectors had sought passengers and cargo, with one minor exception the entire round journey to St. Petersburg was no more than a trial of the practicality of steam for oceanic navigation. In light of that fact, it is hard to understand the common British view that the Americans failed to appreciate the potential of steam on the Atlantic. Rather, they seemed to perceive that potential when it was only prefigured.

Apparently the continuation of the voyage to St. Petersburg was envisioned even before the departure of the *Savannah* from her home port. It is impossible now to determine whether before the sailing there was already an appreciation that the economic realization of trans-Atlantic steaming must lie in the future, so the owners might best recoup their investment by attempting to sell their ship to the Russian Czar, or whether that notion came to Moses Rogers when he reached Europe. Certainly on May 20, 1819, when the ship sailed from Savannah, it was noted under "Ship News" as "Cleared: Steam Ship *Savannah*, Rogers Master St. Petersburg, Scarbrough & McKenne [agents]."[70] Rogers did take his vessel out of Liverpool, through the Irish Sea and North Channel to round the north of Scotland between the Orkneys and Shetlands, on to Arendal in southern Norway and through the Øresund into the Baltic, making the *Savannah* the first ocean-going steamship ever to enter that sea, and on to Stockholm, where a protracted stop was made. During her stay there the Swedish king sought to purchase the *Savannah*; but as he offered only hemp and iron to the value of $100,000 (to be landed free at New York), whereas Rogers and the other owners were by then fairly desperately in need of actual cash, the offer was rejected and the ship sailed on to St. Petersburg with the only passengers she ever carried under steam—a retired British general, Lord Lynedoch (and his nephew) who was going to visit his brother-in-law in Russia, the British ambassador to the czar's court.[71]

That court was greatly interested in the steamship when it arrived, and the czar apparently offered Moses Rogers a monopoly of steam navigation on the Black and Baltic seas if he would remain there and undertake the development. Although virtually no detailed information exists on this invitation, it seems to indicate that Russia—like the United States at best only a partially developed country—could perceive the great contribution that steam navigation on rivers and narrow seas could offer under such conditions. Fulton had already sought such a concession in Russia but had died before it could be negotiated; Rogers was offered it on his arrival on the *Neva* but declined because he and his crew wished to return to the United States.[72]

On October 10 the *Savannah* sailed from Kronstadt, stopping briefly in Copenhagen and reaching Tybee Light at the mouth of the Savannah River on November 30. There is argument whether steam was used at all on this leg of the journey; Frank O. Braynard, perhaps the best authority on the voyage, believes it was.[73]

No doubt for the crew this was a happy return, but for the "elegant steam ship *Savannah*" it was sharply mixed with sadness. Despite the technical success of the voyage, even the effective use of her dismountable paddlewheels, which were assembled and then taken apart to stow on deck in heavy weather, no economic support for her potential service had been forthcoming. Certainly there were economic limits to steaming at this time—it seems doubtful that in 1819

there was any ship that could have crossed the Atlantic entirely under steam—but the *Savannah* had effectively demonstrated that a steam-auxiliary engine had great virtues. It could allow the navigation of a more direct course than was possible for a sailing packet. It could gain reasonable headway, perhaps up to 8 or 10 knots, in a time of calm winds. And it was of very considerable advantage in entering and leaving narrowly confined ports where sailing was difficult or obviated by tides and currents. Even sixteen years after the voyage of the *Savannah*, the British Association for the Advancement of Science held that trans-Atlantic steam navigation was "one of the grandest projects which . . . ever occupied the human mind but perfectly chimerical."[74] So it reflects no lack of courage or ingenuity that the trial of Moses Rogers and his Savannah backers was not met with success. There was too much timidity among passengers and shippers at this time.

THE ADVENT OF THE FORMAL ATLANTIC FERRY

From a physical and economic viewpoint the Atlantic was the place where steam navigation of the open seas had to be pioneered. If its reaches were too wide for economically practicable service by steamships, all other oceans were likely to prove even less amenable to this development. In Europe, as in America, the first salt-water navigation came in coastal services and the transit of the narrow seas of the Mediterranean, Baltic, and Caribbean. The General Steam Navigation Company of Britain established a steamer service from London to Portugal in 1826, and two years later the City of Dublin Steam Packet Company announced their run from Dublin to Bordeaux. The government of India was seeking some form of coasting steamer service from Britain. In 1825, using the auxiliary sail-steam combination initiated by the *Savannah*, the paddle steamer *Enterprise* sailed from London to Calcutta in 113 days. This heavily subsidized undertaking still proved ahead of its time and was not soon repeated.[75] The secret to an Indian service was found in the more limited undertaking of routes in the narrow seas, from Britain to and through the Mediterranean to Alexandria. In 1840 a substantial mail subsidy was awarded to the extended Peninsula Steamship Company to carry mails by steam to Alexandria. Such was the origin of the Peninsula and Oriental Steamship Company, which came to dominate this route when the British East India Company lost the monopoly of eastern trade. But the key was found in the heavy subsidy granted by the British post office to these early steamship lines, money that managed to keep financially undersupported services going until they could gain enough trade to operate with at least marginal profitability. "The important fact . . . is that it was so, that the new mail policy of the British Government remained unique for ten years after 1840 and that in those years it gave British ocean steam shipping a start it never lost" until our time.[76]

Returning to the real testing ground of the steamship, the Atlantic begrudged passage for a generation. In 1822 another steam auxiliary, the British *Rising Star*, crossed the Atlantic and sailed around the Horn to become the first steamship in the Pacific. It was followed two years later by the first French auxiliary, the *Caroline*, and five years later by the first Dutch auxiliary, the *Curaçao*. Not until 1833 did the first true steamship make the Atlantic crossing, and then again as an example of North American determination. Built to navigate in the narrow waters of the Gulf of St. Lawrence, the *Royal William* was a steamship with little more than auxiliary sail, shifting the balance to that side for the first time in these Atlantic crossings. New owners, among them the

Halifax Quaker merchant Samuel Cunard, decided as a result of the cholera epidemic of 1832 that there was not a very profitable trade for the ship in that Gulf of St. Lawrence service. They believed she should be steamed to Britain to be sold there. Sailing from Québec, she took only seventeen days to reach the Isle of Wight and soon thereafter was sold to the Spanish government.[77] The success of the *Royal William* was, like that of the *Savannah*, a technical accomplishment but not an economic one. Because she was in ballast, she could carry more fuel than was feasible on a commercial journey; yet she did demonstrate that a true steamship, with only quite incidental sails, could cross the Atlantic. She was much larger than the *Savannah*, so her fuel capacity was much greater; but there still remained the problem of constructing a ship that could *earn* her passage across the Atlantic. The Americans and then the Canadians had shown how to navigate. It remained for the English to show how to do so *profitably*, if not exactly economically.

At first that demonstration was equivocal, stemming from the larger interests of Britain's great nineteenth-century railroad genius, Isambard Brunel. As chief engineer of the Great Western Railway, Brunel saw no valid reason that his great project should stop at the Bristol Channel. An artery to the West might well follow the desired mercantilist practice of pushing Britain's trading frontier all the way to American shores. To accomplish that, the deity having interposed the Atlantic, a steamship service was needed.

At a meeting of the directors of the Great Western Railway Company in October 1835 it was jokingly suggested that the Paddington-Bristol line be extended to New York by means of a steamship to be named the *Great Western*. Although many at the time believed it impossible to build a steamship with enough coal capacity for that distance the idea took hold and the Great Western Steamship Company was organized early in 1836.

Brunel took charge of the planning, designing a ship of great strength capable of bunkering 800 tons of coal and propelled by cycloidal-type paddlewheels using curved blades that were quieter in entering the water. Fitted out in the grand manner of the time, the *Great Western* sailed from Bristol on April 8, 1838, initiating what became the Atlantic Ferry properly conducted. When she arrived in New York fifteen and a quarter days later, it was to severe and undeserved disappointment. She was beaten by only 4 hours in the crossing by a much smaller ship, *Sirius*, chartered by the British and American Steam Navigation Company from service in the Irish Sea, to substitute for their proper entry in this competition, the *British Queen*, whose engines had not been finished in time. Although the *Sirius* gained the title at first steamship in regular passenger service across the Atlantic, it was Brunel and the *Great Western* that effectively originated the service and established the practice that the largest and fastest ships of the time would be entered upon this run.[78] But even though the *Great Western* was operated until 1846 on the Bristol to New York run, it was not a self-supporting operation, as was demonstrated by the eventual abandonment of service after the Great Western Steamship Company failed to garner the mail subsidy that could mean the difference between marginal profit and deep losses.

The British government decided to advertise for bids for the carriage of the Britain to United States mails that brought forth the greatest competition yet witnessed. It seems to have been appreciated that with this subsidy a steamship company could probably sustain a trans-Atlantic schedule, whereas without it the future still seemed in question. Or, as a New York newspaper phrased it at the time, "Can steam packets be made to pay?" Thornton in his history of British ship-

ping gives the obvious answer. " 'No.' But if a substantial mail contract were obtainable, the outlook was very different."[79] In response to this call for tenders for the conduct of the mail transport there were four contenders: the Great Western Steamship Company, the British and American Steam Navigation Company, the City of Dublin Steam Packet Company, and a new company to be organized in Liverpool and Glasgow and to be made up of ships agents, marine-engine builders, shipbuilders, and Samuel Cunard—the Halifax merchant who was in fact the force behind this entry. To the amazement of all but this latter potential shipping company, their offer was accepted by the Admiralty, the agent for the choice— leaving the Great Western Company, with its established run, the largest and most advanced ship afloat, and its powerful Bristolian supporters, puzzled and angry. A century and a half later we are still puzzled because, although the Cunard Company (as it came to be known) succeeded in its venture, there is no reason to doubt that the established Great Western Company would not have succeeded equally given the same handsome subsidy.

Having won the contract, the Cunard Company had to secure ships to fulfill its commitment to undertake a fortnightly service between Liverpool and Halifax and Boston in summer, reduced to monthly in the winter.

> To carry on this trade four steamers, the *Britannia* (launched February 5th, 1840), *Acadia, Columbia,* and *Caledonia*, were built of wood by Robert Duncan and Co., and others, at Port Glasgow, each being 207 feet long, by 34 1/2 feet broad, and 22 1/2 feet deep, and of 1150 tons . . . having two cylinders . . . driving paddles 28 1/2 feet [in] diameter, which gave an average speed of 8 1/2 knots per hour.[80]

Such ships were certainly larger and more competent than the *Savannah* of twenty

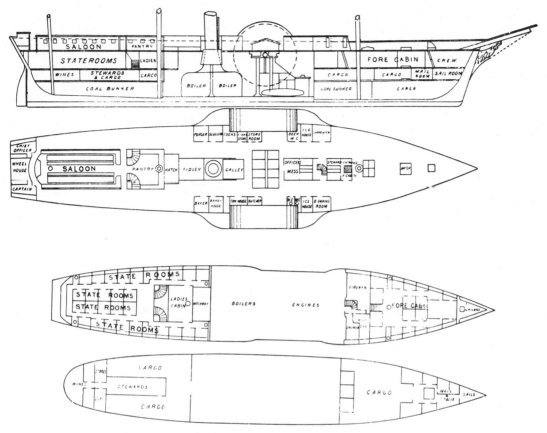

Section and deck plans of the *S.S. Britannia. Source*: A. F. Maginnis, *The Atlantic Ferry: Its Ships, Men, and Working* (London, 1900).

years before, but they were neither much faster nor the most advanced ships of their own time. The *Great Western* of 1838 had been 5 feet longer, with nearly 200 tons greater displacement, and the same speed. The British and American Navigation Company had taken possession of the *British Queen* in 1839 and the *President* in 1840. These were of 275-foot length, 37.5-foot beam, 27-foot depth, and 1,863 tons gross register tonnage. Although larger by half than the Cunard ships, these British and American ships failed to operate long: the sailing of the *President* from New York on March 11, 1841, led to the disappearance of that vessel with no survivors

and the consequent collapse of the company. The *British Queen* was sold to the Belgians, removing almost immediately one of Cunard's two British competitors.[81] The other, the Great Western Company, hung on somewhat longer. The *Great Western* was kept in service to New York until 1845 when she was replaced by the *Great Britain*, a ship of great distinction that is still to be seen in the dock from which she was launched at Bristol in 1843—certainly the most distinguished of the early ships and a most happy survivor to our times. The *Great Britain* designed by Brunel was far in advance of any Cunarders of the time or, for that matter, years to come. She was of iron, strong enough to survive a winter on Rathmullin Point in County Down, Ireland, where she was stranded in September, 1846, and possessed of a screw propeller driven by engines operating at 25 pounds pressure. Her dimensions were: 274 feet long, 48.25 feet broad, 31.5 feet deep, and of 3,270 register tonnage. Built in a dry dock, she remained captured therein for a year (1843–1844) while the Bristol port authorities dawdled about widening the lock gates as they had promised. She remained on the Atlantic Ferry station until 1852, when she was withdrawn and put on the Australian run.[82] With a speed of 11 knots, she could make New York in just over fourteen days; even on the Australia run, she covered the distance via the Cape to Melbourne between August 21 and November 10, 1852. She continued on this station until 1882, when the *Great Britain* was sold again. Storms off Cape Horn forced her in 1886 to Port Stanley in the Falkland Islands, where she was condemned and used as a coal hulk until 1937, when she was beached at Port William.[83] But even that ignominious disposition did not prove fatal. In the early 1970s a group in Bristol set about returning the hulk of the *Great Britain* to the Cumberland Dock where she was built. Using a massive seagoing barge, they carefully raised the hull of the *Great Britain* from the mud on Sparrow Point in the Falklands, loaded it on the barge, and with great caution brought her back to Bristol's Floating Harbor where she has been patiently restored. Obviously her engines and screw are gone, but what remains of this first great iron ship cannot help but fascinate us and cause us to hold her builders, most notably Brunel, in high regard.

The Great Western Company, though the technical leader of its time, was not a continuing financial success. The plodding Cunard Company gained that end while all its early competitors fell away by the early

1850s. Thornton in his history of British shipping looks at the rapid and somewhat improbable rise of Cunard:

> The new Cunard Line invaded the Atlantic trade at a time when no fewer than 100,000 people were migrating annually to the United States and every one of them was doing it in an American ship. It was a direct and obvious threat to the American packet-owners and [he argues] they made the profound mistake of being too proud to admit it. A variety of other reasons have been advanced by experienced writers on the subject, but none have provided any solution to the real problem, which is, as we have seen, that the Americans during the very years when they were failing so signally to respond to the challenge of steam on the Atlantic were developing it with energy and extreme brilliance upon their lakes and rivers. Was it not they who seized upon the new invention of the propeller early in the 1840s and put it into immediate practice, while our own Admiralty experts were still unable to make up their minds about it?

He goes on to argue that two factors explain this course to him:

> First, the future of the steamship lay with the engineer and, in spite of American achievements in new and specialized directions, it was in England and Scotland that were to be found the leaders in the rapidly progressing science of marine engineering. . . . Second, . . . the steamship could not be made to pay. What Congress would have replied to a determined appeal for a subsidy by the established packet-owners we do not know. It was never presented.[84]

The poor maligned Yankee shipowners seem to have been sighted through a reversed telescope. If technical prowess was the key, how then was the Great Western Company—far in advance of the Cunard Line in this regard—forced to quit? The key seems to lie in the subsidy the British Parliament gave to steam-packet lines starting in 1838. By awarding the Atlantic Ferry subsidy to Cunard, the Admiralty consigned the Great Western Company to the same ultimate fate as the early efforts of the Americans. In 1845 the *Massachusetts* was built for Captain R. B. Forbes and other Boston investors (157 feet long, 32-foot beam, 20 feet deep, with a tonnage of 751) as an auxiliary steam-sail packet. She was the first ship in the Atlantic Ferry to use a screw propeller, so there was no lack of ingenuity involved, although the particular arrangement involved proved somewhat ineffective in the rough North Atlantic, and her size was too small for economical operation.[85] Without a subsidy the *Massachusetts* had to be withdrawn from the station in 1846 and sold to the War Department as a troop transport, the only form of subsidy Congress was willing to give to steamshipping at the time.

The chauvinism of dispatching effective American competition as due to the "mistake" made by Yankee packet-boat owners in appraising the importance of steam is matched only by the conceit that marine engineering was a British possession. As another Briton, Tute, tells us:

The Cunard "monopoly" which in 1847 was total, there being no other steamship service in regular operation on the Atlantic in that year, came abruptly to an end in 1850 when the proud *Collins* line swept into the lead. The United States were back in the transatlantic trade with a vengeance. The pace suddenly increased. The new American ships were not only more comfortable than the Cunarders; they were faster. New York was now within ten days of Liverpool.

Punch was generous indeed:

A steamer of the Collins Line—
  A Yankee Doodle Notion,
Has also quickest cut the brine,
  Across the Atlantic Ocean.
And British Agents, no way slow
  her merits to discover,

Have been and bought her—
  just to tow the Cunarder packets over.[86]

The creation of the "Dramatic Line" of the New York and Liverpool United States Mail Steamship Company, to give Collins's firm its legal name, depended on the availability of a mail subsidy of the sort Cunard had enjoyed for a decade. With that in hand, Edward Knight Collins set about securing ships far better engineered than were those of his Liverpool-based competition, disproving the notion that fuzzy thinking had afflicted Yankee shipowners (Collins came from Cape Cod) and technical bungling the East River shipbuilders. Commencing service with a sailing of the *Atlantic* on April 27, 1850, the Collins Line put four identical ships on the run. The *Atlantic, Arctic, Baltic* and *Pacific* (282 feet long, 45 feet broad, 31.5 feet deep, and with a tonnage of 2,860) "were a great advance upon the Cunarders then existing, and were the first to have straight stems, . . . smoking-rooms, . . . bathrooms, and barbers' shops, and on one or two of the vessels the saloons at first were placed amidships."[87] Steam was at 17 pounds pressure, which on a consumption of 85 tons of coal a day gave an average speed of 12 knots, fast enough to outdistance the aging Cunarders. The economic headway was not as distinguished. The high cost of construction and operation of the vessels left the company with little profit, and the collision of the small French Steamer *Vesta* with the *Arctic* off Cape Race on the Banks in September, 1854, led to the loss of that Collins ship and 322 lives, among them the owner's wife, son and daughter. In December, 1857, the last of the great wooden paddle steamers launched by the Collins Line, the *Adriatic*, sailed from Liverpool. The ship (355 feet long, 50 feet broad, and 35 feet deep, with a tonnage of 3,670) was never heard of again.[88] With her loss and the general unprofitability of the operation, and the great slump of 1857 in the

United States, the Dramatic Line disappeared within the month, in January, 1858.

When we seek the durability of the Cunard operation in contrast, it seems that conservative operation (rather than any great service or technical originality) provided the answer. The cautious Nova Scotian and Scottish owners seldom led the industry in technical terms, only slowly adopting what others had pioneered, often at fatal costs, as in the case of the screw propulsion of Forbes's *Massachusetts* or the speed of Collins's *Atlantic*. Not only did the Cunarders oppose speed for its tendency to be gained at the cost of safety, they also shied away from it because of its economic costs. In staying the course they were around to pick up the pieces of other services that foundered either economically or literally. In 1858 they gained from the departure of the Dramatic Line; in 1912 they gained perhaps even more from the collapse in confidence that came with the dramatic loss of the White Star Line flagship *Titanic* on her maiden voyage. Seldom in its long history was the Cunard line either exciting or particularly interesting, but it was eminently durable, never losing a passenger from accidents to its ships in its century and a quarter of effective participation in the Atlantic Ferry.

The result was that most of that century and a quarter, from 1840 to 1965, was taken up with efforts by others to enter and persevere in the Ferry, usually by offering technical improvements faster than the Cunard Company was able or willing to make them. Other British companies were active in this competition and, starting late in the nineteenth century, the shipping companies of other European and North American countries came to take an increasing part. Cunard remained the competitor to beat, however, but mainly from the economic rather than the technical viewpoint. Tute looks on the period before 1870 as the

time for pioneering, "the first wonder of a regular steamship service across the Western Ocean long forgotten, and with the accent about to be thrown more heavily than ever before on speed and comfort. The Cunard Company still had the lion's share of the business but they were being steadily outclassed" both by British competitors and by the French and the Germans who had entered the Atlantic Ferry in the 1850s.[89] The most important foreign competitor to Cunard proved to be the Hamburg-American Line, whose first steamer, the *Borussia*, (an iron screw steamer 317 feet long, 40 feet broad, 28 feet deep, with a tonnage of 2,349) was put on a Hamburg and Cuxhaven to New York, via Southampton, run in 1855.[90] Under the aegis of the company's director of immigrant services (who was to become its principal director), Albert Ballin, Hamburg-American (HAPAG) became by the end of the century the largest shipowning concern in the world and the greatly dominant force in the immigrant trade between Europe and North America. In the process the company managed effectively to work out an economic equation that demonstrated that the immigrant trade could be used to make profitable the sort of service that was distinguished mainly by increases in speed and luxury undertaken to appeal to the first-class passengers.

NATIONAL COMPETITION THROUGH SERVICE DISTINCTION

It is impractical to attempt to chart the detailed course of the competition among British steamship companies and between them and their important foreign contestants. Throughout the last three decades of the nineteenth century the British as a group continued to dominate, even more so in the sense that many of the ships employed by the French and Germans in the earlier years were actually constructed in Britian. But the

Germans in particular began in the 1890s to set the pace that both British operating companies and shipbuilders had to match. Because the great expansion of the British merchant marine under steam, overtaking the American lead in all shipping lost during the Civil War, came through becoming the carrier for many nations, the British (having abandoned the last Navigation Acts in 1849) could not fully protect even their domestic market. The competition came in any and all international connections. Thus the service between England and the United States could be provided by French or German vessels as well as British. Only services internal to a single state—England to Ireland, for example—could be protected under the established law of cabotage that permitted a nation to reserve its coastwise navigation to her own vessels. This accepted practice became the refuge of the American merchant marine in the post–Civil War period with Atlantic coastwise navigation and service from the East to the Pacific Coast becoming the backstay of what American mercantile navigation persisted.

In northwestern Europe, where Germany, Norway, Denmark, the Netherlands, Belgium, France, and Britain all sought to become important steamship powers, the notion of carrying persons and goods from a second to a third country was accepted. In this way the French or Germans managed to enter the major tourist transit, which was between Britain and the United States, while combining it with the immigrant and other services from their own ports. This activity helped to shift the main passenger ports for the Atlantic Ferry in Britain from Liverpool to Southampton, because that south coast port had two distinct geographical advantages: it had a longer period of high tides ("a double high-tide") than most other British ports, as well as a lower tidal range than some such as Bristol; and it lay close to the general navigation lane that passed from the

North Sea (the German Ocean, as it was often called then) toward the open Atlantic. The rise of Cherbourg on the French side of the Channel came from this same ease of calling during passage from elsewhere.

The fierce competition that grew up in the Atlantic Ferry forced on the contestants a constant concern for strategy within a framework with a number of variable conditions. From 1870 to the mid-1890s the most apparent variable was speed, but just below this obvious ranking came the operation of several other orderings. Among the first-class passengers the level of comfort was a matter of distinctions; among the masses the availability of steerage and its cost distinguished among carriers. Frequency and reliability of service, convenience of ports, costs, national and corporate loyalty, and other service factors entered into the competition. The competition was felt mainly in the matter of service. The steamship was a fairly standardized vehicle by the 1870s—the paddle had been replaced by the screw propeller, iron (and later steel) was coming to replace wood for the hulls, and advances by one operator in the size and technology of his latest entrant tended to be matched fairly rapidly by his major competitors. Still, there was a lag while that catching up took place, and there was always a certain cachet compounded of a number of service factors that attached to various companies. Cunard was definitely the line of the timid and the traditional—safe, unflamboyant, staid in the extreme. One wonders how an imaginative genius could have thought up their latter-day motto, "Getting there is half the fun," because the White Star Line of British liners was far more frolicsome and fashionable, and the French Line certainly gave more joy in the dining saloon.

In a summary way the size of vessels was perhaps the most directly competitive feature, because it tended as it rose to provide both greater speed and greater comfort. For

S. S. Great Eastern of 1858. *Source:* A. F. Maginnis, *The Atlantic Ferry: Its Ships, Men, and Working* (London, 1900).

this reason we may use a summary of the growth in the size of vessels as a necessary summary of the evolution taking place during this period of overriding competition. First, however, it is necessary to note Brunel's last contribution to marine engineering—his enormous iron ship the *Great Eastern*, launched in 1858, which stood for nearly forty years as the largest ship ever built, albeit a true freak that found little practical employment. The ship was nearly twice the length of most vessels of its time at 680 feet, wide by comparison at 83 feet in the beam, 48 feet deep, and with a massive tonnage of 18,915. It had ten boilers, a hundred furnaces fired athwartships, that operated two cylinders of 84 inches diameter under 30 pounds pressure. The propulsion was by two paddlewheels as well as a single screw.[91] But the *Great Eastern* was too vast for its time and probably too eccentric in its design. She

served only occasionally and then most effectively as a cable-laying ship for which her vast size was further enhanced by removing one of her five stacks, and the two associated engines, to permit the transport of an entire trans-Atlantic cable. When she went to the wreckers in 1887 there was still no ship of her size; none exceeded her in tonnage until 1901, none in length until the *Oceanic* of 1899, and none in beam until the *Mauretania* of 1907. Some assign her failure not to her being too large for her time but rather to her affront to the sea gods: "The legend that at least one of the reasons for the colossal bad luck and failure of the *Great Eastern* was that she carried around with her the whole of her life, the dead bodies of two riveters who accidentally were sealed up in her double bottom, still today dodges about in the shadows of our minds."[92]

Putting aside the *Great Eastern* as the exceptional proof of the general rule, we may logically begin our summary of size with ships contemporary to the behemoth. In 1857 the Collins Line introduced the *Adriatic* as the latest word in size and style and, unfortunately, the last in their roster. Built in New York, she was 355 feet long, 50 broad, and 35 deep, with a tonnage of 3,670, according to a design of George Steers, who gained lasting fame as the designer of the original yacht *America*, for which the cup has been named in honor of her first victory in that classic race.[93] With such paternity it seems reasonable to assume that the *Adriatic* represented the height of technical excellence for her time. Certainly for luxurious appointments she stood at the forefront, but her hull remained wooden and she was propelled by paddlewheels, with auxiliary sails, for a top speed of 13.5 knots. In light of her qualities she was constructed to carry 316 first-class and 60 second-class passengers, with no steerage allowed.

Five years later Cunard set a milestone in the Atlantic Ferry by putting into service its last trans-Atlantic paddle steamer, the *Scotia* (379 feet long, 48 feet broad, 30 feet deep, with a tonnage of 3,871). Although she was highly successful, the growing experience with screw propulsion finally convinced the company to moderate the continuing conservatism of its Admiralty advisors and adopt a single screw for their ships (as the Inman Line had been doing for several years). By 1869 Inman had launched the *City of Brussels* (390 feet long, 40.25 feet broad, 27 feet deep, and of 3,081 tons) that became the first ship to be awarded a metaphorical Blue Ribbon, which never existed in substance but was constantly referred to until the early 1960s when, with the end of effective trans-Atlantic competition and the speed it engendered, it was also metaphorically retired in the possession of its last holder, the *United States*, the only American ship ever to gain this laurel. Both Inman and Cunard began to respond to the efforts of the Oceanic

Steam Navigation Company, organized in 1870 by Thomas Henry Ismay and adopting the banner of the White Star Line. Thus a three-sided competition within the British steamship community became the main driving force on the Atlantic. The Oceanic Company began its long-running tradition of naming its ships so as to end in *-ic*—just as Cunard did in *-ia* and Inman as the *City of*—by launching the *Oceanic* (420 feet long, 41 feet broad, 31 feet deep, with a tonnage of 3,707), which was particularly luxurious for its time. Screw propulsion permitted it to overcome the former domination of the midships section of the vessel by engines and boilers to operate paddles; the machinery could be pushed aft, allowing the public saloons to extend the width of the ship. Much was to be changed over the years, but the *Oceanic* was probably the next ship after the Collins Line *Adriatic* of fifteen years before to force a major change in the quality of service on the Atlantic Ferry.

Speed and size began to increase quite rapidly even in this period while most of the competition lay among British lines. The French Line, Companie Général Transatlantique, had begun North American service with the sailing of the *Washington* from Le Havre to New York on June 15, 1864,[94] but along with the German steamship lines they played little role in forcing the competitive pace until the turn of the century. Instead it was the British companies that fought the battle for the prestige position to be gained through possession of the record for fastest service in the Ferry. In 1858 the *Adriatic* had established a speed of 13.5 knots; in 1869 the *City of Brussels* had increased the pace to 14.5 knots. The *Oceanic* as fitted with compound engines (those that used the steam twice or more), which were introduced on the Atlantic in 1870, could open a new phase in the race, as the coal could be used more efficiently, effectively reducing the deadweight loading necessary. Also, boiler pressures were creeping up. The flagship of the

White Star Line used 65 pounds pressure and gained a speed somewhat over 14 knots, not yet superior to the single-expansion engines of the *City of Brussels* but providing the potential for rapid advances.[95]

The double-expansion engine managed to cut the fuel consumption per horsepower in half so that higher speeds became practicable even with the same level of coal consumption.[96] It is impossible here to trace the full extent of the race. The White Star Line (Oceanic Steam Navigation Company) forced the pace in the 1870s by building larger and faster ships. In 1874 and 1875 the *Britanic* and the *Germanic*, sister ships, were launched on highly successful careers. They were 455 feet long, 45 feet broad, 34 feet deep, with a tonnage of 5,004, thus raising the standard above that critical figure and making the existing Cunard and Inman ships old fashioned. Compound engines operating at 85 pounds pressure were used so that the speed was increased to slightly over 16 knots.[97] Suddenly the passage from Liverpool to New York was reduced to just about a week's time.

In the 1880s the Inman Line of British steamships came under severe financial pressure, which Ismay of the White Star Line unsuccessfully sought to alleviate. Instead it fell to the capitalists interested in the Pennsylvania Railroad to come to the rescue, and thereby change the ownership and registry of the *City* ships to the other side of the Atlantic, although operations remained located on the Mersey. In 1888 Inman launched the *City of New York*, followed by the *City of Paris* a year later.

The introduction of these splendid ships to the Express Transatlantic Service marks one of those epochs of complete transformation in type of vessel, which, as the years roll by, the demands of the public necessitates, and the advance of engineering science renders possible. In the design and construction of hull and machinery great advances were made, steel being very extensively used; . . . great breadth of beam was adopted, the most minute subdivision into water-tight compartments, effected by numerous transverse and, for the first time, for and aft mid-line bulkheads. These were rendered practicable on account of the adoption, for the first time, in the Express Service, of the "twin screw" system of propulsion. Another great novelty was the adoption of the water chambers, to lessen the rolling in a sea-way.[98]

Triple-expansion engines were employed independently powering each screw and the pressure was raised to 150 pounds. With a speed of twenty knots, the *City of Paris* was the first ship to reduce the Ferry to less than six days duration.

The White Star Line met this challenge by building the *Teutonic* and the *Majestic* (566 feet long, 58 broad, 40 deep, with a tonnage of 9,984), which had their respective maiden voyages in 1889 and 1890. They shared with the Inman ships the speed records on the Atlantic; but at last, in 1893, Cunard overcame its extreme conservatism to launch the *Campania* (600 feet long, 65 feet broad, 43 feet deep, with a tonnage of 12,950) and a sister ship the *Lucania* powered with triple-expansion engines operating at a boiler pressure of 165 pounds. These were the first Cunard ships to be built without any sails and the first anywhere to exceed 600 feet, save for the recently dismantled *Great Eastern*. Finally Cunard had a real ocean greyhound, capable of shrinking the Atlantic Ferry to 5 days and 8 hours.[99]

The pace of the mid-1890s was sufficient to force on the Continental shipowners considerable advances in service if they intended to stay in the trade. The German companies had been very active in the immigrant transport, and the French had earned a reputation they enjoyed to the very end for a level of luxury no other company could match. But speed became the test of

S. S. Oregon of 1883. *Source:* A. F. Maginnis, *The Atlantic Ferry: Its Ships, Men and Working* (London, 1900).

competitive success, particularly in the first-class passenger trade, which then assumed much greater importance than it ever would again in times when far more tourists were to cross the Atlantic in place of the masses of steerage passengers whose numbers declined rapidly after World War I. Although many of the fast liners did carry steerage, no owner gave them much thought in planning his ships: they merely increased profits handsomely at little additional cost. Moreover, although no one would have constructed vast and speedy ships for immigrants, there were advantages in this trade to be gained from increases in speed. Thus the previous flagships of a line might still return good profits to the firm when downgraded to the immigrant trade and transformed to carry large numbers in no great comfort.

The Germans used the late 1890s to shock the British shipping fraternity as no one had been able to do before. In 1858 the North German Lloyd Steamship Company had begun its Atlantic service, but for nearly forty years it had settled for a major role in the immigrant trade as well as a presence in the Germany-to-America express services. In the mid-1890s the company decided it either had to make radical changes or give up the express trade. In 1897 the *Kaiser Wilhelm der Grosse* (627 feet long, 66 feet in the beam, 36 feet deep, with a tonnage 14,350) was launched to become the largest and fastest ship afloat. On her maiden run she clocked nearly 22 knots on her eastbound journey. Within a year the success of this challenge was clear: the North German Lloyd was carrying 28 percent of the passengers landed at New York.[100] In part because of her size, certainly because she for the first time introduced effective international competition for the British in the Atlantic Ferry, and because of the impending change in the Ferry service to place more emphasis on tourist travel and less on the emigrant-steerage trade, we may logically look upon the *Kaiser Wilhelm der Grosse* of 1897 as the first of the modern steamships that for nearly three-quarters of a century dominated the Atlantic Ferry and, thereby, the technical forefront of ocean shipping. Although speeds were to be raised another 10 knots in this fierce race, by reaching substantially above 20 knots, the German flagship reduced the passage sufficiently that, with a sister ship, she could effectively maintain a weekly sailing from either side of the Atlantic.

Taking the late 1890s as the beginning of the last phase of the seaborne Atlantic Ferry, we may note certain general conditions that attached to the trade until its demise in the 1960s. The ports involved had been reduced appreciably, basically to New York in the United States and to a single national port for three of the four active European participants—Southampton (substituting for and replacing Liverpool), Le Havre, and Rotterdam. In Germany for some time longer both Hamburg and Bremerhaven survived, though ultimately the Elbe port became the dominant one for the American trade until the post–World War II political partition of Germany returned Bremerhaven to major importance. Normally each of the four European entrants in the North Atlantic race departed initially from its national port but made an intermediate call at a British or French port, Southampton in the first instance and Cherbourg in the second. After World War I the Italians entered seriously into the race, again heading for New York on a departure from Genoa, with a common call at either Barcelona or Algeciras in Spain. Some second or third-level passenger services did use other ports— Liverpool, Cobh, Zeebruge, Göteborg, Oslo, Bergen, and Amsterdam in Europe and Boston, Halifax, and Montréal in North America. But the epitome of the Atlantic Ferry always was the service from New York to individual national ports in England, France, Holland, Germany, and later Italy.

The 1890s also witnessed the introduction of the last two significant technical advances in steamship operation, although in one case steam was replaced by internal combustion. Nevertheless we will follow common usage in employing the term *steamship* to refer to the general body of mechanized transport by water. The two advances in the 1890s were the introduction of the steam-turbine engine and the diesel engine. As early as 1884 Charles Parsons had introduced his turbine engine for a stationary application and in 1894 a yacht, *Turbinia*, was fitted with a turbine to test its marine application. At first cavitation was encountered around her propeller but improvements overcame that problem, and for the vast 1897 naval review at Spithead she was able to race among the lumbering battleships (powered by reciprocating engines) at a speed of 34.5 knots, proving beyond question that higher speeds in shipping would be most likely to come from adoption of the turbine.

The diesel engine had a slower and less dramatic introduction. Invented in the 1890s, the first ship installation was on a river boat in Russia, where it was coupled to an electric generator as a diesel-electric system because the earliest diesel engines could not be reversed, posing an obvious operational problem unless they were coupled to electric traction motors. This 1903 experiment was successful so in 1912 the *Seelandia*, a Danish freighter, was launched in Copenhagen to become the first oceangoing diesel-powered ship. This began a particular Scandinavian affection for the diesel motor vessel that has characterized ocean shipping down to the present. British and American builders have continued to favor steam turbines, arguing persuasively that their easier maintenance and highly variable operating speeds prove ultimately more economical than do the vaunted diesels. In any event, in the Atlantic Ferry the turbine gained the main attention as it held out immediate prospects of considerable increases in speed over that provided by the best reciprocating steam engines.

In 1899 perhaps the last example of that classic reciprocating engine was employed in the White Star Line response to the German challenge on the Atlantic. The *Oceanic* (of 1899) was 686 feet long, the first ship to exceed the *Great Eastern* in that dimension, though it still was 2,000 tons smaller in gross tonnage at 16,900. It was 68 feet broad and 49 feet deep, able to accommodate 1,500 passengers, 1,000 of them in third class or a slightly improved version of steerage.[101] But its engine did not prove the match for the German's that the builders had promised; so it is not surprising that Cunard, seeking to meet the foreign challenge, took the more drastic step of adopting the steam turbine. Before that came about, however, the Germans upped the ante; the Hamburg-American Line ordered the *Deutschland* that "achieved 22½ knots on her maiden voyage [in 1900] and, as she settled down, added a knot to her regular performance. By now the British were being left far behind in the matter of speed."[102] Thus Cunard was under heavy pressure, as was the White Star Line. To answer that, the conservative firm took an unusually bold step; they decided to build the *Caronia* (1904) and the *Carmania* (1905) as an experiment. The *Caronia* had triple-expansion reciprocating engines, whereas the *Carmania* had Parsons steam turbines. In sea trials the turbined ship gained better than a knot on its sister, so the Liverpudlians decided to make their main challenge with the new form of engine. Partly in response to the success that J.P. Morgan had had in

gaining financial control of the White Star Line, the next year (1903) the British government agreed to subsidize Cunard in building two ships that could maintain 24 or 25 knots, to be made available to the British Admiralty in time of war. What resulted were the *Lusitania* and *Mauretania* in 1907.

Although each was a fine ship, we may best look at the *Mauretania* both because she was the luckier of the two—her sister ship was sunk with heavy loss of life by a German submarine in 1915—and because she was by common agreement the most successful and popular ship ever built. She represented a considerable increase in size for the Atlantic competitors. She could carry 563 first-class, 464 second-class, and 1,138 third-class passengers, in a hull 762 feet long, 88 feet broad, and 57 feet deep. The two ships alternated possession of the Blue Ribbon on the Atlantic until the loss of the *Lusitania*, and the *Mauretania* retained sole possession of it until 1929 when she lost it permanently, first to the German *Bremen* put in service that year. Thus the *Mauretania* held the speed record basically for twenty-two years, from her maiden voyage in 1907 when she averaged 27.4 knots.[103] Even thus vanquished, the greatest lady of the Atlantic remained in service until withdrawn in 1934 just before the *Queen Mary* was put into service. Throughout that nearly thirty years she was an extremely popular ship, granted a high status to be shared only with the French Line's *Ile de France*.

With such compatriots the now well-heeled White Star Line decided it needed something more glamorous than the aging *Oceanic*. At 31,000 tons the Cunard ship had nearly doubled her size. The other British contestant, though owned in the United States, decided on size as its competitive challenge. The Cunarders had also reduced the Atlantic for the first time to less than a five-day voyage, making any contest on speed grounds increasingly difficult. In the

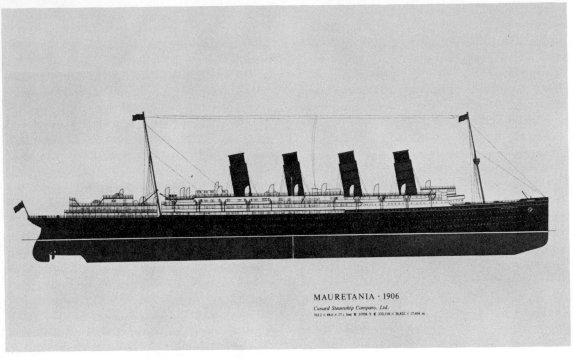

MAURETANIA · 1906

Cunard Steamship Company, Ltd.

The original *S.S. Mauretania* of 1908. Tre Tryckare drawing.

Mauretania and her sister there was still a vestige of the past: "In both ships and indeed in all large passenger vessels built up to 1914 the emphasis was upon the great public rooms of the liners—ornate dining saloons and lofty main lounges and smoking rooms—rather than on the still comparatively neglected sleeping boxes which passed for ordinary passenger cabins."[104] And it might be added that most of the grandeur and space was slaveringly bestowed on the first-class passengers, leaving the ordinary travelers crowded below decks on the voyage and waiting on the deck if recourse to lifeboats was necessary. When the *Titanic* sank in 1912, entrance to those boats was by sex but then class, undoubtedly contributing to the loss of 1,500 lives.

It was size and grandeur that White Star sought. In 1911 their *Olympic* raised the size to 45,324 tons, much the largest ship ever built. That same year a sister, the *Titanic* increased even that figure, measuring out at 46,329 tons (853 feet long, 93 feet broad, and 60 feet deep). She could carry 735 first-class, 675 second-class, and 1,030 third-class passengers, and a crew of 860. Her service speed, however, was only 21 knots, as White Star had settled on a policy of medium speed and greatest emphasis on comfort. There is no need to go into detail about her fate. As the ultimate in luxury, she had a fashionable list of passengers on her maiden voyage in the spring of 1912, as well as a captain who thought her essentially invincible. The sea punished him, and a greatly unfortunate share of his passengers, for such a presumption before the voyage ended. Somehow luxury and size could never justify carrying lifeboats for only 1,178 on a ship with 3,547 passengers and crew.

The final lap in the prewar contest was begun when the German shipowners set about meeting the British challenge. Just before 1914 the Germans launched and put into service for a few months the *Vaterland* and the *Imperator*, very large and fast ships to compete with Cunard's *Aquitania* (launched in 1913, gross register tonnage of 45,647, overall length 901.5 feet) and the White Star *Olympic*, the surviving sister of the *Titanic*. The *Vaterland* and *Imperator* were to be joined by the *Bismarck*, launched in 1914 but not completed until after the war, in providing a weekly trans-Atlantic service. At 56,621 gross register tons, 954 feet long over all, the *Bismarck* was the largest ship afloat at the outbreak of the war. When completed she had accommodation for some 4,000 passengers, 1,000 in first-class, 545 in second-class, and some 2,500 in third. As with most prewar ships her cabins were tiny and little more than boxes, but her saloons were grand indeed. These German ships were taken in 1918 as reparations, becoming the largest ships of the early 1920s—the *Imperator* as Cunard's *Barengaria*; the *Vaterland* at U.S. Lines' *Leviathan*; and the *Bismarck*, when completed, as the White Star *Majestic*. Whether this triad would have provided the mass transit on the Atlantic Ferry that their owners envisioned, capable of handling 3,000 to 4,000 passengers a week in either direction between New York and Southampton and Bremen, was never proved. Certainly the undertaking, if successful, would have made North German Lloyd, their owners, the leading operator in the Ferry. But in the few months of operation in 1914, of only two of the ships, the case was not clearly resolved.[105]

The 1920s differed from the prewar years in a number of ways. There were far fewer immigrants from Europe and far more tourists thence from the United States. The glut of emergency shipping built during the war, plus the German reparations of the three great 50,000-ton liners, seemed to inhibit any notable new construction. During the early years of the decade a number of 20,000-ton ships were launched, some with technical improvements but none seeking a lead in the competition that was largely relaxed as a result of the eviction of the Germans under the Treaty of Versailles. Britain still had Cunard's *Mauretania, Aquitania,* and *Barengaria* and White Star's *Olympic* and *Majestic* in the 40,000- and 50,000-ton class; and the United States from 1923 had the *Leviathan*, at 59,000 tons a giant ship. But such single mammoths have posed scheduling problems since the day of the *Great Eastern* because the pairing with a much smaller vessel leaves the deck sometimes overcrowded on the return journey.

The strong demand for service on the Atlantic Ferry during the 1920s brought the French into the competition in a fashion they had never before adopted. In 1927 the French Line launched one of the greater ships ever entered in the contest, and in 1934 they followed with the finest steamship ever built.

> The advent of the 43,150 ton Île de France on the 22nd of June 1927 marks the start of the last and really modern era in giant Atlantic liner construction. Although in appearance the Île de France seemed to be merely a larger version of the 1913 *Paris . . .* , she had in fact important differences, and in 1927 was the sixth largest liner in the world. She was the first North Atlantic liner to be fitted with gravity davits for her lifeboats, and as these were raised up over the decks, her passengers enjoyed a greatly enlarged deck space. Decorated in what was then the modern French style, she had a large following [particularly] Americans who thought her the most graceful and attractive ship afloat and for many years she carried more first-class

NORMANDIE · 1932
Compagnie Générale Transatlantique
981.5 × 117.7 × 91.8 feet € 83243 T € 299,160 × 35,975 × 27,980 m

The *S.S. Normandie* of 1935. Tre Tryckare drawing.

passengers than any other ship on the North Atlantic.[106]

But as only the sixth largest ship, the queen of the French fleet had to gain laurels rather than ribbons, leaving Cunard still the runner to overtake.

The Germans did just that when in 1928 the North German Lloyd launched on successive days the *Europa* and the *Bremen*. The latter was 938 feet overall in length, with a tonnage of 51,656. Steam in the 1914 *Bismarck* (White Star *Majestic*) had been at 260 pounds per square inch pressure, but with the *Bremen* fourteen years later the figure had risen rapidly to 330 pounds "and superheated to 700°F," signaling the rapid technical advances in marine-engine construction that came after World War I. Such improvements allowed the *Bremen*, on its

maiden voyage in July, 1929, to attain almost 28 knots (later fully reaching that speed) to take the Blue Ribbon away from the *Mauretania*, which had held it for twenty-two years, longer than any other vessel ever possessed it. Yet the *Bremen* was quickly surpassed by other ships and carried the seeds of the destruction of her kind in that she was equipped with a catapult used to launch a small plane that would speed the priority mails from her deck to shore, over distances then practicable for air transport, as she approached the other side of the Atlantic.[107] But in 1929 the German contenders forced on any serious contender for leadership in trans-Atlantic transportation a new undertaking in technical terms.

The French were the first to respond, and in a manner that sought to win under the rules that the Germans had just set as well as those the French had put into practice two years before. What they sought was not merely the most luxurious ship ever built but also the largest and fastest. In this came the unique qualities of the *Normandie* that made so tragic her mishandled foundering less than a decade later. After World War I improvements in marine technology, particularly engines, had permitted both larger ships and more efficient ones, so more space was available for passenger comfort. This trend was further enhanced by the shift of what had at first been known as "steerage" but by the time of the war had become "third class," to an improved and more socially elevated "tourist class" where elemental comfort was increasingly demanded. Cabins were enlarged at the same time that privacy was improved by restricting numbers. The *Île de France*, perhaps the first *grande luxe* liner, had proved a great drawing card for the Comapnie Générale Transatlantique. Thus the company, in seeking to compete with the Germans, began by adding to their own strength qualities equal to their competitors. The *Normandie* had seven distinct classes of accommodation for passengers: "30 grand luxe, 30 de luxe, 790 first class, 16 intermediate, 657 tourist-class, 139 *mixte*, and 135 third-class, a total of 1975." When we compare this with the 4,000 carried in the *Majestic* of a decade before, we can see clearly how much the standard of accommodation for all classes had been raised. Because the *Normandie* had a register tonnage of 86,496 and an overall length of 1,029 feet (a 119-foot beam and a 92-foot depth, with a mean draft of 36.5 feet) the sharp reduction in passenger capacity joined with great increase in tonnage again demonstrates the new standards of space and comfort that were introduced. This advance was joined to an accomplished operating mean speed of 31.2 knots, gained three years after service began in 1935 when she had been refitted with four-blade, rather than three-

blade, propellers.[108] Even more pleasant for the French Line was the fact that in a time of economic depression, when the *Normandie* entered service in 1935, she proved capable of steaming across the Atlantic with an oil consumption no greater than that of her elegant older sister the *Île de France*, despite approaching twice her tonnage and moving at 31 rather than 23.5 knots. In part this efficiency came from the larger ship's use of turboelectric propulsion—electric motors driving the propellers with current supplied by turbine generators.

It is a great misfortune that this most beautiful of all ships had only a four-year working life. Laid up in New York at the outbreak of World War II, she was taken over by the United States government in December, 1941, and the following February was burned at her dock, the result of carelessness that had brought much bedding aboard while refitters were working on structural changes with torches, leading to a fire that passed beyond control, other than by pouring so much water aboard that she capsized and sank. Refloated, she was found to be unsalvageable; in 1946 she was towed to New Jersey and broken up on one of the saddest days in the operation of the Atlantic Ferry.[109]

The role of national pride in this last phase of the Atlantic Ferry is most evident in the speed with which various nations entered the race. In 1929, just as the *Bremen* increased the pace, Mussolini was so piqued that he first forced a consolidation of several companies into the Italian Line and then urged them on to lay down two 50,000-ton liners, the *Rex* (overall length 880 feet, gross register tonnage 51,075) and *Conte di Savoia* (overall length 815 feet, gross register tonnage 48,502). Put in service in 1931, these attractive ships helped first to win the Blue Ribbon for Il Duce, when the *Rex* in 1933 steamed from Gibraltar to New York at a mean speed of 28.92 knots, and to gain for the Italians a role in the Atlantic Ferry much greater than they had held before. The *Conte di Savoia* was always a favorite of the seasick as she was the only large ship equipped with gyroscopic stabilizers.[110] With the Germans, Italians, and French involved, it is not surprising that the British found that their old reliables, the *Mauretania* and the *Olympic*, were too old to run the course. Thus in 1930 Cunard set about the construction of a new giant, their first "thousand-foot ship" to outmatch the Germans. As Job No. 534 work was continued until 1931 when construction was stopped because of the great slump in Ferry travel and the massive decline in shipping in general. The next year saw over 15 million tons of shipping idle for the world as a whole and some 850 ships laid up in British ports.[111] In such a context the British challenge had to wait. Even the Italian and German ships were crossing the Atlantic half or more empty so the urgency of the races was more nationalism than economic competition. The French Line disposed of eight of their liners in this period, the Dutch were only moderately active, and the Americans were suffering in an even more aggravated way the general failure they had experienced in trying to become a major maritime power—on the Atlantic as elsewhere. Their control of the White Star Line was given up in 1926, when it returned to British ownership. But even in those hands the Crash of 1929 threw the British companies operating in the Ferry into rapid contraction of services. Any entry in the thousand-foot liner contest had to be put off. By the early 1930s not only were the liners losing money, but also their plight was being transferred to a degree to tramp freighters seeking to operate on the same runs.

The subsidized national fleets . . . took almost without exception the form of regular liner services and it might have been thought that the tramps would be the last to be affected. The reverse was the case. For the long period of intense competition between the subsidized and unsubsidized services led to a gradual alteration in commercial technique. The liners, finding themselves a third to a half empty owing to the unnatural supply of superfluous tonnage, acquired the permanent habit of filling up with part cargoes—"parcels," as they are called—of the cheap, bulky commodities, such as grain, sugar, rice and maize [sic] which are usually carried in whole cargoes by the tramps.[112]

In order to pursue their desire for a thousand-foot liner, Cunard was forced to help bail out the failing White Star Line. In 1931 the two were joined to become the Cunard White Star Line, and in return the British government agreed to loan the company sufficient money at a low interest rate to complete Job No. 534. Called the *Queen Mary*, she was launched in September, 1934, and as completed and put in service in 1936. She was the fastest and longest between the perpendiculars of any ship, slightly exceeding the *Normandie* in those measures, though not in gross register tonnage or overall length. The *Queen Mary* was 975 feet between the perpendiculars (1,019.5 feet overall), 118 feet in the beam, 92 feet deep, with a load draft of 38.8 feet and a gross register tonnage of 81,235. On completion of her period of modification (by 1938) the *Queen Mary* had settled to an average speed of 31.7 knots, fractionally faster than the French ship. Some measure of the market for which she was built is gained by noting the fact that the most numerous class in her passenger loading was first with 776, followed by 784 in second and 579 in third-class.[113] In contrast to the *Normandie*, the *Queen Mary* saw the first class (originally called "cabin class") amidships, the second (originally "tourist") was aft, and the third was forward.[114]

With the entry into service of the *Queen Mary*, the *Mauretania* and the *Olympic* were retired by Cunard White Star. Attention turned to finding a running mate for the giant ship so that a weekly service might be maintained from either shore. The French Line was finding an awkward disproportion among their ships in operations depending on the giant *Normandie* and the *Île de France* and even smaller sisters. Cunard had to depend on the *Aquitania* and lesser liners, so they decided to go ahead with a second "Queen," launched in 1938 and named for the reigning consort but not fully fitted out when war broke out in 1939. Making a secret voyage to New York in March, 1940, the semifinished ship was, after the United States entered the war, fitted out as a troop ship, the role she fulfilled until rebuilt in 1946. The *Queen Elizabeth* was smaller than the *Normandie*, 83,673 gross register tons, though longer, 1,031 feet over all (987.4 feet between perpendiculars), 118.6 feet broad, with a normal draft of 39 feet. She carried 822 first-class, 668 second-class, and 798 tourist-class passengers. On her maiden voyage as a liner in 1946, she crossed the Atlantic in 4 days, 16 hours, and 18 minutes, for an average speed of 28 knots.[115] For the first time since the last few months before World War I, when the Germans ran their express service with two equivalent ships, a test could be made of the practicality of a weekly service run with departures from either side of the Atlantic. It had been discovered that to allow sufficient time for turn-around of these huge ships, still maintaining a weekly schedule, an operating speed of 28 knots was necessary. This became both the cruising speed of the "Queens" and the design speed of the last generation of great liners.

With the two Cunarders in place in 1946, that last generation of the Atlantic Ferry had been born. The Germans and the Italians were then absent, since all their contending vessels had been destroyed during World War II. The Dutch were able to use the *Nieuw*

Amsterdam (36,000 tons), launched just before the war and a fortunate survivor of that conflict, which they paired wiht a new sister, the *Rotterdam* (38,645 tons, 768.7 feet long), launched in 1958.[116] The French had come out of the war denied their prime entry by the burning of the *Normandie*, but they could attempt a comeback with a reparations vessel, the *Europa* (of 1929), which had survived the war and was in 1946 to become the French Line's *Liberté*. With the *De Grasse* (launched in 1924) and several other smaller ships, a service began. For active participation in the race, however, something better was needed. Several new ships of intermediate size were built in the first decade after the war, but the French Line decided that a modern giant was needed to gain the combination of luxury and speed that was the French objective. In 1960 the liner *France* (978.6 feet between the perpendiculars, 1,035 feet overall, with a tonnage of 66,348) was launched to become the ultimate luxury liner, never effectively matched before the end of the Ferry. She could accommodate 407 first-class passengers and 1,637 in tourist class, second class having pretty much become a casualty of the war. "Designed for a service speed of 31 knots...she attained 34.13 knots...on trials with her turbines developing 90 percent of full power"[117] Considerably faster than the "Queens" and much more luxurious, the *France* became the star of the last act.

For that bittersweet performance she had a leading man, paired with her in one of the few examples of international partnership. At the close of World War II the United States had the largest merchant fleet ever assembled, over 40 million tons, equal to all the world's shipping, steam and sail, in 1910. It was appreciated that such a vast fleet could not be maintained. Admiral Emory Land, the shipping administrator, testified before Congress that the postwar fleet probably should aim at some 16 million tons, a

50 percent increase on the country's 1939 tonnage.[118] As part of this the Americans were interested in becoming a full participant in the passenger competition in the Atlantic. Before the war they had never succeeded in gaining the pace. The *Leviathan* had proved an economic liability, too large at 60,000 tons to pair well with her "sisters" the 24,289-ton *Manhattan* and *Washington*, introduced in the early 1930s. The former *Vaterland* was really a 1914 ship, now badly over age in technical terms. In the mid-1930s the Shipping Administration finally agreed to her withdrawal as long as a third intermediate-size ship was laid down. From this arrangement came the *America*, launched in 1939 as a 26,000-ton ship but one with more capacity than that figure might suggest because technical evolution had given her a higher capacity per ton than older ships possessed.

After the war the United States government and the United States Linc were anxious to build on this considerable technical success. They agreed on a liner of the passenger capacity of the Queens and sought to give it an American twist in the service specialization that was emerging. For an American ship, speed would be the drawing card. As launched in 1951, this giant, the *United States*, was 916.8 feet long and, at 39 feet, of the same draft as the *Queen Elizabeth*, but only 53,329 tons. Nevertheless she carried only 131 fewer passengers than the *Queen Mary*, at considerably higher speeds and with a size 25,000 tons less. On her proving runs she managed to average 35.59 knots eastbound and 34.51 knots westbound, to win the Blue Ribbon from the *Queen Mary*, which had held it uninterruptedly since 1938. During the 1950s the *United States* was the bellwether on the Atlantic and the height of technical advance in fast passenger liners. This was because a great deal of effort had been expended to give her high speeds, long range, and efficient carrying capacity so that

she might be used as a troop carrier in wartime. Many of her technical details remained secret, but there seems no doubt that she was the most advanced turbine liner ever built—essentially the ultimate stage of the steamship in the traditional sense of that term. No ship ever sought to challenge her speed, and the nonexistent yet very real Blue Ribbon, whose possession Cunard figured was worth $10 million a year plus a great deal of general prestige, was retired in her possession. After the French Line put the *France* in service in the early 1960s, a scheduled pairing was maintained with the *United States*, each ship leaving one side of the Atlantic when the other departed the other shore. Thus in the 1960s the final scene of the Atlantic Ferry came with two pairings, the Franco-American one just mentioned and the British one of the Queens. But they could play for only a few years longer.

In 1959 the first jet planes flew the Atlantic demonstrating a reliability, due to flying higher and farther than their piston or turboprop predecessors, and a cheapness of operation that immediately led to the introduction of extensive tourist-class compartments. These planes had few first-class seats, but then the liners of the 1960s had few first-class cabins. The bulk of the trade had become the tourist and the tourists' class. In fighting for this trade, the planes gained an immediate and increasing cost advantage. With the discovery of the true economies of jet propulsion, the airlines could continue to reduce fares to a point the steamship companies could not hope to reach. By the mid-1960s fewer and fewer tourist-class passengers bought steamship tickets. The economics of the liner trade, which by this time was essentially a tourist trade, began to become grim indeed. So grim was this descent that by the end of the decade most operators were seriously considering abandoning their participation in the Atlantic Ferry, turning their ships to the rather ignominious role of floating bars and saunas in the cruise trade.

In 1972 the *United States* was removed from the Ferry run, following on the removal of the Queens several years before when the peculiar *Queen Elizabeth II*, a cruise ship to be used occasionally on the Ferry, entered service. This ship was more modern than luxurious, slower than the stars in the last act, and altogether a depressing sequel to what had been a glorious epic. She earned her laurels as a serious working ship, however, when in 1982 she carried the major part of the British Expeditionary Force that successfully retook the Falkland Islands after the surprise Argentinian capture. As Spratt saw it in 1950:

> While such modern leviathans as the "Queen Mary" and the "Queen Elizabeth" have proved more economical in service than their smaller predecessors, one hesitates to speculate as to whether the ultimate size or speed have yet been attained. In view of the enormous development in the last hundred years, it would indeed be rash to venture upon any prophecies at all. In the "Edinburgh Philosophical Journal" for January 1820, we read: "it seems probable . . . that for general purposes, steam will not be found applicable as a power for propelling ships across extensive seas." Another prophecy, written in 1934, stated that "it is improbable that the Atlantic steam ferry will be supplanted by an air ferry." Subsequent developments in the latter direction have already caused us to reconsider the possibilities; but we may be sure that the great Atlantic Ferry will continue, whether on sea or in the air, or by a combination of both, to maintain commerce and friendship between the peoples of the Old World and the New.[119]

Now, a generation later, we know the current state of the Ferry. A minuscule number travel in the traditional way, and for all intents and purposes the steam Ferry is gone.

In the next chapter we shall see how its job has been taken on by a new air Ferry.

THE GENERAL PATTERN OF SEA TRANSPORT

The Atlantic Ferry is obviously only a small part of world shipping, although in its time it was the laboratory of technical advance and the showcase for the latest accomplishments. We have seen the first introduction of steam in oceanic navigation taking place there, the evolution of the great paddle steamers on those waters, and the final victory there of screw propulsion around the time of the Civil War, never to be significantly changed. The development of the reciprocating engine was similarly an Atlantic undertaking. Starting with low pressures and single expansion of the steam in the 1840s, the years saw a rise in pressures from a few pounds per square inch to 910 for the *France* of 1960. In the nineteenth century the steam came to be used more than once in double, triple, and finally quadruple expansion engines, at that point probably reaching nearly the ultimate efficiency for the reciprocating engine. In the first decade of this century the steam turbine was introduced in large ships to gain both speed and efficiency in the use of fuel. Further economies in fuel were gained by the substitution of bunker oil for coal, mainly in the 1920s, which permitted far smaller stokehold crews and more compact bunkering. For passenger operations the turbine sufficed to the final curtain of the Ferry; but in freighter operations, particularly among Scandinavian, German, and other Continental operators, the diesel engine came into use as early as the first decade of this century and gained particular attention with the increasing shift to petroleum fuels.

Away from the North Atlantic the strictly passenger ship was far less common, with operators commonly combining major working of freight with a reduced space given to the carriage of passengers. Before World War II most scheduled services carried some passengers in the South American, South African, Indian, Australian, and East Asian trades from western Europe and the United States, while frequently earning their wages from cargo operations. Some of these routes offered frequent sailings and had moderately large ships in service. American services to the east and west coasts of South America provided large and quite luxurious cargo-liner schedules, as did British services particularly to southern South America and the Caribbean islands. British services to South Africa and India and Australia were similar, even rising to full liner operations. American services across the Pacific tended to combine cargo and passengers, but on relatively fast schedules at fixed times. Germany before World War I had extensive combination services to its widely scattered colonial possessions in Africa and the Pacific islands. The French, with the second most extensive colonial empire after Britain and as a major maritime power in modern times, had in 1851 created *Les Messageries Nationales*, a postal steamship line to operate in the Mediterranean.[120] Over the decades its services were expanded to reach, after the opening of the Suez Canal in 1869, to the French possessions in India, Indo-China, and the Pacific, and to the east coast of Africa. The first expansion came with the opening of a service to eastern South America, Rio and Buenos Aires, in 1857, to be followed by a coastal service to French entrepôts in West Africa beginning in 1860.[121] In the first years of that decade services from Suez to Saigon, with branches to Réunion; to Calcutta and Chandernagor; to Shanghai; to Singapore and Batavia; and to Manila were started, to be carried all the way to Marseille after the opening of the Suez Canal at the end of the decade.[122]

With the collapse of the Second Empire in 1871, the company lost its imperial adjective,

gaining its present name, *Messageries Maritimes*. It is impossible here to follow all the extensions of routes, but it should be noted that the spread of the company's interests carried it throughout the world, save for the field of operations of the Companie Générale Transatlantique, whose role in the Atlantic Ferry we have noted. With the opening of the Panama Canal in 1915, routes to the French possessions in Oceania ran either easterly via Suez or westerly via Panama, as was the case for British, Dutch, and other northwest European maritime companies in their ties with colonial possessions in eastern Asia and Oceania. There can be no question that, in terms of scheduled marine services, the existence of a colonial empire was a critical matter. The Germans bulked large so long as they had such possessions before World War I. The French, Dutch, and British continued that role until 1939, although it declined considerably after the decolonization epoch of 1945–1965. Even failed colonial powers such as Denmark and Sweden continued to carry their trading frontiers to distant lands through the survival of their merchant marine. The Danes, although they failed in creating a colony in Thailand, have continued down to our time as an important maritime partner of the Thais. American administration of the Philippines after 1898 greatly enlarged United States merchant shipping in the Pacific. To a very large degree established world shipping channels before 1939 reflected these various colonial ties. In Latin America, Thailand, and Japan—the only economically significant countries outside Europe and North America not colonialized in 1939—the pattern of shipping was more diverse, though it did tend to reflect treaty ties and established relationships, such as the Danish-Thai connection already noted.

Only the tramp-steamer operations, trying all ports and accepting all cargoes for transport to an infinite variety of other ports, had such flexibility. Even there the more maritime nations dominated. The British, with their rapid rise to paramount position in steamer operations soon after the American Civil War, tended to dominate tramp operations up to 1939. Norwegian, Danish, Dutch, and German tramps also entered the trade in the nineteenth century. Their lead was followed by Greek shipowners in this century.

As safety requirements, labor conditions, and wages were improved in the leading western countries after World War I, a new aspect of marine operation arose—the flag of convenience, registry of a vessel in a basically nonmaritime nation whose laws were far more lenient in these matters than were those of the leading industrial nations. This shift was particularly important for American operators, whose interests did not decline as drastically as the tonnage figures would indicate. Between 1945 and 1964 U.S. registry of ships declined nearly in half, from over 40 million tons to just 22 million. But in that period Liberian registry rose to half that of the United States, from only 250,000 tons in 1959, and Panamanian from 75,000 to over 4 million in 1964. Not all Liberian and Panamanian ships are American-owned, but a great many are. It is probable that American registry would have dropped even farther except for the considerable importance of coastal and intercoastal shipping in American trade. Under established international practice, trade between ports of a nation is reserved to that nation under the law of cabotage. In the United States the high labor costs still forced on this protected trade the need to gain labor economies. This was done through the pioneering of the container ship.

The container ship had a distinctively North American origin. It was first introduced in its primitive state in the operations of a Canadian-American railroad, the White Pass and Yukon Railway of the Yukon Territory, British Columbia, and Alaska, which started using small container boxes capable of being transported on flat cars of this narrow-gauge rail line and on the decks or in the hold of ships plying between Skagway in the Alaska Panhandle and Vancouver and Seattle. Such working avoided the repeated loading and unloading of package and low-bulk freight consequent on the operation of a railroad totally separated from the North American continental rail system and connected to it only by coastal shipping to the railheads at Prince Rupert and Vancouver in British Columbia or Seattle in Washington. The notion of using a container on a railroad was of much longer standing—the Camden and Amboy Railroad of New Jersey employed them in 1849, the Pennsylvania in 1869, and the Long Island Railroad in the sense of wagons carried on flatcars in 1884; this sort of piggyback was introduced in Nova Scotia in September, 1855; as early as 1842 the Paris-Orleans Railroad in France had begun transporting mail coaches carrying passengers, mail, and parcels by placing them bodily on flatcars drawn in trains.[123] It was the operation of the White Pass and Yukon, which opened in 1900 to serve the Klondike Gold Rush but has remained in service to the present to connect Whitehorse and the mining areas of the Yukon with the outside world, that suggested the logic of containerization of cargo handling on ships, as was done in the 1920s.

A wider use of ship containerization had to await both logical employment and permissive labor conditions. By the time the technology had been reasonably worked out through the introduction of piggyback operations on railroads, which first came on an extensive scale on North American railroads after the end of World War II, port labor was normally so strongly unionized that any change in working conditions tended to meet sharp resistance. Only in the 1950s in

Containership operations in the Port of Oakland. Port of Oakland photograph.

the ports of the San Francisco Bay Area was an opening secured in the context of the mainland-to-Hawaii transport of freight. After 1945 an increasingly large proportion of the passenger flow between the California ports and Hawaii was carried by air services, so the decline in shipping was obvious as was the greater specialization of marine services on freight alone. Even there there was some general concern that air-freight operations would cut into the traditional sea trade. Given these concerns, the longshoremen's union in the Bay Area agreed to movement of containers of freight that

would expedite and cheapen the handling. The success of the undertaking was immediate: it cost considerably less to transport goods through the port functions, there was considerably less pilferage, and damage claims were sharply reduced. Most container boxes were simply lashed on deck for the run to Hawaii and were loaded and unloaded by the ship's cranes.

The law of cabotage meant that the mainland-Hawaii run was completely under the control of American shipping companies, so the impact of labor costs was probably higher there than anywhere else in the world. The same could have been said for the so-called intercoastal trade between the Atlantic and Pacific coasts of the United States if there had been much service of that sort in the early 1950s. At the time of the 1848 Gold Rush in California, a large number of ships had provided such intercoastal runs, passing around Cape Horn until 1854, when a railroad was completed across the Isthmus of Panama. From then on passengers tended to transfer on the Isthmian Railroad to cut the sea journey in half, but freight moved around the Horn for the most part. But in 1869 the completion of the first North American transcontinental railroad began to affect this service to the point it was much reduced by the end of the century. Only the opening of the Panama Canal in 1915 seemed to offer much likelihood of a revival of intercoastal shipping. To make certain that the railroads did not artificially restrain its return, the Panama Canal Act had made it illegal for a railroad to own a shipping company. Even with such a protection, however, the connection by sea between the coasts simply did not transpire as anticipated. There were American companies engaged in the trade before 1939, when most went out of this operation, but they never assumed a very important role in the internal transportation of the United States: handling costs of goods in the ports of the East and the West together in this service tended to dampen any real economic benefits from such a service. The railroads continued to carry the lion's share of intercoastal movements.

The potential for a change came to a critical point in the 1950s when the combination of restriction of the trade to American bottoms, the possible improvement in the matter of port handling costs through potential containerization, and the rapid increase in the economic importance of the West Coast in the American economy was joined by a rapidly increasing use of trucks for the collection and moderate-distance transport of general freight. If some way could be found to tie trucks and ships together, the development of marine intercoastal service seemed potentially profitable and economical. McLean, a trucking firm, organized this operation as Sea Land starting with a service from the port of Newark, New Jersey, to Houston in 1956. Using a converted World War II tanker—adapted to carry fifty-eight truck trailers, with wheels, on deck—this service proved popular and remunerative. Florida was added to this route in 1957 and Puerto Rico in 1958.

With experience in this operation Sea-Land developed the "cellularized" vessel by converting six conventional cargo vessels to carry 226 containers, now shed of their chassis and wheels, thus transportable either by such truck chassis or on rail flatcars. These cellularized vessels were able to carry more boxes because these might be loaded below as well as on deck. The higher carrying capacity thus gained made intercoastal service in the United States a brighter prospect, so service was inaugurated between Port Elizabeth, New Jersey, and a new terminal at Oakland in 1962. Four tankers converted to cellularized containerships, T-3s, were employed on the run and could maintain a speed of 15 knots.[124]

By the mid-1960s there was growing interest both within and outside the United States in container operations. Trans-Atlantic and trans-Pacific shipping lines began to carry a few boxes as deck cargo and to contract for new tonnage, or reconstructions, that would permit cellularized handling of containers. In 1966 Sea-Land began service by containerships from the port of New York to Rotterdam, Bremen, and Grangemouth in Britain. Three years later trans-Pacific service was established from Oakland to Hong Kong, Taiwan, and Singapore. Both American flag and other carriers entered these trades at approximately the same time, so

The major container docks of Oakland. Port of Oakland photograph.

that by the early 1970s the containership was viewed as the basic transoceanic carrier, with the older break-bulk vessel rapidly declining in use and bulk carriers—of oil, grain, minerals, and the like—gaining a more specialized nature alongside the container ships. Supertankers of 100,000 displacement tons and over were constructed, to be followed by super-supertankers of 350,000 to 400,000 tons following in turn. The containership fitted better than the general-cargo ship into the increasing specialization that was affecting the leading merchant-marine nations.

At first the greatest appeal of the con-tainership was its speed and economy in port—ships of considerable size could be unloaded and reloaded in eight to ten hours, rather than the several days that a general-cargo ship of that size would require, through the use of the increasingly large and fast gantry cranes that were being installed on the docks of specialized container ports. Parenthetically it might be noted that such installations in American ports (with the strange exception of a few such as Portland, Oregon) brought those facilities for the first time to a similar stevedoring technology to that found in Europe, where ships' booms and cranes were not employed but rather dockside gantries. But by the early 1970s the more vigorous operators began to think in terms of speeding up the ocean voyage as well. Taking Sea-Land for an example, their first ships of the mid-1950s made 15 knots; ships added in the 1960s only made 1 knot more; but starting in 1972 they put in service AL-7 vessels that were both very large—1,096 boxes either 35 or 40 feet long and capable of containing up to 30 tons—and very fast, with a top usable speed of 33 knots, nearly 5 knots faster than the *Queen Elizabeth II*. These were steam-turbine vessels of the sort typical of the American merchant marine.

The embargo of oil sales to several western countries by the Arab members of the Organization of Petroleum Exporting Countries (OPEC) in 1973 began an increase in the price of petroleum that would reshape world shipping patterns considerably, though perhaps not as radically as it has air travel. The rise in price caused two shifts in maritime operations: (1) sharp slackening off of the anticipated increases in world oil consumption that made the specialized tanker tonnage too large for the market and (2) increasing efforts to make more economical use of fuel in the operation of ships. The slackening of the tanker market was further complicated by increasing disenchantment with the very largest of tankers. These enormous ships found many channels too shallow for transit, many ports unapproachable, and the fabric of their construction rather weak in critical ways. At least for the foreseeable future, the ceiling for tanker size seems to have been reached and possibly even exceeded in an economic sense. In the matter of fuel consumption, the drive for speed seems to have been stopped even more certainly. Just as the *United States* ended the competition among passenger liners at just under 35 knots, the *Sea-Land McLean* of 1972 and her sisters seem to have won a pyrrhic victory in cargo operations at 33 knots. By the late 1970s containerships were being

operated well below their rated cruising speeds to reduce fuel consumption. In 1979 I crossed the Atlantic eastbound on a Farrell Line containership, the *Austral Endeavor*, capable of over 28 knots but run on this voyage between a high of 25 knots on departure and 8 knots when in the narrow seas of western Europe.

The rise in fuel costs was not the only contributor to this shift in operating procedure. Experience with loading and unloading operations showed shipowners by the late 1970s that runs must be laid out in anticipation of the time of arrival and tailored to reach the objective port at just the right moment. This comes from the very high cost of stevedoring: the standard twenty-one-man crew on the Baltimore docks in the spring of 1982 received $795 an hour straight pay ($1,200 an hour on Saturdays and $1,590 an hour on Sundays) and received that pay starting at 8:00 A.M. on the day contracted for whether the ship was in dock or not, up to eight hours.[125] Although container operations do make the labor input much more productive than was the case with traditional break-bulk ships using a sling-loading of individual units, labor remains a very high-cost item and one that is rigidly applied because of strong union rules. Similarly, the extremely high cost of gantry cranes on the docks, now running at above $2 million apiece for the most modern types, means that no port has that many and all must use them extremely efficiently to amortize their cost.[126] Thus increasingly ships have had to run on computer-derived courses and speeds that get the ship to the dock just when a gantry is available and a crew has been called.

CONCLUSIONS

In the early 1980s several features of the geography of ocean transport stand out. The passenger ship in a serious sense is gone: only the cruise vessel remains. Similarly, the race for dominance through speed in container operations seems to have ended. Now fuel economy has gained a major place in operators' concerns, along with a continuing effort to make cargo handling in port ever more economical. Finally, the trend toward increasing specialization of vessels, not merely to freight handling but to specific freights as well, continues. But the frantic rise in the size of oil-carrying vessels seems to have stopped and may well reverse itself until the most efficient large, but not supergiant, tanker is found. Ocean navigation reached its technical peak at the time when it was a ubiquitous and absolutely essential service, with strong monopolistic qualities. Today ocean navigation is merely one of a number of specialized services in world transportation. The specialization continues, but within a more narrowly defined frame than was the case only a generation ago. That specialization has assured the survival of the ship and the merchant marine, as it has all other forms of transportation with which people have experimented during the evolution of the historical geography of transportation. Gone is the passenger, but certainly not the mariner.

NOTES

1. Frederick Chapin Lane, *Venetian Ships and Shipbuilders of the Renaissance* (Baltimore, Md.: Johns Hopkins University Press, 1934), p. 1.
2. Loc. cit.
3. Charles Singer et al., *A History of Technology*, vol. 2: *The Mediterranean Civilizations and the Middle Ages, c. 700 B.C. to c. A.D. 1500* (Oxford: Oxford University Press, 1958), p. 585.
4. Ibid., p. 587.
5. Ibid., p. 588.
6. Ibid., p. 569.
7. Ibid., p. 575.
8. Ibid., pp. 272–273.
9. Lane, op. cit., p. 36.
10. Singer, op. cit., p. 574.
11. Quoted in C. Ernest Fayle, *A Short History of the World's Shipping Industry* (New York: Dial Press, 1933), p. 169.
12. Ibid., p. 128.
13. Quoted in ibid., p. 120.
14. Ibid., pp. 210–211.
15. Ibid., pp. 170–171.
16. Passim.
17. Ibid., p. 148.
18. Ibid., p. 127.
19. Pieter Geyl, *The Netherlands in the Seventeenth Century* (New York: Barnes & Noble, 1964), part 2, pp. 372–373.
20. R. V. Coleman, *The First Frontier* (New York: Charles Scribner's Sons, 1948), p. 97.
21. Robert G. Albion, William A. Baker, and Benjamin W. Labaree, *New England and the Sea* (Middletown, Conn.: Wesleyan University Press [for Mystic Seaport], 1972), pp. 21–22.
22. Ibid., p. 25.
23. Samuel Eliot Morison, *The Maritime History of Massachusetts* (Boston: Houghton Mifflin, 1961 [first published 1921]), p. 14.
24. Lawrence A. Harper, *The English Navigation Laws: A Seventeenth-Century Experiment in Social Engineering* (New York: Columbia University Press, 1939), p. 38.
25. Ibid., p. 39.
26. Ibid., p. 55.
27. Ibid., p. 57.
28. Morison, op. cit., pp. 50–51.
29. Ibid., pp. 64–65.
30. Albion, Baker, and Labaree, op. cit., p. 59.
31. Ibid., pp. 60–61.
32. Morrison, op. cit., p. 206.
33. Albion, Baker, and Labaree, op. cit., p. 99.
34. Ibid., p. 161.
35. For a detailed discussion of blockade running during the Civil War, see Stuart L. Bernath, *Squall across the Atlantic* (Berkeley: University of California Press, 1970).
36. Ibid., p. 4.
37. Ibid., pp. 11–12.
38. Albion, Baker, and Labaree, op. cit., p. 154.
39. Ibid., pp. 159–160.
40. W. A. Baker and Tre Tryckare, *The Engine*

Powered Vessel (New York: Grosset & Dunlop, 1965), p. 11.

41. Ibid., p. 12.
42. John H. Morrison, *History of American Steam Navigation* (New York: Stephen Daye Press, 1958 [first published in 1903], p. 11.
43. Ibid., pp. 19–21; Baker and Tryckare, op. cit., pp. 13–14.
44. Baker and Tryckare, op. cit., p. 13.
45. Morrison, op. cit., p. 258.
46. Ibid., pp. 366–370.
47. Ibid., p. 376.
48. Ibid., pp. 192–202.
49. This letter is quoted at length in ibid., pp. 226–238.
50. William E. Lass, *A History of Steamboating on the Upper Missouri* (Lincoln: University of Nebraska Press, 1962).
51. Randall V. Mills, *Stern-wheelers up Columbia* (Palo Alto, Calif.: Pacific Books, 1947).
52. Morison, op. cit., p. 213.
53. R. H. Thornton, *British Shipping* (Cambridge: Cambridge University Press, 1959), pp. 4–5.
54. Ibid., pp. 6.
55. Ibid., pp. 6–7.
56. Morison, op. cit., p. 233.
57. Albion, Baker, and Labaree, op. cit., p. 127.
58. Ibid., pp. 143–146.
59. Morrison, op. cit., pp. 435–436.
60. Ibid., p. 436.
61. Quoted in Frank O. Braynard, *S.S. Savannah: The Elegant Steam Ship* (Athens: University of Georgia Press, 1963), p. 2.
62. Ibid., p. 13.
63. Quoted in ibid., p. 28.
64. Quoted in ibid., p. 36.
65. Ibid., p. 37.
66. Ibid., p. 113.
67. Ibid., pp. 109, 120.
68. Ibid., p. 138.
69. Quoted in ibid., p. 139.
70. Quoted in ibid., p. 111.
71. Ibid., p. 154.
72. Ibid., pp. 174–176.
73. Ibid., pp. 183–184.
74. Ibid., p. 210.
75. Thornton, op. cit., p. 16.
76. Ibid., p. 22.

77. G. P. DeT. Glazebrook, *A History of Transportation in Canada* (Toronto: McClelland and Stewart Ltd., 1964), vol. 1, p. 95; Thornton, op. cit., p. 23.
78. Baker and Tryckare, op. cit., pp. 42–43.
79. Thornton, op. cit., p. 23.
80. Arthur J. Maginnis, *The Atlantic Ferry: Its Ships, Men, and Working* (London: Whittaker and Company, 1900), pp. 25–26.
81. Ibid., pp. 15-16.
82. Ibid., pp. 16-22.
83. Baker and Tryckare, op. cit., pp. 45–46.
84. Thornton, op. cit., p. 28.
85. Baker and Tryckare, op. cit., p. 47.
86. Warren Tute, *Atlantic Conquest: The Men and Ships of the Glorious Age of Steam* (Boston: Little, Brown, 1962), pp. 49–50. Tute, though British, happily avoids Thornton's rather chauvinistic analysis.
87. Maginnis, op. cit., p. 44.
88. Ibid., p. 47.
89. Ibid., p. 86.
90. Maginnis, op. cit., p. 126.
91. Ibid., p. 124.
92. Tute, op. cit., p. 120.
93. Maginnis, op. cit., p. 47; Baker and Tryckare, op. cit., p. 58.
94. Baker and Tryckare, op. cit., p. 75.
95. Ibid., p. 80.
96. Tute, op. cit., p. 93.
97. Maginnis, op. cit., pp. 94–95.
98. Ibid., pp. 65–69.
99. Ibid., pp. 43–44; Tute, op. cit., pp. 138–139.
100. Baker and Tryckare, op. cit., pp. 100–101.
101. Ibid., p. 102; Maginnis, op. cit., pp. 104–105.
102. Tute. op. cit., p. 148.
103. Baker and Tryckare, op. cit., pp. 118–119.
104. Tute, op. cit., p. 158.
105. H. P. Spratt, *Outline History of Transatlantic Steam Navigation* (London: Science Museum, 1850), pp. 45–46.
106. Tute, op. cit., p. 208.
107. Baker and Tryckare, op. cit., p. 151.
108. Ibid., pp. 168–169, 176–177; Spratt, op. cit., pp. 50–51.
109. Tute, op. cit., pp. 213–214.
110. Spratt, op, cit., pp. 49–50.
111. Tute, op. cit., p. 210.
112. Thornton, op. cit., pp. 85–86.

113. Spratt, op. cit., pp. 51–52.
114. Baker and Tryckare, op. cit., p. 172.
115. Spratt, op. cit., pp. 52–53.
116. Baker and Tryckare, op. cit., pp. 232–233.
117. Ibid., pp. 224–225.
118. Tute, op. cit., p. 227.
119. Spratt, op. cit., p. 53.
120. Roger Carmour, *Sur les Routes de la Mer avec les Messageries Maritimes* (Paris: Éditions Andre Bonne, 1968), p. 27.
121. Ibid., pp. 59–64.
122. Ibid., p. 81.
123. John Marshall, *The Guinness Book of Rail Facts and Feats* (Enfield: Guinness Superlatives Ltd., 1975), pp. 72–73; J. Tham, *The Pictorial Encyclopedia of Transport* (London: Hamlyn, 1979), p. 110.
124. Sea-Land Industries Investments, Inc., investment brochure, ca. 1981, p. 12.
125. *Christian Science Monitor*, February 25, 1982.
126. On June 30, 1979, I witnessed considerable consternation on docking on another containership, the *Young America*, at Baltimore (from Le Havre). The ship had arrived at the appropriate berth at 7:00 A.M., the hour for most efficient labor use, by means of a careful modulation of speeds, most well below her planned cruising range. In the next berth, however, a tornado the previous evening had totally crumpled a brand-new $2 million gantry, exposing one of the dangers of these cranes, which can be as tall as a ten-story building.

THE ROAD IN TRANSITION III: THE RISE TO DOMINANCE

For a society seemingly dominated by road transportation, two things may be hard to understand: how relatively recently such a domination came about and how relatively slowly it took place. No doubt in the totality of transport the Middle Ages were a time when road traffic surpassed all other forms of movement; but in transport over any distance, water would then have been the "prime mover." With the canal era that suzerainty was increased after a fairly short interregnum—of the turnpike in England and the *route royale* in France during the early eighteenth century—when roads assumed a temporary ascendancy. Although the canals lost their hierarchical position by 1840, their role was taken over by the railroad, not the road.

It would be incorrect to portray the nineteenth century as a time without roads. We have seen that where the more developed, capital-costly forms of transportation could not be justified, roads continued to be built

and remained the backstay even of long-distance transportation. The migrants' trail, the traders' track, and the military road were widely if not very intensively used in the last century. But each came, in due course, to be replaced throughout most of its length by rails. The Oregon Trail had as its neighbor, and then its replacement, the Union Pacific; General Wade's roads in the Highlands were paralleled, and then substituted for, by the railroads to the northern and western coasts of Scotland. The roads remained, of course; but, as their ancient ancestors the Roman roads had become disarticulated into local tracks, so did the turnpikes, *routes royale*, migrant trails, and traders' tracks become functionally discontinuous. The glimmerings of the past purpose were still there, but virtually no one understood any longer that they had been routes to capture the horizon.

The nineteenth century was for the road a time of contraction to purposes of a very

A mountain plank road in the American West.

local scale. We must seek the first evidence of change on that parochial level. People in communities, particularly the smaller or less densely settled examples, depended most fundamentally on roads. Farmers had no choice but roads until they reached the whistle-stop where they might load their grain, cattle, cotton, or wives and children for distant journeys. Similarly, the rise of the suburbanization that developed so strongly in the United States (from the mid-nineteenth century on) left families in a road-dependent state once they went out through the door of their suburban rail depot. This was not the case in cities: the mainline station normally provided the meeting place of steam railroad with horse-car, cable-car, or (later) electric-car line. Private provision could work in both directions in this situation, even to the extent that the franchises extended to many electric-traction companies required them to pave and plow the streets on which they operated. But the suburban and rural railroad depots, if even a building existed, were the meeting place of private with public transportation, and of the dominant and evolving facilities with those laid aside and dormant. It is no surprise, then, that it was in the suburbs and the countryside that the first efforts to change the situation were begun, through arguments for both better facilities and new technologies.

The need for that improvement is clearly recorded right down to the last decade of the nineteenth century. The polymath N. S. Shaler, writing on *American Highways* in 1896, held,

> In the present condition of this country the resources which favor distant transportation are well organized. The development of the railway and interior steamboat transportation has provided for these needs in a measure which has been attained only in some of the richest European states. It is otherwise with the ways which serve for local intercourse:

these have been so far neglected that their ill condition operates as a distinct check on the social relations upon which the character of our local communities intimately depends. The politcal life of our commonwealths, as well as their economic advance, is to a great extent determined by the readiness with which the people obtain that association with one another which leads to the development of a public spirit. Important as are the effects of good acquaintance in the communities of any state, whatever be its system of government, they are particularly important in a democracy; for there the unending task of holding fast to the good which has been won, and of winning gains for the future, is to be effected only by means of an intense social life such as will give the able men of each neighborhood an opportunity to affect the motives of their weaker fellow-citizens.

The reasons above given should make it evident that the interest of a democracy in good roads should rest on a deeper foundation than mere commerce or commercial needs. Account should be taken of the value of these ways of communication to a people from the point of view of their place in the intellectual development of their communities. Thus viewed, good roads will be seen to have a very important relation to the mechanism of a democratic state.[1]

The then dean of the Lawrence Scientific School at Harvard held that the contemporaneous sad state grew from two roots: the method of constructing and maintaining roads in our states, and the climate, terrain, soil, and bedrock of the country. His first complaint referred to what he found clearly a vestige of feudalism, the corvée: "It has bred, in a systematic manner, a shiftless method of work; it has led our people to look upon road-building as a nuisance. There is no situation in which the American workman makes so unsatisfactory an appearance as when he is endeavoring to do the least possible amount of labor which is to count as a day's work on the highways of his district."[2]

The survival of the corvée, with its uninformed notions about how roads should be constructed, its tendency to lead the local men to treat it as a social gathering, and its perpetuation of the idea that nature's surface of the land needs no more than clearing of trees and stones to make a quite usable highway, stemmed at least in part from the nineteenth-century American idea that important accomplishments were those won by private effort and ingenuity, whereas the efforts of government should come only in those matters of lesser importance in which practical-minded investors could see no great return on their money. Even Shaler did not question the dominance of American transportation by the privately constructed and operated railroads:

> The changes in the methods of transportation which have been effected during the last half-century have made ordinary roads mere adjuncts to the railways. It rarely occurs that merchandise is wagoned for more than thirty miles. There is no systematic communication between the States by ordinary roads. In no one case is the intercourse between the capitals of two of these units in the federal Union kept up by the use of highways. In case of war, whether it were internecine or with a foreign power; all distant transportation would commonly be accomplished by the railways or rivers, as it was, indeed, during the [recent] Rebellion.[3]

The absence of a national system of roads, of even a practicable system of mail routes, much as it might aid the latter service, was accepted philosophically. Shaler, as an enlightened observer of American transportation at the end of the last century, spoke for his time in accepting much of that condition:

> This is hardly enough of an advantage [the provision of an integrated road system] to warrant the institution of a national work, which would prove extremely costly, after the manner of all federal constructions, and which would require an army of public servants for its administration. However effected, the people have in the end to pay for what they get from the powers above them. The price is the dearer the further these powers are removed from local inspection. It therefore does not seem advisable to seek federal aid in the work of constructing our ways.[4]

In 1896 he and other informed observers believed that the states should be the focus of road-building initiative and that the likely "progress of invention" would make two changes in the wagon and carriage transport then available: "The first of these relates to the probable effect of the application of some form of mechanical energy to the propulsion of carriages; the other to the adoption of steel tramways for the use of ordinary freight-wagons."[5]

The tendency to localize road use and provision is easy to understand. In terms of technology there was no clear perception of the potential for any long-distance use of roads. The powered-carriage and the freight-wagon supported and guided by a grooved steel track were seen as parochial in scope, as improved adjuncts to the increasingly comprehensive national system of railroads (built by private initiative). That effort was so availing that by the time of World War I the United States possessed some 250,000 miles of railroad, which were adequate even in a country of 3 million square miles to provide interregional arteries of movement and an extensive local-distribution system in the more densely settled regions. We should not overlook the fact that the Interstate Highway System of our time is only one-sixth that length.

Today we appreciate that the earlier efforts at road improvement in the United States sought merely to bring this country up to the level of the more advanced countries of western Europe. Throughout the writing on road improvement in the 1880s and 1890s, re-peated reference is made to the more ad-vanced state of road building in France, Bri-tain, and elsewhere in Europe, while America was literally in a nontraversable morass. From Shaler's comments quoted earlier we know this to be a reasonably ac-curate appraisal. What it overlooked, how-ever, was that on both continents roads had become relegated to the local-service role: railroads had become the long-distance car-rier in all of Western culture. The very much smaller size of European countries, their much more populous nature, and the con-siderable infrastructure of roads inherited from the prerailroad era all contributed to the better state of things. There was as well the beginnings of scientific road building in France and Britain before the coming of the railroad, which was combined with a na-tional responsibility for roads in France and other Continental countries that meant that much more money was available for their construction and upkeep than could be found under the extremely localized provi-sion by towns and counties in the United States.

Perhaps we should also reflect on the role that wars played in that superiority of roads in Europe. The French system, the Prussian system, the Continental system pioneered under Napoleon with its first military roads across the Maritime Alps to Piedmont, and even Wade's roads in Scotland all came from this military concern, which among other things shifted the cost from the locality to the central government. Although Shaler saw the railroad as the main avenue of war, closer attention would remind us that during his Rebellion the Confederate and Union forces fought desperately along—and over possession of—the turnpikes and plank roads of northern Virginia and adjacent Maryland. But such land warfare was un-common in American experience. In essence the contrast we should draw is that roads, the backstay of local transport on either conti-nent, were very much better in Europe in the second half of the nineteenth century.

The main question we face is: What brought the improvement of local transpor-tation in America such that in the century between 1850 and 1950 the United States came to take the lead in road construction and highway transportation? I wish to sug-gest that it was on this parochial stage that we shall find the answer. It was in trying to satisfy that demand for local transportation that Americans wrought the Automobile Revolution. To understand that revolution, and to avoid any suggestion of chauvinism, let it be made clear that Americans certainly did not invent the automobile—but who would deny that they showed the world the versatility and comprehensiveness of its use? To detach America from that revolution on the grounds of the European invention of the automobile would be as foolish as argu-ing that Britain and Germany worked the Marxist revolution because it was in those two lands that the ideas were hatched.

Again, to understand this evolution we must distinguish provision of facilities from technology of operation. The period we should look at is that just after the close of the Civil War in America and the Franco-Prussian War in Europe, the 1870s, when two vehicles were introduced that reshaped local transportation through giving, for the first time, an individual access to mechanization. In this way it was technology that came before facility, although in Europe, as we have already seen, local roads were in a reasonably good state. The result was that as Europe sought to innovate in local, personal transportation, it was mostly a vehicular im-provement that was attempted; but in Amer-ica both that advance and one in the state of local roads had to be carried on in harness.

THE MECHANIZATION OF
INDIVIDUAL TRANSPORTATION

The poor state of local roads in the United States accentuated the unimproved state of local travel, making it hard to move around save on the specially laid rail pavements of the railroad, the street railway, and the cable and elevated car lines just being introduced. The steam road carriages and tractors for heavy loads, experimented with in England and France from the beginning of the century, were unusable on the soft and miry roads of America, even in cities, where the surface was normally little better than in the countryside. The cost of goods away from the railroad station was increased by heavy charges for the difficult road transport involved. In American cities wholesaling establishments clung to the track side as the only place in the system of transportation where goods could easily and cheaply be handled and transferred from one vehicle to another, from the boxcar bringing in commodities to the express or less-than-carload lot assembler's car moving it farther by rail to ultimate retail customers in other towns.[6] And similarly visitors to the city arrived by rail, stayed at hotels near the station, visited offices on streets leading away from it, and shopped in retail stores still limited to its immediate vicinity. That clustering was even further advanced when mass transit for the city was developed in the last third of the nineteenth century. Its focus of intracity movement joined that of regional or interregional movement in the heart of the city, the *downtown*, which remained the nexus of efficient, mechanized transportation both nationally and locally.

Yet the nature of American settlement was constrained by that excessive focus on efficient transportation and its sharp distinction from the difficult movement found away from the rails or, in more limited areas, the waterways. The constraint was felt particularly in the suburbs of the city and in the agricultural countryside. Each might be approached by train; in fact, the suburbs developed first because of that possibility of train connections starting in the 1840s and 1850s.[7] But beyond the bead-pattern of suburban depots strung outward along the railroads converging on the city, local travel became awkward. The nineteenth-century railroad suburb was nearly as tightly clustered as the central city, though surrounded by open fields, because once off the train pedestrian movement was the norm, and that on streets and sidewalks were often little more than the natural surface. The health benefits of more isolated housing were fully appreciated; the stark reality of its isolation was not. No wonder the central-city department store, places of entertainment, and public institutions drew so many suburban people: given the existence of the suburban railroads, it was far easier to reach to the heart of the city than to move far within the suburbs themselves.

The isolation of the suburb in its hinterland of poor natural roads was real for all who lived there, though hardest on the women who stayed there most of the time. Men went to central-city employment; children commonly have tended to find perverse pleasure in the rigors of the natural landscape. But even the men, when they were at home on the weekend, might find the functional immobility frustrating. A similar sense of isolation existed in the farming areas, although two factors probably made its impact more economic than social: farms were composite production-residential entities, so none of the gender contrasts found in the suburbs existed; and farms normally had horses or mules that could cope with the poor natural roads, even if they did introduce high costs of transportation. In the suburbs, however, once the railroad failed to serve, as it could not in local movement, there was virtually no family mobility.

In the period after the Civil War, suburbanization became very popular in American cities. Their populations, particularly in the truly large industrial cities such as Boston, New York, Brooklyn, Newark, Philadelphia, Baltimore, Pittsburgh, Cleveland, Cincinnati, Chicago, and St. Louis, was expanding very rapidly and becoming noticeably more diverse. Crowding in the core area tended to deteriorate the public-health conditions, and the polyglot nature of that burgeoning population encouraged those seeking to establish or maintain a so-called native culture to move away to suburbs. The railroads had made such a residential transfer possible; but beyond the journey-to-work or the more occasional journeys to shop or for cultural activities, these suburban families were effectively parochialized to their physically distinct suburb. As suburbanization in America appealed to the economically fortunate, there was a pent-up demand for local mobility that was joined with a considerable ability to buy the instrument of its accomplishment if the latter were to become available. The more wealthy did keep carriages or other horse-drawn vehicles, but we should not overlook the fact that owning and keeping a horse and carriage was always far more relatively expensive than automobile ownership has been since the creation of the Model T Ford in the first decade of this century. The middle-class residents of the peripheral districts of the central city were similarly stymied: they were not really in the carriage set, but they lived in a situation where what public transportation there was—horse-car lines, cable-car lines, or possibly steam railroads reaching to the city core—were similarly unusable for local circulation because of the strongly radial pattern of their routes. Thus the more affluent both in the city and in the suburbs had a real need for local transportation and the potential ability to pay for it.

The search for mobility in local transportation came along two lines: the effort to develop a motorized carriage or buggy and the search for an entirely new vehicle that might be propelled by human muscle power. The first led to what Henry Ford called "the family horse" when he developed the Model T; the second led to the sport bicycle and through it to the safety bicycle of the latter part of the last century.[8]

Before we examine these technological developments a word should be said about the geographical examples employed, because it is geography to a great degree that determines the logical area of consideration. As we shall see, the bicycle was of European origin; so was the first successful motorized road vehicle, whether we consider the "steam locomotive" or the gasoline-engined automobile. But it was in the United States that both the bicycle and the automobile first came into widespread use, being developed as practical conveyances for a mass market rather than as sporting contrivances for a small wealthy class. Once taken up, these vehicles so transformed American life that the United States became the exemplar of the automotive life for the world at large. In 1929 it was determined that the United States had 3,727,393 miles of road (47.7 percent of the world total of 7,805,629) and 24,629,921 automobiles (70.6 percent of the world total of 32,028,584).[9] Thus there is no question that America was the place to observe the great automotive transformation. Although these figures do not make the appropriateness of that area for the consideration of the bicycle obvious, we may justify that conclusion by adding the fact that the first call for the improvement of American roads came in the arguments of the bicyclists of the 1870s.

The first efforts to mechanize individual transportation came, as did most mechanization, in the effort to devise a machine that might magnify the muscle power of a single individual. In the Middle Ages efforts to create a manumotive machine already had begun leading Giovanni Gontana, rector of the Faculty of Arts in the University of Padua, to make designs to that end in 1418–1419. His plans, like those that followed for several centuries, were for a primitive equivalent of the so-called hobby-horse, a four-wheeled contrivance driven by thrusting the feet to the ground to drive the device forward. In 1696 Dr. Elie Richard of La Rochelle in western France invented a pedal-operated version of this form that was reported to be "light and easy to drive." Other Frenchmen, particularly the Comte de Sivrac, experimented further but it remained for the German Charles, Baron von Drais de Sauerbrun, to develop the first practical application in the early nineteenth century. This *Draisienne*, coming to be known in English as "Hobby-horse," was a two-wheeled frame driven forward again by thrusting the feet to the ground and pushing forcefully to give forward motion. Considerable speeds were reached. "Journeys such as from Beaune to Dijon, a distance of 37 kilometres, were made with the 'Draisienne' in 2½ hours at an average speed of 15 k.p.h."[10] With this machine the advantages of speed became the main force in popularization, because the effort required to push the Draisienne by thrusting the feet was considerable. By 1819 this primitive bicycle had been taken from France and Germany, where it was introduced, to Britain and America; but it failed to catch on as more than a curiosity.

In that same year the Reverend Mr. Edmund Cartwright, who had in 1784 invented the first workable power loom, devised a pedal-operated quadricycle. In the first half of the last century a number of inventors, particularly in Scotland, made improvements that began the approach to the modern bicycle. In 1839 Kilpatric Macmillan advanced the principle that two wheels in line could maintain balance and be driven by cranks and levers working on the rear wheel.[11] Sometime in the early 1860s Pierre and Ernest Michaux, baby-carriage makers in Paris, fitted two pedals to the hub of the front wheel of what was there known as a *vélocipède*, adding yet another essential to the bicycle. By then the front wheel, very large in relation to the rear one, was pivoted to allow for steering. One of the assistants in the Michaux works, Pierre Lallement, who claimed that he actually thought of using pedals, left in dissatisfaction for the United States, "where in association with James Carrol of Ausonia [probably Ansonia] Connecticut, he patented...the velocipede in that country; this was the first bicycle patent to be granted in the United States."[12] Meanwhile in France the vélocipède was the rage, with the first race being held at St. Cloud in 1868 and the first bicycle road race run between Paris and Rouen in 1869. Ever since this certainly eccentric pastime has gripped the French to a degree that totally denies their self-perception of rationality. From that passion came most of the technical improvements that made the modern bicycle.

In 1867 Rowley B. Turner, the Paris agent for the Coventry Sewing Machine Company of England, convinced that firm to begin the production of the Michaux vélocipède, leading not only to a considerable production of that machine but the foundation of the great Coventry bicycle industry, which ultimately became the largest in the world.[13] English improvements were made on this basically French invention throughout the 1870s and 1880s, as well as American perfections on Lallement's version being manufactured in Connecticut. By 1875 the ordinary bicycle had become the one with a very large front wheel, directly driven by pedals, and a very small rear wheel. These were quite unstable and of little practical value, though they made a great impression of bravery on observers. These "penny-farthing" machines had definite upper-class connotations, with the largest club promoting them being found at Cambridge University.

A different line of advance began again in France, where in 1869 Andre Guilment began work on what became the safety bicycle, one in which the wheels were made equal in size and the powering was transferred to the rear wheel through the use of an endless chain connected to the pedals. This system was taken up in England particularly in the 1880s, and a machine of much wider appeal than the penny-farthing ordinary or sport bicycle was finally available. "A cycling boom occurred in the middle of the 1880's [in England] based chiefly upon the development of the safety bicycle, during which the cycling movement spread considerably not only among the middle and lower classes, but also among both men and women of the upper classes."[14] The introduction of the Rover safety bicycle in 1885 joined John B. Dunlop's development of the pneumatic tire in 1888 to make cycling finally a popular undertaking, in both senses of the word.

As early as 1877 Colonel Albert A. Pope of Boston began the production of ordinary (penny-farthing) bicycles and soon thereafter of safety bikes. Pierre Lallement had returned to the United States to work with Pope, and quickly the bicycle became far more than a toy for sport. It was in this period that the city population began to take it up for recreational purposes, and those in suburbs found it useful as well for everyday local movement. Hiram Maxim, one of the important automobile pioneers, explains the change the bicycle wrought:

> I had been spending the evening with an attractive young lady in Salem [Massachusetts] . . . . I thought about transportation. I saw it emerging from a crude stage in which mankind was limited to the railroad, to the horse, or to shank's mare. The bicycle was just becoming popular [in the summer of 1892] and it represented a very significant advance, I felt. Here I was covering the distance between Salem and Lynn on a bicycle. Here was a revolutionary change in transportation. My bicycle was propelled at a respectable speed by a mechanism operated by my muscles. It carried me over a lonely country road in the middle of the night, covering the distance in considerably less than an hour. A horse and carriage would require nearly two hours. A railroad train would require only half an hour, and it would carry me only from station to station. And I must conform to its time-table, which was not always convenient when calling upon an attractive young lady in Salem.[15]

In this way suburban swains, which we assume Maxim to have been, could expand their areal scope along with their temporal one, giving for the first time an individual mobility to those living without call on a carriage.

The bicycle was at first little more than a toy and the sporting vehicle of moderately affluent young men. It was in this context that it first began to influence American transportation, along with that of Europe. In North America the impact was more direct and immediate because to ride the sorts of ordinary bicycles available in the 1870s required considerable balance and skill, both faculties enhanced by good road surfaces. The rutted rural road and suburban street were hard on cyclists, who, like most recreation enthusiasts, were both intense in their interests and extremely vocal. We should not forget that this thing they rode was called a *hobbyhorse*, or *hobby* for short, giving us our popular word for "a pursuit outside one's regular occupation engaged in for recreation" (Merriam-Webster). All that need be added is that hobbyists have commonly been more earnest and demanding in relation to that change from their normal occupation than in their regular work itself. Certainly such was the case with the hobby riders when it came to road improvements.

The call for improvement, the first relatively concerted effort, came from the League of American Wheelmen organized in 1880.[16] One of the League's officials, Isaac B. Potter, wrote in *Harper's Weekly* in 1896,

> Every cyclist is an unswerving believer in the need for better roads. He knows no more of the misery of a mud road, perhaps, than all the horses and all the mules knew a thousand years ago, but the gift of speech has blessed him with the privilege of telling about it. And so it shall come to pass when all our farmers ride bicycles the country road will reach the full splendor of its excellence . . . then will the great mission of the bicycle have due acknowledgment, and the efforts of the wheelmen for better roads be placed in the schedule of things that are not altogether selfish.[17]

So clearly did the Wheelmen see the need for improvements that their first official publication was the *Good Roads Magazine*, begun in November, 1891, which reached a circulation of a million three years later.[18] But by the end of the decade the craze for bicycles had largely passed, leading the *New York Times* to editorialize on September 13, 1900: "The bicycle will not wholly disappear. The misfortunes of those who suffer from bicycle accidents will not deter many others from experimenting with a method of locomotion that has its charms and advantages. But it will probably find a place with such relics of former crazes as the game of croquet."[19] That doom was not quite so complete as the journal of grey wisdom would have had it, but certainly the political power of the Wheelmen was reduced. Still, during the 1880s and 1890s their impact had been considerable, and a beginning was made toward improving roads. The effort for the farmer was small, but in the suburban penumbra around cities accomplishments were more observable. The fundamental instrument of change came with the creation of a new method of building and financing highways.

THE GOOD ROADS MOVEMENT AND TAXATION

The standard way to construct and maintain roads in the United States right down to the end of the last century was through the corvée of ancient origin. In cities, street construction and maintenance had shifted during the nineteenth century to being planned by engineers and carried out by paid workers supported by local property taxes. The countryside, even in the environs of suburban railroad depots, still got its roads at the hands of men "working out their taxes" in a very sociable but not very constructive fashion. It was in transforming that provision that the League of American Wheelmen, and those who came to join them in the Good Roads Movement, saw the greatest progress. Starting with the state of New Jersey in 1889, highway legislation was adopted that permitted counties to issue bonds for road construction, thus allowing them to make substantial investments for materials and labor.[20] In 1858 Eli Whitney Blake of New Haven had invented a stone crusher that greatly facilitated this first phase of improvement, which was particularly characterized by the construction of "rock roads"—that is, roads with a substratum of crushed rock to promote drainage.[21] With the subsequent development of the steam shovel and the steamroller moderate mechanization was at hand to create what were essentially macadam pavements water-bound with a surfacing of sand and clay. Essex County, New Jersey, was the pioneer in improving its clearly suburban roads, but soon thereafter other counties in New Jersey followed the practice. The effort was facilitated by the formation of a state highway department in the Garden State in 1894 to make available state aid enacted in 1891. In 1892 Massachusetts became the second commonwealth to shift some of the financial responsibility for road provision to the state, followed in 1895 by California and Connecticut, and in 1898 by Vermont and Maryland. Generally it was the more urban states that provided state aid for roads at an early date; but by 1917, with the adoption of the practice by Indiana, South Carolina, and Texas, all states had shifted much of the responsibility away from the local areas, where it had lain under the corvée, to the states, where it rested under tax support.[22]

The twenty-six years taken up with creating the state responsibility for roads were the time of the Good Roads Movement. Initiated by the Wheelmen, the movement was taken up in the late 1890s by promoters of the automobile. Colonel Albert Pope, Lallement's last employer, had been interested as a cycle manufacturer and remained so when, in the last years of the nineteenth century, he shifted his efforts to automobile manufacture. In 1892 a National League for Good Roads was founded comprising diverse elements interested in road improvement.[23] There was no constitutional problem raised with state involvement, as those governments, as the ultimate repositories of powers under the United States Constitution were clearly entitled to support improvements within their areas. The federal government, however, was seen perhaps by a majority as restrained from financial involvement. Thus, in the 1890s the proponents of road improvement had to content themselves with quite indirect federal participation. This came in 1893 when, through its concern for the interests of farmers, the Department of Agriculture established an Office of Road Inquiry to provide professional advice on road-building, ostensibly in what came to be seen as farm-to-market rural roads.[24]

Needless to say, this was the camel's nose; but it took until 1916 to gain full federal participation in road building, and even then only in the guise of caring for the farmer's interest, which kept the federal government out of road-building in cities until after World War II.

Specifically, the Office was instructed at first to carry out inquiries into the methods of highway construction and management throughout the country, and to aid agricultural colleges and experiment stations by publishing the results of these investigations. In 1897 the function of studying road-building materials in the various states was added to the Office.[25]

At this period in the historical geography of American transportation, interest in roads lay mainly in securing economical and enduring surfaces. The location of the roads came from an earlier time. The first phase of the Good Roads Movement was specifically and narrowly that of creating artificial roads where before there had only been "natural" ones, but leaving the geography alone.

The effort toward paving roads had two theaters: the urban and the rural. The initial efforts were made in the first, though not before the period we are considering. European cities had had paved streets even in Napoleonic times, in American cities there were few treated surfaces before the Civil War. The street railway, introduced in 1832 in New York, made up for that absence; the availability of those lines tended to slow down American efforts at street paving. Only at the end of the century did the larger and more prosperous cities begin to lay stone and wood blocks in their streets to give a firm surface. That shift was encouraged by the increasing number of automobiles with pneumatic tires that sucked dust from unpaved streets, rendering the life of pedestrians upleasant and deteriorating the street surface. By the time of World War I most arteries in cities were paved, but back streets still had low-grade pavements, if any.

As here we are primarily interested in the creation of the road as a long-distance artery of transportation, we may concentrate on rural mileage and its pavement. The first Portland cement pavements were laid around the courthouse in Bellefontaine, Ohio, in 1891, the same year that the brick pavement on a rural road was laid on the Worcester Pike in Cuyahoga County outside Cleveland.[26] The progress was very slow; as late as 1914 less than 1 percent of the surfaced rural road mileage in the United States had cement pavements. In fact, less than 6 percent were what we today would think of as surfaced—that is, given a rigid artificial surface. Of the quarter million miles of surfaced roads, nearly half (45 percent) were merely treated with gravel, another quarter with water-bound macadam, and 17 percent with a sand-gravel mixture.[27] Even then, no more than 10 percent of the rural road mileage in the United States had been given any surface—that is, changed from the natural road found for the full length of human history.

THE ARRIVAL OF THE AUTOMOBILE

Before we look at the creation of the modern highway, so very different from that in use for millennia, we must stop to take account of the other form of mechanized individual transportation—the automobile, already mentioned. As John Rae begins his history of the automobile, he tells the essence of the matter:

> The automobile is European by birth, American by adoption. The internal-combustion engine, upon which most automobile development has been based, is unmistakably of European origin, and both the idea and the technique of applying it to a highway vehicle were worked out first in Europe. On the other hand, the transformation of the automobile from a luxury for the few to a convenience for the many was definitely an American achievement, and from it flowed economic and social consequences of almost incalculable magnitude . . . . The American economy and American life is organized predominantly on the basis of the universal availability of motor transportation. All this would have been an impressive accomplishment over a period of centuries: as it was, it took place in two generations.[28]

As this is not a history either of sport or of the economic elite, I have no intention of spending more than a few words on the origin and early history of the automobile. Rae argues that Cugnot's 1769 steam tractor for drawing artillery was the first operational ancestor of the automobile, and that Oliver Evans's self-propelled dredge *Oruktor Amphibolos* in 1805 was the first American forebear.[29] The first practicable internal-combustion engine was that patented by the Belgian mechanic Étienne Lenoir in France in 1860. The German, Nicholas Otto, patented the four-cycle engine in 1878. The fuel for both was manufactured coal gas, though after 1859, and the increasing production of petroleum, a fraction removed in the making of kerosene, gasoline, came into wider use.[30] Although Lenoir actually built a vehicle to be operated by his two-cycle engine, this 1860 experiment in Paris was not followed up by any further action. Only in 1885, and in Germany, was a successful automobile developed that had a continuous evolution down to the present time. In that year both Karl Benz and Gottlieb Daimler built such vehicles, though Daimler began with a motorcycle and Benz with a motorized tricycle. In France Emile Levassor was building a primitive automobile in 1891, one that was more a prototype for the present-day car in having its motor at the front, ahead of the seat. By the 1890s Europe had begun to build cars in modest numbers, all by hand and according to a fair number of different plans. France led, with Germany not far behind.[31]

Why weren't Americans part of this vanguard? This was a particularly active period for invention in America—the trolley, the electric locomotive, the phonograph, the electric light, and a number of other fundamental and useful inventions came into being here, but automobiles did not. The first American experiment came only in 1893, in Springfield, Massachusetts, and the car built there by the Duryea brothers was far behind European practice even for that year. In the context of this transitional section it should not be difficult to understand why such a tardy development took place. Virtually nowhere in America were there streets or roads as good as those in the metropolitan areas of France, Germany, Austria, and England: the appeal of an expensive toy to run about in over reasonably good surfaces could hardly be great where few miles of such pavements existed. Rae holds, "It may [have been] that American talent was slow to get interested in motor vehicles because of the discouraging prospect for highway travel in a land of vast distances and poor roads."[32] That seems as reasonable an explanation as any for the slow experimentation with automobiles, though one added point should probably be made: American ingenuity tended to be focused on fairly democratic needs rather than on those of an élite. After all, it was apple pie that was the glory of American cooking. We should not forget that it was almost without European help that Canadians and Americans had introduced the trolley-car to transportation and, through it, transformed the life of the working class in both North America and Europe. That forceful impact was withheld from the automobile until, almost entirely in North American hands, the car was democratized.

THE FIRST PHASE

Before we look at that popularization, it is useful to summarize what was accomplished in the first generation of road improvement in the United States. As the effort was first engendered by the promotional efforts of the wheelmen, the first tangible results came in the vicinity of cities. Although the bicycle was viewed as a possible emancipator of the farmer, it never took on that role, mainly because rural roads were so badly rutted as to make bike riding dangerous and unappealing. In fact, the countryside came to look upon the bicycle and its rider as an urban scourge visted on the innocent agriculturalists. Hilles tells us that "even though a farmer might admit the need for better roads, he resented outsiders telling how to improve it."[33] Writing in the journal *Independent* in 1896, George C. French argued that farmers could bear no additional cost for road-building; that "to take from them the privilege of working their highway tax, under the present system, would be a serious addition to their present burdens, if required to pay the value thereof by a tax in money, as proposed by those who demand this change"; that the highway tax "can now be worked out by the farmers at a time in the season when other farm work is not pressing." In conclusion, he accused bicycle and carriage users from the cities of "clamoring selfishly for fine highways" while not understanding "the burdens they seek to impose upon the impecunious farmer[s] who need rather their sympathy and to be relieved from heavy taxation."[34] Clearly, the countryside would have remained in its mire if left to its own devices.

The efforts at road improvement in the penumbra around cities did yield results that encouraged the expansion first of bicycle ownership, and then of auto purchase. The first improvements tended to be modest; a single lane of a wider road might be surfaced, leaving approaching vehicles (when cars were introduced) to pass each other by use of the adjacent shoulders. As Shaler saw it in 1896,

> One of the most important results of [recent efforts in road building] is the evidence that the hardened part of the way, as it is usually built in this country as well as in most parts of Europe, is much wider than it is necessary to have it . . . [T]he present needs can often be met in a very satisfactory manner by ways not more than from ten to twelve feet in width, with graveled or grassed shoulders having a width of four feet on each side of a macadamized strip. It therefore seems desirable, where, as is generally the case, there is need of extreme economy in the construction, to build very much narrower hardened ways than our people are accustomed to accept.[35]

In some cases the narrowing of the hardened way reached the point that only the tracks of the wheels were paved, leaving a grassed median between the two.

The overriding concern became that of connecting as many places as possible with paved roads, an objective that guided American road building until quite recently.[36] This first phase might, in fact, be termed one of maximum extension of the most basic pavement, with little notion that there would be specializations in roads. As Shaler saw it in the beginning of the era, the distinctions were not so much in width or engineering of the road as they were in level of pavement. He envisioned first farm roads on which,

> . . . the means for construction and repair have naturally to be sought near at hand. it is not practicable to spend much money in preparing them for use. It is not usually possible to incur much expense in drainage. In farm roads, because of the fact that it is rarely practible to keep the surface in a smooth state, it is desirable carefully to consider the matter of grades and to maintain the surface in such a condition that it will not rut to any depth. Where a stone for road-making in the manner of Macadam can be had at small cost, it will generally be found profitable to cover the main farm ways with such material to a depth of six inches and to the width of eight feet. [But often that would not be the case and] The fact is that, until broken up by the repeated tread of the wheels [of heavy wagons], a thick coating of sod affords sufficient support for a tolerably heavy vehicle. It is possible on many farm ways to make use of such sod as a road covering. Where ruts form to any depth they can be closed by cutting a wedge-shaped section from the sod on either side, which has commonly been forced up above the trough, so that the channel may be closed. If this is done in the springtime, the detached sods rammed into place, and the surface strewn with any fertilizer, the effect is quickly to restore the turf.[37]

Lest we look upon this "farm road" as unbelievably archaic in its form, we should note that in 1921, when the automobile era in America was just underway, there were 2.5 million miles of "unimproved and partially graded" roads, a total larger than all the roads in all of Europe at the time.[38] And this was the body of roads that the farm advocates sought to have maintained by perpetuation of the ancient corvée.

The other two classes of road that Shaler envisoned in 1896 were the neighborhood road and the main highway. The first of these, "which the French call vicinal routes, generally require, because of the increased traffic, much more extended care than farm ways." These he believed were to be macadamized (that is, in water-bound macadam) where extensively used but in agricultural areas where "the aggregate of teams passing does not usually exceed forty in a day, . . . a narrow road, such as is above described, will well serve the needs. No serious inconvenience will be found from the narrowing of the way, save that in the night the drivers of wagons may not be able to perceive each other at a sufficient distance to make sure of a turnout place."[39]

The main highways in Shaler's view were the only routes "of a country district [that] should, wherever conveniently possible, be made of broken stone in the manner of Macadam." But "On the highest-grade country roads, those which immediately connect with the great arteries of cities, pavements made of broken stone are apt to prove insufficiently enduring for heavy traffic. In these cases it is often necessary, or at least cheaper, to pave the road with stone blocks. In such instances the road may, even if it be in the country, be regarded as a part of the city streets."[40]

From this analysis it seems appropriate to draw the conclusion that just before the coming of the automobile the only rural highways that could be envisaged as having any justification for what we would, today, call a true pavement were those in the suburban band around major cities and, even then, only if they were extensions of the urban arterial system. This point must be taken because I wish to argue that it was the city and its transportation objectives that first shaped the effort toward modern highways. This was true both at the beginning of the century and in the shaping of the superhighway that came in the late 1920s and early 1930s. Although the League of American Wheelmen had been instrumental in creating the Good Roads Movement, it remained for the adoption of automobiles to make that effort more availing than merely the shaping of some suburban and closely adjacent rural main roads. Shaler's description of "neighborhood roads" and "farm ways," as seen in 1896, demonstrates that what we today consider a paved road was still in the future.

The Popular Automobile and the Model T

This is not the place to recount the development of the automobile; rather, here we are concerned only with its impact on actual transportation. The earlier cars, in the United States as well as Europe, were mainly playthings of the prosperous and wealthy rather than vehicles of serious and continuing transportation. The impact on the main body of travel was relatively small until just before World War I. In 1905 there were only 78,000 motor vehicles licensed in the United States, though by 1910 that figure had risen to 472,000. For reasons that we shall see presently, the increase was rapid thereafter, reaching 1 million in 1912, 2.5 million in 1915, 5 million in 1917, and 10 million in 1921.[41] Only five years later the figure had doubled before the rate of increase slowed markedly. Thirty million vehicles were registered for the first time in 1937, 40 million only in 1948, 50 million by 1951, and 60 million by 1955.[42] Clearly there were three periods of massive and rapid growth in vehicle ownership. The first—numerically the least, though relatively the greatest—period was from 1908 to 1913. Numbers changed rapidly again in the 1920s going from 7.5 million in 1919 to 26.7 million in 1929. Again in the late 1940s and the late 1950s the figures ballooned rapidly from 37 million in 1947 to 67 million in 1957.

Each of these great ratchets of vehicle ownership in the United States can be related to distinct phases of the historical geography of road transportation. The first, between 1908 and 1913, related not so much to the improvement of facilities as to the improvement in the vehicles operating on the roads. In that period the surfaced road mileage grew from 183,000 miles to 244,000, but the increment is not large enough to account for the increase in vehicle ownership.

The Model T Ford. Ford Motor Company photograph.

If we look at the number of passenger cars built, however, we find the answer. In 1908 American manufacturers constructed 63,500 cars; in 1913, 461,500.[43] Between 1915 and 1917 the number nearly doubled, from 895,930 to 1,745,792. Obviously it was the rapid expansion of the American automobile industry that worked the change. Even more than that, it was the expansion of a single builder that truly ushered in the modern automobile era. Certainly no one so reshaped our lives constructively in this cen-

tury as did Henry Ford. When he began shipping his first Model T Fords in 1908, the necessary preconditions for our modern settlement and transportation patterns were largely in place.

Several features made the Model T the car that started the automobile era. It was cheap when first produced and became cheaper over the years, until it could be bought for as little as $290 (1923). The motor was reasonably powerful, 20 horsepower, though easy to keep in repair, even by most owners—not an inconsiderable advantage when gas was bought from blacksmiths in many places and those honest workmen were the only mechanics available on many roads. Particularly significant was the three-point suspension of the Model T, which allowed it to pass over almost any firm and moderately smooth surface that was not over 8 or 10 percent in slope. That ability to cope with the atrocious roads of the car's youth was further enhanced by the high clearance of the car, making it seem ungainly in height but allowing it to be what Ford and his engineers wanted—"the family horse." In 1908 Ford was still making a few cars on other models, but by 1909 he decided to concentrate his production entirely on the Model T. The result was that in the nineteen years of its production over 15 million Model Ts were built. In 1920 half the automobiles in the world as a whole were those Flivvers. The durability of the vehicle came in part from Ford's innovative adoption of vanadium steel for its construction, the first use in America of that tougher alloy.

The massive sales of the car came from Ford's realization that having totally standarized its form—the basic model was set and only modest options could be bought, such as a windshield on the earlier models, to be mounted by the owner—his sales could be greatly increased if he could produce the car more cheaply. The joke went that you could buy the Tin Lizzie in any color you wanted, so long as it was black, but in that constraint lay a far more important transformation of society: by creating the conditions for mass production, Henry Ford also created the ability to sell cars to people in no way approachable by the salesmen of the more stylish and mechanically complex cars of his American and European competitors. During its first full year of production, 1909, the Model T came from the factory as 18,664 identical cars, only about 8 percent of

American car production. In 1913, when the company produced a quarter of a million cars, the Model T was accounting for 40 percent of American production.

This striking increase was due to the realization on the part of Henry Ford and other officers of his company that the standardization of production on one model had established the conditions for mass ownership of cars—his car in particular. To gain that end the price had to be reduced, and the only way they could see to do that was to reduce the time taken to make the car. In early 1913, when that objective was adopted by the Ford Motor Company, it took 12 hours and 28 minutes to assemble a Model T. By introducing the assembly line, which Ford had pioneered for the assembly of magnetos, to the assembly of chassis, by 1914 the Model T was being assembled in an hour and a half. Between 1913 and 1916 the price was dropped from $550 to $380 (the 1908 cars had cost $850), and production had tripled. With a continuing slight decline, in the face of general price inflation, 1921 saw 1 million Model Ts produced, and in 1922 2 million new Flivvers came on the road. Upkeep was equally cheap. Even a front spring cost only $4 and a front fender just $3.75 *installed*. Finally, the durability of "the family horse" as sired at Dearborn was such that "From the end of World War I until 1925 approximately half the cars made in America were Model T Fords, and because they were so rugged, they represented far more than half the cars on the road [in the latter year]."[44]

The impact of the Model T was perhaps more in the countryside than in the city and its suburbs. Where earlier automobiles, particularly those of European provenance, were the recreational vehicles of the prosperous, the Model T became a true workhorse. Farmers bought it in increasing numbers because it could negotiate any road, even a muddy or sandy one, and could operate without roads for field work. The agitation for roads usable by the range of cars available before World War I came mostly from the city and its suburbs: farmers, convinced they could not pay for those roads, tended to oppose efforts at rural road improvement beyond a rather low standard. Thus it would be hard to explain the rapid spread of car ownership in the country save for the advent of the Model T, a vehicle that could operate on the roads already available in rural areas—such as those discussed by Shaler in 1896. Farmers, finding they could benefit from the use of automobiles, began to relent somewhat on their view that all the agitation for good roads was a conspiracy by city people to saddle the overburdened farmer with yet higher taxes. Once rural interests could see that they might benefit from road improvement, that activity, in a time when the countryside was heavily overrepresented in legislatures, became politically feasible. Thus, not only did the Model T make the automobile democratic, it also made the roads for its operation on a regional scale politically practicable.[45]

That political support came through the Department of Agriculture, which joined with the frankly urban agitation of the Good Roads Movement to promote what were essentially regional highways that would tie the farm to its market and the city to its immediate hinterland. The relatively limited growth in miles of surfaced road that we have already noted before World War I came mostly before that active collaboration between the urban and rural interests. The results were almost entirely in what are now called low-grade pavements: sand, gravel, water-bound macadam, and the early oil-bound macadams comprising sand and gravel. Even lumping rural roads and municipal streets, the surfaced road mileage of the United States was less than its railroad mileage until about 1915, though it grew moderately rapidly thereafter reaching

350,000 miles in 1919, 500,000 by 1925, and a million miles in 1935.[46] By that time there was obviously an expansion beyond the regional system toward a truly national highway network.

To understand that change, it is necessary to consider the shifts under several headings: the groups involved, the qualities of pavements sought, the location of roads in relation to settlement, and the overall geographical purpose of various undertakings. Taking the first of these, we find that the heavily recreation orientation of the earliest proponents of Good Roads continued throughout the period before World War II. The role of bicyclists obviously declined rapidly as car ownership came to much the same group, shifting their attention to providing roads for automobiles used for weekend driving and getting about the suburbs. With greater ownership of cars and improvements in the durability of those vehicles, that recreational impulse came to be expressed over greater distances. The Sunday drive was supplemented by the motoring trip during a vacation. The parkway systems of Westchester County, New York; around Boston, Chicago, and Kansas City; and in some rural park areas were first undertaken at this time. Because the long-distance trip for recreation passes over stretches of road surfaced for much more local purposes, no absolute classification of roads is practicable. Instead, it is more rational to look at the various promotional groups operating in the creation of what became the world's largest integrated highway system.

Because the recreationists were historically the first proponents of Good Roads, we may begin with them. The parkways mentioned in the last paragraph represented their first contribution. In the 1880s Boston, through its Metropolitan District Commission, had already begun to provide carriage and bicycle-riding parkways laid out by Frederick Law Olmsted in a girdle around the city. Similar systems in the suburbs were developed in Chicago, and then Cook County, in Kansas City, and in Westchester County north of New York. So long as the unreliable early automobiles and bicycles were the main recreation vehicles, the confined geographical scale of these undertakings sufficed. But as cars improved, particularly as the "automobilists" sought to prove their cars, races and rallies were run over great distances. Those directly interested in automobile manufacture began to undertake longer journeys to demonstrate a possible utility for their cars: "In 1897 Alexander Winton drove one of his cars from Cleveland to New York in 78 hours and 43 minutes actual running time. The whole trip including stops for repairs, took from July 28 to August 7 and covered 800 miles via Rochester, Syracuse, Utica, and Albany." By 1903 three separate journeys were undertaken between San Francisco and New York, each taking about two months.[47] Certainly the most arduous and spectacular of these proving trips was that undertaken in the 1908 road race from New York to Paris via Alaska and Siberia, although Alaska was ultimately dropped from the route. An American car, the Thomas Flyer, won the race, forcing Europeans perhaps for the first time to perceive that American manufacturers may not have used as elaborate engineering as did the Europeans, but they consistently created more durable cars.[48]

EFFORTS TOWARD THE DEVELOPMENT OF A NATIONAL HIGHWAY SYSTEM IN THE UNITED STATES

Once automobile ownership in the United States had become widespread with the advent of the Model T, there was considerable support for shaping a road system of more than regional importance. As early as 1898 a journey from Los Angeles to New York was reported, and in 1902 a large city party made

a fifty-one-day trip from San Francisco to New York via Emigrant Gap, Reno, Lovelock, Winnemucca, Wells, Promontory, Salt Lake City and central Colorado, to Denver and eastward to Gotham. Even as late as 1908 it was stated that "sixty to ninety days was good time for the average non-professional driver to make from the Atlantic to the Pacific."[49] The period before the First World War was one in which attempts at long-distance motoring were undertaken but one in which most of the actual efforts at road improvement were aimed at relatively local goals. The more urban states, those generally most oriented toward cars in this period, had begun to form state highway departments, to shift increasingly away from local labor and taxes for construction and maintenance toward state funding and professional construction, and to license and tax motor vehicles themselves as well as the fuel they consumed. Thus user fees and taxes were increasingly the basis for road improvement.

The state highway systems failed in two definite ways: they obviously were fairly parochial in their scope and interests, and they were not comprehensive. States that were predominantly rural, particularly in the South and Southwest, tended to do little about road improvements. It was in this context that the basically promotional efforts before the war had to operate. As a result of the Good Roads Movement, the national government began to take an interest in rural roads in the guise of farm-to-market routes. Professional advice about road improvement was rendered to states and counties, and a general educational function was undertaken to overcome the myopic view of many countrymen that good roads were a heavy burden on the farmer and of use only to city people. But those efforts of the Department of Agriculture's Office of Public Roads (1901) were still largely parochial, even if collectively it might be hoped that eventually those local interests might coalesce into some sort of regional and interregional network.

It remained for the cities and the makers of automotive products to propose the first interregional highways. During the first decade of this century several car manufacturers, particularly Winton and Packard, actively promoted test runs that showed how bad and discontinuous were the existing highway systems. A run between Cleveland and New York, held by Winton in 1901, was forced off the roads onto the towpath of the Erie Canal in upstate New York for a distance of 150 miles.[50] As late as 1924 a Packard-financed trip from Winnipeg to Victoria was forced to fit railroad wheels to its car to gain transit of the Fraser River Canyon, using the Canadian National tracks.[51] Lest these seem instances of ancient history, we should not forget that it was impossible to cross the United States on any rational route that was fully paved as late as the attack on Pearl Harbor in 1941, and it was physically impossible to cross Canada by road at the outbreak of World War II.

Still, there were interregional connections long before that time, and it was agitation by city motor enthusiasts and car makers that brought them into existence. The first important proposal came from the automotive manufacturers, who through their promotion of test runs knew more about the "roadability" of the United States than any other group. In 1912 Carl Fisher of Prest-O-Lite, Henry Joy of Packard, and Frank Seiberling of Goodyear Rubber became the prime proponents of something originally called the Coast-to-Coast Rock Highway Association, engendered in part from the desire to make it possible "that a corps of 25,000 automobiles can be taken over this road to the opening of the Exposition in San Francisco either in May or June, 1915".[52] That goal was far too optimistic—it came closer to making such a migration possible

for the successor Golden Gate Exposition of 1939–1940—but the effort was begun. In its earliest stages the work was almost entirely promotional and was aimed at uniting the efforts of others toward creating such a national highway. Because at this time a memorial to Lincoln was under discussion, the Rock Highway Association thought in terms of encouraging their road as such a tribute. Congress thought otherwise and Bacon's impressive building was authorized. Once intrigued by the idea, however, the coast-to-coast road promoters decided to go ahead and name it for Lincoln, gaining rights to the term from an earlier group seeking merely a road from Gettysburg to Washington.[53]

The newly renamed Lincoln Highway Association met with state officials in a tier of states between New Jersey and California, seeking agreement on a line of route and a concerted effort at construction. In the area east of Omaha there were sufficient natural roads for their purpose; it was mainly a question of deciding which to improve and getting on with the job. There had been a flurry of interest in Congress with the resumption of federal control of the National Road, stranded at Vandalia in Illinois and considerably neglected by the states to which it had reverted before the Civil War, and a call for its completion to the Pacific. But the time was too early for that, so the Association settled on its private endeavors. There were certain thorny problems. Denver and Colorado wanted the route, but crossing the Rockies in that latitude was too formidable for the time. Instead, what the Association erroneously referred to as the Great South Pass Route was adopted. This was essentially the alignment of the Overland Trail, which replaced the Oregon Trail that *did* pass through South Pass, and the Union Pacific Railroad. Colorado was not happy, but they were hardly involved in the Lincoln Highway so that did not matter greatly.

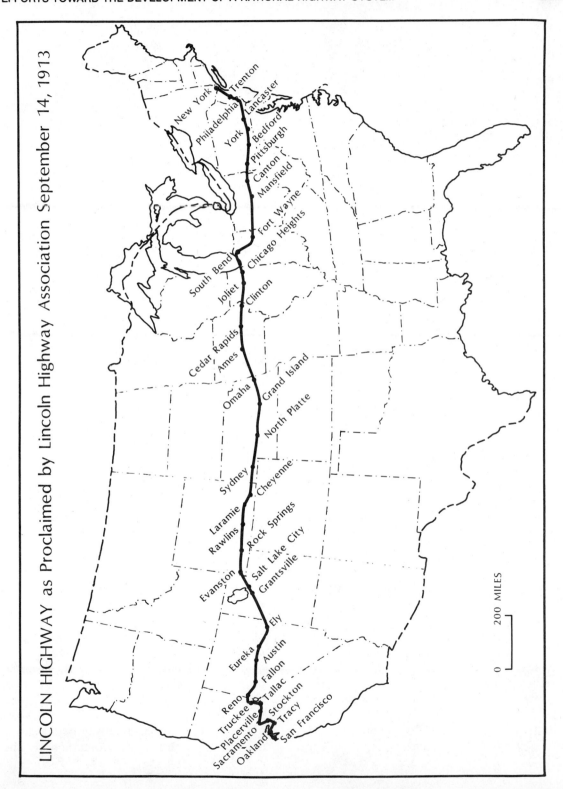

LINCOLN HIGHWAY as Proclaimed by Lincoln Highway Association September 14, 1913

200 MILES

The proponents had decreed that the Highway must be as direct as possible between New York and San Francisco. Where west of Omaha no very definite route was established by existing roads, the Association adopted the Platte Valley to the forks of that river, then up the south branch to Julesburg, Colorado, where the route began its rise over the High Plains, running alongside the Union Pacific through Cheyenne, over Sherman Hill, to Laramie. Between Laramie and Rawlins there was an argument in favor of a route different from the railroad, a discussion that was to be repeated forty years later when the Interstate Highway System was begun, though in the second instance unfortunately resolved differently. The Lincoln Highway stuck to the railroad all the way across Wyoming, though it diverged in the Wasatch to pass directly to Salt Lake City, rather than Ogden. The greatest problem of the whole promotion came in selecting the route west of Salt Lake City. The association wanted to have the road run southwestward to Ely, Nevada, and thence westward along what is U.S. Route 50 today to Sacramento. Utah had other ideas, wishing to have the road head directly west across the Great Salt Lake Desert to Wendover, Utah, and then either to Ely or along the Humboldt River across Nevada. The Beehive State won when the Secretary of Agriculture finally adopted the Wendover route for the later federal highway system, relegating the original Lincoln Highway alignment to a minor federal road that was not even paved until the early 1960s.

Once a route for this coast-to-coast highway had been adopted in 1913, though the Utah-Nevada section was not finally decided on until Secretary of Agriculture Henry Wallace issued his decision in June, 1923,[54] cooperative work among the states commenced. Before World War I reasonable progress had been east of Omaha. "Seedling miles" were constructed at the expense of the Association to demonstrate the virtues of rigid pavements, proper widths, and reasonable alignment. The eastern states were shaping roads that by the early 1920s could provide through connections. In the West, however, actual gaps remained. The stretch across the Salt Lake Desert was not begun until 1925, and it seems to have been the end of the decade before a reasonably usable route was available between the Missouri and the Bay Area. Even then most of this western mileage lacked rigid pavements, and some remained that way as late as 1940.

The Lincoln Highway was merely one of some two dozen major "highways" promoted by private groups. It was the only one that actually invested money in construction—of the seedling miles and of stretches in Wyoming, Utah, and Nevada that did not have very high priority in the state highway budgets. Perhaps the most important contribution of these various highway associations came in discerning logical regional and interregional routes, erecting signs to guide travelers on them, and agitating with the federal government to adopt these as federal routes and provide the improvement that flowed from that designation. By the early 1920s most of this private agitation had run its course, the routes were determined, and what residual importance the associations had was in the way of advertising to encourage tourists to pass their way.

Finally in 1916 a constitutional basis was found for federal involvement in public roads within the states. The Federal Aid Road Act of that year "would accomplish some of the objectives sought by the framers of the Constitution, namely: establish post roads, regulate commerce, provide for the common defense, and, above all, 'promote the general welfare'."[55] With that justification Congress appropriated $75 million to be spent over a five-year period in allocations only to states having highway departments that might supervise the construction. The skew of the agency in the federal government may be judged by its title: the Office of Public Roads and Rural Engineering, still lodged in the Department of Agriculture. At first there was no definite pattern for federal aid, but a supplemental act in 1921 established the Federal Aid System, to comprise 7 percent of the rural road mileage then existing in the several states.[56] In selecting the roads to be improved under the Federal Aid System, the various states essentially adopted for inclusion the main intercity and rural highways of the state in question. The 7-percent figure proved inadequate to cover all roads used for farm-to-market, rural free delivery mail routes, and public school bus routes; so the Congress in 1936 created the supplemental Federal Aid Secondary System to add mileage to cover those routes. Between 1916 and 1943 over $3 billion of federal funds were spent improving these two systems, mainly the original Federal Aid System.[57] Yet given the 3 million miles of rural road in the conterminous United States, clearly a high level of selectivity was necessary. A matter of particular pertinence to the historical geography of transportation is the basis used for that selection.

ESTABLISHMENT OF A NATIONAL HIGHWAY SYSTEM

"In 1909, peak year for horse traffic, some 26,000,000 horses and mules traveled 13,000,000 miles."[59] By 1930 there was an equivalent number of motor vehicles in the United States, but by then that fleet was traveling some 206 billion miles, over half (54 percent) in urban travel. By 1940 the travel had risen above 300 billion miles, and the share for rural travel had grown to just over half. A 50-percent growth in miles traveled took place in the 1940s, although mileages dropped during the depths of

World War II (the 1950 figure was 458 billion miles). The share of rural travel had grown slightly, to 52 percent; but fairly consistently throughout the automobile era the American pattern of driving has meant a somewhat variable spilt between urban and rural driving. With a rapid increase in urbanization, the total miles driven in urban areas has gained on rural mileage despite all the improvements in interstate highways. But this may also be seen from that rural viewpoint: despite the massive movement of American population to cities, rural travel has increased in total mileage sufficiently nearly to keep up with urban. The answer lies in the rapid increase in the number of cars, not in more miles per car per year, a figure that has changed little since 1940 when it reached 9,000 miles per year.[59]

The contribution of motor-vehicle passenger transport has obviously increased over the years, though data are hard to come by. Since 1950 cars and buses have provided about 90 percent of the domestic intercity transportation, with cars accounting for more than 90 percent of that figure. There can be no question that a national system of highways has been created and has continued to compete effectively not merely with the railroads that were its first competitor but equally with airways, which began to gain importance after World War II and achieved major dominance of public transport-over-distance with the introduction of jets in 1958. Airlines today carry only about one-tenth the intercity passenger-miles that cars and buses do; in number of passengers, given their long stages, those airliners are distinctly the vehicle for a small minority of Americans. The disruption of an airline strike can be highly visible, and its victims extremely vocal, but the democratic impact is small.

How was this impressive national highway network shaped? The federal government became the dominant force in regional and interregional highway improvement already soon after World War I. The county road had been the backstay of integrated highway development up to that time, seeking to provide the main arterial streets of cities and the intertown roads of the countryside.[60] States, when they established highway departments, tended to take over some of those road functions from their major administrative subdivision, so that by the end of World War I there were state highways in a number of states comprising rather coincidental alignments laid out originally for local needs.

World War I proved to be the first catalytic period in the development of a national system. Perhaps other than the rather specialized tank, the main technical advances made during the war were in airplanes and motor trucks. We shall see the role of the war in airline development, but here we should look at the truck. These vehicles had been around since nearly the beginning of the automotive era, but they played a minor role until the war forced their adoption, both in domestic transport and in warfare at the European fronts. Trucks used on Pennsylvania highways during the war so deteriorated the thin surfaces of existing roads that emergency efforts were required to keep those ways open. Other states had similar experiences.

In Europe the truck came in as the prime mover of materiel and personnel. Many of those trucks became surplus after the war, and it is not surprising that as late as 1914 there were fewer than 100,000 trucks registered in the United States, but by 1920 there were over 2 million.[61] With car registration rising equally rapidly, it became apparent to military planners that the day of the horse and mule was gone. After the war they began to examine the notion of the motor vehicle as a strategic weapon in the defense of the United States. Already in 1916, when a punitive army expedition was sent into northern Mexico seeking Pancho Villa, it was transported in Dodge trucks.

The Second Phase

In the early 1920s the various federal and state highway officials were involved in selecting the "seven per cent of rural road mileage" to be designated as the Federal Aid System (F.A.S.). As a major constitutional justification for federal participation had been that of national defense, the War Department was asked to designate those roads it considered should be included in the Federal Aid System for defense purposes. In 1922 General John J. Pershing submitted a map showing what stands as the first integrated highway system based on consistent criteria. Because some 200,000 miles of highway could be designated in the F.A.S., the Pershing Map included a number of roads in border areas that lacked interregional importance, though obviously having strategic importance in terms of potential defense in the early 1920s. As the Federal Aid System came into being during the 1920s, it included most of the routes designated by the War Department in 1922.[62] In the context of road development in the period, only modest improvement was envisioned; as higher-grade pavements were extended, between the wars, it seemed that the national defense highway needs had been cared for under the F.A.S.

The activity on the Federal Aid System in the interwar years began with the designation of roads for inclusion, and by the mid-1920s the basic routes had been established. Once part of the aid system, the federal government paid half the cost of improvement on designated routes. This investment was intended to provide a national highway network within a reasonable period of time. In 1923 some 169,000 miles had been designated, and that figure rose slowly until in 1940 some 235,000 miles were included in the

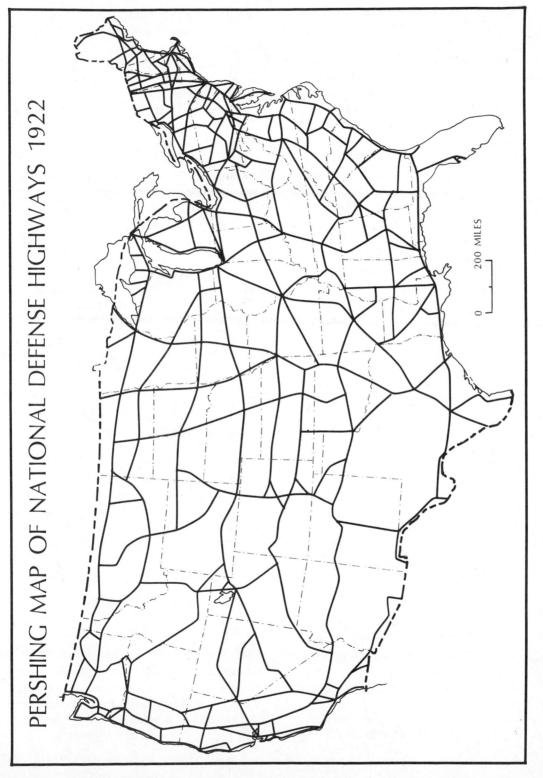

PERSHING MAP OF NATIONAL DEFENSE HIGHWAYS 1922

200 MILES

0

Source: "Highway Needs of the National Defense," House Document 249, 81st Congress.

F.A.S. The following year the total increased sharply with the establishment of the Federal Aid Secondary System. By the late 1950s the total mileage had risen to 750,000. During the interwar period some 8,000 to 10,000 miles of highway a year were improved, save for the period 1933–1937, when totals rose in several years to more than 20,000 miles as a result of relief programs aimed at highway improvement. At the outbreak of World War II our federally aided national highway system was essentially the same length as our railroad network—some quarter of a million miles.[63]

With such an extensive system it became necessary to establish continuous routes and to post signs showing their course, in large part in the beginning because the components of any long-distance federal route had been built as quite separate roads, the full articulation of which was not often obvious on the ground. It was decided that north-south routes should be given odd numbers, ranging from U.S. Route 1 on the Atlantic coast to U.S. Route 101 on the Pacific coast. East-west routes, with even numbers, ranged from U.S. Route 2 along the Canadian border to U.S. Route 98 along the Gulf Coast (through U.S. Route 90 west of Mobile). With the various diagonal routings, these three components of the U.S. Numbered Route System comprised some 156,000 miles, the true national system of highways before World War II—still less than the total railroad mileage but certainly somewhat greater in extent than the trunk-line rails of the country.[64]

There was, of course, a much more extensive system of state numbered highways. Total mileage for that system is not readily available, but it is safe to say that it measures at least three or four times as long as the federal system. In 1940 over 500,000 miles of rural road were under direct state administration, and that figure has risen by perhaps a quarter since then. The outcome of the se-

cond phase of highway improvement—that between the establishment of a federal interest in 1916 and the late 1920s—was the rapid expansion of paved roads of a modest sort. We have already seen that in the first phase, that initiated by the Good Roads Movement and carried on between about 1890 and 1916, the proponents often urged against seeking wide pavements, too high a level of construction, or the massive transformation of the natural road so as to avoid restricting the effort to a small mileage. Even in the second phase, when the federal contribution was to be $75 million over five years for a start, to be matched by the states, a similar search for ubiquity guided the undertaking. Narrow, relatively thin pavements were spread widely in geographical terms, seeking to give "hard roads for all Americans." This outcome was essentially ensured by the first positioning of the effort in the Department of Agriculture and the strong legal justification of the work in terms of farm-to-market roads, post roads, and national defense routes. The upshot of the matter was a rather undifferentiated system of dominantly rural roads numbered as highways of national interest but still mainly of utility in local transportation. City streets and arteries were specifically excluded from federal funding—even from state funding in many states—so a clear distinction was established in funding source and, it turned out, in highway morphology. Between 1916 and 1954 we may accurately distinguish an urban and a rural approach to highway improvement.

The City Shapes the Modern Highway in Efforts Between the Wars

The rather undifferentiated quality of the improvements during the second phase of American highway building can obviously be exaggerated: federal routes in the Great Basin were constructed to a lower standard than Route 1 in the Northeast. But the American norm was still the two-lane rural road with modest shoulders, level intersections, and following an alignment determined by local interests. Even as late as 1939 a major statement of federal concern for highway development adopted the two-lane highway as the objective for three-quarters of a national trunk-road system.[65]

Cities in the 1920s began to experience automobile traffic jams, not constantly but rather at peak periods during the week that tended to grow out of the increasing dependence on cars for two of the common journeys: the journey-to-work and the occasional journey for recreation. In our consideration of mass transit in cities (chapter 5) we have seen that directly after World War I trolley systems in many American cities began to collapse financially, leaving a considerable number of suburban residents with deteriorating or even abandoned electric-car service. To deal with the problem of getting to work, many turned to the automobile, increasingly cheap in cost as a result of Henry Ford's efforts. Throughout the 1920s, save for the recession year of 1921, car sales ranged from just under 2 million in 1920 to 4.5 million per year in 1929.[66] In that growth came the first highway congestion outside the core of cities and, in response to it, metropolitan areas, particularly those with complex settlement patterns of numerous residential suburbs and intermixed industrial satellites—Boston, New York, Philadelphia, Detroit, Cleveland, Chicago, St. Louis, Los Angeles, and the Bay Area in particular—began to search for a solution. In 1939 the U.S. Bureau of Public Roads determined that in designing a national highway system a density of 1,500 cars per day in 1960 should be the break between two- and four-lane construction.[67] Already in the 1920s extensive mileages of metropolitan arteries had such traffic, and some greatly exceeded that figure in daily movements.

The obvious relief for congestion was seen in increasing the width of pavements to allow several lanes of traffic to move parallel in the same direction permitting variations in speed without holding up those wishing to move rapidly. It came to be understood that the capacity of a road was in part a function of the average speed that might be maintained on it, so there was considerable interest in this "speedup."

In the last 1920s cities and metropolitan counties began to construct some stretches of four-lane highway; and some of three lanes with the idea that the shared center lane might be used for passing vehicles overtaking vehicles in their own driving lane. The obvious potential conflict of cars passing in opposing directions and seeking simultaneously to occupy the same, single center lane seems to have been greatly, and lethally, overlooked. Within a decade the three-lane road was seen for the killer it was in America, though it still continues in use in parts of England and on the European continent. The four-lane highway did speed up traffic and considerably reduce the blocking effect of slow vehicles in the curb lane. At first it seemed that this modification of the traditional, narrow rural road might solve the problem.

Speed, however, is not merely the product of clearer lanes through their multiplication; it comes as well from the clearing away of conflict from intersecting traffic, both that seeking to enter the flow and that merely crossing it. By the late 1920s highway engineers in the more urban, or perhaps more precisely suburban, areas began to see that two problems remained in the shaping of the specialized facility necessary for free flow—which meant rapid flow and the absence of congestion—on metropolitan roads. These problems were those already noted: entering the flow and crossing it. What this boiled down to was the clear-cut discipline of movements on heavily traveled highways, to

Superhighway from 1930s, Rotary Traffic Circle at Eastern Approach to Benjamin Franklin Bridge, Camden, N.J., Courtesy of New Jersey Highway Department. Note the Mid-1920s Airport in the Foreground.

be accomplished by engineering works of two kinds: works that permitted continuous movement without periodic interruptions and works that constrained and channeled potentially conflicting movements.

Italy under Mussolini had actually worked out the way to accomplish these two goals. When Il Duce came to power in 1922, his bombast included the notion of restoring Italy to the grandeur that was Rome's, and he soon appreciated that part of that prestige came from the quality of the Roman road system. In the modern renaissance this meant shaping an appropriate highway for automobile traffic, an effort realized in 1924 with the opening of the first *autostrada* from Milan to the Alpine lakes. These were roads built by private capital, to be repaid through tolls, intended to care for the first time entirely for fast automotive traffic. "They did not reach the high standards of later work, but could reasonably be claimed as the world's first roads designed exclusively for motor traffic, since they incorporated the two basic principles of limited access and the elimination of grade crossings."[68] Those incorporations may have been rather derivative, from the need to control access to the *autostrada* so as to recoup private investment through charging tolls. To do that, entering traffic must be restricted to a few manned stations where tolls might be charged, so access must be severely limited and crossing traffic kept off the toll road. Still, the outcome was highly beneficial, demonstrating what was needed in the way of engineering works to create fast, free flow. The success of these *autostrade* was immediate; by 1929 some 320 miles had been constructed.[69]

The Germans contest this initiation of the free-flow roadway in Italy, arguing that in 1922 the 9.8-kilometer *Avus* in Berlin was free of crossings and built entirely for cars gaining access by paying tolls; though it stood as part of a racing circuit, it had median dividers and was used normally for fast suburban traffic.[70] In 1930 it was proposed that a German equivalent of the *autostrade* be undertaken in a system of *autobahnen* from Köln to Bonn, Halle to Leipzig, and Mannheim to Heidelberg.[71] In 1933 the Nazis began their rearmament efforts in part by proposing a system of military highways, still called *autobahnen*, to reach to the critical national frontiers and to provide rapid routes of approach from all parts of the country. By 1942 they had completed some 1,310 miles in what was certainly the first integrated system of fast, free-flow roads to be essentially accomplished.[72]

There can be no question that the modern free-flow, divided highway originated in Europe with these Italian and German developments. Yet it is hard to consider them as the full predecessor of the modern freeway based on civilian needs. Certainly the *autostrade* came closer to providing that base than do the *autobahnen*, although their status as toll roads somewhat limits the analogy. When we seek the origin of free, civilian controlled-access highways, metropolitan America seems to be the site.

Before looking at that initiation, special note should be taken of the two qualities for improvement in dense metropolitan traffic flows cited earlier: control of access and channeling of potentially conflicting movements (both those entering the flow of the highway and those crossing it). To understand the problems encountered in gaining these qualities, the legal bases for road and highway provision should be recalled. The traditional source of construction and upkeep labor had been the corvée, determined by residency in the locale where the road was being built. In the 1890s the attempt to find a better quality of labor for construction and maintenance had led the various American states to substitute "betterment" charges levied against abutting property when a road was to be improved and, a decade later, user charges on gasoline to provide funds to keep roads in repair. With that basis for road support, a distinct legal problem was raised in trying to limit access to the highway. If abutters had had to pay for the road, no notion of equity would allow the access to the road from their property to be restricted. Furthermore, given the nature of the first and second phases of road improvement in America—essentially the reconstruction of existing roads first constructed for local purposes and still fundamental to them—there were practical problems in seeking limited-access highways. The German and Italian precedents did not really apply, as even in those instances control had been exercised only on totally new roads on new alignments—roads free of prior establishment of access and open to users only on payment of a toll. To understand the third phase of American road-building, which we shall consider directly, it is important to separate the two qualities of improvement desired. Control of flow and of conflict of flows might be attempted, but control of access from abutting properties remained impossible.

The Avus Highway outside Berlin. City of Berlin photograph.

The Third Phase

That third phase began in the very late 1920s and picked up speed during the 1930s, partly as a result of the work-relief projects that came with the New Deal. The new effort toward road improvement began in attempts to separate crossing flows and to channel entering and departing flows of traffic. The notion of separations of roadways by superposing one above another on a viaduct was hardly new. The Holborn Viaduct in London had been constructed in part to avoid the congestion on Farringdon Street where the traffic from High Holborn intersected it. The bridge creating a separation of flows was completed in 1869, obviously well before automobiles made such structures even

more necessary. Frederick Law Olmsted had used stone arches on his Boston parkways and in Central Park in New York to isolate the ordinary street traffic from that of recreational purposes in these park constructions. So the idea of grade separation was well understood before the vast increase in vehicular traffic of the 1920s made their wider use desirable. Those previous efforts had come mostly in full isolation of one flow from the other, but on automobile highways the desire arose to separate crossing flows while permitting motorists to turn from one route into the other. The result was the cloverleaf intersection, a simple and logical extension of the nineteenth-century viaduct. First built on automobile highways in New Jersey in the mid-1920s, this complex interchange had been proposed as early as 1906 by the French engineer Eugene Henard. The Grand Boulevard in the Bronx had had crossing streets depressed below it just after 1910, and in a number of cities there were odd examples of the grade separation before the famous Woodbridge Cloverleaf was constructed in New Jersey to launch the grade-separated intersection on metropolitan arterial highways.[73]

In England a contemporaneous movement was underway to introduce a particularly British form of the supposedly free-flowing intersection. A Gyratory Traffic Regulation system was proposed by Holroyd Smith before 1907, when as the president of the Civic and Mechanical Engineers Society he gave a speech promoting the system. At the same time William P. Eno, the famous American traffic engineer, introduced the system at Columbus Circle in New York City. Obviously both these efforts were modeled at least in part on Haussmann's plan for L'Etoile in Paris. The British were so smitten with the *roundabout*, as it came to be known, that most cities in the United Kingdom were dotted with these intersections. Even in the 1960s, when Britain belatedly took up freeway construction, British engineers tended to reject the cloverleaf in favor of a roundabout superposed on the "motorway," forcing the construction of two overpasses (rather than the single one characteristic of the original American structure) to channel entering and exiting flows. Those used to the typical pattern of cloverleaf intersections found on American and Continental freeways and toll roads tend to find the roundabout both confusing and subject to virtually congealed traffic, a situation not relieved by the recent tendency to use "gyratory traffic regulations" at some intersections where the appropriate term for the circle is not "roundabout" but rather "pimple." Other countries adopted the form in the paleocene period of highway development—when the Benjamin Franklin Bridge was built across the Delaware River between Philadelphia and Camden in the 1920s, the Camden Traffic Circle was constructed at its eastern end—but most of these constructions have long since been abandoned as malfunctioning given today's increased traffic volumes.[74] Foreign visitors tend to blame roundabouts for the appalling traffic congestion of London, but the natives remain enamored of their distinctive system.

The grade separation, which became the norm in America and on the Continent, could be built under existing practices of access from abutting land to highways. In the early 1930s several "Super-highways" were proposed in New Jersey, Massachusetts, Pennsylvania, New York, Illinois, and California. These were roads on which major conflicting flows were crossed at grade separations and where the limited or complete cloverleaf was used to handle the interchanges. Commonly at least four lanes of driving ways were present, and a median divider was introduced, although, as on the *Avus* in Berlin a decade before, gaps in the median permitted U-turn or left-turn movements. Perhaps most destructive of the purpose of permitting free and safe flow of traffic was the absence of effective control of access from abutting property, such that cars were repeatedly holding up traffic in the curb lanes by slowing to turn into driveways, or in entering from them. The Super-highway was designed in general understanding of what was needed to speed up flows and increase capacities of highways, but it failed to carry that understanding to its logical conclusion. Major intersections were carried on grade separations, but minor ones tended to be allowed at grade and with left turns from the fast inner lane of the highway. The chance for grisly accidents was great. By the mid-1930s the earlier cases of such roads—the Worcester Turnpike in Massachusetts, for example—had begun to demonstrate that more was needed. The third phase had consisted of the upgrading of previous roads, particularly those nineteenth-century turnpikes that had run straight across the landscape between the two major termini, with little attention to intervening settlement. It was thought that the long-distance nature of the older turnpikes made them particularly appropriate for improvement to Super-highway status, but experience proved that to be only a partial truth. While traffic was light, they did serve well; but with secular increases in flow and with periodic jams of traffic, the lack of access limitation, the left-turning movements on minor roads, and the use of these arterial highways as the site for commercial development all worked both against their basic purpose and its survival.

There was a strong impermanence in these Super-highways and expressways growing out of their very distinction from the mass of earlier rural-road construction. Because they represented the introduction of a considerable differentiation in metropolitan highway construction, with substantial improvement on the previously rather uniform norm of two-lane so-called ribbon roads, these multilane highways tended to concentrate traffic more than had previously been the case. In the absence of controlled access, land adjacent to the improved highways became prime for developments. For the first time there was sufficient differentiation to encourage the outward spread of commercial premises to take advantage of the now rather large flow of cars on these highways. The roadside restaurant was introduced and certain retail establishments began to gravitate to these highways—notably nurseries, commercial recreation facilities, automobile dealers, fruit and vegetable stands, and others that could profit from the heavy flow of potential customers on the fast-deteriorating Super-highways.

That self-destructive quality of the early Super-highways meant that their contribu-

tion was considerable in the search to devise a new form of motor highway, but at best only transitional toward the ultimate shape of those routes. It was quickly appreciated that the investment in multiple lanes, grade separation of intersecting routes, and various channelizing facilities could be wasted unless some way of preserving the free-flow qualities of the road could be found. Residential zoning was resorted to in some places, although it usually proved transitory against the economic returns of the shift to commercial use. It was ultimately appreciated that the only reasonable defense against deterioration was to be found in carrying channelization of access to its logical conclusion—that is, restricting it to a few designated intersections where flow could be carefully guided.

To make that change from the partial transition of the earlier rural road, which the Super-highway represented, a full replacement of that earlier model was the answer; but even then a change in fundamental law was required. Under notions of due process it was accepted that abutters could not be denied access to a road they might have paid for, or at least one to which they had established normal entrance, without very heavy compensation for lost property rights. There had been some early examples of functionally derived constraint of access, such as the four depressed roadways crossing Central Park carrying ordinary street traffic and a number of parkways wherein there was public ownership of the abutting land so that public policy could use that land as a buffer against vehicular access to the road. The Olmsted parkways in Boston had that quality already in the nineteenth century. In 1929 a federal undertaking, the Mount Vernon Memorial Highway connecting Washington's home with the national capital, was opened with full restriction of access, but again only by maintaining a park strip along the road. Other than on parkways such a device led to excessive land taken for road construction and extremely high costs. When in the early 1930s a major artery was proposed across the Hackensack Meadows between Jersey City and Newark to provide an approach to the Holland Vehicular Tunnel under the Hudson, constraint of access was secured through the elevation of that road—mainly to pass over railroads, other roads, and the marshes themselves but indirectly to extinguish any assumed right of access from adjacent property.[75] This Pulaski Skyway, built at a cost of $21,000,000, and another access road to the tunnel from Elizabeth, which was carried in a cutting depressed below the level of the city streets adjacent to it and thus shut off from access, were engineering rather than legal solutions to the problem.

The legal solution came in 1937, when in Rhode Island an amendment to the state constitution was adopted establishing the right to deny access from abutting property to a road on a new right-of-way, other than at intersections where all persons and their vehicles would have that right. The principle was that there was no vested right for adjacent landowners on this fully new construction. New York State adopted similar legislation that same year, and within a decade most urban states had done so making the truly limited-access highway a legal possibility.[76]

The limited-access highway had been introduced in America even before this fundamental change in the legal status of roads, ending the common-law right of access from adjacent property. Those early examples have already been cited. In 1933 Chicago constructed the Lakeshore (Outer) Drive on lakefill, in a situation where the eight lanes of roadway were protected from random access by their location. Elevated highways along rivers were built in New York City and Pittsburgh to gain the same end. Starting in 1916 parkways had been built in Westchester

County, New York, that ultimately reached to the Connecticut line. In 1934 Connecticut let contracts for an extension, still basically a parkway, for the distance remaining to New Haven, creating in this Merritt Parkway the first modern toll road in America. Although the road was constructed with state highway funds, tolls were charged to gain funds for further Super-highway construction.[77] The notion of toll-road financing was advanced a step further when the Commonwealth of Pennsylvania undertook to build a modern divided-lane and limited-access highway across the Appalachians between the outskirts of Harrisburg and those of Pittsburgh. Originally financed by the Reconstruction Finance Corporation as a job-creation program during the Great Depression, the Pennsylvania Turnpike was permitted to levy tolls to cover further construction and the maintenance of the highway after it opened in 1940.

This 160.5-mile route took advantage of some railroad construction undertaken by Andrew Carnegie and New York Central interests beginning in 1883. The South Pennsylvania Railroad was promoted by William H. Vanderbilt in response to the efforts of the Pennsylvania Railroad to construct the West Shore Railroad up the Hudson from Jersey City. His "natural territory" having been violated, Vanderbilt decided to invade Pennsylvania territory by undertaking to construct a more direct and less steep line from Pittsburgh to Philadelphia. In the process the line was laid out with eight tunnels—one of 6,600 feet, one (through the crest of the Allegheny Front) almost 6,000 feet long, and four others of more than 4,000 feet. Even though the South Penn Railroad was eventually dropped, when the West Shore was sold by the Pennsylvania to be leased by the New York Central, much of the tunnel boring had been completed.[79] When in the 1930s a road for the increasingly heavy motor-truck traffic across the Pennsylvania Ap-

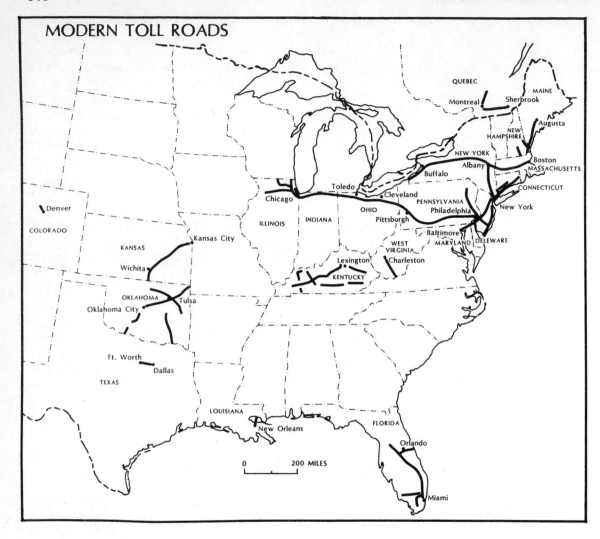

MODERN TOLL ROADS

palachians was bruited, it was decided to adopt much of the alignment of the South Penn Railroad, to finish the third of the tunnel length yet to be bored, and to create a remarkably straight highway across mountain terrain. One hundred miles of the Pennsylvania Turnpike were straight, and grades were remarkably gentle for the terrain. The road was limited in access, partly because of its toll collections, divided be-

tween opposing directions of flow; and totally separated from all crossing roads and railroads. It is generally conceded to be the first modern long-distance highway in the United States, with its original 70-mile-an-hour speed limit. Only the tunnels, which were still the fairly narrow railroad bores, were reduced in width to two lanes of undivided traffic running at lower speeds.

The Fourth Phase

With the construction of the Merritt Parkway and the Pennsylvania Turnpike, the fourth phase of American highway improvement can be said to have begun. The long-distance controlled-access highway was at hand, particularly in the turnpike, which permitted trucks and buses, as the earlier parkways had not. The studies of the economics of operation over these greatly improved highways, particularly for trucking, led almost immediately to calls for a great proliferation of such constructions. In the late 1930s the federal government was urged to study the problem and present a proposal for a national system of toll roads. But there were those who opposed such construction on the notion that highways should be free for all to use. California became the citadel of their campaign. There, in 1940, the first *freeway* (aggressively termed to show its absence of tolls as well as its dedication to creating the free-flow of traffic) was completed between Pasadena and Los Angeles (the Arroyo Seco Freeway). Thus the lines were drawn for a major contest between the advocates of toll roads, staunchly entrenched in Megalopolis, and of free roads, particularly resident in the Los Angeles Basin and California at large.

The federal government made the required study, and in 1939 the Bureau of Public Roads issued its seminal report, *Toll Roads and Free Roads*.[79] When Roosevelt sent that report to Congress, he characterized it as covering the "Feasibility of a System of Transcontinental Toll Roads and a Master Plan for Free Highway Development." He said:

> It emphasizes the need of a special system of direct interregional highways, with all necessary connections through and around cities, designed to meet the requirements of the national defense and the needs of growing peacetime traffic of longer range. It shows

that there is a need for superhighways, but makes it clear that this need exists only where there is congestion of the existing roads, *and mainly in metropolitan areas* [emphasis added].[80]

Thus in 1939 the long-standing distinction between the special needs of the metropolises and the general needs of the countryside remained in the cannon of highway improvement.

This report contained, among other things, the first detailed traffic-flow map of the United States, demonstrating persuasively that the superhighway as it had evolved in the previous decade had come in response to the dense flows of traffic found entirely in those metropolitan regions. The countryside was still fighting the battle of "ribbon construction"—the provision of rigid pavements on reasonably direct routings among the major settlements dotting the national landscape. Surprisingly, the advent of the legal limitation of access begun in Rhode Island two year before was not seen as the logical defense of longevity for those urban superhighways. Instead, Roosevelt's letter of transmittal called for a British practice of fairly recent origin, the notion of "excess-taking," aimed not at preserving the investment but rather at capturing from abutters what Henry George had termed "the unearned increment." The president argued:

> Under the exercise of the principle of "excess-taking" of land, the Government, which puts up the cost of the highway, buys a wide strip on each side of the highway itself, uses it for rental of concessions and sells it off over a period of years to home builders and others who wish to live near a main artery of travel. Thus the Government gets the unearned increment and reimburses itself in large part for the building of the road.[81]

Perhaps it is fortunate that this self-destructive scheme, greatly appealing in economic terms but fatal in morphological ones, was kept from implementation by the onset of World War II. Evidence from the North Circular Road in London can do nothing but convince us that the normally otherwise-minded citizens of Rhode Island understood more of the needs of modern highway development than did British planners and their masters in Westminster.

In physical terms the limited-access highway became the solution, but it had to wait for the winning of the war. Meanwhile, the information contained in *Toll Roads and Free Roads* had time to be digested. Its strongest recommendation was that there were very few sections of any interregional highway network that could earn back their cost and upkeep from tolls. Between Boston and Washington, and in small stretches in the Los Angeles Basin, it was thought a break-even point might be found: elsewhere, densities of traffic were not high enough to allow toll roads to solve the American highway problem. The report, instead, recommended building an interregional network, tentatively some 14,336 miles, forming a basic national network of free roads to provide the most important long-distance connections.

The speed and safety of the system would come from limiting access and determining to use four-lane pavements where the daily flow of vehicles would exceed 1,500. It was thought that where flows were below that figure, two lanes would suffice to assure reasonably free-flow at speeds up to 70 miles per hour, the design speed of the system.

The intent of this 14,000-mile system was that of interregional transportation but not transcontinental movement:

> Facts developed by the highway planning surveys definitely and conclusively show that there is no fully transcontinental travel, none of even semicontinental range, that could be accumulated in sufficient amount on any one or several highways traversing the breadth of the country, either to justify the construction, or to any considerable extent determined the character or location of such a highway or highways.[82]

Thus argued *Toll Roads and Free Roads*, establishing for the first time the general nature of American automotive travel. The report held that most journeys were short; most drivers had low incomes; and the primary needs of a national system of highways were to afford basic paved, all-weather, and fast roads across the country for the few long-distance drivers and in the interests of national defense but to do so at the minimum reasonable expense while concentrating what was then called super-highway construction in the urban corridors outlined and the metropolitan environs of some of the larger cities. This report did depart from previous proposals in that it included within the national system necessary connections through and around cities, rather than excluding any urban construction as had the Federal Aid Primary System.

Preparation for World War II, which broke out in Europe only six months after *Toll Roads and Free Roads* was published, diverted any serious attention from a national highway system until 1944. During American engagement in the war, attention turned to meeting problems of wartime transportation; but as the fighting appeared to be drawing to a close in Europe, thought was given to a postwar highway construction intended certainly to attain many of the goals outlined in *Toll Roads and Free Roads* and, in addition, to guard against a postwar recession of the sort that had affected the United States in the early 1920s. Road construction has ever been a favorite pump-primer in times of economic difficulty. The medium by which to gain these goals was a system of interregional highways proposed

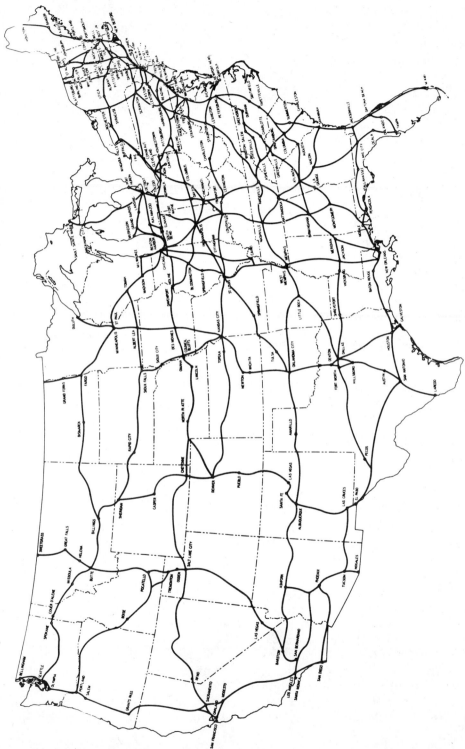

National system of interstate highways. *Source:* House Document 249, 81st Congress.

in a letter from Franklin Roosevelt to Congress in 1944.[83]

That report presented the evolution of American road improvement efforts succinctly:

> Construction of the present main highway system of the United States began in the later years of the horse-and-buggy era of highway transportation. At that time the Nation possessed a rural road network almost as extensive as at present, but it was almost wholly unimproved. By necessity all travel by road was on the shortest range.
>
> In the cities, on the other hand, most of the streets were paved, some with cobble but many with smooth asphalt and brick. It was mainly the desire of the new-fledged motorists in the cities for the comfortable ride into the country beyond the reaches of their paved streets, the similar deferred hope of more humble cyclists, and the competing aims of merchants in each town and city to enlarge or at least to hold, each his own rural trade, that prodded a long-talking "good roads movement" into actual construction.
>
> The construction of roads begun, years of promiscuous building followed. Finally, the builders awakened to the hopelessness of ever joining the thousands of disconnected little pieces of roads those years had produced. They began to realize the need for systematically classifying the vast road network and giving preferential order to the improvement of the portions of greatest use potential.[84]

The improvement even under a system of "preferential order," as was introduced with the Federal Aid System in 1921, "was less than the costly ideal which, by consuming much revenue on little mileage, would have delayed longer the improvement of other sections." Thus the first objective was extending the benefits of improvement as widely as possible. "At ... the beginning of [this] century's third decade, the unimproved sections of roads chosen to make up the newly designated Federal-aid system

were still far longer in the aggregate than the length of those that had been in some manner constructed."[85]

The system proposed in *Interregional Highways* was definitely national in scope, although the use was still perceived as normally much more localized in individual extent. The emphasis lay strongly on speed, with the report arguing for a design that would permit speeds up to 75 miles per hour in rural sections, and never less than 40 even in the most crowded sections. The network was not yet thought of in terms of uniform morphology: the major routes in the area bounded by the Canadian border, the Ohio and James rivers in the south, and Milwaukee–Chicago–St. Louis on the west were largely to be four lanes in width, as was the north-south main highway on the West Coast, except between Sacramento and Eugene; all other sections of the network were proposed as two-lane but limited-access and grade-separated routes.[86]

Perhaps for the first time the role of cities in generating heavy traffic flows was recognized and dealt with effectively in the plan. Interconnection of the major cities was a prime objective because "nearly 90 percent of the traffic moving on main highways has either or both its origin and destination in cities," and studies found "that traffic steadily increases with increased proximity to cities, that on trans-city connections of main routes traffic mounts to volumes far greater than the general levels on rural sections, and that the heavily traveled sections of the proposed interregional system lie mainly within relatively narrow zones of traffic influence about cities of 10,000 or more population."[87] For the first time, as a result of the early comprehensive traffic surveys (undertaken beginning in 1937), some measure of the geographical influence of cities was available. The 1944 report presented the radius of the zone of traffic influence for cities.[88]

City Population	Radius of Zone of Traffic Influence
3,000,000 and more	35 miles
1,000,000 to 3,000,000	30 miles
500,000 to 1,000,000	25 miles
300,000 to 500,000	20 miles
100,000 to 300,000	15 miles
50,000 to 100,000	12 miles
25,000 to 50,000	9 miles
10,000 to 25,000	6 miles

These data, made available by the pioneering traffic surveys of the late 1930s, permitted national highway policy to overcome the earlier rural bias in allocation of highway improvement funding.

In the main component of metropolitan America, that area east of the Mississippi and north of the Ohio and Potomac, funds for construction of free-flowing roads were totally insufficient. Instead, the metropolitan Northeast turned toward a nineteenth-century device, the toll turnpike, to gain road improvements while waiting for a federal program delayed in part by the overrepresentation of rural areas in Congress. Connecticut and Pennsylvania had already used the toll-road solution before the outbreak of World War II, so the model was at hand. Immediately after the war Maine and New Hampshire decided to build coastal toll roads to handle the great summer surge of tourist traffic coming from the more metropolitan parts of the Northeast. New Jersey, the archetypal bridge-route state, took up the form—arguing, as had New Hampshire earlier, that it was possible for much of the traffic transiting the state to do so without ever buying even gasoline while within its borders. Delaware and Maryland took up that argument, as did West Virginia later with respect to the Middle West-to-Florida traffic, to justify building toll roads.

By the early 1950s toll roads extended from central Connecticut in an essentially unbroken line to Baltimore. In this same period New York State, hardly either a bridge state or an impoverished one, decided that an arterial between Buffalo and New York City could only be undertaken as a toll road. In part they had the model of Pennsylvania in its crossing of the Appalachians, although nature had saved the Empire State the excessive costs of such a mountain crossing.

Once New York undertook its "Thruway" and Pennsylvania completed its Turnpike from Philadelphia to Pittsburgh, Ohio could see that there would be a buildup of interregional traffic sufficient to clog its main east-west roads. Faced with that situation, Ohio and then Indiana to the west decided on east-west toll roads to handle the anticipated increase in traffic between the East Coast and the Chicago area. Illinois reasoned that there would be problems of passing that now heavily focused flow around Chicago, allowing it to move westward or north and northwestward toward the trans-Mississippi states and the Upper Midwest. Thus the Illinois Tristate Toll Road was built as a circumferential highway around metropolitan Chicago as far as the Wisconsin boundary. At that juncture—certainly partly on the basis of the two major federal studies on interregional highways—it was decided that the traffic basis for recovering costs through tolls was probably missing farther to the north and west. Some states did not believe that assembled evidence: Kansas undertook to build a turnpike from the edge of Kansas City through Wichita to the Oklahoma boundary, and Oklahoma went wild in turnpike promotion. In this same period of toll-road florescence, Massachusetts, after vigorously resisting the northeastern rush to build toll roads, succumbed, undertaking a toll facility between downtown Boston and the New York boundary. Kentucky, West Virginia, Virginia, and Florida all turned toward the toll road as a solution to arterial highway construction, particularly for tourists traveling between the North and Florida. Colorado, in a seemingly irrational fit, built a toll road between Denver and Boulder, but that road soon became free. Elsewhere in North America the free road, improved through the application of user taxation, was seen as the only practical solution.

The halcyon days of the toll road had been passed by the mid-1950s, when Congress finally took up the provision of a truly integrated national system of interregional highways. It had become apparent that the toll road was at best a limited solution to the problem of providing a national network of limited-access, grade-separated long-distance highways. The major interregional flows in the more metropolitan parts of the Northeast might be handled on turnpikes, but even there truly comprehensive interurban highway connections could not be gained through toll collections. Away from the metropolitan Northeast—save for the rather peculiar systems in Kentucky, Kansas, and Oklahoma, whose justification has always been cloudy—public funds became the obviously essential source for a comprehensive interregional highway construction.

As a result of consideration of the findings of the 1944 report on *Interregional Highways*, Congress that year authorized a national road system, comprising about 1 percent of the nation's mileage of rural roads and city streets. As designated some 37,800 miles of existing streets and highways were assembled into this network, intended to provide interregional connections as the National System of Interstate Highways.[89] The original assumption was that improvements on these existing streets and highways could, if carefully planned, create such a national system. But by 1949, when *Highway Needs of the National Defense* was submitted to Congress, it was becoming increasingly clear that a true interregional highway network would

have standards so different from the older highways of the United States, that upgrading the existing routes to the desired level might prove impossible and would most assuredly be extremely expensive. The Bureau of Public Roads in this 1949 report held:

> Recent research and development have provided definite guides which determine in detail the standards of design required for the adequate service of specific volumes and classes . . . . The determined conditions of the [designated] interstate system have been weighted against these standards, and the system has been found seriously deficient. It is most deficient in sight distances and in the width of pavements, shoulder, and bridges. The sight-distance deficiencies are the result of defects of alignment and vertical curvature. These are fundamental defects. Their correction involves the necessity of much relocation and the obtainment of new or enlarged rights-of-way, accounting in large measure for the high cost of essential improvements.

It was estimated then that the correction of these deficiencies would cost over $11 billion, $5.33 billion of that in metropolitan areas.[90]

The Fifth Phase

In 1949 thinking in the United States had not yet evolved to the acceptance of the need for a totally new, morphologically distinctive system. Congress urged continued effort on the designated interstate system, with considerable relocations but certainly no universal acceptance of the need for new alignments, absolute control of access even in quite rural areas, total grade separation, or a uniform minimum of four lanes divided by a median strip. In the next five years those concepts gained increasing support as a result of the postwar revolution in travel habits. The late 1940s and early 1950s were the Era of the Suburb. The pressing housing needs felt at the close of the war, the onset of what is still referred to as the Baby Boom, and the very rapid decentralization of employment all contributed to a shift in commuting to automobiles. That in turn led to marked increase in car ownership, to the point that by the mid-1950s California and several other states were approaching the point where there was almost one registered vehicle for every adult citizen. Events thus quickly overtook the plans of the 1940s. It came to be appreciated that there was now much more frequent and extended intrametropolitan travel, thus requiring both more geographically extensive and more accommodating metropolitan routes. And in the rural sections of the proposed system, the rise in interregional and truly transcontintental traffic was striking. Trucks were used more commonly than before the war, and their operators sought to extend the economic range of motor-freight operations. In the same way, traffic was strangling the intercity bus industry: routes were so clogged and slow that buses lost in competition with even the far from modern examples of mainline railroads. Ordinary citizens were interested in a new, free-flow system intended for long-distance movement: trucking and bus lobbyists were exigent in their "demands." Even the normally conservative Eisenhower administration was swept into forceful proposals. In 1954 the president called for a national system of interstate highways to be constructed in the interests of long-distance road transportation, though with a much more ample provision of urban connections, bypasses, and so-called defense links than had ever before been contained in a federally funded plan.

The existing 37,800-mile designated interstate highway system became the base on which this new network was to be formed in a geographical, though not a morphological,

sense. New alignments were called for wherever practicable, grade separation was to be absolute, four-lane divided pavements were standard (except where widened to handle greatly concentrated metropolitan traffic), and access was to be sharply limited. It was accepted that some incrementation to the system would be in order. In the legislative consideration of the system its length slowly rose from 37,800 to 40,000 miles, then to 42,000, and finally to an aggregate of about 44,000 miles. Construction began in the mid-1950s and has continued down to the present, although in the thirty years since commencement of construction the system has been nearly completed, just in time to require major reconstruction as authorized under an act of 1982.

The excessively heavy use of the system by motor-freight and intercity bus companies has overtaxed the original pavements producing a more rapid deterioration than had been expected. Trucks, in particular, have been permitted heavier legal axle loadings in some states and increasingly have operated illegally in other states at that level. If the interstate highway system is to survive, trucking must take up more of the bill for constructing and maintaining the system. It is generally accepted that trucks do something like twenty times as much damage to the highway as do cars, so equity would argue that truck operators should shoulder much more of the cost of this system that has become increasingly advantageous in relative terms to truck and bus operators. The rise in the cost of gasoline since the early 1970s has meant that transcontinental car travel has dropped, and longer-distance movement in general by car has probably declined. In the early 1980s gasoline consumption dropped by nearly 15 percent, suggesting more a decline in longer movements than the abandonment of the use of cars in short, intrametropolitan daily movements.

The commonly held informed view is that the Interstate Highway System has been a particular boon to the trucking and bus industries. Some argue that intercity bus operations would have disappeard if the system had not been built when it was.

In Europe the general state of roads before World War II was higher than in America, but in the first two decades after 1945 little was done to improve highways while the vast wartime losses to the railroads were being repaired. Since the late 1950s, however, Britain, France, the Low Countries, Germany, Austria, Switzerland, and Italy have undertaken the construction of great mileages of divided-lane, grade-separated, and limited-access highways. In Britain the undertaking has been less complete than in Germany, Italy, and the Low Countries, though rather ahead of France. In a peculiar reversal of a long tradition, France has come to depend virtually entirely on toll facilities, *péages*, whereas Britain has shunned them completely, creating a partial system of freeways (motorways) that has accomplished considerable improvements, save in the glaring exception of London, which remains the most backward of European cities in dealing with the automobile. As might be anticipated, France has concentrated on a long-distance system strongly dominated by radials from Paris, whereas Germany, in the absence of any primate city after the partition, has created an excellent system of interregional highways. More than any other country on earth, Belgium has adopted the freeway and made it the main form of any significant arterial highway. In the Alps and in Italy the massive engineering necessary to shape high-speed free-flowing highways has led to some of the more spectacular highway structures to be found anywhere. Because these undertakings have been so very expensive, all these mountainous countries, other than Switzerland, have imposed a toll to pay for this work.

NOTES

1. N. S. Shaler, *American Highways: A Popular Account of Their Conditions and of the Means by Which They May Be Bettered* (New York: The Century Company, 1896), pp. 26–27.
2. Ibid., p. 24.
3. Ibid., p 252.
4. Ibid., p. 253.
5. Ibid., p.254.
6. For a discussion of the transportation of wholesale goods, see James E. Vance, Jr., *The Merchant's World: The Geography of Wholesaling* (Englewood Cliffs, N.J.: Prentice-Hall, 1970).
7. For a discussion of the rise of a rail suburb, and those features in general, see James E. Vance, Jr., "Labor-shed, Employment Field, and Dynamic Analysis in Urban Geography," *Economic Geography* 36 (1960): 189–220.
8. Frank Donovan, *Wheels for a Nation* (New York: Thomas Y. Crowell, 1965), p. 61.
9. Highway Education Board, *Highways Handbook, 1929* (Washington, D.C.: Highways Education Board, 1929), pp. 67–70.
10. The source for this section is C. F. Caunter, *The History and Development of Cycles,* part I: *Historical Survey* (London: Science Museum, 1955). The quotation is from p.3.
11. Ibid., p.5.
12. Ibid., p.9.
13. Ibid., p.10.
14. Ibid., p.33.
15. Hiram Percy Maxim, *Horseless Carriage Days* (New York: Dover Publications, 1962 [originally published by Harper's, 1936], pp. 1–2.
16. Jean Labatut and Wheaton, J. Lane, *Highways in Our National Life*, (Princeton, N.J.: Princeton University Press, 1950), p. 89.
17. Isaac B. Potter, "Bicycle's Relation to Good Roads," *Harper's Weekly* 40 (April 11, 1896), quoted in William C. Hilles, "The Good Roads Movement in the United States," M.A. thesis, Duke University, 1958, p.31.
18. Hilles, op. cit., p. 32.
19. Quoted in ibid., p. 38.
20. Labatut and Lane, op. cit., p.90.
21. Ibid.,p. 89.
22. *Highways Handbook,* op. cit., p.25.
23. Hilles, op. cit., p. 40.

24. Ibid., p. 49.

25. Ibid., p. 53.

26. Labatut and Lane, op. cit., p. 85.

27. *Highways Handbook*, op. cit., p.22.

28. John B. Rae, *The American Automobile: A Brief History* (Chicago: University of Chicago Press, 1965), p. 1.

29. Ibid., p. 2.

30. Ibid., p. 3.

31. Ibid., pp. 7–8.

32. Ibid., p. 8.

33. Hilles, op. cit., p. 65.

34. Quoted in ibid., p. 66.

35. Shaler, op. cit., pp. 247–248.

36. In 1953, in discussions with Oklahoma highway officials, I was told that the main guiding principle in determining highway planning in the Sooner State was the effort to place "every county seat on a paved road."

37. Shaler, op. cit., pp. 47–48.

38. Data from *Highways Handbook*, pp. 23, 69.

39. Shaler, op. cit. p. 51.

40. Ibid., pp. 52–53.

41. *Highways Handbook,* op. cit., p. 27.

42. *Historical Statistics of the United States, Colonial Times to 1957* (Washington, D.C.: U.S. Government Printing Office, 1960), p. 462.

43. Ibid., p. 462.

44. Frank Donovan, *Wheels for a Nation* (New York: Thomas Y. Crowell, 1965), p. 103.

45. The information on the Model T is taken from Rae, op. cit., pp. 58–62, and Donovan, op. cit., pp. 99–120.

46. *Historical Statistics of the United States,* op. cit., p. 458.

47. Rae, op. cit., pp. 30–31.

48. T. R. Nicholson, *Adventurer's Road: Story of Pekin-Paris, 1907 and New York–Paris, 1908* (New York: Rinehart and Company, 1958).

49. Lincoln Highway Association, *The Lincoln Highway: The Story of a Crusade That Made Transportation History* (Dodd, Mead and Company, 1935), pp. 6–7.

50. Rae, op. cit., p. 32.

51. Lincoln Highway Association, op. cit., pp. 267-268.

52. Ibid., p.11.

53. Ibid., p. 24.

54. Ibid., p. 188.

55. Labatut and Lane, op. cit., p. 91.

56. Loc. cit.

57. Ibid., p. 92.

58. Ibid., p. 96.

59. These data are derived from the *Statistical Abstract of the United States.*

60. Labatut and Lane, op. cit., p. 98.

61. *Historical Statistics of the United States*, p. 462.

62. The Pershing Map is included in House Document No. 249, 81st Congress, 1st Session, 1949 *(Highway Needs of the National Defense)*, facing p. 70.

63. *Historical Statistics of the United States*, p. 458.

64. Labatut and Lane, op. cit., p. 99.

65. *Toll Roads and Free Roads*, 76th Congress, 1st Session, House Document No. 272, p. 42.

66. *Historical Statistics of the United States*, p. 462.

67. *Toll Roads and Free Roads*, p. 41.

68. Geoffrey Hindley, *A History of Roads* (Secaucus, N.J.: The Citadel Press, 1972), p. 98.

69. Loc. cit.

70. Hans Hitzer, *Die Strasse: Von Trampelpfad zur Autobahn, Lebensadern von der Urzeit bis heute* (Munich: Verlag Georg Callwey, 1971), p. 300.

71. Ibid., p. 307.

72. Hindley, op. cit., p. 99.

73. Labatut and Lane, op. cit., pp. 105–106.

74. Ibid., p. 106.

75. Ibid., p. 103–104.

76. Ibid., p. 110.

77. Ibid., p. 108.

78. Alvin Harlow, *The Road of the Century: The Story of the New York Central* (New York: Creative Age Press, 1947), pp. 328–334.

79. *Toll Roads and Free Roads*, House Document 272, 76th Congress, 1st Session, Washington, D.C., 1939.

80. Ibid., p. vii.

81. Ibid., pp. vii, viii.

82. Ibid., p. 5.

83. *Interregional Highways: A Report of the Interregional Highway Committee Outlining and Recommending a National System of Interregional Highways*, House Document 379, 78th Congress, 2d Session, 1944.

84. Ibid., p. 1.

85. Ibid., pp.1–2.

86. Ibid., p. 103.

87. Ibid., p. 40.

88. Ibid., p. 43.

89. *Highway Needs of the National Defense*, House Document No. 249, 81st Congress, 1st Session, p. 2. This report, along with *Toll Roads and Free Roads*, April 1939; *Highways for the National Defense*, February, 1941; and *Inter-* *regional Highways*, January, 1944, provides a detailed picture of the emergence of the Interstate Highway System finally undertaken with federal funding.

90. Ibid., pp. 2–3.

chapter 7

The Ultimate Ubiquity

The Evolution of Commercial Aviation

In the beginning human beings could walk, swim, and float on buoyant objects to move around the earth's surface, but they could not fly. For that reason the historical geography of transportation has two distinct time scales: that for other forms of transport and that for flying. Even the railroad has classical and certainly medieval roots; flying has none that are other than mythical. Aspiration remained completely divorced from accomplishment until the 1780s, when the two lines of experiment that were ultimately to become practical were first rewarded with any success. These might be divided between the heavier-than-air vehicles and those raised from the ground by the buoyancy of a gas lighter than the normal atmosphere. In 1781 the architect to the prince of Baden, one Karl Friedrich Meerwein, apparently succeeded in flying an ornithopter (a flapping-wing device) that was combined with a glider at Giessen in Hessen, perhaps appropriately discerning one of the classic centers of glider

flight to be found in the nearby Vogelsberg.[1]

Far more important in the history of flying were the early experiments of the Montgolfier brothers, paper manufacturers, undertaken around Annonay in the Ardeche of France just south of St. Étienne in 1783. On June 4 that year the Montgolfiers gave their first public demonstration of a hot-air lofted balloon, a technology quickly accepted and modified by the Académie des Sciences in Paris. Using hydrogen, that institution encouraged ascents around Paris, first carrying only animals—a cock, a duck, and a sheep, in what must seem a particularly Gallic trial—on September 27, and then men, on November 21. This initial human flight extended for some 5 miles from the Chateau de la Muette on the edge of the Bois de Boulogne. Rather quickly thereafter the French advanced this balloon technology, both hot-air and hydrogen-filled, to the extent that by the end of the eighteenth century much of the basic technical experience was in hand for lighter-than-air flying.[2] What remained to be done was not the lofting of vehicles but, rather, directing them toward specific geographical goals. The balloon for the first time allowed humans to fly, but it did so in the absolute sense of the soap bubble rather than in the practical sense of a bird.

Direction had, of necessity, to be the basic objective in all practical flight. Floating above the surface was as fascinating then as now, but undirected movement could hardly pass beyond the realm of sport—or, as was soon to prove the case, beyond certain limited reconnaissance activities in wartime. Before taking up the search for geographical control, we might look briefly at the use of free-floating balloons during the remainder of the last century. By 1785 the first aerial crossing of the English Channel was made from Dover to the forest of Guiines near Calais, using a Montgolfier balloon. Ascents in Belgium and Germany were first made in this decade and in the United States in 1793, using a gas-filled Charles-type bag. The next year the French army, during the Battle of Maubeuge, devised the "captive balloon"—a balloon held in place aloft by a long line anchored on the ground but permitting good visual surveillance of activities at the surface, to allow J. M. J. Coutelle in the *Entréprénant* to become the first aerial observer.[3] This sort of captive balloon was used increasingly frequently in subsequent wars, perhaps most notably the American Civil War. Count von Zeppelin became interested in military ballooning when he served as a volunteer officer in the Union Army during the Civil War. When he observed a free balloon ascent at St. Paul, Minnesota, his fascination was cemented, to long-lasting effect.[4] Free balloons became more reliable, in operation but not in direction, through experimentation and improvement mainly in the envelope to contain the gas. The hot-air bal-

loons were reasonably safe, save when mishaps might set the usually flammable bag alight from the burner that produced the hot air; but gas-filled balloons were dangerous by their nature because hydrogen and illuminating gas were commonly used. Nevertheless, distances increased. In 1835 H. H. Clayton sailed his balloon from Cincinnati some 350 miles in nine and a half hours to Monroe County, Virginia (now West Virginia), passing over the rugged Appalachian Plateau for most of the distance. The next year a balloon sailed from London to Weilburg in Nassau, Germany, a distance of 480 miles but at a more leisurely pace, taking eighteen hours.[5] The Alps were first crossed, from Marseille to Turin, in 1846, while the Austrians became the originators of aerial warfare when they sent pilotless hot-air balloons carrying bombs activated by timing devices against Venice in 1849. Fortunately, no one was killed and little damage was done. More constructive was the first air photograph, taken from a balloon, of Paris in 1858. The increasingly sturdy nature of these vehicles allowed Henry Coxwell and James Glaisher to rise over Wolverhampton to a height thought to have been about 20,000 feet in 1862. In America the Union Army developed the first "aircraft carrier" to which to moor their observation balloons in the Potomac, holding them captive and connecting them by telegraph wire with the ground.[6] Thus did significant but highly specialized use of the free and captive balloon evolve.

The next practical step in flying took place in the search for a way to control the balloons' direction. There were a number of attempts before the mid-nineteenth century, one of which—by Monck Mason in England in 1844—became the believable basis for a reporter's hoax that Edgar Allen Poe perpetrated to earn a bit of money from the newspapers of New York. But Mason and the others failed to create a functioning *dirig-*

ible, the French term that became universal for a steerable airship. In 1852 Henri Giffard conducted a successful trial of a steam-powered airship operating at 6 miles per hour for the 17 miles from Paris to Trappers—the first dirigible to fly successfully, albeit highly tentatively. Still, one of the mysteries of this effort was the seemingly successful operation of a "gravity-powered" airship by its inventor, Solomon Andrews, a physician from Perth Amboy, New Jersey, as a contribution to the Northern effort during the Civil War. His airship comprised three cigar-shaped gas-bags, possibly copied from Giffard's but, unlike his airship, capable of sailing effectively into the wind and gaining ground.

Others added various forms of motive power in attempts to construct the successful dirigible. Steam was applied but only with most marginal success: instead, the first almost practicable airship, *La France* of Charles Renard and Arthur Kerbs (using an electric motor), was flown 5 miles at 14.5 miles per hour at Château-Meudon in 1884. Gasoline engines were substituted in Germany in 1888, signaling the obvious transition that assured ultimate success.[7] The Woelfert airship used in this latter test was further refined and the more advanced *Deutschland* built, only to crash at Tempelhof (Berlin) in 1897, killing the inventor. But this German effort was soon taken up by others, most notably Count von Zeppelin, whose advancing age made further foreign military engagements impractical.

It was a Brazilian living in France, Alberto Santos-Dumont, whose efforts were first met with success. As Santos-Dumont tells his story:

> Returning to Paris by rail, I gave up the ambition to continue Giffard's trials, and this state of mind lasted with me for weeks. I would have argued fluently against the dirigibility of balloons! Then came a new period of temptation, for a long-cherished idea dies hard.

> When I took account of its practical difficulties, I found my mind working automatically to convince itself that they were not. I caught myself saying "If I make a cylindrical balloon long enough and thin enough, it will cut the air ..." and, with respect to the wind: "Shall I not be as a sailing yachtsman who is not criticized for refusing to go out in a squall?" At last an accident decided me. I have always been charmed by simplicity, while complications, be they never so ingenious, repel me. Automobile tricycle motors happened to be very much perfected at the moment. I delighted in their simplicity, and, illogically enough, their merits had the effect of deciding my mind against all other objections to steerable ballooning. "I will use this light and powerful motor", I said, "Giffard had no such opportunity!"

> Giffard's primitive steam engine, weak in proportion to its weight, spitting red-hot sparks from its coal fuel, had afforded that courageous innovator no fair chance, I argued. I did not dally a single moment with the idea of an electric motor, which promises little danger, it is true, but which has the capital ballooning defect of being the heaviest known engine, counting the weight of its battery.[8]

It was the availability of a light motor, with a light and efficient fuel, that made Santos-Dumont's efforts effective. Starting in 1898, he built several experimental "dirigibles" that carried him to heights of 1,000 feet or more above Paris and could be directed in a specific course he chose. Still, Santos-Dumont favored merely hovering above the ground. "The place of the airship is not in high altitudes, and it is better to catch in the tops of trees, as I used to do in the Bois de Boulogne, than to risk the perils of the upper air without practical advantage!"[9] For him, the dirigible was a sports vehicle, not to be used in heavy winds, to be kept dry by avoiding rainy spells, and to be cruised at a modest speed just above the treetops. Through experimentation he succeeded in developing a dirigible that won the Deutsch Prize offered for a flight from St. Cloud to and around the Eiffel Tower (a distance of 5.5 kilometers) and return within the period of half and hour to the Aero Club grounds where the race began. Santos-Dumont No. 6 accomplished this flight with 30 seconds to spare on October 19, 1901.[10] Even in his success and worldwide acclaim, which came in 1901 and succeeding years as he continued his directable-balloon experiments, Santos Dumont recognized that what he was was an "aerostatic sportsman"and that his dirigibles probably had very limited practical applications. He ended his book with a symbolic argument between two young men:

> "Our only hope to navigate the air," continued Pedro, . . . "must, in the nature of things, be found in devices heavier than the air, in flying-machines or aeroplanes. Reason by analogy. Look at the bird . . . "
>
> "Once you desired me to look at the fish," said Luis. "You said the steamboat ought to wriggle through the water . . . "
>
> "Do be serious, Luis," said Pedro, in conclusive tones. "Exercise common sense. Does man fly? No. Does the bird fly? Yes. Then if man would fly, let him imitate the bird. Nature has made the bird. Nature never goes wrong."[11]

The Brazilian turned his attention to the experiments with heavier-than-air craft—aeroplanes, as they were then called—and he obtained some successes. But already when he imagined the conversation between Pedro and Luis, men had fully imitated birds, and had flown, in December the previous year, although Europe seemed to take a long time to learn of and then to accept the accomplishments of the Wright brothers in 1903. In that ignorance and in line with the trend of development of the steerable balloon, other Europeans continued the efforts of Santos-Dumont. Most notable among them was Count von Zeppelin, long since returned to his home on Lake Constance and retired by

age from his quixotic pursuit of cavalry warfare. Still in his mind was the observation in St. Paul of the excitement of free ballooning. In the late 1890s he began thinking in terms of a dirigible as the main practical application of lighter-than-air technology. On July 2, 1900, near Friedrichshafen on Lake Constance, he undertook the first trial of his airship (*Luftschiff*). This Luftschiff Zeppelin No. 1, LZ-1, flew for 17 minutes before it sank toward the lake surface, impaling itself on a buoy to puncture the gas bag. During the next eight years Zeppelin thought up modifications and had them built; a few proved to be improvements. In 1908 he was ready to seek to obtain a government subsidy offered to the builder of a dirigible that could remain constantly in the air and under direction control for twelve hours. On July 1st the 446-foot-long LZ-4 (with 519,000 cubic feet of hydrogen in its cells) was successfully flown on a course passing over central Switzerland at 40 miles per hour for the full 12 hours. The count wanted more, a 24-hour flight, so on August 4 it was attempted. Flying down the Rhine to Basel, a course was steered to Strasbourg and then onward to Worms and Mainz, where the airship turned back toward home. Forced several times to land for adjustments to the engines, the trip continued all night until, in the early morning, nearly 24 hours after leaving Lake Constance, another landing was made to repair the engines at Echterdingen. While on the ground a sudden wind tore the dirigible loose, leading to its crash into a clump of trees and destruction by an explosion of the half million cubic feet of hydrogen it contained.[12]

The count's experiments had finally caught the interest of the Kaiser, so money became available and improvements were made that created airships able to cruise considerable distances at reasonable speeds. The greatest contribution of von Zeppelin came in his adoption of and considerable improvement in the notion of giving rigidity to the dirigible. Santos-Dumont had experienced constant problems with his airships because their structure depended on internal pressure (causing them to be termed *pressure* or *nonrigid* airships) that had to be maintained at all times despite changes in temperature, gas content, and outside pressure. This was done by inserting an air bag, ballonet, inside the outer skin and inflating or deflating it to compensate for changes in the volume of the lifting gas. But success in maintaining the constant pressure on the skin evaded most of the early aeronauts, so the notion of building a dirigible with an aluminum skin on a rigid frame was undertaken. Already in 1897 David Schwartz had designed and launched such an aluminum-sheathed airship, but it crashed on its trial at Templehof as a result of poor airmanship.[13] Since it had flown before that mishap, the buoyancy of such a rigid vehicle had been proved, suggesting the line of approach that Zeppelin would take.

> For his first airship, 420 ft long and 38 ft in diameter, he used an aluminium [sic] framework like Schwartz, but he covered it in fabric and divided it into seventeen compartments each containing a lined gas bag holding a total of nearly 400,000 cubic feet of hydrogen . . . Zeppelin's emerged from its shed and moved out over the water of Lake Constance in July 1900 and *it is at this point that the stories of the balloon and the rigid airship diverge* [emphasis added][14].

The lifting properties of gases—really the difference between the weight per unit volume of various gases and that of the atmosphere—was accepted and used to give the dirigible ascension.[15] What were needed to make it a useful vehicle of transport were the maintenance of an airworthy shape and the attachment of engines to give it headway and steerage. The rigid frame offered the best hope of securing those two qualities in addition to the well-established ascension of the lifting gas envelope.

Count von Zeppelin's first airship, the LZ-1, had a capacity of 388,140 cubic feet contained within a structure made rigid by twenty-four longitudinal girders extending from nose to tail and held in a cylindrical form by sixteen transverse frames, all of this of aluminum and cross-braced with wires. The cover was of cotton cloth, the internal cells of ruberized cloth. Its fairly weak motors managed to draw the airship, with tractor action, at a speed approaching 20 miles an hour. From this beginning the count worked toward longer and more capacious Zeppelins, better structured and drawn by more powerful motors. The LZ-4 that made the successful endurance runs to Switzerland and Mainz was only 20 feet longer than the LZ-1 at 440 feet; but its capacity, and thereby its lift, was considerably expanded to 519,000 cubic feet, giving theoretically nearly 5 tons more weight that could be lofted.

Starting with the LZ-5—built to replace the airship Zeppelin lost at Echterdingen and using funds supplied by the government and other German sources—an airship of some economic potential existed. Speeds were up to 40 miles an hour, the frame of the Zeppelins was becoming perfected, and experience in handling these massive airships was improving their maneuvering. In 1910 von Zeppelin and others formed the Deutsche Luftschiffarts–A.G., Delag, to construct and operate such airships in commercial service. During the five years before the outbreak of World War I the company constructed and operated five small airships that made 1,588 flights carrying 34,228 passengers, all in safety, both in short tourist circuits and over considerable distances among the air harbors established at Frankfurt, Hamburg, Berlin, and Dresden. These airships—the *Deutschland, Schwaben, Viktoria-Luise, Hansa* and *Sachsen*—covered some

170,000 flying miles to establish beyond doubt the practicality of the Zeppelin.[16] The war led to the very rapid development of the dirigible. Germany built eighty-eight airships on Zeppelin's design during the four years of hostilities, using them for bombing Britain, observing for naval warfare, and sneaking through the Allied blockade. In 1917 a daring effort was made to relieve the hard-pressed forces in German East Africa by dispatching the LZ-59 to carry medical supplies, munitions, and messages by air from Yamboli in Bulgaria. Slipping across the eastern Mediterranean at night, the airship flew some 2,800 miles, 400 short of its goal, when it was ordered to return to base on the mistaken information that the German forces in East Africa were being defeated. Some 4,225 miles were flown without a stop, but the airship still had fuel for another 3,750 miles.[17] It was the ability to fly long distances with relatively little consumption of fuel that really recommended the dirigible even over the heavier-than-air craft that were then being developed. At this time the speed difference between the two forms was not particularly significant. Zeppelins could fly at 45 to 50 miles and hour; utilitarian heavier-than-air planes could not fly more than 30 to 40 miles an hour faster, and were held to very short practical stages in their flying.

It was after World War I that the Zeppelin came into its own as a practical vehicle. For a time Delag, as a German company, was forbidden to return to its prewar commercial ventures. By the mid-1920s conditions had changed, and the construction of a new commercial airship was undertaken. As launched in 1928, the LZ-127 (most of the numbers having been taken up for the eighty-eight airships the company built during the war) was enormous by comparison with the five small prewar Zeppelins that served the world's first commercial aviation company. The LZ-127, soon named the *Graf*

Zeppelin, and completed in 1928, was 775 feet long, with a capacity of 3,308,600 cubic feet of hydrogen. She followed fairly directly on the LZ-126, built by the Germans as reparartions for World War I and flown across the Atlantic for delivery to the Americans in October, 1924. This 2,470,000 cubic foot airship became the U.S. Navy's *Los Angeles*, greatly heightening American interest in dirigibles, though never leading to any significant commercial development beyond the sturdy and simple blimps built by Goodyear Rubber Company starting in 1911. In the end only the Germans ever pursued the airship as a scheduled carrier of passengers and priority freight.

The *Graf Zeppelin* left on her maiden voyage, across the Atlantic to New York, in the fall of 1928. Despite a potentially fatal navigational error by an inexperienced crewman that tore her covering, forcing mid-ocean repairs and the dangerous descent of the airship, she reached New York to jubilation with twenty passengers and 66,000 pieces of mail. Service was continued both to New York (Lakehurst, New Jersey) and the Mediterranean in 1929, but as a publicity venture an around-the-world trip was announced for August. Setting out from Lakehurst on August 29, this circumnavigation was completed in 21 days, 5 hours, and 54 minutes, for an average speed of 70.7 miles per hours. Only 47 hours had been spent on the ground. During the next decade the *Graf Zeppelin* navigated over 1 million miles in complete safety, despite its enormous load of explosive hydrogen. It was used for a scientific expedition to the Arctic Ocean off the Siberian coast, as well as for numerous trips across the North Atlantic to Lakehurst and the South Atlantic to Rio. This airship conclusively demonstrated the reasonably low cost of propulsion of the Zeppelins and their great range without refueling. No other aircraft of the time could have come close to providing commercial air service across an ocean as wide as the Atlantic, and no other means of transport could have maintained speeds of 75 miles an hour.

The success of the LZ-127 led to a proposal under the Third Reich for an even larger Zeppelin, the LZ-129, with a cruising speed of 78 miles an hour and a capacity of over 7 million cubic feet of gas. The very size of the Zeppelin meant that fairly commodious accommodations could be afforded to some fifty passengers. When launched in 1936, the ship, now named *Hindenburg*, was the epitome of Zeppelin technology. During that summer she carried 1,000 passengers across the Atlantic. On her inaugural flight in early May, 1937, all went well until she docked at Lakehurst, where soon after tying up at the mast there on May 6, the airship burst into flame, burning rapidly with the loss of thirty-six lives. With that explosion went the hopes of dirigible navigation for commercial purposes. So many military and naval versions of the rigged airship had failed that the crash of the one significant commercial dirigible was fatal. Service was never resumed, even though the *Hindenburg* would almost certainly have survived had it been filled with helium, as had been all American dirigibles after 1922. Given the military potential of the blimp and dirigible, the United States, the main producer of helium, was unwilling to export the millions of cubic feet of the nonexplosive gas to Hitler's Reich that would have been needed to loft these monstrous Zeppelins. Without it, the consequences of an explosion were fearsome—so much so that, despite the fact that there was no other air services across the Atlantic in 1937, the *Hindenburg* was never replaced. The history of airship service died with the last embers at Lakehurst on that May evening.

THE TURN TO HEAVIER-THAN-AIR CRAFT

We must go back in time at least to 1903, the year of Santos-Dumont's great success. By then he was fairly convinced that the future of aerial navigation, as it was then called, lay in copying not the soap bubble but rather the birds. The former rises by displacement, the latter by muscle power. In the dirigible we deal not with powered flight but instead with powered traction and direction. A floating object is moved and steered, but it is not lofted by that power. In powered flight that force not only pulls (or pushes) the airplane, it also raises it. Without power there is no sustained lift (as there is in an airship). So in devising an airplane (that is, a heavier-than-air craft), power must be employed to lift and to propel. At first this was not seen to be the case. The earliest effort at heavier-than-air flight came from using the lifting power of air currents to give ascent, much as the lifting property of certain gases gave lift to an airship. As with the early balloons, the use of air currents meant essentially that direction could not be demanded in this earliest phase. Any aeroplane had to go where the wind took it; otherwise it would not be held above the ground. Thus, in looking at the beginning of heavier-than-air vehicles, we must look at these wind-supported craft— that is, at gliders.

The analogy with the bird at first interfered with the development of a functioning heavier-than-air craft, because of the failure to understand the difference between the sailing or hovering function of the bird wing and its role in the forward propulsion of the body. The result was the attempt to create a flapping-wing aeroplane modeled on the immediate perception of how a bird flies, rather than how it actually succeeds in that act. Before much could be accomplished, considerable analytical observation, leading to theoretical formulations, had to be undertaken. With the work of Cayley between 1799 and 1809, much of the fundamental theory of aerodynamics was worked out, leading to the appreciation of the difference between lift in the wing and forward propulsion. The flapping-wing *ornithopter,* though engaging the attention of amateur aeronauts throughout the nineteenth century, was increasingly abandoned by the more serious investigators in favor of what we now call *gliders*—craft using the power of the wind to support themselves. "Cayley first formulated the basic problem of mechanical flight in these words: 'to make a surface support a given weight by the application of power to the resistance of the air.' On a little silver disc now preserved in the Science Museum [in London], and dated 1799, is an engraved diagram showing the forces of lift, drag and thrust."[18] With the concept of lift in hand, the glider could be developed either by using speed supplied by some sort of catapult system or by launching from a cliff into open air to give the initial thrust to force the air at speed over the wing surface. By 1809 Cayley had constructed and flown a full-size glider and before his death in 1857 he had made many contributions to the successful design of gliders such that what remained was mainly to discover a way of controlling the direction and maneuver of flight and a light and powerful enough engine to give sufficient power to use "the resistance of the air" effectively to lift the wings. Cayley during his lifetime discovered "that there exists a region of low pressure ('vacuity') on the upper surface [of a wing] which provides powerful lift" once that wing is effectively inserted into a strong stream of air.[19] Gliders and gliding resulted. It remained for the engine developments, largely in Germany in the last quarter of the nineteenth century, and the Wrights' experiments with aircraft control, in the United States at the turn of the century, to complete the effective evolution of the aeroplane into a commercial vehicle.

Gliders, essentially experimental and sport vehicles, do not truly concern us, though their evolution is intrinsically of great interest. We may logically begin our story of the aeroplane with the first success-

ful experiments with powered flight. It was that application of power, and concomitantly the effective development of aircraft control, that made available lift of economic significance.

> Wilbur and Orville Wright were the first men to make powered, sustained and controlled flights in an aeroplane, and land on ground as high as that from which they took off. They were also the first to make and fly a fully *practical* powered aeroplane, one that could take off and land without damage to itself or its occupant, and could fly straight, turn, and perform circular flights with ease. Finally they were the first to make and fly a practical passenger-carrying aeroplane.[20]

It is necessary to cite those facts, and on European authority, to overcome what was for many years a chauvinistic myopia on the questions involved. Santos-Dumont and others working in Europe actively discounted the word coming from America about successful, sustained, and powered flight, arguing that the Brazilian's flight in 1906 was the first ever accomplished by a heavier-than-air craft, which it was not, rather than the first in Europe, which it was.

Turning to the Wrights, we should appreciate that the first piloted and controlled gliders had been those of Otto Lilienthal, who worked in Germany from 1891 to 1896, when he was killed in a gliding accident,[21] so their efforts even in gliding were contemporaneous with those of the successful pioneers. The first manned glider had been Cayley's machine of 1852–1853, but the person on board was carried where the winds took him with locked controls, and that similarity to the conditions of the free balloon remained until Lilienthal's first success. What the glider did was to show the way to secure mechanical lift, using the power of the air flow, leaving still to be solved the matter of control of the machine and independence of direction in its movement. Wilbur Wright wrote later "my own active interest in aeronautical problems dates to the death of Lilienthal"—that is, to 1896. In the next several years the brothers sought to learn as much as was known about the flight of birds and what had been accomplished in glider operation. They became convinced that birds corrected for wind deflection and other distortions of their intended flight by the torsion of their wing tips, a practice the Wrights introduced to their gliders beginning in 1900. They tested these at Kitty Hawk on the Outer Banks of North Carolina, a site chosen from a list supplied them by the U.S. Weather Bureau of the places in the United States possessed of the strongest and most constant winds. At this point the force of the wind was still perceived as a necessary positive element in gaining powered flight. As Wilbur saw it at this time, "When once a machine is under proper control under all [wind] conditions, the motor problem will be quickly solved."[22]

Such was the case. In 1903 the Wrights set about building their first powered aeroplane, which, prophetically, they called the *Flyer* after the brand name of the bicycles they manufactured for a living. Throughout the fall of that year they conducted experiments at Kill Devil Hill at Kitty Hawk, and on December 17 they accomplished their immediate goal. This biplane, with a 40-foot, 4-inch wing span and a wing surface area of 510 square feet, had a 12-horsepower engine driving two pusher propellers of the Wrights' design. In a wind varying between 20 and 27 miles per hour, at 10:35 on that Thursday morning, Orville Wright became the first man ever to fly in an aeroplane, covering a distance of 120 feet in 12 seconds of sustained flight. During the same day other experiments increased the distance covered by this machine, operating at about 30 miles per hour, first to 175 feet and subsequently, in a fourth trial, to 852 feet in 59

seconds. Stowed for the night, the machine was wrecked by the heavy winds of that late December day on the Outer Banks. The Wrights gave up for the year and returned to Dayton, where they began constructing a new plane that might incorporate improvements based on their trials that wintry day. On May 26, 1904, at Huffman Prairie outside Dayton, they commenced trials of *Flyer No. 2*, and during that summer they accomplished 105 takeoffs. By November flights of 5 minutes duration, covering up to 2.75 miles in a circular course, had been accomplished. No considerable elevation was sought to minimize the dangers to the pilots of these first manned flights.[23]

The Wrights, as the only successful plane builders and aviators at this time, were careful to maintain considerable secrecy about the technical details of their several planes. This worked against them: the press published only modest and sometimes skeptical accounts of their activities. After further experiments in 1905 they gave up active trials for three years; by then they had secured patents on the fundamental improvements they had introduced. In 1907 they broke their secrecy when Wilbur Wright went to France to promote their latest plane; the next year actual flights were resumed, with startling results. Europeans had been experimenting with aeroplanes during the same years the Wrights had been laboring at Dayton and Kitty Hawk, but with very different results. A few short jumps had been accomplished; and, as Gibbs-Smith sees it, "One can only say that—for reasons unknown—there was, and there remained for a decade, a lamentable lack of vision amongst those Europeans in whom one would have expected to find it."[24]

Their lack of knowledge and experience, added to their impatience, bred a "slap-dash" and undisciplined approach which, over the years 1905 to 1908, resulted in a prodigious waste of effort, fruitless construction and testing of abortive machines and a multitude of blundering efforts to get off the ground. It is a melancholy duty to record that, with all the European pioneers continuously at work, they were still not able to construct and fly practical aeroplanes in any real sense until after Wilbur Wright had flown for all to see in France in the summer, autumn and winter of 1908.[25]

So does the leading British authority on the aeroplane summarize what came before Wilbur Wright's demonstrations of 1908.

Once he had shown the way, however, Europeans were quick to learn. The Wright machine was a biplane depending on the warping of the wings to give control and direction to the flight. A separate European approach grew up employing the monoplane, first externally stressed; but by 1910 Hugo Junkers in Germany had patented his thick-section cantilever wing that worked without external bracing by struts or wires.[26] The *aileron*, at first called a horizontal rudder, a hinged flat surface used to control lateral balance, was more widely applied in Europe than in America, although "There is now also no doubt that the modern invention of ailerons stems directly from the Wrights' warping, as the brothers had always maintained."[27] Still, the European refinements of the aeroplane produced the basic configuration that became virtually universal by 1940—a low-wing monoplane, cantilevered and controlled by ailerons as to lateral balance and directed by a vertical rudder in turning movements. The French aeronaut Louis Blériot began the development of the monoplane with his plane No. VII in 1907; two years later, in an improvement of that machine, he accomplished the first airplane crossing of the English Channel and gave the monoplane a lasting popularity.

The work of the Wrights in America and of Blériot, Henri Farman, and Gabriel Voisin in France represented the main successful elements in the creation of an economically significant aeroplane. By 1908 that utility had been demonstrated when the Wrights created the first two-seater plane that might be used for specialized commercial operations (the first passenger ever lofted was Charles W. Furnas of Dayton, at the Kill Devil Hill on May 14, 1908). A three-seater was developed and used by Blériot in June, 1909, setting the stage for the increase in passenger capacity that would make air transport a possibility.[28] Only five years later the first scheduled passenger air service was introduced over the 22-mile crossing of Tampa Bay between that city and St. Petersburg and was run for some weeks.[29] By then another American, Glenn Curtiss, had entered the ranks of the significant commercial pioneers. A bicycle maker, like the Wrights, Curtiss had participated during the first decade of this century in a consortium, which included Alexander Graham Bell, under the title Aerial Experiment Association, in an attempt to produce practical aeroplanes. In 1909 Curtiss had developed what proved to be a remarkably successful plane, the "1909 type" that won the Reims air race of that year with spectacular success. Striking out on his own, Curtiss, at Hammondsport, New York, began to build planes distinctive for their powerful engines. By 1914 he was working on a twin-engined seaplane that he intended to enter into the attempt to fly the Atlantic. Unfortunately, World War I interrupted that effort.[30] Still, before the outbreak of war in August of that year, the aeroplane had reached a stage of technical development that meant that the air-transportation industry was clearly in prospect. Only the Zeppelins were flying regularly, but the Tampa Bay aeroplane service had signaled the advent of heavier-than-air transport on a practical, continuing basis. No doubt that development would have continued apace without the war; because of it, the change came more rapidly.

This is not the place to consider the role of the aeroplane in World War I. We need note only that the demands placed on those machines for aerial warfare were such that significant improvements were wrought, particularly in the matter of providing striking increases in the power of the engines used to secure flight. In 1919 a Curtiss NC-4 flying boat accomplished the first aerial crossing of the Atlantic, between Newfoundland and Lisbon, with a stop in the Azores, under the command of Lieutenant Commander A. C. Read. A month later, in June, a nonstop flight from Newfoundland to Galway in Ireland was completed by British Captain J. Alcock and Lieutenant A. Whitten-Brown in 16 hours and 27 minutes for an average speed of 118.5 miles per hour in a converted Vickers *Vimy* bomber.[31]

During the 1920s the focus was on designing avowedly commercial aircraft, distinct from the warplanes of the beginning of the decade. Fokker in Holland sought to advance through the use of wooden, stressed-skin, high-wing monoplanes that gained wide acceptance. Junkers pushed the evolution of the metal stressed-skin monoplane, with a low wing that permitted a lighter undercarriage. But it was in the United States in the late 1920s that the most significant plane of the decade came from the builders. This Lockheed *Vega* of 1927 had radial engines of either 220 horsepower or 425 horsepower that could transport a pilot and six passengers at speeds between 110 and 135 miles per hour over distances ranging between 500 and 900 miles. The use of a wooden stressed skin permitted a 35-percent decrease in weight over the previous framework structure, with no loss of interior height and width. "The *Vega* set the fashion and the pace for this general-purpose type of aircraft,

and inspired a world-wide development, and its influence spread also to the design of larger aircraft."[32]

Once hostilities were ended, the demand for aircraft came from the emergence of a civil aviation industry. The Germans led the way with the Deutsche Luftreederie, which began service from Berlin to Leipsic and Weimar on February 5, 1919, followed only three days later by the French Farman Company, which started a Paris-London service using a converted *Goliath* bomber. In August the first daily service was established on this latter route, from Hounslow to Le Bourget, with a schedule of 2 hours 30 minues and a fare of £21.[33] This undertaking was carried out by a British firm, Aircraft Travel and Transport Company, using four-passenger versions of wartime aircraft. In October of that same year Albert Plesman established a Dutch airline, K.L.M., which in 1920 undertook a joint service with Aircraft Travel on the Amsterdam-London route.[34] Farman Airlines, the French operation, had flown the first trans-Channel service in 1919, and several other French companies had been among the first commercial aviation undertakings with diverse routes, among them a service from Toulouse to Barcelona flying across the Pyrenees.

Outside Europe this same period saw the creation of the Queensland and Northern Territory Aerial Services Limited in 1920, the base from which grew the Australian national airline, Qantas. In most European countries the 1920s witnessed the creation of subsidized national airlines—Sabena in 1923, Finnair (Aero Oy) in 1924, Lufthansa in 1926, and LOT, the Polish airline, in 1929. The major exception was the creation of a Swiss national carrier but by private owners, the formation of Swissair in 1931, which as a result of its nongovernmental status became the first European airline to purchase American-built planes.

The pattern of European civil air transport

was one of a functional intermixing of aircraft development and manufacture, largely in the interests of national defense, with airline operation to give a market for those aircraft in their civilian version. The British, French, and Germans in particular conceived their policies in these terms, though the Germans had to mask their interest in military planes after the Treaty of Versailles. Anthony Fokker, the Dutch engineer who had been the greatest designer of planes for the Kaiser's forces, in the early 1920s moved his operations to Hasbrouck Heights, New Jersey, across the river from New York City where the potential for plane manufacture seemed brighter.[35] In America, despite a considerable effort during 1917 and 1918 to build large numbers of planes and, even more important, the *Liberty* engines to power them, the peace brought no clear national policy for civil or military aviation. The Wrights and the companies associated with their interests, Glenn Curtiss, and several others continued to build planes—more for sport than for practical purposes as at least for several years the cheap availability of war-surplus planes depressed the market. Still, in America the absence of a national civil aviation policy and of an aggressive program of military aviation meant that free competition among plane builders was assured, along with a totally laissez-faire entrée to air transportation.

The contrast between Europe and the United States was striking: in Europe the emphasis was on international commercial flying, given the small territory of most states, and on the national subsidized airline as a market for the nation's planes. In the United States, in the absence of a subsidy, a policy, and a chosen set of aircraft builders, little coherent air transportation development took place. What did occur was of highly local significance. We have already noted the first of all civil aviation undertakings, the St. Petersburg-Tampa Air Boat Line organized by Thomas Benoist using a Curtiss flying boat that started the very first scheduled passenger transport on January 1, 1914, and in five months on a twice daily schedule carried some 1,200 passengers, at $5.00 each, and with complete safety.[36] After the war this pattern persisted. In June, 1920, Aero Limited (Aeromarine) began what proved a short-lived service between Miami and Bimini, Nassau, and Havana that carried some 2,200 people.[37] But an accident by a Miami taxi carried in which five passengers were killed effectively discouraged the market, leaving Aeromarine in a shambles. Other local services were started between Detroit and Cleveland. There appeared to be a strong preference in the United States among passengers for the use of flying boats, whose forced landing seemed less potentially fatal, so the earliest routes were usually restricted to overwater operation. This skew was further encouraged by the lack of appreciable capital costs in providing for flying-boat facilities and the relatively large payload that might be carried by these craft in an era when the weak undercarriages of land-based planes limited their size. In Europe this problem was less obvious because the existence of coherent national aviation policies meant that land facilities were more plentiful, and the high operating subsidies made larger payloads less essential.

In Europe the bilateral arrangements of the sort worked out between Aircraft Transport and Travel in Britain and K.L.M. in the Netherlands, when the Amsterdam-London service was inaugurated, became common. Most countries had a primate city that served as their point of attachment to an international network of flying. These could be, and usually were, quite different from the points attaching previous national systems of transportation together. Where Dover, Harwich, and Southampton had fulfilled that role for British rail operations, and

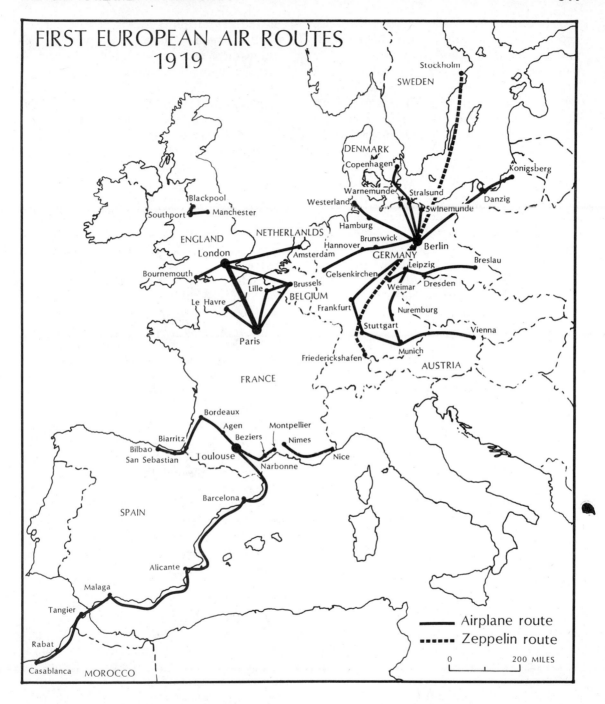

FIRST EUROPEAN AIR ROUTES 1919

SWEDEN
Stockholm

DENMARK
Copenhagen

Konigsberg

Blackpool
Southport Manchester

Warnemunde Stralsund
Westerland Swinemunde Danzig

Hamburg
ENGLAND NETHERLANLDS Brunswick
London Hannover Berlin
Amsterdam GERMANY Leipzig Breslau
Bournemouth Gelsenkirchen Weimar Dresden
Lille Brussels
BELGIUM Frankfurt Nuremburg
Le Havre Stuttgart Vienna
Munich
Paris Friederickshafen AUSTRIA

FRANCE

Bordeaux
Agen Montpellier
Biarritz Beziers Nimes
Bilbao Toulouse Nice
San Sebastian Narbonne

SPAIN Barcelona

Alicante

Malaga
Tangier

Rabat
Casablanca MOROCCO

——— Airplane route
▪▪▪▪ Zeppelin route

0   200 MILES

Calais or Le Havre accommodated France in the same way, now London (Hounslow) and Paris (Le Bourget) were directly reached; as were Amsterdam, Brussels, and Madrid as they never had been in a simple way by rail or sea. But the European pattern was a long-distance one only in a relative sense. The air distance from London to Paris is 209 miles, that to Amsterdam 230 miles—values little different from those between Boston and New York or Washington and New York, journeys we consider virtually local in scale. Even London to Berlin is only 591 miles, similar to the flight from New York to Detroit. Thus, what we are dealing with in the airways pattern of Europe in the 1920s is a much more rapid development of a comprehensive system, but still one with fairly short legs, and those largely both subsidized and restricted to a single, or at most a couple of cities in each country. There can be no doubt that modern air transport came first in Europe, but most of its problems were not very effectively solved there. Aircraft tended to be costly to operate, small in capacity and mostly derivative from military planes rather than designed mainly for commercial operations. The national subsidies got the service started in a very effective way: national restrictions tended to leave it technically cramped.

THE ADVENT OF AMERICAN CIVIL AVIATION

The American experience was quite different, apparently slow and awkward. Once the war was over, the United States joined all the other advanced countries in envisaging a rapid onset of air transportation. Without financial assistance from the central government, however, no passenger system of the sort Europe witnessed grew up. Instead , the American effort comprised two quite dissimilar efforts. There was the weak and faltering effort at the private development of passenger transportation by air, the fits and starts of which we have already noted. In addition there was a reasonably concerted effort directly by the government to introduce air-mail service. Between 1919, when it began, and 1925, the United States Post Office operated that flying service directly, hiring the pilots, providing the facilities, and operating the planes. Within a short time after service started, the routes were extended, to San Francisco from New York, to Miami and Havana from Boston, and with feeders from cities not on these two fundamental airways. At first the service could only operate during daylight hours, but given American distances that restriction severely curtailed the actual utility of air mail. Only as the Post Office came to install light beacons, at a spacing of about 20 miles, could night flying be introduced.[38] Because American air service was made up of these two separate components—private passenger companies and governmental air-mail lines—it was in the United States that much of the early development of both bad-weather and night flying took place. In Europe the joint passenger-mail operation, commonly by national carriers, meant that in questionable conditions or at night the planes remained grounded as passengers showed great reluctance in undertaking such journeys.[39] The need for operation under all conditions in America forced the development of instruments to give nonvisual guidance to these air-mail pilots, and causing them, in turn, to learn what came to be called blind-flying—that is, navigation by instruments rather than the observation of a relationship to the horizon.

By the mid-1920s a number of conditions were changing that rapidly brought forward the development of civil aviation. By then most of the wartime aircraft had been worn out or had crashed, and there was an increasing understanding that the secret of all-weather flying lay in stronger engines and airframes to hold them. Fokker developed the trimotor plane on the argument that two engines were twice as reliable as one, and three half again better, even disregarding the power they collectively produced. Western Air Express, a non-air-mail operation between Los Angeles (Glendale) and Oakland organized in 1925, was one of the first to employ these trimotors when they received a $180,000 grant from the Guggenheim Fund for the Advancement of Aeronautics that permitted the company to experiment with its equipment and the running of an airline totally dependent on earnings rather than subsidy.[40] All told, about a hundred of the Fokker trimotors were sold to airlines, and they began to create an industry with equipment sufficiently strong to undertake the very taxing job of providing long-distance, all-weather air transportation in the United States.

Another change that came in the mid-1920s fundamentally influenced the evolution of the American air-transport industry. That was the decision to open up air-mail transport to private carriers. This was done in part from a philosophical viewpoint—America was perhaps most favorably impressed by free enterprise in that decade—and in part from an increasing interest in securing a national passenger air transportation system, and in another part from the realization that the ultimate scale of air service was likely to be beyond the competence of any single organization. In 1925 Congressman Kelly of Pennsylvania introduced a bill calling for the opening of air-mail routes to private bidding. As the Kelly Act, this legistation became the cornerstone of the American civil aviation industry. Before its passage the United States cast a relatively small shadow on that industry worldwide, but after its enactment a number of airline companies were quickly founded in the United States that still stand as the largest in the Free World. At first their lineaments were

not clear, and certainly some did not survive as appreciable operations, but within a decade most of the trunk carriers of the present were operating over routes that are still distinguishable even in this time of airline laissez-faire. Perhaps even more strikingly, an outgrowth of the opening of civil aviation to private development in the United States was the sharp ratchet it applied to airplane development and construction. Up to 1925 Europe was certainly ahead in engineering and building, although Americans had even by then created the reputation for strength and adaptability in aircraft that they had earned for railroad engines and equipment during the preceding century. Once the transfer of the subsidized air-mail transport to private carriers took place under the Kelly Act, the American airframe and airplane-engine industries gained a lead in commercial craft construction that has held good for half a century.

Certainly Europeans were active both in airframe construction and in the operation of airlines. The French and British were beginning the evolution of very extensive networks of air service to serve their colonial empires, alignments that could be shaped earlier in the development of the airline industry than could those across the broad oceans because the *stage,* the length of practical single segments of any route, was still short enough to require numerous intermediate landings for fuel and servicing at a frequency too great to be accomplished in the broad ocean basins. "By the end of this decade, the larger three-engined airliners—biplanes and monoplanes—could carry some 15–20 passengers, a crew of two or three, and a small amount of freight, at cruising speeds of 90–110 m.p.h. over stages of 500 miles."[41] In 1919 approximately a million miles were flown, a figure that rose to 57 million at the end of the next decade, while the passengers increased from 5,000 in 1919 to 434,000 in 1929.[42] Largely as a result of

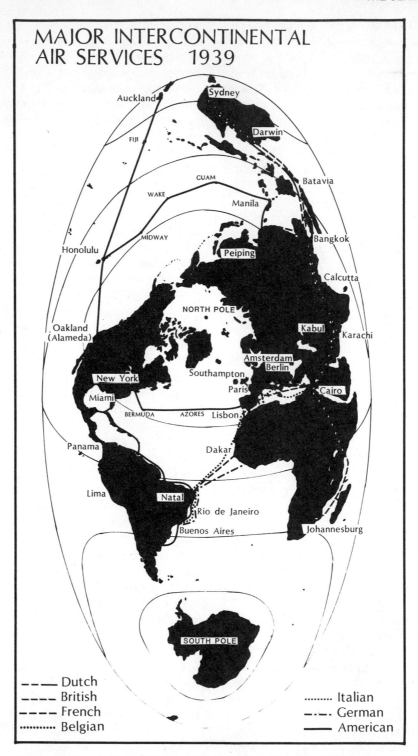

MAJOR INTERCONTINENTAL
AIR SERVICES   1939

Auckland
Sydney
FIJI
Darwin
GUAM
Batavia
WAKE
Manila
MIDWAY
Bangkok
Honolulu
Peiping
Calcutta
NORTH POLE
Oakland
(Alameda)
Kabul
Karachi
Amsterdam
Berlin
New York
Southampton
Miami
Paris
Cairo
BERMUDA   AZORES   Lisbon
Panama
Dakar
Lima
Natal
Rio de Janeiro
Buenos Aires
Johannesburg

SOUTH POLE

– – – Dutch
– – – British
– – – French
········· Belgian

········· Italian
–·–·– German
——— American

Source: R. E. G. Davies, *A History of World Airlines* (London, 1964).

Sperry's work in the United States, instrument flying became a reality by the end of the decade. "[O]n September 24th 1929, Lieut. James Doolittle, in a Sperry-equipped Consolidated NY-2 biplane, was able 'to take off, fly a specific course, and land without reference to the earth.'"[43] Instrument flying as it evolved between 1925 and 1935 served to make all airlines more reliable in their scheduling, a factor perhaps of greatest importance in the stormy and more overcast regions of the world where so many of the industrial nations lay.

Geographically most important in this technical evolution of the airlines was the matter of stage. So long as its upper limit remained around 500 miles, Britain and France held a strong position in the pioneering of long-distance routes. With convenient colonial possessions in North Africa, France could develop air service connecting the metropolitan country with its possessions even in Equatorial Africa. Britain was even better served by its territorial possessions. With Gibraltar and Malta as crown colonies; Palestine as a mandate; Trans-Jordan, Iraq, and the Gulf emirates as client states, the air passage to India by Imperial Airways, organized in 1924, could be created. Thence to Australia control of Burma and Malaya gave further usable stepping stones, leaving the ultimate key to through service to the lengthening of the stage sufficient to permit a hop from Singapore to Northern Australia. K.L.M. developed a similar route from Amsterdam to Batavia in the Dutch East Indies. By the 1930s these long-distance routes to central and southern Africa and southern and southeast Asia from Europe were opened, although the short stage of the planes kept schedules to a number of days and encouraged overnight stops in several places. Within Europe the distances were so relatively short that the technical demands on planes were fairly easy, a gentle condition that permitted domestic producers of aircraft

to fill the market even with what were planes not in the forefront of development. Germany probably had the most advanced aircraft industry, but restrictions on German aviation combined with the loss of its prewar empire to give a peculiar twist to her efforts at creating an international air system. Germany turned particularly to Latin America, notably to Colombia, shaping there what were equivalent to the colonial airways of Britain, France, and the Netherlands but doing so in what were privately owned—that is, German-owned—companies flying routes internal to Latin American countries. These were connected to Germany by the Zeppelin operations from Rio across the narrowest part of the Atlantic to Africa and Europe.

THE EVOLUTION OF THE MODERN AIRLINES IN AMERICA

Space forbids a detailed examination of all airlines. In making a selection among them for more extensive consideration, the tie between the airline industry and aircraft development serves as a useful sorting device. There is no question that the modern commercial airliner evolved in the United States, for the most part, and that its evolution and standardization in various periods can most succinctly be followed there. We have already seen the critical onset of this evolution in the Kelly Act of 1925, which opened the flying of mail to private operators, affording to them a government subsidy that gave both capital and stability to the industry. It is no accident that by about 1930 the state of the art in the production of commercial airliners was normally represented by the most economically successful American plane of the time. Europeans continued to make considerable technical contributions—the jet engine and the turboprop plane, for example—but they were very seldom able to shape an outstanding commercial aircraft from these contributions. And the Americans made so many perhaps less fundamental but collectively crucial technical contributions to aircraft design that not only was their business sense more advanced than Europe's, but they also tended to fill the technical gaps that lay between a fundamental invention and its practical utilization. We have already seen the basic contributions of Americans to instrument flying—that is, to the creation of all-weather airlines. Similarly, they contributed engines that, though perhaps not the most theoretically advanced, were by far the most powerful for their weight, cost, and operational simplicity. In the final analysis, geographical competence in airlines came from being able to fly in any weather and over longer distances, which could comprehend routes where closely placed stepping stones were not available, for either geographical or political reasons. Power also gave greater reliability and safety, speed and directness of routing, all commercial as well as competitive advantages, particularly in the first need of any airline—that is, to divert passengers from established means of transportation.

Starting with the Kelly Act, contractors were permitted to fly the feeders attached to the main trunk air-mail route, that from San Francisco to New York; in 1926 the trunk itself was advertised for private airline bids. To operate these contracts, it was desirable that better aircraft be used than were generally available. William Boeing, an aircraft builder from Seattle, who had some experience in operating between that city and Victoria, entered an extremely low bid, $1.50 per pound of air mail, for the western segment of the trunk, Chicago to the Bay Area. To accomplish that transportation for such a figure, it was necessary for him to improve on his experimental air-mail plane, the number 40, by installing better power. This was found in the newly developed Pratt & Whitney *Wasp* engine of air-cooled radial design.[44] The combination proved effective,

and the rapid and competitive improvement of commercial aircraft had begun. Because Boeing was interested in plane manufacture, he sought to make his profit as much from that operation as from the running of the Boeing Air Transport Company that successfully bid on the trunk-line contract. Such a transfer of costs was common in American wholesaling but was novel in transportation, a fact that led within a decade to the forced separation of aircraft builders from airline operation because of fear of monopoly power.

The same bidding practice that gave Boeing Air Transport the western half of the trunk line shaped the rest of the original civil aviation network of the United States. "Of the handful of major laws Congress has passed relating to aeronautics, the Kelly Act is the most important in one respect: it fathered the airlines. It provided aviation interests with the incentive to form operating companies, and it encouraged capital to invest in them. . . . The first five contracts were awarded by Postmaster General New on October 7, 1925."[45] Yet it was not one of those contractors who started the first airline. That honor went to Henry Ford, who had been building a plane for several years and had been employing it in an operation that tied Detroit eastward to Cleveland and westward to Chicago. With that experience and a sturdy trimotor to do the job (some say remarkably similar in many details to the Fokker trimotor that Admiral Byrd parked in the motor builder's Dearborn hangar one night), Ford could establish scheduled operations on the route he was already flying but now with an air-mail contract. By the end of 1926 there were twelve air-mail routes on which commercial carriers were providing service, some of them carrying a few passengers in the process. By the following year the "Columbia Route," the trunk line, had been let in its two segments, the western to Boeing Air Transport, as we have seen.

Fundamental change came in 1929, when Walter Folger Brown was appointed postmaster general by Herbert Hoover. Hoover's son was involved in Western Air Transport; and while the Great Engineer was previously serving as Secretary of Commerce in the second Coolidge administration, he had been instrumental in the appointment of the Morrow Commission, given the job of making recommendations as to American aviation policy. One of the basic recommendations of that commission had been that the federal government should encourage civil aviation, as it essentially had not done up to that time. The lighting and marking of the commercial and mail airways, a job given the Lighthouse Service, was undertaken. In addition, intermediate emergency landing fields were constructed.

The successful solo trans-Atlantic flight that Lindbergh accomplished in 1927 so fired the popular imagination that both capital and passengers were volunteered to the airline industry in unheard of amounts in the last two years of the decade. To encourage the development of commercial airlines as distinct from air-mail contractors, Postmaster General Brown came up with the proposal, adopted by Congress in 1929, that subsequent contracts be given not in terms of so much money per pound of air mail carried but instead on the basis of the carrying capacity made available for the transport of mail.

The net effect of Brown's proposal was to shift the interests of the nascent airlines toward larger planes, ostensibly able to carry great amounts of air mail but, that not availing, usable for the transport of passengers, if they offered themselves. And in the Lindberg euphoria they were doing so in increasing numbers. With the flood of capital into airlines, encouraged by the organization of three aviation holding companies during the frantic last year of the Boom, there was for the first time the money to spend on absolutely modern and powerful planes. These holding companies were typical of their time: they tied together a number of the previously segmental airlines and united them to major manufacturers of aircraft and their components. The United Aircraft and Transport Company organized in late 1928 comprised Boeing Airplane, Pratt & Whitney engines, Hamilton propeller, and Boeing Air Transportation, to which were soon added Sikorsky, Northrup, and Stearman aircraft, Standard Steel Propeller, and Stout Airlines.[46] This arrangement created the cross-subsidization of operation by manufacture that had proved so fertile in the growth of wholesaling.

The three holding companies adopted somewhat different strategies, each with a distinct geographical rationale. United Aircraft and Transport sought to shape the first transcontinental airway, using its western holdings, of the Chicago–San Francisco segment of the Columbia Route and a north-south route along the West Coast, as the base. Through astute stock manipulation the company gained control of National Air Transport, contractor for the eastern half of the trunk. That carrier had not been notable for its passenger operations, charging a very heavy $150 to carry a passenger from Chicago to New York in 1927.[47] But in the hands of the transformed Boeing interests, National gave them both control of the most important air-mail contract and the first effective transcontinental passenger route. Out of the five airlines came a single company, United Airlines, with headquarters in Chicago that set about developing the passenger business along the Columbia Route of the air-mail network. This integration of aircraft production and air-transport operation became the model others sought to emulate, most notably the financiers of Wall Street who saw in the "aviations" a new bonanza to reward speculation on the pattern of the railroad of the nineteenth century and the "traction" mag-

The Sikorsky S-42 Flying-boat. Pan American World Airways photograph.

nates of the earlier twentieth century. The rather adventitious combination of companies that United Aircraft and Transport had assembled gave to United Airlines a particular goegraphy. The trunk air-mail route was the main stem of the company. To that was added a north-south line from Vancouver on the north to Los Angeles on the south, and some other feeders that had fallen under their contol. But in substantial measure the central trunk route was the basis for the airline, extending from New York across Pennsylvania through the northern Middle West to Chicago, Des Moines, Omaha, Cheyenne, Salt Lake City, Elko, Reno, and the Bay Area.

The other major holding companies were the Aviation Corporation, which combined North American and Curtiss aircraft builders with an assortment of lines that came to be known as American Airways; and North American Aviation, controlled by General Motors, which held a 47.5 percent interest in Transcontinental Air Transport and a controlling one in Eastern Air Transport. Taking the latter holding company first, Transcontinental Air Transport had been conceived of as the companion of the Pullman car on the route from New York to Los Angeles when it entered service in the summer of 1929. The president of the Pennsylvania Railroad, General W.W. Atterbury, had cooperated en-

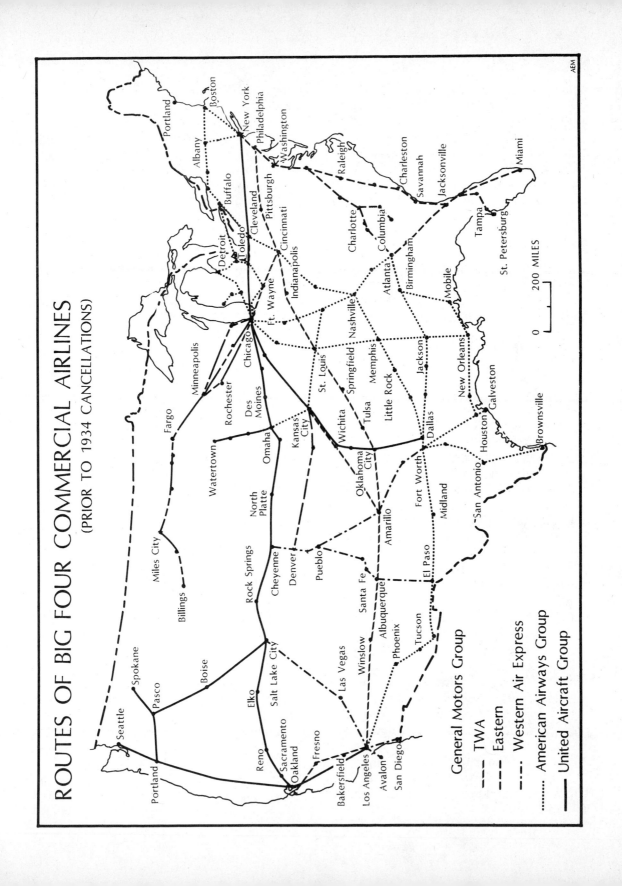

ROUTES OF BIG FOUR COMMERCIAL AIRLINES
(PRIOR TO 1934 CANCELLATIONS)

General Motors Group
- TWA
- Eastern
- Western Air Express

American Airways Group
United Aircraft Group

0   200 MILES

AEM

thusiastically in the conception of the service along with its originator, Clement Keys. The fundamental strategy they had adopted was based on two logical assumptions for the time: that night flying was not practical for passengers and that the crossing of the Appalachians, and probably the Rockies, was so dangerous as to be beyond the competence of a passenger airline. Given those assumptions, the plan was worked out, calling for a departure from Pennsylvania Station, New York, on the "Airway Limited" at 6:05 P.M. reaching Port Columbus, Ohio, at 7:35 A.M. using Pullman sleepers as transport. Air travel was commenced at the Columbus Municipal Airport at 8:15 A.M. using Ford Trimotor planes carrying ten passengers with stops at Indianapolis, St. Louis, Kansas City, and Wichita, to the airport at Waynoka, Oklahoma, at precisely 6:24 P.M. There passengers would board the Santa Fe Railway's "The Missionary" at 11:00 P.M. on sleepers for an arrival at Clovis, New Mexico, at 8:20 A.M. With the return of daylight, air travel was resumed at 8:10 A.M. at "Portair" in Clovis, the seeming discrepancy resulting from the fact that the railroad counted its arrival in Central Time, whereas the T.A.T. plane left on Mountain Time. Waystops were made at Albuquerque, Winslow, Kingman, and Los Angeles, with the final destination of the plane at San Francisco at 7:45 P.M. The initial rate was $338.10, with meals charged extra.[48]

The third holding company, Aviation Corporation, had assembled a disparate group of airlines extending from Cleveland southwesterly to Garden City, Kansas, and San Angelo, Texas, in late 1929. This assemblage was further enlarged in the next several years. Colonial Air Lines, the original contractor for Air Mail Route No. 1 between Boston and New York, had been organized by Boston capitalists in league with Juan Trippe and several other recent graduates of Yale interested in flying. On June 18, 1926,

they had commenced a service that earned $1,000 per trip from the Post Office, but the enthusiasts, eager to develop passenger business, ordered some Fokker trimotors to provide both more comfort and more power and reliability. That aggressive approach led Trippe to seek to bid on the eastern segment of the Columbia Route when it was opened for private operation, but his capitalist backers would not hear of it, so he parted company with this incipient domestic carrier and turned his driving attention to service outside America's borders. Colonial Air Lines remained a local operation until it was swept up in the mergers of the early 1930s by the Aviation Corporation, which sought to match the consolidations of United Aircraft and Transportation and North American. A similar fate befell Robertson Aircraft Corporation, the contractor for Air Mail Route No. 2 between Chicago and St. Louis. In 1930 the collection operation had been sufficiently successful for the organization of American Airways and the formal promulgation of a policy calling for a third transcontinental airway along a fairly southern route.[49] At first there were no through connections either to New York or to Los Angeles, the chosen termini, so Universal Air Lines (as it was called in late 1929) established a schedule similar to that of T.A.T., save for the fact that common cause was made with the New York Central and Boston and Albany. Trains were used from Boston and New York to Cleveland where air service commenced at 7:10 the next morning, passing via Chicago and Kansas City to Garden City, Kansas, reached at 6:20 P.M. Thence the Santa Fe Railway was used all the way to Los Angeles, though a branch airway continued via Universal Air Express from Kansas City to Wichita and Tulsa, and a connection through a captive Braniff Air Lines to Dallas. When organized in 1930, American Airways, as the Aviation Corporation's chosen instrument, aggressively extended this network, seeking to force all air lines in the southern United States into the American compound. Some, however, managed to escape, among them Braniff, which had an independent existence until May, 1982, when it fell into bankruptcy. At that time Braniff had sought a court injunction against American Airlines, arguing that American was using unfair practices to try to force Braniff into receivership.[50] Such was the legacy of the rather buccaneering efforts of the Aviation Corporation in the early 1930s.

Within a couple of years the three trunk carriers—T.A.T., United, and American—had accomplished their objective of shaping this triad of airlines. In that effort they were greatly aided by Walter Folger Brown as postmaster general. In that office he made it extremely clear that he wanted a few very strong carriers; he awarded air-mail contracts, and thereby subsidies, to gain that end. The result was that most of the pioneering operation fell into four big companies: United, Transcontinental and Western (a merger between T.A.T. and Western Air Transport forced by Brown), American, and Eastern Air Transport (a line serving the East Coast route from New York to Miami). Elsewhere there were some small outfits serving local demands—Braniff in Texas, free of American's clutches; Northwest between Chicago and Minneapolis; and Delta centered in and around Birmingham at that time. But the evolution of aircraft and of the practices of American flying came mostly at the hands of the Big Four and their foreign-service peer, Pan American Airways.

As conceived by Walter Folger Brown and the financiers of the three large holding companies, concentration was the rationale in this first phase of commercial air development. The same philosophy affected international connections. No doubt influenced in part by European practice, where the national airline was the instrument of most commercial development, with a large part of the operation falling within the scope of international flying due to the small extent of the nations, Postmaster General Brown enunciated the concept of the "chosen instrument" for American air ties with other nations. But before taking up that policy we should examine the origin of foreign flying by American companies. We have already noted that one of the first American air lines to be attempted at the close of World War I was the Aeromarine operation between Key West and Havana. The Caribbean offered unusual opportunities for flying in that the weather was normally reasonably good, the islands were close enough together so the short stage of the aircraft of the 1920s still provided practical service, and the existence of Prohibition in the United States encouraged tourist travel to this area. It was not until the late 1920s, however, that serious and sustained efforts occurred in this area. The same interest on the part of financiers that shaped the three domestic airline holding companies in these years led, with fits and starts, to the shaping of an overriding holding company in hemispheric commercial air navigation. That company, Aviation Corporation of the Americas, was an outgrowth of the same interested group of northeastern "aerial sportsmen" and investors who had created Colonial Air Transport to fly between Boston and New York, a group focusing on Juan Trippe. When he and his supporters failed to interest the conservative Boston bankers in bidding for the Chicago–New York segment of the Columbia Route, the young sportsmen sold out and turned their attention toward finding a new route to conquer. Eventually they settled on the Caribbean and on the prospective air-mail contract from Key West to Havana. Starting in 1927 they sought to tie up that route, but they found that another group of adventurous capitalists had organized Pan American, Incorporated, with designs on the tropical service. After considerable financial buccaneering, the Aviation Corporation of the Americas group gained the field by securing exclusive landing rights in Cuba, an obvious necessity for any such operation, thereby forcing a merger on Pan American. That title seemed definitely preferable to the other, which might easily be confused with what became the "American" route across the South, so in 1930 the successor company adopted it. It was the air-mail contracts that made these Caribbean operations possible, and it was the considerable Republican political connections of the aerial sportsmen and their Wall Street backers that secured them those contracts. Under Postmaster General New in the Coolidge administration, the group that gained control of Pan American secured first the Key West–to–Havana air-mail contract, later extended to Miami and interconnection with the domestic network of air commerce, and then a route onward to Haiti, the Dominican Republic, and Puerto Rico.

With the active encouragement of the Post Office, as the instrument for developing commercial aviation in the United States, Juan Trippe and his Pan American airline rapidly expanded the American aviation network across the Caribbean—to Panama via Nicaragua and Costa Rica; to Guatamala via Mexico from Brownsville, Texas; and from Miami via Havana, Haiti, the Dominican Republic, Puerto Rico, and the Lesser Antillies to Trinidad and the Guianas. This had been accomplished during the late 1920s, leaving Pan Am on the northern approaches to South American but with only very limited operations there. In this same period the potential competition between W. R. Grace and Company, the American mercantile-shipping giant on the West Coast of South America, and Pan Am had been overcome by the creation of Panagra airlines, a joint company. Their field of operation lay south of Colombia, while Pan Am's lay north thereof, leaving a gap across

that republic that viewed American proposals with very great reserve after Theodore Roosevelt's activities in Panama. To tie the West Coast Route together, Pan Am had somehow to gain transit of Colombia. That was done by secretly purchasing 80 percent of the locally operated but German-owned airline SCADTA's stock, removing their opposition, and gaining Colombian acceptance of the completion of an American-operated airline extending from Panama to Chile. Through the Kellogg-Olaya Pact of 1929, the first bilateral aviation treaty of the United States, both Colombia and the United States were permitted to operate flights from one country to almost any point in the other—a most generous provision that the Americans assumed was unlikely to be exercised by the Colombians.[51]

The East Coast Route in South America had been developed in a less friendly fashion. Other New York interests had organized the New York, Rio, and Buenos Aires Airways (N.Y.R.B.A.) which in January, 1929, proposed a weekly service over the 7,000 miles between its announced termini using "nine-ton, twin-engine flying boats that could carry a three-thousand pound load six hundred miles without refueling." Possessed of the Argentine, Uruguayan, and Brazilian air-mail contracts to the United States, N.Y.R.B.A. thought its route established. But they reckoned without Juan Trippe, who viewed South American air space as reserved commercially for Pan Am. After much infighting in the halls of the Post Office and the skies of South America, Pan Am succeeded in forcing N.Y.R.B.A. to sell out to them, and the East Coast Route was established in concert with the other American foreign services. The principle of the "chosen instrument" of international commercial flying for the United States was firmly established.

The most striking geographical constraint on the extension of American domestic routes came in transoceanic flying. Although the first trans-Atlantic flight was made in 1919 and the initial trans-Pacific one in 1924,[52] there was no commercial plane capable of flying stages of sufficient length to contemplate transoceanic flying at this time. We should not forget that the N.Y.R.B.A. flying boats first used on the East Coast of South America Route had a stage of only 600 miles, nowhere nearly sufficient to permit oceanic service. For the Atlantic the stage had to be increased to at least 1,800 miles for successful operation, whereas on the Pacific it seemed that a stage of at least 2,400 miles was required. In a later section we shall discuss this specific problem of oceanic flying. For now it is necessary to look at the evolution of aircraft in terms of land flying and with much more restricted stages.

In America the scale of the domestic market, both geographically and in potential plane sales, was such that planes capable of dealing with long-distance and long-stage flying (and many of those craft that were successful) became a potentially profitable undertaking. No European country could have anticipated effectively developing such a market. Britain and France each had an empire that might be served with such craft, but neither would have wished to purchase many planes from the other. The German operations in South America were seen as a market for German-built aircraft. It is hard to believe that Postmaster General Brown made his decisions as to subsidies on the basis of careful analysis of the situation, particularly as the main motivation seems to have been to avoid the early problems of American railroads with their short and locally oriented (first- and second-phase) lines. But he obviously made a lucky decision, if not a wise one. By encouraging capacity rather than actual transport of mail and by sacrificing Post Office objectives to those of passenger transportation, he gave the critical boost to American commercial

aircraft production. For half a century the lead gained then has been held, and only in the last few years has there been even any serious challenge to that supremacy.

The American lead was not immediately acknowledged. During the 1930s European countries sought to protect and advance their own aircraft companies, probably mainly to give the basis for the construction of military craft, which during that decade were the prime concern of Europeans. But the European planes of the 1930s were on the whole ineffective technical competition for American builders. Even in the later part of the decade Britain was unable to join in the necessary bilateral agreements with the Americans to permit trans-Atlantic flying because there was no British plane capable of commercial operation on the route, whereas there clearly was such an American craft after about 1935. So when we here discuss the evolution of the commercial plane almost wholly in American terms, we are examining what is for us fundamentally a geographical question in its most appropriate terms.

THE ADVENT OF THE MODERN AIRLINER

By the mid-1920s a distinctive commercial airliner was emerging in the first of a series of conjunctions that have characterized aircraft building. The explanation is not hard to find for these general agreements: given the close relationship between the technical competence of a plane and the sort of service that may be offered and the competitive nature of the industry, it is not surprising that the introduction of a technical advance allowing improved service—in speed, comfort, stage length, ability to fly at night or in bad weather, or cost—makes all operators anxious to offer that improvement. This anxiety exists far more in the United States than in most countries because here the absence of a chosen or a national domestic instrument has meant that service is often the main difference between one company's flights and those of its competitor's. And there have been competitors in domestic service since the late 1920s. At first the competition came only on very long-distance connections, such as between the coasts, but before very many years subcontinental links, such as Chicago to New York, also were characterized by choice. This was an ideal climate for innovation and for its rapid dissemination.

The plane that transformed air service in the late 1920s was the trimotor, a craft of greater reliability and safety in a time when engines were notably cranky. The combination of multiple engines and low landing speeds meant that the failure of an engine, or even two, was not necessarily fatal. The maneuverability of the plane could be maintained by a single engine, and the slow landing speed meant that only a relatively short field was needed to survive a forced landing. So important was this development that it has been said that "The first big improvement in the airplanes used came around 1924–25, with the introduction of trimotors that could fly after one engine had failed." As German routes were gaining passengers faster than the costly British runs to India, the smaller Junkers and Fokker monoplane trimotors were the most commonly used. Still, they cruised at around 90 to 95 miles per hour and it was only with the building of the Ford Trimotor, copied from these European prototypes but somewhat improved with an all-metal skin and better aerodynamic qualities, that speeds above 100 were reached—105 miles per hour with the 1926 model and 120 with the 1928 model. "American radial engines were already superior to European designs,"[53] so advances in Europe were won mostly at the cost of three- and four-engine planes while in the United States the powerful single-engine plane, such as Lindberg's Ryan monoplane

Spirit of St. Louis, offered the hope of avoiding much of the complication of the multi-engined planes of Europe. But in the mid-1920s, when Henry Ford decided to get into aircraft construction, he did it by copying the latest in European notions; he merely made his copy a better commercial craft than had the originators.

The commercial success of the Ford Trimotor encouraged the first efforts at passenger transport in the United States. That plane, however, lacked several commercially desirable qualities. By 1929 the production of civil aircraft in the United States had risen to 5,500 from only 60 five years before, and the next year the Watres Act provided bonuses for the number of passenger seats available on air-mail planes and the use of multiple engines.[54] Those bonuses began the rapid expansion of airlines and the purchase of advanced aircraft, those that began to make up some of the deficiencies of the early trimotors. The Lockheed Vega of 1927 was a "more advanced design—a high-wing cantilever monoplane, it came close to modern designs in aerodynamic efficiency, and brought the cruising speed of a commercial airplane up to 150 m.p.h. The Vega was made of plywood and could carry only four to six passengers...."[55] But the existing stock of Ford Trimotors depressed the market for new planes, so it was only in 1930 (with the provisions of the Watres Act) that matters began to change. The Northrop Alpha and the Boeing Monomail had demonstrated the virtues of all-metal, low-wing monoplanes, the latter with a retractable landing gear by 1930, but only in 1933 had the market developed sufficiently to encourage the marketing of planes with those qualities.

Most experts view the Boeing 247 as the first of the modern generation of airliners. As designed it accepted the fact that had been established, that twin-engine planes were actually safer than trimotors— because they not only could be maneuvered but actually could be flown on a single engine—and it incorporated most of the technical improvements accomplished in the five years before it was first built in 1933. Carrying ten passengers, at a speed of 155 miles per hour, this all-metal, low-wing monoplane appealed to United Air Lines, which ordered sixty from its then fraternal aircraft builder. Transcontinental and Western Air Lines immediately sensed a competitive improvement in service and asked Boeing if it might gain some access to the first planes to be built. The builder refused, and the carrier on the Los Angeles to New York route turned to another aircraft company, Douglas, thus launching a second and competitive model seeking to reflect the state of the art in commercial airliner construction. From that competitive effort came the DC-1, produced later in 1933. That craft gained speed, cruising at 170 miles per hour; and its production model, the DC-2 of 1934, increased the payload to 14 passengers. As the later plane, the DC-2 gained an advantage that still often is found in aircraft construction—the chance to incorporate improvements in the later plane, the need or nature of which is learned from the earlier entrant in a marketing race. As a result, no more than 75 Boeing 247s were sold, but 220 DC-2s entered service.[56] The rapid introduction of new planes in 1933 and 1934 forced the competitive pace in an industry where private corporations visualized loss of business if they failed to make changes and change came to be seen largely in terms of service. It was in that context that the greatest of all airplanes, the DC-3, came into production and use.

THE GREAT DC-3

The geographical conditions in American commercial flying proved the sire of this monumental plane. The key lay in the desire to shape an aircraft that could offer service advantages in transcontinental flying, something crucial in the formation of an American pattern in contrast to a European one. In such long-distance service over land, the actual stage length was not as important as speed and all-weather, all-hour flying ability. The prototypical DC-1, built for sale as the DC-2, used a stressed-skin metal construction that gave unusual strength in relation to weight, which increased the energy efficiency of the plane, cheapening its operating costs. To understand the genesis of this and other contemporary planes under construction by American aircraft builders, we must reiterate that in the early 1930s the United Aircraft group, specifically its United Air Lines and Boeing aircraft construction components, had gotten together on the design of such a stressed-skin, all-metal, low-wing monoplane. The Boeing 247 that emerged in service in 1933 was a sleek plane capable of carrying ten passengers across the country in 19 hours. The retractable landing gear improved the appearance as well as increasing the aerodynamic efficiency, as did the N.A.C.A. cowl covering the two radial engines set into the wing. Thus, "The year 1933 marked a milestone in air transportation when United put the revolutionary Boeing 247's into service. They immediately outmoded all passenger airplanes then in service. . . ."[57]

Unable to buy 247s from Boeing, Jack Frye, vice-president of Transcontinental and Western, on August 2, 1932, sent a letter to the other major American aircraft builders "exploring the possibilities of an aircraft to use on its transcontinental routes in place of the Ford and Fokker Trimotors then in service." Douglas aircraft quickly picked up on this enquiry and "On July 1, 1933, eleven months from the date of Frye's letter, the prototype DC-1 was flown."[58] It proved even more advanced than the 247s, so it was quickly put in production as the DC-2, and 220 were ultimately built. The speed of development—less than a year—and the development costs—only $306,778—must startle us today in an era when years and hundreds of millions of dollars are involved in the launching of a fully new model. Before quantity production was undertaken the Wright engine company had improved the original 1820-F engine used in the prototype, building the 1820-F3 with increased power. That accomplishment allowed the DC-2 to loft a heavier payload and operate at a lower cost. So successful was the production model that many were sold in Europe, particularly to K.L.M., with its greater independence of national aircraft monopolies. It was that operator which entered a DC-3 in the 1934 McRobertson Air Race from London to Melbourne, coming in second (after a specially built deHavilland Comet racer) despite carrying a crew, six passengers, and 400 pounds of mail, in a time of 90 hours and 17 minutes.[59]

This demonstration gave the Douglas company a great lift as a commercial aircraft builder (the DC-1 was the first they had ever attempted). Their initial order by Transcontinental and Western had been for 26 planes, subsequently enlarged to 41, and other lines quickly followed after the Australia race. The first DC-2 was put in service on the Newark-Pittsburgh-Chicago run for Transcontinental, and that company bested United's time to Chicago, in 247s, by half an hour at 5 hours. United replaced their own engines by more powerful models, but still the Douglas craft held the edge. And they were cheaper to operate, as had been demonstrated when both the DC-2 and the 247 competed in the Australian air race. It was in that favorable circumstance that the aircraft builder was approached by C. R. Smith of American Airlines asking for the first clear example of what has become a common practice: the "stretching" of aircraft. The term implies the maintenance of the basic design qualities of a craft but their enlargement to gain various ends. In this first instance, what Smith sought for his company was a plane sufficiently enlarged to permit the installation of berths for overnight flights, such that the transcontinental run could be made to seem shorter to the sleeping passengers. To gain the space for berths, the fuselage had to be widened to a dimension similar to that of the Curtiss Condors the operator had introduced in a sleeper service between Chicago and New York in 1934. As those planes were considerably slower than the DC-2s, they did not seem competitive on the much longer transcontinental run.

The Douglas efforts led to the DST, Douglas Sleeper Transport, a plane with an improvement in operating cost, due again to improved engines (the Wright 1820-G2 or Pratt and Whitney 1830, each with 1,000 horsepower). "This was . . . the first American transport to show a favorable net difference between costs and revenues at reasonable load factors and for a substantial spread of operating ranges."[60] The specialized sleeper version of the stretch had a limited market, but the twenty-one-passenger regular version was an immediate success. Miller and Sawers have shown that this ordinary version, called the DC-3, had seat-mile operating costs that ranged from 33 to 50 percent below those of planes operating in 1935. American Airlines was the first to buy and fly the DC-3, putting it in service on the Chicago–New York run on June 25, 1936. The experience of the carrier was so favorable that C. R. Smith held that "The DC-3 freed the airlines from complete dependence upon government mail pay. It was the first airplane that could make money by just hauling passengers."[61] With the possible exception of the first American jet, the Boeing 707, no plane's success was so immediate and so complete. Within two years DC-3s were carrying 95 percent of all air passengers in the United States and were in use on thirty foreign airlines. With these aircraft, nonstop service between Chicago and New York was

The DC-3. Trans-World Airlines photograph.

introduced, though it did not prove a commercial success, because of the extra fare of $2.05! The success of the DC-3 came certainly from the quality of its airframe design but as well from the improved engines it used, the variable-pitch propeller incorporated, and improvements in fuels.[62]

AMERICAN FLYING BECOMES MORE OPEN

The geographical pattern of flying introduced by the DC-3 had two crucial components. The first came from its great improvement in operating costs, which allowed air service to reach to a greater number of places, those previously submarginal in the working by more costly planes. The other was the result of the introduction of practical commercial flying independent of air-mail payments, an innovation we have already noted in the words of American Airline's president. For the first time companies that had been frozen out by Walter Folger Brown's policy of lending Post Office aid only to the few strongest operators could try to enter commercial aviation. It is not without significance that the last increment to the body of trunk-line carriers in domestic service in the United States came between 1936 and 1938, the period of the introduction of the DC-3. Only when federal regulation of airlines was virtually abolished in 1978 was there any resumption of the founding of these mainline air carriers. It was the early trunk carriers—United, Transcontinental and Western, American, and Eastern—and the group founded or significantly enlarged with the onset of practical passenger transport by air—Delta, Northwest, Continental, Western, and Braniff—that shaped the commercial air network of the United States. Some of the second group had been founded in the late 1920s as had the original Big Four—Delta, for example, had then been a local service and crop-dusting outfit centered on northern Mississippi and Alabama from a base at Birmingham; Northwest had garnered the Chicago–Minneapolis air-mail route; and Braniff had been founded in 1928 with the hope of gaining the Dallas to Atlanta airmail route. But the large aviation holding companies in cooperation—some said collusion—with the Post Office Department had pretty much restricted their scope. Before they could gain much of a role in the American airline industry, two things had to happen. The first was the development of a plane that could make passenger flying without subsidy feasible, and the DC-3 handsomely provided that.

The other necessity was an opening up of the industry to easier entrée and to competitive bidding for air-mail routes, with their attached subsidies. It was the New Deal that accomplished this second requisite. When Franklin Roosevelt entered the White House in 1933, he and his aides gave a critical examination of many of the acts of the Coolidge and Hoover administrations with respect to big business, which after 1927 clearly included the "aviations." A Senate committee under the chairmanship of Hugo Black of Alabama began examining the matter of

Post Office subsidies to the airlines. Without going into detail, it may be noted that the conclusion was that Postmaster General Brown and the representatives of the Big Four had gotten together, perhaps technically legally under the antitrust laws, but obviously seeking to structure the industry oligopolistically. Responding to this conclusion, F.D.R. ordered the suspension of all air-mail payments and the flying of the mail by the Army Air Corps. Thus in late January, 1934, the structure that Brown had imposed on the aviation holding companies was ostensibly in a shambles. The Black Committee had clearly demonstrated the paternity of the American network by forcing Vice-President L. H. Brittin of Northwest Airways to read a copy of a letter he had sent but destroyed (the copy reconstructed from scraps taken from a search of three hundred bags of wastepaper). That letter described the situation in Washington:

> The airmail contractors are having a desperate time in Washington. The Postmaster General was not able to get the necessary legislation in the Watres Bill [of 1930] to enable him to grant airmail contracts to the passenger-carrying airlines without competitive bids. He has made up his mind to do this anyway, and has hit upon a plan that is causing the operators no end of trouble. He has conceived, probably in iniquity, a plan for three main transcontinental routes competitively operating, and several north-and-south lines as well. To work things out he called the operators together, handed them this map and instructed them to settle among themselves the distribution of these routes. They have been meeting every day for two weeks and to date they have arrived nowhere. The Postmaster General meets with them about once a week, stirs them up and keeps them going.[63]

But in the end Brown had his way. United held on to its existing transcontinental route; and what was then Transcontinental Air

Transport, the pioneers of the central route with their air-rail combination already detailed, engaged in a shotgun marriage with Western Air Transport, between Salt Lake City and Los Angeles, with Brown holding the arms, to form Transcontinental and Western Air to provide a second coast-to-coast operator. In the South conditions were chaotic, although the Aviation Corporation had gobbled up a number of short-line companies and held such a dominant position that Wall Street would not countenance the rise of a competitor.

Aviation Corporation had grown out of a collaboration between Averell Harriman, seeking in the aviations to match his father's accomplishments in rails, and Robert Lehman of the banking family. After Lindberg's flight they had accumulated $38 million through the sale of stock and set out on a shopping spree for an airframe company, one making engines, control of airports, and a number of small airlines. Subsequently they lost control to E. L. Cord, and it was he who brought some order to the route network. Still, it was awkward, and Postmaster General Brown exerted pressure, such as that on Braniff and Delta, to try for a better alignment for this holding company. But in the end, after the painful bargaining session in Washington, American Airlines (as it had become) gained the only transcontinental route that might also be thought of as pan-American, as it touched both Canada and Mexico, the former at Buffalo and the latter at El Paso.[64] In such a circuitous fashion American set out to serve the "southern trans-continental route."

Here we must introduce a parenthetical note. American, because of this geographical circuity had to seek some service innovation to compete with United and Transcontinental and Western in the coast-to-coast market. The instrument they used was the sleeper plane, the theory being that they would make a virtue of their much longer schedules

by flying much of the distance at night. Curtiss Condors were fitted out with berths and a lumbering service begun. Using the upstate New York air-mail route via Buffalo, the Chicago–New York run was made to take all night. In similar fashion, the route from Chicago to Los Angeles via El Paso in crossing the Guadalupe Mountains of west Texas often encountered clouds, and the Condors were so underpowered that they were forced to land passengers on the eastern side of the crest; American would then bus them to the west, where flight might be resumed. Such was the jerry-built nature of American Airways even after it had won its route in the political halls of Washington.

It was to overcome those problems that C. R. Smith (the president of American) went to Donald Douglas in 1935 seeking a new plane that could carry fourteen berths and fly over the Guadalupes. From that request grew the DC-3 [DST], which changed American from a politically derived, Rube Goldberg contrivance to the largest transporter of air passengers in the United States within two years of the initial purchase. The airline industry as a whole gained great advantages through its introduction, notably in the standardization of maintenance to a single plane—80 percent of all commercial airliners in the United States in the late 1930s came to be DC-3s—and of parts to that same craft. In addition, the greater speed (175 miles per hour) and size of this plane meant that the number of commercial craft could be reduced from 460 before its introduction to 358 in United States passenger service five years later.[65]

With the arrival of the DC-3, practical daytime transcontinental flying in the United States had arrived. Schedules were 15 hours eastbound and 17 hours westbound, with the time difference in the westbound flight more than compensated for by the gain in clock time due to the passage over three time-zone boundaries. Also, the normal stage had been increased. With fewer than the full twenty-one passengers the plane normally carried, the Chicago–New York run could be made nonstop; with even more reduction the Los Angeles-Chicago leg was flown without intermediate landing. But the common commercial operation called for refueling stops about every 500 to 600 miles, and a practical ceiling of some 7,000 to 8,000 feet. The plane could, however, fly across the Rockies even in bad weather, though it was forced to fly dogleg routings via the basins and power passes. The problem was partly that of operational ceiling for the engines of the plane, but also the physical comfort of the passengers in an aircraft that was unpressurized and thus reflective of the atmospheric conditions of the altitude at which it was flying. Above 8,000 feet many passengers experienced considerable shortage of oxygen if subjected to the normal atmosphere at that elevation. Still, the DC-3 combined a reasonable stage length—with schedules such as New York, Cleveland, Chicago, Omaha, Cheyenne, Salt Lake City, Reno, and San Francisco quite practicable— to a speed that permitted 5-hour flights from New York to Chicago and operating costs that made passenger transport, even without air-mail payments, generally profitable.

THE ARRIVAL OF THE FOUR-ENGINE PLANE

The DC-3 permitted North Americans to widen their lead over other nations in commercial aviation in two ways: our totals of passengers grew faster than any other continent's, and with that expansion came the possibility of specialization of service. In the same way that innovation in ocean shipping tended to be found in the Atlantic Ferry because there there was such a large volume to be transported, in North American commercial aviation significant and rapid evolu-

tion was most likely to take place. The remaining constraints felt once the DC-3 had proved itself in service were twofold: that the stage was too short for an effective speed-up of long-distance services, and that the ceiling was still too low to permit direct, great-circle routings over mountainous terrain. When facing those constraints, operators and aeronautical engineers soon appreciated that the solution lay in increasing the power of the planes. As by the mid- to late 1930s the piston engine (as manufactured in the United States) had reached a level of perfection that suggested further advances might come more slowly, the solution to more power came through multiplying the engines. As early as 1913 Igor Sikorsky, then in Russia, built the *Bolsche,* the first four-engined plane, establishing a tradition of multiple engines that he maintained for many years.[66] Europeans, particularly the British, had favored four-engined planes even in the interwar years. The Germans, for example, had built a twelve-engined Dornier DoX flying-boat in 1929, while the British had the Handley-Page H.P. 42 land plane with four engines put in service in 1930, following with the famous Short Empire class four-engined flying-boat in 1937. The reason for these multi-engined planes was the limited power that a single engine might contribute—around 1,000 horsepower in the mid-1930s. In land planes the reasoning was that it was desirable to keep the weight of planes down in order to limit the length of runway needed. That desire effectively constrained both the deadweight load of the plane and the weight of fuel, reducing the demand for multi-engined planes. But with flying boats these constraints were absent. Long takeoffs could be accomplished in protected still waters, so heavy planes—that is, multi-engined craft—and heavy fuel loadings could be envisaged. For that reason most of the early four-engined craft were in the flying-boat category, even in the United

States. The great competitive advantage of American aircraft in the 1930s came on land and from the superior engines with which they were fitted. Those land planes operated very effectively with two engines while several European makers were experimenting, seldom successfully from a commercial viewpoint, with four-engined planes. The Americans gained a notable victory when they applied their more powerful engines to flying-boats; these possessed a weight-to-power efficiency that permitted long-stage flying over water earlier than for any other nation.

The success of the DC-3 was in considerable measure the result of its ability to fly through "weather", given its sturdy construction and powerful engines. Even so, the airlines appreciated that it would be better still to be able to fly over the worst of the weather. That meant building a plane that could fly much higher than had been the practice.

Planes had flown above 20,000 feet within little more than a decade of Kitty Hawk, but only at the expense of great oxygen hunger to those on board, or else a supplemental supply thereof. It was only when the all-metal monocoque design began to emerge during World War I that a possible commercial solution was suggested. No one envisioned supplying passengers with individual oxygen masks, so the obvious solution had to be in pressurizing the cabin to the extent its pressure and oxygen level could be held to that of no higher than 8,000 feet. To do so meant both sealing the cabin and making its walls and windows strong enough to handle a pressure of 2.5 pounds per square inch or more. The stressed-skin, monocoque airframe was the only one that held much hope to gain those ends. And it was the American developments, represented by the DC-1, DC-2, and DC-3, that showed the way. None of those planes was pressurized, but each had a structure basically strong enough to accomplish that end. If

planes were to fly above the weather, they also required a supercharger to enrich the oxygen in the air going to the piston engines, as the thin air at high altitudes tended to cause the normal carburetors to malfunction and the engines to die.

The particular situation in American aviation—four large companies competing with each other over long routes—led to the effort to produce a high-flying plane. American Airlines had asked Douglas to develop the DST, later modified for day use as the DC-3, to meet that company's particular competitive needs given its circuitous routes. First by operating at night, and then by adopting longer stages that helped to overcome the sinuous pattern of the company's initial airmail routes simply by flying directly across some of the meanders, American gained the largest share of the American passenger market. Transcontinental and Western found itself at an increasing disadvantage, particularly because, in the reshuffle of contracts that grew out of the New Deal attack on the pattern that Walter Folger Brown had originated, TWA (as it was coming to be known) suffered the greatest loss. When F.D.R. was forced in 1934 to call the airlines back into the transport of air mail, much of the prior pattern was restored, but competitive bidding was introduced and more carriers were allowed to enter the ranks. In that situation, TWA found itself crowded by new companies and pressed by American Airlines' competitive advantage gained by the straightening of some of its routes.

To compete effectively, Jack Frye, the president of TWA, reasoned that offering a service that might fly above the worst clouds, rather than merely through them as the DC-3 could do, would appeal to passengers. He sought to interest the Wall Street investors who had taken over from the earlier holding company, but they refused to risk the capital. So Frye turned to a great flying enthusiast who, exceptionally, was also very rich. Howard Hughes saw the great advantage to be gained from what was then called stratospheric flying, so he quietly began buying up TWA stock until he had a sufficient block to force the Wall Streeters to sell out to him. At that point Frye was given the go-ahead to contract for high-flying, pressurized planes. The undertaking was handled with great secrecy to avoid tipping off either American or United airlines to what the next competitive entry would be. But once Hughes owned TWA, Boeing was approached and asked to evolve from the B-17 bomber (of sturdy construction for high-altitude flying and possessed of a supercharged engine) a "Stratoliner." The plane that resulted could cruise at 14,000 feet and at a speed of 200 miles per hour, 25 faster than the DC-3, allowing a 13 hour 40 minute eastbound crossing from Los Angeles to New York, with only one intermediate stop at Chicago. Unfortunately for TWA, however, the Stratoliner came into service only in 1940, not long enough before American entry into World War II to permit its commercial virtues to be fully demonstrated.[67] Still, this plane was to prove itself in an important way during that conflict, as it was the only commercial plane that could effectively and economically fly the Atlantic with a jump from Newfoundland to Ireland. The potential for intercontinental flying was at hand.

Once launched in commercial aviation, Howard Hughes did not stop at the Stratoliner. "Even before TWA took delivery on its first Stratoliner, Hughes was talking to Frye about a bigger, stronger, and faster plane for their transcontinental service." Their search was encouraged by the development of stronger engines for military aircraft, then receiving great attention. With these, Hughes and Frye believed a major increase in airliner speed was possible, allowing more direct routes with fewer stops. Although an airline could have located its intermediate stops entirely for technical reasons, almost

none did so because, once on the ground, it made sense to be able to use that stop for commercial purposes. So the desirable operational pattern would be one wherein the company could fly easily from California to Chicago, the self-evident interior Junction City. TWA approached Lockheed Aircraft, asking them to attempt to come up with an entirely new craft, perhaps using some of the developments of the B-24 bomber they were constructing but not truly patterned on it. The builder's president replied, "The way to start is with the biggest engine in the world," the Wright 3350.[68] This 1939 contract began the development of what became the first postwar plane, the delay because that war intervened and only prototypes could be produced before the end was near in 1944 and 1945.

Before taking up the *Constellation* that resulted from TWA's cooperation with Lockheed, note should be made of the evolution that was taking place among other builders and operators, and even in American foreign flying. The signal success of the DC-3 had given both the Douglas company and American airframe builders in general a leading role in commercial aviation. Thus the conditions found within the American airline network came to make a distinctive contribution to the evolution of the industry even well outside the United States. The conditions that had the greatest impact were the rapid growth in passenger totals, the fact that in the United States only a part of the network carried an air-mail subsidy and the increasing importance of transcontinental services. The absence of subsidy, or its relatively modest scale, meant that actual operating costs weighed particularly heavily on domestic American carriers. The rapid increase in passenger totals gave to those carriers the notion that larger aircraft could be justified by market conditions, particularly if their operating costs per seat mile could be held to the favorable levels attained by the

DC-3, or even improved over those figures. And the emergence of a considerable transcontinental demand suggested to the carriers that planes capable of making the coast-to-coast flights with only a single intermediate stop, as opposed to the minimum of three necessary in commercial use of the DC-3, would gain the service edge that was beginning to play such an important role in the evolution of competitive aviation in the United States.

Almost no other country had set about to secure domestic competition among airlines, and that initial situation in the United States was further accentuated by the philosophy of the New Deal imposed when air-mail contracts were renegotiated in 1934 after the fiasco of the Army Air Corps transport of this mail. F.D.R. was forced to turn to the Big Four and their foreign-flying brother, Pan Am, to end the slaughter of pilots consequent upon giving the Air Corps a responsibility it was unable to handle, but he, in turn, forced those carriers to transport the mail for more realistic payments and to compete effectively among themselves. No other country had such a policy and it is significant that the airframe builders of no other nation succeeded in constructing planes as economical to operate as those coming from Santa Monica, Seattle, and other American aircraft plants. The efforts of the British, Germans, and French before World War II can justly be disregarded for the most part with respect to commercial aircraft because the results were of less lasting importance and even of little current interest except to the antiquarian of airplanes.

What followed the DC-3 in the United States was the four-engined plane. In the hands of Douglas, very much the dominant producer (as more than four out of five American commercial planes were DC-3s by the late 1930s), the basic components of that success were simply enlarged—*stretched*, as the industry term became—from the DC-3.

The squarely oval fuselage of the earlier plane was adapted to the larger successor, producing a craft with two seats on each side of the aisle. The stressed-skin, low-wing monoplane had become an absolute norm. What changed were the length of the fuselage, the width of the wings, and the wing-loadings, that is the pounds of plane per square foot of wing surface involved. Those loadings could be, and were, greatly increased through the use of more complex wing structures—using wing flaps, then slotted flaps, and other technical devices of cross-section, configuration, and movable section—and of more powerful engines. In the 1930s the United States became the premier engine builder, repeating for aircraft engines the history of locomotive building, through the creation of tractive power unmatched in Britain or Europe to the extent that being American became synonymous with being more powerful, durable and adaptable. American aircraft builders invaded the European markets, save in those countries where nationalistic and defense objectives kept them out. K.L.M. became a major purchaser of these planes—we should not forget that Dutch company that had entered a DC-2 in the London–Sydney air race—and even the British European Airways operation bought DC-3s. With those external markets to add to the already most substantial domestic markct, a successful American commercial aircraft could anticipate a total sale sufficient both to recover developmental costs and return an actual profit. Almost no foreign builder enjoyed those prospects.

Even before the earliest production models arrived at the airline maintenance bases, Douglas began to think about stretching the DC-3, using four instead of two engines, widening, lengthening, increasing wing loadings, and installing more powerful engines that were being developed for the military bombers then on the drawing

The DC-4.

boards. The first result was a plane that Douglas called the DC-4E, and it taught a lesson that has not always been remembered in subsequent developments: that a plane is built either for an existing or a potential market, but no market that is too conjectural is wisely relied on by a company seeking to remain in business. The larger Douglas plane, though encouraged by actual seed money from the Big Four and Pan Am, came out too large for the perceptions of the market of the 1940s, and only six were ordered (by United Airlines). A number of in-novations designed for this experimental model were subsequently incorporated in the production model, the DC-4, which was somewhat reduced in size. Actually no production models of the DC-4E were ever built; the prototype was sold to Japan, and it soon crashed there.[69] As constructed the DC-4 was 117 feet long, with a wing span of 96 feet, using wing loadings in the range of some 31 or more pounds per square foot (in contrast to 24 pounds for the DC-3), capable of a stage of 2,100 miles, and cruising at 200 miles per hour. The passenger load ranged between 44 and 66 depending on permissible takeoff weights and the desired stage length. This complex of abilities was seen as the desirable one to tap the domestic American market as it was perceived in the late 1930s. But given the necessary construction time the DC-4 did not fly until 1942, and no civilian use was made of the plane until the close of World War II. Thus, even though the five major American carriers had sought and subsidized the construction of a larger airliner as early as 1936, it was only nine years later that they gained possession of any of those planes, and even then mainly as war surplus when the armed services began to release the craft they had secured between 1942 and 1945. Throughout this trying period the superb DC-3 flew generally safely, always most sturdily, and certainly most profitably on virtually all the land-based air routes flown by Americans, as well as many outside the country.

That war may have delayed the introduction of planes specifically intended for transcontinental and intercontinental flying, but it did make significant contributions to the evolution of commercial aviation. Although transoceanic flying had begun before 1939, mainly by Pan American, the war forced its rapid improvement and enlargement. To gain that end considerable advances in aviation meteorology were made, as well as the beginning of the use of radar both for weather and navigational purposes. Technically required airfields in Newfoundland, Labrador, and Iceland in the Atlantic and on a number of islands in the Pacific were constructed for military purposes but remained for civilian use in 1945. And the general state of the aeronautical technology was greatly advanced by exigent demands of wartime flying. Most important, however, may have been the rising appreciation among an increasing number of persons of the advantages of air transport. By 1940 two and a quarter million passengers annually

were being carried by the airlines of the United States, more than for the rest of the world combined. That lead continued through the war when the Air Transport Command of the U.S. Army accomplished prodigious feats both in numbers of men transported and in the geographical reach of its operations. In particular, the experience of flying land planes across the Atlantic became widespread, thus opening the horizon for postwar commercial flying. But more of that later.

In June of 1939 Howard Hughes, by then firmly in control of the destiny of TWA, decided that his airline needed a high-altitude plane capable of flying across the continent with only one stop and above most of the "weather" that the earlier planes had had to contend with in scheduled operation. Because Hughes and Donald Douglas had fallen out over a racer that the Santa Monica firm was modifying for him in the 1920s, TWA was forced to turn to other builders, in this instance to Lockheed. From that inquiry came a proposal for "a plane with a 3000-mile range" and capable of carrying up to sixty passengers, a vast increase on the DC-3 that had begun service less than two years before. At Lockheed's suggestion the scale of the craft was increased in line with the rapidly improving engines that were coming as a result of the preparation for the war that seemed imminent. It is difficult to pin down the precise specifications of this great Lockheed plane, perhaps the most strikingly beautiful ever built, because it got no farther than the planning stage before war came even to the United States, and construction had to be shifted to a rather desultory undertaking. At first Lockheed and TWA kept the undertaking intensely secret, but the outbreak of war in Europe ended that when the Army Air Corps took over control of all aircraft production. To rationalize production they forced TWA to allow Pan Am to join in this project, the latter dropping its own plans for a slightly different plane, but even then the aftermath of Pearl Harbor stalled much further progress until 1944 when victory was in sight. That year a prototype of the *Constellation* was flown by Howard Hughes and Jack Frye, the president of TWA, accomplishing a transcontinental flight in 7 hours 30 minutes, for a cruising speed of 280 miles an hour, more than 100 miles an hour faster than the DC-3s. TWA could clearly hope for a tremendous competitive edge once peace came, as their contract specified that they could purchase the first forty *Constellations* built.[70]

Thus by 1940 the two planes that were to account for most of the long-distance aviation by American companies before the advent of jets were well advanced in development. The DC-4 and the Constellation became the rootstalk from which were developed the full array of postwar four-engine planes in America. From the DC-4 came the postwar DC-6s and DC-7s that were essentially stretched versions of that basic design with an egg-shaped cross-section and straight sides, a single tailfin and four engines. From the *Constellation* of 1944 came all the stretches of that plane, with a distinctive droop at nose and tail and a three-finned tail to present the second prototype for a four-engine craft. The stretches came mostly in response to shifts in the specifications of the purchasing airlines but were timed particularly to make use of advances in engine design for which Pratt and Whitney and Wright became renowned. World War II contributed mightily to that rapid advance in engine power, so the delay in the construction of civilian models of these two four-engine prototypes was far from totally lost time. The basic engines—for American planes mainly the Pratt and Whitney R-2800 and the Wright R-3350—had been designed before the war—(the R-2800 was planned jointly for the emerging *Constellation* and military craft in 1939), so it was mostly mod-

ification that took place in the late 1940s and the 1950s. The only significant postwar engine, the Wright turbocompound version of the R-3350, carried piston-engine design to what seems to have been the ultimate, particularly because these large, complex engines were awkward to maintain, requiring major overhaul as frequently as once every 1,000 hours.[71]

The way stretching worked was for the basic wing and fuselage designs to be maintained but with extra panels of similar design inserted to give greater length or wing span. The changes in the *Constellation* tended to be more radical but less frequent than those made in the Douglas planes, with the result that the Douglas planes proved more adapted to airline needs and thus were better sellers. The stretching did not greatly enlarge these planes, though it was on occasion critical to the payload. For example, by widening the fuselage of the DC-2, to permit sleepers, the DC-3 had been created. That widening process could, however, pose considerable problems as more powerful engines were required to maintain even the same speed. But lengthening the plane tended not to change the speed, though more power might be required to lift a greater weight off the runway. Still, a wider plane, such as the *Constellation* that was 6 inches wider than the DC-6, might allow a significantly greater number of seats—a fifth row in this instance—that more than paid the cost of more powerful engines. The tradeoffs were complex, but the right combination might make the difference between an economical plane and one that could not earn its keep in a competitive market.

Every [airline headquarters] had file cases full of data on which type of plane—taking into consideration the purchase price, flight-crew pay, fuel and food cost, and the rest—flew each trip most economically. The statisticians liked to divide the number of revenue pass-

The original (049) *Constellation*. Trans-World Airlines photograph.

engers by the sum of these charges. The final result was the average per-mile performance of the airliners, and by this measure the DC-6B was a more economical performer than the Lockheed *Constellation*, more economical indeed than any piston plane ever built, including the legendarily profitable DC-3.[72]

The most significant concern in this complex equation, from our point of view, was the contribution of geographical conditions both to the market and to technical operation. Two particular expressions of that geography were the drive for transcontinen-

tal service and that for transoceanic flying. Obviously the shortest distance between any two points on the earth's surface is a great circle route—a fact that was just beginning to emerge at that time, as previous planes had been so constrained by short-stage operation that they had to find a route that provided many intermediate landing facilities, preferably with local airline markets that could be served in the operation of the long-distance services. But such way-stops did increase the distance flown as well as the time taken for the full journey, to the extent the DC-3 required 18 or 19 hours to pass between the coasts. Such timing was tolerable westbound because the elapsed clock time was perhaps only 15 hours. Eastbound, however, an 18-hour flight tied to a 3-hour time change meant that the better part of a full day was taken, explaining the interest in sleeper planes at that state of airliner operation. In Europe the problem was not fully appreciated, as only the Soviet Union had enough east-west extent to experience a similar problem, and there passenger convenience counted for little. Thus it was the Americans who had to face and solve this problem if anyone was to do so.

The *Constellation* was designed to do two things: add over 100 miles an hour to the speed of the DC-3 and increase the stage to the point where one-stop transcontinental flying became possible. Given the distance from Los Angeles to New York, it was thought necessary to consider an intermediate stop, in TWA's case in Kansas City, their operating headquarters. Even with that stop, a service in 10 hours became possible east-bound using the *Constellation,* always a relatively fast plane. In the immediate postwar years the Lockheed planes had an 80-mile-an-hour advantage over the Douglas four-engine entry, the DC-4, so the latter company quickly stretched that parent craft, adding 7 feet, and substituting Pratt and Whitney R-2800 engines that could make slightly better speed than the engines in their arch-rival. With this greatly increased power the stage could be lengthened, and United Airlines introduced transcontinental service with what was essentially no more than a technical stop in Lincoln, Nebraska, to refuel, using the DC-6, a stretched version.[73] The engineers at Lockheed were impatient with the TWA management because they refused to operate the *Constellation* in nonstop transcontinental service, of which the planes were capable, on the argument that no one would wish to travel sitting for 10

hours at a time without a walk around on the ground to break the monotony and restore the circulation. Having frequently made the 10-hour flight from San Francisco to western Europe, I can understand their reasoning, but the market thought otherwise when such nonstop transcontinental service was introduced. TWA, using a *Constellation* stretched 19 feet to become a *Superconstellation*, introduced nonstop transcontinental service on October 19, 1953, to be followed by American Airlines service using the DC-7 a month later.[74] The certain ability to operate coast-to-coast came from the introduction in both these planes of the Wright turbocompound engine, the monster of its breed and so complicated that maintenance was ever a problem. Still, under ideal conditions these engines could propel aerodynamically sophisticated planes at something around 350 miles an hour, essentially the ultimate in piston-engine performance in civil aviation. These two ultimate stretches of the four-engined workhorses of American and Free World aviation also allowed the introduction of trans-Atlantic nonstop flying. Pan Am put the DC-7 in that service in 1957, soon to be followed by TWA with a *Super-Superconstellation* that weighed twice as much as the 1940 version of the plane but accommodated no more passengers. Needless to say, the economics of the latter craft were most unfavorable, so its short life before the advent of jet aircraft two years later was not as sad as one might think.[75]

Although the *Super-Superconstellation* and the DC-7 were used in nonstop service across North America or the Atlantic, most services were conducted in a more modest way. The older DC-4s and DC-6s and the various earlier models of the *Constellation* were used to provide transportation between pairs of cities that were less than a continent or an ocean apart, or else for the cheaper long-distance runs that were sold as "economy" or "coach" starting in the early 1950s.

The stretched *Constellation* (1049G). Trans-World Airlines photograph.

These were operated more economically by employing shorter stages that required less powerful engines and lower fuel consumption. By economically employing such larger craft, the airline companies could obviously undertake to provide service at reduced fares in order to enlarge the travel market. By the mid-1950s the 4-cent-a-mile fare was a reality, and several airlines, notably American, were aiming for a 3-cent-a-mile fare that began to approach the 2-cent level that American railroads adopted to encourage rail coach travel during the Depression of the 1930s. But the airlines never reached the 3-cent fare, and soon even coach fares began to increase, though it was only after the 1973 oil embargo that tickets began to become much more costly, reaching highs of 20 cents a mile or even more on some short-haul flights in the Northeast in the mid-1980s. In the 1950s low fares proved very effective in rapidly increasing the number of passengers. By 1955 planes were carrying more people between American cities than were trains, and those numbers increased at a rate of about 15 percent a year in some years. From about 1955 on most towns of any size in the United States were served by airlines, either the trunk carriers, which numbered around a dozen by that time, or feeder airlines specializing in supplementing the work of the "trunks" so that it became possible to fly from most separate settlement clusters of 10,000–20,000 to others of the same scale in other parts of the United States. Even though the greatest number of points were served in the 1950s, still the great mass of travel was accomplished among the fifty or so truly metropolitan traffic generators.

In some significant ways the 1950s were the halcyon days of American air travel from a geographical viewpoint. With planes that carried between twenty-one (the DC-3, still in very wide use on feeder routes) and sixty (the *Constellations* and DC-6s employed on the most important trunk routes) service had to be repeating, and thus practicably fairly frequent. Also, because most planes still had fairly restricted stage lengths, the numerous intermediate stops afforded a rather dense network of through services to major air hubs, even if there were very few runs of continental or transoceanic length. The density of good service thus secured, along with very reasonable fares, meant that it was in the 1950s that air transport began to have a great impact on American life and economic activity. Business flying grew massively. Some said it made up 85 percent of all flying, as it was likely to be so repeating, bringing into existence the cluster of airport hotels that removed much of the distinctive qualities of a "place" for many travelers. Very long journeys might be accomplished in which the traveler never left the air milieu, never saw more than a handful of "natives," and was denied the taste of local—that is, regional—foods, accents, and customs. Perhaps most notable a loss was the decline of intervening experience in travel. High above the ground, often obscured from it by clouds, the air traveler tended to journey with denizens of his home town and the one he was visiting, but no others. The transcontinental nonstop routing exaggerated this pattern, perhaps contributing to the rise of a coastal culture in the United States that tended to look upon "Middle America" as certainly a deprived, most likely a benighted place, and one increasingly unseen.

THE YEARS OF IMPERIAL ADVANCE: 1920-1940

To understand the "water jump" from one continent to another across the broad oceans, we must first look at the spread of integrated commercial air service from the two hearths of development in western Europe and in North America. As we have seen, it was in France, Germany, and Britain in Europe and in Canada and the United States in North America that the main body of aircraft evolution took place, and the major development of airlines came into being. There were air services elsewhere—notably in Australia, the Soviet Union, and parts of Latin America—but the shaping of an industry was the work of Europe and North America. Once that industry had been perceived, in Europe by national carriers and in America after about 1930 by the Big Four, there was a strong desire on the part of these generally well capitalized and actively promoted lines to spread beyond their country of origin. This was particularly the case in Europe because of the small extent of most of the countries involved. Taking the Netherlands as a case in point, it can easily be seen that any Dutch airline, to have a rational existence, must be engaged in international flying. Thus it is not surprising that the Hollanders were among the very first to seek an advance outside their own borders, though clearly within the context of the extensive Dutch empire then in existence. The situation was less extreme in the instances of France and Britain, the national space being

The DC-7. American Airlines photograph.

somewhat more extensive, but to gain the advantages of air transport in full measure it was essential to turn to servicing an empire.

It is impractical here to attempt to follow in detail the growth of these imperial airlines. Suffice it to note that Britain had air service to India by 1929, which required seven and half days: by plane from London to Basle; by train thence to Genoa; by means of a flying boat to Port Said in Egypt; and then by landplane service via Palestine, Iraq, and the Trucial Coast of Arabia to Karachi (now Pakistan, but then British India). Compared with this Heath Robinson creation, Transcontinental's air-rail route from Los Angeles to New York was efficient and elegant with its two-day service.[76] The Dutch began a fortnightly service to the East Indies via the Middle East and India in 1929. Imperial joined with the Australian airline, QANTAS, to shape a through route that opened on December 8, 1934, between London and Brisbane, for the first time deleting the London-Brindisi (Italy) rail connection. The twelve-day flight covered 12,722 miles, certainly the longest scheduled service by one carrier (QANTAS Empire Airways) on earth. But even before that K.L.M. had begun Amsterdam-Australia service with a DC-2. This American craft was so superior to the de Havilland equipment that Imperial and QANTAS Empire were operating that the Dutch captured much of the trade between England and India and Australia as well as dominating the connection with the Dutch East Indies.[77] The order for fourteen DC-2s that the Dutch placed in Santa Monica began the American invasion of European airlines. The six-day schedule for the five-passenger planes gave K.L.M. a strong commercial edge, which was further enhanced in March, 1936, when they put eleven-passenger DC-3s on the run. While all this was going on, Imperial started down a backward track by ordering large four-engined flying-boats in disregard of the considerable success that the Dutch line had had in using landplanes on this obviously land-hopping route.[78]

While the Dutch and British were concentrating on the route to southeast Asia via India, the French were also looking toward Indo-China. In 1929 a flying-boat service was established between Marseille and Syria (then a French mandate); this was extended to Baghdad in December of that year. In January, 1931, the service was pushed on to Saigon, though with only airmail service beyond Baghdad. During the 1930s passengers began to be carried after Air France was organized as the chosen national carrier in 1933.[79] The German Lufthansa also entered the Middle East competition with flights to Baghdad in 1936. In 1939 this service was continued on to Bangkok, but only three fortnightly flights were carried out before the outbreak of World War II stopped the service. Using four-engined Focke-Wulf planes, this German run reduced the Berlin-Bangkok journey to two and a half days.[80]

The African imperial services were of similar form: the stringing together of air, sea, and rail segments to create a through route, with the air services operating across the least developed of these portions. From 1932 on this jury-rigged arrangement was available from London to Cape Town but eventually an all-air routing was forged and the time was reduced from the initial eleven days.[81] The French developed similar services via the Saharan colonies to Equatorial Africa and Madagascar, substantially in cooperation with the Belgians who traded landing rights in the Congo for those in west Africa. The Italians during their vicious advance into the Horn of Africa shaped a limited network tying Ethiopia with Rome. The African network of airlines at the outbreak of World War II comprised two elements: the long imperial routes projected across the continent to reach to the most distant British, French, and Italian colony, combined with specialized nets of local airlines, often operated by private carriers, in contrast to the nationalized trunk routes, within the individual colonies. South Africa, as a dominion, had its own national carrier (South African Airways) organized in 1934, which two years later took over part of the responsibility for the Cape to Cairo airway from Imperial, just as QANTAS had done from the beginning on the London-to-Sydney run.

South America saw a rather different version of imperialism, that of two American companies that shaped their own "empires," one on South America's east coast and the other on the west.

The Pan Am dominance of Latin American aviation and of American foreign flying was largely complete during the 1930s. Juan Trippe advanced the notion of the "chosen instrument" of American foreign services, no doubt following the lead of the nationalized airlines of western Europe that enjoyed monopolies on the routes radiating from their capital cities save for the necessary quid-pro-quo routes that had to be granted bilaterally to the national airline of the paired country. There is little doubt that in the 1930s to have shared the somewhat meager market among several American carriers would probably have caused all to fail, or at least to require even greater subsidies than were needed for that chosen instrument. At the same time, there is little doubt that the actual service suffered from the absence of competition. Pan Am had a remarkable record for anticipating the need for and the nature of technical improvements in aircraft. The company had planes far more capable than those of other foreign carriers, with the probable exception of K.L.M., and it was these technical superiorities that strained relations with Britain in the effort to fly the Atlantic. But the American carrier proved very conservative in operating practices. Long after domestic carriers were flying overnight from coast to coast, Pan Am would only operate in daylight, and it was the joke among airmen that the company would allow its planes to fly only on moonlight nights, and then only across Miami Bay.

With Latin America in hand and commencing (with air-mail subsidies) to yield profits, Pan Am began to think about intercontinental flying where there were no such convenient strings of islands, or isthmian stops, that allowed service in planes with rather short stages of operation.

THE TRANS-ATLANTIC JUMP

In the nineteenth century the transit of the North Atlantic became the most heavily traveled oceanic route, as we have already seen with respect to the Atlantic Ferry. It was clear that commercial aviation could envision this as potentially the most profitable oceanic route that might be developed. As early as 1919 special pioneering leaps were made across the North Atlantic using the few stepping stones that existed to make the journey less demanding. Newfoundland in the northeast, Bermuda and the Azores in mid-ocean, and Ireland in the farther east, viewed from North America, allowed the maximum stage to be kept to some 1,900 miles, 500 miles shorter than the minimum stage in crossing the central Pacific, the 2,400 miles between California and Hawaii. In both the Atlantic and the Pacific there was a northerly rim of land—Labrador, Greenland, the Faeroes, and Norway in the Atlantic; Kamchatka, the Aleutians, and Alaska in the Pacific—but given the virtually unknown qualities of Arctic weather and the general use of flying boats in the pioneering phase of ocean crossing (thus making the frozen seas of the north perhaps even more of a barrier), the more southerly latitudes were the obvious realms of aviation. Oddly enough, the Pacific, though much wider than the Atlantic, was far less of a problem in terms of weather. Even in terms of stepping stones to allow for refueling en route, the Pacific was no more difficult save for the one great gap that lay between California and Hawaii. But once flying boats had been improved to the extent they could undertake stages of 2,400 miles, even that jump became possible.

It was a political matter that finally determined the first transoceanic flying—or, rather, a combination of technical constraints and political geography. Britain, given the interwar extent of the British Empire, obviously controlled "landing rights" more widely spread than those of any other country. France came second in this regard, with other major Western powers far less naturally favored. In particular the United States, Germany, and Italy, the other major promoters of commercial aviation, were badly served, except for the distribution of American possessions in the mid-Pacific. In the 1920s Germany had, through the use of dirigibles, somewhat sidestepped that constraint. In 1928 the *Graf Zeppelin* made a dramatic and successful commercial flight across the middle North Atlantic, and two years later an experimental British dirigible—the R-100, built by Vickers aircraft—successfully completed a round trip to Canada that was a technical success but in no real sense a commercial venture.

The Germans sought another resolution of the technical and political problems of oceanic flying. They developed the catapult principle to permit the refueling of the Dornier 18 air-mail plane in mid-Atlantic independent of landing rights. The arrangement was that a flying boat (the Dornier 18) would depart from Europe and fly to a point in the ocean near the Azores, where it would land on the sea surface, protected in part by a great canvas sheet laid on the sea to calm the waves (in some cases oil was also added to lower the crests). Once it was floating there, a small catapult tender, the *Westfalen*, would hoist the plane on board for refueling. When that operation was completed, the plane was then made airborne by a catapult that gave a very rapid increase in speed to reach the necessary lift in a short takeoff.[82] Thus, refueled, the aircraft continued on to New York, completing a trans-Atlantic flight in a plane with too short a stage to do the job and in the service of a country that had no landing rights anywhere in mid-ocean. The trip was a success, but it is extremely doubtful that the operation was commercially so during the few experimental flights made in 1936.

It became ever more clear that there was a sharp distinction between the once-off experimental flight and sustained commercial operation. The Italians, Germans, French, and English all undertook experimental Atlantic flights in the 1930s, but none of these was a commercial undertaking. It was only the Americans who possessed that capability in that decade, and they were forfended from exploiting it by political restraints interposed by the British, because

Pan Am and Imperial Airways had agreed in 1930 not to begin service before the other was ready to do so. The British government had forced upon Imperial a Buy British policy that meant they had to operate with British aircraft. Without going into detail, it seems accurate to hold that neither in flying boats nor in landplanes were these craft of British provenance up to sustained commercial service on the Atlantic. By dint of what was euphemistically called "composite" construction (that is, attaching a smaller plane to the larger one to give added power in takeoff without sustained fuel consumption in flight once the two separated soon after takeoff), there were several oceanic crossings accomplished by the underpowered British craft. But the risk involved in this sort of Rube Goldberg arrangement was sufficient to rule it out for passenger service, and make it difficult even for mail operations. In contrast, by the mid-1930s Pan Am had planes that were technically able to fly the Atantic, if use of the closest stepping stones could be obtained. As Newfoundland and Bermuda were directly controlled from Westminster, that use was not available until British aircraft builders managed to assemble a commercially viable plane for the water jump. That they did not succeed in doing before the outbreak of World War II.

Possessed of a plane, in fact two, that could accomplish the minimum stages of the North Atlantic, but unable to employ them there, Pan Am first turned its oceanic-flying attention to the Pacific. American possessions were strategically spread across that vast ocean at distances close enough, though still wider than those on the Atlantic, to permit an island-hopping schedule from North America to Asia.

As early as 1931 Pan Am sent letters to U.S. plane manufacturers inviting them to build a four-engine flying boat capable of carrying mail and passengers on trans-oceanic flights.

In 1932 Trippe entered into one contract with Sikorsky to build a seventeen-ton flying boat, and a second with Glenn Martin to construct an even bigger one—a twenty-six ton giant capable of carrying a payload across the twenty-five-hundred-mile distance between San Francisco and Honolulu.[83]

When those planes became available, Pan Am commenced exploratory flights, first to Hawaii from Alameda, California, and then in stages farther across the Pacific until Manila was reached. Gaining information from those trials, procedures were adjusted; on November 22, 1935, the first air-mail flight left Alameda heading across the broad jump to Hawaii and on to Manila. The plane involved was the Martin M-130, the China Clipper, a giant for its time with a wing span of 130 feet (equal to the 727 jet of a generation later). It was powered by four 850-horsepower Hornet engines that gave the lift that permitted cruising at 130 miles an hour carrying mail and from sixteen to thirty-two passengers. And the maximum stage of 2,500 miles was enough to cover the great leap to the Islands from the Bay Area.[84] At first only mail was carried, but in 1936 passenger service was begun and for the first time a complete transoceanic route stood in a developed condition.

The faltering British efforts to secure an operable aircraft for Atlantic service bore upon the gentlemen's agreement that Juan Trippe and Imperial Airways had entered into in 1930. In 1937 the British had received sixteen Empire flying boats, the craft they intended to use in the water jump, but "eight had crashed or been wrecked by November 1938" and a larger prospective replacement was "nowhere near complete."[85] Imperial Airways was obviously in no condition to fly the Atlantic, so Trippe was forced by prospective competition from other Europeans, and even other American companies, to leave the British to sort out the technical and political maze in which they found themselves.

The French had managed to fly the Atlantic in a six-engined flying boat, the *Lieutenant de Vaisseau Paris,* on August 30, 1938, using the Azores as a stepping stone; and the German Condor flight from Germany to New York, though only exploratory, suggested further Continental efforts. In America, American Export Lines, the young and aggressive steamship line serving the Mediterranean from New York, had begun to look at trans-Atlantic air development. In this climate Pan Am was desperately anxious to begin service. They even had a new flying boat, the Boeing 314A, weighing some 42 tons and capable of transporting thirty-five passengers at 145 miles an hour in considerable luxury, to use in the service. So denying themselves use of the British islands in the Atlantic, Pan Am on March 27, 1939, began the first scheduled trans-Atlantic service flying from New York via the Azores to Lisbon and thence to Marseille and Southampton, flying the 2,750 miles at an average speed of 160 miles per hour in seventeen and a half hours.[86] George Woods Humphrey, the managing director of Imperial, wrote to his chairman, J. C. W. Reith, that the Pan Am 314 "intends to miss out Bermuda, and that is done intentionally to avoid British 'stepping stones.' [He added] I know that they will not be able to do so very often—if at all—westbound, but the desire and perhaps the determination to do so if necessary, or eventually, is there."[87] But they did do so, and the strange nationalistic myopia that seemed to grip British civil aviation at this time was confounded. Humphrey even coolly went on to tell Reith that if Britain were to gain an entry into the trans-Atlantic service it would have to be via Portugal and the Azores, and he asked "for authorisation to approach Pan American to use their facilities on the islands." This at the same time landing rights in Newfoundland and Bermuda were being denied until a British entry could be made to stay aloft commercially.

In June, 1939, Pan Am finally won the right to land in Newfoundland, so it commenced passenger service on two routes to Europe—that of the *Dixie Clipper* via the Azores and Lisbon and that of the *Yankee Clipper* via Newfoundland, on the 24th of the month on the northerly route and the 28th on the southerly.[88] To counter that success, Imperial began a series of experimental flights using in-flight refueling of Empire flying boats, at Shannon in Ireland and Hattie's Camp (which came to be known as Gander) in Newfoundland. Although Woods Humphrey exalted in the better on-time performance of these fourteen experimental flights than Pan Am's actually commercial flights, he had to note that on a number of occasions gasoline had leaked into the bilges of the plane or other misfunctions in refueling had taken place to the point that "Flight refuelling in connection with a passenger service would be out of the question."[89]

The acute embarrassment of Britain, with its self-serving denigration of American successes, fortunately came to an end once war broke out in September. The failures in commercial aircraft production were more than compensated by the critical success of British military craft in the Battle of Britain, the first air war. That same prescience can be found in the report of one of the pilots of the in-flight refueled flights. Captain Jack Kelly-Rogers wrote that speed is "a vital necessity in the operation of a successful Atlantic service," because the North Atlantic is characterized by a very strong westerly wind and in flying, the slower the plane, the greater the headwind effect. Given its aerodynamic qualities, "the all-round performance needed would probably be difficult to obtain in a flying boat, and it appears that a successful service is much more likely to be operated by landplanes. [Even for safety in a

forced landing at sea] it appears that a well-constructed land aircraft would probably be as safe as a flying boat."[90] The forced landing of a British flying boat that met with severe damage to the plane and loss of life confirmed that point, leading the thought of most operators toward the landplane.

With the onset of hostilities in 1939, the advantages of ferrying planes directly from the American aircraft plants to Britain became great, and major efforts were made to accomplish that feat. It was done first by building airfields in Bermuda, Newfoundland, and Iceland for the North Atlantic air ferry and in Brazil and West Africa for that across the South Atlantic. But as time passed and planes were enlarged in size, by special loading of fuel it became increasingly possible to make longer water jumps, bypassing certain of the stepping stones. During the early years of the war the enlarged, four-engined Douglas transport, the DC-4, proved the only commercial transport in Allied hands capable of the trans-Atlantic water jump. Using the newly constructed airport at Gander in Newfoundland, the DC-4 could hop eastbound to Prestwick in Scotland, providing a fully adequate test first of the wisdom of the use of landplanes on the North Atlantic and then of the weather conditions that were likely to be encountered in year-round flying in such high latitudes. Fortunately, the more laden flights tended to be eastbound, with a normally strong tailwind, whereas the less heavy westbound flights had to buck that wind, sometimes requiring an intermediate stop at Keflavik in Iceland, where an airport was constructed during the war.

CIVIL AVIATION AFTER 1945

World War II developed two machines that had immediate impact on the postwar world—the bulldozer and the four-engined plane—and two whose impact was somewhat delayed—the jet plane and the rocket. For the moment only the four-engined plane need concern us.

The wartime experience with long-distance flying and the potential availability of craft capable of such operation combined to suggest that the new component of postwar civil aviation would be international competition of the sort that had before the war been mainly found in the United States domestic airline industry. In the years before 1939 there had been joint operation of services between European capitals by the national airlines of the two countries involved. There had been some competition between Imperial Airways and K.L.M. on the run to India and Singapore. Otherwise most services in international flying were essential monopolies. But by 1943 the British had made it clear that after peace they intended to attempt to develop the North Atlantic air jump much as the Atlantic Ferry by steamship had evolved: with the conflux of local European services on Britain and the domination of the trans-Atlantic jump by Britain. This was seemingly possible because the critical stepping stones were still in British hands.

The United States government had evidently learned quite a bit from the delay in the commencement of trans-Atlantic air service, correctly perceiving that it was the stranglehold of Britain in a time when she was without a plane to enter the joint service with Pan Am (envisaged by the gentlemen's agreement of 1930) that had held up American efforts. So in 1944 a conference on civil aviation was assembled in Chicago seeking to rationalize postwar flying. At that conference, held between November 1 and December 7, 1944, two opposing viewpoints emerged: an "open skies" doctrine advanced by the Americans and a "national sovereignty" doctrine of the British.[91] The State Department advanced the idea of the freedom of the skies, to go along with the much

older notion of the freedom of the seas. The British argued in contradiction that there are actually five freedoms of the skies and that these are quite separable, with national sovereignty attaching particularly to the "fifth freedom" in an almost inseparable fashion. Those freedoms were:

1. The right of transit—that is, to pass through the air space of a country without landing, rather analogous to the freedom of the seas.
2. The right to make a technical stop in a country, to pick up fuel or to make mechanical repairs.
3. The right to discharge passengers at an airport in the country involved.
4. The right to pick up passengers in that country to return them to the country of origin of the airline.
5. The right to discharge passengers in that foreign country and then to pick up passengers originating there and carry them on to a third country.

With respect to the fifth freedom Solberg notes, "the way the British talked about this made it so rare and remote that no greater concession could ever be bestowed by a sovereign nation."[92]

The intransigence of the British, joined by the Dutch in the interests of K.L.M. left the Chicago convention with precious little international freedom granted. It was finally conceded by the European narrow-freedom advocates that the right of free, peaceful passage in the air space of another and the right of landing for technical purposes were essential to orderly development of postwar civil aviation. But no more international rights were granted. Instead, it was left to bilateral treaties arranged by individual nations to determine which of the other three freedoms might be granted. The establishment of any air service between two countries would be subject to such joint agree-

The interior of the B-314 *Yankee Clipper*. Pan American World Airways photograph.

ments; and they must, of necessity, grant to one party, normally to both, the third and fourth freedoms. It was impractical to envision such a connection without the right to discharge and pick up passengers in the other country. Normal air connections have been so widely established that for most of the industry the third and fourth freedoms can be thought to exist operationally. There are, of course, exceptions. Cuba and the United States do not exchange these rights; nor do Czechoslovakia, Vietnam, North Korea, or Albania do so with the United States. Before the imposition of martial law in Poland in December, 1981, which led to the suspension of Soviet flights to New York, a peculiar situation had obtained whereby Pan Am, the American participant in the joint service, found it virtually impossible to sell tickets in Moscow, whereas the Russians could do so easily in New York. The result was a great imbalance in the third and fourth freedoms such that it seems to me highly unlikely that the United States will ever permit the restoration of Russian flights unless there is some much stronger guarantee of functional reciprocity in the future.

It was the fifth freedom, the right to pick

up passengers in a foreign country and carry them on to a third country, that became the rarest privilege and the one most jealously granted. At first it was seldom needed in intercontinental flying because there was a tendency to concentrate service on one or two "gateways"—New York or Miami on the East Coast; Los Angeles or San Francisco on the West Coast; London, Paris, or Amsterdam in western Europe. And planes were small enough—the DC-4 carried some thirty-five in trans-Atlantic service—that separate planes were used to fly between single pairs of these gateways. But as planes increased in size, and particularly as the maximum stage was lengthened so interior cities in North America could be reached, there were routes on which it was desirable to have several destinations in Europe to combine so as to gain a viable passenger load. Once having stopped at the closer, there was a strong commercial urge to be able to board passengers there in order to keep the load factor up on the subsequent leg of the journey. Bilateral agreements between the United States and other countries brought much of the fifth freedom into play, but mainly because the value of landing rights in the United States was so extreme that this country had a good bargaining point. In working out those agreements after jets were introduced—and interior American cities began to be served directly from Europe—Britain, France, Germany, and the Scandinavian countries gained unusually generous rights to overfly the whole domestic airlines system of the United States, loading passengers on the West Coast for Europe. Japan gained equally advantageous rights with respect to the East Coast. All the United States gained in return was the right to land at Prestwick in Scotland, or at Nice and the three Scandinavian capitals rather than Copenhagen alone.

The rapid evolution of international civil aviation, the fundamental structural change that came with jets, and the intensely nationalistic nature of the industry—as became clear even from the British and Dutch stand at the Chicago Conference—all have created strains that were not foreseen. The vastly greater value of overflight privileges in the United States as compared with America's benefits from the operation of the fifth freedom in Europe has created a potentially disruptive element. Decisions made in the immediate postwar period have not disadvantaged the United States alone: informed opinion in Norway now views the benefits gained by joining with Sweden and Denmark in the creation of the Scandinavian Airlines System in 1946 as a mixed blessing. A worldwide airline clearly resulted but there is little doubt that Denmark gained most from the consortium, even though its interest is identical with the Norwegian (two-sevenths of the total, with Sweden holding three-sevenths). The choice of Copenhagen as the junction city for northern Europe has left Oslo, in particular, rather in an aviation backwater with little nonstop service to the rest of Europe or trans-Atlantic service to the United States, save on an American airline. There seems to me little doubt that in these times of straitened airline circumstance and much intensified competition there will in the next decade be considerable pressure to reexamine, and potentially revise the basic structure of international flying that was established very quickly, and somewhat casually, in the years right after 1945.

In the years between 1945 and 1959 that pattern evolved quickly, with most national airlines seeking to expand their services to all adjacent capitals and to London and New York. Britain, France, West Germany, the Netherlands, the Scandinavians, Japan, Australia, and Canada sought, generally successfully, to establish worldwide air services to match those being projected by American companies. The Roosevelt administration had already decided at the close of the war

The DC-6. American Airlines photograph.

that Pan Am would lose its chosen-instrument status. American Airlines entered the field as it purchased American Export Airlines when the latter was found to be operating against the law because it was owned by a shipping company, an organization forbidden to own a competing medium of transport. TWA immediately jumped into European and North African markets on the basis of its vast experience as a military contract flier during the war. Braniff Airways took over from Panagra when this embargo of shipping company ownership of an air-

line was also applied to the Grace Lines interest in that carrier. Eastern and American rapidly expanded services to the Caribbean and Mexico, even to the northern tier of South America; and Northwest commenced service across the Pacific to compete with Pan Am and TWA, which had entered the service after the war. United Airlines remained the only one of the Big Four that did not get into international operations, perhaps in response to the thinking of its president, Pat Patterson, who in 1944 stated his view that in postwar flying twenty-three airliners would be able to carry all the people flying across the Atlantic in the year 1955.[93] No doubt his thinking was influenced by a government report that had noted that some 20,000 persons crossed the North Atlantic by steamship in peacetime and that maybe 4,000 to 6,000 of them might be diverted from first class to flying, an equivalent in cost at the time.

The great advances in aircraft performance came as a result of the ever-improving power of American engines. This successful effort was already apparent before the war, when in 1939 the British built the Armstrong-Whitworth *Ensign,* a plane that was unsatisfactory in its service to Imperial Airways until it was refitted, during the war, with more powerful American engines.[94] The war moved engine development forward with great speed, so the DC-4 and *Constellation* designed for prewar engines became in one sense obsolete when they were first made available to the airlines in 1945. To overcome that situation, the aircraft builders started designing modifications that became essentially new planes from a commercial viewpoint. "The first new design to enter service after the war was the DC-6, which began scheduled flying in 1947. Differing from the DC-4 mostly in its size and speed—it cruised at 280 miles per hours instead of 200—" its basic design was merely a stretch of the prewar plane, though one critical enough to permit nonstop journeys across the United States under ideal conditions.[95] The speed advance also allowed the DC-6s to operate a westbound New York–Los Angeles service in 10 hours, 50 minutes, where the DC-3, with three stops, had taken 17 hours, 40 minutes, and the DC-4 had required around 15 hours. This speedup was a result of two improvements; that in cruising speed is self-evident but there was also a sufficient increase in maximum stage length (consequent on more powerful engines, with greater lift, and more fuel-carrying capacity)

to permit a reduction in the number of technical stops required. The change had begun in 1946 with the placement in service of the Lockheed *Constellation* (1-049) that reduced intermediate stops to one in transcontinental service and advanced the speed to 270 miles per hour. The DC-6 had increased that speed only marginally, 10 miles per hour, but it had removed the intermediate stop westbound. The DC-7, introduced in 1953, advanced the speed 25 to 40 miles per hour and increased the fuel capacity sufficiently so that consistent nonstop service either east- or westbound became possible, reducing the journey time to 8 hours westbound and 7 hours, 40 minutes east-bound. This represented the ultimate accomplishment of piston-engined planes.[96]

THE TURBO PROP AIRLINERS

Before looking at that geographical pattern, note must be taken of a line of aircraft development that tells us a great deal about the continuing success of the American aircraft builders—the development of the turboprop engine wherein the fuel was burned to operate a turbine geared to the propeller. This transitional technology had come about because theoretical studies had indicated that jet engines (basically turbines) could not operate as efficiently at intermediate speeds as could a propeller. It was appreciated that airframes, flying practices, and other factors made the high speeds of the pure jet impracticable for efficient operation. To resolve this dilemma using a turbine hitched to a propeller seemed to offer advantages, among them the cheaper upkeep of the turbine engine and the higher power-to-weight ratio it enjoyed. It was the British who saw the most advantage in the development of the turboprop, and then considerably because the American engine manufacturers seemed to have a virtual stranglehold on the making of high-efficiency piston engines and the planes that used them.[97] The Vickers *Viscount*, using Rolls-Royce Dart engines, was first flown by 1948 and was put in experimental service in 1950, when British European Airways ordered twenty. These were the first turboprops, and they proved most effective on fairly short-distance operations.

The American operators were very hesitant in shifting to the new technology, for several reasons. They had large numbers of fairly new planes that had been designed and built to the particular geographical demands of American civil aviation—that is, rather long legs in interregional and transcontinental service. There was also the anticipation that the pure jet airliner was only a few years in the future and that the turboprop was at best only a transition. American aircraft builders adopted that argument, holding that while they waited for the jet, the retrofitting of turboprops to existing planes was the logical course. Both Douglas, with the DC-7D, and Lockheed, with a new variant of the *Constellation,* held out the prospect of a turboprop evolution from the two basic American planes. The result was that only American Airlines looked covetously at turboprops, perhaps because it was then the largest American carrier and the one with the greatest number of short to intemediate-length services. At their behest Lockheed designed and built an American turboprop, the *Electra,* to compete with imported *Viscounts* used by Capital Airlines in similar service in the Northeast. The *Viscount* turned out to be the British DC-3, and just about the only commercially successful British plane in the postwar period. Its success came from a felicitous combination of a relatively simple and proven turboprop engine and a fairly simple evolution from existing airframes. In other words, there was no element of experimentation where failure could hold up the introduction of the plane

to commercial service, thus foregoing the advantage of being the first in the market.

Even so, the rapid development of the commercial jet was such that the turboprop had a short life. The problem turboprops posed was that they were great fuel consumers, giving up to the piston planes an advantage that began to weigh more heavily as airline competition increased, reducing load factors and making operating costs a critical concern. American aircraft builders gained much of the value of increased power-to-weight ratios through the introduction of the turbocompound engine on the DC-7C and the later *Super Constellations*. The turboprop revolution never came in America, probably because the geographical pattern of American civil aviation placed more emphasis on longer flights, and the first generation of turboprop planes were not good in that field. Only the later British derivatives of the *Viscount,* the *Vanguard,* and particularly the *Britannia* had stage lengths useful in the longer American operations. The 40- to 50-mile speed advantage, over the DC-7, was not a sufficient inducement, and by the time of their introduction—1957 for the *Britannia* and 1960 for the *Vanguard*—the jet was on the scene, so the turboprop proved one of the several ingenious but hardly commercially important British innovations in postwar transportation.

CIVIL AVIATION ON THE EVE OF THE JET

When we turn to the geography of civil aviation just before the introduction of jets, certain features stand out. The first among these was the introduction of nonstop flying over great distances—the Atlantic, major stretches of the Pacific, and transcontinentally. It was with the DC-6 that S.A.S. began Polar Service from Copenhagen to Los Angeles via Sondre Stromfjord in Greenland and Winnipeg in 1954.[98] The Great Cir-

The Lockheed *Electra*. American Airlines photograph.

cle Route began to be used more frequently because by this time the maximum stage of aircraft was sufficient to allow the overflying of previously uncrossable areas, such as the Barren Ground of Canada, Amazonia, and the North Pacific. With the adoption of what were considerably shortened routes, the fact that the DC-7 gained no speed advantage of any moment on its predecessor did not destroy its competitive advantage. With easier long-distance flying, passenger movements increased, particularly by encouraging the

shift from transcontinental trains in North America and steamships on the North Atlantic, the Pacific, and the Indian Ocean (to Australia).

This trend was advanced rapidly by the adoption during the 1950s of the practice of running so-called air coaches. United Airlines had toyed with the idea of reduced fares on planes flying at the less desirable hours as early as 1940, but the war delayed any serious consideration of the practice. Only in the early 1950s was there equipment sufficient to reconsider the question. Domestic carriers began to run what were variously called "coach" or "night coach" flights in 1952 and Pan Am introduced "tourist" flights on the Atlantic at that time. Both actions were a response to the rise of the "non-scheduled" airline—basically a charter carrier normally using fairly old and slow equipment and flying only when a full load was on hand. Given those conditions, the fares were sharply reduced over the single, basically first-class fares then charged by the airlines. "Nonsked" operation could work only on fairly heavily traveled routes flown over moderately long to great distances. The result was the creation of a true economy of scale in flying, wherein it was not unusual for the cheapest fare over a short distance to be as large as the cheapest over a considerably greater distance for which economy fares were available. At first the economy services were in separate planes but eventually the demand was so great that the larger planes coming into use during the 1950s could not be filled with those continuing to fly first class. The outcome was the joining of the two groups in a single plane, with considerable distinctions in on-board services but none in the basic transportation provided. In the beginning the first-class passengers were placed in the rear of the craft, which was both safer and smoother in flight; but in one of those quirks of ostentation it was discovered that the economic élite prefered to ride in front, so the class sections came to be reversed.

The effect of economy-tourist class service was striking. By 1955 the domestic airlines of the United States were carrying more passengers than did the railroads in intercity service.[99] At the same time the North Atlantic carriers overtook and passed the companies in the Atlantic Ferry that had ruled both the waves and the service for almost a hundred years. This rise in patronage was not alone the result of reduced fares, though that was almost certainly the dominating influence. Faster schedules gained from longer stages and nonstop operation also contributed, as did the increased altitude of flying. Pressurization of planes, introduced in the Boeing planes of the late 1930s, made widely available with the immediate postwar *Constellation,* and introduced in the Douglas aircraft with the DC-6, had permitted flying at or even above 20,000 feet, where weather was likely to be better and speeds could be increased. All these factors contributed to the greater popularity of flying and the enlargement of the market, which in turn allowed for the operation of tourist class and the lowering of fares. In that enlarged market the geographical pattern of service could be both ramified and intensified. Routes from North America to southern Africa and Australia and New Zealand, from Africa to Australia via the Indian Ocean and South America to New Zealand and Australia, and from Europe to the Far East via Canada and Alaska could be proposed.

THE ADVENT OF JET AIRCRAFT

The jet engine was proposed in theoretical terms already in 1927–1928, when Frank Whittle was a British Royal Air Force cadet. The search was for a way in which flight could be speeded up through experimentation along two lines of advance: a simple rise in the speed given by the engine and a lifting of the altitudinal ceiling for flight that would increase the speed. By 1929 Whittle had settled on the use of a gas turbine to create the jet. In the mid-1930s Hans von Ohain at Göttingen took up the search for a practical jet engine with the support of the Heinkel company, who were also backing Werner von Braun's initial efforts to produce a rocket-propelled plane. In 1936 both the German and the British efforts to build a jet engine began in earnest, though in the British instance hardly at a fast pace. By 1937 Whittle

The mix of planes at La Guardia Airport around 1950. Port Authority of New York and New Jersey photograph.

had an operating engine, but it was only in 1939 that he was allowed by his service to engage in development research full time. In August, 1939, Heinkel and von Ohain had the first jet plane to fly, the He 178. Fortunately for the Allies, bureaucratic interference in this development so slowed the further development that by the end of the war the British effort had caught up and passed the German one. Military jet aircraft of German and British construction began to appear during the last year of World War II, so in 1945 the stage was set for considering this engine for civil aviation.[100]

The fundamental difficulty was that this was an engine designed for high speed at a time when the airlines could not clearly envisage operating at any such speeds. The fuselages and wings of commercial aircraft were not appropriate to jet power at high speeds. As these basic designs were stretched over the next ten years, from the DC-4 to the DC-7 and the *Constellation* to the *Super-Super-Constellation,* speeds were increased from 200 miles an hour for the DC-4 to 359 miles per hour for the DC-7C. To utilize the jet engine efficiently, operating speeds must be raised a hundred miles an hour over the maximum then attained,[101] and seemingly to do that an entirely different fuselage and wing were needed. Thus the shift to jet power required not the simple stretching in which the aircraft builders had been engaged for more than a decade in 1945, but instead so much technical innovation that the characteristics of the resulting plane were very much in doubt. This was particularly the case with respect to the economic characteristics of the craft, which would determine whether the airlines could operate them once built. It seems to me significant that it was in the heavily subsidized, strongly nationalistic framework of British civil aviation that the first efforts at building a jet passenger plane took place. Britain still clung to the Buy British doctrine and was rightly proud of its accomplishments in the development of the jet engine. In this, quite unlike the situation in piston engines and planes to employ them, Britain was ahead and might profit from its lead.

It was the British who had the faith to pursue the true jet and the engine to power it. The Rolls Royce Avon engine, designed in 1944 and introduced in 1949, was available for use in the prospective jet passenger aircraft.[102] De Havilland in England began to design a jet passenger plane in 1946 and had the *Comet I* flying in 1949. But this enterprise seems to have been somewhat lonely.

> The greater willingness of the American [aeronautical] scientist and designer to try new ideas gave them an advantage over their British counterparts in the years immediately after the war.... Comparing the technical achievements of the British and American industries, so far as their ability to produce economical jet-powered airliners was concerned, the American industry seemed to be ahead from 1945 to 1950 in airplane design, but behind in engine design; in the early 1950's the British industry seemed to catch up in airplane design while the American industry caught up in engine design. But the dif-

ference between the technical achievements of different companies in the same country was still greater than that between the industries of the two countries, on the average, so British and American airplanes of the mid-fifties cannot be so crudely evaluated. All this comparison can suggest is that the technical possibility of producing successful airliners was roughly equal in the two countries; what was actually built depended on political and commercial factors, too.[103]

It was the availability of superior Rolls-Royce engines that made the *Comet* possible: it was the failure of adequate innovation in aircraft design that made it ultimately a disaster. Similarly, it was the absence of an adequate American jet engine in the late 1940s that delayed an American jetliner until the late 1950s, but when it flew it demonstrated again the superb ability of U.S. companies in the production of commercially successful aircraft.

The *Comet I* began flying in 1952. To accomplish that feat so early, the de Havilland Company had made two fateful decisions: to build the body of the plane as close to that of existing airliners as possible, and to use a jet engine that they had developed for military craft rather than wait for the introduction of the Rolls-Royce Avon that was expected only in 1954. Using that engine limited the *Comet I's* speed to 460 miles per hour, its stage to no more than 2,000 miles, and its passenger load to thirty-six.[104] Even more limiting was the fact that its operating costs were three times those of the DC-6. The geographical pattern that the *Comet I* might effectively operate was strikingly similar to that that had characterized the early European intercontinental services. The first run began from London going to Johannesburg on May 2, 1952. This was followed soon after by the establishment of the route to Cairo, Karachi, Bombay, Colombo, Calcutta, and Singapore, which was continued on to Tokyo in April, 1953. Air France also bought *Com-*

ets that they operated to Rome, Beirut, and Algiers; UAT ran them from Paris and Marseilles to Casablanca, Dakar, Abidjan, and Brazzaville.[105] These were essentially long-distance runs that might be operated using short hops across the Mediterranean and then across the continental masses in easy stages. The plane was expensive to operate and appealing only where long journeys were carried out across those great land masses. "The surprising feature of de Havilland's conduct seems, in retrospect, that they should have built an airplane that carried too few passengers to be economic, and which they would soon make obsolete."[106]

Fate was to accomplish that process even more rapidly. Three *Comets* had been lost because there were "handling difficulties at landing and take-off." A further plane was lost near Calcutta when it "broke up in the air in a tropical storm in circumstances which were never fully explained." But the coup de grace came when a BOAC *Comet* also "broke up" soon after takeoff from Rome on January 10, 1954. When a South African Airways *Comet* suffered a similar fate on April 8 off the coast of Sicily, all *Comets* were grounded.[107] Parts of the BOAC plane that were recovered off Elba ultimately yielded an answer to what happened. "The *Comet*'s cabin had burst as a result of metal fatgue under stress of repeated pressurization cycles."[108]

With the withdrawal of all *Comet I*s, the status of jetliner development had to be reappraised carefully. There was no doubt that the airframe used by de Havilland needed considerable improvement, thus destroying the British planemakers' lead in jet-engine construction. By the time the *Comet IV*, which proved a safe plane, began to fly in 1958, the advantages of being the first to build jetliners had been lost. The plane that resulted represented 1945 technology somewhat updated more than it did the current state of the art as represented by the Boeing

jets just then coming into service. There is no doubt, however, that the lessons learned from the *Comet* were invaluable in permittig the aircraft builders and the airline operators to work a true jet revolution in the course of little more than five years, after the Boeing 707 entered service in 1958.

We may now turn to the late 1950s phase of the propeller-jet transition. The Americans and the British were the main competitors throughout this transitional period, with the Americans trying hard to catch up with the British jet-engine technology and their European cousins seeking to come abreast in airframe construction. The severe setback with the *Comet* airframe so delayed de Havilland that it was unable to introduce an airworthy successor until 1958, the same year that the American Boeing Company succeeded handsomely in introducing their 707. Boeing rapidly pulled up to de Havilland and then well ahead of them when Pratt and Whitney introduced their J-57 jet engine that offered more power than any available in Britain and with operating costs similar to those for piston engines.[109] The J-57 became the basis from 1952 on for the design of a truly large jetliner, and it was with that power that Boeing could build the 707, the aircraft that played much the same role with respect to jet operation that the DC-3 had in piston planes: it was the first jetliner that was commercially viable, and, like its predecessor twenty years before, it demonstrated an economic productivity of the sort that no earlier craft had approached. The 707 as it was improved with fan-jet engines became so much more efficient than the best piston planes, even the fabled DC-6s, that the revolution was on and the shift to jet power was extremely rapid.

The principle of the fan jet had been proposed by Frank Whittle in the 1930s and taken up by Rolls-Royce in the 1940s. They had diverted about 5 percent of the air entering the engines into a bypass around the

The inaugural flight of the Boeing 707, October 26, 1958. Pan American World Airways photograph.

burner to provide better cooling and some additional thrust. Pratt and Whitney had at first scoffed at this practice, but when General Electric showed interest in the idea and American Airlines asked for the fan-jet engine because it was quieter, Pratt and Whitney succumbed.

What had happened? Pratt and Whitney had done it again. They had taken the principle that Whittle had enunciated and Rolls had cautiously executed and expanded it almost beyond recognition. If Rolls had thought to send a little bit of air through the engine un-

combusted, Pratt & Whitney turned its model into a veritable fresh-air machine. Less than half the thrust would be produced by the combustion core of the engine. [The speed of the fan blades was raised] to the point where they compressed and expelled the air that provided 60 percent of the planes forward thrust.[110]

There were two great advantages of these fan-jets in comparison with the pure combustion-thrust engines they replaced: they were very much quieter, avoiding the deafening whine of the earliest jets, and they were considerably cheaper to run. With them, the operating costs of jets were dropped well below the level of the last, large piston-engined planes.

This is not the place to attempt a full summary of the evolution of jetliners. It is sufficient to note several of the principal changes they experienced. The next to come after the introduction of fan jets in the early 1960s was the move to shift the location of the jet engines from the wing, in the position that had become virtually universal for piston planes, to the fuselage in the rear. The idea had first been applied by the French in the building of the *Caravelle* in 1959, and was soon taken by up Boeing (in the 727) and Douglas (in the DC-9) once United Airlines ordered twenty *Caravelles*. The advantages of the rear engines were much quieter cabins for the passengers and better aerodynamics for a wing uncluttered by engine pods. In developing the 727 and the DC-9, the American aircraft builders also changed the take-off and landing angles to a much steeper altitude, allowing the planes to rise to the economical cruising altitude of 30,000 feet or more quite quickly and, in turn, to descend rapidly into the airport at the end of the hop. These shifts made shorter-distance jet operation more practicable, thus further speeding up the jet transition.[111]

The next great change in jetliners came in the opposite direction, in the search for the ultimate in long-distance jet aircraft. That development, as was the case with most of the evolution of the craft and, in turn, with the geography of air transport, came from improvements in engines. The virtual monopoly of high-powered aircraft engines by American builders continued during this evolutionary stage. It was the availability of larger engines, commonly more economical in operation and in power in relation to weight, that permitted the shift. The introduction of the fan jets of the early 1960s had raised by fifty to sixty the number of passengers that might be carried by the 707. The 727 when it came along in the early 1960s could carry as many passengers in its stretched version as could the four-engined 707, but with only three engines. Thus the designers' experience was that power increases meant profit increases, and the harnessing of the larger engines being designed and built became the next goal in aircraft construction.

That goal was reached with the adoption of the *wide-bodied* fuselage. The favorable experience with the jetliner once the engines had been made stronger and more economical, as well as quieter and commercially productive over shorter stages than had first been envisioned for jets, was to encourage the development of the airborne equivalent of the superliners of the 1920s and 1930s. These were to be planes capable of carrying between 350 and 450 passengers and of making the water jump across any ocean.

Boeing was the first to enter the competition when Juan Trippe for Pan Am made the largest aircraft order ever placed, $525 million for twenty-five Boeing "jumbo-jets" to be denominated the Boeing 747. When these came into service in the late 1960s, they could carry up to 500 people, though in normal operation with first-class as well as economy they carried between 400 and 425. The 747 was half again as long as any previous plane and wide enough to have nine or ten rows of seats as well as a second aisle. This stretching in both dimensions gave the 747 a passenger capacity two and a half times that of the largest 707s and DC-8s.[112] Once in operation the wide-bodies proved sufficiently more economical with a full passenger load to permit the transport of mass groups of passengers at unheard-of low fares.

The favorable response to the 747—craft were sold to most of the important international airlines as well as to most of the major trunk carriers in North America—

encouraged the other airplane builders to enter the contest. By this time the Europeans had been fairly effectively excluded from the general market for large planes, leaving only Douglas and Lockheed to contest with Boeing. By then, Boeing had become the dominant aircraft builder in the world at large, gaining that rank entirely from its successful development of jetliners, starting with the 707 and building even more heavily on the 727 that became the best-selling airliner since the DC-3. With a short-range jet, the 737, Boeing developed the concept of a "family of planes," no longer direct stretches as had been the practice in the 1940s and 1950s, but now specialized airframes for specialized services. The 707 remained, until the 747, Boeing's long-range jetliner, and the development of the 727, with several stretches, was for the regional and inter-regional market. The 737 came about to serve those airlines, and those routes that were intraregional, requiring jets that could carry fairly small numbers of passengers, though many more than most piston planes ever carried (as the air passenger market had grown so massively), over distances of a few hundred miles per stage. The 747 completed the geographical specialization of the airliner to the extent that any serious aircraft builder had to seek its own entry in this size and range of service.

Douglas had developed the DC-8 as the competition for the 707, offering it for introduction in 1960. It, like the 707, cost about a third less to operate than the piston planes it replaced, and flew 40 percent faster.[113] Douglas expanded its family by introducing the DC-9 in the late 1960s to carry about 110 passengers over fairly short stages. The premier airframe builder of the piston era sought to regain its position among jets by developing the DC-10, introduced in 1970, whose capacity was in the 250- to 260-passenger range. The plane proved a strong competitor for Boeing, as it was a wide-body in many ways better suited to domestic flying in Canada and the United States, where frequent and highly ramified services seemed to call for planes in the 250-passenger range more than in the 400–500 range useful mainly on the New York–Los Angeles run. The DC-10 suffered an unfortunate stigma when improper maintenance by American Airlines caused one to crash on takeoff from O'Hare Airport in Chicago. After correcting those practices and strengthening the members that gave way to provide more insurance, the DC-10 has resumed its popularity with the airlines for its cheaper operating costs and appropriate size for most markets, including a number of trans-Atlantic services.

The 747 has as a result been increasingly restricted to very heavily traveled routes or those requiring extremely long stages, such as flights from the western United States to western Europe, or across the Pacific. This specialization has been further enhanced by the development of an ultra-long-distance plane, the Boeing 747SP, capable of flying almost any commercially practicable route nonstop. South African Airways, with its inability to land in most of black Africa, has adopted this plane, as has Pan Am for nonstop services to Australia from the West Coast of the United States. Not possessing so large a family of planes as Boeing, and having gained a far smaller part of the market, Douglas has not sought to play tag with the Seattle plane builder in this small and specialized ultra-long-distance market.

Lockheed, the other American aircraft builder to survive into the jet era, demonstrates the problems of survival today. After very successful development of the *Constellation,* as one of the two prime competitors for world markets in the halcyon days of piston-plane operation, Lockheed sought to enter the jet age in the manner that the Europeans were doing so, by the creation of a turboprop aircraft that could compete with

The inaugural flight of the Boeing 747, 1970. Pan American World Airways photograph.

the proposed Vickers *Viscount* that the British had announced for 1953. But by following the British lead, Lockheed had diverted effort and money from the main chance, which was in the early development of a pure jet. In that way the company missed out on the first stage of jetliner construction, that represented by the 707 for Boeing and the DC-8 for Douglas. It was only when the next major rachet in the evolution of the craft was under discussion, that toward the wide-bodied plane, that Lockheed managed to extricate itself from the blind alley of the turboprop. Again the

British lead proved almost disastrous. In the late 1960s Rolls-Royce began flogging a new jet engine that they had on the drawing board. This RB211 was to be highly advanced, efficient in fuel consumption, and possessed of more pounds of thrust than anyone else's engines. So satisfied were Rolls and their countrymen that the *Observer* did not hesitate to crow "Britain is better than anyone else in the world" in aircraft-engine production when Lockheed signed a contract to buy the engine for their new wide-bodied plane on March 29, 1968.

Experience was to smite Britain for its

The Lockheed L-1011. Trans-World Airlines photograph.

shameless assertion and to bring Lockheed to the edge of bankruptcy for believing its reality. The airframe they designed, the L-1011, was perhaps the finest wide-body built, but the engines they selected for it were not. "Lockheed's design for the L-1011 was considerably more sophisticated than any previous design, and many of the airlines also judged the RB211 to be half a generation ahead of both the Pratt & Whitney and the G.E. engines. Customers of the L-1011 knew that they would be well served if both the airframe and the engine upheld the promise of their design. The airframe did, but the engine did not."[114] It took Rolls-Royce ten years to evolve their engine to the point that it delivered on its promises, and they on theirs. By then Rolls was bankrupt, and it was only by herculean efforts of Lockheed and a loan guarantee by the United States government that the aircraft builder survived, and by their survival and agreement to a revision of the Rolls contract upward that the smug British engine builder remained in business.

THE AIRPORT, THE GEOGRAPHICAL ANCHOR

In the earliest phase of flying, taking off and landing were accomplished through the use of racecourses and reasonably flat pastures.

Even in the late 1920s and early 1930s, when commercial aviation was firmly underway, grassed or graveled runways were the order of the day. With the advent of the DC-3 and the rapid rise in the volume of passengers and frequency of flights, some better system was needed. It was provided by paving the runways to overcome the softening of the surface by repeated landings in wet weather. Bromma, the airport for Stockholm, and Schiphol (Amsterdam) were the first to be paved in Europe; La Guardia Airport in New York was one of the first in the United States. These early pavings were relatively thin concrete or tar, but over the years the increasing weight of planes has forced constant strengthening to the point that the 775,000-pound 747 requires a runway pavement some 2 feet thick.

The design complexity of the airport has increased along with the improvement of paving. As takeoff weights have risen, the length of the runway has had to be lengthened until today it may require a runway of up to 13,000 feet to take off the largest jets at high-elevation airports such as Denver, Johannesburg, or Mexico City. The introduction of the jetliner forced the reconstruction of most airports seeking to cater to scheduled carriers, as the weight of these turbo-fan planes was considerably increased over the weights of the piston planes they replaced in various types of service. Runways had to be lengthened and strengthened; when the wide-bodied jets were introduced between 1970 and 1972, new unloading facilities had to be introduced to deal with planes with floors up to 18.5 feet above the surface of the runway. The "jetways" became a distinguishing feature of those airports engaged in trunk-line service, separating them from the more regional and local airports where stairway ramps remained common. Today about the only personages seen descending theses ramps are dignitaries arriving in private 707s or the

like; the rest of us depart through an aluminum conduit with all the glamor of arrival by Parisian sewer-boat.

The earlier airports, those built between the advent of the DC-3 and that of the jet, tended to be much more complex than their modern replacements. What is commonly considered "the world's most-overcrowded airport," Heathrow in London, was originally constructed with six runways in mind, but the arthritic nature of the original plan and the introduction of jets have forced (and permitted) the dropping of two of those landing ways.[115] The general point is that the power of jets has made possible to land "cross wind," whereas in the past craft were forced to land into the wind. Even today, as the windshear-related crash of Pan American at New Orleans in July, 1982, bore out, there may be some reasons for moderating landings and takeoffs because of the wind. But up to now that moderation has not been a matter of selecting a particular runway so much as one of delaying the movement until the wind itself moderates. This attempt to gain independence from the wind direction also has introduced the so-called hard landing in times of severe and variable winds, when jets land as quickly and determinedly as possible to avoid being blown off the runway by locally strong gusts. But the cost of jet-weight runways is such that no airport can afford more than a choice between two directions as a result of the up-to-two-mile length of the facility and its extremely costly pavement.

The physical structure of airport terminals has become a controversial subject among advocates of radically different forms. The poles are the decentralized facility, with a number of separate terminals rented to individual airlines and the linear type of straightforward rectangular integrated terminal. Most of the small and medium-size airport facilities fall in the second category, while most of the giant intercontinental air-

The runways at La Guardia in the late 1930s. Port Authority of New York and New Jersey photograph.

ports tend toward moderate to extreme eccentricity and indulgence of planners' and architects' hunches. Because most European airports handle considerably fewer passengers, and often fewer airlines, than the larger American facilities, they tend toward the linear rectangular form. The introduction of jets has caused most to develop the finger pier attachment by which jetways can be reached that make contact with the actual planes. Some of these terminals are large and complex—Schiphol in Amsterdam and Frankfurt's airport—but others are fairly plain as Manchester Ringway, Oslo Fornebu, and Helsinki Vantaa.

Only Heathrow and the two larger Parisian airports are eccentric, London because of historical mischance and Paris because of the French obsession with high technology. In both instances the traveler is the loser. Heathrow began as a military project when it was thought that British troops would have to be airlifted to the then "Far East" to defeat the Japanese, but the rapid defeat of those Imperial Forces made the project unnecessary. Still, the original planning had been done by the British Royal Air Force, an organization with a fixed notion that an airport had to be designed with the facilities in the center of a number of separate runways wrapped around to permit takeoffs and landings on a choice of azimuths. The result was ultimately disastrous for a commercial airport as it confined the space available for the construction and enlargement of terminals, and the functional nature of airports constrained the development of tall buildings that might provide the necessary space. When joined with a poorly thought-out design for those terminals that the confined space did permit, the result was the "most overtaxed airport" already mentioned. Crowding and confusion are the result, and the vexed question of a third London airport arises as much because of the atrocious teminal conditions at Heathrow as because of any absolute inability of an airport to handle so many flights or passengers. O'Hare Airport in Chicago demonstrates that a single facility may be considerably busier than Heathrow and still function reasonably efficiently.

The Parisian airports, though considerably less busy than Heathrow, are still among the world's busier facilities. Orly, to the south of the city, was the first modern airport, developed after World War II from a former naval flying school, As it evolved it became two tall, boxy terminals possessed of mechanized internal passenger movers, predicting the extreme development of those facilities in the futurist Charles de Gaulle Airport opened at Roissy north of Paris in 1974. CDG, as it has tended to become known by its airport symbol, consists at present of a central circular terminal, highly developed with motorized walkways ascending in Plexiglas tubes that carry people around rather like a standardized commodity, which of course in airline practice they are. The system is subject to difficult interruption because of mechanical failures or strikes, and it tends to be unforgiving once one has started along the wrong path, leaving little choice but to accept one's fate until spewed out at the curbside where the brave

can seek to retrace their steps and start with fresh hope and a different direction. For all its rigidities in handling passengers, CDG does have splendid flexibility in treating with nature, as I discovered in December, 1979, when landing in a TWA plane from Cairo that arrived in an empty airport in mid-morning because of a fog so thick that it was necessary to crawl to the terminal once on the ground. Only TWA among American, or for that matter most airlines, and Charles de Gaulle among most airports had the ability to handle totally blind landings. Such can be the advantages of high technology, but the imprecision and indecision among passengers in terminals can make its application to ordinary human beings disintegrative.

In North America the airport has been treated rather differently from the way it has in Europe or some other countries where a single facility may serve the long-distance needs of an entire country. In the United States no single airport has ever played the dominant role that Heathrow or Schiphol plays even today, and the trend has been toward a greater regional balance. Cities such as Seattle or Philadelphia that had virtually no air service of any importance before 1945 today stand as major national and international destinations. American cities, fully appreciating the modern application of urban mercantilism, have invested hundreds of millions of dollars each in gaining a modern jet airport. Even within a state this rivalry may exist. St. Louis and Kansas City; Philadelphia and Pittsburgh; Los Angeles, San Diego, San Jose, Oakland, and San Francisco demonstrate this situation. Only small, compact states, such as Massachusetts, Rhode Island, and Connecticut, have been able to have a single airport and airport commission at work. Elsewhere there is too much awareness of the prime virtues of easy and good access to the civil-aviation network to permit the restriction of service to a single major airport.

The difference between the United States and most developed countries other than Canada and Australia is that by far the vast majority of intercity travelers by public transportation move by air. Currently it is about 85 percent of the travelers, and they move in about 3,000 civil aircraft in regular service. This represents about half of all the airliners flying the world today, so the scale of American aviation is so vastly greater than any other country that it is difficult to compare the United States–Canadian system, highly internally integrated, with the air system anywhere else.[116] With such a large system and market the number of airports required is very great, and the absolute necessity for any sizable city to have an airport and air service is obvious. Thus, in discussing airports in the United States and Canada, most must be summarized as small to moderate in size; of simple integrated design; and tied by a few airlines to other cities of similar size nearby and to one or two hubs where interregional, transcontinental, or intercontinental connections may be made. Beyond that generalization there is less consistency that can be perceived when viewing the dozen or so major air terminals and half dozen hubs. Boston, New York, Washington, Atlanta, Miami, Chicago, St. Louis, Dallas–Fort Worth, Houston, Denver, Los Angeles, San Francisco, and Seattle in the United States and Montréal, Toronto, Edmonton, and Vancouver represent the great airports of North America. Of those only Chicago, Atlanta, St. Louis, Dallas–Fort Worth, and Denver (plus smaller junctions at Salt Lake City and Las Vegas) are operated as organized hubs where a major airline brings together many of its routes, there interchanging passengers from one flight to another so as to provide one-change service to virtually all other destinations on its company network. Delta Airlines pioneered this practice, using Atlanta; its direct

competitor, Eastern Airlines, followed suit exactly in also using Atlanta, making that airport the world's second busiest in number of passengers handled, after Chicago O'Hare. Subsequently American Airlines made Dallas–Fort Worth its hub; United used both Chicago and Denver for its hubs, Continental Airlines and Frontier Airlines used Denver; Northwest employed Minneapolis; TWA adopted St. Louis; and Western Airlines used Salt Lake City in similar fashion. As a result, these airports have become congested both with the near-simultaneous arrival and departure of many flights and with the floods of passengers they bring.

The hub-and-spoke system represented by these confluxes of planes and passengers on a single airport and the general interchange function that the largest American metropolises perform in air travel have meant that eight of the first ten airports in the world ranked by passengers handled are American. Only Heathrow (number 4 in the world) and Tokyo Haneda in 1977 (number 5) broke the highest ranks. Los Angeles International ranked third, John F. Kennedy in New York sixth, San Francisco seventh, Dallas–Fort Worth eighth, Denver ninth, and La Guardia in New York tenth in that year; Miami was thirteenth, Washington National fourteenth, Honolulu seventeenth, and Boston eighteenth. Of these, only Washington and Boston were minor interchange points, but the two were the southern and northern anchors of the vast air shuttle in the American Northeast, which by some measure stands as the world's most heavily traveled air route. Frankfurt (eleventh), Osaka (twelfth), Paris Orly (fifteenth), Toronto (sixteenth), Rome Fiumicino (nineteenth), and Madrid (twentieth) completed the world's twenty largest airports in terms of passenger flows. In terms of aircraft movements the rankings changed somewhat: Philadelphia,

St. Louis, Detroit, and Kansas City joined the top twenty; Tokyo, Osaka, Honolulu, and Madrid fell below that mark.[117]

The pattern of the largest airports in the United States tends to be individually distinctive. Boston was perhaps the first of the extremely linear terminals with separate structures, leading one into another, arranged around a great open U in which a multistory parking garage has been built. John F. Kennedy, first opened in 1957, carried that design to an awkward extreme by separating the airlines into buildings somewhat remote from each other, occupied by single carriers, sometimes with lesser tenants.[118] Washington Dulles, a similarly new site opened in 1962, carried remoteness to the ludicrous limit first by being located on a long, unapproachable access highway at a point 27 miles from the White House and then by forcing the loading and unloading of planes in slow, rigid, and awkward mobile lounges that make the most vigorous and provident passenger travel at the speed of the most infirm or feckless. The isolation of Dulles has meant that the resurrected National Airport, just across the Potomac from downtown Washington, has nearly five times as many passengers in a facility that was the height of design in 1940. Atlanta, as a result of its hub function for two of the large airlines as well as its major regional significance, has been forced into a massive reconstruction and enlargement program that has produced the largest terminal in the world, spread over such a large area that internal transportation has had to be provided.

The interior hubs are, with the exception of Dallas–Fort Worth, airports with less exceptional physical layout. O'Hare Airport in Chicago began as a private airfield for the Douglas Aircraft Company during World War II called Orchard Place, thus the airport symbol for Chicago—ORD. The airfield was purchased by the city of Chicago after the war, and construction of a major jet airport was begun in 1949 and completed in its first phase in 1955, eclipsing the older Midway Airport closer to The Loop, which was shut down for a time. As American civil aviation expanded, O'Hare grew apace until it now handles the greatest number of landings and takeoffs of any commercial airport, some 1,900 arrivals and departures each day. With seven heavily utilized runways, O'Hare is by some measure the largest and most complex airport in existence and capable of handling nearly twice as many passengers as does Heathrow, and with far less confusion and clutter. As the present Jefferson Park subway-elevated line has been completed to O'Hare, it shares with the Cleveland airport the distinction of having the easiest access of any American terminal.[119] The layout of this vast facility is simple and straightforward, three massive rectangular terminals with piers leading to the vast number of gates that project jetways to reach the dozens of planes constantly loading and unloading there.

In sharp contrast is the other great interior hub, Dallas–Fort Worth, which is as complicated as Chicago is simple, and irksome to the transfer passenger in proportion. Intended as the terminal for a 17,000-acre facility, compared with O'Hare's 7,000, as opened in 1974 Dallas–Fort Worth Airport had three massive runways and four distinct semicircular terminals tied one with the other by a slow-moving automated train. Based on the notion that one could drive to within a couple hundred feet of the departure gate, the layout at Dallas–Fort Worth has proved sprawling but inconvenient for the hub function it has increasingly undertaken. This airport is certainly one of the great disasters of planning rigidity. Its elegant and elaborate layout must have appealed in plan form: its execution can hardly satisfy any rational person. Only that modular "design patron," driving up to the entrance in his large Texas car and walking directly to his close-in flight, is satisfactorily served. Anyone changing airlines must allow a lot of time to deal with the automated, but hardly very activated, subway; and even making a hub connection can require a lot of walking and a fair block of time.

Two other interior hubs have been far more successful as physical systems. Lambert Field in St. Louis was an early postwar facility with a great arched main terminal that has aged very well and permitted the projection of piers to provide more boarding gates. Denver's Stapleton Field, with a single comprehensive terminal, has risen into the top ten of the world's airports by service as a hub for United, Frontier, and Continental airlines. On the Pacific Coast, Los Angeles International is the dominant airport both in volume of traffic, being exceeded only by Chicago and Atlanta among the world's air facilities, and in its role as the fundamental junction city for access from California to western Europe and Latin America. As a physical structure, Los Angeles International is distinctive, standing as a terminal with two parallel ranks of buildings divided by a massive mall largely filled with parking structures and service facilities. The distinctive feature of the layout is that there are seven satellites, each reached by a tunnel from the ticketing buildings surrounding the mall, thus permitting the loading of planes completely around the circumference of the satellite. The arrangement reduces the excessive linearity found in Boston and the cramp and chaos of Heathrow.

San Francisco International Airport ranks along with Kennedy in traffic but provides service in a much more compact structure, three integrated terminals ranged in a U around a massive parking garage. As the Bay Area City's dominant airport, this terminal originates and terminates a very large volume of traffic, but its junction functions are far less than for Dallas–Fort Worth, Atlanta, or Denver. Seattle, with a terminal of three units physically separated one from the other and interconnected by a reasonably prompt subway system, shares with the Bay Area this originating-terminating characteristic, though each does serve as a jumping-off point—San Francisco particularly for Hawaii and the Pacific, and Seattle for Alaska and the Polar Route to Japan.

A final aspect of the airport that deserves some notice is the proximity to the central city. No other great city is so well served as Boston, whose Logan Airport is merely across a narrow harbor and reached by subway. Cleveland, Chicago, New York, Paris, and London share the subway access, but at a considerably greater distance from the core. Zurich, Frankfurt, and Amsterdam have main-line rail connections. At the opposite end of the spectrum, places like Prince Rupert, British Columbia, have airports that may be reached only by ferry from the mainland. Most cities have arterial highway approaches to their airports, commonly over a distance of ten to fifteen miles. In the 1960s in a rash of unbalanced futurism the planners in several cities designed over-sized and overly-isolated terminals. Mirabel Airport thirty-four miles north of Montréal is perhaps the extreme case, though Dulles twenty-six miles from Washington, Kansas City International eighteen miles out, and Buenos Aires some thirty-two miles from the Argentine metropolis all are rather isolated. For the airline traveler it is fortunate that the planner's notion of building an "inter-continental" airport at Palmdale, seventy-five miles north of Los Angeles, has been dropped for now.

In the consideration of the historical geography of air transportation the airport has increasingly become the main literally defined geographical feature. With the general adoption of jetliners, even for quite short hops, the former constraints imposed by mountain barriers have virtually disappeared. Almost any jetliner can fly over the world's highest mountains, and with the increasing efficiency of jet engines, the world's oceans no longer interpose severe barriers. The 747 can fly most oceans in one hop, and its specialized long-distance model can fly any ocean and most oceans and continents combined. The result is that today every place on earth approachable by jet planes is within less than twenty-four hours of any other place on earth, using the most direct route. For a very considerable part of the reasonably-settled world scheduled services do, in fact, provide schedules that permit interconnection of most places, even using connecting flights, within a twenty-four hour period. So for the average travelers the geography of air transport is getting to their local airport and getting to their ultimate objective from the airport on the other end. It is for that reason that we become increasingly concerned not with the conditions of actual flight, which have tended to become quite standardized, but rather with the geography of airports and the access to those facilities that in some cities have taken over from the central business district as the main site of human conflux within the metropolis, and certainly within its region, on any continuing basis. Metropolitan areas have tended to become most widely known by their football stadiums and their airports.

The next great change in jetliners came in the opposite direction, in the search for the ultimate in long-distance jet aircraft. That development, as was the case with most of the evolution of the craft, and in turn with the geography of air transport, came from improvements in engines. The virtual monopoly of high-powered aircraft engines by American builders continued during this evolutionary stage. It was the availability of larger engines, different from the jet airliners that had already been built. For a time Boeing, as by far the world's largest civil-aircraft builder, made detailed design studies for an SST. The company's economic studies found that only with a massive public investment in development could any private company undertake to build such a craft. When Congress turned down such a subvention, the American SST went into limbo, leaving the British and French consortium to pursue that goal with a massive subsidy of more than £1 billion. Possibly in a world of cheap jet fuel the resulting *Concorde,* which first flew commercially in 1976, might have made its mark; but it arrived in service three years after the Arab oil embargo imposed in 1973 as a response to the outbreak of war with Israel. In the succeeding times of drastic increases in the cost of fuel, which has risen in price over ten times in less than a decade, the *Concorde* has become a commercial pariah. Using something on the order of four times as much fuel per passenger mile as the wide-bodied jets, and even more in relation to the new energy-efficient jets that are now beginning to fly, the Boeing 757 and 567, the *Condorde* has been kept aloft only by a large subsidy from the French and British governments to their respective national airlines. The British subsidy is reported to be of the order of $100 million a year, and the French subvention is likely to be of similar scale. All this for a few flights a week between Europe and New York, and Washington and Mexico City, in planes that average load factors of less than two-thirds of the small capacity of around one hundred passengers. The general conclusion after some nine years of operation is that, whatever the price of fuel, the *Concorde* is too small a plane ever to be economic to operate, and one that is becoming frighteningly costly to maintain as the prestige symbol it has become.

CONCLUSIONS

Today the plane has lost most of its cachet by becoming the standard way for people to move over any considerable distance, in the United States or in the world at large. Eighty-five percent of intercity public travel in the United States is now by air. Our airports have become huge assemblages of service personnel as well as great confluxes of travelers, usually representing the most concentrated locale for economic activity and employment outside the downtown of the metropolis itself. In many cities the newer and more active hotels concentrate around the air terminal, and office and wholesaling activities increasingly cluster there. The vast size of civil aviation in America has meant that there is a full range of specialization—from air taxis bringing travelers from small outlying towns to great airports for trunk-carrier service, through those major general airlines to specialized mass-transporters of people, such as World Airways in Oakland, which flies a few heavily developed routes such as Oakland, Baltimore, Newark, and Boston; Oakland to Frankfurt; and Oakland to Honolulu; leaving the more extensive network development to the trunk carriers.

The deregulation of route assignments in the early 1980s has further encouraged this level of specialization by allowing the rise of a number of new carriers, which often begin as small feeder airlines in a particular region only to go national with deregulation and a hunch that there is a need for a particular service, such as cheap flights by Texas International from it namesake to Los Angeles. This specialization of flight has encouraged the entrance of what were at first called third-level carriers, those that fed the trunk carriers at major regional air junctions with passengers carried in small two-engined piston planes from most of the small cities in a region. The air taxi has taken over most of that function while the former local-service airlines—Frontier, for example—have tended to become at least regional, with some becoming seminational. The outcome of all this is that air transport is now the backbone of public transport among the cities of the United States. To attempt to sketch the pattern of American air service today is impossible in this small compass. With the use of automobiles and local buses to feed the diversity of air carriers at various levels of airport terminals, this is a fully sufficient system, save in the rail corridors of the Northeast, around Chicago, and in California and the Portland-Seattle belt in the Pacific Northwest.

Outside the United States and adjacent parts of Canada, no such elaborated and ramified air net exists. Some of the New Lands, such as Australia and New Zealand, approach the pattern. Most other countries use air transport much more selectively, employing it for interregional and international flights. In Europe this is because land transportation is so highly developed and so relatively modern that governments (which run most of the airlines) have established a restraint on the competition with railroads (also run by those governments). Only a very small proportion of Europeans move about Europe by air. It is mainly when they set out on very long journeys, particularly intercontinental trips, that they use civil aviation. The result is that European governments heavily subsidize international flying conducted by their national airlines, in which they capture customers from foreign airlines, while starving domestic operations that would compete with the nation's chosen instrument of national transport, the railroad.

It is only in the underdeveloped world that flying gains the universality that it does in North America, but then only in a peculiar way. Many Third World countries have found employment for their often overly large populations by encouraging them to work in other countries as so-called guest workers. Egyptians work in the Persian Gulf, as do East Asians. The result is that flights to "the Gulf" are strange combinations of the very poor, but usually fairly young, crowded into the rear of the plane with their bedrolls and scant baggage, and the very rich or institutionally exalted riding comfortably in first class forward. These are lands where integration into the world economy came in the era of civil aviation; thus the guest worker and the manager both must go by air, if in distinctly different parts of the plane.

The future of that civil aviation is uncertain. What does appear likely is that the trend toward mass transport by air will continue. Growth will decline as fuel costs and the greatly increasing price of new aircraft are reflected in the relative increase in the cost of flying. But the absence of any large-scale investment in alternative forms of public long-distance transportation means that for the predictable future air transport will dominate outside of Europe and Japan, and internationally from those areas. Efforts will continue to make aircraft more energy-efficient as well as able to squeeze a few more seats in to help pay those costs. Speed will probably remain much as at present, as to move much higher means moving into supersonic flying, and no one today is going to spend the money to build the SST large enough to be a commercial success. In air transport the ironic situation exists that there is probably a much closer approximation of stability in the newest form of transport than there is in most of the historically older forms of moving people and goods about the earth's surface. The technology is not likely to change too much in a generation, but the geography of this activity without roots in the earth can shift with lightning speed and with dire consequences for those carriers that fail to understand that evolving geography.

NOTES

1. C. H. Gibbs-Smith, *Flight through the Ages* (New York: Thomas Y Crowell, 1974), p. 35. Other centers of glider operation are found in the United States around Elmira, New York, and in Fremont, California.
2. Ibid., pp. 37–44.
3. Ibid., p. 43.
4. John Toland, *Ships in the Sky: The Story of the Great Dirigibles* (New York: Henry Holt and Company, 1957), p. 41.
5. Gibbs-Smith, op. cit., p. 51.
6. Ibid., pp. 67–69.
7. Gibbs-Smith, op. cit., pp. 76–77.
8. Alberto Santos-Dumont, *My Airships* (New York: Dover Publications, 1973), pp. 29-30. Reprint of 1904 English translation of 1904 French original, *Dans l'Air,* pp. 29–30.
9. Ibid., p. 71.
10. Ibid., p. 74.
11. Ibid., pp. 121–122.
12. Toland, op. cit., pp. 39–44.
13. Gibbs-Smith, op. cit., p. 84.
14. L. T. C. Rolt, *The Aeronauts: A History of Ballooning, 1783–1903* (New York: Walker and Company, 1966), p. 223.
15. At 32 F. and 29.92 inches pressure, the atmosphere weighs 80.72 pounds per thousand cubic feet of dry air. Under the same conditions a like quantity of hydrogen weighs 5.61 pounds and of helium 11.14 pounds. Thus a thousand cubic feet of hydrogen will lift 75.11 pounds and of helium 69.58 pounds. "Airships," *Encyclopaedia Britannica,* 1967, vol. 1, p. 458.
16. Toland, op. cit., p. 49; C. H. Gibbs-Smith, *A Brief History of Flying from Myth to Space*

Travel (London: Her Majesty's Stationery Office, 1967), p. 35.

17. Toland, op. cit., pp. 55–56.
18. Charles H. Gibbs-Smith, *The Aeroplane: An Historical Survey of Its Origins and Development* (London: The Science Museum, 1960), p. 10.
19. Loc. cit.
20. Ibid., pp. 35–36.
21. Ibid., p. 197.
22. Quoted in ibid., p. 38.
23. Ibid., pp. 41–42.
24. Ibid., p. 48.
25. Ibid., p. 50.
26. Ibid., p. 93.
27. Ibid., p. 180.
28. Ibid., p. 332.
29. Ibid., p. 87.
30. Ibid., pp. 68–69, 87.
31. Ibid., p. 96.
32. Ibid., p. 97.
33. Ibid., pp. 98–99.
34. Kenneth Hudson, *Air Travel: A Social History* (Bath, Avon: Adams and Dart, 1972), pp. 11–33.
35. Carl Solberg, *Conquest of the Skies: A History of Commercial Aviation in America* (Boston: Little, Brown, 1979), p. 35.
36. Ibid., p. 9.
37. Ibid., p. 31.
38. Ibid., p. 25.
39. Loc. cit.
40. Ibid., p. 38.
41. Gibbs-Smith, *The Aeroplane,* op. cit., p. 100.
42. Loc. cit.
43. Ibid., p. 104.
44. Solberg, op. cit., pp. 55–58.
45. National Committee to Observe the 50th Anniversary of Powered Flight, *Fifty Years of Aviation Progress* (Washington, D.C., 1953), p. 25.
46. Solberg, op. cit., p. 61.
47. Ibid., p. 106.
48. Information from the timetable in *The Official Guide of the Railways,* January, 1930.
49. Solberg, op. cit., pp. 33–36; Ben Butterfield, *Aviation in America* (New York: American Geographical Society and Nelson Doubleday, 1957), pp. 33–34.
50. On an American flight three weeks before Braniff's collapse I experienced the gratuitous attacks on Braniff when, in a complaint about American's poor service, I was told by one of the company's supervisors in Dallas that I should realize how much better they were than Braniff, hardly the matter at issue.
51. Ibid., pp. 84–85.
52. Gibbs-Smith, *The Aeroplane,* op. cit., p. 103.
53. Ronald Miller and David Sawers, *The Technical Development of Modern Aviation* (New York: Praeger Publishers, 1970), p. 14.
54. Ibid., p. 17.
55. Ibid., p. 18.
56. Ibid., pp. 18–19.
57. Ibid., pp. 98–99. The quotation is from *Aviation* 89 (September, 1940): 104.
58. Loc. cit.
59. Ibid., p. 100.
60. William Littlewood, "Technical Trends in Air Transport," *Journal of the Aeronautical Sciences* 20 (April, 1953): 231. Quoted in ibid., p. 101.
61. Quoted in ibid., p. 102.
62. Ibid., pp. 102–103.
63. Quoted in Solberg, op. cit., pp. 141–142, paragraphing removed.
64. Ibid., pp. 162–167.
65. Ibid., p. 172.
66. Gibbs-Smith, *The Aeroplane,* op. cit., p. 86.
67. Solberg, op. cit., pp. 177–189.
68. Ibid., pp. 189–190.
69. Miller and Sawers, op. cit., pp. 131–133.
70. Carl Solberg, op. cit., pp. 190–193.
71. Ibid., pp. 142–143.
72. Ibid., p. 315.
73. Ibid., p. 314.
74. Ibid., p. 353.
75. Ibid., p. 356.
76. R. E. G. Davies, *A History of the World's Airlines* (London: Oxford University Press, 1964), pp. 172–173.
77. Ibid., pp. 174–175.
78. Ibid., p. 175.
79. Ibid., p. 179.
80. Ibid., p. 180.
81. Ibid., pp. 180–182.
82. David Beaty, *The Water Jump: The Story of Transatlantic Flight* (New York: Harper & Row, 1976), p. 118.

83. Solberg op. cit., p. 229.
84. Ibid., pp. 232–234.
85. Beaty, op. cit., p. 140.
86. Ibid., p. 140.
87. Letter quoted in ibid., p. 142.
88. Ibid., p. 145.
89. Ibid., p. 147.
90. Quoted in ibid., p. 148.
91. Davies, op. cit., p. 426.
92. Solberg, op. cit., p. 286.
93. Ibid., p. 288.
94. Miller and Sawers, op. cit., p. 133.
95. Ibid., p. 40.
96. Ibid., p. 214.
97. Solberg, op. cit., p. 357.
98. Davies, op. cit., p. 280.
99. Solberg, op. cit., p. 346.
100. Miller and Sawers, op. cit., pp. 157–161.
101. Ibid., p. 153.
102. Ibid., pp. 161–162.

103. Ibid., pp. 175–177.
104. Ibid., pp. 179–180.
105. Davies, op. cit., p. 452.
106. Miller and Sawers, op. cit., p. 180.
107. Davies, op. cit., pp. 453–454.
108. Loc. cit.
109. Miller and Sawers, op. cit., p. 185.
110. Solberg, op. cit. , pp. 402–403.
111. Solberg, op. cit., p. 403.
112. Ibid., p. 404.
113. Miller and Sawers, op. cit., p. 3.
114. John Newhouse, "A Reporter at Large: A Sporty Game, IV; A Hole in the Market," *The New Yorker,* July 5, 1982, p. 53.
115. Roy Allen, *Major Airports of the World* (London: Ian Allen, 1979) p. 73.
116. Newhouse, op. cit., p. 66 passim.
117. Ibid., p. 27.
118. Ibid., p. 90.
119. Ibid., p. 41.

chapter 8

CONCLUSIONS
The Morphogenesis of Transportation

Our consideration of the historical geography of transportation during the last five centuries may seem greatly complex and highly episodic as presented in its progression. Yet there is a distinct and relatively consistent evolution to it, shared by all the forms of transportation and running through the entire semimillenium. Consistency is found in the constant operation of morphogenetic processes, cyclical in nature but ever bearing on the shaping of the facilities and technology of transportation. The driving force has consistently been the human desire to carry the innate mobility of mankind to its logical limits, to frontiers that have grown more distant with advances in human knowledge and the technology that puts it to work. In seeking to conclude these extensive and necessarily categorical observations on the creation of modern transportation, it seems appropriate and efficient to consider those morphogenetic processes as a group and briefly to demonstrate their bearing on the creation of the diverse transportation of the present.

The story we have seen is that of increasing complexity, starting with the pack-trails of the late Middle Ages and ending with the wealth of mechanical transportation of the late twentieth century, a worldwide set of systems of movement whose similarity of evolution may not be instantly apparent. It may be suggested, however, that essentially all the forms of transportation we have used, and still employ today, have grown under a shared ontogeny and that it is in that sharing of staged process that we may find an explanation of the structural relationship of all possible forms of transportation. The stages in the ontogeny seem to account for the course of the morphogenesis that is the main dynamic of the historical geography of transportation.

There is much that is simple and logical, essentially self-evident, in the ontogeny of transportation; yet I think there is considerable value in trying to tie together the whole evolutionary process as a guide in the effort to relate all forms of transportation. The clear stages in the evolution of forms can be perceived, but they are far from contemporaneous in history; in fact, the cycle begins for the earlier forms in the late Middle Ages and for the later ones only in this century.

EXPERIMENTATION

Because mobility is innate to human beings, it is unnecessary to explain why we seek to render it either more geographically competent or physically less demanding. As rational beings we must always have observed the world around us and have looked at its conditions with a mind to gaining easier or more distant movement. The movement of brush being transported on the surface of a stream, of birds flying above our heads, and of wild horses cantering across an arid plain would all cause us to think of emulation or harnessing. Both those activities would require experimentation, as anyone who has ever watched bronco-busting in a rodeo would know. Boats can be built, but not all float either reliably or respond in direction to our will. Icarus showed even in antiquity that flight is liberating but is hard to sustain. So every form of transportation, even that innate to human life, is at first experimental—as the efforts of any baby teach us.

Experimentation relies on envisaging a successful technology and greatly depends on the availability of certain conditions of nature and of resources. Icarus would still be in prison had he not had some source of wax; if, in turn, he had had a more durable adhesive, the Greeks might have flown before the French. So environment and what we call the factor endowment play significant roles in engendering experimentation. As we have seen, canals came where water had artificially to be managed, either

because it was too plentiful or because it was not sufficiently so. In similar fashion, it was when the nations of Atlantic Europe began to move onto the sea that great technical advances in sailing were both required and accomplished. In the development of the railroad a mining experience seems to have been nearly essential, although in America we demonstrated that a great need for transportation and a mechanical ingenuity could quickly lead to innovative efforts that were themselves distinctive because the factor endowment was different.

Throughout the evolution of the complex solutions to the demand for transportation each has had its experimental phase. For canals most of the technical requisites were created experimentally between about A.D. 1200 and 1600. Certain limited experiments in improving the natural road, particularly in the creation of highway engineering in its basic tenets and in introducing user charges for securing funds for construction, came in the seventeenth and eighteenth centuries. The railroad was in its experimental phase for a similar time, with the first efforts falling entirely in the realm of facilities, though the developments leading to the application of mechanical power were worked out successfully in little more than a third of a century, 1804 to about 1840. The rise of mechanical propulsion of ships was similarly rapid, taking place during the first half of the nineteenth century, though the creation of effective ocean navigation was quite drawn out, from the fifteenth through the nineteenth century. But in general the more recent innovations in transportation have come more quickly. The Montgolfiers worked in the late eighteenth century, but little advance was made in flying for a century, and then progress was very rapid. The first heavier-than-air flight was in 1903; only a decade later, aerial warfare became a grim reality. The automobile, with its subsequent fundamental transformation of highway

Wooden covered bridge on the Boston and Lowell near Lebanon, New Hampshire. Photograph in author's collection.

transportation, did not exist before the 1880s; but within less than fifty years most American families with steady incomes owned and actively emloyed cars in their daily lives. Rapidity of development in the more modern forms can often be matched with a similar relative decline in significance: the electric trolley came only in the late 1880s, but within a half century it had been relegated to a significant but geographically very restricted role.

INITIATION

Experimentation is an intellectual undertaking, but in a study of historical geography we must be concerned with the geographical consequences of such trials. This is the initiation of actual service on a sustained and economically significant basis. Some innovations have been applied to actual commercial transportation quickly and widely; others either have been slow to be put to use or have affected only a confined area. The canal was slow indeed in making widespread contributions. Born in Italy and Holland in the thirteenth century, the canal did not greatly affect France until the seventeenth century, Britain until the eighteenth, and America until the nineteenth. Even when adopted, the canal could have only a narrow application. In Britain, though the canal was of signal importance, most were built in a relatively confined area bounded by Liverpool, York, London, and Bristol. France somewhat denied this rule, but only at the cost of a massive two-century program of public works.

Quite consistently the place of initiation of new forms of transportation was where existing forms were taxed—in other words, where the advantages to be gained from successful innovation could match or exceed the potential costs. Canals came in the most economically advanced parts of Europe at their time of birth—Flanders and the Po Basin. Railroads matched that economic centrality by emerging in the mining areas of Germany, Britain, and France, and in the environs of the centers of American mercantilism and capital accumulation in the era of the dominant American merchant marine—Boston, Philadelphia, Baltimore, and Charleston (New York was a glaring but understandable exception to this rule). Automobiles came into use first in the suburbs, which became the home of the most economically favored element of society at the turn of the century. The rise of the steamboat and steamship followed in kind: the steamboat came first in the Great Republic, where the initial potamic phase of transportation had been constrained by the problem of establishing retributive flows of boats back toward the headwaters of streams; and the steamship came first on the North Atlantic, which by the 1840s was the main marine artery of the mercantile world. Even air service showed a specific "locale" for its initial service: on a short route, heavily traveled, that was made difficult by a natural barrier to rail transportation—London to Paris, Toulouse to Barcelona, Key West to Havana. These places of stress on earlier transportation became characteristic for the initiation of fledgling forms. Sometimes they seem to have experienced stunted growth. The initiation of air-cushion Hovercraft across the Solent and the English Channel seems after a generation to have become little more than a curiosity. This vaunted innovation has remained remarkably uninspiring beyond its native heath.

AMPLIFICATION AND EXTENSION

For a form of transportation to gain wide use, two things seem necessary: that its initial, usually rather tentative employment be strengthened through amplification of purpose, and that through that enlargement of utility extension of routes takes place. The early railroads, for example, were as local and specific in purpose and technology as the mineral plateways that sired them. But even the Stockton and Darlington became an important passenger carrier, though its promoters had given that purpose little thought. With the Liverpool and Manchester an interurban function was added, allowing the creation of the typical British railroad constructed to serve an existing market. In the United States the Boston and Lowell Railroad fell in that mold; but very quickly a further amplification of purpose was shaped, the developmental railroad, which led to the creation of an equally characteristic American railroad. It was this American type that pioneered railroad service in much of the world, leading to by far the greatest mileage of railroad extension.

These two processes are intimately interrelated, to the point it is commonly impractical, and probably unnecessary, to distinguish the amplification from the extension: one may precede the other in either order, or they may be essentially contemporaneous and interacting. It should be appreciated that amplification of the utility of a form of transportation essentially ensures the extension of its routes. The pound lock amplified the utility of the earlier single-level waterways, making the ascending and watershed canals possible and greatly extending the canal to reach throughout France, the Low Countries, Germany, and England in Europe, and the Northeast and Middle West in the United States. In similar fashion, the amplification of railroad technology, in

American hands, to permit its use where markets are little developed and where stiff grades and sharp curves were either an economic or a physical necessity, meant that railroads could breast the Alps, using American-type locomotives, or spread across Canada and Siberia, using American-style construction. It was the amplification of the European-invented automobile, through its democratization in America, that led to its adoption as the common and daily transport of the masses not merely in North America and other New Lands but in western Europe as well. The forms of transportation that have been evolved into different but closely related expressions of a common root have tended to be both enduring and of surpassing importance. The canal could not be so readily and so widely amplified as the railroad or the automobile, so its role in the historical geography of transportation was, of necessity, both more minor and less perpetuated. Some forms, the Hovercraft and the supersonic transport plane, in all probability have largely defied amplification; in the great sweep of transportation evolution, theirs has been a walk-on part, and quite possibly one that will be dropped during a long run.

GENERALIZATION

The experience with transportation forms has passed through a fairly consistent cycle, several stages of which have already been noted. Perhaps the least obvious of these is generalization, a process under which the form is taken up and viewed as the most technically advanced, whereupon a considerable effort is subsequently undertaken to make use of that status. Several examples will serve best to show how generalization has influenced the historical geography of transportation. The canal represented the first broad-scale form of transportation to be

generalized. Its origin as a fundamentally technical improvement on nature came in two narrow geographical areas where the conditions were favorable for experimentation and initiation. The success in those efforts led to an amplification of the functions expected of canals and an extension of the technology to other areas. The successes in these early stages strengthened the notion that the canal was the most advanced form of transport and the one that should be the objective of any efforts at improvement. In France in the early nineteenth century a national system of canals was called for, with a belief that it was the most advanced technology of the time (the French passion for high tech is not just a new thing). Only where that level of technical accomplishment seemed wildly impracticable, from an economic viewpoint, would those plans of the 1820s admit of compromise, the building of some sort of railed road. In the same decade the Commonwealth of Pennsylvania generalized the notion of the canal as the forefront of transportation improvement into the call for the canalized Mainline System. The fact that it was wildly impractical was overlooked in the belief in the efficacy of the latest technical achievement. This characteristic of transportation developers did not stop with the canal builders; the proponents of the railroad came closer to the truth, but, still, they called for railroads down city streets and in other situations where environmental conditions would have been severely deteriorated or economic limits greatly overreached. In our day the helicopter, the Hovercraft, and the supersonic plane has each been touted beyond reason by those unaware of the rational limits to the application of the process of generalization.

Not all that has resulted from that over-enthusiasm is bad: the rational limits to the employment of a form of transportation could hardly have been found if strong promotion had been lacking. The transcontinental railroad in the United States would not have been built little more than a third of a century after the initial railroads had not the process of generalization been at work. The vast morphogenetic change in American cities that came in the generation before World War I would never have been accomplished if the trolley, subway, and elevated had not been seen as vastly powerful and infinitely extensible forms of transportation. It was Henry Ford's almost messianic view of the "family horse" provided by the automobile that led him to design a car that could operate virtually without roads and to build it for almost any family's budget. Thus his generalized view of the automobile shaped modern transportation in the developed world. Only recently have we begun to discover the limits to generalization of the car. Those limits are always there, and in that fact we discover the interrelationship that generalization introduces to the historical geography of transportation. Because high technology is seemingly ever-changing, there is no freezing of the solution to the improvement of transportation. The canal was adopted as the desideratum in the period between 1500 and 1830, but then the limits to its generalization were overreached, and it was discovered that a new, ultimately even higher technology was needed. The railroad, by first coming as a successful substitute for canal-building (as in the Stockton and Darlington), was taken up as the new technology and was pushed to, and a bit beyond, its rational limits—beyond them in the interurban systems that sought to replace railroads in those activities that the older steam carriers had very effectively undertaken. This process of generalization has led first to the finding of the limits for the development of a form, and once found, to the experimentation with substitute forms that might better serve those unsatisfied demands, starting again the cycle of experimentation, initiation, amplification, and extension. If it were not for the limits to generalization of all forms of transportation, there would certainly be much less rich and varied historical geography of transportation than there is.

UNIVERSALIZATION

The process of generalization was largely one of function—the search to apply a technology to the widest possible set of demands. Paired with that effort was one of distinctly geographical nature, the attempt to create the most areally extensive system possible—what we have observed repeatedly as the attempt to create ubiquity for the form or the transportation company. These may seem very much the same thing, the push to the limits of utilization, and of course they are. But there is an important difference when it comes to historical geography. Technology is basically subject to historical accounting, though obviously there are spatial and environmental forces shaping that history along with a host of cultural and social ones. In a geography, however, we must focus more precisely on the morphological evolution of the application of those technologies. To do that effectively, I believe we must distinguish generalization of technology from universalization of facilities, a geographical measure.

The process of universalization is driven by the assumed benefits of ubiquity in transportation systems. The efforts to shape a comprehensive French canal system, the drive to provide turnpike roads in all of England and Wales, and the program for ribbon pavements to the remotest corners of most American states all grew from the effort toward ubiquity. In railroad development in many regions, notably in the Trunk-Line Territory of the Northeast and Middle West of the United States and in all of Canada, there was a fierce competitive search for ubiquity. The Pennsylvania and New York Central railroads were gripped in such a contest until after World War I. In Canada the search for universalization shaped three fully transcontinental systems by the years of that war—systems so fragile that two were bankrupt before they were essentially complete. Even in Britain the contest between the London and North Western and the Great Western railways took on the qualities of a search for ubiquity by the Stephenson gauge and the wide gauge, respectively.

It is clear that the process of universalization did not die with the discovery of its limits for railroads. Air transport, with its great ease of entrance into the competition (due to the natural provision of routes and the necessary national provision of air traffic control), has become a grim battlefield of universalization. Once the Chicago Convention was in hand at the end of World War II, with its assertion of the Fifth Freedom that permitted the stringing together of long air routes by any country possessed of enough areal extent or traffic generation to have a chip to play, there was a great entrance into the North Atlantic water jump by competitive airlines from all western European countries, and many others as well, and of course by nine American and three Canadian carriers. Although not all national carriers have been able to gain true terrestrial universalism, many have tried and a number have succeeded. Britain, France, West Germany, Scandinavia as a unit, the Netherlands, Italy, Greece, Israel, India, Japan, the Soviet Union, Australia, Brazil, South Africa, and several carriers in Canada and the United States have all succeeded in shaping essentially world airlines. Other countries have come close, notably Belgium, Switzerland, Saudi Arabia, Jordan, Thailand, China (both mainland and Taiwan), Finland, South Korea, and Argentina. It is the relative ease with which universalization has

taken place in the airline industry that has contributed to the considerable overcapacity in commercial air transport today.

In the United States the deregulation of airline routings and service introduced in the late 1970s has led to similar national universalizing trends. Regional carriers before deregulation have become transcontinental in several cases, oversupplying seats for the market demand. Braniff Airlines was the most bemused by universalization, spreading (after the beginning of deregulation in 1978) from a regional carrier in the American interior, with an important international route down the west coast of South America, to become a fledgling world airline with routes across North America, to Chile in the south, Japan in the west, and western Europe in the east. As part of this grander view of its corporate role, Braniff engaged in a financially disastrous interchange arrangement to fly trans-Atlantic *Concordes* onward from New York to Dallas. That extravagance lasted only fifteen months (January, 1979, to May, 1980) before it was dropped, but the siren appeal of universalization could not be undone so easily. Braniff survived only two years longer, becoming the first major airline to go into bankruptcy in May, 1982, with a startling debt of $733 million.[1]

Reality usually has set the limits to universalization, if normally less cataclysmically. Those boundaries, though geographical in location, have normally been set in economic terms. The French could not complete their canal system as planned in the 1820s because costs for the later segments became exorbitant for any anticipated use that might be made. The railroads also realized about the time of World War I that lines yet to be built usually held little financial appeal, and cars and trucks, interurbans, and even airlines were making an increasingly empty victory of any rail universality. So far airline companies have acted as if such a denouement does not face them—

as if they can gain universality for many national airlines, and for private corporate carriers in North America. To me that notion seems unsound. The level of national subsidy involved is high, and the taxing of the resources of the private carriers is severe, so it is most unlikely that some will not flinch in this strange game of chicken in the air. Much as there may be few technical limits to ubiquity in airline operation, certainly there are many economic ones. In the end private companies must operate at a profit across the board, and even public carriers must begin to limit their subsidies. Considerable fear exists concerning the survival of several American carriers; it seems that eventually the financial hemorrhage sustained in chauvinistic interests by the French and British in running the *Concorde* must be stopped, and the high cost of subsidizing a number of national airlines must be moderated. It seems highly improbable that the process of universalization in air transport will have a history very different from the story of that process in other forms of transportation. In the end, all other forms have found their economic and functional limits, learning to live within their rational budget and doing the job for which they enjoy a great comparative advantage.

LIMITATION AND SPECIALIZATION

That balance among the various forms stems from two other processes found in this ontogeny. The first grows out of the obvious limits to functional utility and to geographical extent that have characterized all forms of transportation. As the forms themselves have evolved, they have encountered these boundaries; and as limitations came to be perceived, new cycles of development were initiated, creating competitive or, more precisely, supplemental forms of transportation. In such a situation the limits to utility in one means of transport tend not only to create its

supplement but also to cause its own specialization, thus introducing these concomitant processes. Limitation by its very nature implies acceptance of a partial role, one wherein an area, a time, or a function will be served in a specialized fashion.

In the case of canals the geographical and temporal boundaries are clear; yet the survival of the form cannot be questioned. What happened in Europe beyond its broad Atlantic fringe was an economic constraint on canal building, due in considerable measure to the late economic development of the more easterly and interior parts of Europe such that modest development and late inclusion in the industrial world encouraged the initiation of a specialized form better suited to those conditions than were the costly canal constructions of the seventeenth and eighteenth centuries. The railroad could better serve this less developed part of Europe than could the canal. And it was the particularly American form of the railroad, rather than the British, that tended to influence construction in Germany, Russia, and other parts of central and eastern Europe. Yet ultimately canals were carried as far east as the Oder and Silesia when industrialization in this century reached the level that required cheap bulk transport. Thus the canal was limited both in time, by the introduction of competing specialized forms, and in space, by economic boundaries. Only as those economic boundaries were pushed backward by development could the specialized cost advantages of the canal engender its construction, even in our century.

In America this collateral relationship of limitation and specialization is constantly reestablished. In the last century even that particularly developmental device, the American railroad, reached a conditional boundary at the edge of established agricultural settlement. Beyond that limit a specialized, less costly, and admittedly far less competent form, the wagon road, had to

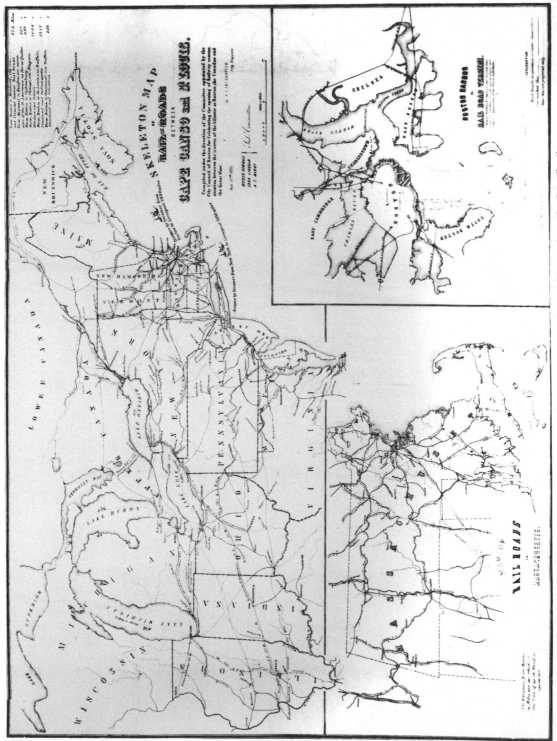

Map of railroads proposed between Cape Canso, Nova Scotia, and St. Louis, Missouri. 1851 map in author's collection.

be employed. Only as economic activity beyond the continuous frontier—the various gold rushes to the Sierra Nevada, Cascades, and Rockies—gave anticipation of greater economic support, and as political exigencies—in the matter of maintaining the Union in the Civil War—urged immediate action, was the railroad boundary pushed beyond the settlement frontier. That action proved primarily a political act, causing the actual bankruptcy of the Union Pacific in little more than a decade after its completion and the approach to that condition in the Central Pacific, averted probably more by lack of interest by others in taking it over rather than by any greatly more profitable state of the operation. Only slowly were the geographical limits for railroads effectively pushed outward, forcing the range-cattle industry in the Great Plains to depend on the great cattle drives for yet another generation, and even a gold rush, such as that in the Black Hills in the 1870s, to depend on wagon roads for their external connections.

The history of the electric-traction industry in America is graphic indeed in its demonstration of the collateral nature of limitation and specialization. When Henry Whitney in 1888 adopted the five-cent fare for the West Boston Street Railway it seemed as if there were few, if any, limits to the spread of the trolley. Streetcar suburbs sprang up even well out into the countryside, and it seemed that the economic constraints to urban movement had been totally removed. The traction industry seemed an even greater bonanza than the steam railroad had been in the second half of the nineteenth century. Managers of traction companies could see the direct relationship between the extension of their lines and the rise in their receipts. What they tended to overlook was the accompanying rise in their costs and, as repair became necessary, the even steeper climb in that rate. By the early 1920s the limitation of electric traction was

brutally clear, leading to a decline in that industry even more precipitous than its previous growth. The trolley was seen at last as a specialized form of transport, fine for its particular realm but economically disastrous beyond it. The resurgence of interest in latter-day trolleys, in the ever-shiny neologisms of planning now called Light Rail, can be integrated in our tale when we realize that what we have done, rather belatedly, is come to grips with the limits of utility of the form and its special contributions.

The poor suburbanites, lured out of town by the trolley wire, in the mid-1920s began to find themselves beyond the frontier because of the tie between specialization and limitation. In dire need they created the automotive underpinnings of American metropolitan society and began, in turn, a further outward push of the urban frontier. Only the cost America paid for its uncritical support for Israel, engendering the Arab oil embargo of 1973, demonstrated the limits that attached to this new attempt at universalization. When crude oil began its rapid rise from around $2.50 a barrel to $36 a barrel within a decade, the limitation existing in automotive transportation became clear. But in an assertion of the strength of the public's belief that cars represent the form of transportation most capable of generalization, many workers began to think in terms not of giving up automobile commuting but, instead, of seeking jobs in the suburbs that might still economically be reached by car. Shopping journeys took on a similar revision, elevating suburban centers to a dominant role to decrease distances traveled under newly increased transportation costs. Obviously, under the very generalized form of the automobile, with most people able to make direct decisions about routings and extent, the operation of the process of limitation will proceed, but its nature will be less self-evident. Because so many of us still favored automobile transportation, we proved willing to change the journey-to-work perhaps more than the way we engaged in it.

There is, however, growing evidence of the interaction of specialization and limitation in commuting. As a result of increasing doubts about the economic feasibility of the car commute in the traditional city-center employment situation, a new movement for mass transit to the center has arisen. The outcome has been the greatest economic delusion of our time. It is perceived that it is cheaper to substitute buses and rapid-transit service for cars, thus repealing the geographical limitation that the rise in gasoline prices seemed to impose on the journey-to-work. All this appeared to bear out the relationship between specialization of transport and the actual location of the limitation of utility—in other words, the geographical boundary of economic use of the form. If the return to mass transit had been in terms of the original phase of mass transit—that is, when the rider ostensibly paid for the service he was rendered—then the renaissance would have been real and desirable. But we know from our analysis that even that first phase of transit development was economically unreal: there was a strong subsidy from the investors in traction securities to the riders who were not, in fact, paying an economic fare. Yet because those fares had been low, when the transit renaissance of the 1970s came about, it was expected that transit fares must be, if not obviously so low, at least not astronomically higher. But the actual operating costs were clearly that much elevated, such that given the expectations of the transit commuters, a very large public subsidy had to be built into all metropolitan commuter fares, whether by bus, traction, or railroad. In such a situation we can logically argue that there is no repeal of the interaction of limitation and specialization, but there can be a distinct distortion of its perception through political intervention. That same political fogging of the processes operating in transportation comes as well in the very considerable subsidy that buses receive from the likes of the Interstate Highway System, barges gain from toll-free public waterways, airlines capture from a massively subsidized air-navigation system, and international airlines pick up from the participation of heavily subsidized national airlines. Thus, although there may be a still present concomitance between limitation and specialization, political intevention tends repeatedly to seek to deny it on the basis of uninformed assumptions. The relationship of forms of transportation in the service they are asked to render is badly disrupted by this intrusion of political interest.

PARALLEL AND COMPLEX DEVELOPMENT

Not all is evil in that political intrusion; clearly, social objectives must frequently intervene against economic determinism. To argue for an unrelieved application of limitation and specialization as processes shaping the complexity that is modern transportation would be far too deterministic. There is, however, a need to understand the degree of intervention and its effects. In the United States, since 1971 when Amtrak was formed as the National Railroad Passenger Corporation, there has been a strident campaign by the Greyhound Bus organization to depict that nationalized carrier as the privileged recipient of almost unlimited public subsidies and thus in a uniquely favored position. Yet informed thought is strong that had not the vast Interstate Highway System been constructed after 1954, Greyhound and other intercity buses would probably have been out of business by now. Recently it has become much more accepted that those bus companies, and their motor-trucking neighbors, have received a vast subsidy, both in the construction of roads to the higher level made necessary by their heavy vehicles and

The transportation articulation point in West Oakland. Port of Oakland photograph.

in the rather low level of user taxation they pay. The Surface Transportation Act of 1982 sought to correct some of that radical favoritism toward buses and trucks, only to be met with impassioned cries from those industries. If subsidies exist, as they do in all forms of public transportation—the car being virtually the only vehicle that basically pays its way—no public carrier can pretend to abstemiousness on the subject. In addition, we should take account of the fact that such subsidies are most usually justified on the argument that national welfare is advanced by the creation of the parallel and complex development of transportation.

Diversity has become a national goal that grows out of the acceptance of the processes of limitation and specialization. Complexity is assured in most developed countries not only by functional advantages to be gained from specialization of forms of transportation but also by policies that seek through that range of choice in transport to accomplish social objectives. The young cannot drive, the elderly may not wish to, and the very poor cannot afford to do so. Thus public transport is a social necessity, however uneconomic it may be. Air transport has come to serve long-distance, particularly business travelers, but commonly fails to

The T.G.V. High-Speed Rail Line on French National Railroads (S.N.C.F.) Crossing the Escarpment Between Cluny and Mâcon. French National Railroads Photograph.

provide access to small rural places; for that, bus travel has been considered essential. Yet recently the Greyhound Company has proposed dropping a number of smaller rural places from its schedule of stops, so we may find the problem of rural access surfacing for public consideration. Some have argued that passenger trains are unnecessary in the United States, so it should not be overlooked that even the vastly truncated passenger rail service run by Amtrak does serve more stops in the United States than all the stops on all the airlines combined. The need for complexity is not so much economic as it is social.

Even so, there are good economic reasons for that complexity. Heavy commodities could never bear the cost of air transport, a fact attested to by the extremely small role that airlines play in freight movements. The duplication between railroads and inland waterways is more direct, some arguing that given the bulk of the trade, railroads could move many mass commodities nearly as cheaply as do inland barges, save for the considerable federal subsidy given in waterways construction and maintenance. Even

so, it is doubtful that railroads could move all the bulk that passes by waterway without a massive improvement and enlargement that might prove beyond the abilites of railroad companies to finance, given their low rate of earnings on capital. The story of the evolution of transportation presented in the previous chapters should obviate the need to specify in detail the argument for complex development. We have seen repeatedly that a new form of transport brings qualities that are in demand, or soon come to be when the process of amplification sets in. Certainly no developed country today can hope to function efficiently and acceptably without access to specialized transportation. Those who have emergencies or engage in business commonly need plane travel; those who fear flying cannot accept it; and those who move large families on a small budget can hardly hope to do so except in their own car, however old and unkempt it may be.

Parallel development also plays its part. Although there has been a progression in the various cycles of transportation evolution, none of these forms of movement has been totally abandoned when its successors were introduced. In fact, there has been a co-evolution among all the forms, mainly because limitation and specialization are among the advanced stages in the ontogeny of transportation. Parallel development means that relationships are ever-changing; for a hundred years, technical advance in ocean shipping came primarily as a result of innovations first introduced in dominantly passenger service. Since the advent of the jetliner, however, passenger transport by sea has virtually disappeared, save for cruises, which hardly lead to much technical improvement. In long-distance transportation today, improvement is essentially induced by competition among airframe builders and among airline operators, all within a single industry. Yet improvement does take place in merchant shipping, particularly in reducing energy consumption, because parallel development has meant that air freight has tended to win in a simple contest of speed, whereas shipping is victorious in terms of the economic measure of cost. This has not meant, however, the abandonment of efforts to speed up ocean shipping. This is done today not by running vessels as fast as those of twenty years ago but instead, through container handling, by greatly reducing the time taken in terminal operations.

Evolution seems to have been enhanced by competition among the forms of transportation. The basic technology of each was initiated when it stood as technically the most advanced for its time. When the deficiencies of a specific medium became obvious, efforts were made to overcome those, normally leading both to the change in the original form and to the creation of distinctly new forms of transport that avoided the previous failings. Railroads, for example, could greatly ramify the networks of movement possible with canals. In turn, however, the suburbanization of population and in-

dustry showed up sharply the failings of the steam railroad, leading to the rapid expansion of the use of automotive transportation. But clogging in the flows of automobiles has reduced their lead, giving to the airlines, even in fairly short-distance transportation, certain advantages that they have effectively exploited. But the competition among both forms and carrier companies, through unceasing efforts at parallel evolution, have aided human movement very greatly. The result has been both the parallel evolution and a complex development of the facilities of transportation.

COMPREHENSIVE EVOLUTION

The cycle of processes here considered has a suggestion of neatness not absolutely true in actual experience. Experimentation and initiation as much as limitation and specialization do not occur only in set stages of the cycle of evolution. When the French began work on their high-speed railroad technology, the T.G.V., in the 1970s, they were fully as experimental as Marc Seguin had been a hundred and fifty years before when he undertook to mechanize the Stephanoise mineral lines. And as those T.G.V. lines were introduced, there were proposals for amplification and extension similar to those attaching to the French railroads under the July Monarchy. The very longevity of the various forms of transport has meant that evolutionary cycles have recommenced several times during their existence. The very nature of the American system of railroad building was based on a real, if probably unconscious, acceptance of the notion of comprehensive evolution—that is, repeating and permanent technological adaptation to the great driving force of transportation, the search for more efficient, economical, rapid, comfortable, and competent movement through the harnessing of natural and mechanical forces. America could not afford

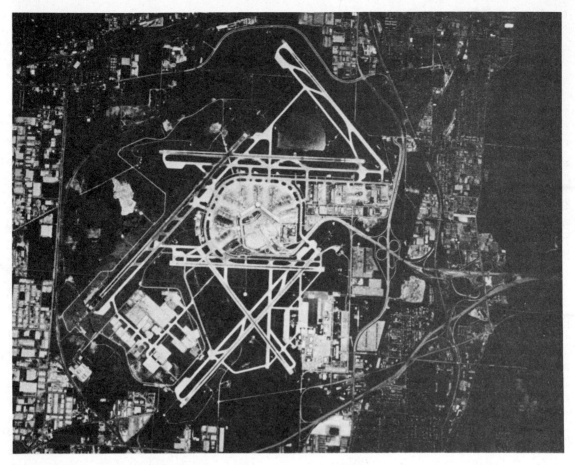

The approach to O'Hare Airport. Chicago Transit Authority photograph.

British railroads, so she bought American ones for the time being, planning to seek a higher standard sometime later in her cycle of economic development.

The relative position in development has always been critical in determining what transportation can be had. The Romans, with great flows of booty and continuing tribute, could manage to construct and maintain a road system denied to later Europeans until the French, in the seventeenth century, gained the numbers and national wealth to match those resources of the Roman Empire. Canals and roads could thereby enjoy a simultaneous cycle of evolution, rivaling the efforts of the ancient empire. National wealth in England could not match the treasury of the Most Christian King, though her mercantile capital could, so the turnpike was evolved as a contemporaneous solution to transport, again through a cycle that extended from the mid-seventeenth to the mid-nineteenth century. At that point mercantile capital, now joined by industrial capital, began to shape British railroads entirely within the private sector, in contrast to the French practice of public construction of the railroad infrastructure. Each had its cycle of evolution, but the historical timing of initiation and the agency of accomplishment varied with the stage of development when the processes were begun.

As we look at transportation today, we are observing this comprehensive evolution, with some forms hardly underway even as others seem to have reached the stage of limitation that leads to extreme specialization. From standing as the most universal and advanced forms of transport in the beginning of our story at the onset of the sixteenth century, ocean shipping has become highly specialized, not geographically but functionally. Few reaching maturity today have had any experience with ocean passenger transport, and that condition seems likely to persist. The current ferment in the airline industry suggests that the degree of specialization in that operation, with its functional and geographical limitation, is still to be determined. It does seem, nevertheless, that such a specialization will become established. Already there seem to be two parallel airline systems emerging, one for long-distance transportation at a fairly economical cost and one for short movement at a high per-mile charge. The first seems the vested property of the few large geographically extensive airlines; the second seems much more open to experimentation with service and even initiation of new companies. Transportation is as evolutionary as it ever was, and its processes exist within a developmental cycle that has long-standing antecedents.

THE HISTORICAL GEOGRAPHY OF TRANSPORTATION

That evolution is best considered under two headings: the *temporal,* primarily its history, and the *spatial,* primarily its historical geography. The two are clearly strong in their interrelationships, but they differ in their disciplinary interest and in the grist for their methodological mills. The temporal account is one of human experimentation and its consequential acts, whereas the spatial account is one of specific acts of location of facilities and the adjustment of those facilities to space, surface conditions, the existing settlement pattern, and the locational pattern of extant social and economic activities. Strongly influenced by time, history has shown particular concerns for ontogeny, and in this historical geography must have similar concerns. The latter, however, must have a concern not merely for the cycle of evolution but also for its shaping by the exogenous factors of physical, social, and economic environment. There is no absolute line between history and historical geography in this matter; rather, the differentiation is one of emphasis and degree of urgency in the consideration. History can quite well satisfy its intellectual curiosity by considering human acts and institutions; historical geography cannot, for it must add a strong morphological curiosity as well.

The addition of morphology is required because exogenous forces and their effect are hard to reconstruct. Nature does not write; payment for construction is more likely to be recorded in minute books, which tend to survive, than are the multifarious small decisions, commonly made far from the corporate treasurer's and secretary's offices where records are kept; and book and record keeping were skills developed in the late Middle Ages, whereas spatial analysis is hardly able to talk even today. Yet the morphology had to be shaped for the form of transportation to come into effective existence. If we learn to read morphology, particularly in its evolutionary sense, we may well establish information about spatial structure and process that was never written down and, in any case, has seldom survived to our time. This morphological analysis, leading to a conjecture as to process, can succinctly be called *morphogenesis,* the origin of the physical forms that characterize a specific pattern having observable areal extent.

Morphogenesis is a totality that must be broken down in most cases for human comprehension. The morphogenetic processes outlined in this concluding chapter are suggested to that end. As has been strongly pointed out, they are not exclusive either in time or in place. Cycles begin, progress, are renewed, and evolve again, to a state that is no more than current when it is observed. There is no finality to the cycle; certainly there is little absolutism to it as well because there can be a number of parallel cycles in progress, which are advancing with different stages obtaining at a specific time.

The morphogenetic processes are proposed primarily as a pandect useful in the comparative analysis of the evolution of transportation. Up to the present there has been far too little attention given to the comparative morphology of transportation. Highly important beginnings were made by Edward Ullman in his study of the American railroad network and by Jay Appleton in his appraisal of the geography of communications in Britain. Harold Mayer has greatly advanced our understanding of the pattern of shipping and railroads. There have remained the problems of international comparative analysis; of handling the full range of land-, sea-, and air-based forms of transportation; of dealing with the full story of the comprehensive evolution since the Transportation Revolution of the period between 1500 and 1800. In such comparisons, I believe, are to be found the evidence of the broadly general processes shaping the complexity that is modern transportation. Here I have sought in both a temporal and a spatial frame to carry out such comparative studies seeking to establish the morphogenetic processes.

THE IMPACT OF MORPHOLOGICAL EVOLUTION IN TRANSPORTATION

The technology of movement is an innately interesting subject, one combining the fascination of innovation with the excitement of improved access to distant lands. Consideration of the evolution of human travel compounds that intellectual appeal by adding the dynamism of a successful struggle and the improvement of human condition. Carrying the tale one step farther, to include the morphogenesis of transportation, the essential contribution of the historical geography of transportation, provides us with a measure and an understanding of the impact of advancing technology and its proliferating facilities on other aspects of life, of human geography.

Without elaborating on this final step in our tale, it should be clear from the half millennium of temporal change and the vast extent of the Western, developed world here considered—even if primarily its European and North American hearths of innovation have had to serve as examples—that that morphogenetic progession goes far toward explaining much that has happened in the same period in the social, cultural, and economic life of the West. And by recent adoption and extention the affect on the rest of the world, and the total human condition. It seems patent that the economic geography of our planet is now so integrated that prosperity or decline sets in by the world unit alone. The "Reagan recession" of the early 1980s was a pandemic because there are few effective economic isolates any longer. The creation of an advanced system of worldwide transportation has led to an equal system of worldwide trade, such that even a capitalistic downturn has caused considerable shuddering in the state-planned engine of the Soviet Union and its client states. And in turn the economic cartel among oil producers, which contributed to the crisis in Western economies, has itself fallen prey to the universalization of transportation, and thereby of trade.

The current chauvinistic cries of the French minister of culture about "American cultural domination" are joined with efforts in Canada to assure the "Canadian content" of magazines, television, and other aspects of culture, again aimed directly at American impact. The less developed world is less pointed in its demonology, but equally as xenophobic. It adds up to an increasing feeling that in some unspecified way a world culture is emerging that is destroying the parochialized cultures of the past. It will be argued that bigness should not overpower greatness and refinement, that the crass new culture should not decimate traditional and tested accomplishment. In other words, we are beginning to have "One World," and many do not care for it. Lest it seem that this is the American conquest and deterioration of older cultures, it should be pointed out that those areas have a similar impact on America. Anyone comparing the level of cooking, of wine making, of opera performance, and a dozen other cultural activites and attributes in the modern United States with the situation fifty years ago could not avoid seeing the (most fortunate) cultural invasion of America that has gone along with its largely quiet role as a cultural hearth.

What this tells us is that since 1945 more people have moved internationally, particularly intercontinentally, than ever before; quite probably more people have moved that way in the last forty years that in all of human history before 1945. There need be no campaign to instill one's culture in another, as the French seem to think the Anglo-Saxons seek doggedly to do, when there is an interconnected world. The auditory horrors of the discotheque were not a deliberate Gallic implantation on American soil; the seeds came in on the feet of returning Americans. Sleeping on a cold floor, dousing good natural food with the chemical MSG, and sitting in anatomically unrealistic Scandinavian-modern chairs all became part of American life when air travel became a mass undertaking. There are two schools of thought on culture—that inbreeding weakens the stock and that outbreeding does—but there can be no question that culture has never been the same since travel became a widespread human activity.

Other examples could be given of how our modern world is shaped by the great changes in transportation that have come since the beginning of the Transportation Revolution. These seem so widely perceived and understood that they need not be specified. All that remains to be said is that when human beings first became human they had two qualities that assured the ultimate arrival of the present state of affairs: human beings had an innate mobility that so engaged their other and more distinctive quality, inquisitive intelligence, that they have spent every intervening period, and much of their time, in trying to gain greater mobility further to satisfy that geographical inquisitiveness. The insatiable curiosity of human beings has lain not merely in an intellectual realm, of knowing about the world at large, but as well in using that world for their own satisfactions. It was this search for goods that projected European migrations to other continents, thereby bringing the earlier phases of the Transportation Revolution that were to allow a more complex satisfaction of curiosity such as we have today. It is in many ways paradoxical that the economic integration of the world came before its cultural integration. That coming together could, however, have been foreseen as the logical

One horizon captured: Promontory, Utah Territory, on the morning of May 10, 1869. Union Pacific Railroad photograph.

realization of the most primordial urges to improve on innate mobility. Earliest people found their view constrained by the hills of their home site, and intelligent curiosity would have given them the strongest of desires to learn what lay beyond. The Mercantile Revolution that was contemporary with our Transportation Revolution, and certainly a significant source of it, merely whetted that interest in what was unobservable from the homestead. There grew up a third characteristic of humans in this specific context: an impatience with the constraints of their original condition and geographical realm. The ever-earnest belief in the perfectability of mankind had tucked away in a corner a very specific geographical effort: this was the accomplishment of the ultimate human mobility that became the historical geography of transportation, the human effort of capturing the horizon.

NOTE

1. R. E. G. Davies, *Airlines of the United States, since 1914* (Washington, D.C.: Smithsonian Institution Press, 1982), pp. 677–678.

A Ford dealer in Portland, Oregon, decided to illustrate the Model T's "mountain-goat ruggedness" to potential customers by sending this 1921 centerdoor sedan model up the steps of Benson Polytechnic High School. Ford Motor Company photograph.

Postface to the 1990 Edition

Events commonly overtake the plans of individuals, frequently to their discomfiture. The publication of this book is a clear measure of extrinsic factors at work in the realm of ideas and of the alternation of fortunate and unfortunate timing. In 1977 a long-established American publisher, Harper and Row, brought out the first of a pair of books seeking to understand one of the central relationships of human geography—transportation development and fixed human settlement. This association of major human activities has engaged my interest since the mid-1940s, the earliest years of my career in geography. By the early 1970s I had shaped an integrated proposal about the force of human morphogenesis. At that time Harper's was seeking to draw closer together the activities of commercial publishers in the college field and work usually reserved for university presses. Harper's College Press was created, and in 1977 it published *This Scene of Man: The Role and Structure of the City in the Geography of Western Civilization,* which enjoyed modest academic and mild commercial success.

During this period when the first abutment, concerned with the creation and evolution of cities, was publicly on view, I worked on the plan of the second, the statement of the processes shaping the evolution of transportation. By the mid-1980s I had proposed a process model for transportation evolution and had almost completed explication of historical examples. I returned to Harper's in the hope that it might be published along with a reprinting of its companion, *This Scene of Man.* But events had changed conditions. Harper's College Press and its editor were gone, and geography was regarded as too small a field for much continued interest. As a kindness to me, the new book, *Capturing the Horizon: The Historical Geography of Transportation since the Transportation Revolution of the Sixteenth Century,* was published in a modest printing. By the time it became available, Harper and Row had been sold, and the second abutment of the bridge tying together transportation-settlement relationships collapsed.

The chance of a joint consideration of the transportation-settlement relationship came to life again when the Johns Hopkins University Press accepted the revised edition of *This Scene of Man,* now retitled *The Continuing City,* for publication. With this return of favorable events, I was encouraged to attempt the rescue of *Capturing the Horizon,* whose copyright had reverted to me. Now, for the first time, these two intimately related books have become available at the same time.

I had hoped that typographical errors in *Capturing the Horizon* might be corrected, but financial considerations led us instead to insert a list of corrigenda. George Thompson, as acquisitions editor at Johns Hopkins, has given great and most valuable support to the project, as have all involved there. Logan Campbell, my original editor, and George Thompson deserve considerable thanks. In addition, Harold Mayer, Bill Wallace, and Don Meinig were of great encouragement in bringing forth this, the other abutment intended to explain and support my analysis of the transportation-settlement relationship.

Finally, I wish to comment briefly on two questions that might logically arise with respect to this reissuance of *Capturing the Horizon* after the elapse of three years. The first question concerns changes that might have taken place in my thinking with respect to the evolution of transportation. Obviously there have been numerous changed circumstances and thus it would be appropriate to cover, for example, the failure to approve the merger of the Southern Pacific Railroad and the Santa Fe Railway and the substitution therefore of a merger of the S.P. with the Denver and Rio Grande Western Railroad, but the exigencies of returning this book to print and the heavy costs involved make revisions impracticable. In similar fashion, it would be desirable to present an analysis of the very rapid rise in planning for, and operation of, high-speed rail services in western Europe and Japan. But because that evolution is as yet only partially revealed, such an analysis must wait for a few more years. I hope to publish a book on the subject when the future pattern becomes clearer.

The second question arises from the simultaneous publication of this book and *The Continuing City.* What is to be gained from reading the volumes at the same time? Because both their organizations fall naturally into stages of evolution, it becomes possible to build a picture of transportation-settlement relationships and to establish the processes involved. These are mentioned briefly in each book, and a far more ample explanation is to be secured from considering the co-evolution of settlement and of the instrument then currently in use to enhance human mobility. That instrument is suggested by the structural needs of the settlement, whereas the geographical pattern of the settlement is heavily shaped by the operational nature of the instruments of mobility.

Index

Corrigenda to the 1986 Edition

Key: L = left column; R = right column; M = map

PAGE	CORRECTION
xiiR	*This Scene of Man* was completely revised and reissued by the Johns Hopkins University Press in 1990 as *The Continuing City: Urban Morphology in Western Civilization.*
9R	actually, not actualy
11L	incomparable, not imcomparable
14R	Britain, not Britian
17L	geographical, not geogtagical
25R	ubiquitous, not ubiquitoius
27L	varied, not varried
45L	transshipped, not transhipped
46R	Naviglio, not Naviglia
48R	Naviglio, not Naviglia
50R	Naviglio, not Naviglia
50L	grandiose, not gradiose
73M	Montluçon, not Montluçan
82R	Naviglio, not Naviglia
96L	emerging, not emergining
97L	Smethick, not Smethwich
97R	Coventry, not Conventry
134R	berm, not bearm
142R	martello, not martelo; of, not af
210R	Wolverhampton, not Wolver Hampton
211R	unappreciated, not unappreicated
235R	parlement, not parleament
248R	Siena, not Sienna
249L	narrow-gauge, not narrow-guage
249L	Chambéry, not Chambery
252L	Neapolitan, not Neopolitan
255L	Should read from line 30 "It speaks well for the great advances in engine design

PAGE	CORRECTION
	that all four succeeded in the basic task, with *Bavaria* gaining the first prize."
255R	well, not wet
290R	line 6 missing, "stations and division points."
305R	garbled section from last line on page continuing on 306L: replaced by: "Also, it was intended that a number of 'branches' of the Union Pacific be built between railroad termini ultimately located on the Missouri River between Kansas City, Missouri, and Sioux City, Iowa, and the legal 'starting point' of the Pacific Railroad found on the (p. 306L) 100th meridian . . ."
327R	split, not spilt
328R	Subsequently the Southern Pacific Railroad and the Santa Fe Railway were denied permission to merge. Instead the S.P. commenced a merger with the Denver and Rio Grande Western Railroad.
339R	journeys, not journies
348L	route, not routes
353L	line 14, the, not they
362L	Staffordshire, not Strafordshire
425L	Pythias, not Pytheas
426L	Carrack, not carack
445L	Halley, not Haley
464L	Britannic, not Britanic
467L	Île de France, not Ile
471L	Compagnie, not Comapnie
495R	unpleasant, not upleasant

659

PAGE	CORRECTION	PAGE	CORRECTION
497R	visited, not visted	543L	legislation, not lefistation
519R	canon, not cannon	548L	geography, not goegraphy
529R	Ardèche, not Ardeche	560L	line 13, lower, not power
533R	rubberized, not ruberized	587L	fatigue, not fatgue
534L	Yanboli, not Yamboli	593L	these, not theses